WHO'S WHO

IN THE

TWENTIETH CENTURY

First published in 1993 by
Brompton Books Corp.
15 Sherwood Place
Greenwich, CT 06830
USA

Copyright © 1993 Brompton Books
Corp.

ISBN 0-86124-798-1

Printed in Hong Kong

THIS PAGE, CLOCKWISE FROM TOP LEFT:
Richard Nixon; Mary Quant; Bette Davis;
Sean Connery; Moshe Dayan; Spencer Tracy
and Katharine Hepburn; Carl Lewis;
Mahatma Gandhi.
OPPOSITE PAGE, ANTICLOCKWISE FROM TOP
LEFT: Martina Navratilova; Ronald Reagan;
Hideki Tojo; Fred Astaire and Ginger Rogers;
Pope John Paul II.

WHO'S WHO

— IN THE —
TWENTIETH
CENTURY

Brompton

The following authors contributed to *Who Was Who in the Twentieth Century* (entries are concluded with the relevant author's initials):

EB   **Dr E J Borowski** MA (Hons), BPhil (Oxon)
Senior Lecturer, Department of Philosophy, University of Glasgow

MB   **Marina Benjamin**
Freelance writer

MBe   **Dr Mark Berelowitz** MPhil, MRCPsych
Consultant child psychiatrist, Maudsley Hospital

DC   **David S Carter**
Freelance writer

MC   **Maria Costantino**
Lecturer in Cultural Studies and author

JC   **John Crossland**
Historian and author

DD   **Dougal Dixon** BSc (Hons), MSc

MD   **Marty Dobrow**
Editorial consultant

DE   **Doreen Ehrlich**
Writer and teacher of History of Art, Architecture and Design at Hillcroft College, Surrey, and Cultural Studies at Epsom School of Art

NF   **Nigel Fryatt**
Executive Editor, *Cars and Car Conversions, Off Road and 4 Wheel Drive, MiniWorld*, and author

CH-M   **Clare Haworth-Maden**
Freelance writer and editor

JH   **Jessica Hodge**
Freelance writer and editor

RJ   **Robert Jameson** MA

IJ   **Ian Jeffrey**
Freelance writer and critic

DK   **Damian Knollys**
Freelance writer

GL   **Dr Ghislaine Lawrence**
Senior Curator, Clinical Medicine, The Science Museum, London

ML   **Dr Mark Loughlin** MA, PhD
Teacher of History at The Edinburgh Academy

AM   **Alison Mark** MA
Writer and editor

JM   **Judith Millidge**
Freelance writer and editor

FM   **Frank Milner**
Walker Art Gallery, Liverpool

JPi   **Dr J L Pimlott**
Deputy Head of the Department of War Studies, Royal Military Academy Sandhurst, and author

JP   **Dr James Pullé**
History Teacher, Bishop Heber High School, Malpas, Cheshire

AR   **Aileen Reid**
Architectural researcher

CR   **Caroline Richmond**
Medical writer and historian

IR   **Ian Ridpath**
Astronomy author

SR   **Simon Rockman**
Deputy Editor, *Personal Computer World*

ER   **Elizabeth Rose** MA

NS   **Neil Sinyard**
Lecturer in English Literature and Film, Hull University

DSl   **Don Slater**
Lecturer in Sociology, Goldsmiths' College, University of London

DS   **Donald Sommerville**
Editor and author

EMS   **Eleanor M Stillwell**
Freelance writer and editor

ES   **Dr Eleni Stylianou**
Research biochemist, Cytokine Biochemistry Group, Strangeways Research Laboratory

MT   **Michael Taylor**
Aviation author and editor, Assistant Editor *Jane's All the World's Aircraft*

PT   **Peter Thresh**
Historian

CW   **Dr Carol Watts**
Lecturer in English, Birkbeck College, London University

JW   **Dr John Westwood**
Formerly Senior Lecturer in History at Sydney University

PW   **Peter Wymer** BSc, CN
Freelance science writer

The publisher would like to thank Ron Callow of D23 for designing this book, Judith Millidge and Clare Haworth-Maden for editing it, and Duncan Clarke, Dave Carter and Aileen Reid for proofreading. The following individuals and agencies provided photographic material:

The Bettmann Archive: pages 2 (center left), 10 (top), 12, 13 (top), 15 (left), 18 (all three), 21 (bottom), 29 (top), 30 (right), 31 (top), 38 (top), 39 (center), 40, 42 (bottom), 43 (right), 46 (right), 50 (top right), 52 (left), 53 (both), 56, 57 (right), 59 (right), 63, 64 (right), 65 (bottom), 66 (right), 69 (left), 73, 78 (right), 80, 81 (top), 84 (left), 85 (bottom), 87, 88 (bottom), 92 (top), 102 (center), 108, 122 (bottom), 136 (top), 147, 148, 150, 156, 158 (top left), 163 (top), 166 (left), 170 (both), 173 (all three), 179, 186 (top left and bottom), 188, 190, 193 (left), 198 (center and right), 201 (bottom), 202 (bottom), 206 (bottom), 211 (left), 212 (right), 215 (all three), 220 (right), 222 (bottom).

The Bettmann Archive/Hulton Picture Library: pages 2 (top center), 17 (top), 23 (top), 25, 34 (both), 124, 125 (bottom), 127 (right), 155 (top left), 158 (top right), 159 (top), 189 (top and bottom), 203 (bottom), 206 (top left), 220 (left).

Brompton Books: pages 2 (four in right-hand column), 3 (center left and bottom), 8 (top), 9 (bottom), 13 (bottom), 14 (top), 21 (top), 22, 30 (left), 33, 37 (bottom), 45/46, 51, 52 (right), 55 (right), 57 (left), 62 (bottom), 68, 69 (right), 74, 76 (right), 77 (bottom), 89 (top), 92 (right), 95 (bottom), 98 (bottom), 107 (top), 110 (bottom), 112, 114 (bottom), 118, 119, 128, 135 (top), 145 (bottom), 160, 167 (top), 175 (top), 176 (bottom), 177 (both) 197, 205 (bottom), 206 (top right), 208, 216 (top).

Brompton Books/AP/Wide World Photos: page 216 (bottom).

Brompton Books/Chicago Historical Society: page 183 (bottom).

Brompton Books/Collections of the Library of Congress: pages 67 (right), 92 (left), 178 (right), 218.

Brompton Books/Editions Stock, Paris: page 142 (top).

Brompton Books/Federal Bureau of Investigation: page 98 (top).

Brompton Books/John Fairfax & Sons Ltd: page 139.

Brompton Books/JFK Library: page 111.
Brompton Books/LBJ Library: page 105.
Brompton Books/The Museum of Modern Art/Films Stills Archive, NY: pages 38 (bottom), 67 (left), 202 (top), 213 (bottom).
Brompton Books/National Film Archive, London: pages 85 (top), 95 (top), 97 (left), 109 (bottom), 110 (center), 126, 136 (bottom), 194 (right), 200, 209 (bottom).
Brompton Books/Jerry Ohlinger: page 207 (bottom).
Brompton Books/Schomberg Center for Research in Black Culture, New York Public Library: pages 65 (top), 97 (right).
Brompton Books/Wisconsin Center for Film and Theater Research: page 17 (bottom).
The Walt Disney Company: page 58.
Pedro E Guerrero: page 221 (bottom).
Robert Hunt Library: page 224 (top).
Israeli Government Press Office: pages 24, 182 (top).
National Baseball Library, Cooperstown NY: pages 57 (top), 181.
New York Public Library: page 50 (left).
Reuters/Bettmann Newsphotos: pages 2 (bottom left), 3 (top left and below right), 14 (bottom), 15 (right), 26 (right), 27 (bottom right), 28, 37 (top), 42 (top), 55 (left), 59 (left), 76 (left), 77 (center), 78 (left), 83 (bottom), 90, 96, 99, 100/101, 109 (top), 117, 122 (top), 129 (right), 131 (right), 133 (left), 134, 141 (top), 144 (both), 149, 162 (bottom), 186 (top right), 199 (right), 203 (top), 205 (top), 223.
Billy Rose Theater Collection: page 174 (right).
Karl Schumacher, The White House: page 23 (bottom).
Springer/Bettmann Film Archive: page 165.
UPI/Bettmann Newsphotos: pages 3 (bottom left), 5 (both), 6 (both), 7, 8 (bottom), 9 (top and center), 10 (bottom), 11, 16 (both), 19 (all four), 20 (both), 23 (left), 26 (left), 27 (left and top right), 29 (center), 31 (bottom), 36, 39 (top and bottom), 41 (top), 43 (left), 44 (left and center), 45 (right), 46 (left), 47, 48, 49 (both), 50 (bottom right), 54 (both), 60, 61 (both), 62 (top), 66 (left), 70, 71 (both), 72, 75 (all three), 81 (bottom), 82, 83 (top), 84 (right), 86, 88 (top), 89 (bottom), 91, 93 (both), 100 (left), 101 (top and bottom right), 102 (top), 103 (both), 104 (both), 106, 107 (bottom), 110 (top left and right), 113, 114 (top), 115, 121, 123, 125 (top), 127 (top), 129 (top and bottom), 130 (both), 131 (left), 132, 133 (right), 135 (bottom), 137, 138, 141 (bottom), 142 (bottom center and right), 143 (both), 145 (top), 146 (both), 151, 152 (both), 153, 154 (both), 155 (top right and bottom), 157 (both), 159 (bottom), 161, 162 (top), 163 (center left and right), 164, 166 (right), 167 (bottom), 168 (both), 169, 171 (both), 172 (both), 174 (left), 175 (bottom), 176 (top), 180 (both), 182 (bottom), 183 (top), 184, 185, 187 (both), 189 (center), 191 (all three), 192, 193 (right), 194 (left), 195, 196, 198 (left), 199 (left), 201 (bottom), 204 (both), 207 (top), 209 (top), 211 (right), 212 (left), 213 (top), 214, 219, 221 (top), 222 (top), 224 (bottom).
US Army Photographs: pages 32 (SC197145), 64 (left, S355355).
The White House, Washington: page 41 (bottom).
Wide World Photos: pages 35, 178 (bottom).

AALTO, ALVAR
1898-1976
Finnish architect and furniture designer

After graduating from Helsinki Polytechnic in 1921, Aalto established his first office in Jyväskylä and after 1925 worked with his wife Aino Marsio. Early works were in a stripped-down classical style, but after moving to Turku in 1927 he soon began his 'white period', producing masterly functionalist designs. These include the Municipal Library, Viipuri (1927-35), and the sanatorium at Paimio (1929-33). Also from 1927 Aalto designed modernist furniture, often using novel techniques for shaping plywood, and from around 1935 he and Aino Marsio founded the Artek furniture company to manufacture his designs. In the 1950s Aalto was occupied in rebuilding his native land, including his designs for Rovaniemi, capital of Lapland, and Säynätsalo Town Hall. His strikingly expressive designs using bright-red brick in simple geometric shapes have led this time to be dubbed his Cézanne period. Aalto is among the very greatest of twentieth-century architects; while never abandoning the principle of functionalism, Aalto mastered a wide variety of new and traditional materials and formal solutions, and even on huge projects he never lost a sense of human scale, or neglected the detail of his buildings. **AR.**

AARON, HENRY LOUIS (HANK)
1934-
American baseball player

With one strong, fluid swing in 1974 Hank Aaron of the Atlanta Braves broke the most sacred record in American sports: Babe RUTH's lifetime home run mark of 714. 'Hammering Hank' finished his sensational 23-year-career with 755 homers and 2297 runs batted in, figures that still top the major league charts. He was remarkably consistent, never cracking more than 50 homers in a season but still assaulting Ruth's record with steady totals year after year. Aaron was not just a slugger; he finished his career with 3771 hits, third on the all-time list, and a .305 batting average. **MD.**

ABBAS, FERHAT
1890-1989
Algerian statesman

Abbas published *A Manifesto of the Algerian People* in 1943, demanding independence from France. Elected to the French National Assembly in 1946, and the Algerian Assembly in 1948, initially he attempted to co-operate with the French. He joined the FLN (Front de Libération Nationale) in 1956 in order to achieve autonomy by revolution and became Prime Minister of the provisional government in 1958. After a bitter struggle with France, Abbas became President of independent Algeria in 1962 but was deposed a year later. **JC.**

ABDUL-JABBAR, KAREEM (b. LEW ALCINDOR)
1947-
American basketball player

The basketball career of Kareem Abdul-Jabbar was epitomized by the elegant, deadly shot he perfected, the 'sky hook'. This 7-foot-2 inch center for the Milwaukee Bucks and Los Angeles Lakers was a blend of graceful intensity throughout his 20 years in the NBA, playing more games (1560) and scoring more points (38,387) than anyone in league history. He also stands alone with six MVP trophies, 237 playoff games, and 5762 playoff points. Six times he helped his team to the league championship. In college (he was then known as Lew Alcindor) he led UCLA to three straight national titles. **MD.**

ABERNATHY, RALPH DAVID
1926-
American civil rights leader

His quiet authority complemented Martin Luther KING's charisma in the leadership of the US civil rights movement. Taking his Master's degree in Atlanta, Georgia, he made the city's West Hunter Street Baptist Church, from 1961, a stronghold in the pas-

ABOVE: Civil rights activist Ralph Abernathy.

sive struggle for Black rights, and both his church and home were dynamited by extremists in 1971. His first blow for civil rights was to coordinate the Montgomery, Alabama, bus boycott in 1955, though his organizational skill was seen to greatest effect in the Poor People's Campaign in Washington in 1968. As chairman of the Commission on Racism and Apartheid, he addressed the United Nations on these issues in 1971. **JC.**

ACHEBE, CHINUA
1930-
Nigerian writer

Born in Igboland, Achebe studied in Ibadan, then worked for the Nigerian broadcasting company in Lagos. Active in his support for Biafra in the civil war, Achebe had stated that the writer should be at the forefront of 'the big social and political issues of contemporary Africa.' In his first novel, *Things Fall Apart* (1958), he explored the communal culture of a tribal village, a culture challenged in the novels *No Longer At Ease* (1960) and *Arrow of God* (1964) by the effects of British colonialism. Achebe has won numerous prizes for his work, which includes short stories and poetry. **CW.**

ABOVE: US Secretary of State Dean Acheson.

ACHESON, DEAN
1893-1971
American statesman

Secretary of State during the Korean War, Acheson's cool judgment helped to limit a potentially worldwide conflict. A lawyer, he was appointed private secretary to Justice BRANDEIS of the Supreme Court in 1919, and served as Under-Secretary of the Treasury under ROOSEVELT in 1933, returning to his old law practice later that year. He was Assistant Secretary of State throughout World War II and Under-Secretary from 1945 to 1947, where his astuteness in the opening moves of the Cold War won him the Secretaryship under TRUMAN. **JC.**

ADAMS, ANSEL
1902-1984
American photographer

Born and brought up in San Francisco, Adams visited Yosemite Valley in 1916, and from 1920 onwards was closely associated with the Sierra Club. He decided on photography after meeting Paul Strand in 1930, and in 1932, with Edward Weston and others, he founded the f/64 group, dedicated to the promotion of pure photography. His work was admired and exhibited by Alfred STIEGLITZ at An American Place in 1936. In his landscapes he celebrates a grandiose, undisturbed country, presided over by mountains and a wide sky. In 1940 he was instrumental in setting up the first department of photography as a fine art, at the Museum of Modern Art, New York. **IJ.**

ADAMSON, JOY
1916-80
Austrian conservationist

Joy Gessner dabbled in music and medicine before finding her vocation in life. Working as a botanic illustrator in Kenya she met British game warden George Adamson who became her third husband. In 1956 she met lion-cub Elsa, immortalized in her book and subsequent film *Born Free*, and became dedicated to conservation. Sadly she was murdered in 1980. **MB.**

ADDAMS, CHARLES
1912-1988
American cartoonist

Most famous as the creator of a long-running series of usually one-frame gags for *The New Yorker* about a group of vampires, ghouls, and monsters known as 'The Addams Family'. But for their inversion of every usual decency, they live as a normal American family. Ironic, but rarely dark, Addams' morbidly gentle humor flirts

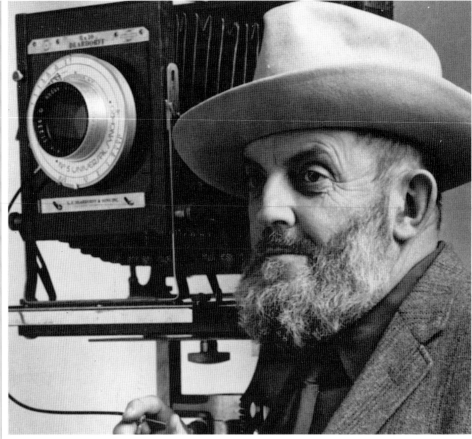

ABOVE: *Ansel Adams and the tools of his photographic trade.*

with the public's love of incongruity and our enjoyment at the parody of earlier horror movies. **FM.**

ADENAUER, KONRAD
1876-1967
German statesman

Founding father of the democratic postwar Germany at 69, he had no political experience other than as mayor of Cologne. Backed by the Western powers, he became the first Chancellor of the Federal Republic in 1949, remaining in office for 14 years, during which time he took Germany into the EEC and Nato, with full sovereignty. **JC.**

ADLER, ALFRED
1870-1937
Austrian psychologist

An early disciple of FREUD, Adler disagreed with him about the importance of the sexual drive in young children. Adler believed that the child was driven to the development of self-assertion, mastery, and domination, and that these factors played a greater part than did sexuality in the development of the personality. This drive was usually in compensation for the individual's real or perceived feelings of inferiority or lack of power. Adler's contribution has been underrated: he contributed to the development of self-psychology, and to our understanding of cultural influences on disorder. **MBe.**

ADRIAN, EDGAR DOUGLAS, BARON
1889-1975
British physiologist

Educated at Cambridge University and St Bartholomew's Hospital, London, Adrian's life-long study was the function of the nervous system. After a residency at the Hospital for Nervous Diseases, Queen Square, Adrian began research at Cambridge in 1919, carrying on work begun with Keith Lucas on the nature of the electrical impulse in nerves. He shared the Nobel Prize (1932) with C S SHERRINGTON for investigations into neuromuscular co-ordination. In 1934 he began to study the electrical activity of the brain, making important contributions to electroencephalography. **GL.**

ABOVE: *West German Chancellor Adenauer (left) and Premier Bulganin.*

ABOVE: Playwright Edward Albee deep in thought.

AGNELLI, GIOVANNI
1866-1945
Italian motor manufacturer

Founded in 1899, Fabbrica Italiana Auto-mobile Turino was a family affair and has grown to being one of the largest companies in the world which is still run by the founding family. Much of the success of Fiat has been due to Agnelli's management style which has covered commercial as well as mass-production vehicles and specialist companies like Ferrari. **NF**.

AGOSTINI, GIACOMO
1943-
Italian motorcycle champion

Giacomo Agostini won a total of 122 Grand Prix and 15 world titles at both 350cc and 500cc between his first success in 1965 and his retirement in 1977. For most of his career he rode for the Italian MV Agusta team and his rivalry in the late 1960s with the British rider Mike Hailwood is particularly remembered. **DS**.

AIKEN, CONRAD
1889-1973
American poet and novelist

Earth Triumphant (1914) was his first verse collection. Always interested in the themes of self-knowledge and self-transcendence, his edition of Emily Dickinson helped bring her to prominence. He also wrote critical essays and short stories, and *The Collected Novels* appeared in 1964, of which the autobiographical *Ushant* is the best known. **AM**.

AKHMATOVA, ANNA
1889-1966
Russian poet

Akhmatova brought to the Russian lyric, according to fellow Acmeist Osip Mandelstam 'the wealth of the nineteenth-century Russian novel.' Raised outside St Petersburg, she married Nikolai Gumilev, organizer of the Guild of Poets, in 1910. Her collections of poetry, from *Evening* (1912) to *Anno Domini MCMXXI* (1921), noted for their frank delineation of women's passion, won her great fame. Increasingly denounced after 1923, her work was banned until 1940. The arrest of her son in 1934 prompted her cycle on the Stalinist terror, *Requiem* (1963), while *Poem Without a Hero* is a 20-year meditation on the suffering of her time. She was rehabilitated in 1956. **CW**.

al-BANNA, SABRI [ABU NIDAL]
1937-
Palestinian revolutionary

Born in British-ruled Palestine, al-Banna fled to Gaza in 1948 when the state of Israel was created. He joined *al-Fatah*, the Palestinian freedom-fighters, in the 1960s and in 1970 was sent to Iraq as representative of the Palestine Liberation Organization. Trained in North Korea and the People's Republic of China, he became a fighter dedicated to the destruction of Israel. Taking the name Abu Nidal ('Father of the Struggle'), he founded a terrorist group of the same name (originally 'Black June'), and organized a number of operations, notably grenade attacks on Rome and Vienna airports in December 1985. **JP**.

ALBEE, EDWARD
1928-
American playwright

Albee's first Broadway success was *Who's Afraid of Virginia Woolf?* (1962), the ferocious portrayal of a night of drunken mutual abuse between a middle-aged professor and his wife, which became a memorable film. *A Delicate Balance* (1966) won a Pulitzer Prize, as did *Seascape* (1975). He has also dramatized the work of other authors. **AM**.

ALBERS, JOSEPH
1888-1976
German painter

Albers trained as a teacher before enrolling, in 1920, in the Bauhaus, formed the pre-vious year. His imaginative use of materials led to teaching posts on the preliminary course and as head of the stained-glass and furniture workshops. After the Bauhaus was closed by the Nazis in 1933 he emigrated to the USA and taught at the Black Mountain College, North Carolina, and Yale University. An important link between European and American abstract traditions, from 1950 his work centered on a series of paintings, *Homage to the Square*, which explored color relationships through a single compositional form, squares set within squares. His theories, published in *The Interaction of Color* (1963), had a strong influence on Op Art. **ER**.

ALCOCK, SIR JOHN WILLIAM
1892-1919
British pilot

Qualifying as a pilot in 1912, Alcock joined the Royal Naval Air Service and saw action in World War I before being taken prisoner by Turkish forces in 1917. After leaving the service in 1919, he became chief test pilot for Vickers. On 14-15 June 1919 he and Arthur BROWN made the first non-stop Atlantic crossing by aeroplane (a Vickers Vimy), taking 16 hours 17 minutes to fly from Newfoundland to County Galway. On 18 December that year he was killed in an accident in France, caused by bad weather, while delivering a Viking amphibian. **MT**.

ALEXANDER OF TUNIS, HAROLD, 1ST EARL, FIELD MARSHAL
1891-1969
British soldier

An Ulsterman, commissioned from Sandhurst into the Irish Guards in 1910, Alexander saw distinguished service in World War I, winning the DSO and MC. In 1939-40, at the beginning of World War II, he commanded the British 1st Infantry Division in France and was reputedly the last man to leave Dunkirk. After command in North Africa (1942-43), he was appointed Supreme Allied Commander in Italy. Despite strong German resistance and difficult terrain, Alexander's forces slowly drove the enemy northwards and liberated Italy in April 1945. He was Governor-General of Canada 1946-52, after which he served as Defence Minister until his resignation in 1954. **JPi**.

ALEXANDERSON, ERNEST
1878-1975
American electrical engineer

Born in Sweden, Alexanderson settled in America in 1901 and worked in communications at General Electric. He was the principal developer of the high-frequency alternators used for radio transmitters in the days before valves took over. Alexanderson was a prolific worker with a most inventive mind and had some 300 patents to his credit. **PW**.

ALI, MUHAMMAD (b. CASSIUS CLAY)
1942-
American boxer

A poet and a pounder, Ali captured the imagination of people across the globe with his wicked charm, his fierce bravado, and his masterful boxing. He held at least a piece of the world heavyweight championship on several occasions, most impressively from 1964 to 1967 and from 1974 to 1978. Then known as Cassius Clay, he first gained acclaim in the 1960 Olympics, capturing the gold medal in the light heavyweight division. In 1964 he won a stunning upset victory by knocking out heavyweight champion Sonny Liston. His rhyming prediction of victory, his graceful 'Ali Shuffle,' and his vicious punching power made him a charismatic champion, but he was stripped of his title in 1967 when he refused to enter the US military because of religious convictions. When Ali's appeal was honored by the Supreme Court in 1971 he resumed his career, but lost his title to Joe Frazier. He regained it in 1974, stunning then champion George Foreman with his 'rope-a-dope' tactics. In 1978 Ali lost to Leon Spinks, regained the championship, then retired. He tried a comeback in 1980, but lost his final title bid to Larry Holmes. **MD.**

ALLEN, WOODY [ALLEN STEWART KONIGSBERG]
1935-
American film director and actor

Allen is America's most original movie actor, writer, and director all rolled into one. On screen, he is the epitome of the modern bungler tormented by self-doubt, neurosis, and unswervable lust. He co-wrote and appeared in *What's New, Pussycat?* (1965), his first film, and *Play It Again, Sam* (1972) was the plaintive cry of a man who never got the girl and a tribute to Bogart, who usually did. Renowned for producing funny pictures with a serious side, such as *Annie Hall* (1977) which won three Oscars, his recent work such as *Crimes and Misdemeanours* (1989) is a little more thoughtful. **DC.**

RIGHT: Boxing heavyweight Muhammad Ali towers over Sonny Liston.

ABOVE: Comic director Woody Allen (right).

ALLENBY, EDMUND, 1ST VISCOUNT, FIELD MARSHAL
1861-1936
British soldier

At the beginning of World War I in 1914 Allenby, a soldier with wide experience of cavalry actions in colonial campaigns, was given command of the British cavalry in France. By early 1917 he was commanding Third Army in the costly Battle of Arras. On 17 April 1917, however, Allenby was transferred to command British and Imperial troops in Palestine, fighting the Turks, and it was here that his reputation was made. By 9 December he had captured Jerusalem and in September 1918 he conducted an epic attack at Megiddo which opened the way to Damascus and Turkish surrender. **JPi.**

ALLENDE [GOSSENS], SALVADOR
1908-1973
Chilean politician

Allende's attempt to create a viable people's republic through his proudly proclaimed 'first freely elected Marxist government in the West' was crushed by the Chilean Army, with CIA support. He led a coalition of left-wing parties to power as President in 1970 but his socialist reform program, including land reform and income equalization, failed. Overthrown by General PINOCHET in 1973, his democratic experiment was followed by savage military repression. **JC**.

ALVAREZ, LUIS WALTER
1911-88
American physicist

Studied at Chicago and Berkeley, becoming Professor of Physics there in 1949, Alvarez's main field of research was in sub-atomic particles, and he identified a number of very short-lived types. As a practical scientist he was involved in the development of radar, microwave navigation beacons, and the atomic bomb during World War II, and the building of the first proton linear accelerator in 1947. To the general public he is better known as the scientist who, with his son Walter, suggested that the dinosaurs were wiped out by climate changes produced by the fall of a giant meteorite some 65 million years ago. **DD**.

ABOVE: Brutal Ugandan dictator Idi Amin.

AMIN, IDI
1928-
Ugandan politician

A bloodthirsty buffoon who tyrannized his country for eight years, he was responsible for the murder of an estimated 300,000 people. A veteran of the King's African Rifles, he overthrew Milton Obote and expelled Uganda's 70,000 Asians in 1971. Deposed after Britain broke diplomatic relations and Tanzania invaded (1979), he fled to exile in Saudi Arabia. **JC**.

AMIS, SIR KINGSLEY
1922-
British novelist and poet

First associated with the 'Angry Young Men' of the 1950s, his first and very funny novel *Lucky Jim* (1954) was a popular success. Amis has written and edited several volumes of poetry, in addition to his prolific output of increasingly jaundiced fiction, and won the Booker Prize for his novel *The Old Devils* (1986). **AM**.

AMUNDSEN, ROALD
1872-1928
Norwegian explorer

The polar explorer Roald Amundsen is famed for two major achievements: he was the first person to navigate his way through the fabled North-West Passage, and he beat Captain Robert SCOTT to become the first man to reach the South Pole in December 1911. Amundsen died heroically – he was never seen again after setting off to rescue Umberto NOBILE. **RJ**.

ANDERS, WLADYSLAW, GENERAL
1892-1970
Polish soldier

Captured by the Russians in 1939, Anders was released in 1941 to raise an army of Poles to fight the Fascists. They joined the British Eighth Army in Italy, where, under Anders' command, they took Monte Cassino in May 1944. When the war ended, Anders chose to live in London. **JPi**.

ABOVE: Norwegian Roald Admunsen.

ANDERSON, MAXWELL
1888-1959
American playwright

Maxwell Anderson began as a journalist before the immense success of his war play *What Price Glory?* (1924). His work ranges from prose and verse drama, to radio plays and musical comedies, from satires on the New Deal (with Kurt Weill) to historical dramas such as *Anne of the Thousand Days* (1948). **CW**.

ABOVE: US playwright Maxwell Anderson (right) and Kurt Weill.

ANDERSON, SHERWOOD
1876-1941
American novelist and short-story writer

One of America's foremost naturalistic writers, Anderson made his name with his book *Winesburg, Ohio* (1918), short stories exploring the frustrations of small-town existence. His novels include *Dark Laughter* (1925), which depicts racial themes with a formal simplicity that owes much to Gertrude STEIN, and the semi-autobiographical *Tar, A Midwest Childhood* (1926). **CW**.

ANDRE, CARL
1935-
American sculptor

A pioneer of Minimalism in the 1960s, Andre conceives his works as 'real' rather than 'symbolic' objects. They consist of horizontal mathematical arrangements of identical commercially produced units and have aroused controversy, particularly his arrangement of 'bricks' bought by the Tate Gallery in 1972. He also pioneered 'earthworks,' where the land itself becomes the art object. **ER**.

ANDROPOV, YURI
1914-84
Russian politician

Head of the KGB Andropov became President of the USSR in November 1982. From ensuring political correctness in newly occupied Karelia, and playing a murky role, as Ambassador to Hungary, in defeating the 1956 uprising, he was elected to the Supreme Soviet in 1962. In 1967 he became chairman of the State Security Committee and a member of the Presidium in 1982. **JC**.

ANGELOU, MAYA
1928-
American novelist and poet

One of Black America's most important writers, Angelou was born in Missouri and raised in Arkansas and California. In the following years she has been a waitress, singer, actress, Black activist, editor, and academic. In her twenties she toured Europe and Africa in *Porgy and Bess*; in New York acted in Genet's *The Blacks*, and joined the Harlem Writer's Guild. In the 1960s she was active in Black struggles, becoming editor of *African Review* during her years in Ghana. Her extraordinary life, her resilience and rich resources for hope, are collected in five volumes of autobiography beginning with *I Know Why the Caged Bird Sings* (1984). **CW**.

ANOUILH, JEAN
1910-1987
French playwright

Author of some 40 works, Anouilh is one of the most popular playwrights in France. He is noted for his reinterpretations of Greek myths, *Eurydice* (1942) and *Antigone* (1944), and for his plays dealing with historical figures such as Robespierre and Becket, and most famously, Joan of Arc in *The Lark* (1953). **CW**.

ANQUETIL, JACQUES
1934-87
French cyclist

Jacques Anquetil is regarded as one of the all-time greats in his sport and shares the record of five wins in the Tour de France, including four in a row (1961-4). A Norman by birth, he excelled both in individual time trials and in powerful attacks during conventional race stages. **DS**.

ANTONIONI, MICHELANGELO
1912-
Italian film director

Antonioni sprang to prominence when his film *L'Avventura* (1959) was booed off the screen at the Cannes Film Festival but then rapidly established itself as an art-cinema classic, to be followed by *La Notte* (1961) and *L'Eclisse* (1962). He had a commercial hit with the English-speaking *Blow-Up* (1966), but he is still most associated with arty studies of alienation. **NS**.

APOLLINAIRE, GUILLAUME
1880-1918
French poet

Apollinaire was a legend of his time – half-Polish, half-Italian, supposed son of Pope Leo XIII and descendant of Napoleon. A

ABOVE: French poet Guillaume Apollinaire, by Pablo Picasso.

celebrant of the modernist spirit, Apollinaire was a friend of PICASSO and BRAQUE, his fascination with Cubism expressed in *The Cubist Painters* (1913). The collections *Alcools* (1913) and *Calligrammes* (1918) include experiments with concrete poetry and punctuation, and works of extraordinary lyricism, such as 'Zone'. He coined the term surrealism, which he used to describe his play *The Breasts of Tiresias* (1918). **CW**.

ABOVE: US author Maya Angelou.

APPEL, KAREL
1921-
Dutch painter

Co-founder, in 1948, of Cobra, a group dedicated to free expression of the unconscious, in his paintings Appel uses strident colors, violently applied; they contain distorted vestiges of human and animal figures. His controversial 1949 mural for the City Hall, Amsterdam, was whitewashed over but he achieved international recognition in the 1950s, receiving the UNESCO prize for his work at the 1954 Venice Biennale. **ER.**

APPLETON, SIR EDWARD VICTOR
1892-1965
British physicist

Appleton's most notable achievement was the identification of a number of layers in the atmosphere, one of which bears his name. The Appleton layer is a band in the ionosphere containing ionized gases and can reflect radio signals, as is the Heaviside layer, another that he identified. An interest in radio, sparked off by service as a signals officer in World War I, inspired this research. The discovery helped the development of radar. He was awarded the Nobel Prize for Physics in 1947 for his discoveries. He was also involved in the initial research that led to the building of the atomic bomb. **DD.**

ARAFAT, YASSER
1929-
Palestinian nationalist

Born in Palestine when the country was ruled by the British, Arafat was 19 years old when his homeland was split into Arab and Jewish areas, the latter becoming the state of Israel. Preferring exile, he moved to Kuwait, where he worked as an engineer and, in 1958, helped to found the guerrilla group *al-Fatah*, later absorbed into the Palestine Liberation Organization (PLO). In 1969, using *al-Fatah* as a base, Arafat became chairman of the PLO. As such, he was effective leader of the Palestinian people, gaining international credibility and recognition despite a series of political and military setbacks. In 1970, as terrorist groups under the PLO umbrella mounted attacks on Israeli and Western targets, the PLO was expelled from Jordan, moving to Lebanon. From there, more direct attacks were made on Israel, leading to counter-strikes which culminated in the Israeli invasion of Lebanon in 1982. The PLO was forced by this action to disperse and Arafat was both heavily criticized and strongly opposed as leader. He survived, but realized that political dialogue was potentially more productive than armed confrontation, renouncing terrorism in 1988 and supporting peace initiatives in the aftermath of the Gulf War in 1991. **JP.**

ARAGON, LOUIS
1897-1982
French writer and political activist

Louis Aragon was a Dadaist before becoming an exponent of Surrealism. With André BRETON he founded the review *Littérature* in 1919 and *La Révolution surréaliste* in 1924, publishing his first collections of poetry, *Feu de joie* (1920) and *Le Mouvement perpétuel* (1925) and his major surrealist novel *Le Paysan de Paris* (1926). In 1927 he joined the Communist Party. Visiting the Soviet Union in 1930 he was so impressed with the system that he broke with Surrealism and turned to writing Socialist-Realist novels. During World War II he became one of the most popular poets of the Resistance. **CW.**

ARBER, WERNER
1929-
Swedish microbiologist
NATHANS, DANIEL
1928-
American microbiologist
SMITH, HAMILTON OTHANEL
1931-
American microbiologist

Awarded the Nobel Prize in 1978, Arber, independently of Nathans and Smith, discovered the restriction enzymes. These special enzymes cleave genes at predefined sites on the DNA molecule to form specific gene fragments. They have been used extensively to analyse the chemical structure, organization, and expression of genes in viruses and animals. In 1981 their use enabled the first genetic disease, sickle-cell anaemia, to be diagnosed antenatally. **ES.**

ARBUCKLE, ROSCOE (FATTY)
1887-1933
American actor

'Fatty' Arbuckle was the grown-up fat boy of the silent era. After a spell as a Keystone Cop he formed his own company in 1917. But after being acquitted of manslaughter in 1921 his movies were withdrawn and he became difficult to work with, dying in 1933 after an abortive attempt to relaunch his career. **DC.**

ARBUS, DIANE
1923-1971
American photographer

Diane Arbus contributed hugely to the acceleration of photographic history in the 1960s and 1970s. Although she worked as a fashion photographer in the 1950s, she became celebrated, and even notorious, for pictures of the gauche, the curious, and the stressed. Previous documentarists were interested in conversation and disclosure; Arbus was content to register encounters with often grotesque and marginal figures. This crucial move towards a confrontational portraiture might have been stimulated by her encounter in 1959 with the photographer Lisette Model, who worked in the pitiless realist style of the German New Objectivist painters. **IJ.**

ABOVE: *PLO Chairman Yasser Arafat (left) greets Saddam Hussein.*

ARCARO, EDDIE
1916-
American jockey

Too short to live his boyhood dream of playing baseball, Eddie Arcaro dominated US horseracing for more than 30 years. No one else has ever won the Triple Crown twice. In fact, no jockey has won *any* of the Triple Crown races more times than Arcaro. All told, he rode 4779 winners. **MD.**

ARCHIPENKO, ALEXANDER
1887-1964
Russian sculptor

Born in Kiev, Archipenko moved to Paris in 1908 and in 1923 to the USA. His style developed through Cubism to a purely abstract art which rejected all imitation of nature in the search for an autonomous plastic language. Among the first to use voids as positive elements in his designs, he also revived the use of polychromy and considerably influenced European sculpture. **ER.**

ARENDT, HANNAH
1906-1975
American political theorist

A student of Husserl and Jaspers, and twice a refugee from the Nazis, Arendt worked for Jewish organizations and publishers in Paris and New York before her first academic appointment in 1963. She traced the totalitarianism of HITLER and STALIN to the collapse of the nation state, compared the American and French revolutions, and is best known for her controversial views contained in *Eichmann in Jerusalem* on responsibility for the Holocaust and 'the banality of evil'. **EB.**

ARMANI, GIORGIO
1935-
Italian designer

Armani's first work as a designer was with Nino Cerruti in 1961 and later with Emanuel Ungaro. Following the establishment of his own company, Armani rose to become one of Italy's most acclaimed designers of ready-to-wear, and one of the few to move successfully from the field of menswear to womenswear. **MC.**

ARMSTRONG, EDWIN
1890-1954
American electronic engineer

In 1920 Armstrong patented what became the standard radio receiver, the superheterodyne, which allowed a radio to be tuned by the use of a simple knob. An innovative engineer with over 42 patents to his name, he also devised a means of reducing static on broadcasts by using frequency modulation, or FM. A rich man by the 1930s, he used vast sums of his own money in the struggle to get FM radio established, and was involved in bitter legal battles over royalties on his patents after World War II. **PW.**

ARMSTRONG, LOUIS
1900-71
American jazz trumpeter and singer

After gaining early experience in Joe (King) Oliver's band, Armstrong was working with the best outfits in Chicago by 1926, and was soon recording. His warmth of tone and inventiveness (he was instrumental in developing the technique of soloing over a repeated verse pattern) meant that he was in great demand first as a soloist and then as a bandleader. Soon he was fronting a band for the Broadway Revue 'Hot Chocolates' and found himself increasingly at home in a big-band context. He toured Europe and the UK in the early 1930s and began to feature treatments of popular tunes rather than the blues numbers that had hitherto been his staple fare. In the mid-1940s he began to use smaller ensembles, a format which brought him greater critical acclaim, and was soon firmly established as a key figure in the American jazz establishment. His growling voice certainly lacked most of the traditional qualities, but he brought to it the same warmth which characterized his tone on the trumpet. His sense of rhythm and early pioneering work earned him a place in the annals of jazz, despite the fact that by the 1950s he was more of a popular entertainer than an innovator. **DC.**

ARMSTRONG, NEIL
1933-
American astronaut

As the commander of Apollo 11, Armstrong became the first man to walk on the moon. A veteran of the Gemini space program, Armstrong and his colleagues Collins and Aldrin blasted off from Cape Canaveral on July 16 1969 in their rocket Saturn V, which carried Apollo 11 and the inner module, nicknamed Eagle. Once in lunar orbit Armstrong and Aldrin climbed into Eagle for the descent on to the moon's Sea of Tranquility on 20 July. As the world watched Armstrong descended the ladder and with the words: 'That's one small step for a man – one giant leap for mankind', set foot on the moon. With Aldrin, he spent two hours collecting some 20 kg of rock and soil samples and setting up equipment, and they returned to earth international celebrities. **PT.**

ARNOLD, EVE
1913-
American photographer

After war work in a photo-finishing plant Arnold studied at the famed New York School for Social Research. In 1952 she became a member of Magnum, the photographers' co-operative. Noted for her work in Hollywood during the 1950s, and in China during the 1970s, she was faithful throughout to the humane idioms of postwar reportage. **IJ.**

ABOVE: Jazz legend Louis Armstrong.

ABOVE: *Astronaut Neil Armstrong, the first man on the moon.*

ARNOLD, HENRY, GENERAL
1886-1950
American airman

As a serving US Army officer, Arnold was taught to fly by the Wright brothers in 1911. Six years later he joined the Aviation Section of the Army's Signal Corps, organizing and commanding the 7th Aero Squadron in 1917-18. During the interwar period, he became a strong advocate of airpower in future war, and in 1942 was appointed Commanding General of the US Army Air Force, with a seat on the Joint Chiefs of Staff Committee. As such he ensured that the USAAF played a leading role in the defeat of the Axis powers in both Europe and Asia. **JPi**.

ARP, JEAN
1877-1966
French sculptor

Born in Strasbourg, Arp studied in Paris. Associated variously with the expressionist Blaue Reiter group, the Zurich Dada group, formed in 1916, and the Surrealists, he experimented with collage, abstract paintings, and reliefs before turning to sculpture around 1930. Drawing on the work of BRANCUSI, he developed a sensual, organic style, evoking human anatomy. **ER**.

ARUP, OVE
1895-1988
British engineer

Arup's name is associated with innovative building projects worldwide from the Sydney Opera House to small bridges of revolutionary design. Just after World War II he founded what is now one of the world's largest civil and structural engineering partnerships, specializing in bringing together all the skills necessary for technically demanding assignments. **PW**.

ASHCROFT, DAME PEGGY
1907-1991
British actress

A thorough British dramatic training made Ashcroft a leading Shakespearean stage actress before her sporadic film appearances, from a supporting role in Hitchcock's *The Thirty-Nine Steps* (1935) to the Academy Award winning performance as Mrs Moore in David Lean's *A Passage to India* (1984). She also appeared in British TV series including *The Jewel in the Crown*. **DC**.

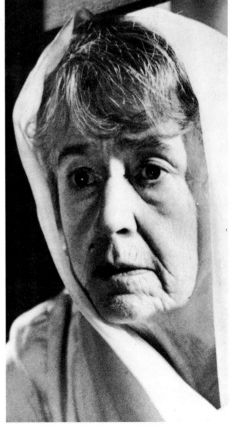

ABOVE: *Oscar-winning actress Peggy Ashcroft.*

ASHE, ARTHUR
1943-1993
American tennis player

With class and dignity, Arthur Ashe became a tennis pioneer and a moral force in the world of sports. A black man in an almost completely white game, Ashe won 33 tournaments, including the US Open (1968), the Australian Open (1970), and Wimbledon (1975). At UCLA he won the NCAA singles title in 1966. **MD.**

ASHTON, SIR FREDERICK
1904-1988
British dancer and choreographer

Born in Ecuador, Ashton decided to become a dancer after seeing Anna PAV-LOVA dance in Peru in 1917. In the early 1920s he studied with MASSINE in London, and later with Marie RAMBERT, who encouraged his early efforts at choreography. He began his association with Margot FON-TEYN at the Vic-Wells Ballet in 1935, and created leading roles for her in most of his ballets over the next 25 years. Prewar ballets included *Baiser de la Fée* (1935) and *Patineurs* (1937), and during the war he served with the RAF. When Sadlers-Wells Ballet moved to Covent Garden in 1946, Ashton created his first postwar ballet, *Symphonic Variations* followed by, among others, *Scene du Ballet* (1948) and *Ondine* (1958), all of which continued to provide Fonteyn with leading roles outside the classical repertoire. Ashton also created ballets around the talents of the new generation of dancers: *The Dream* (1954) for Antoinette Sibley and Anthony Dowell, *Two Pigeons* (1961) for Lynn Seymour and Christopher Gable as well as cementing the partnership of Fonteyn and Nureyev with *Marguerite and Armand* (1963). In 1963 Ashton succeeded de VALOIS as Director of the Royal Ballet, retiring in 1970, the same year he choreographed and danced in the film *The Tales of Beatrix Potter*. Ashton continued to produce pas de deux and solos during the 1970s, but it was not until 1976 that he returned to choreographing a full length ballet, *A Month in the Country*, again for Lynn Seymour. While most of Ashton's work was for the Royal Ballet, he also worked as guest choreographer in Monte Carlo and with American Ballet Theater. Many of his ballets are in the repertoire of companies throughout the world. Ashton's greatest success as a performer must surely have been opposite Robert Helpman as an Ugly Sister in his own *Cinderella*. **MC.**

ASIMOV, ISAAC
1920-1992
American novelist

Born in Russia, at age three Asimov emigrated to the United States with his parents. A brilliant biochemist, he has been a great popularizer of science, but his greatest renown has come from his science-fiction writings, especially the *Foundation* series, and the famous collection *I, Robot* (1950). He won four Hugo awards. **AM.**

ASPLUND, ERIK GUNNAR
1885-1940
Swedish architect

Trained at the Stockholm Academy of Art, Gunnar Asplund effected the change from his much-admired severe classical style (Stockholm City Library, 1924-27) to a Modernist one only in 1930. He became equally adept at handling steel and glass (Stockholm Exhibition Buildings, 1930) and concrete, as in the becolumned Forest Crematorium, Stockholm (1935-40), which, although unquestionably Modernist, has a Greek austerity and monumentality. **AR.**

ASQUITH, HENRY HERBERT, 1ST EARL OF OXFORD AND ASQUITH
1852-1928
British politician

Tactically adroit and willing to harness the talents of LLOYD GEORGE and CHURCHILL, Asquith ensured that the combination of timely social intervention by government and continuing commitment to free trade that was New Liberalism, dominated the turbulent days of Edwardian politics. The challenge of total war, however, required energetic leadership rather than cultivated chairmanship, a war economy rather than 'business as usual', and Asquith was eventually toppled from power in 1915 along with the remnants of New Liberal ideas. Embittered by the experience, instead of allowing the postwar reconstruction mood to heal Liberal divisions, Asquith pursued his rivalry with Lloyd George to the extent that Labour replaced Liberal as the alternative party of government. **JP.**

ABOVE: *Syrian leader Hafiz al Assad.*

ASSAD, HAFIZ AL
1928-
Syrian politician

Former anti-Western hawk who adopted a more pragmatic approach in the nineties, Assad dropped overt support for guerrilla groups in favor of playing middleman with the Islamic fundamentalists and the West, particularly in the hostage negotiations. The driving force of the Ba'ath Party, he has been successively Minister of Defense, Prime Minister and, since 1971, President. **JC.**

ABOVE: *Fred Astaire with Judy Garland.*

ASTAIRE, FRED
1899-1987
American dancer, actor, and choreographer

With very little formal dance training, Fred and his sister Adele were launched as a child vaudeville act in 1906 and toured the US until 1916. They continued to dance together in a number of musicals in New York and London until their last show together, *The Band Wagon* (1931), when Adele retired to marry. Astaire's first film appearance was in *Dancing Lady* (1933), briefly partnering Joan CRAWFORD. The same year he made his first film for RKO, *Flying Down to Rio* in which he was teamed with Ginger ROGERS. The partnership of Astaire and Rogers soon became one of Hollywood's most popular and they made ten films together. Although Astaire arranged all of his own dances he usually worked in tandem with his dance director, Hermes Pan. Following the break-up of the Astaire-Rogers partnership, Astaire went on to dance with some of Hollywood's leading ladies, although he always maintained that his favorite partner was Gene KELLY. In 1949 Astaire received a special Academy Award for his outstanding contribution to the technique of musical motion pictures. In later years, as well as writing an autobiography *Steps in Time*, he continued to appear in films in acting roles such as in *The Towering Inferno* (1974). **MC.**

ASTON, FRANCIS WILLIAM
1877-1945
British physicist and chemist

From 1910 Aston worked in the Cavendish Laboratory in Cambridge and, with F W Soddy, developed the concept of isotopes, in which atoms with the same chemical properties may have different chemical weights. This comes about because the nuclei of the atoms may have the same atomic number – the number of protons in the atom's nucleus – but will have different numbers of neutrons. He received the Nobel Prize for Chemistry for this work in 1922. He also developed the mass spectrometer, a device that separated isotopes by projecting them through a magnetic field. **DD**.

ABOVE: Kemal Atatürk, Turkish statesman.

ATATÜRK, KEMAL [MUSTAFA KEMAL]
1881-1938
Turkish statesman

Revolutionary soldier, Atatürk created modern Turkey from the ruins of the Ottoman Empire as a secular, non-aligned state. President for life, he gave Turkey the Latin alphabet, and with it the basis for a modern educational system, Western-inspired law and female emancipation. His successors have had difficulty living up to his model and, despite division of mosque and state, the problem of Islamic fundamentalism is still not solved. **JC**.

ATLAS, CHARLES
1894-1972
American body builder

Charles Atlas transformed himself from a meek and meager youngster into a muscled and monied man. An unimposing youth in Italy, Atlas changed his nationality, his name (from Angelo Siciliano), and his physique. He opened a gym in New York and

ABOVE: Canadian author Margaret Atwood.

later developed a mail-order program that brought bodybuilding to the masses, turning 97-pound weaklings into flexing fanatics. **MD**.

ATTENBOROUGH, SIR RICHARD
1923-
British actor and film director

Attenborough made his film debut in the Noel Coward film *In Which We Serve* (1942), going on to play character roles and leads in British and American movies. It is as a director of films such as *Oh What A Lovely War!* (1969) that he is best known today. He won an Academy Award for *Ghandi* in 1982. **DC**.

ATTLEE, CLEMENT, 1ST EARL,
1883-1967
British politician

Modest and mild-mannered, Attlee appeared a surprising victor over CHURCHILL in 1945, yet his was one of the most successful reforming governments of the century. Elected a Labour MP from London's East End in 1922, the combination of barrister's skills, privileged education, and social idealism offered by Attlee brought him the party leadership in 1935. If shrewd opposition increased his internal authority, by securing the War Coalition's reconstruction portfolios for Labour ministers he prepared the way for electoral success. Eclipsed in public by such figures as BEVIN, Cripps, and BEVAN, in private Attlee was the man who made them a team. As he tired so they bickered, bequeathing Labour 13 years in opposition. **JP**.

ATWOOD, MARGARET
1939-
Canadian novelist and poet

The Circle Game, Atwood's first volume of poetry, was published in 1966, and her first novel, the comic Gothic *The Edible Woman* in 1969. Several volumes of poetry and a series of novels have followed. *Surfacing* (1972), which became a cult novel, owes much to her early years spent in Northern Ontario and Quebec, and like much of her fiction, deals with female self-discovery and emancipation. *Lady Oracle* (1976), *Life Before Man* (1979), and *Bodily Harm* (1981), were succeeded by the bleakly dystopian *The Handmaid's Tale* (1985). She has been writer-in-residence at several North American universities. **AM**.

AUCHINLECK, SIR CLAUDE, FIELD MARSHAL
1884-1981
British soldier

Joining the British-Indian Army in 1903, Auchinleck spent World War I in Egypt and Mesopotamia. Returning to India in 1918, he served on the North-West Frontier, where he gained a reputation for mountain fighting. In 1940 he commanded the British expedition to Norway before returning to India as Commander-in-Chief. In July 1941 he was appointed C-in-C Middle East and in November 1941 his forces relieved Tobruk, but then retreated before a renewed Axis onslaught. At Alamein in July 1942 Auchinleck fought a successful holding action, but was then relieved of his command. He returned to India. **JPi**.

ABOVE: *W H Auden (right) and Isherwood smile for the camera.*

AUDEN, W[YSTAN] H[UGH]
1907-1973
British poet

Born in Yorkshire, Auden first came to notice as an Oxford student. *Poems* (1930) was well received. In addition to further volumes of poetry, several of his plays were produced by Rupert Doone's Group Theatre. The poem 'Spain' (1937) commemorates his brief stint as an ambulance driver for the Republicans in the Spanish Civil War. In 1939 he left Britain for America with Christopher Isherwood, and later became a US citizen; there he met his lifelong companion Chester Kallman. Unpopular in Britain for a short time for his wartime 'desertion', his talents were eventually rewarded by the post of Professor of Poetry at Oxford in 1956, where he continued writing and editing anthologies. **AM**.

AUSTIN, HERBERT, 1ST BARON
1866-1941
British motor manufacturer

Austin began as a designer and racing driver for Wolseley before establishing his own company. The Austin Seven, which he produced in 1922, did for his company what the Model T Ford had done in America. The Seven was an important vehicle and was built under license in Germany by BMW. The Austin company merged with Morris to form the British Motor Corporation in 1952. **NF**.

AVEDON, RICHARD
1923-
American photographer

Like so many American photographers Avedon was a student of Alexey Brodovitch in New York. From 1945 he worked for *Harper's Bazaar*, before becoming a staff photographer for *Vogue* in 1966. Celebrated primarily for his hieratic portraits of American people, which can be seen most notably in *Portraits* (1976) and *In The American West* (1985). **IJ**.

AVERY, OSWALD
1877-1955
Canadian biologist

A physician by profession, he joined the Rockefeller Institute Hospital in 1913 when lobar pneumonia was being investigated. His work showed that the products of the pneumococcus bacterium found in human serum and urine were polysaccarides that were specific to each pneumococcoal type and thus demonstrated that bacteria could be identified biochemically. He began his most famous work in 1932 on the isolation and analysis of the factor that permanently transformed non-virulent pneumococci to disease-producing organisms in vitro. Avery's evidence, published in 1944, that this factor was deoxyribonucleic acid (DNA) was fundamentally important. He had identified the mediator of cellular inheritance and set the stage for the elaboration of its structure and function. **ES**.

AYCKBOURN, ALAN
1939-
British playwright

Ayckbourn is a writer of popular, almost farcical comedies of middle-class values and relations, with an edge to the humor. *Relatively Speaking* (1967) was his first major success, followed by many more, including *The Norman Conquests* (1974). Well-observed and impeccably crafted, his plays have become increasingly pessimistic. **AM**.

AYER, A[LFRED] J[ULES], SIR
1910-1989
British philosopher

One of the key figures in the development of British philosophy in the twentieth century, Ayer was advised by Gilbert Ryle to study in Vienna after he graduated from Oxford in 1932. There he was greatly influenced by the positivism of the 'Vienna Circle', led by CARNAP and Schlick, and on his return to Oxford he popularized their views in his best-known work, *Language, Truth and Logic* (1936). This is a highly rhetorical attack on a wide range of 'metaphysical' discourse, which he held to be 'literally meaningless' because incapable of direct verification. He tempered his views somewhat in a second edition in 1946, and developed them more reflectively in later works as he successively held the Grote Chair of Philosophy in London and the Wykeham Chair of Logic in Oxford. **EB**.

AYUB KHAN, MOHAMMED
1907-1974
Pakistani politician

President of Pakistan from 1958 to 1969, Ayub Khan was the first commander in chief of the Pakistan army after independence (1951-58). Ruling through martial law until 1962, he established a stable economy, but abolished civil liberties. His opposition to India over the Kashmir problem and his autocratic style of government led to his downfall in 1969. **JC**.

ABOVE: *Noted US photographer Richard Avedon.*

BAADE, WALTER
1893-1960
American astronomer

During World War II Baade used the Mount Wilson 100-inch (2.5-meter) telescope in California to discover that stars in the nearby Andromeda Galaxy fell into two age groups – older stars in the center and younger ones in the outskirts. Further observations with the Palomar 200-inch (5-meter) telescope after the war confirmed that these two populations were of different brightnesses. Previous estimates of the distance to the Andromeda Galaxy had been based on incorrect values of the brightness of its stars. Baade's revised figures showed that galaxies were twice as far away as previously supposed, thereby doubling the size (and age) of the known universe. **IR**.

BABEL, ISAAK
1894-1941
Russian writer

Babel is regarded by many as the most significant of all post-revolutionary Russian prose writers. Growing up in an Orthodox Jewish community in Odessa, his childhood figured semi-autobiographically in his stories, the first of which was published by GORKY in 1916. From 1917 Babel served as a soldier, first for the Tsar, and then as a member of the notorious and, paradoxically, anti-semitic, Cossack regiments. From this experience came his exceptional collection of stories *Red Cavalry* (1923-5), which depict the violence and passion of Cossack life. Denounced in the late 1920s, he was arrested in 1939 and died in prison. **CW**.

BACALL, LAUREN
1924-
American actress

Lauren Bacall made her screen debut with BOGART in *To Have And To Have Not* (1944) after director Howard HAWKS spotted her on the cover of *Harper's Bazaar* and signed her to a seven-year contract. The Bogart-Bacall chemistry was box-office magic; they were married in 1945 and made three movies subsequently – *The Big Sleep* (1946), *Dark Passage* (1947) and *Key Largo* (1948). Her finesse in comedy was showcased in *How To Marry A Millionaire* (1953) when she deftly stole scenes from Marilyn MONROE and Betty Grable. She became the toast of Broadway in *Cactus Flower* (1967) and *Applause* (1970), a musical adaptation of the movie *All About Eve*, in which she won a Tony Award. **DC**.

BACON, FRANCIS
1909-1992
Irish painter

Bacon first achieved renown in 1945, on ex-

ABOVE: Irish artist Francis Bacon.

hibiting his *Three Studies for Figures at the Base of a Crucifixion* (1944). Their twisted, animal-like bodies with human heads were a disturbing reminder, to a postwar audience, of human bestiality, and Bacon's work was continually to focus on the most repulsive and frightening aspects of mankind. His 1951 versions of Velázquez's dignified portrait of *Pope Innocent X* convert him into a screaming figure on the verge of madness, and the highly expressive style Bacon developed, blurring and contorting the flesh, exerts a horrid fascination which partly accounts for his popularity. He himself observed that nobody had ever bought one of his paintings because they liked it. **ER**.

BADOGLIO, PIETRO, MARSHAL
1871-1956
Italian soldier-politician

After widespread military service, Badoglio was Governor of Italian Libya (1928-33); he then commanded the invasion of Ethiopia (1935-36). Promoted to Chief of Staff, he resigned over Mussolini's invasion of Greece in 1940. Three years later, Badoglio negotiated Italy's surrender to the Allies, and served as Prime Minister until June 1944. **JPi**.

BAEKELAND, LEO HENDRIK
1863-1944
Belgian-born American chemist

In 1909, while looking for a substitute for shellac, Baekeland produced a resin-like substance which, under certain conditions of temperature and pressure, would flow into a mold and set hard. Once set, this substance could not be melted again. It was the first artificially produced thermosetting plastic and he named it bakelite. Its lightness, strength, durability and electrical resistance made it the basis of the earliest plastics industry. He also contributed to the development of photography by inventing the first photographic paper – which he named Velox – that could be developed in artificial light. **DD**.

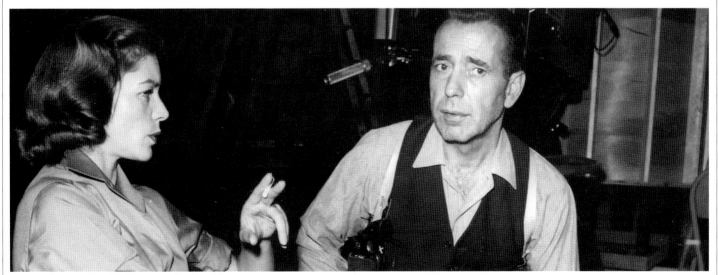

ABOVE: Lauren Bacall with co-star/husband Bogart.

ABOVE: *Singer-songwriter Joan Baez.*

BAEZ, JOAN
1941-
American folk singer

Baez spearheaded the resurgence of folk music in the USA during the late 1950s and early 1960s, after long neglect. Her pure, silvery soprano and simple treatment of traditional ballads made her first solo albums, on which she accompanied herself on guitar, among the first major successes of the folk boom. She made the Pete SEEGER song 'We Shall Overcome' the anthem of the Civil Rights and anti-Vietnam movements, in which she was closely involved. She had a long-running but spasmodic professional and personal relationship with Bob DYLAN. **JH**.

BAILEY, DAVID
1938-
British photographer

Britain's most charismatic fashion photographer joined the staff of British *Vogue* in 1960, and went on to help establish the shape and look of that decade. He associated fashion with some of Britain's more vivid sub-cultures, and helped publicize some of the energy of those cultures. **IJ**.

BAIRD, JOHN LOGIE
1888-1946
British electronic engineer

A graduate of Glasgow university, after war service Baird tried to attract commercial backing for his experiments using radio waves to transmit pictures. In 1924 he transmitted the silhouette of a Maltese cross and in 1926 Baird repeated his 'seeing by wireless' demonstration of television to members of the Royal Institution. The pictures were of poor quality, and Baird's mechanical system was beaten by EMI's electronic system for the BBC contract in 1937. **PT**.

BAKER, JOSEPHINE
1906-1975
American-born dancer and singer

Baker had her main success in Europe after appearing in Paris in 1925 with the show *La Revue Nègre*. She was famed for her lissom legs, exotic looks and skill as a comedienne, plus her risqué costumes. She was awarded the rare Medaille de la Résistance by President de GAULLE for her work during World War II. **JH**.

BALANCHINE, GEORGE [GEORGI BALANCHIVADZE]
1904-1983
Russian dancer, choreographer, and ballet master

Arguably one of the most prolific and influential choreographers of the twentieth century, Balanchine was associated principally with the New York City Ballet, where he was Artistic Director from 1934. He was also ballet master of DIAGHILEV's Ballets Russes (1924-29), the Ballets Russes de Monte Carlo (1944-45) and created works for many ballet companies around the world. He devised dances for operas, Broadway musicals, films, and television.

For more than 50 years he collaborated with Igor STRAVINSKY and produced some 26 works, among these some of his undoubted masterpieces: *Apollo, Orpheus, Firebird, Agon, Violin Concerto*. Taking classical technique as his base, Balanchine went on to extend and 'distort' it resulting in a greater dynamism of movement, often at the expense of traditional 'correctness'. He has been criticized by many (including some of his dancers) for producing mechanical, soulless, and gymnastic ballets. Often plotless, with little decor and few costumes, Balanchine's ballets are an expression of his individual artistic beliefs in the primacy of dance. **MC**.

ABOVE: *The Scottish inventor John Logie Baird.*

BALDWIN, STANLEY, 1ST EARL OF BEWDLEY
1867-1947
British politician and statesman

The first manufacturer to make it to 10 Downing Street, Baldwin constructed his domination of interwar politics out of an unexciting but reassuring combination of honesty, commonsense, and affability. These proved attractive qualities to an electorate uneasy about the mercurial talents of LLOYD GEORGE and unsure about the ultimate intentions of the rapidly growing Labour Party. To Baldwin, then, fell a leading role in easing the traumas of the General Strike of 1926, abandonment of the Gold Standard in 1931, and the Abdication Crisis of 1936. Unfortunately he did not demonstrate the same sureness of touch in international affairs and his passive approach to the dictators has cast something of a shadow over his reputation. **JP**.

ABOVE: *British Prime Minister Arthur Balfour.*

BALFOUR, ARTHUR, 1ST EARL
1848-1930
British politician and statesman

The century saw two distinct and contrasting phases to Balfour's political career. The first, between 1902 and 1911, saw him unhappily cast, both in government and opposition, as leader of the Conservative Party. Although a gifted administrator, Balfour found it hard either to manage his parliamentary supporters or to understand the ordinary person. Divisive and unpopular stands followed over tariff reform, the People's Budget and the House of Lords. With the outbreak of war in 1914, however, Balfour's sharp intellect and great personal charm was more successfully applied to imperial and international affairs. The 1917 declaration on Palestine and 1926 report on Dominion status that bear his name testify to the strength of his influence in these fields. **JP**.

BALL, LUCILLE
1911-1989
American comedienne

Ball left New York at 15 to be a bit player in Hollywood, including a stint as a Goldwyn Girl. She was first noticed in *Follow the Fleet* (1937) with Ginger ROGERS and Fred ASTAIRE. After switching to television in 1951 for *I Love Lucy* she established herself as America's favorite comedienne for many years. **DC**.

BANDARANAIKE, SIRIMAVO RATWATTE DIAS
1916-
Sri Lankan politician

The world's first woman Prime Minister, serving two terms, from 1960 to 1965 and from 1970 to 1977, she succeeded her husband, S W R D Bandaranaike after his assassination in 1959. Completely inexperienced in politics, as President of the Sri Lankan Freedom Party, she nevertheless carried on her husband's socialist and nationalist policies. Returned to power in 1970, she established the Republic of Sri Lanka, but her inability to resolve ethnic tensions led to a massive defeat in the 1977 elections. **JC**.

ABOVE: Film and TV comedienne Lucille Ball.

RIGHT: Roger Bannister, the first sub-four-minute miler.

ABOVE: Sri Lankan Premier Bandaranaike.

BANNISTER, SIR ROGER
1929-
British track athlete

Roger Bannister was the first man to run a mile in less than four minutes. The four-minute barrier had been a great target for athletes for years until Bannister's run of 3 min 59.4 sec at Oxford on 6 May 1954. He was assisted by two other leading British athletes, pacemakers Chris Chataway and Chris Brasher. Bannister is now a distinguished neurologist and university administrator. **DS**.

BANTING, SIR FREDERICK
1891-1941
Canadian surgeon

Banting began the experiments with J J R Macleod and C H Best which led to the discovery of insulin (1922) for which they shared the Nobel Prize. Banting's achievement ended 30 years of failed attempts to extract the supposed pancreatic hormone. Embarassed by public adulation, Banting subsequently turned to wide-ranging research problems, including silicosis and, at the time of his death in a flying accident, aviation medicine. **GL**.

ABOVE: Dr Banting, co-discoverer of insulin.

BARBER, SAMUEL
1910-81
American composer

Despite the prospect of a successful career as a singer, the predominantly romantic side of Barber's character steered him towards concentrating on composition. This path proved to be extremely fruitful and resulted in many prestigious awards. Barber rose quickly to popularity: unlike most twentieth-century composers, his music is almost immediately accessible. Many composers found that their efforts to explore new ideas in tonality and form served only to estrange them from their listeners, but this was never the case with Barber. He worked with familiar tools and wrote in familiar forms to create his own intensely romantic style. **DK**.

BARDOT, BRIGITTE
1934-
French actress

Spotted by Roger VADIM on the cover of *Elle* magazine in 1950, Bardot acted in a series of supporting roles before her first starring role in Vadim's *And God Created Woman* (1956) brought her international recognition. She won critical acclaim for *The Truth* (1961). Her career has dimmed in recent years as she lends her time to a variety of worthy causes. **DC**.

ABOVE: Pioneer heart surgeon Christiaan Barnard (left).

BARNARD, CHRISTIAAN
1922-
South African surgeon

As a student, Christiaan Barnard was a well-liked man, but not an academic or surgical star. Trained at Cape Town University, he went to Minneapolis in the 1940s to train under Walter Lillehei, the foremost American heart surgeon. After his return to South Africa, Barnard was experimenting on transplanting hearts into dogs, who reject transplanted tissues less readily than humans, when another American surgeon, Walter Shumway, announced his intention of transplanting a human heart. Barnard had already established the necessary surgical principles, including keeping the patient's tissues supplied with oxygen during the period when the old heart had been removed and before the new heart was plumbed in. On hearing Shumway's announcement, he performed the first human heart transplant on 3 December 1967. That patient died after a few days, but his second patient lived for nearly two years. Barnard performed other transplants, but international fame and rheumatoid arthritis have combined to alter his career to that of medical guru and jetsetting playboy, and nowadays he is noted for his enthusiasm for controversial 'rejuvenating' injections. **CR**.

ABOVE: French film star Brigitte Bardot.

BARRYMORE, LIONEL
1878-1954
American actor

From the early 1930s Barrymore was a famous and well-beloved member of the MGM stock company, often playing churlish millionaires and sentimental grandfather figures in films such as *Rasputin and the Empress* (1932) and *David Copperfield* (1934). From 1938 until the end of his career, terrible arthritis and a couple of falls forced him to do all his performing in a wheelchair, and he began to concentrate on directing. He won an Academy Award for *A Free Soul* (1931), but is today best remembered for playing Dr Gillespie, the kindly yet stern mentor of the callow Kildare, in the Doctor Kildare films. **DC**.

BARTH, KARL
1886-1968
Swiss theologian

One of the most radical Protestant theologians of the century, Barth's condemnation of the Nazi regime as manifest in the Barmen declaration of 1934 ended a glittering theological career in German universities. His reputation had been made long before through his theocentric *The Epistle to the Romans* (1919), although his Church Dogmatics provide perhaps the best appraisal of his theology which emphasizes the discontinuity between man and God. A practically minded Christian Socialist rather than an aloof academic, Barth maintained a lifelong campaign for social justice opposing the nuclear and conventional arms race. **ML**.

BARTÓK, BÉLA
1881-1945
Hungarian composer

Although Bartók's music is highly original in style, he by no means cut himself off from the influences of the world around him. Inspiration came from many sources, most notably studying national folk music with KODÁLY. He even used notated bird and insect sounds as a basis for his so-called 'night music' passages. However perhaps his most interesting ideas stem from his study of form and its relationship with symmetry and mathematical relationships such as the 'golden section.' His music ranges from highly rhythmically charged passages compressed with chromatically displaced melodic phrases to passages of the most mysteriously mesmerizing quality, leaving one almost spellbound.

Like many composers advocating a new approach to composition Bartók had an upward struggle to be recognized. Sadly his struggle was made even worse due to the political climate in Hungary at that time, especially when his only ballet *The Miraculous Mandarin* was banned and labeled 'expressionistic,' 'too erotic,' and 'too violent.' The beauty of Bartók is that while some of

his works remain a challenge for even the most learned musicians, his music is not elitist. His *Mikrokosmos* has been hailed as the first major set of didactic piano pieces since J S Bach. **DK**.

BARUCH, BERNARD
1870-1965
American financier and public servant

As a young broker, Baruch also speculated on his own behalf and was a rich man by the age of thirty. Taken into government service in World War I he swiftly rose to become director of the War Industries Board, making him virtual controller of the US economy. He continued to advise the government on economic matters, and in World War II addressed the problems of mobilization. The 1946 Baruch Plan for limiting the danger of nuclear war was frustrated by Soviet opposition. Unlike so many others whose wealth brought political influence, his advice was good and his actions well thought-out. **JW**.

BARYSHNIKOV, MIKHAIL
1948-
Latvian-American dancer and actor

Born in Riga, Baryshnikov studied in St Petersburg and joined the Kirov Ballet as a

ABOVE: Hungarian composer Béla Bartók.

soloist in 1960. While on tour as a guest artist with a group from the Bolshoi in Canada in 1974, Baryshnikov decided to stay in the West, so that he could extend his repertoire to include modern ballets. An incredible virtuoso performer, he joined American Ballet Theater dancing often with ballerina Gelsey Kirkland, and appeared as guest artist with the Paris Opera Ballet. In addition to making his choreographic debut in 1976 with his version of the *Nutcracker*, Baryshnikov has also ventured into acting with roles in *The Turning Point* and *White Nights*. **MC**.

BASIE, COUNT [WILLIAM]
1904-1984
American jazz pianist and composer

It was in the Reno Club in Kansas that Basie was spotted by critic John Hammond and brought to New York and overnight success, recording with an expanded outfit which included the great tenor sax player Lester Young. A gentle and unassuming man, his initial robust style, influenced by Fats WALLER, soon gave way to increasingly sparse and laconic contributions which became his trademark. Although over the years his musicians came and went, he maintained a top-class line up of soloists, producing records of a superb and consistent quality. **DC**.

BAWDEN, SIR FREDERICK
1908-1972
British biologist

Graduating from Cambridge (1928) Bawden joined the Rothamsted Experimental Station in 1936, becoming Director in 1958. His demonstration with N W Pirie (1936) that tobacco mosaic and other viruses were nucleoproteins was a fundamental contribution to molecular biology. Bawden became an international figure in agricultural research. **GL**.

ABOVE: The Beatles. From left to right: Harrison, Starr, Lennon and McCartney.

THE BEACH BOYS
WILSON, BRIAN
1942-
WILSON, CARL
1946-
WILSON, DENNIS
1944-83
JARDINE, ALAN
1941-
LOVE, MIKE
1941-
MARKS, DAVID
1948-
JOHNSTON, BRUCE
1942-
American pop group

One of the most influential American bands ever, their 1963 album *Surfin' USA* launched the Beach Boys on the road to success, although ironically only one of the band, Dennis Wilson, surfed. By the third album they had switched focus from surfing to cars and hot rods, other key elements in the emerging teen culture. Brian Wilson, producer and writer of most of their material, retired from touring after a nervous breakdown, but was back with the single 'Barbara Ann' and the 1966 hit 'Good Vibrations', their most successful. However in 1967 he abandoned work on a new album after hearing the BEATLES' *Sergeant Pepper*, and their popularity declined. An unsuccessful comeback attempt in the mid-1970s was followed by two solo albums from Brian Wilson which earned moderate success, but their output has been patchy ever since. **DC.**

BEADLE, GEORGE WELLS
1905-1989
American geneticist

Beadle's early enthusiasm for genetics led to a doctorate at Cornell University on the genetics of maize. He later investigated eye color in the fruit fly *Drosophilia*. In the 1940s he worked with TATUM on gene function, and their work formed the basis of biochemical genetics. He received the Nobel prize for Medicine in 1958. **EMS**.

THE BEATLES
LENNON, JOHN
1940-80
McCARTNEY, PAUL
1942-
HARRISON, GEORGE
1943-
STARR, RINGO
1940-
British pop group

The biggest single influence on sixties rock and pop, the Beatles, led by the songwriting team of Lennon and McCartney, served their apprenticeship in clubs in Hamburg after local success in their native Liverpool. There they developed their own songwriting style distilled largely from cover versions of numbers by artists such as Buddy HOLLY and Chuck BERRY. Their chart breakthrough came with the single 'Love Me Do' in 1962, followed by 'Please Please Me', the first of many # 1s, early in 1963, the year 'Beatlemania' was born. They were the first UK group to break the US stranglehold on writing original material, leading the way for other groups in Britain. Through continued recording as well as work on films such as *Help!* and *Yellow Submarine* they continued to be the prime innovators of the decade. Playing a lead role in flower power and psychedelia, they made pioneering use of the modern recording studio, inspired by producer George Martin, on the 1967 album *Sergeant Pepper's Lonely Hearts Club Band*. After this album, however, they pursued increasingly separate interests, and their break-up in 1970 was surrounded by financial wrangles. After the split they each went on to individual success, although constant speculation as to a possible reunion was only quashed by Lennon's tragic death in 1980. **DC.**

BEATTY, WARREN
1937-
American actor

One of Hollywood's more complex talents, Beatty is an innovative director and producer, and a more than competent actor. He first broke into movies opposite Natalie Wood in *Splendor in the Grass* (1961); a series of less than memorable films followed until he produced and starred in *Bonnie and Clyde* (1967) with Faye DUNAWAY, a movie that introduced a new level of violence to the screen. *McCabe and Mrs Miller* (1971), with Julie CHRISTIE, got some notice, as did *Shampoo* (1975), although it was labeled as sexist, which Beatty denied. Even more popular was the delightful comedy *Heaven Can Wait* (1978), which was nominated for an Academy Award as best picture. He at last won an award as Best Director for *Reds* in 1982, and *Dick Tracy* (1990) was an elaborate production, every detail of which Beatty personally oversaw. **DC.**.

DE BEAUVOIR, SIMONE
1908-1986
French novelist and journalist

In 1929, while studying philosophy at the Sorbonne, de Beauvoir met Jean-Paul SARTRE. Together they became the foremost exponents of existentialism, later founding the review *Les Temps Modernes*

(1945). These years, and her relationship with Sartre, are documented in her auto-biographical trilogy. Her first novel, *L'Invitée*, was published in 1943, and she was awarded the Prix Goncourt for *Les Mandarins* (1954). De Beauvoir's *Le Deuxième sexe* (1949) is a powerful and important feminist treatise, in which she argues that marriage and motherhood are feminine submissions to male domination. **CH-M**.

BECKENBAUER, FRANZ
1945-
German soccer player and coach

Franz Beckenbauer was West Germany's leading soccer player in the late 1960s and for much of the 1970s. He won numerous domestic trophies during his long career with the Bayern Munich club and played in three European Cup winning sides. As an international he captained the West German team to the European Championship in 1972 and the World Cup in 1974. He completed his playing career with New York Cosmos. He retired from playing in 1977. He became coach of the West German national team in 1984 and led them to World Cup victory in 1990. **DS**.

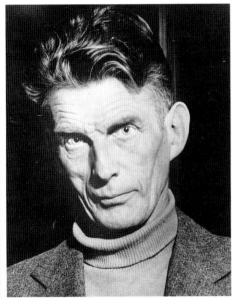

ABOVE: *Irish novelist and playwright Samuel Beckett.*

BECKETT, SAMUEL
1906-1989
Irish writer

Irish-born Beckett first visited Paris in 1929 and finally settled there in 1933, befriending James JOYCE. During World War II Beckett joined the Resistance, and was forced to flee to Free France in 1942. The period after the war saw him write prolifically. The trilogy *Molloy* (1951), *Malone meurt* (1952) and *L'Innommable* (1953) was outshone by his best-known work: *En attendant Godot* (1952). This play demonstrates his existential beliefs and his disillusionment with the human condition. He was awarded the Nobel Prize for Literature in 1969. **CH-M**.

ABOVE: *French novelist Simone de Beauvoir.*

BECKMANN, MAX
1884-1950
German painter

Beckmann's experiences as a hospital orderly during World War I led him to abandon his earlier conservative impressionism. Using angular shapes, influenced by Gothic art, he recorded the moral decay and disorientation he saw in modern society. After his work was included in the Nazi 'Degenerate Art Exhibition' of 1937, he emigrated to the Netherlands and in 1947 to the USA. **ER**.

BECQUEREL, ANTOINE HENRI
1852-1908
French physicist

Becquerel was born into a family of physicists, and became Professor of Physics in Paris in 1895. His famous discovery was an accidental one – that a salt of uranium would produce discoloration on a photographic plate that was still wrapped. For his work on radiation that followed, he shared the 1903 Nobel Prize for Physics with the CURIES. He was first to recognize that radiation had an effect on living tissues when he found that radium in his pocket burned him. The SI unit of radioactivity is named after him. **DD**.

BEEBE, CHARLES WILLIAM
1877-1962
American naturalist and explorer

Beebe had an early interest in natural history, and was curator of the ornithological collection of the New York Zoological Society at the age of 22. His later books on the subject, such as *Galapagos* (1923), were great popular as well as scientific successes. Perhaps his most famous adventure as an explorer was the trip he made in a bathysphere down to a depth of 1000m in 1934. **RJ**.

BEECHAM, SIR THOMAS
1879-1961
British conductor

Born in Lancashire, the son of pharmaceutical tycoon Sir Joseph Beecham, 'Tommy' Beecham decided against a career in his father's firm and went on to become one of the most celebrated conductors of the age. A largely self-taught musician, he created and directed a number of orchestras during his lifetime, most notably the London Philharmonic and Royal Philharmonic. A roguish figure with a sharp wit, Beecham inspired numerous anecdotes, but his musical prowess should never be underestimated: a champion of Mozart, Delius, Strauss, and SIBELIUS, his legacy is still very much apparent in the field of symphonic performance today. **DK**.

BEGIN, MENACHEM
1913-1992
Israeli politician

Begin took the Likud Party to victory in 1977 after 30 years in the political wilderness and promptly signed a peace treaty with Egyptian leader Anwar SADAT giving back Sinai. The Nobel Peace Prize resulted. His invasion of Lebanon in 1982, planned to last 72 hours, lasted three years and forced his resignation. **JC**.

ABOVE: *Israeli leader Menachem Begin (left) with Carter and Sadat.*

BEHAN, BRENDAN
1923-1964
Irish dramatist

Brendan Behan was born in Dublin. After his arrest in 1939 for involvement with the IRA, he turned his experience of detention into his first play *Borstal Boy* (1958). His most famous plays, *The Hostage* (1958) and *The Quare Fellow* (1959), deal with aspects of the Anglo-Irish conflict, often to tragi-comic effect. **CW**.

BEHRENS, PETER
1868-1940
German architect, designer, and industrialist

Behrens was an important catalyst in the development of Modernist architecture and industrial design, although he began his career as a painter in an Art Nouveau style. In Darmstadt (1901) he designed his own house and fittings in a MACKINTOSH-influenced style. Behrens was employed from 1907 by the great electrical combine AEG in Berlin to design everything from electrical equipment to catalogues, shops and factories. AEG promoted products which were not only functionally efficient but also creatively and sensitively designed, projecting the brand image of an industrial power and making Behrens one of the first industrial designers. His AEG Berlin turbine factory (1908) was the first steel-and-glass building in Germany, although most Behrens buildings are simplified classical in style. **AR**.

BÉJART [BERGER], MAURICE
1927-
French dancer and choreographer

The son of philosopher Gaston Berger, Béjart made his debut in Vichy in 1945 and danced with various classical and modern European companies. With the critic Jean Laurent, he founded the Ballet de l'Etoile in 1954, and with Henriques Pimental in 1957 the Ballet Théâtre de Maurice Béjart, which soon became one of the finest troupes performing original works. Following the success of his *Sacré du Printemps* in 1959, Béjart was commissioned by the director of the Théâtre Royal de la Monnai in Brussels. Béjart's company was dissolved and reformed as the Ballet of the 20th Century, which he used for his somewhat eclectic explorations of dance. He presented pure dance, total spectacles with lyrics, dramatic pieces, and ballets set to orchestral masterpieces. On the one hand receiving acclaim and the 1966 Prix de la Fraternité from the anti-racist and pro-peace movement for *Romeo and Juliet*, Béjart also managed to scandalize with works such as *Erotic*. Often critics were scathing in their attacks, but nevertheless public enthusiasm for Béjart and his company remains enormous. **MC**.

BELL BURNELL, JOCELYN
1943-
British radioastronomer

Discoverer with Anthony Hewish of pulsars, for which they were awarded the Michelson Medal from the Franklin Institute (1976), Jocelyn has held research posts at Southampton University, UCL, and SSO. Since 1989 she has been based at the Royal Observatory, Edinburgh. **MB**.

BELL, DANIEL
1919-
American sociologist

Bell is a leading conservative sociologist and futurologist largely famous for his account of the transformation from industrial society to a post-industrial society in which information and expertise rather than manufacturing are now crucial. Bell also attacked modernist culture through the concepts of 'the end of ideology' and 'the cultural contradictions of capitalism,' claiming that the work ethic which created industrial society has now given way to a culture of pleasure which is destabilizing it. **DSL**.

BELMONDO, JEAN-PAUL
1933-
French actor

Sexy, charming, and appealingly homely, this French leading man began with supporting roles until he rocketed to fame in *Breathless* (1959), soon symbolizing the 'New Wave' antihero and young rebel to international audiences. Belmondo has since worked with many famous French movie directors, including Jean-Luc GODARD, François TRUFFAUT and Louis MALLE. **DC**.

BELOW: Ben-Gurion, Israel's founding father.

BENEŠ, EDVARD
1884-1948
Czechoslovak statesman

Co-founder with Tomáš MASARYK, of Czechoslovakia in 1918, Beneš served as Minister for Foreign Affairs (1919-35) before succeeding Masaryk as President. He resigned the presidency in 1938 in protest against the Munich Agreement which led to loss of the Sudetenland to Germany, but was leader of the Czech government in exile during World War II and returned to the presidency after the defeat of Nazi Germany until his death. **JC**.

BEN-GURION, DAVID
1886-1973
Israeli statesman

WEIZMANN's executive in the creation of Israel, Ben-Gurion established the Haganah Defense Force and the Histadruth, the Labor Federation, under the British Mandate, and provided the means and the will for national survival against the odds in two wars, in 1948 and 1956. As Israel's first Prime Minister he read the country's Declaration of Independence and was President until 1963. **JC**.

BENNETT, ALAN
1934-
British playwright and actor

Bennett first attracted attention as a student with *Beyond the Fringe* (1960), the satirical revue. His plays range from political comedy in *Forty Years On*, and farce in *Habeas Corpus*, to more serious dramas based on the modern British traitors BURGESS, Maclean and Blunt; he has increasingly written for television, including the brilliant series of monologues *Talking Heads*. **AM**.

BENNY, JACK
1894-1974
American comedian

Benny's inimitable reproachful look, his pretense of stinginess, and his much-maligned violin playing were trademarks which kept this comedian popular for forty years. Although films were possibly his least successful medium, he scored a comedy triumph in *Charley's Aunt* (1941) and his performance in *To Be or Not To Be* (1942) was touchingly funny. **DC**.

BENTON, THOMAS HART
1889-1975
American painter

Born in Neosho, Missouri, Benton worked as a cartoonist before studying at the Art Institute of Chicago and traveling to Paris. His abstract paintings failed to find success and around 1920 he abandoned Modernism. Spokesman for the Regionalists, who included WOOD, he is best known for his energetic murals satirising urban life and celebrating rural and small-town America. **ER**.

BENZ, KARL
1844-1929
German Motor manufacturer

Benz produced a three-wheeled gasoline-powered vehicle in 1886, often claimed to be the first 'car', and in 1894, the Velo, said to be the world's first series production car. Benz was not a great motorsports enthusiast, yet ironically he built the Blitzen Benz which won many races and in 1909 took the World Land Speed record at 141.7mph. During World War I Benz factories built military vehicles and aero-engines. A merger with Daimler produced the Daimler-Benz company in July 1926. **NF**.

BERG, ALBAN
1885-1935
Hungarian composer

Berg is perhaps the most approachable of all the atonal and serialist composers. He chose to follow in the footsteps of his teacher SCHOENBERG by abandoning the traditional use of key relationships; yet he was less rigid in his use of the twelve-note system, allowing a freer, more romantic element to enter his work. By adapting the principles of the twelve-note system rather than taking them to their extremes, Berg introduced an intrinsic quality into his work which helped realize his sense of drama. Many feel that this is the reason why his works are more popular than those of his contemporaries. **DK**.

BERG, PAUL
1926-
American biologist

Best known for the method he perfected of using bacteria to produce the first recombinant DNA molecules, Berg's technique allowed the use of bacteria to manufacture proteins of medical importance such as human insulin. Aware of the potential dangers of such research, if uncontrolled, he became a well-known campaigner for restrictive guidelines on genetic engineering experiments, which were published in 1976. **ES**.

BERGIUS, FRIEDRICH KARL RUDOLPH
1884-1949
German chemist

Bergius worked in industry for a period spanning both World Wars and developed the process for converting coal into oil by treating it with hydrogen under high pressure. Petrol thus produced was widely used in Germany during World War II. He received the Nobel Prize for Chemistry in 1931. He also developed a technique for converting wood into sugar. **DD**.

BERGMAN, INGMAR
1918-
Swedish film director

Bergman established his international reputation during the 1950s with a trio of masterly works, *Smiles of a Summer Night* (1955), *The Seventh Seal* (1956), and *Wild Strawberries* (1957). A grim trilogy on the themes of religious doubt and psychological torment, *Through a Glass Darkly* (1960), *Winter Light* (1962), and *The Silence* (1963) gave him a reputation as the starkest purveyor of Scandinavian gloom since August Strindberg, and he achieved his zenith of creativity at this time with *Persona* (1966). His career faltered in the following decade, but he made a remarkable comeback with *Fanny and Alexander* (1982). **NS**.

ABOVE: *Hungarian composer Alban Berg.*

BERGMAN, INGRID
1915-1982
Swedish-born American actress

Bergman had a natural beauty and a warm smile that allowed her to outshine all of Hollywood's female stars. Born in Stockholm, she was a well-known screen actress in Sweden before David O. SELZNICK brought her to Hollywood for the 1939 US version of the Swedish film *Intermezzo*. She became a star overnight. *Casablanca* (1942), in which she starred with BOGART, further enhanced her reputation. In 1946 she won a Tony Award for her Broadway interpretation of Joan of Arc in Maxwell Anderson's *Joan of Lorraine* two years before she starred in the film version. Her wholesome image was tarnished, however, in 1950, when she left her husband to live with Roberto ROSSELLINI, her director in *Stromboli* (1950), and bore him a son and a daughter, the actress Isabella Rossellini. The American public did not forgive her, and it was not until her Academy Award for *Anastasia* (1956) that she was welcomed back to the fold. **DC**.

BERGSON, HENRI
1859-1941
French philosopher and diplomat

Reacting against contemporary scientific accounts of time, Bergson developed his own conception of experienced duration as a continuous flux of 'becoming'. Only appearance was static; the true reality was dynamic, infused with a 'vital force', and not subject to the deterministic outlook of science. Married to a cousin of Proust, Bergson became a cult figure, and in 1928 was awarded the Nobel Prize for Literature. After diplomatic work during World War I, he became a member of the League of Nations and, although not a practising Jew, declined the offer of the Vichy government to exempt him from their discriminatory laws. **EB**.

BERIA, LAVRENTI
1899-1953
Russian police chief

Rapidly promoted by STALIN as 'the promising fellow Georgian,' Beria became, for Russians but later for the peoples of Eastern Europe, the arch-demon in the Kremlin. He organized the vast slave labor system of the Gulags and ensured the subservience of satellite states by the application of state terror. Throughout World War II he was Stalin's deputy but on the latter's death in 1953 he was charged with espionage by his rivals for power and summarily shot. **JC**.

BERIO, LUCIANO
1925-
Italian composer

Although Berio is totally devoted to serialism, he uses techniques in both his compositions and in the performance of his works which are more akin to the so-called 'avant-garde' school of musicians. A good example is his *Circles* where the singer merges and separates from the instrumentalists as she moves around the stage. **DK**.

BERKELEY, BUSBY
1895-1976
American choreographer and director

Busby Berkeley was Hollywood's top choreographer during the 1930s and 1940s. He dazzled cinema audiences with lavish extravaganzas of mass choreography, employing dozens of dancers in a spectacular array of kaleidoscopic movements in films such as *42nd Street* (1933) and *Gold Diggers of 1935*. An inventive cameraman who used daring shots and impeccable cutting techniques, he went on to direct his own films. **NS**.

ABOVE: *Hollywood choreographer Busby Berkeley.*

BERLIN, ISAIAH, SIR
1909-
British philosopher and political theorist

A leading figure of 'Oxford philosophy' and of British artistic life, Berlin stressed the historical dimension of philosophical analysis in contrast to the formality of logical positivism. He wrote studies of key figures in the development of Western thought towards artistic and political liberalism, and in *Two Concepts of Liberty*, argued against doctrines which, by 'forcing men to be free', actually enslave them. He was the first Jewish Fellow of All Souls, and the founding President of Wolfson College Oxford. **EB**.

BERLUSCONI, SILVIO
1936-
Italian media magnate

Berlusconi started out as a building contractor but in 1976 began to diversify into newspapers and later became the publisher of *Il Giornale*. In 1978, during the chaos caused by the deregulation of Italian broadcasting, he set up a television station in Milan and in 1980 took over two television channels in Italy. He bought a 25 percent holding in the French television station, La Cinq, which folded in 1992. **DSL**.

BERNSTEIN, CARL
1944-
American journalist

From working as a copyboy on *The Washington Star*, Bernstein eventually joined *The Washington Post* in 1966. He became famous for breaking the story behind the Watergate burglary with Bob WOODWARD with whom he co-wrote *All the President's Men* and *The Final Days*. Since then he has worked as an ABC news correspondent (1981-84). **DSL**.

BERNSTEIN, LEONARD
1918-90
American conductor and composer

Bernstein's greatest asset lies in his sheer versatility. It is quite remarkable how this much-loved figure is remembered in so many different guises, for not only is he regarded as an exceptionally gifted conductor, he is also much admired and equally respected as a composer, pianist, and author. This versatility continued to spread throughout his compositions producing such diverse works as *West Side Story* and *Chichester Psalms*. Aside from academic talents, he radiated a special warmth to listener and fellow musician alike. This rapport blossomed in his relationship with the New York Philharmonic which he conducted from 1959 until his death.

BERRY, CHUCK
1926-
US rock singer and guitarist

A huge influence on sixties rock, Berry was the pioneer of the essential riff-based rock guitar style. He took rhythm'n'blues and adapted it to the teenage consumer culture of the fifties with juke-box hits such as 'Johnny B. Goode' and 'Roll Over Beethoven'. Trouble with the law dogged his private life, however, and a slack period in the early sixties was followed only briefly by renewed interest in his songs after cover versions by rising artists such as the BEATLES and the ROLLING STONES, since when little has been heard of him. **DC**.

BERTONE, GIUSEPPE
1922-
Italian coachbuilder

The first Bertone-bodied vehicle was the Spa 9000 in 1921 but it was not until Guiseppe took over from his father and designed the Alfa Romeo Guilietta Sprint in 1954, that the styling house was firmly established. The sensational Lamborghini Muira in 1966 fully stamped Bertone's reputation as one of the century's most influential designers. **NF**.

BELOW: *Leonard Bernstein, composer and conductor.*

LEFT: One of the legends of rock 'n' roll, Chuck Berry, in action.

about the emotional needs of children. In his later life he wrote a cogent criticism of the English translation of FREUD's work, and of what he saw as the mechanistic approach of modern analysis. **MBe**.

BEUYS, JOSEPH
1921-1986
German artist

Born at Kleve, Beuys studied at Düsseldorf Academy and served as a Luftwaffe pilot during World War II. Shot down over the Crimea, he was rescued by the local Tartars, who kept him warm using felt and fat which, with iron and copper, became key symbols in the personal mythology he created, one of the central themes of his art being the generation and understanding of energy. In 1961 he was appointed Professor of Sculpture at Dusseldorf Academy, which enabled him to disseminate his ideas widely before his dismissal in 1971. As the leader in West Germany of the worldwide Anti-Form movement, he rejected the concept of art as an object for aesthetic contemplation and with a commercial value, emphasizing the creative process rather than its end product. Deeply influencing Performance Art in the 1970s, his famous 'Actions' included *How to Explain Pictures to a Hare*, (1965), in which he covered his face with honey and gold leaf, and *Coyote*, (1974), a week spent locked up and in 'dialogue' with a live coyote. He saw speech as a form of invisible sculpture and staged political debates or 'social sculptures', in which he attempted to revolutionize people's thought and mobilize their creativity in order to transform society. **ER**.

BEVAN, ANEURIN
1897-1960
British politician

A powerful political outsider from Wales, Bevan's contrasting commitment to principle ensured that the creation of the National Health Service was his only great governmental achievement. Role model for the left, Bevan's legacy to the Labour Party was the ideological conflict that kept it out of power from 1951 to 1964. **JP**.

BEVERIDGE, WILLIAM, 1ST BARON BEVERIDGE OF TUGGAL
1879-1963
British economist and social reformer

Beveridge established a national system of labor exchanges before World War I and forged the London School of Economics' preeminence in social science during the interwar years. His greatest achievement was his 1942 Report on Social Insurance which provided the blueprint for, and created the consensus behind, Britain's postwar welfare state. **JP**.

BETHE, HANS ALBRECHT
1906-
American physicist

Bethe left a teaching post in his native Germany for Britain with the rise of Hitler in 1933 and worked at the Universities of Manchester and Bristol, before moving to the USA in 1935 where he became Professor of Theoretical Physics at Cornell University. On the outbreak of World War II he was appointed head of the theoretical division of the Manhattan Project that designed the atomic bomb. Thereafter he became a notable peace campaigner. His work on the energy generated in stars – fusion energy – gained him the Nobel Prize for Physics in 1976. **DD**.

BETTELHEIM, BRUNO
1903-1990
German psychoanalyst

Bruno Bettelheim used both his appalling experiences in Dachau and Buchenwald, and his psychoanalytical training in his work with severely disturbed children in Chicago. He set up the Orthogenic School to try to reach out to children with whom other people could not communicate. An effective communicator himself, he wrote eloquently about his own experiences, and also

ABOVE: British Labour politician Ernest Bevin.

BEVIN, ERNEST
1881-1951
British trade union leader and statesman

Originally a farm laborer, Bevin was transformed by trade-union work into an international statesman. Rising through the ranks he created the massive Transport and General Workers Union in 1921. Essential to industrial mobilization, when war came he was made Minister of Labour in 1940. With Labour's election victory in 1945, Bevin became Foreign Secretary; his greatest triumph was to help commit American economic aid to Western Europe. **JP**.

BHUTTO, BENAZIR
1953-
Pakistani politician

The first Muslim woman to lead her country, Bhutto came straight from Oxford University to head her father, Zulfikar Ali Bhutto's party after he was hanged by the military junta in 1979. Emerging from several years in jail, she campaigned vigorously for a return to democracy and, after dictator ZIA ul-Haq's death in an air crash, she won the 1988 election. Accused of tolerating corruption, however, she lost her leadership in 1990. **JC**.

BELOW: Pakistani politician Benazir Bhutto.

BIKILA, ABEBE
1932-1973
Ethiopian marathon runner

Abebe Bikila holds the unique distinction of winning (Rome, 1960) and successfully defending (Tokyo, 1964) the Olympic marathon title. Both wins were achieved in what were then the best-ever marathon times. Although he was not the first African to win a major distance running event, his triumph in Rome proved to be the inspiration for many successes by African runners. He also, remarkably, ran that race barefoot. **DS**.

BIRD, LARRY JOE
1956-
American basketball player

The 'Hick from French Lick (Indiana),' Larry Bird was a total sophisticate on the basketball court. Despite limited speed and leaping ability, Bird was one of the best forwards ever to play the game. He did it all: shooting, rebounding and uncanny passing. A three-time MVP, he led the Boston Celtics to three NBA championships. **MD**.

BIRDSEYE, CLARENCE
1886-1956
American inventor

It was during a hunting trip in the Arctic in the 1920s that Birdseye's attention was drawn to the possibilities of food preservation at extremely low temperatures. Noting that the food tasted better if frozen rapidly, he spent six years developing an industrial process to do this. By 1930 the first frozen-food packets were on the market and his empire was born. **PT**.

BIRO, LADISLA
1900-1985
Hungarian inventor

In the mid-1930s Biro devised a pen that would not blot and used quick-drying ink. Having patented the design in 1938, he set up a company to manufacture it. During World War II the ballpoint pen was issued to the US armed forces and the RAF, where its capabilities of working at high altitude and on wet paper and difficult angles were especially appreciated. Exremely expensive, when first sold to the public in 1945, Biro had sold his interests in their manufacture in 1944 and was not to reap the rewards of the remarkable invention. **PT**.

BJERKNES, VILHELM FIRMAN KOREN
1862-1951
Norwegian meteorologist

Born into a mathematical family, Bjerknes became Professor at Stockholm and Leipzig, and founded the Bergen Geophysical Institute in 1917. He applied hydrodynamic principles to the atmosphere and oceans, and developed a theory of weather fronts – in which the atmosphere could be visualized as discrete masses of air of different properties with unstable weather produced at the boundaries, or fronts, between them. This has become the mainstay of modern weather forecasting. **DD**.

BLACK, SIR JAMES WHYTE
1924-
British pharmacologist

Sir James Whyte Black is the most creative designer and developer of major new classes of drugs the century has seen. He has invented the first members of two new classes of drugs: beta-blockers, and H2 antagonists. Beta-blockers block the beta-effects of noradrenalin by blocking their access to their receptor sites within cells, and are used primarily to treat high blood pressure, angina, and disorders of heartbeat. H2 antagonists block the secondary effects of histamine and thus prevent or greatly reduce the output of hydrochloric acid in the stomach, allowing ulcers in the stomach and duodenum to heal and alleviating oesophagitis. Black's research is based on the meticulous study of the molecular nature of normal and abnormal physiological processes; as a result of which drugs are designed to block these processes. Born and educated in Scotland, he was a university lecturer in St Andrews, Malaya, and Glasgow before joining ICI Pharmaceuticals in 1958, where he developed the first beta-blocker. In 1964 he moved to Smith, Kline, and French (now Smith, Kline, Beecham) and developed the first ulcer drug, cimetidine. After a period as Professor of Pharmacology at University College, London, Black moved to the Wellcome Research Laboratories for a further 12 years and during that time he shared the 1982 Nobel Prize for Medicine or Pharmacology. He is now head of the James Black Institute, a commercially based institute linked with King's College London, where he heads an innovative drugs research team. **CR**.

BLANCO, SERGE
1958-
French rugby union player

Born in Caracas, Venezuela, Serge Blanco won a record number of 93 international appearances for France between 1980 and 1992. He took some time to settle to his best position of full back and on some occasions seemed to suffer from an over-excitable temperament, but more often his brilliant and unorthodox skills won matches and delighted crowds. **DS**.

BLANKERS-KOEN, FANNY
1918-
Dutch track athlete

Fanny Blankers-Koen is best remembered for her four gold medals in the 1948 Olympics in London (100 meters, 200 meters, 80 meters hurdles, 4×100 meters relay). In addition she was also at that time the world record holder in the high and long jumps but did not compete in those events at the Olympic Games. In total she held, at various times, world records in seven events. **DS**.

ABOVE: Nobel Prize-winner Sir James Black.

ABOVE: Louis Blériot, the first man to fly the English Channel.

BLÉRIOT, LOUIS
1872-1936
French inventor and aviation pioneer

Well-known for his flying accidents, Blériot nevertheless contributed greatly to the early development of powered airplanes. Having made his fortune inventing car accessories, he turned to aviation; his Type VI *Libellule* of 1907 was the first to fly with cantilever wings, and the Type VII of the same year introduced the classic tractor monoplane layout. On 25 July 1909 he piloted the first airplane (Type XI) across the English Channel, winning a £10,000 prize. Mass-produced examples of this airplane and subsequent types were widely used for sport, military and commercial flying before, during, and after World War I. **MT**.

BLOCH, MARC
1886-1944
French historian

It is difficult not to eulogize about this truly heroic character. His gifts as a historian were matched only by his bravery in two world wars. A fierce patriot of Jewish descent, Bloch received the *Légion d'honneur* in World War I, and died in 1944 fighting for the French Resistance. With Lucien Febvre, he founded the historical journal, *Annales*, which in turn influenced an entire new school of French and International history aimed at a general audience as well as scholars. Chiefly a medievalist, his great work being *Feudal Society* (1935), the range of periods on which he could write authoritatively was phenomenal. **ML**.

BLUM, LÉON
1872-1950
French politician

In 1936 Blum's attempts to reform and re-arm France in the face of growing German

ABOVE: French politician Leon Blum.

might were frustrated by the right wing, though he introduced the 40-hour week and nationalized France's war industry. Resigning in 1937 over Senate opposition to his fiscal reforms, he was later arraigned by the puppet Vichy regime for war crimes, was convicted but survived to be appointed provisional President-Premier of the Fourth Republic. **JC**.

BOCCIONE, UMBERTO
1882-1916
Italian painter and sculptor

Boccione joined the Futurists in 1909, becoming a leading member of the movement. From 1912 he absorbed the lessons of Cubism, developing a style of painting which depicted both human subjects and their motion. His sculpture used combinations of non-traditional materials and merged figures with their surroundings. Boccione died during World War I. **ER**.

BOFF, LEONARDO
1938-
Brazilian theologian

Along with Gustavo GUTIERREZ Boff is one of the leading exponents of Liberation Theology. Yet his advocacy of the preferential option for the poor and the positive redress of the appalling poverty and social deprivation of the Third World brought him into conflict with the Catholic Church culminating in 1992 with his resignation from the Franciscan Order and the Priesthood. Influenced by Marxist dogma, Boff seemed more authoritarian than the Vatican, and continues his teaching unimpeded by Rome. **ML**.

BOFILL, RICARDO
1939-
Spanish architect

Bofill's 'model making' approach to design can be seen in such developments as Le Viaduc Housing at St Quentin-en-Yvelines, France (1974) where the clusters of seemingly simple modular forms are typically post-modern; he draws on a wide vocabulary of architectural forms and allusions. **DE**.

BOGARDE, SIR DIRK
1920-
British actor

Elegant, handsome, and gifted Bogarde has consistently turned in first-rate performances, even in second-rate films. He began work as a scenic designer and commercial artist, but he really wanted to act, and made his debut with a small suburban London theater in 1939. After service in the war his career began in earnest, and a stage play, *Power Without Glory*, won him a contract with Rank. The subsequent string of pictures included *The Blue Lamp* (1950), and *Doctor in the House* (1953), the first in the successful 'Doctor' series. Hollywood beckoned, although Bogarde resisted, remaining at home as the top British box-office draw throughout the 1950s. In the 1960s he began to get the kind of leads needed to display his subtlety and sensitivity as an actor. In *Victim* he played a gay character at a time when homosexuality was still taboo, and his performance as the decadent valet in *The Servant* (1963) won him a British Film Academy Award. His performance as the dying composer obsessed with a young boy in *Death in Venice* (1971) was a remarkable tour de force. One of his finest later performances was in Alain RESNAIS' complex *Providence* (1977). In recent years Bogarde has also proved himself to be an accomplished novelist. **DC**.

worked on the Manhattan Project and helped to develop the atomic bomb, but in 1944 began to act against the proliferation of nuclear weapons. As a result he organized the first Atoms for Peace Conference in Geneva in 1955. At about that time in Geneva he helped to set up CERN, the European Council for Nuclear Research, the world's foremost establishment for research into high-energy physics. **DD**.

ABOVE: *Humphrey Bogart (right) in* Treasure of the Sierra Madre.

ABOVE: *Danish physicist Niels Bohr.*

BOGART, HUMPHREY
1899-1957
American actor

After a classical education and a spell in the navy, where an injury to his lip may have accounted for the distinctive lisp, Bogart became a stage manager, gradually turning to acting in Broadway farces and making five films in the early 1930s which sank without trace. He got his break in *The Petrified Forest* (1936) alongside Leslie HOWARD, and played mostly gangster roles. Director John HUSTON developed his cynical good-guy persona in the 1941 films *High Sierra* and *The Maltese Falcon*, and the ultimate Hollywood movie of all time, *Casablanca* (1942) with Ingrid BERGMAN. It was on the set of *To Have and To Have Not* (1944), that he met Lauren BACALL, whom he later married. Bogart finally won a much-deserved Academy Award for Best Actor for his role in *The African Queen* in 1951. **DC**.

BOHR, NIELS HENRIK DAVID
1885-1962
Danish physicist

Bohr gained his doctorate in Copenhagen in 1911 and then moved to Britain to work in Cambridge and then Manchester. There he modified RUTHERFORD's concept of an atom consisting of a positive nucleus surrounded by negative electrons by postulating that the electrons could only exist as multiples of certain fixed values. This concept became known as the Bohr nuclear atom. This work gained him the Nobel Prize for Physics in 1922, the year of the birth of his son Aage who was himself to become a Nobel prize-winner in physics in 1975. He returned to Copenhagen as the Director of the Institute of Theoretical Physics, but fled to America when Germany occupied Denmark. Before leaving, he dissolved his Nobel medal in acid to hide it, waiting until his return to precipitate the gold and recast it. In America he

BOLAN, MARC
1944-1977
British pop singer

The original duo behind T Rex were regulars at 'happenings' in the late 1960s and had built up a dedicated following by 1971 when they achieved chart success with 'Get It On' and 'Hot Love'. But by 1973 Bolan was losing out in the glam-rock stakes, his faltering career finally halted by a car crash in 1977. **DC**.

BÖLL, HEINRICH
1917-1985
German writer

Böll was one of the most prolific and translated of all postwar German writers. Born in Cologne, he was a bookseller before being conscripted into Hitler's army. After the war he began to write short stories (influenced stylistically by HEMINGWAY), radio plays, and novels such as *The Train Was On Time* (1949) and *Billiards at Half-Past Nine* (1959), on the effects of wartime experience and postwar guilt. Recent work has dealt with contemporary themes – the amorality of tabloid journalism in *The Lost Honor of Katherina Blum* (1974), and terrorism, in *The Safety Net* (1979). Böll won the Nobel Prize for literature in 1972. **CW**.

BONDI, HERMANN, SIR
1919-
British mathematician and astrophysicist

One of the authors, with HOYLE, of the steady-state theory of the universe, which accounts for its expansion by postulating that new matter is constantly being created, Bondi was also a prominent educationalist and scientific adviser to both the Ministry of Defence and the Department of Energy. **EB**.

BONG, RICHARD IRA, MAJOR
1920-1945
American fighter pilot

The most successful US fighter pilot, Bong gained 40 'kills' in the Pacific theater by 1944, while flying a P-38 with the 49th Fighter Group. Returning home in December 1944, he became a test pilot with Lockheed, but was killed on 6 August 1945 when the jet engine of his P-80 failed. **MT**.

BONHOEFFER, DIETRICH
1906-1945
German Lutheran pastor and theologian

One of the most outstanding and inspiring Christians of the century, Bonhoeffer's outspoken opposition to Hitler earned him his death in Flossenburg concentration camp in 1945. Educated at Tübingen and Berlin he was a signatory to the Barmen declaration of 1934 which founded the Confessing Church, a direct protest to the support given to the Nazis by some German Protestant Churches. He was Head of the Seminary of the Confessing Church which although outlawed by Hitler continued its work underground. He was arrested in Berlin in 1943 after an unsuccessful mission to Stockholm to inform the Allies of the Resistance plot to kill Hitler. Theologically, he emphasized a Christianity which reflected the practicalities of life in contemporary society. His moving *The Cost of Discipleship* (1937) is an inspiring exhortation of the trials and tribulations a Christian must embrace as a genuine disciple. **ML**.

BOOT, JESSE, LORD
1850-1931
British businessman

At the age of 13 Boot took over his father's herbalist shop. Studying pharmacy in his spare time he became a chemist and devoted himself to expanding his business. By the 1890s his chain was big enough to justify building factories at Nottingham to produce its own drugs. He added a circulating library to his shops and this, like his provision of drugs and health items to an ever-wider clientele of ordinary people, had a big social impact. He made substantial gifts to good causes, especially in his native Nottingham, and Nottingham University was founded with his assistance. **JW**

BOOTH, HUBERT CECIL
1871-1955
British engineer

An engineer of catholic talents, Booth's most ubiquitous monument to posterity is the humble vacuum cleaner. This universal boon to cleaners everywhere was described in a patent which he took out in 1901. His idea of causing dust to be sucked up and then collected by a filter is the basis of all such machines. **PW**.

BOREL, ÉMILE
1871-1956
French mathematician and statesman

One of the founders of real-value function theory, and the author of results which greatly influenced complex analysis, Borel was also Minister for the Navy until he was imprisoned by the Vichy government and later joined the Resistance; he was decorated after both World Wars. He developed an account of the measure of sets of points, a theory of divergent series, integrated probability theory with measure theory, and was one of the founders of game theory. **EB**.

BORG, BJÖRN
1956-
Swedish tennis player

Björn Borg was the leading men's tennis player of the 1970s. His game particularly featured powerful ground strokes and great concentration. He is also remembered for winning the Wimbledon championships five times in a row (1976-80) and for six successes in the French Open. He retired in 1983 but briefly attempted a comeback in 1991. **DS**.

BOULEZ, PIERRE
1925-
French conductor and composer

Boulez is undoubtedly one of the leading interpreters of contemporary music. He began his career by composing works according to his own complex mathematical formulae before turning to SCHOENBERG's theory of serialism. Many of his later works include chance and choice elements where, for example, music is determined by throwing dice. **DK**.

BOULT, SIR ADRIAN
1889-1983
British conductor

Throughout his career Boult always maintained his enthusiasm for contemporary music in all its forms whether ballet, opera, choral, or orchestral. He held many prestigious posts including Director of BBC Music (1934-42) before training and conducting the newly formed BBC Symphony Orchestra (1931-50). He also wrote the popular autobiography *My Own Trumpet* and two textbooks on conducting. **DK**.

ABOVE: English composer Sir Adrian Boult.

LEFT: Swedish tennis sensation Bjorn Borg at Wimbledon.

BOURGEOIS, LOUISE
1911-
American sculptor

Born in Paris, Bourgeois studied painting under LEGER before emigrating to the USA in 1938. Her first sculptures date from the late 1940s. She has experimented with materials as diverse as wood, bronze, latex, and stone. Much of her work appears sexually descriptive and occasionally has feminist connotations, for example *Destruction of the Father* (1974). **ER**.

BOURKE-WHITE, MARGARET
1904-1971
American photographer

Margaret Bourke-White trained in photography at the influential Clarence H White School of Photography at Columbia University, New York. From its inception, in 1929, she worked for Henry Luce's *Fortune* magazine, and then from 1929 until 1957 for his magazine *Life*, which used her picture of a dam in Montana on the cover of its first issue. Always a compassionate and progressive reporter, her first book was *Eyes on Russia* (1931), and her most celebrated, *You Have Seen Their Faces* (1937), with a text by Erskine Caldwell. Her greatest picture, and one of the most complete news pictures ever taken, is of a line of refugees queuing at a relief station in Louisville in 1937 under a poster of an idealized white family with matching slogans. **IJ**.

BOWIE, DAVID [DAVID JONES]
1947-
British pop singer

Although 'Space Oddity' charted in 1969, it wasn't until the 1971 album *Hunky Dory* that Bowie began to establish a wide following. The bold follow-up, *Ziggy Stardust and the Spiders from Mars*, provided a role model for glam rock with the first of Bowie's stage incarnations as Ziggy, and he remained a trendsetter rather than a follower in music and fashion throughout the 1970s. Acting roles in the early 1980s earned him praise, and in 1983 the disco-oriented album *Let's Dance* signaled a fresh rise in popularity which subsequently fell back. In 1989 he founded a hard-rock quartet, the Tin Machine, which received guarded praise. **DC**.

BOWLBY, JOHN
1907-1990
British child psychiatrist

John Bowlby was a child psychiatrist and psychoanalyst who contributed greatly to thinking about children's needs for secure, reliable, and loving relationships. He sought to introduce more empirical verification in a field that suffered from an excess of theory, and wanted to examine the psychological impact of external experience. In his influential monograph, *Maternal Care and Mental Health*, published after World War II, he concluded that the relationship between mother and young infant is of importance in its own right, and acts as the fundamental building block for the proper development of personality. This theory was quite revolutionary, and has not only influenced the way children are cared for in hospitals and children's homes, but also therapeutic practice, especially family therapy. Bowlby's ideas are summarized in his hugely influential trilogy on Attachment, Separation and Loss. **MBe**.

BOYCOTT, GEOFF
1940-
British cricketer

Geoff Boycott was one of the finest batsmen of recent times. He made his Test debut in 1964 and eventually retired from playing in 1986. He scored his 100th century fittingly on his home Yorkshire ground against Australia. Single-minded in his devotion to the game, he was often also criticized as being too outspoken and self-centered. Towards the end of his career he was involved in various disputes at the Yorkshire club but remains active in the game as commentator and coach. **DS**.

BOYD, WILLIAM
1895-1972
American actor

With film appearances as early as 1919, Boyd was a star of the early talkies, until after a few years of high living, drinking, and gambling his popularity began to fade. Then in 1935 he signed a six-picture deal to play Hopalong Cassidy, a role he would play for the rest of his life. Hopalong, dressed in black and riding his white horse, Topper, didn't drink, smoke, swear, hardly ever kissed the heroine and was an enormous hero to millions of youngsters. Boyd shrewdly bought the television rights and took the character to the small screen where he soon became a hero to a whole new generation. **DC**.

BOYER, HERBERT WAYNE
1936-
American biochemist
COHEN, STANLEY
1922-
American biochemist

Two of the pioneers of genetic engineering, they independently (Boyer with Robert Helling in 1973 and Stanley Cohen with Annie Chang) constructed functional DNA from two different sources. These chimeras could be inserted into bacteria which replicated and expressed traits derived from both original DNA sources. Thus the first practical methods for systematically cloning (and thus mass producing) specific DNA fragments were achieved. **ES**.

BRADBURY, RAY[MOND]
1920-
American novelist

Bradbury is a prolific short story writer, and one of the foremost practitioners of science fiction, or more properly, science fantasy. Wonderful depictions of small-town America mingle with bizarre creatures drawn from a nightmare carnival. Among his many novels and collections *The Martian Chronicles* (1950) deals with Earth's efforts to colonize Mars, and reflects Bradbury's underlying concern with social and political issues; these re-emerge in *Fahrenheit 451* (1953), set in a future totalitarian state where books are burned. *Something Wicked This Way Comes* (1963) is a chilling depiction of a more subtle kind of evil that gains power from our inner desires. **AM**.

BRADLEY, OMAR, GENERAL
1893-1981
American soldier

Commissioned into the infantry in 1915, Bradley spent his early career in training and staff appointments, but in 1942 was given command of an infantry division and

BELOW: General Omar Bradley (left) with Generals Weyland and Patton.

sent to North Africa. Promoted to corps command, he took part in the 1943 invasion of Sicily, after which he was transferred to England in preparation for D-Day. A popular commander and skilled tactician, he commanded US forces in the Normandy breakout (July-August 1944), before assuming command of the huge 12th Army Group, which liberated Paris in August 1944, and fought on to the Elbe in 1945. He was the first Chairman of the US Joint Chiefs of Staff, 1949-53. **JPi**.

BRADMAN, SIR DONALD
1908-
Australian cricketer

Don Bradman's stature as cricket's most successful batsman can best be judged by a single statistic. Only five players in the history of the game have a batting average in test cricket greater than 60. Four of those have averages between 60 and 65; Bradman's figure is 99.94. In all first-class games he made 117 centuries – passing 100 in better than one innings in three. He was a punishingly quick, as well as a prolific scorer and such was his dominance that the England team visiting Australia in 1932/33 devised the intimidatory 'Bodyline' bowling tactic solely to combat him (an event so unprecedented as to embitter relations between the two countries for a time). Bradman's test career spanned the years 1928-48 and his record might have been even more remarkable without the interruption of the war years and an earlier season lost to illness. Remarkably a medical examination at the start of his military service revealed below-average eyesight. After his playing career he remained prominent in the administration of Australian cricket. **DS**.

BRAGG, SIR WILLIAM HENRY
1862-1942
British physicist

Bragg was a latecomer to the field, his first work in physics being done after he was 40. His most important work was on X-ray diffraction – the analysis of crystal shapes by examining the reflection of X-rays from them. For this, he gained the Nobel Prize for Physics in 1915, which he shared with his son William Lawrence Bragg. **DD**.

BRAIN, DENNIS
1921-1957
British horn player

Born in London, the son of a horn player, Dennis Brain made a name for himself as a performer of masterful technique and immense sensitivity. The dedicatee of many contemporary works, his recordings of the Mozart and Strauss horn concertos remain legendary. A fatal car accident ended his short career. **DK**.

BRANCUSI, CONSTANTIN
1876-1957
Romanian sculptor

Originally a cabinetmaker, Brancusi received formal art training in Bucharest and Paris, where he arrived in 1904. His facility in traditional, naturalistic modeling techniques attracted the attention of Rodin, who offered him a position in his studio. This Brancusi refused, from a growing certainty that traditional sculpture could only render surface appearances without ever penetrat-

ing the true essence of its subjects. His formative years had been spent in a peasant community with a strong tradition of wood carving and from 1907 he abandoned modeling for direct carving in limestone and marble. He had a deep empathy for his materials, often allowing them to dictate stylizations and gradually, by eliminating distinguishing features by which members of a type are individuated, he achieved the reduction of organic forms to their most essential generic qualities. Seeking perfection in his highly polished forms, he would make several versions, often including bronze casts. His best-known works include *Bird In Space* (1923-40) and *The Seal* (1936-43), and his radical simplifications had an immense impact on twentieth-century sculpture. Increasingly interested in primitive sculpture, from 1914 he also produced rougher, fetishist wood carvings, including the large *Endless Column* (1920), reminiscent of a tribal totem pole. **ER**.

BRANDEIS, LOUIS DEMBITZ
1856-1941
American lawyer

The first Jew to be appointed to the Supreme Court (in 1916), Brandeis was renowned for his liberal judgments. He was known as 'the people's attorney' for waiving his fees for poor but deserving clients, and was fond of saying 'We must be ever on our guard lest we erect our prejudices into legal principles.' **JC**.

BRANDO, MARLON
1924-
American actor

Expelled from military school, the young Brando headed for New York and became a pupil of Stella Adler at the Actors' Studio; he became the first Stanislavsky method actor to make an impression in films. On Broadway he played the role that would catapult him to stardom on both stage and screen: that of Stanley Kowalski in *A Streetcar Named Desire*. *On the Waterfront* (1954) brought him an Academy Award, and he began to emerge as the image of non-conformity when this was still a rare commodity. But in the 1960s his movies went downhill amid a stormy personal life and a reputation for being temperamental; his own attempts at producing and directing led to financial disaster. He then made a brilliant comeback in *The Godfather* (1972) for which he won an Academy Award, although he refused to accept it. He created a stir in the bold and sexually explicit *Last Tango in Paris* (1972) and played the cruel Commander Kurtz in *Apocalypse Now* (1979). For his first role in years as an African lawyer in *A Dry White Season* (1989) he was nominated for another Academy Award as Best Supporting Actor. **DC**.

LEFT: Marlon Brando in The Wild One.

BRANDT, BILL [HERMANN WILHELM]
1904-1983
British photographer

Although born in Hamburg and schooled in Germany, Switzerland, and Vienna, Bill Brandt is known as one of the great photographers of British life. He began to photograph in Vienna in 1927, and spent three months in the studio of MAN RAY in Paris in 1929. He settled in London in 1931 and his first major work was *The English at Home* (1936). His vision of his adopted homeland, with its cast of policemen in darkened London streets, barmaids, holidaymakers, and the gentry with their servants, was more Edwardian than modern, and has affinities with the surrealist styles of the painters Giorgio de CHIRICO and René MAGRITTE. The film-maker Alfred HITCHCOCK was another influence, especially in the dramatic tableaux which appear in *A Night in London* (1938). In the late 1930s he worked for the picture magazines *Lilliput* and *Picture Post*, and in 1940 began to record bomb-damaged London. His culminating image of a haunted land was *Literary Britain*, published in 1951. His literary landscapes, strongly marked by tracks and stones, prefigure the conceptual landscapes of Richard Long. In *Perspective of Nudes*, his last major book (1961), he sculpts with light, in the manner of a Seurat or a Henry MOORE. **IJ**.

ABOVE: *Willy Brandt pictured as Mayor of Berlin.*

BRANDT, WILLY
1913-1992
German politician

Principal exponent of postwar *Ostpolitik* (reconciliation with the Eastern bloc), Brandt returned to Germany after working with the Norwegian Resistance during World War II and entered politics, serving as Chancellor in 1969-74. As such he backed integration into NATO and the EEC, while his efforts for detente with the East brought him the Nobel Peace Prize in 1971. He later chaired the Brandt Commission which reported on the world economy in 1980. **JC**.

BRANSON, RICHARD
1950-
British entrepreneur

With a knack for publicity, the affable Branson built his empire on the youth culture of the 1970s. While still only a teenager, Branson set up a mail-order record company and soon attracted a number of big names to his own Virgin label. The launch of Virgin Atlantic airline in 1984, a £200-million stockmarket flotation in 1987, and crossings of the Atlantic in balloons and boats have kept the 'happy hippy' millionaire in the spotlight. **PT**.

BRAQUE, GEORGES
1882-1963
French painter

Braque studied at the Ecole des Beaux-Arts, Paris, and from around 1906 began painting in a Fauvist style influenced by MATISSE and André Derain. But the 1907 Cézanne Memorial Exhibition in Paris changed his life and he began experiments with geometrically analytical paintings which he and PICASSO developed together as Cubism. Braque was the first to introduce (1911) stencilled lettering and papier collé into his paintings, where printed papers such as newspaper, marbled paper, or wood-grain paper were stuck to the canvas. Braque's work became much less angular after World War I and he diversified to produce book illustrations, decorative designs, and stage sets. **AR**.

BRAUDEL, FERNAND
1902-1985
French historian

As editor of the *Annales* from 1957 to 1968, Braudel can rightly be regarded not only as a worthy successor to BLOCH and Febvre but as an epoch-making historian in his own right. *The Mediterranean and the Mediterranean World in the Age of Philip II* (1949) has been described as the most important historical work since World War II. Interested in large themes covering long time spans, Braudel minimized the importance of individuals' actions, depicting them as prisoners of the longer biological, climactic, and geological framework of events. **ML**.

BRAUN, WERNHER VON
1912-1977
German engineer

Born in Germany, von Braun was an expert on liquid-fueled rockets. At the age of 25 he was technical director of the German experimental weapons research center at Peenemunde and his design for the V2 rocket – the first ballistic missile to carry a warhead – set the pattern for future Russian and American liquid-fueled rockets. After World War II he developed rockets for the US Army, adapting his work for the space race of the 1950s and 1960s. At NASA von Braun designed the enormous Saturn V launch vehicle that launched the Apollo 11 mission to the moon in 1969. **PW**.

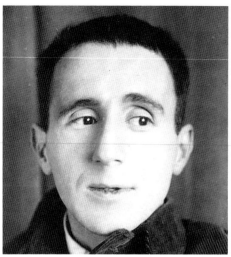

ABOVE: *German dramatist and poet Bertolt Brecht.*

BRECHT, BERTOLT
1898-1956
German dramatist and poet

Born in Bavaria, and left-wing in politics, Brecht emigrated from Nazi Germany to America, and only returned to settle in East Berlin in 1949. Prior to the war, at the time of the Weimar Republic, his experimental plays owed much to Expressionism. His version of John Gay's *The Beggar's Opera* (first performed in 1798), *Die Dreigroschenoper (The Threepenny Opera)* incorporated music by Kurt WEILL, and was a major success when it was staged in 1928. True to the principles of his vision of epic theater, his plays were typically constructed of short, loosely-linked scenes; attempted to eschew the charisma of individual characterization and audience identification; and were strongly didactic. His most celebrated plays include *Leben des Galilei (The Life of Galileo*, 1937-9), subject of a legendary interpretation by Charles Laughton, *Der gute Mensch von Sezuan (The Good Woman of Sechuan*, 1938-41), *Mutter Courage (Mother Courage*, 1941), and *Der kaukasische Kreidekreis (The Caucasian Chalk Circle*, 1948). On his return to Germany he founded his own theatrical company, the Berliner Ensemble, of which he was director until his death. The influence of his radical theories of theater and style of presentation on the modern theater cannot be overestimated. **AM**.

BREL, JACQUES
1929-1978
Belgian singer/songwriter

Brel began his career singing in Paris cafés in the late 1940s and established himself as a leading French romantic singer. He made his US debut at Carnegie Hall in 1965, and his songs were much covered by British and US performers. His last album, in 1977, sold 650,000 copies in a day. **JH**.

BRENNER, SYDNEY
1927-
South African-British molecular biologist

Born and educated in South Africa, Brenner was one of the pioneers of genetic engineering. He discovered the single-strand messenger RNA, a link between DNA and ribosomes where proteins are synthesized, in 1960. His work proved vital in further research into the genetic code. **ES.**

BRETON, ANDRÉ
1896-1966
French poet and painter

Primarily noted as a writer and poet, Breton was the founder of the Surrealist movement, becoming known as 'The Pope of Surrealism' through his controlling influence. He wrote a series of Surrealist Manifestos including, with Leon TROTSKY, *Towards an Independant Revolutionary Art.* He also produced 'Poem-objects', assemblages of surrealistically juxtaposed objects. **ER.**

BREUER, MARCEL
1902-1981
Hungarian-American furniture designer and architect

Breuer joined GROPIUS's Bauhaus at Weimar in 1920, and influenced the school's shift from arts and crafts to art and technology. He was head of furniture at the Bauhaus from the age of 22, and by 1925 he was designing ruthlessly functional yet elegant tubular steel furniture, including the S-shaped cantilever chair of 1928. Breuer emigrated to the US in 1933 and taught a whole generation of American architects at Harvard – JOHNSON, Landis Gores, Paul Rudolph – enthusing them with his purist, functionlist aesthetic. The clear distinction and separation of functionally different elements in Breuer's furniture and buildings (eg UNESCO Headquarters, Paris, 1952-58), means they sometimes sacrifice aesthetic cohesion to functionalist integrity. **AR.**

BREZHNEV, LEONID ILICH
1906-1982
Soviet politician

The last real Stalinist to hold power in the Soviet Union, Brezhnev was leader of the coup which toppled KHRUSCHEV in 1964. The grim conservatism of his rule was best exemplified by the crushing of the 'Prague Spring' in 1968. He proclaimed the right of Soviet intervention in any client state where Communism was threatened, but also signed the Helsinki Accord in 1976. He is remembered for the persecution of dissidents like Sakharov, the Afghanistan embroilment, and a legacy of widespread industrial decay. **JC.**

RIGHT: Soviet President Leonid Brezhnev.

BRIAND, ARISTIDE
1862-1932
French politician

Prime Minister of France nine times between 1909 and 1929, Briand was a socialist statesman and co-author of the 1925 Locarno Pact. His work for European peace and influence in the League of Nations earned him the Nobel Peace Prize in 1926. **JC.**

BRITTEN, (EDWARD) BENJAMIN, BARON
1913-1976
British composer and pianist

Born in Lowestoft, Suffolk, Britten had a distinguished musical education under Frank Bridge and John Ireland. A gifted pianist who accompanied some of the world's finest performers (including the tenor Peter Pears, who became Britten's lifelong companion), his fame attaches more to the evocative compositions which survive him. His first opera, *Peter Grimes*, is one of the century's masterpieces, but he produced works in a wide range of other media besides: choral works, works for children and chamber music. Co-founder of the Aldeburgh Festival, Britten's is the richest of musical legacies. **DK.**

BROOKS, LOUISE
1906-1985
American actress

Primarily a dancer until her film debut in 1925, Brooks' striking good looks and distinctive brunette bob created the image of just another flapper, but her 1928 performances in *A Girl in Every Port* and *Beggars of Life* showed that she had real acting talent. She made her best films under G W Pabst in Germany, but on her return to Hollywood she found life in the movie capital intolerable, eventually abandoning show business altogether and becoming a recluse. In the 1950s she was rediscovered by movie buffs and wrote a critically acclaimed autobiography entitled *Lulu in Hollywood*. **DC.**

BROOKS, MEL
1926-
American actor, writer, and director

A talented comedian and writer, Brooks won an Oscar for his 1968 screenplay for *The Producers.* He begun his career writing TV comedy, initially for Sid Caesar's *Your Show of Shows.* Brooks specializes in broad often vulgar slapstick humor, best exmplified in films such as *Blazing Saddles* (1974). **DC.**

BROWN, SIR ARTHUR WHITTEN
1886-1948
British engineer and pilot

An engineer before joining the Royal Air Force as a pilot in World War I, Brown was navigator on the famed first non-stop Atlantic crossing of 14-15 June 1919, accompanying Captain John ALCOCK aboard the Vickers Vimy. Having received a knighthood, he subsequently became general manager of Metropolitan Vickers. **MT.**

BROWN, JAMES
1928-
American soul singer

James Brown's 1965 hit, 'Papa's Got a Brand New Bag', was the song which marked the birth of modern funk. After the black consciousness anthem, 'Say It Loud, I'm Black And I'm Proud' and the 1970 dance classic 'Sex Machine', he was less popular until rap artists of the mid-1980s revived his material. **DC.**

BRUSILOV, ALEXEI, GENERAL
1853-1926
Russian soldier

After a relatively undistinguished military career, Brusilov took command of the Russian 8th Army in 1914. He achieved major successes against the Austrians in Galicia in 1916, but in 1917 he could do nothing to prevent defeat. In 1920 he commanded the Red Army and drove the Poles as far as Warsaw before being repulsed. **JPi.**

BRYAN, WILLIAM JENNINGS
1860-1925
American politician

Bryan was a silver-tongued orator in more than one sense, for his rallying call was the freeing of the dollar from the silver standard. Leader of the Democrats for 30 years, Bryan was thrice defeated for the presidency but became Secretary of State under Woodrow WILSON when he tried to organize machinery for international peace-keeping on the eve of World War I. He died shortly after prosecuting the famous 'Monkey Case,' in which a Tennessee schoolteacher was prosecuted for denying the Divine Creation. **JC.**

BUBER, MARTIN
1878-1965
Jewish philosopher and German literary figure

Although he was educated in the German tradition at the universities of Berlin, Leipzig, Zürich, and Vienna, Buber's main intellectual activity was within the Jewish world, although he was not a practising Jew and opposed the particularity of religious observance. Among the founders of the Zionist movement, he edited its newspaper, and led the campaign for Jewish cultural renaissance as well as political sovereignty. He founded a publishing company, the intellectual periodical *Der Jude*, and an ecumenical journal *Die Kreatur*, and translated the Hebrew Bible into German. His study of Hassidism imparted a mystical aspect to his early works, out of which he later developed his doctrine of the distinction between functional 'I – It' interactions and the dialogue of 'I – Thou' relationships with other beings, through which God, the 'eternal Thou', is glimpsed. In the early days of Nazi rule, he became director of the German national Jewish adult education organization, but his outspoken criticism of the regime was silenced, and in 1938 he emigrated to Palestine, where he founded a similar adult education network and was appointed to the Chair of Social Philosophy at the Hebrew University. **EB.**

BUBKA, SERGEI
1964-
Soviet track and field athlete

Sergei Bubka has dominated pole vaulting since the mid-1980s. He was the first man to surpass 6 meters and the first also over 20 feet. He did not compete at the 1984 Olympics because of the Soviet boycott but set four world records that summer. He won gold in 1988 and his failure to retain his title in 1992 was one of the greatest sporting surprises. He was one of the first Soviet athletes to benefit from the liberalization of the system and collect the financial rewards of outstanding performance. Later in his career he moved to live in Germany. **DS.**

BUCKLEY, WILLIAM [FRANK]
1925-
American political journalist

The son of a selfmade millionaire, Buckley articulated his inherited suspicion of government interference with economic individualism. After publishing a vigorous attack on liberalism at Yale, he founded the journal *National Review*, which he used as a vehicle for his own outspoken conservative political views. He became an influential voice in American politics, stood unsuccessfully for Mayor of New York, and was briefly a delegate to the United Nations. **EB.**

BUGATTI, ETTORE ARCO ISIDORE
1881-1947
Italo-French motor stylist and manufacturer

Born in Italy, Bugatti was the son of a silversmith, and built his first car in 1901. A perfectionist, not interested in mass production, he concentrated on lightweight, fast cars. The famous name has been revived in 1992 with a new sports car. **NF.**

BUNCHE, RALPH JOHNSON
1904-1971
American diplomat

Bunche's attempts on the UN Palestine Commission to reconcile the Arab-Israeli conflict won him the 1950 Nobel Peace Prize. A founding member of the UN, in 1957 he became UN Under-Secretary for Special Political Affairs, mediating in the Congo débâcle of 1960. From 1967 to 1971 he was Under-Secretary General of the UN, and was increasingly involved with the Civil Rights Movement. **JC.**

BUÑUEL, LUIS
1900-1983
Spanish film director

Buñuel established his reputation with surreal, iconoclastic films such as *Un Chien Andalou* (1928) and *L'Age d'Or* (1930). He worked briefly in Hollywood, but failed to reconcile commercial needs with his audacious style. *Los Olvidados/The Young and the Damned* (1950) restored his reputation, but

BELOW: Surrealist film director Luis Buñel.

he achieved most notoriety with *Viridiana* in 1960, an overtly blasphemous film. His later works, *Belle du Jour* (1967) and *The Discreet Charm of the Bourgeoisie* (1972), were sly dissections of middle-class morality, and to the end he was cinema's foremost surrealist, the scourge of the conventional, the commonplace, and the complacent. **NS.**

BURGESS, ANTHONY [JOHN ANTHONY BURGESS WILSON]
1917-
British novelist

Author of critical works, notably on JOYCE, Burgess is also an orchestral composer, even a polymath. His prolific output of fiction includes the desperately bleak dystopian vision of *A Clockwork Orange* (1962), the Kubrick film of which achieved cult status, the comic Enderby novels, and *Earthly Powers* (1982), an ambitious depiction of twentieth-century life and letters. **AM.**

BURGESS, GUY FRANCIS DE MONCY
1911-1963
British spy

Educated at Eton and Cambridge, and an outrageous homosexual and drunkard, Burgess must have seemed an unlikely candidate for recruitment to the KGB. However, having gone over to the Russians as a student, Burgess made himself most useful by obtaining a post at the Foreign Office, and was then appointed to the Washington embassy. Aware that his deception was about to be discovered, he fled to Russia with his co-spy Donald Maclean in 1951. **RJ.**

BURNET, SIR (FRANK) MACFARLANE
1899-1985
American immunologist

Burnet shared the Nobel prize with Sir Peter MEDAWAR in 1960 for work on immunological tolerance. His theories focused on antibody production, for which he developed the adaptive enzyme concept (1941) then, with Frank Fenner, the indirect template theory (1948) to explain body mechanisms of self/non-self recognition. **GL.**

BURTON, RICHARD
1925-1984
British actor

Burton's reputation as a fine actor was based primarily on his stage career; his brooding good looks and magnificent voice did not bring him immediate film success. Shakespearean roles and the 1960 Broadway musical *Camelot* kept him in the public eye until his role as Mark Anthony in *Cleopatra* (1962). His off-screen romance with Elizabeth TAYLOR made hot news. *Who's Afraid of Virginia Woolf*, which they made together in 1966, was a tour de force for both, but Burton went on to star in increasingly inferior films until his death. **DC.**

BUSBY, SIR MATT
1909-
British soccer manager

Matt Busby had a successful playing career in the years before World War II, but became famous as manager of the Manchester United club in 1945-71. He was injured in the air crash at Munich in 1958 when virtually his whole, highly promising team were killed. He was able to rebuild his side to success in the 1960s and won the European Cup in 1968. He remains a much-loved senior figure in the British game. **DS.**

BUSH, GEORGE HERBERT WALKER
1924-
American politician and president

Vice-President since 1981, Bush inherited with the Presidency in 1988 the problems which Ronald REAGAN had begun to find intractable: a weakening economy and a dangerously unstable Middle East. The failure of the first to respond to limited treatment eroded Republican support which not even the success of the lightning desert campaign against Saddam HUSSEIN, could reverse, and Bush was defeated in his 1992 re-election attempt. **JC.**

BUSH, VANNEVAR
1890-1974
American scientist and administrator

As one of the most influential scientific advisers to President F Roosevelt, Bush was a major administrative driving force behind the mammoth wartime project which produced the first atom bomb. He was particularly concerned with the tricky task of coordinating the British and US lines of research to speed up the achievement of their joint objective. **PW.**

BELOW: Richart Burton in Anthony and Cleopatra *with future wife Elizabeth Taylor.*

ABOVE: Ex-President George Bush with General Schwarzkopf.

BUSHNELL, NOLAN
1943-
American inventor

Creator of the video game, Bushnell had enjoyed night-long games on his college $4M mainframe computer during the 1960s and the development of microcomputer technology in the 1970s enabled him to realize his dream and market a video game. After two false starts, he launched Atari in 1972, and set about marketing 'Pony'; he created a new industry which, by 1982, far surpassed both the pop music and film market in the US. **PT.**

BUTLIN, SIR WILLIAM
1899-1980
British holiday tycoon

'There are lots of Sir Williams, but there will only be one Sir Billy'. Butlin set up a holiday camp in Skegness in 1936, providing a holiday village with outdoor and indoor activities. He was, as he said, the first man to make money out of the traditional British summer weather and 20 years later his empire catered for a million holidaymakers. **PT.**

BUTTERFIELD, HERBERT
1900-1979
British historian

A veritable institution of Peterhouse College, Cambridge, it is for the historiographical lambast, *The Whig Interpretation of History*, that Butterfield will be best remem-

bered. He attacked the unfortunate tendency of historians to produce a ratification, if not a glorification, of the present, being particularly suspicious of a Protestant, Establishment bias in British History. **ML.**

BUTTS, ALFRED
1900-1993
American innovator

Long periods of unemployment led Butts to devise 'Scrabble' during the 1930s. His game initially enjoyed modest sales, but once adopted by Jack Strauss of Macy's in 1952, sales rocketed to 4.5 million sets within two years. With the mixed attractions of crosswords, anagrams, and good luck, 'Scrabble' is still extremely popular. **PT.**

BYRD, RICHARD EVELYN, REAR ADMIRAL
1888-1957
American naval pilot and polar explorer

Best remembered for his polar flying, Byrd led a two-airplane expedition to the Canadian Arctic in August 1925. On 9 May 1926, accompanied by Floyd Bennett, he made the first flight over the North Pole and then, with three crew members, led the first flight over the South Pole on 28-29 November 1929. Meanwhile a successful transatlantic flight of 29 June to 1 July 1927 had ended in a sea-ditching off the French coast due to fog. Continuing his polar explorations before and after World War II, Byrd was in charge of postwar US *Deep Freeze* operations in the Antarctic. **MT.**

CAGE, JOHN
1912-1992
American composer and pianist

Cage was quite an eccentric figure in the musical world, described as a 'tireless experimenter and musical nonconformist.' He invented the concept of the prepared piano where objects are placed on the strings inside the piano thus drastically altering the sound produced. His compositions include examples of aleatory, electronic, and even 'silent' music. His most famous works include *Imaginary Landscapes* for twelve radios, *4′ 33″*, a silent piece which was followed ten years later by his *0′ 0″*, another silent piece designed to be performed 'in any way to anyone.' **DK**.

CAGNEY, JAMES
1899-1986
American actor

Cagney was America's favorite tough guy, a pugnacious, punchy Hollywood legend. After working as a waiter and a racker in a pool room, he broke into vaudeville as a female impersonator and chorus boy, eventually making it to Broadway. Films followed, and in *The Public Enemy* (1931) he lit up the screen by shoving a grapefruit into Mae Clark's face. He made a series of cheap, quick but popular tough-guy pictures, but proved the depth and sensitivity of his acting playing Bottom in *A Midsummer Night's Dream* (1935), and in *Angels with Dirty Faces* (1938) was cast alongside BOGART. Cagney then attempted a series of changes of direction, first to romance, then comedy, where he revealed a masterful sense of timing. His popularity was ensured when, drawing on his vaudeville background, he played George M Cohan in *Yankee Doodle Dandy* (1942). In the 1950s he tried directing, continuing to act in *Man of a Thousand Faces*

(1957) and showing a deft comic touch in the hilarious *One, Two, Three* (1961). Retiring that year, Cagney received the American Film Institute's Life Achievement Award in 1974; he made a final film, *Ragtime*, in 1981. **DC**.

CALDER, ALEXANDER
1898-1976
American sculptor

Originally trained in engineering, Calder studied at the Art Students' League, New York, 1923-25. His line drawings of the circus, made in 1925, were the inspiration for his lively sculptures 'drawn' with wire and also spawned a miniature mechanized circus made from scrap materials (1926-31), with which he gave performances in his studio. Increasingly convinced that 'art was too static to reflect our world of movement', from 1930 he produced mechanized abstract constructions and in 1932 invented the mobile. Organic shapes cut from tin were suspended on wire, producing infinitely variable, graceful compositions and, similarly, his static abstract works, or 'stabiles', reveal dramatically different aspects from successive viewpoints. **ER**.

CALLAGHAN, JAMES, BARON CALLAGHAN OF CARDIFF
1912-
British politician and statesman

Having held all the great offices of state during the Labour governments of 1964-70 and 1974 onwards, Callaghan was the natural successor to WILSON in 1976. These were difficult days to govern Britain, but Callaghan boosted his public standing by skilfully implementing the IMF loan and Lib-Lab Pact. The 1978-9 'Winter of Discontent' undid all this and opened the way to Conservative electoral victory. **JP**.

ABOVE: *Opera star Maria Callas.*

CALLAS, MARIA
1923-1977
Greek-American opera singer

A coloratura soprano who almost singlehandedly revived the early nineteenth-century operatic repertoire with her performances of Rossini, Bellini, and Donizetti. Her first professional appearances were in Athens, where she concentrated on Verdi and Wagner, but her powerful, expressive, and wide-ranging voice and extending repertoire took her to La Scala, Milan, with additional seasons at Covent Garden and the New York Met in the mid-1950s. Despite her intelligent musicality, Callas was an inconsistent and occasionally unreliable performer; her famous liaison with Greek shipping millionaire Aristotle Onassis coincided with a vocal crisis that effectively ended her career. **JH**.

CALVINO, ITALO
1923-1985
Italian writer

Born in Cuba, Calvino grew up in San Remo, Italy. He became a leading figure in the neo-realist movement in Italy with *Il sentiero dei nidi di ragno* (*The Path of the Nest of Spiders*, 1947), his first novel. He was also an essayist and journalist. His later fiction, which explores the possibilities of fantasy and myth after the fashion of BORGES, stretches the bounds of realism to such an extent as almost to place him among the Magic Realists. In 1973 he won the prestigious Premio Feltrinelli. The whimsical, entertaining, hyper-postmodern *Se uno notte d'inverno un viaggiatore* (*If On a Winter's Night a Traveller*, 1979) is his best-known novel. **AM**.

ABOVE: *James Cagney in* Yankee Doodle Dandy.

CAMP, WALTER CHAUNCEY
1859-1925
American football player, coach, and innovator

Walter Camp has long been called the 'father of American football.' At Yale University he played, coached, and wrote about the game. Truly, he helped to define it, establishing some of football's basic rules and strategies. Each year a Walter Camp All-American team is named to honor top collegians. **MD**.

CAMPBELL, DONALD MALCOLM
1921-1967
British World Land Speed Record Holder

Motivated by his father's numerous World Land Speed records in the late 1920s and 1930s, Donald Campbell brought the record back to Britain in 1964 when he drove Bluebird Proteus to a speed of 403.10mph. He held the World Water Speed Record seven times and died making a further record-breaking attempt. **NF**.

CAMUS, ALBERT
1913-1960
French writer

Born and educated in Algeria, as a philosophy student Camus became involved in left-wing theater, and in 1934 briefly joined the Communist Party, leaving because of its attitude to the Arabs. He was an active member of the Resistance. His great existentialist novels – *The Outsider* (1942), *The Plague* (1947) and *The Rebel* (1951) – explore an absurdist universe, in part a reaction to the condition of colonial Algeria. Attacked for his anti-communism by some on the Left, Camus was nevertheless acknowledged by SARTRE as 'one of the principal forces in our cultural domain'. He received the Nobel Prize in 1957. **CW**.

CANNON, WALTER
1871-1945
American physiologist

Cannon's career centred on Harvard University. An immensely influential figure, he was an 'all-round' physiologist of the old school. His researches ranged from zoology to innovative methods using radio-opaque meals to study the gut with x-rays (1898). Research during his military service (1917-19), in collaboration with Sir William BAYLISS, led to a new understanding of traumatic shock. **GL**.

CAPONE, AL(PHONSO)
1898-1947
American gangster

Capone was initiated into organized crime in New York and went on to head the most notorious crime syndicate in Chicago during the 1920s. He controlled much of Chicago's gambling and sex industry and supplied the city with illegal drink. He was certainly a murderer and an extortioner, but was jailed for tax evasion in 1931. He was released in 1939 as a result of a nervous breakdown. **RJ**.

ABOVE: American novelist Truman Capote.

ABOVE: A smiling Al Capone.

CAPOTE, TRUMAN
1924-1984
American writer

Alabama-born Capote's early novels, *Other Voices, Other Rooms* (1948) and *The Grass Harp* (1951) are essentially novels of the American South, although they also contain many fine surrealist and gothic moments. *In Cold Blood* (1966) deals with a Kansas murder case - this 'non-fiction novel' proved a bestseller. **CH-M**.

CAPRA, FRANK
1897-1991
American film director

Capra's heyday as a director was in the 1930s, when he excelled at comedies with a strong moral message. He won three directing Oscars – for *It Happened One Night* (1934), *Mr. Deeds Goes to Town* (1936), and *You Can't Take it With You* (1938) – but his most complex, enduring film is probably *It's a Wonderful Life* (1946), a dark, Dickensian fantasy on the inspiring theme that no man is born a failure. **NS**.

CARDIN, PIERRE
1922-
French fashion designer

Born near Venice to French parents, Cardin began his career in Vichy as a tailor's assistant. He moved to Paris where he worked with Elsa SCHIAPARELLI and made costumes for Jean COCTEAU's film *Beauty and the Beast* (1947). Always an innovator, his first collection in 1957 featured bubble skirts, and his 1964 collection, with cat-suits and helmets, was called 'space age'. During the 1960s he raised hemlines to four inches above the knee, while necklines plunged to the waist both at the back and front. Cardin is particularly associated with the use of knitted fabrics and bias-cut 'spiral' dresses. **MC**.

ABOVE: Designer Pierre Cardin with actress Jean Moreau (right).

CARDOZO, BENJAMIN
1870-1938
American lawyer

An eloquent interpreter of the extent of federal powers, Cardozo started his career in the New York Supreme Court acting against the Tamany Hall interest. Appointed an Associate Justice of the Supreme Court in 1932, he became known for his liberalism and particularly for his decisions on social reform. He described himself as 'a judicial evolutionist.' **JC.**

CARLSON, CHESTER
1906-1968
American inventor

The inventor of the xerographic copier which for the first time made possible cheap and simple copying of documents, Carlson had appreciated the need for such a copier while working in the patents department of a New York electronics firm where he had needed copies of blueprints and patent descriptions. Disposing of wet chemicals, he relied instead on the combination of electrostatics and photoconductivity and in 1938 produced his first xerographic copy. Six years later he obtained commercial backing from the Haloid Company (later Xerox Corp) for his invention. **PT.**

CARNAP, RUDOLF
1891-1970
American philosopher

After being educated in Germany as a physicist, and studying mathematics under FREGE, Carnap was invited to Vienna where he collaborated with Schlick in the work which led to the school of empiricism known as 'logical positivism' (which was popularized in English by A J AYER). Later, in *The Logical Syntax of Language*, Carnap argued that philosophical questions are only capable of resolution if they can be interpreted in terms of logic. With the rise of the Nazis, Carnap moved to Chicago whereafter his main work was concerned with the philosophy of science and, in particular, probability. **EB.**

CARNARVON, GEORGE, 5TH EARL
1866-1923
British Egyptologist

Carnarvon funded, and helped Howard CARTER conduct, the excavations in the Valley of the Kings that brought to light the fabulously rich tomb of the Pharoah Tutankhamen in 1922. Carnarvon died soon after, thus contributing to the myth of 'Tutankhamen's Curse'. **RJ.**

CARNEGIE, ANDREW
1835-1919
American industrialist and philanthropist

Scottish by birth, Carnegie's story is a classic one of rags to riches. Working his way up in the US from bobbin boy to railroad superintendent, Carnegie made a fortune from speculation and iron, seeking the total integration of the mining, shipping, smelting, and production of steel in America. He sold the Carnegie Steel Company in 1901 to GI Pierpoint Morgan for $480 million, and distributed his wealth in the US and UK through the creation of endowments and trusts in the areas of education, world peace, and teacher training. **PT.**

ABOVE: *Industrialist and philanthropist Andrew Carnegie.*

CARO, ANTHONY
1924-
British sculptor

Caro trained in engineering before studying at the Royal Academy Schools, London, 1947-52. He was an assistant to Henry MOORE, 1951-53, and his early work was figurative. In 1959 he met David SMITH while visiting the USA, and began making large-scale sculptures from prefabricated metal elements such as I-beams and propeller blades, welded and bolted together. Painted in a single resonant color, they convey a particular mood, often emphasized by the title, as in *Early One Morning* (1962). Latterly he has favored weathered, rusted surfaces. His works usually sit on the floor and present very different formal compositions from different viewpoints. **ER.**

CAROTHERS, WALLACE
1896-1937
American chemist

A teacher's son, he was himself a teacher until 1929 when he joined the Du Pont Company as a research chemist. He studied polymerization – the linking together of atoms to form very long chains – and in 1932 produced the first synthetic rubber which was called Neoprene. He also developed a substance that could be drawn out into a fine strong filament with similar properties to silk. In 1937 this was manufactured as Nylon, the first synthetic fiber. Carothers often suffered from depression and, despite his successful career and recent marriage, committed suicide at the age of 41. **DD.**

LE CARRÉ, JOHN
1931-
British novelist

Born David Cornwell, Le Carré is a writer of thrillers and grimly realistic spy stories from *The Spy Who Came in from the Cold*, and the series of novels featuring George Smiley, spymaster and master spy, to *The Little Drummer Girl*, many of which have been successfully filmed or serialized for television. **AM.**

CARREL, ALEXIS
1873-1944
French surgeon

Carrell gained his medical degree at Lyon in 1902. He was a pioneer in the methods of blood-vessel surgery and organ transplantation. He was the first person to publish details of a successful surgical method for joining major blood vessels, and much of his method remains the basis for present day surgery. He was awarded the Nobel Prize for Medicine or Physiology in 1912, for his work on organ transplants in animals, and his recognition of the immune reaction that caused the rejection of such transplants. In 1935 he also devised a mechanical heart capable of keeping isolated organs alive outside the body. **EMS.**

CARRERAS, JOSÉ MARIA
1946-
Spanish opera singer

With DOMINGO and PAVAROTTI Carreras is one of the three great tenors of the late twentieth century. His sweet, warm voice and handsome stage presence at first brought him mainly romantic roles, such as Alfredo in Verdi's *La Traviata*. The 1970s and 1980s saw him tackling heavier Verdian parts, and he has returned triumphantly to the international scene after overcoming leukaemia. **JH.**

CARTER, ANGELA
1940-1992
British novelist

Angela Carter was originally a journalist, (*Nothing Sacred* [1982] is a collection of some of her journalism), but was also a short-story writer of considerable power, and is most highly regarded as a novelist. Frequently considered a practitioner of magic realism, Carter was highly literate and her works are typically humorous, often blackly, and in style range from gothic, pastiche and science fiction to the picaresque. Interested in myth-making, folk and fairy tales and very much a feminist, until her tragic early death Carter was one of the finest writing talents in Britain, although never a prize winner. *Nights at the Circus* (1984) and *Wise Children* (1991) were her last novels before her death. **AM.**

CARTER, ELLIOTT COOK
1908-
American composer

New Yorker Elliott Carter has been one of the century's most distinguished composers. A reticent performer, his orchestral, choral, and chamber works draw together techniques as diverse as those of the Renaissance madrigal, jazz, and modern serialism, supporting his expressive elements in complex and shifting rhythmic structures. **DK**.

CARTER, HOWARD
1874-1939
British archaeologist

In November 1922, after many seasons largely unrewarded work at the Valley of the Kings near Thebes (Luxor) in Egypt, Howard Carter located the tomb of the Pharoah Tutankhamen. Most of the valley's tombs had been robbed in ancient times, but the tomb of Tutankhamen had preserved intact the greatest treasure ever recovered by an archaeologist. The find so caught the public imagination that he and his sponsor, Lord CARNARVON, can be said to have begun the modern popularization of archaeology. **RJ**.

ABOVE: Archaeologist and Egyptologist Howard Carter (with cane).

CARTER, JIMMY [JAMES EARL]
1924-
American politician and president

As Governor of Georgia (1970-74) Carter proved a strong defender of civil rights. His 'zero-based budgeting system' ensured exact financial accountability by departmental heads. Carter won the Democratic nomination for President in 1976, winning the campaign in the wake of Richard NIXON's disgrace. He branded the tax situation 'a national disgrace' and fought to improve the economy. He signed the first SALT agreement and brokered the peace treaty between Israel and Egypt in 1979 but had no answer to the militancy of Iran or to REAGAN's presidential campaign. **JC**.

ABOVE: Former US President Jimmy Carter (left).

CARTIER-BRESSON, HENRI
1908-
French photographer

Cartier-Bresson, the greatest of all European human-interest photographers, studied painting with the cubist André Lhote in Paris in the late 1920s before turning to photography in 1930. His reputation was fully confirmed in 1952 with the publication of his first major book *Images à la Sauvette (The Decisive Moment)*. In 1955 *Les Européens (The Europeans)* was published, as well as books on Moscow and China. Cartier-Bresson emphasized the importance of being in the middle of things, absorbed by events, to the point of being able to reproduce 'the organic rhythm of forms'. Surrealism stressed absorption in the 'creative process', and at the same time sports photographers, aided by new lightweight cameras, such as the Ermanox, scrutinized events for 'the psychological moment'. Cartier-Bresson applied this process to reportage in general. He was also impressed by the irreverent, wry humor of André KERTÉSZ. Together they worked for Lucien Vogel's illustrated magazine *Vu*. In addition he lived in a culture which attached importance to psychological realism, and his achievement was to extend this from literature into photographic art. In the years after the war he projected a recuperative idea of France as a land of continuities and character, as an example to itself and to the rest of the world. In 1947 he helped found the cooperative picture agency Magnum Photos. **IJ**.

CARUSO, ENRICO
1873-1921
Italian opera singer

With his exceptionally beautiful mellow voice, Caruso's early roles were lyric ones, and his regular appearances at the Met between 1903 and 1920 included the role of Dick Johnson in the world premiere of Puccini's *La Fanciulla del West*. As his voice matured, he acquired an almost impeccable technique, and extended his repertoire into dramatic roles such as Samson in Saint-Saens' *Samson et Dalila*. He was the first tenor to make numerous recordings, which contributed both to his own and to the medium's success; his 'Una furtiva lagrima' from Donizetti's *L'Elisir d'Amore* is operatic singing at its greatest. **JH**.

CASLAVSKA, VERA
1942-
Czechoslovak gymnast

Vera Caslavska won three gold medals at the 1964 Olympics and had further success at the 1966 World Championships but her most notable performances were en route to four gold medals at the Mexico games in 1968. Her grace and elegance were held to be particularly touching since her country had recently suffered from the Soviet invasion. **DS**.

CASTRO, FIDEL
1926-
Cuban politician

Creator of the only Communist state in the New World to date, Castro was a student agitator imprisoned under the Cuban dictator BATISTA. He trained as a guerrilla in Mexico, landed in Cuba in December 1956, and brought his revolution to a triumphant conclusion in January 1959. He beat off a direct US challenge at the Bay of Pigs (1961) but became increasingly isolated by American economic blockade and hence dependent on the USSR, which settled the missile crisis (1962) without consulting him. His charisma has been the only answer he can give latterly to his increasingly restive and impoverished people. **JC**.

CATHER, WILLA
1893-1947
American novelist

Though born in Virginia, Willa Cather was brought up among the immigrant communities in Nebraska. In novels such as *O Pioneers!* (1913), *My Antonia* (1918), and *A Lost Lady* (1922), Cather evokes life on the frontier with a lyricism and classical lucidity that marks her work, exploring the tension between domesticity and creative freedom in women's lives. *Not Under Forty* (1936) contains her theories of fiction. **CW**.

RIGHT: Cuba's Fidel Castro addresses the UN.

ABOVE: Dictator Nicholae Ceauçescu.

CEAUÇESCU, NICOLAE
1918-1989
Romanian politician

Ceauçescu was the last of the postwar Communist dictators to be overthrown, shot on Christmas Day 1989 after a summary trial. The violence of the Romanian counter-revolution, in contrast to elsewhere in the old Eastern bloc, testified to his mad intransigence and the loathing he inspired. General Secretary of the party from 1965, he looked to MAO for inspiration rather than Moscow and his cult of personality reached bizarre depths, buttressed partly by Western flattery. **JC**.

CHADWICK, SIR JAMES
1891-1974
British physicist

Chadwick's specialty was atomic structure and after graduating from Manchester in 1911 he went to Berlin to work with Hans Geiger. There he was interned at the outbreak of World War I. After the war he went to Cambridge where he discovered the neutron – the particle with no charge in an atom's nucleus. He was awarded the Nobel Prize for Physics for this in 1935. He held a number of academic posts at Cambridge and at Liverpool, where he built the first cyclotron in Britain. He headed the British contingent in the Manhattan Project. **DD**.

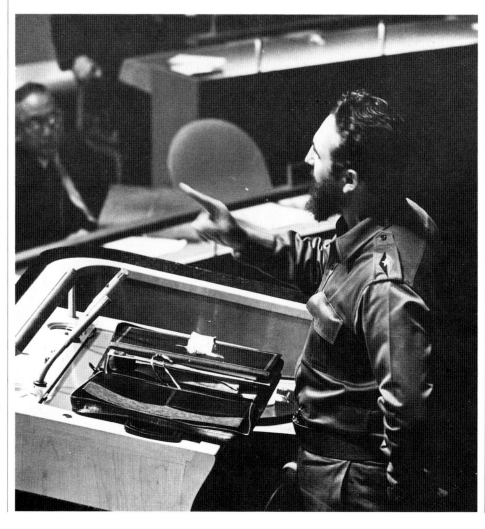

ABOVE: French Expressionist artist Marc Chagall.

CHAGALL, MARC
1887-1985
French painter

Chagall studied in St Petersburg under Leon Bakst before traveling to Paris in 1910. While absorbing elements of Cubism he retained a debt to Russian folk art, developing a highly individual, imaginative style. His richly colored, dreamlike images, with their irrational juxtapositions of realistically drawn objects, were based on memories of his Russo-Jewish childhood. Returning to Russia in 1914, he became Commissar of Arts in Vitebsk, his home town, after the 1917 revolution but resigned following disagreements with MALEVICH. After working in Moscow for the Jewish State Theatre, in 1923 he returned to France where he found the artistic atmosphere more congenial. Hailed as a precursor of the emergent Surrealist movement, he refused to be associated with it, specifically repudiating its doctrine of automatism. He took French citizenship in 1937 but in 1941 was forced to leave occupied France for the USA. There he executed designs for the ballet, returning to France in 1948. During the 1960s and 1970s his monumental works drew on the bible, war, mythology, and the circus, which he saw as a metaphor for life. A prolific artist, he also practiced printmaking, book illustration, stained-glass design, and wall painting. **ER**.

CHAMBERLAIN, NEVILLE
1869-1940
British politician

Although perhaps the most able and energetic minister of the interwar years, both as Minister of Health and Chancellor of the Exchequer, Neville Chamberlain is more often portrayed as either a naive peacelover for trusting Hitler or a 'guilty man' unwilling to confront aggressors. Recent research findings show, however, that his policy as Prime Minister (1937-40) was driven by the strategic imperative to avoid war on European, Mediterranean, and East Asian fronts simultaneously, and the diplomatic need to maintain unity between Britain and the self-governing Dominions. Nevertheless revelations that Chamberlain became almost obsessive about appeasement and sought to manipulate public opinion by management of the press continue to raise questions about his judgment. **JP**.

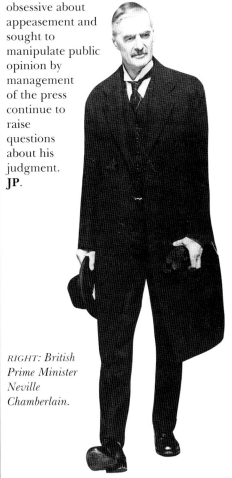

RIGHT: British Prime Minister Neville Chamberlain.

CHAMBERLAIN, WILT [WILTON NORMAN]
1936-
American basketball player

A truly dominating force in the National Basketball Association, the 7-1 center was enormously agile for his size, a combination that made him almost impossible to stop. As a member of the Philadelphia Warriors in 1961-1962, Chamberlain averaged an astonishing 50.4 points per game. In one contest against the Knicks he scored a record 100 points. He is the league's all-time leading rebounder and its second leading scorer. 'The Stilt' also played for the Harlem Globetrotters and the University of Kansas. **MD**.

CHANDLER, RAYMOND
1888-1959
American novelist

Born in Chicago, Chandler was educated in England at Dulwich College, and returned to America in 1912 where he settled in California. He was already an established writer of crime stories in big city settings when his first novel, *The Big Sleep*, was published in 1939. This introduced Philip Marlowe, his hard-boiled private eye, master of the ironic observation, cynical but vulnerable to women. Many of his stories were translated to film, like *Farewell, My Lovely* (1940) and *The Long Goodbye* (1953). He was also something of an authority on the genre, as well as a highly successful screenwriter. **AM**.

ABOVE: *Crime novelist Raymond Chandler.*

CHANDRASEKHAR, SUBRAHMANYAN
1910-
Indian-American astrophysicist

Chandrasekhar studied in England before settling in the US in 1936. His most celebrated work was done at Cambridge, England, in the 1930s concerning the peculiar physics of white dwarfs – 'dead' stars in which matter is crushed to ultra-high density. He calculated that a white dwarf could not have a mass of more than about one and a half times that of the sun, otherwise gravity would collapse it into something even smaller and denser. That 'something' is now known to be either a neutron star or a black hole, and the limit to a white dwarf's mass is termed the Chandrasekhar limit. He won the Nobel Prize for Physics in 1983 for this work. **IR**.

CHANEL, COCO [GABRIELLE BONHEUR]
1883-1971
French fashion designer

Chanel's clothes and accessories have become a lasting symbol of elegance. Her earliest patterns were revolutionary; designed to be worn without corsets, they had fewer linings, and were thus less rigid than contemporary fashions. In 1916 she began to work with jersey which proved so successful that she began to manufacture the material herself. Having introduced the twin set, designed to be worn over her wide-legged 'yachting pants', she threw a succession of new fashion ideas at the world during the 1920s such as collarless cardigan jackets and quilted handbags on gold chains. She was the archetypal 'garçonne' in this period: slim, flat-chested with a short haircut. In the mid-1930s she concentrated her energies on manufacturing and closed her salon. In 1954, at the age of 71, she shocked and delighted the fashion world with a show of re-vamped prewar designs. **MC**.

LEFT: *Coco Chanel.*

CHANEY, LON
1883-1930
American actor

Chaney, 'The Man of a Thousand Faces', suffered more for his art than any other actor. In order to look like a vampire he wore a set of huge false teeth which kept him in constant pain and metal rings inside his eyelids to give him the characteristic stare. He broke into films in *The Miracle Man* (1919) playing a bogus cripple, and followed this with a series of mainly grotesque parts. His make-up was so inventive that he often played two parts in one film. His greatest success was in *The Hunchback of Notre Dame* (1924), but he is equally remembered for *The Phantom of the Opera* (1925). **DL**.

ABOVE: *Screen legend Charlie Chaplin.*

CHAPLIN, SIR CHARLES
1889-1977
British actor and director

Chaplin was a legendary figure in his own lifetime despite a comparatively limited output. At the age of 17 he joined the Fred Karno Company and toured Britain, and on tour in the US in 1912 he began making movies for Mack SENNETT, 35 in his first year, evolving the tramp character as he went along; the funny walk, the bowler hat, the cane and moustache, the baggy pants. In 1920 *The Kid* was an enormous box office smash, and he became an international star. Having co-founded United Artists in 1919, Chaplin resisted sound as long as he could; *City Lights* (1931), with a score he composed and conducted, and *Modern Times* (1936) are essentially silent movies, and though there are great moments in later films, the use of sound revealed flaws, chiefly a tendency to become excessively sentimental. *A Countess from Hong Kong* (1966) was already dated on its release. Nor was praise for his earlier work universal; conservatives attacked him for not fighting in World War I, for his left-wing politics, for his refusal to become an American citizen, and his alleged fondness for teenage girls, and he and his family were forced to move to Switzerland during the McCarthy era, but in 1971 he returned to the United States in triumph to receive a special Academy Award. **DC**.

CHAPMAN, COLIN
1928-1982
British designer and motor manufacturer

Probably the most creative and innovative race-car designer of his generation, Chapman built his first 'Special' in 1947 and went on to win seven World Championships for Constructors and six World Championships for drivers titles. He established the Lotus Cars manufacturing concern with exceptional, if somewhat fragile, sports cars like the Elan and Esprit. It was no secret that Chapman's heart was in racing and he divorced himself from the factory to concentrate on Formula One. An experienced pilot and yachtsman, Chapman died at the controls of his own light plane, while still firmly at the peak of his innovative powers. **NF**.

CHARDIN, TEILHARD DE
1881-1955
French Jesuit theologian and palaentologist

This truly remarkable man entered the Society of Jesus in 1899, was awarded the *Légion d'honneur* for his work as a stretcher-bearer in World War I and in 1922 completed his Phd in palaentology. This was to be the field in which he would really make his mark, with his seminal discovery of Peking Man in 1929. He combined his palaentological and theological expertise to offer a startling view of Christian evolution, which provoked much scientific debate and brought him into conflict with the Catholic Church. **ML**.

CHARLES, RAY
1930-
American singer, composer and performer

Charles is perhaps the most successful soul singer of all time. Blind from the age of six, he taught himself to arrange and compose from braille and had his first rhythm and blues hits in the early 1950s; 'I Got a Woman' was covered by Elvis PRESLEY. His first number one was 'Georgia on my Mind' with Hoagy Carmichael, soon followed by 'Hit the Road Jack' with his female quartet the Raelets and 'I Can't Stop Loving You'. His unique mixture of gospel power, everyday subjects, and smooth, straightforward delivery ensured that hits and world tours continued well into the 1980s. **JH**.

CHARLTON, BOBBY
1937-
British soccer player

Bobby Charlton played 106 international soccer matches for England and scored a record total of 49 goals. From a well-known soccer family (his brother Jack was also a noted player and is currently a successful manager), Bobby played throughout his career with the Manchester United club being one of the survivors of the air crash at Munich (*see* Matt BUSBY). He was one of the heroes of England's World Cup win in 1966 and scored twice in Manchester United's European Cup success in 1968. Less successful as a coach after his retirement in 1973, he remains a much-respected commentator on his sport. **DS**.

CHARNLEY, SIR JOHN
1911-1982
British surgeon

Charnley's career lay in orthopaedic surgery, to which he brought a flair for mechanical engineering. By the late 1960s he had perfected the first successful hip replacement operation, using the Charnley prosthesis. A related interest was in devising clean-air systems for operating theaters. **GL**.

CHEEVER, JOHN
1912-1982
American writer

Massachusetts-born Cheever's ironic and sophisticated short stories and novels – in particular *The Wapshot Chronicle* (1957), *The Wapshot Scandal* (1964), and above all *Falconer* (1977) – stage an often shocking encounter between affluent, middle-class white America and a world of psychic and historical nightmare that it attempts to shut out. **CW**.

CHESHIRE, LEONARD, BARON
1917-1992
British pilot and charity founder

Cheshire enjoyed two outstanding careers: one as 'probably the greatest bomber pilot of any airforce in the world' and the other as the founder of over 270 nursing homes in 47 countries. As a pilot Cheshire was awarded the VC for his relentless courage in guiding low-level sorties over Germany during World War II. Somewhat lost for a cause after the war, Cheshire took into his home an incurable patient. This patient kindled in him a Catholic faith and led to his life's work in setting up hospices for the incurable of any age or creed. In this he was assisted by his wife Sue Ryder. **PT**.

CHEVALIER, MAURICE
1888-1972
French actor and singer

Chevalier's early song, 'Valentine', about the delights of a mistress established his niche as a charming roué with a trademark straw hat. Hollywood stardom followed; he returned to Paris in 1935 a world figure and had a second string of successes in the 1950s, above all *Gigi* (1958), receiving a personal Oscar that year. **JH**.

CHIANG KAI-SHEK
1887-1975
Chinese statesman

Chiang was heir of SUN YAT-SEN's revolution, but his reforms were first stalled by steady Japanese annexation of China in the 1930s, and then by the corruption of the ruling clique. He was forced to unite with the Communists by his own Manchurian troops who kidnapped him in 1936, and stemmed the Japanese tide by costly tactics. World War II, when he was one of the big four, was his finest hour. After losing the Civil War which followed, he was unable to prevent the Communists splitting the broad coalition of the Kuomintang. The founding party of modern China was driven into the offshore bastion of Taiwan. Chiang turned Taiwan into a successful capitalist enclave with American backing and remained its President until his death. **JC**.

ABOVE: Chinese Nationalist Chiang Kai-Shek.

CHILDE, VERE GORDON
1892-1957
Australian archaeologist

The most influential archaeological theorist of his generation, Childe was the first to bring the rather remote world of prehistoric studies to popular attention with his best-selling *What Happened in History* (1942). He first came to prominence in 1920 as supervisor of the excavations at Skara Brae in Orkney, possibly the most significant prehistoric find of the century, but it was his first book in 1925, *The Dawn of European Civilisation*, that really made his reputation. Childe revitalized the field of prehistoric studies with his revolutionary attitude to the subject. His willingness to embrace a more geographical approach, so long resisted by earlier archaeologists, and his wider concept of a culture actually representing an entire people, established him as an international force. **ML**.

CHIRICO, GIORGIO DE
1888-1978
Italian painter

Born in Greece, de Chirico went to Italy in 1909, in 1910 producing his first 'enigma' paintings, empty Italian townscapes in which a solitary figure or statue appeared. Moving to Paris in 1911 he developed a theory of 'metaphysical insight' into a mysterious reality behind ordinary things. His strange iconography substituted tailors' dummies and statuary for humans, juxtaposing them with incongruous objects. The dream-like quality of these mysterious associations was heightened by their stillness and unreal perspective. Returning to Italy in 1915, in 1917 he founded the Metaphysical school, which prefigured Surrealism. From 1930 he abandoned modern art, concentrating instead on imitating the Old Masters. **ER**.

CHOMSKY, NOAM AVRAM
1928-
American linguist and political activist

Chomsky developed a theory of generative grammar which made him internationally famous at the age of 40. The son of a Hebrew scholar, Chomsky studied mathematics and philosophy at the University of Pennsylvania. He moved on to linguistics, which he taught at Massachusetts Institute of Technology, where he now holds a chair. In his books, *Syntactic Structures* and *Aspects of a Theory of Syntax* he provided an account of the way humans are able to generate enormously diverse languages and expressions from an innate capacity for speech. Chomsky has since become widely known as a political activist, particularly for his opposition to American involvement in Vietnam and to US foreign policy. **DSl**.

RIGHT: Linguist and activist Noam Chomsky.

CHOU EN LAI
1898-1976
Chinese politician

MAO's intellectual right-hand man, Chou fled from post-Manchu China to found the Chinese Communist Youth Group in Paris in 1922, returning in 1924 to become head of political training at the Whampoa Military Academy. He organized the abortive Communist rising in Shanghai in 1927 and joined Mao in 1931, becoming Political Commissar of the Red Army in 1932. Chief Communist negotiator for the release of CHIANG KAI SHEK after his kidnap in 1936, he was also Mao's representative in negotiations with the USA, who were trying to intervene in the civil war. Once the People's Republic was established in 1949, Chou became Foreign Minister until 1958 and played an important part in enhancing Chinese influence in the third world. He was Prime Minister from 1958 until his death and was a moderating influence during the Cultural Revolution, doing much to maintain amicable relations between China and the West. **JC**.

CHRISTIE, DAME AGATHA
1890-1976
British novelist

English creator of such well-known detectives as Hercule Poirot and Miss Marple, Agatha Christie is internationally held to be a master of the literary whodunit. The author of more than 60 novels, including *Murder on the Orient Express* (1934) and *Death on the Nile* (1937), her formalist ability to manipulate plot and character in an apparently simplistic way makes her work as immediately accessible as a crossword. Her novels, which expound the new, yet conservative suburban values of the interwar years, are widely adapted for film and television. Her play, *The Mousetrap*, has been running in London for over 30 years. **CW**.

CHRISTIE, JULIE
1941-
British actress

Christie's film debut came in 1962 in *Crooks Anonymous*, and in *Darling* (1965) she won an Academy Award for Best Actress for her portrayal of a self-centred model. Critics were unimpressed with subsequent films, although *Doctor Zhivago* (1965) and *Shampoo* (1975) were great commercial successes. Few roles have allowed her to display her great range as an actress. **DC**.

CHRISTO [CHRISTO JAVACHEFF]
1935-
American sculptor and designer

Born in Gabrova, Bulgaria, Christo settled in the USA in 1964. He is best known for his packaged objects, whereby familiar objects, ranging from trees to architectural monuments, are wrapped in canvas or semi-transparent plastic to enhance awareness of the fundamental forms below. He also makes assemblages of oil drums. **ER**.

ABOVE: US motor manufacturer Walter Chrysler.

CHRYSLER, WALTER
1875-1940
American motor manufacturer

Starting as a railway engineer, Chrysler bought his first car in 1905 and joined General Motors in 1912. He left to work for the Maxwell company, which he turned around from loss to profit, and purchased outright in 1925, forming the Chrysler Corporation. He produced the Airflow which, although a commercial mistake, emphasized commitment to research in vehicle aerodynamics. Chrysler actually overtook Ford in production terms and stayed there until 1950. The company has had a troubled recent history but now has some interesting four-wheel drive machines, as well as the outrageous Viper sports car. **NF**.

CHUIKOV, VASILI, MARSHAL
1900-1982
Russian soldier

Joining the Red Army in 1918, Chuikov rose to command a regiment during the Civil War (1919-21). In 1942, as the Germans entered Stalingrad, he took over defense of the city. His success assured him a leading role in the counter-offensives of 1943-45, culminating in the seizure of Berlin. **JPi**.

CHURCHILL, SIR WINSTON
1874-1965
British politician and international statesman

Churchill probably deserves description as the greatest Briton of the century. Not for being the most versatile holder of Cabinet office – that was perhaps R A Butler. Not for length of service as Prime Minister – many have served longer. Not even as the manager of a war effort – LLOYD GEORGE was the more skillful. But because his spirit persuaded the nation when it stood alone in 1940 that victory could still be won and that it would be worth whatever sacrifice.

From the start Churchill was driven by a heroic view of history and his place in it. Thus the daring journalist of the Boer War became the principled defender of free trade, forceful social reformer, outstanding Minister of Munitions, and farsighted opponent of appeasement. Unfortunately this view was not universal. Distrusted for changing party so often, despised as a class warrior after Tonypandy and the General Strike, demonstrated as reckless by Gallipoli, and derided for obstructing Indian reform, Churchill appeared an unlikely architect of national unity. Yet he was the people's choice when threatened with military humiliation or worse. The purposeful leadership and inspirational oratory that followed did not disappoint.

Although cast aside in 1945, his warnings about the Iron Curtain and Conservative electoral success in 1951 brought him an 'indian summer' in Downing Street. On his death Churchill was honored with the century's only state funeral for a civilian. The nation had thanked its savior. **JP**.

CITROËN, ANDRÉ
1878-1935
French motor manufacturer

Apart from establishing a major motor manufacturing company, André Citroën was famous for some very innovative marketing ideas. For nine years in the 1920s the company's logo hung in electric lights from the Eiffel Tower. He introduced front-wheel drive to the mass market with the Traction Avant, but financial problems lost Citroën control of his company in 1934. **NF**.

RIGHT: Prime Minister Churchill (right) pictured with President Truman.

CLAPTON, ERIC (ERIC JONES]
1945-
British blues guitarist and singer

First gaining public attention with the Yardbirds in 1963, Clapton began as a blues purist in the Muddy Waters mold, fitting well into John Mayall's Bluesbreakers, whose 1966 *Bluesbreakers* album confirmed him as the best blues guitarist of his age. With 'supergroup' Cream he played to rapturous audiences until he became disillusioned with touring at the end of 1968, and in 1970 he recorded the classic hit 'Layla' with Derek and the Dominos, also beginning to guest on other people's albums. But tragedy in his personal life and heroin addiction kept him out of the public eye until 1974 and the release of the album *461 Ocean Boulevard*. Less successful albums and publicity surrounding a drink problem continued to dog him, but since his 1985 appearance at Live Aid he has increasingly enjoyed cult status, with sell-out concerts in 1990 and 1991 at London's Royal Albert Hall evidence of his continuing popularity. **DC**.

CLARK, JAMES
1936-1968
British racing driver

A driver of phenomenal talent across a variety of different machines, Jim Clark not only won the Formula One World Championship, twice, but also took America's premier race, the Indianapolis 500 in 1965 – each time at the wheel of a Lotus. A natural driver, he was often seen in sedan cars, notably a Lotus Cortina. He crashed fatally at Hockenheim. **NF**.

CLARK, MARK, GENERAL
1896-1984
American soldier

After service in World War I, Clark climbed the ladder of promotion in the US Army until, in 1942, he was appointed to assist General EISENHOWER to plan the invasion of French North Africa. In September 1943 he commanded the Allied landings at Salerno in Italy, after which he led the Anglo-US 5th Army northwards towards Rome. His conduct during the near-disastrous Anzio landings in January 1944 has been criticized, but this did not prevent his promotion to command the Allied 15th Army Group in Italy 1944-45. In 1952-53 he commanded United Nations forces in Korea. **JPi**.

CLARKE, ARTHUR C
1917-
British writer

Most famous for *2001: A Space Odyssey* (1968), Clarke wrote the screenplay for that spectacular film in collaboration with Stanley KUBRICK, and has written many non-fiction works on space travel. His novels are a curious amalgam of the visionary and the pessimistic, all backed up by substantial technical knowledge. **AM**.

CLAUDEL, PAUL
1868-1955
French writer

Paul Claudel passionately testified in his work to the strict Catholicism he embraced in 1886. His versification, drawn uniquely from the prose of Rimbaud and the Old Testament, and his major plays such as *Le Soulier de satin* (1919-24) exerted a strong influence over the succeeding generation of poets. **CW**.

CLEMENCEAU, GEORGES
1841-1929
French statesman

Nicknamed 'the Tiger,' Clemenceau took over the French premiership in November 1917, at the age of 76, after army mutinies had threatened the country's ability to continue World War I. He ensured victory and made sure that French interests prevailed in the Versailles Treaty. In 1920 he was defeated first for the presidency and then his government lost office, whereupon he retired. De GAULLE instituted the tradition of saluting the Tiger's statue in the Champs Elysées. **JC**.

CLIFT, MONTGOMERY
1920-1966
American actor

Nominated for an Academy Award for Best Actor for his film debut in *The Search* (1948) and *From Here to Eternity* (1953), Clift was a promising star who generally played introspective heroes. Drink and drugs and the strain of having to conceal his homosexuality made him a tragic figure, and he died of a heart attack at the age of 45. **DC**.

CLINTON, WILLIAM JEFFERSON BLYTHE
1946-
American politician and President

The youthful Democrat Governor of Arkansas defeated George BUSH in the 1992 presidential elections, offering Americans economic and social reforms at home and a maintenance of US military might abroad. Although he has inherited the large Republican budget deficit, Clinton is the first President for many years to have a compliant Congress and Senate to assist his legislative program. **JC**.

COBB, TY [TYRUS RAYMOND]
1886-1961
American baseball player

Cobb was known as 'the Georgia Peach,' but there was nothing sweet or fuzzy about him. His ferocious competitive spirit made him one of the greatest baseball players of all time and one of the least popular. He was known for inciting opposing players with his acid tongue and his vicious spikes-up slides. As a member of the Detroit Tigers he won 12 American League batting titles in 13 years, including a remarkable nine in a row. Three times he hit over .400. His lifetime batting average of .367 has never been approached. **MD**.

COBHAM, SIR ALAN
1894-1973
British long-distance pilot

First working as a farm-hand and in a warehouse before enlisting in the army in 1914, Cobham secured a transfer to the Royal Flying Corps three years later. In 1919 he began a joy-riding and photography business but in November 1924 took off on the first of many long-distance return flights, between London and Rangoon. Subsequent epic return journeys included Zurich in a day, Africa, India, and Australia, establishing routes for Imperial Airways' Empire operations and becoming a national hero. He also founded Flight Refuelling Ltd. His National Aviation Day barnstorming circuses of 1932-36 gave many people their first experience of flying. **MT**.

COCHRAN, EDDIE
1938-1959
American singer and guitarist

One of rock's early singer/songwriters, Eddie Cochran first enjoyed chart success with the 1958 top ten hit 'Summertime Blues'. In 1959 a second single, 'C'Mon Everybody', made it to the top ten in the UK too, and he was still gaining in popularity when he was tragically killed in a taxi later that year in London. **DC**.

COCHRAN, JACQUELINE
1906-1980
American record-breaking pilot

Cochran became the first woman to participate in the Bendix Trophy races in 1935. During World War II she joined the UK's Air Transport Auxiliary and later led the American Women's Air Force Service Pilots. She set a vast number of records, while flying a Lockheed JetStar, but she is best remembered for becoming the first woman to fly supersonically on 18 May 1953, piloting a F-86 Sabre fighter. **MT**.

COCKERELL, SIR CHRISTOPHER
1910-
British engineer

Born and educated in Cambridge, Cockerell originally worked as an electronics engineer developing airborne navigational equipment at Marconi during the 1930s and 1940s. A keen sailor, he became interested in the effects of an air 'cushion' under a boat's hull in reducing friction. In 1955 he demonstrated the hovercraft principle – where a boat 'floats' on a cushion of air – and in 1959 Cockerell crossed the English Channel on a full-size prototype. He founded Hovercraft Development Ltd to promote his invention, and saw it enter regular cross-channel service in 1968. Since 1953 he has had 56 patents granted concerning hovercraft design. **PW**.

COCKROFT, SIR JOHN DOUGLAS
1897-1967
British physicist

Cockroft studied the acceleration of atomic particles in a magnetic field and, in 1932, working with Ernest Walton, he was the first to split the atom. For this achievement they shared the Nobel Prize for Physics in 1951. He became the first Director of the Atomic Energy Research Establishment at Harwell in 1946. **DD**.

COCTEAU, JEAN
1889-1963
French writer and director

Poet, novelist, artist, playwright, film director, Cocteau was born in Maisons – Lafitte, near Paris. Mainly remembered for two of the cinema's most poetic fantasies, *Beauty and the Beast* (1946), and *Orphée* (1950), both starring Cocteau's favourite actor and intimate friend, Jean Marais. **NS**.

ABOVE: Jean Cocteau, writer and director.

CODY, SAMUEL FRANKLIN
1861-1913
British aviation pioneer

Texas born, Cody worked at Farnborough in England helping develop various flying apparatus for the British army, including a glider, airship, and the British Army *Aeroplane No 1* that made the first officially recognized airplane flight in Britain on 16 October 1908. His *Cathedral* biplane won the first British military aeroplane trials in August 1912. **MT**.

COHN-BENDIT, DANIEL
1945-
German student leader

A student at Nanterre University (Paris), Cohn-Bendit was spokesman for the 22 March [1968] Movement, created to oppose the 'repression' of the Establishment. Although barred from entry to France, 'Danny the Red' appeared in Paris to lead the May Revolution in 1968, posing a significant threat to the government. **JP.**

COLE, NAT 'KING'
1917-1965
American singer and jazz pianist

Cole began his career as a big band leader and then formed the King Cole Trio in 1939 with himself on piano. His smooth and mellow vocals became increasingly popular and the trio had number one hits in the 1940s with 'I Love You for Sentimental Reasons' (1946), 'Nature Boy' (1948) and 'Mona Lisa' (1951). A solo artist from 1951, Cole had over 40 hits in the next 15 years, including 'Too Young' (1951), 'Answer Me, My Love' (1954), and 'Stardust' (1957), one of America's best loved songs. A target for racial abuse in the 1950s, Cole went on to make several films and a series of extremely successful albums. **JH.**

COLETTE, SIDONIE-GABRIELLE
1873-1954
French novelist

Essentially a fin-de-siècle writer, her own music-hall experience colored her portraits of the demi-monde; her descriptions of the natural world are sensuous, skirting sentimentality. The Claudine stories, her first books, were signed by her husband Willy, her Svengali. *Chéri* (1920) and *La fin de Chéri* (1926) are her best-known novels. **AM.**

COLLINS, MICHAEL
1890-1922
Irish nationalist and soldier

A member of *Sinn Fein* ('Ourselves Alone') and the Irish Republican Brotherhood, Collins participated in the abortive Easter

ABOVE: *Irish Nationalist leader Michael Collins.*

Uprising in Dublin in 1916. Imprisoned by the British, he was released without trial in December. Between 1919 and 1921 he organized a highly effective guerrilla campaign against the British in Ireland, accompanying Arthur GRIFFITH to London in 1921 to negotiate the Irish Free State Treaty. In the ensuing civil war against Republican forces, Collins commanded the Free State Army and, on the death of Griffith, became head of the Free State government. He was ambushed and killed by Republican forces 10 days later. **JP.**

COLLINS, PHIL
1949-
British rock drummer and singer

Collins' first break came as drummer with rock group Genesis. When Peter Gabriel quit in 1975, Collins took over as lead singer and worked hard to expand the band's appeal into the 1980s. A confirmed workaholic, Collins guested constantly on albums as well as pursuing a solo career which began in 1981 with *Face Value*. In 1985 he characteristically played in both London and Philadelphia for the Live Aid project via Concorde. In 1988 he turned to the screen, playing the lead in the box office hit *Buster*, a film about the Great Train Robbery. **DC.**

COLTRANE, JOHN
1926-1967
American jazz saxophonist

The contemplative meandering style derived from modal structures developed with Miles DAVIS in the late 1950s made Coltrane one of the most influential sax players of the new generation. Although initially dismissed, records with his own quintet from 1959 best exemplify what is now recognized as a major contribution to the development of jazz. **DC.**

COMANECI, NADIA
1961-
Romanian gymnast

Nadia Comaneci was the finest female gymnast of modern times. Her style developed the daring acrobatic moves introduced by KORBUT and she took them to new standards literally judged to be perfect. She scored maximum possible marks in some routines on her way to the Olympic overall title in 1976 and added to her tally of gold medals at Moscow in 1980. Her personal life was troubled under the harsh Romanian regime of the 1980s and she settled in the USA after 1989. **DS.**

CONNERY, SEAN
1930-
British actor

In the early 1960s Connery, a relative unknown, was given the sought-after role of Ian FLEMING's superspy James Bond. *Dr No*

(1962) was a huge success, and Connery as Bond was soon an international phenomenon. But in 1971 he announced he was giving up the part for good, and went on to deliver solid performances in films such as *The Man Who Would Be King* (1976) and *Outland* (1981). In 1986 he gave a brilliant performance as a balding medieval monk turned detective in *The Name of the Rose*, and won the Academy Award for Best Supporting Actor playing a tough Chicago cop in *The Untouchables* (1987). **DC.**

CONNORS, JIMMY [JAMES SCOTT]
1952-
American tennis player

Feisty and tenacious, Jimmy Connors has been an irrepressible force in the tennis world for more than 20 years. After a star-studded college career at UCLA, he turned pro in 1972. By 1976 he was the top-ranked player in the world. He has won over 100 professional tournaments, including eight grand slam titles. **MD.**

ABOVE: *Noted jazz saxophonist John Coltrane.*

CONRAD, JOSEPH
1857-1924
British writer

Teodor Josef Korzeniowski, born in the Ukraine, adopted the name by which he is now known on the publication of his first book, *Almayer's Folly*, in 1895. He had begun writing while still working as a seaman, eventually becoming a master mariner, a life which provided the settings for most of his fiction and from which he retired to full-time writing in 1894. He had become a British subject in 1886. A masterly novelist, his work remained unpopular for some

ABOVE: Ukrainian-born novelist Joseph Conrad.

years, despite the publication of, among other works, the classics *The Nigger of the Narcissus* (1897), *Lord Jim* (1900), *Nostromo* (1904), and *The Secret Agent* (1907), one of his political novels. During this period he also co-wrote *The Inheritors* (1900) and *Romance* (1903) with Ford Maddox Ford, and short stories, including the powerful 'Heart of Darkness' (1902), the major inspiration for the film *Apocalypse Now*. Popular and hence financial success eventually came with *Chance* in 1913, followed by other works, none of which is considered his best novel. Innovator and modernist, stylist and moralist, it is remarkable that his total mastery of written English far exceeded his grasp of the spoken language, and that a man who had learnt the langauge as an adult should come to be considered one of the greatest twentieth-century novelists. **AM**.

COOLIDGE, (JOHN) CALVIN
1872-1933
American politician

A New England lawyer, he was guided as President by the maxim, 'more of the office desk and less of the show window.'. As Vice-President, he succeeded to the White House on HARDING's death in 1923 and for the next six years presided over a seemingly prosperous nation – for which his pragmatic but ill-founded fiscal policies took the credit. Only six months after his retirement before the 1928 election, the Wall Street Crash ushered in the Depression. *JC*.

COOPER, GARY
1901-1961
American actor

The Virginian (1929), an early talkie and prototype Western, was the beginning of Cooper's enduring persona as the straight-shootin' man of few words. Sometimes he played the role in a war setting, as in *Sergeant York* (1941), for which he won his first Oscar. He also starred in sophisticated comedies, including *Design for Living* (1934), and was least convincing as the intense intellectual in *The Fountainhead* (1949). But it is for his

Oscar-winning performance as the marshal who reluctantly goes forth to kill those who threaten society in *High Noon* (1952) that he is best remembered. **DC**.

COOPER, JOHN
1923-
British racing constructor and tuner

Credited with pioneering the rear-engined Formula One design, Cooper won two World Championships in 1959 and 1960. He was the first to tune the humble Mini and helped develop its popularity and international sporting success with the Cooper and Cooper S models. **NF**.

COPLAND, AARON
1900-1990
American composer

Born in New York, Aaron Copland was influenced by a variety of musical styles, which led him to create some of the most distinctive and best-loved American music ever written. A student of Nadia Boulanger, he brought together neoclassical and jazz elements, as well as more traditional themes: Quaker hymns, folk songs, cowboy tunes, and Latin-American styles. Among his best-known works are the *Fanfare for the Common Man*, *Appalachian Spring*, *Rodeo*, *Billy the Kid*, *El Salón México*, and his *Cuban Overture*. His chamber music, clarinet concerto, and film music are also highly regarded. **DK**.

COPPOLA, FRANCIS FORD
1939-
American film director

Coppola has become a kind of father-figure to the modern generation of film-makers, particularly after his success with *The Godfather* (1972) and *The Godfather Part II* (1974), mature and masterly movies that combined the sweep of a dynastic gangster melodrama with a political analysis of corporate America. His subsequent films have

ABOVE: Film director Francis Ford Coppola.

generally failed, artistically or commercially, to live up to their grandiose ambitions, though *The Conversation* (1974) is an ingenious, post-Watergate thriller and *Apocalypse Now* (1979) is an undeniably impressive war movie in which America's incursion in Vietnam is interpreted as a mad, metaphorical journey into the primitive evil of man. **NS**.

LE CORBUSIER, [CHARLES-EDOUARD JEANNERET]
1887-1965
Swiss architect, painter, and designer

Le Corbusier was the single most influential architect in the mid-twentieth century, as much for his theoretical writings as for his buildings. His first training was as a painter and the influence of his reductive, Cubist-inspired Purist painting can be seen in his architecture. Periods in the offices of PERRET and BEHRENS reinforced his interest in standardization and mass-production, and contributed to his theories as expressed in *Towards a (New) Architecture* (1923) and *Decorative Art Today: Urbanism* (1925). He saw the house as a 'machine for living in' (Dom-Ino project house, 1914; Villa Savoie, Poissy,

ABOVE: US composer Aaron Copland.

1927) and extended this concept to a whole city of three million inhabitants, divided into different areas for work, living – in multi-story blocks of flats for efficiency – and leisure, all linked by transport networks. After World War II Corbusier was able to put many of his ideas into practice, in individual buildings such as the apartment block of Unités d'Habitation at Marseilles (1947-52), and in whole cities such as the Capitol at Chandigarh in the Punjab (begun 1950). While always faithful to the machine ethic, Corbusier often utilized local materials, favoring that modern and potentially unexpressive material, concrete, creating rough finishes or sculptural shapes, as at the church of Notre-Dame du Haut, Ronchamp (1950-54). Corbusier is often blamed for the postwar planning blight, but this has more to do with his imitators' inability to master his subtlety in planning and in handling scale to create a humane environment. **AR**.

CORI, GERTY
1896-1957
Czech chemist

Gerty Radnitz studied chemistry at the German University at Prague and gained her MD in 1920. She married fellow student Carl Ferdinand Cori that year, and by 1922 the couple were exploring new career horizons in Washington DC. The Coris solved one of the major problems of the day in physiology, that of unravelling the metabolism of sugar. They isolated and characterized the principal enzymes involved in the breakdown and synthesis of glycogen. For effecting the first synthesis of glycogen in a test-tube, they shared the Nobel Prize in Medicine in 1947. That year Gerty was made Professor of Biochemistry at Washington University School of Medicine. Gerty's solo research was equally groundbreaking. In 1954 she chemically determined the molecular structure of glycogen. Though she suffered from myelosclerosis, which meant she needed regular blood transfusions, she continued to study the nature of glycogen storage diseases in children until her early death. **MB**.

COSTA, LUCIO
1902-
Brazilian architect

Costa, the leading Brazilian Modernist architect after the revolution of 1930, influenced a new generation of architects. His designs for the Ministry of Education and Health in Rio de Janeiro of 1937-43, with its huge piloti and the Brazilian Pavilion for the New York World's Fair of 1939, show the influence of Le CORBUSIER. **DE**.

COURRÈGES, ANDRÉ
1923-
French designer

Following a brief career as a civil engineer, in 1949 Courrèges joined Balenciaga where he remained until he opened his own house in 1961. He became known as the 'Space-Age' designer because of his futuristic yet functional designs, which included see-through and cut-out dresses. **MC**.

COURT, MARGARET (NÉE SMITH)
1942-
Australian tennis player

Margaret Court is one of a select band of tennis players who have achieved (in 1970) a Grand Slam of wins in the four leading singles tournaments. Raised in a small town in New South Wales, she played much of her early tennis with men and adopted their serve and volley style, which she matched to natural athletic skills. Her first major success was in the Australian championship in 1960 and her victory over Billie-Jean KING in the 1970 Wimbledon final was one of the finest matches ever. **DS**.

COUSTEAU, JACQUES YVES
1910-
French conservationist

Cousteau graduated from the French naval academy in Brest and served in the French Navy. While on leave following a car accident, he borrowed a pair of goggles and was immediately hooked on underwater exploration. During World War II he served in the French Resistance, and afterwards was appointed head of the Underwater Research Group of the French Navy. From a technological viewpoint his important work was the invention, in 1943, with Emile Gagnan, of the aqualung – a self-contained breathing system that allowed a diver to swim freely underwater. He worked with Auguste Piccard on the first bathyscaphe – a submersible capable of diving to great depths. With these devices, and his research ship *Calypso*, he was able to pioneer the exploration of the ocean floor. He founded the Cousteau Society – a conservation group dedicated to the preservation of the underwater world – in 1974, and became director of the Oceanographic Museum in Monaco. To the public, he is best known for his ground-breaking films and television programs that brought the wonders of the underwater world to a wide audience. **DD**.

COWARD, SIR NOËL
1899-1973
British playwright

Playwright, screenwriter, composer, novelist, director, and producer as well as actor, Coward was one of the bright lights of the 1920s and 1930s, the ultimate sophisticate, with in his own words, 'a talent to amuse'. His first major success as a dramatist was *The Vortex* (1924); this was followed by *Hay Fever* (1925), the first of several social comedies which became his trademark. *Private Lives* (1930) and *Blithe Spirit* (1941) were also successful films, and during the 1940s Coward showed himself to be an accomplished film producer and actor working with David LEAN on patriotic movies such as *In Which We Serve* (1942) and *This Happy Breed* (1944) as well as the popular *Brief Encounter*. He continued to appear in cameo roles until the 1960s. **DC**.

RIGHT: Noel Coward.

CRAWFORD, JOAN
1906-1977
American actress

Crawford was the movie star the public loved to hate. A stint in the chorus line of the Broadway show *Innocent Eyes* led to her screen debut in *Lady of the Night* (1925). In *Our Dancing Daughters* (1928) she became a symbol of the Jazz Age and took over as 'Number One Flapper' from Clara Bow. Her first talkie was *Hollywood Revue of 1929*, and after hounding MGM for more substantial parts, she won an Oscar for *Mildred Pierce* (1945). In the 1950s she played ageing femme fatales, and in 1962 she played opposite rival Bette DAVIS in the psychological drama *Whatever Happened to Baby Jane?* **DC**.

CRICK, FRANCIS
1916-
British molecular biologist
WATSON, JAMES
1928-
American molecular biologist
WILKINS, MAURICE
1916-
New Zealand biophysicist

Their demonstration of the structure of DNA is generally considered to be the most important discovery in biology this century. Watson and Crick worked on elucidating the detailed structure of DNA at the Cavendish Laboratory, Cambridge. They used what was known about the composition of nucleic acids, Wilkins' results at King's College, London as well as those of his colleague Rosalind FRANKLIN. Her X-Ray crystallographic studies of the hydrated form of DNA pointed to it being a helical structure and she had also shown that phosphate groups were situated on the outside of the helix. Their proposed model of DNA (published in 1953) was a double helix consisting of two parallel strands of alternate sugar and phosphate groups linked by pairs of organic bases. Watson and Crick built several accurate molecular models before eventually making one that incorporated all the known features of DNA and which gave the same diffraction pattern as that found by Wilkins. Their proposed semi-conservative nature of DNA replication was later confirmed by Messelsohn and Stahl. Crick, Watson, and Wilkins were awarded the Nobel Prize in 1962. **ES**.

CROCE, BENEDETTO
1866-1959
Italian historian and philosopher

After the death of his parents in an earthquake, Croce engaged mainly in private study, developing his 'Philosophy of Spirit', in which he distinguished between logic and aesthetics as the subjects of distinct intellectual activities. He was much influenced by his study of Marx and Hegel, and held that the only true knowledge was that of historical propositions. He published his work in four volumes between 1902 and 1917, and also founded the intellectual journal *La Critica*, much of which was occupied by his own work in progress. He entered politics after World War I, and became Minister of Education; after MUSSOLINI assumed power, he became the leading intellectual opponent of Italian Fascism, making his position clear in his histories of Naples, Italy, and Europe. Although he was again briefly a Cabinet Minister after the war, he mainly returned to his studies, and on his 80th birthday founded the Italian Institute for Historical Studies in his home, where it remains to this day. **EB**.

CRONKITE, WALTER
1916-
American television newscaster

Cronkite dropped out of college to become a reporter and covered the fighting in World War II for United Press International. He reported on the Nuremberg War Trials after the war and in 1950 joined CBS news as a correspondent. For 20 years he was the anchorman for CBS Evening News and one of the most familiar and respected personalities in American public life. He also published books on international relations and current affairs. Since leaving CBS in 1981 he has continued to write books, give lectures, and narrate documentaries. **DSl**.

ABOVE: *Bing Crosby (left) and Fred Astaire.*

CROSBY, BING
1903-1977
American singer and actor

Crosby's mastery of the microphone gave him his first radio show in 1931. To the current melodic style he added his characteristically casual delivery and husky voice, becoming one of the founders of pop singing. His first record to sell a million was 'Sweet Leilani' in 1937; he had 46 top ten hits in the 1940s alone, including the perennial 'White Christmas' (1942), 'Swingin' on a Star' (1944) and 'Alexander's Ragtime Band' (1947). Movies include *Pennies from Heaven* (1936), *Going My Way* (1944), which won him an Oscar, and the classic *Road* series with Bob HOPE. **JH**.

CRUYFF, JOHAN
1947-
Dutch soccer player

Johan Cruyff has achieved considerable success both as a player and later as a coach.

ABOVE: *Crick and Watson with the DNA structural model.*

He helped win three European Cups with the Ajax club of Amsterdam in 1971-73 and was the star of the Dutch team that were runners-up in the 1974 World Cup. Later in his career he played with Barcelona and also in the North American Soccer League. As a coach he has achieved domestic and European success with first Ajax and later, at Barcelona. **DS**.

CUKOR, GEORGE
1899-1983
American film director

Cukor came to Hollywood after directing on the New York stage. Noted for his impeccable taste, and a fondness for theatrical subjects, he excelled at extracting remarkable performances from actresses, such as Greta GARBO in *Camille* (1937), and Judy GARLAND in *A Star is Born* (1954), and won an Oscar for *My Fair Lady* (1964). **NS**.

CUMMINGS, E[DWARD] E[STLIN]
1894-1962
American poet

Highly technically innovative, typographical and linguistic experimentation were the hallmark of his brief but often emotionally subtle poems, which frequently attracted more attention on that account, rather than for their undeniable lyric power. A prose piece, *The Enormous Room* (1922), was based on his brief and mistaken 1917 incarceration in a French detention camp. **AM**.

CUNNINGHAM, ANDREW, 1ST VISCOUNT, ADMIRAL
1883-1963
British sailor

In September 1939 Cunningham was appointed Commander-in-Chief of the Mediterranean Fleet and, except for a short time in Washington DC in 1942, was to remain in that theater until the Italian surrender in 1943, having created and maintained naval supremacy under adverse conditions. From 1943 until 1945, Cunningham was First Sea Lord. **JPi**.

CUNNINGHAM, MERCE
1919-
American dancer and choreographer

Since the mid-1950s Cunningham has maintained his position as one of the world's leading personalities of the avant-garde, and as a major influence on young choreographers. He began as a soloist with Martha GRAHAM's company in 1939, creating leading roles until his departure in 1945. His first independent concert was in 1942 and included music by John CAGE, a lifelong collaborator. The first performance of the Merce Cunningham Dance Company took place in 1953 and, to date, Cunningham has choreographed nearly 100 works for his company. **MC**.

CURIE, MARIE
1867-1934
Polish-French scientist

Because of the lack of educational facilities in Poland, she moved to Paris in 1891 and graduated in physics from the Sorbonne in 1893. She decided to study the rays given off by uranium and its ore – a phenomenon recently discovered by Henri BECQUEREL. Working with her husband Pierre, whom she married in 1895, she isolated the new elements polonium and radium in 1902. For their work on radioactivity they were jointly awarded the Nobel Prize for Physics in 1903, along with Henri Becquerel. After Pierre's accidental death in 1906, she took over his professorship in physics at the Sorbonne. She was awarded the Nobel Prize for Chemistry in 1911 for her discovery of polonium and radium, and became the first person ever to be awarded two Nobel Prizes. With the outbreak of World War I she instigated X-ray services in military hospitals. She eventually died of cancer, brought on by exposure to the radioactive elements with which she worked – the hazardous nature of the phenomena she studied were not recognized in those days. Her notebooks are still too radioactive to handle. She was the first woman scientist to gain worldwide acclaim and the unit of radioactivity of a substance was named the curie (ci) after her. **DD**.

CURTISS, GLENN HAMMOND
1878-1930
American aircraft engineer and pioneer pilot

Curtiss began his career constructing engines and later joined Alexander Graham Bell's Aerial Experiment Association. Flying the AEA's *June Bug* on 20 June 1908, he became the first American to fly after the

ABOVE: Madame Curie in her laboratory.

Wrights, and on 4 July won the *Scientific American* trophy for the first official US public flight of over 1 km. He received the first pilot's license from the Aero Club of America, established the first US airplane factory, his airplanes were the first to take-off and land on ships (in 1910-11), and Curtiss flying-boats and trainers were widely operated thereafter. He retired in 1921 and died after an appendicitis operation. **MT**.

CUSHING, HARVEY
1869-1939
American neurological surgeon

Cushing is best known for his work on the pituitary gland, culminating in the identification of Cushing's Syndrome, the overproduction of cortisol by the adrenal gland. He also made important contributions to the understanding of cerebral and intracranial tumors. Many surgical techniques he developed for brain surgery in Boston, 1912-1932, remain standard today. **GL**.

ABOVE: US dancer and choreographer Merce Cunningham.

DALADIER, EDOUARD
1884-1970
French politician

One of the leaders who helped sign away Czech independence at Munich in 1938, he also led France in the early part of World War II before being replaced by Paul Reymond. Arrested by the puppet Vichy government in 1942, he was convicted of war guilt and deported to Germany in 1943. Surviving the war, he served as a member of the National Assembly from 1946 until his resignation in 1958. **JC.**

ABOVE: French statesman Edouard Daladier.

DALAI LAMA [TENZIN GYATSO]
1935-
Tibetan Buddhist leader

Aged five when recognized as the reincarnation of the 13th Dalai Lama who had died in 1933, the Tibetan Buddhist has achieved universal respect in his quest for world peace. The Dalai Lama remains the most poignant symbol and victim of Chinese aggression in the 1950s and the cowardice of the international community in the face of the ruthless conquest of Tibet in 1951. Since 1959 he has lived in exile working ceaselessly for the liberation of Tibet. He was awarded the Nobel Peace Prize in 1989 in recognition of his non-violent protest. **ML.**

DALE, HENRY
1875-1968
British physiologist
LOEWI, OTTO
1873-1961
German physiologist

Dale and Loewi shared the Nobel Prize in physiology in 1936 for their separate but complementary work on the chemical transmission of nerve impulses. Loewi's elegant experimental evidence for chemical neurotransmitters led Dale and his colleagues to identify that one of these was acetylcholine, released at nerve endings in voluntary muscles and throughout the autonomic nervous system. This discovery revolutionized neurophysiology. **ES.**

DALI, SALVADOR
1904-1989
Spanish painter

Dali's training at the Madrid Art School prefigures his career; earlier suspended for inciting the students to riot, in 1926 he was expelled for 'extravagant behavior'. Becoming increasingly interested in the metaphysical painting of de CHIRICO and the meticulous realism of the Pre-Raphaelites, in 1929 he joined the Surrealist movement, collaborating with the Spanish director Luis BUÑUEL on the first Surrealist films. He developed a theory of 'critical paranoia', wherein genuine delusion, as found in clinical paranoia, was cultivated, while remaining residually conscious of the deliberate suspension of reason. His paintings depicted dreams and paranoid hallucinations with an incongruously exact, photographic accuracy. Their highly finished, glossy surface adds to the eeriness of his world of melting watches, giant ants, and figures from which half-open drawers protrude. His increasingly mannered work and his support for the Spanish dictator Franco became unacceptable to the Surrealists and in 1938 he was expelled from the group, but for the public at large his work remained synonymous with Surrealism and he achieved international notoriety. Between 1940 and 1955 he lived in the USA and devoted himself largely to self-publicity, in 1942 publishing his autobiography *The Secret Life of Salvador Dali* which was followed in 1965 by *The Diary of A Genius*. **ER.**

ABOVE: Surrealist painter Salvador Dali.

D'ANNUNZIO, GABRIELE
1863-1938
Italian writer

An ardent nationalist, much influenced by Nietzsche, D'Annunzio saw dramatic service in World War I and later led the occupation of Fiume, of which he was dictator from 1919-21. He was a controversial figure, decadence being a keynote of his work, such as the novel *Il piacere* (1890), and the play *Le Martyre de Saint Sebastien* (1911), set to music by DEBUSSY. **AM.**

DARROW, CHARLES
1889-1967
American innovator

During the Depression, Darrow, an unemployed heating engineer, found himself unable to afford a trip to the movies. He invented a game to while away the evenings, naming it 'Monopoly'. A game with a neat manmade world and an element of risk, it was a huge success and Darrow received royalties on all sets sold. **PT**

DAVIES, [WILLIAM] ROBERTSON
1913-
Canadian writer

Journalist, critic, publisher, and writer, Davies was Professor of English at Toronto University and Master of Massey College. The Canadian small-town life of his invention, Salterton, and the academic world are the most notable settings for his massive trilogies of novels. A slightly ponderous wit and erudite humor are their major features. **AM.**

DAVIS, BETTE
1908-1989
American actress

In more than 80 films during her career, Davis often played a flinty, acid-tongued woman who could speak words as though spitting nails. Her toe-to-toe combat in the front offices of Hollywood film companies made her a force to be reckoned with, too. She made her Broadway debut in *Broken Dishes* in 1929, and by 1930 she was in Hollywood, her first performances unnoticed. Not a classic beauty, she was the electrifying bitch in *Of Human Bondage* (1934), and *Dangerous* (1935) won her an Academy Award for Best Actress, making her a major box office attraction. Audiences liked her best when she was bright and bitchy, but she was also effective in weepy soaps. *Jezebel* (1938) won her a second Academy Award. In the late 1940s her career took a dive, but she fought back with *All About Eve* (1950), possibly her finest film. When her career faltered again she took out advertisements announcing her availability and took work in horror pictures and on television. *Whatever Happened to Baby Jane* (1962) with Joan CRAWFORD was a huge success; she continued acting, and in 1977 was the first woman to receive the American Film Institute Life Achievement Award. **DC**.

DAVIS, JOE
1901-1978
British snooker player

Joe Davis held the world professional snooker championship from its inception in 1926/27 until 1946 when he relinquished the title, although continuing to play successfully until 1963. Far more than any other of his generation, he developed the art of controling the cue ball to build large scores. **DS**.

ABOVE: Jazz maestro Miles Davis.

DAVIS, MILES
1926-1991
American jazz trumpeter and composer

First coming to prominence with a nine-piece band in the late 1940s, Davis's contribution was immediately original, with a fragile tone, often muted, and much subtler than the contemporary sound. It was at the Newport Jazz Festival in 1955 with a band featuring John COLTRANE on tenor sax that he made it big, ushering in a new style which began to challenge the preeminence of bebop. Later orchestrations by Gil Evans showed off his poignant phrasing to the full, and his increasingly sparse style made him the fashionable and chic 'King of Cool'. He made a series of stylistic changes in subsequent album releases, first developing a modal style in contrast to the contemporary

preoccupation with chord patterns and structured phrasing, and then launching the jazz-rock movement with the 1969 album *In A Silent Way*, packing out rock venues at a time when jazz had begun to lose popularity amongst the young. **DC**.

DAVIS, SAMMY, JR
1925-1991
American singer, dancer, and actor

Davis overcame racial barriers to become a major star and a member of the Sinatra clique. A string of hits in the 1950s including 'That Old Black Magic' (1955) was followed by stardom in Gershwin's *Porgy and Bess* (1959) and Weill's *Threepenny Opera* (1964). Later he concentrated on television and cabaret. **JH**.

DAY, DORIS
1922-
American singer and actress

Remembered for her wholesome 'girl next door' image, Day's private life did not always live up to it. Her first film, *On the High Seas* (1948), also gave her her first solo hit, 'It's Magic'. *Calamity Jane* (1953) established her as a movie star and *Love Me or Leave Me* (1955), with Jimmy Cagney, showed she could act as well as sing. She won an Oscar for Hitchcock's *The Man Who Knew Too Much* (1956), but is perhaps best remembered for the series of light comedies, including *Pillow Talk* (1959), which she made with Rock Hudson. **JH**.

BELOW: The original 'Rebel Without a Cause', James Dean, whose successful film career was cut short by an automobile accident.

DAYAN, MOSHE, LIEUTENANT-GENERAL
1915-1981
Israeli soldier-politician

Born in Palestine, Dayan fought with the Haganah, the Jewish militia force, during the 1930s. In 1941 he participated in the British invasion of Vichy-French Syria, where he was badly wounded, losing his left eye. After service in the Israeli War of Independence (1948), he was appointed Chief of Staff to the Israeli Defense Force in 1953, and led the IDF to victory in the Sinai campaign of 1956. In 1960 he entered the Knesset, serving as Minister of Defense during the stunningly successful Six Day War (1967) and the more difficult Yom Kippur War (1973). **JPi**.

DEAN, JAMES
1931-1955
American actor

A cult figure to the young and angry, Dean was a symbol of vulnerability, sensitivity, and doomed rebellion. Despite his slight build and far from perfect features, his charisma launched a meteoric rise to fame, playing the bad son with whom the audience identified in *East of Eden* (1955). *Rebel Without a Cause* (1955) became the theme film of the affluent, but apolitical 1950s generation. But that same year he died when his new Porsche crashed on the way to an auto race. The response to his death was astonishing; nothing like it had occurred since the death of Valentino. James Dean fan clubs sprouted across America, filled with fans for whom he epitomized the idea of rejection and victimization by the unfeeling adult world. **DC**.

DEBS, Eugene
1855-1926
American labor leader

Debs co-founded the American Railway Union (1893), serving a jail sentence for 'obstructing the US mails' in the Pullman strike. A militant socialist, he also founded the Social Democratic Party and was the Socialist presidential candidate four times (1900-1912), polling nearly a million votes against Woodrow WILSON. A pacifist, he was imprisoned in 1918 for sedition, and stood again as presidential candidate while a convict. **JC.**

ABOVE: *Claude Debussy at the piano.*

DEBUSSY, Claude
1862-1918
French composer

Although Debussy disliked the term 'impressionist', his music has often been likened to Impressionist paintings. There are certainly similarities in that both parties were trying to break away from the orthodox use of tone, color, and form to produce a freer and more imaginative composition. Even as a student at the Paris Conservatory Debussy rebelled against orthodox harmony preferring to experiment with 'forbidden' progressions and unrelated chords. Like the painters his work became more colorful and less rigid in its form. Another important influence in Debussy's life was that of the literary symbolists including Mallarmé, Verlaine, and Baudelaire. It was a poem by Mallarmé which inspired Debussy to write his famous *Prélude a l'après-midi d'un faune.* Historians often cite this work as being the first real break away from orthodox forms. **DK.**

DEBYE, Peter Joseph Wilhelm
1884-1966
Dutch-American physical chemist

Debye pioneered the technique of X-ray crystallography – the analysis of crystalline substances by the deflexion of X-rays passing through them. He was awarded the Nobel Prize for Chemistry in 1936, before he left for America, and eventually became Professor of Chemistry at Cornell University in 1950. **DD.**

DELBRUCK, Max
1906-1981
German biophysicist

Delbruck moved to California to work on bacteriophages (viruses that live in bacteria) and showed, independently of Alfred Hershey, the ability of viruses to exchange or recombine their genetic material inside the same bacterial cell. No-one previously had shown genetic recombination in such primitive organisms. For this work, Delbruck, Hershey, and Luria received the 1969 Nobel Prize for Physiology or Medicine. **ES.**

DEMPSEY, Jack
1895-1983
American boxer

Heavyweight champion for more than seven years, Jack Dempsey is best remembered for a fight he lost. After Dempsey surrendered his crown to Gene Tunney in 1926, the two fighters met again in 1927 in Chicago. In the seventh round Dempsey floored Tunney, but did not go to a neutral corner. The resulting 'long count' lasted only to 9; Tunney got up and won the decision. The 187-pound Dempsey had won the title in 1919, knocking out 245-pound champion Jess Willard. Known as 'the Manassa Mauler,' Dempsey was one of the world's most popular athletes in the 1920s. **MD.**

DENG XIAO PING
1904-
Chinese statesman

A survivor of the 'Long March' (1934-35), Deng has endured many vicissitudes in his career. He rose to become General Secretary of the Communist Party in 1956, but fell from power during the Cultural Revolution (1966-69). He returned to favor in 1973 as Vice-Premier, but was removed by the Gang of Four shortly before MAO's death in 1976. Returning to power the following year, he supported improving relations with the USA, viewing with suspicion the activities of the Soviet Union. Regarded as the elder statesman of Chinese politics, Deng continues to hold the reins of power in the People's Republic. **JC.**

DERRIDA, Jacques
1930-
French philosopher

One of the key figures of the Deconstructionist movement, Derrida directs attention to language itself, rather than to any supposed reality behind the language, and holds the written language to be conceptually prior to the spoken. Two key aspects of language are *différences* and *différance*: meaning arises only from the differences between expression and the reader must defer judgement between conflicting expectations set up as a sentence unfolds until a decision can be made. **EB.**

DEWEY, John
1859-1952
American philosopher and educationalist

One of the founders of philosophical Pragmatism, Dewey taught science and classics in high school before beginning his career as an academic psychologist. He founded the experimental laboratory at the University of Chicago, where he tested the theories of learning which he derived from his opposition to the 'spectator theory of knowledge'. Knowledge, for him, required the agent's experimental effort, and the role of the teacher was to guide the inquiries of the child. Truth was no more than 'warranted assertability', a view which he went on to apply in a variety of areas of philosophy. He was an active civil libertarian, wrote extensively on social and political matters, and was greatly in demand as a lecturer throughout the world. **EB.**

DIELS, Otto Paul Hermann
1876-1954
German organic chemist

Most of Diels's work was done in the University of Kiel where his research showed that all steroids had the same carbon structure. Along with Kurt Alder, he won the Nobel Prize for Chemistry in 1950 for the synthesis of organic compounds containing two double bonds in the Diels-Alder reaction, first perfected in 1928. **DD.**

DIETRICH, Marlene
1901-1992
German actress

Beautiful, aloof, sophisticated, demanding, generous, and world-weary, Dietrich exercised a fascination on the world for over fifty years. She began acting in the theater in Berlin for, among others, the famous Max Reinhardt, and she was a well-known theater actress by the 1920s. Director Josef von Sternberg cast her as the sexy vamp Lola Lola in *Blue Angel* in 1930, and having outshone the presumed star, Emil JANNINGS, went to Hollywood where she was an immediate success. A handful of mediocre films in the mid-1930s were rectified with *Destry Rides Again* (1939) in which she sang 'See What the Boys in the Back Room Will Have'. Opposed to Nazism, she defied Hitler, refusing to return to Germany and instead became an American citizen. However she remained an outsider in Hollywood, intrinsically cosmopolitan with strong European ties and a pantheon of intellectuals and international celebrities as friends. After the war she launched a new career as a night-club and cabaret performer, and movies such as *Stage Fright* (1950) and *Witness for the Prosecution* (1958) kept her film career alive. A loving retrospective of her work, entitled *Marlene*, produced by Maximilian Schell, was released in 1986. **DC.**

DiMaggio, Joe [Joseph Paul]
1914-
American baseball player

Performing with stoic grace, Joe DiMaggio was one of baseball's all-time greats. DiMaggio played his entire 13-year career with a dynastic New York Yankees team, which made it to the World Series 10 times in that span (winning nine of them). His greatest feat came in 1941 when he got at least one base hit in 56 consecutive games, a record that still stands. This streak was finally broken by the Cleveland Indians, but then 'Joltin' Joe' ran off another streak of 16 games. DiMaggio finished his career with a .325 batting average and 361 home runs. He was also one of the best defensive players ever to play the centerfield position. Three times he won the American League's Most Valuable Player award, and he was elected to the Baseball Hall of Fame in 1955. His brothers Vince and Dom also played in the Major Leagues. After DiMaggio's retirement he stayed in the public eye by marrying Marilyn Monroe, and, later, by having his name invoked in a memorable song by Simon and Garfunkel. **MD**.

BELOW: German-born actress Marlene Dietrich.

Dior, Christian
1905-1957
French designer

Dior had a relatively late start in the fashion industry: he gave up his studies in political sciences to study music but instead spent much of his time traveling and running an art gallery. In 1935 he began selling fashion sketches to Paris newspapers and gained experience in design working with Lucien Lelong until, in 1942, cotton magnate Marcel Boussac offered him the chance to open his own couture house. Dior's first collection in 1947, originally called the 'Carolle Line' was nicknamed 'The New Look' and featured huge skirts on tiny waists with boned bodices which exaggerated the female form. Subsequent collections introduced the stand-up collar, coolie hats, and the popular 'Princess' line which gave the illusion of a high waist. In 1954 Dior named his collection the 'H' line; the 'A' and 'Y' lines followed in 1955. Favoring black, navy blue, and white, Dior accessorized his clothes with brooches pinned at the waist, neck, and shoulders and in the fifties introduced the fashion for several ropes of pearls wound around the neck. He was also at the vanguard of a revival of men's suiting. His last collection in 1957 was based on the 'Vareuse', a garment with a stand-away collar and cut to hang loosely on the hips. **MC**.

LEFT: Baseball legend Joe DiMaggio.

BELOW: French designer Christian Dior.

ABOVE: Walt Disney and his most famous creation.

DISNEY, WALT
1901-1966
American animator and film producer

The man who became the most famous name in film animation began working as a commercial artist in Kansas City in 1919. Having produced a series of animated cartoons and commercials for a local theater, Disney set up in partnership with his brother Roy and his creative collaborator Ub Iwerks in Hollywood in 1923. In 1928 he created his most famous character Mickey Mouse, who became a household name after his first talkie, *Steamboat Willie*, in which Disney provided Mickey's high-pitched voice. Mickey's success spawned a menagerie of other cartoon characters - Minnie Mouse, Goofy, Donald Duck, and Pluto. Always an innovator, by the mid-1930s the entire studio output was in technicolor, and in 1937 Disney realized his dream of creating a feature-length cartoon, *Snow White and the Seven Dwarfs*. The Disney organization had grown and during World War II produced a large number of morale-boosting films. Disney diversified further with forays into television during the 1950s as well as opening the Disneyland theme park in California in 1955. The entertainment empire he created continues to dominate the field. **JM**.

DIX, OTTO
1891-1969
German painter

Dix was profoundly affected by his front-line service in World War I. His etchings, *Der Krieg* (1924), are a powerful testimony to the horrific nature of war. His veristic montages, such as those of war cripples, contributed to the Berlin Dada Fair (1920), deliberately incorporated ugly materials, paralleling his refusal to ignore the ugly realities of life. During the 1920s he chronicled the squalor of Berlin night life with merciless realism, particularly prostitutes, who symbolized for him the moral decay of the Weimar Republic. In 1933 he was dismissed from his teaching post at Dresden Academy by the Nazis, who declared his work degenerate and forbade him to exhibit. **ER**.

DOENITZ, KARL, GRAND ADMIRAL
1891-1980
German sailor

In 1916, six years after entering the German Navy, Doenitz joined the submarine (U-boat) service, seeing action against Allied merchantmen. When the U-boat arm was restored under Hitler in 1935, Doenitz was given command and conducted a successful campaign against enemy shipping after 1939. By early 1943 it seemed that the British were facing defeat, Doenitz was appointed Commander in Chief of the German Navy in March 1943; in April 1945 he was appointed Hitler's successor and, as such, authorized Germany's unconditional surrender. Tried as a war criminal, Doenitz was imprisoned until 1956. **JPi**.

DOESBURG, THEO VAN
1883-1931
Dutch painter and architect

Doesburg's early paintings were expressionistic but in 1915 he met MONDRIAN, whose severe geometric abstraction he began to emulate closely. During the 1920s he utilized more dynamic elements in his 'Contra-Compositions'. Doesburg was the driving force behind De Stijl, an association of painters and architects founded in 1917 and dedicated to creating a new artistic language of extreme aesthetic austerity. **ER**.

DOLMETSCH, ARNOLD
1858-1940
French-British musician

Born in Le Mans, Dolmetsch followed his family trade and became an expert craftsman of musical instruments, using traditional techniques. He became a major figure in the resurgence of early music performed in near-authentic style, the source of much debate today. He is also highly significant for almost single-handedly reviving the recorder after 150 years of neglect. **DK**.

DOMAGK, GERHARD
1895-1964
German bacteriologist

Domagk's study of an azo dye synthesized by his colleagues, called prontosil rubrum (red) revealed it was an effective anti-streptococcal agent in mice. Published in 1935, his discovery, at a time when little progress had been made in the search for antibacterial agents, was received with great skepticism. A year later however, his findings were confirmed. Although FLEMING had discovered penicillin a few years earlier, he did not have the chemical expertise available to Domagk to develop it into an antibiotic. Thus Domagk's discovery resulted in the production of the first antibiotics. **ES**.

DOMINGO, PLACIDO
1941-
Spanish opera singer and conductor

Domingo's strong, wide-ranging lyric-dramatic tenor and quick musical intelligence have led to immense operatic versatility. After early work in Israel, singing in Hebrew, he made his Met debut in 1968 in a lyric role. He has returned regularly since and extended his repertoire to Berlioz (Enée in *Les Troyens*) and Wagner (the

ABOVE: Spanish opera star Placido Domingo.

eponymous hero in *Lohengrin*); Otello and Don Carlos are among his most famous and frequent roles. Operas he has conducted include *La Traviata* and *Tosca*, and *La Bohème* at the Met. **JH**.

DONEGAN, LONNIE
1946-
British singer and guitarist

Donegan was the founder of skiffle music, played mainly on guitar and improvised percussion such as tea chests and washboard; hits included 'My Old Man's a Dustman'. He vanished from the pop scene in the early 1960s with the emerging Mersey sound, which was partly inspired by his do-it-yourself approach. **JH**.

DOOLITTLE, JAMES HAROLD, LT GENERAL
1896-
American military, record-breaking, and racing pilot

Best remembered for leading 16 carrier-borne B-25s in the first air attack on Japan on 18 April 1942, Doolittle had previously made the first coast-to-coast US crossing in a day (4 September 1922), won the 1925 Schneider Trophy race, performed the first outside loop, pioneered blind-flying instrumentation, won other races and set a 294 mph (473 km/h) speed record for land-planes in 1932. He commanded US air forces in North Africa and Europe during the war and after, as a civilian, became President of the Institute of Aeronautical Sciences. **MT**.

DOUGLAS, KIRK [ISSUR DANIELOVITCH]
1916-
American actor

It was after a stint on Broadway that Douglas appeared in his first film, *The Strange Love of Martha Ivers* (1946), playing opposite Barbara STANWYCK. But it was not until *Champion* (1949), in which he played an immoral prizefighter, that the Douglas intensity was put on display, and it made him a star. He turned down flashier films in order to make *Young Man with a Horn* (1950), the life story of Bix Beiderbecke, rapidly establishing himself as one of the new postwar breed of masculine movie idols. In 1956 he formed his own company which gave him new freedom to make films such as *Paths of Glory* (1957) and *The Vikings* (1958), with Ernest Borgnine and Tony Curtis. Despite his movie success, Douglas retained an interest in the Broadway stage, and in 1963 he appeared in *One Flew Over the Cuckoo's Nest*. He continues to be a forceful presence in the film industry today, and is also an author. **DC**.

DOUGLAS-HOME, ALEC, BARON
1903-
British politician

MACMILLAN's surprise successor after renouncing his title, Douglas-Home is often dismissed as a caretaker Prime Minister; yet he almost won the 1964 Election. Honest and uncomplicated, preferring state affairs to party management, Douglas-Home is best judged on his many years of Cabinet responsibility for foreign policy between 1955 and 1974. **JP**.

DOWDING, HUGH CASWALL TREMENHEERE, 1ST BARON
1882-1970
British Air Chief Marshal

An RFC/RAF Squadron Commander in World War I, he took postwar staff and training positions in Britain, Asia, and the Middle East. In 1930 he joined the Air Council for Supply and Research, taking particular interest in the development of fighters and radar. Becoming Air Officer Commander-in-Chief of the new RAF Fighter Command in 1936, he organized fighter and radar defenses into a nationwide coherent force which defeated the Luftwaffe in the 1940 Battle of Britain. That November he joined a Ministry of Aircraft Production mission to the USA and retired two years later. In 1943 he was created a baron. **MT**.

ABOVE: American author Theodore Dreiser.

DREISER, THEODORE
1871-1945
American novelist

Theodore Dreiser was born in Indiana to a poor German Catholic family. He left home for Chicago to begin his career as a journalist at 15. His first novel *Sister Carrie* (1900) was withheld from circulation because of its frank portrayal of the ambition of a young working girl, who achieves social success thorugh her sexuality. Here, as in his famous *An American Tragedy* (1925), Dreiser develops a naturalist account of the often violent impact of the modern social environment upon individual identity. His later work increasingly moved towards a socialist solution to the naturalist predicament. **CW**.

DREYFUSS, HENRY
1903-1972
American designer

Dreyfuss's functional design for the 1933 Bell telephone is the very essence of anthropometrics or 'human engineering,' later defined in Dreyfuss's influential *Designing for People* (1955). Dreyfuss later produced the radically compact Trimline telephone (1965). His innovative industrial designs included influential work for RCA television, Goodyear tyres, and Hoover vacuum cleaners. **DE.**

DUBČEK, ALEXANDER
1921-1992
Czech politician

Seemingly a careerist in the Czech Communist Party, Dubčeck, appointed as First Secretary in place of Novotný during January 1968, initiated a liberalizing regime that was to lead to his downfall at the hands of the Russian-dominated Warsaw Pact in the following August. Ambassadorial and minor postings followed, but he shot to prominence as a figurehead during the successful Czech pro-democracy movement in the late 1980s, and was appointed speaker of the Federal Assembly under HAVEL's presidency. **JC.**

ABOVE: *Alexander Dubcek, the Czech politician.*

DUBOIS, WILLIAM
1868-1963
American writer

An active worker for race reforms, DuBois dedicated his magazine *The Crisis* to the encouragement and celebration of black culture. His novels, sketches, and verses focused on life in the black community. He described his *Dusk of Dawn* (1940) as 'not so much my autobiography as the autobiography of a concept of race'. **CW.**

DUBUFFET, JEAN
1901-1985
French painter

Dubuffet trained in Paris from 1918 but in 1924 largely abandoned painting for the family wine business. When he began to paint seriously in 1942, his concerns lay outside the accepted realm of 'Fine Art.' Interested in child art, naive art, psychotic art, and graffiti, for which he coined the term 'Art Brut,' he attempted to bring their direct, unfettered approach to his own work. Using plaster, glue, asphalt, and broken glass, he created thickly impasted images which he scratched and scribbled on. Although in the Dadaist tradition, Dubuffet had a more positive approach to art, nurturing interest in areas previously despised. **ER.**

DUCHAMP, MARCEL
1887-1968
French artist

In 1912 Duchamp became a founder member of Section d'Or, a group of artists sharing an interest in Cubism and the dynamism of the modern machine age. In *Nude Descending A Staircase* (1911-12), Duchamp attempted to inject movement into the Cubist idiom and in 1912 used machine forms for paintings on the theme of Virgin or Bride. In 1913 he began making constructions which looked like machines without functioning as such, and carried this concept into his 'ready-mades', everyday objects which functioned as 'art objects' because he so designated them. He became infamous for ready-mades like *The Fountain* (1917), a urinal 'signed' R Mutt, and his bearded and moustachioed *Mona Lisa* (1920), entitled L.H.O.O.Q., (elle a chaud au cul: she has a hot arse). These attempts to debunk 'High Art', had an enormous impact on twentieth-century art, from Dada to Pop Art and beyond. In 1915 he moved to the USA, beginning his most famous work, *The Bride Stripped Bare By Her Batchelors, Even*. Essentially a wry comment on sexual frustration, it was created from wire and tin foil on a large sheet of glass and incorporated 'ready-mades', for example a coffee grinder. Abandoning it in 1923, he also largely abandoned his career as an artist but remained justly famous, as one of the few artists to revolutionize concepts of art. **ER.**

DUFY, RAOUL
1877-1953
French painter

Born in Le Havre, Dufy moved to Paris in 1900. Drawn to the pure color of the Fauves and later the quality of Cézanne's composition, by the late 1920s he had evolved a distinctive, decorative style of his own. Using color as a foil for lively drawing, he created charming oils and watercolors of race-meetings, fashionable resorts, and flowers. **ER.**

DULLES, JOHN FOSTER
1888-1959
American diplomat

A Republican statesman, Dulles became Secretary of State in 1953, after a distinguished diplomatic career. He helped formulate the UN Charter in 1945, and negotiated the 1951 peace treaty with Japan. Opposed to Soviet expansion he worked to strengthen the USA's position in the Cold War, and developed the policy of 'brinkmanship' in his negotiations. **JC.**

DUNCAN, ISADORA
1877-1927
American dancer and teacher

The American pioneer of 'Free Dance', Duncan developed her own anti-balletic philosophy and dances. Although they lacked a systematic basis, Duncan considered them to be a revival of the Greek dances of antiquity, and as such abandoned the formal leotard and tights to perform in loosely flowing tunics, barelegged and barefoot. Two of Duncan's dance principles were in direct opposition to the tenets of ballet: she believed the solar plexus to be the source of the body's power and that all dance rhythms were determined by either yielding to or resisting the force of gravity. Acclaimed in Europe, she received a cool reception in the USA, not least for her political and moral beliefs: she was a fervent supporter of the young Soviet state and had several much-publicized affairs. Faced with poverty following the death of her lover Essenin (who went mad and committed suicide in 1925), Duncan settled in Nice and began her autobiography *My Life*. She still gave occasional performances even in her fifties, the last being in Paris in 1927. Shortly afterwards, in Nice, she was killed when her scarf tangled in the wheel of her open car. **MC**.

DUPONT, PIERRE
1870-1954
American industrialist

Dupont became president of the family chemicals business in 1915 and supervised its great expansion during World War I. When war orders declined, he decided that the company should invest heavily in the then uncertain future of General Motors. In 1920-23 he was GM President and encouraged a reorganization that transformed the prospects of that company. **JW**.

ABOVE: Pierre Dupont, the US industrialist.

DURKHEIM, EMILE
1858-1917
French sociologist

Durkheim is considered to be the founding father of modern sociology. Born in France to a Jewish family, he got his first teaching post at the University of Bordeaux in 1887. Durkheim argued that sociology must have its own unique object and methods of study. This was possible because social institutions exist above the level of the individual, and can be explained in terms of social patterns rather than the actions of individuals. Durkheim advanced this view in *The Rules of Sociological Method* (1895) and demonstrated it most dramatically in *Suicide* (1897). Here he argued that suicide – which seems the most individual of acts – can be explained as the product of social forces. In the process, Durkheim made major advances in statistical analysis. Durkheim's other major theme was social solidarity and the crisis of common values under the impact of industrialisation. In 1897 he founded a famous review journal *L'Annee sociologique*, through which he established sociology as a recognized discipline. Durkheim moved to Paris in 1902, becoming full Professor at the Sorbonne in 1906. In 1912 his last major work *The Elementary Forms of Religious Life* argued that religious symbols were expressions of social solidarity. **DSl**.

ABOVE: Bob Dylan, the singer-songwriter, with Joan Baez.

DÜRRENMATT, FRIEDRICH
1921-1990
Swiss playwright

Dürrenmatt's grotesque absurdist dramas – in particular his most famous black comedies *The Visit* (1956) and *The Physicists* (1962) – deal with issues of power and responsibility in a postwar world where tragedy is no longer a relevant category. He was also author of many radio plays and some critical essays. **CW**.

DWORKIN, ANDREA
1946-
American feminist

Dworkin is an American radical feminist who is an aggressive critic of all aspects of male sexuality and patriarchy. Her stance rests fundamentally on a subtle, but contentious understanding of the political nature of language and the function of symbolism. She is equally lauded and reviled by critics and participants of the feminist/anti-feminist debate. Dworkin is more of a sensationalist than a historian of fact, and her semi-autobiographical novel, *Ice and Fire* (1986), attracted much attention as it details violent male sexuality so realistically that some readers found it pornographic. **EMS**.

DYLAN, BOB [ROBERT ZIMMERMAN]
1941-
American singer and songwriter

A seminal influence in white rock music from the Beatles to David Bowie, Dylan's writing ranges from melting love songs to complex allegory. Early singing was influenced by folk singer Woody GUTHRIE, but the 13 songs (almost all his own) on his second album, *The Freewheelin' Bob Dylan* (1963), established a new musical genre and included such classics as 'Blowin' in the Wind', 'Don't Think Twice, It's All Right', and 'A Hard Rain's A-Gonna Fall', which became a protest anthem. Dylan adopted a more rock-related idiom in 'Bringing It All Back Home' (1965), much to the horror of folk purists, but shot to the top ten with 'Lay Lady Lay' in 1969. Always a spasmodic artist, Dylan made another comeback in 1974 with *Blood on the Tracks*, sometimes hailed as his best album, although *Desire* (1975) is his bestseller to date. His music in the 1980s reflected his interests as a born-again Christian and found a smaller audience. **JH**.

DZERZHINSKY, FELIX
1877-1926
Russian secret police chief

The founder of the Cheka (the secret police) and architect of the Soviet system of repression, Dzerzhinsky was born a Polish aristocrat and became a fanatical Christian before converting to Bolshevism. A veteran of the abortive 1905 Revolution, he formed LENIN's secret police initially to prevent 'social hooliganism,' but he soon honed it into the sinister, all-powerful machine for eliminating the state's enemies which BERIA would later inherit with such terrible consequences. **JC**.

EAMES, CHARLES
1907-1978
American designer and architect

Born in St Louis, Missouri, Eames trained as an architect and worked from 1939-40 in Eliel Saarinen's office. Together they won a New York Museum of Modern Art (MOMA) competition for 'Organic Design for Home Furnishing' with complex three-dimensional molded plywood seating and rectilinear modular storage cabinets. The Herman Miller Furniture Company manufactured Eames-designed metal-framed plyformed chairs; another 1948 MOMA competition-winning stamped-metal chair was manufactured as molded glass-fiber-re-inforced polyester shells with metal-rod legs; and woven-wire, stacking and upholstered versions followed. Eames' work during the 1960s and 1970s included the famous swivel chair of three rosewood shells upholstered in leather, and he was widely honored for his many everyday classic designs. **AR.**

EARHART, AMELIA
1898-1937
American aviator

Considered the greatest of the American pioneer aviators, Amelia Earhart was the first woman to gain a pilot's certificate from the US National Aeronautic Association in May 1923. Her greatest triumph came on 21 May 1932 when she landed in Northern Ireland at the end of the first solo Atlantic flight by a woman. The crossing from Harbour Grace, Newfoundland, had taken 14 hours 54 minutes and also set a world non-stop distance record for women. Again in a Lockheed Vega, she made the first solo flight by a woman from Honolulu, Hawaii, to California, USA, on 11-12 January 1935. She disappeared near Howland Island in the South Pacific on 2 July 1937 during an around-the-world attempt. **MT.**

EARL, HARLEY J
1893-1969
American motor stylist

Within American automobile styling, Earl is credited with responsibility for the tail fin so prevalent in US car designs of the 1950s and 1960s. Earl was head of the 'art and color' section of General Motors in 1927, which became 'Styling' in 1937. Earl became Vice President GM in charge of styling in 1940. **NF.**

EASTMAN, GEORGE
1854-1932
American businessman

A Scotsman, Eastman owned a photographic plate factory in Rochester, NY and in 1887 introduced his Kodak No 1 box camera, which, unusually, used a roll of sensitized paper to take 100 shots instead of

ABOVE: The air pioneer Amelia Earhart.

photographic plates. When the roll was finished the camera was returned to Eastman, who developed the pictures and reloaded the camera. Soon transparent nitrocellulose film replaced the paper roll, enhancing the image clarity. With his slogan 'You press the button, we do the rest' this and succeeding cameras found a mass mar-

LEFT: Actor Clint Eastwood.

ket. Despite a successful suit brought against him for patent infringement, the Eastman Kodak Company prospered, as did photography as a hobby. In 1904 the 'Brownie' box camera was introduced. Priced at $1.00 (the original No 1 had been $25.00) it was for children and the film could be easily removed for local processing. Much of Eastman's profit was ploughed back into research and during his lifetime Kodak produced a successful color film. He gave away much of his wealth to US higher education. **JW.**

EASTWOOD, CLINT
1930-
American actor and director

It was in the TV western series *Rawhide* that Eastwood first came to public attention. It also brought him to the attention of Italian director Sergio LEONE, and Eastwood was soon starring in the now legendary 'Spaghetti Westerns', beginning in 1964 with *A Fistful of Dollars*. Eastwood was quickly an established star who could pick and choose roles at will, although his thin-lipped, unemotional style was perfect for the scruffy brutal hero of these early films. Since then he has tightly managed his career, also directing films such as *Breezy* (1973) and *Bird* (1988) with an efficiency and economy rare in Hollywood, and almost all his pictures have been big money makers. **DC.**

EATON, CYRUS
1883-1979
American industrialist

Canadian-born, Eaton made an early fortune from share dealings and founded the Republic Steel Corporation in 1930. In his later years he campaigned for nuclear disarmament and US-Soviet cooperation. From 1957 he was one of the sponsors of the Pugwash conferences, where Western and communist intellectuals could discuss problems privately and without propaganda. **JW.**

ECCLES, SIR JOHN CAREW
1903-
Australian neurophysiologist

Sir John Eccles shared the 1963 Nobel Prize for Medicine or Physiology for his work on the transmission of nerve signals across synapses – the junctions where one nerve cell interacts with another. He was educated in Melbourne and Oxford, and held senior academic posts at British, Australian, and New Zealand universities before moving to Chicago in 1966. Eccles has also performed important research on the cerebellum, the lobed organ at the base of the skull concerned with coordination and balance. He is the author of many books and scientific papers, but is most famous for his widely read book, *The Neurophysiological Basis of Mind*. **CR.**

Eco, UMBERTO
1932-
Italian academic and novelist

Academically more renowned as a world famous semiotician, Eco is also a distinguished scholar of James JOYCE, and a historian and philosopher with a particular interest in the Middle Ages. His taste for obscure and occult material, heresiology and Masonic lore has drawn comparisons with the great Argentinian writer Jorge Luis Borges. He was appointed Professor of Semiotics, a newly fashionable subject, at the University of Bologna in 1971. The erudite medieval detective story, *The Name of the Rose*, his first novel, was published in 1980 and became an international bestseller and source of a film. *Foucault's Pendulum* appeared in 1989. **AM**.

Eddington, SIR ARTHUR
1882-1944
British astronomer

Eddington was a champion of the theories of Albert EINSTEIN, and led an expedition to the total solar eclipse of 1919 which proved, as Einstein predicted, that starlight is bent as it passes through the sun's gravitational field. This was one of the first triumphs for the theory of relativity. Eddington was noted for his own theoretical work on the structure and energy output of stars. **IR**.

Eden, ANTHONY, 1ST EARL OF AVON
1897-1977
British politician

Having been appointed Foreign Secretary at a remarkably young age, Eden's resignation early in 1938 over the appeasement of dictators made him one of the figures of national resistance when war broke out. With his popularity untouched by Conservative defeat in 1945, Eden returned to the Foreign Office in 1951 where he pulled off some remarkable diplomatic coups. Within a year of becoming Prime Minister, however, ill-health and temper produced the fatal misjudgements that led to the Suez Crisis and a humiliating retirement. If later events in the Middle East perhaps proved him right, it was small comfort. **JP**.

Edward VIII, KING
1894-1972
British monarch, later Duke of Windsor

Eldest son of King George V, he succeeded to the throne in 1936 after an apprenticeship which included naval service and extensive travel. However, he declared his intention to marry an American divorcee, Wallis Simpson, triggering a constitutional crisis which led to abdication in favor of his brother George VI. **JP**.

Edwards, GARETH
1947-
British rugby union player

Many commentators would describe Gareth Edwards as the finest all-round scrum half ever to play his sport. He played 53 times for Wales from 1967-78, never being dropped nor missing a match through injury. An explosive runner, his total of 20 international tries is far and away the best by a scrum half, and long and accurate passing and kicking, relative weaknesses in his early career, soon became features of his style. He also played on three British Isles tours, including the only series victory in New Zealand in 1971. **DS**.

Ehrlich, PAUL
1854-1915
German medical scientist

Ehrlich studied medicine at the University of Leipzig and his early studies with aniline dyes to stain body tissues laid the foundations for the science of haematology. He discovered a technique for staining the tuberculosis bacillus that was vital for the diagnosis of TB in 1882, and later developed a diagnostic test for typhoid. While working with Emil von Behring he developed a serum against diptheria. He founded the George Speyer Haus for Chemotherapy in 1907, and started his important work on syphilis, which culminated in the production of Salvarsan, a cure that has also been used in the treatment of other diseases caused by a spirillium. He received the Nobel Prize for Medicine or Physiology in 1908 for his work on immunology. He was also awarded honorary degrees from Oxford, Chicago, and Athens and was made a Privy Councillor, Prussia's highest honor. **EMS**.

Eichmann, ADOLF
1906-1962
German functionary

Eichmann ran 'the Jewish Evacuation Department' of the SS and convened the Wannsee Conference in January 1942, which sealed the fate of European Jewry. This followed the failure of his attempts, through a personal visit to Palestine, to resettle German Jews with Zionist help. Personally supervised shipments to the death camps, despatching 400,000 Hungarian Jews in two months alone. Using a Vatican passport, he escaped at war's end to Argentina, where he was kidnapped by the Israelis, returned to Israel for trial, and hanged in 1962. **JC**.

Einstein, ALBERT
1879-1955
German-Swiss-American physicist

Born in Germany, Einstein was educated in Switzerland when his family moved there. He took Swiss nationality when he graduated at the age of 17. Thereafter he had difficulty in pursuing a higher education and took work at the Swiss Patent Office in Berne. This gave him enough free time to do research and in 1905 he published three famous papers. The first was on Brownian motion – the random movement of particles – and paved the way for later molecular theory. The second was on the photoelectric effect and became crucial in the development of quantum theory. The third was on the special theory of relativity in which mass and energy were equated. It was the second of these that gained him the Nobel Prize for Physics in 1921. The outbreak of World War II found him in America where he stayed, becoming instrumental in the development of the Manhattan Project to build the first atomic bomb. Afterwards he actively promoted disarmament, and turned down the offer of the Presidency of Israel. His later work included the development of the general theory of relativity which involved the constancy of the speed of light, and the attempt to find a theory that unified electromagnetic and gravitational fields – a theory that is still elusive. **DD**.

ABOVE: *Albert Einstein, winner of the 1921 Nobel Prize for Physics.*

EINTHOVEN, WILLIAM
1860-1927
Dutch physiologist

William Einthoven was the inventor of the first clinical electrocardiogram. He began his work in 1901 by adapting a string galvanometer so that it would record the variations in electrical impulses associated with the heartbeat. He was able to mimic the tiny action currents of the heart and use them to solve problems of rhythm. The electrocardiogram has since been of great value to physicians for the diagnosis of coronary artery disease. Einthoven's research has formed the basis of modern electrocardiography. He was awarded the Nobel Prize for Medicine or Physiology in 1924. **EMS**.

EISENHOWER, DWIGHT, GENERAL
1890-1969
American soldier, politician, and president

After graduation from West Point in 1915, Eisenhower served with the US Army in France as a staff officer and held senior positions thereafter until the outbreak of World War II. In 1942 he was appointed US commander in Europe and was Allied commander in North Africa and Italy, 1942-43. As Supreme Commander of the Allied Expeditionary Force from January 1944 he held together a disparate alliance of US, British, Canadian, and French troops, launching the Normandy landings on 6 June 1944 and leading the Allies to victory in May 1945. Eisenhower resigned from the army in 1952 to stand as the Republican Presidential candidate; he was elected 34th president of the USA, and repeated this triumph in 1956. A natural conservative, Eisenhower used troops to enforce racial segregation in Arkansas, and his administration endorsed the anti-communist witch-hunt of Senator MCCARTHY. Foreign affairs were dominated by the Cold War, and although his administration took a firm line against the Soviet Union, Eisenhower himself favored a more conciliatory approach. This attitude made possible the end of the Korean War in 1953 and he also refrained from intervening in the Hungarian uprising of 1956. One of America's most popular Presidents, 'Ike' retired in 1960. **JPi**.

EISENSTEIN, SERGEI
1898-1948
Soviet film director

Eisenstein was the most important early Soviet film artist. His use of montage in his films electrified audiences, critics and fellow film-makers, particularly the renowned Odessa Steps sequence in *Battleship Potemkin* (1925). After an unsuccessful time in Hollywood, and a number of abortive projects in his own country, Eisenstein returned to international prominence with two historical epics, *Alexander Nevsky* (1938) and the two-part *Ivan the Terrible* (1944-46), the latter incurring Stalin's wrath for its unflattering portrait of a tyrant. His theory of montage (where meaning is built up from a collision, or clash of images) was to be profoundly influential; and his films, in their expression of brotherhood, collectivism, and conflict, are an invaluable document of post-Revolution ideology. **NS**.

ELGAR, SIR EDWARD WILLIAM
1857-1934
British composer

Elgar is a musical colossus who stands astride the turn of the century. Brought up in Victorian Worcestershire, he drew inspiration from his beloved native landscape to produce music of global importance. Able to wallow in the jingoism of Empire, as in his *Pomp and Circumstance* marches, he was equally able to reach deep into the soul and create such masterpieces as the *Dream of Gerontius, Enigma Variations, Sea Pictures*, and his incomparable cello concerto. His organ, chamber, and orchestral pieces all show sparks of the genius which pervades his greatest works. **DK**.

ABOVE: British composer Sir Edward Elgar.

ELIOT, T[HOMAS] S[TEARNS]
1888-1965
American poet

Born in St Louis, Missouri, and educated at Harvard, the Sorbonne and Oxford, Eliot settled in London in 1915 at the suggestion of Ezra POUND, joined the High end of the Anglican church, and became a British subject in 1927. He taught, worked for Lloyds Bank until 1925, reviewed books, and edited the journal *The Criterion*, which published *The Waste Land* in its first edition in 1922. He became a director of Faber and Faber in 1925, nurturing a roster of younger poets. Equally influential as a critic and literary figure and as a poet, his importance for twentieth-century literature is enormous. *Prufrock and Other Observations* (1917) was his first collection; 'Prufrock' itself had been first published two years earlier. Other volumes of poetry were succeeded by his masterpiece, *The Waste Land*, perhaps the central text of modernism, the final version of which was much influenced by, and dedicated to POUND. He published highly regarded critical essays throughout his career, and in the Thirties a series of verse dramas and plays had some success, the finest being *Murder in the Cathedral* (1935), the rest at best

ABOVE: General Eisenhower (seated, right) with senior NATO officers.

uneven. The major achievement of his later poetry, *The Four Quartets* (1935-42) was first published in its entirety in 1943. He was awarded the Nobel Prize and the Order of Merit in 1948. **AM**.

ELIZABETH II, QUEEN
1926-
British monarch

Elder daughter of the Duke and Duchess of York (later King George VI and Queen Elizabeth), she came to the throne in February 1952, being crowned at Westminster in June 1953. Since then, she has visited every part of the Commonwealth and acted as a symbol of British tradition worldwide. **JP**.

ELLINGTON, DUKE
1899-1974
American jazz composer and pianist

The predominant jazz composer of all time, Ellington began his career in the 1920s at the Cotton Club in Harlem after encouragement from Fats WALLER. He grew steadily in popularity, making recordings and composing scores, his first popular success being the 1930 tune 'Mood Indigo'. It was in the 1940s that his band, now with Billy Strayhorn as arranger, whose tune 'Take The A Train' had become the band's theme, produced their finest recordings. By 1950, however, he was less in evidence as a creative force. His place in jazz history rests with the legacy of his songs, a huge influence on twentieth-century songwriting. **DC**.

ELLIS, HAVELOCK
1859-1939
British writer, psychologist, and physician

After qualifying as a doctor in 1889, Ellis preferred to pursue his literary predilection, editing the Mermaid Series of Old Dramatists and the Contemporary Science Series, in which his first book *The Criminal* was published in 1890. His seven-volume *Studies in the Psychology of Sex* (1897-1928), which examined human sexual impulses, caused him to be prosecuted for obscenity. Indeed, until 1953 the studies were only available to doctors. **CH-M**.

ENDER, KORNELIA
1958-
East German swimmer

Kornelia Ender was one of the most powerful competitors produced by East Germany during that country's period of prominence in world swimming. She won four individual gold medals at the 1976 Olympics and added four silvers in other events at the 1972 and 1976 celebrations. She set numerous world records particularly in the 100m freestyle and 100m butterfly at which she excelled. Whether her preparations were free from the abuses common in East German sport can be debated. **DS**.

ABOVE: The great Duke Ellington pictured with his orchestra.

ENDERS, JOHN FRANKLIN
1897-
American biologist

Educated at Yale and Harvard, Enders' pioneering work provided a method for culturing viruses in quantity outside the human body. Research on viruses had been greatly hindered by scientists' inability to grow them in nutrient substances. In 1948 he developed a growth medium containing penicillin to suppress the growth of bacteria and used it to culture the mumps, and later the polio virus. Together with his colleagues Frederick Robbins and Thomas Weller, he produced a vaccine against the measles virus; all three shared the Nobel Prize in 1954. **ES**.

ENO, BRIAN
1948-
British synthesizer player and producer

Synthesizer pioneer with Roxy Music in the

BELOW: Jacob Epstein at work.

1970s, Eno was the guru who worked with such artists as BOWIE, U2 and David Byrne as well as producing his own 'mood-music'. Latterly an important pioneer of New Age music, he has also been in demand as a producer throughout his career. **DC**.

EPSTEIN, JACOB, SIR
1880-1959
British sculptor

Born in New York, Epstein studied in Paris and became deeply interested in ancient and primitive sculpture. In 1905 he settled in Britain, taking citizenship in 1907. In 1907-08 he produced 18 figures for the façade of the British Medical Association (now Zimbabwe House), London. Their nudity and distortion was considered indecent and similar controversy arose over his tomb for Oscar Wilde, Paris (1910-12). Around 1913-18 he employed a more geometric, mechanistic style, exemplified by *Rock Drill* (1913-14). The uncouth primitivism and expressive distortion of his monumental carvings continued to raise controversy throughout his career, in contrast to his many sensitively modeled portrait busts which were widely admired. **ER**.

ERHARD, LUDWIG
1897-1977
German politician

An anti-Nazi businessman, he became the German Federal Republic's first Minister of Economics, in which post he made possible the 'Economic Miracle.' He coupled economic flair with a strong feeling for public relations, taking union leaders into his confidence and maintaining a balance between wages and prices. He enjoyed the complete trust of Chancellor ADENAUER, but the latter's carping brought his own Chancellorship to an untimely end. **JC**.

ABOVE: Surrealist painter Max Ernst.

ERNST, MAX
1891-1976
French painter

Born in Cologne, Ernst studied philosophy at Bonn University. A self-taught painter, in 1919 he founded the Cologne Dada group. After meeting André BRETON he moved to Paris in 1922, becoming a founder member of the Surrealist movement in 1924. He adapted Dadaist techniques to Surrealist uses, producing whimsical collages and photomontages, and in 1925 invented frottage, a technique akin to brass rubbing. Childhood memories were an important source for his work, particularly his *Forest* paintings. He left the Surrealists in 1938 but without changing style. He spent the years 1941-48 in the USA before returning to France, taking citizenship in 1958. **ER**.

ESCOFFIER, GEORGES AUGUSTE
1846-1935
French chef

Escoffier helped to prepare dishes for Napoleon III during the Franco-Prussian war of the 1870s, but his real fame and fortune were made in London. Escoffier worked at its two premier eating places: the Carlton and the Savoy. Many of the original dishes (such as Peach Melba) that he invented for London's high society are still reproduced today. **RJ**.

EULER, ULF VON
1905-
Swedish physiologist

The son of a Nobel laureate, he won the Nobel Prize for isolating noradrenaline, the first neurotransmitter to be identified. In 1935 he had identified the first prostaglandin so-named because he assumed it came from the prostrate gland. Later these important inflammatory mediators were in fact found in many other human tissues but his deduction that they were fatty acids was correct. **ES**.

EUSEBIO, SILVA FERREIRA DA
1942-
Portuguese soccer player

Born in Mozambique, Eusebio became one of the stars of Portuguese and European soccer in the 1960s. He won European Cup medals with the Benfica club in 1961 and 1962, was European Footballer of the Year in 1965 and was one of the highlighted players of the 1966 World Cup. **DS**.

EVANS, SIR ARTHUR
1851-1941
British archaeologist

Between 1899 and 1907 Evans funded and directed a series of excavations on Crete, primarily at Knossos. Some of Evans's archaeological interpretation is now discounted, and his restoration work is too enthusiastic for today's taste, but his achievement in almost single-handedly bringing to light the glories of the Minoan palace civilization was extraordinary. **RJ**.

ABOVE: British actress Dame Edith Evans.

EVANS, DAME EDITH
1888-1976
British actress

Commanding plumby-voiced actress, born in London, Dame Edith was more renowned for her work on stage than on screen (particularly for her legendary performance as Lady Bracknell in Oscar Wilde's *The Importance of Being Earnest*). She was sometimes seen to great effect on film, notably in *The Queen of Spades* (1948), *Tom Jones* (1963) and *The Whisperers* (1967). **NS**.

EVANS, WALKER
1903-1975
American photographer

Evans, the most influential of all American modernist photographers, began to work in 1928 after a short period in Paris. In 1930 his pictures were used to illustrate Hart Crane's *The Bridge*, and between 1935 and 1938 he photographed for the Farm Security Administration in the Eastern United States. His first and greatest book was *American Photographs*, published in 1938. His subject was society in construction, and in decay, seen in public spaces and in relation to advertising stereotypes. The dispassionate, modernist style which he developed in the 1930s fell into disfavor in a subsequent age of humanist reportage, but in the 1960s his influence became paramount among social documentarists and artists of a new generation. **IJ**.

EVANS-PRITCHARD, SIR EDWARD
1902-1973
British anthropologist

Evans-Pritchard was a pioneer of social anthropology, and one of the most influential of anthropological field workers. His most famous piece of ethnography was perhaps his study *Witchcraft, Magic and Oracles among the Azande*, published in 1937, which gave a detailed and fascinating account of the supernatural beliefs of the African Zande tribe. Evans-Pritchard also lived among the Nuer in Africa, publishing in 1940 an influential study of kinship structures; this work has been much criticized, however, both for theoretical reasons and because it bears only a limited relationship to how the Nuer themselves perceive their lineages. **RJ**.

EYSENCK, HANS
1916-
British psychologist

From 1942 German-born Eysenck practiced as a psychologist in London. In 1950 he became Director at the Psychological Department of the Institute of Psychiatry, University of London, becoming a Professor at the university in 1955. Eysenck was deeply critical of Freudian psychoanalysis, instead advocating behavior therapy – treating the symptoms of mental disorder rather than the root causes. Eysenck's *Race, Intelligence and Education* (1971) is the most controversial of his many works. **CH-M**.

ABOVE: *Douglas Fairbanks in* The Thief of Baghdad.

FAIRBANKS, DOUGLAS
1883-1939
American actor and film director

Fairbanks' career took off in the 1920s when most of his famous costume adventures were made, and he swashbuckled his way through classics such as *The Mark of Zorro* (1920) and *The Three Musketeers* (1921). It was his age, not his voice, which hurt Fairbanks when the talkies came, and he had all but retired by 1930. **DC**.

FANGIO, JUAN-MANUEL
1911-
Argentinian racing driver

Still thought by many to be the greatest-ever racing driver, Fangio first raced in 1934 in his own Model T Ford. He won numerous events in South America before coming to Europe in 1948. He drove for Maserati, Alfa Romeo, Ferrari, and Mercedes-Benz, winning the World Championship five times before retiring in 1958. **NF**.

FANON, FRANTZ
1925-1961
West Indian political theorist

Born in Martinique, Fanon studied medicine in France and was assigned to a hospital in Algeria during the nationalist rising. His experiences led him to condemn the evils of Western imperialism in a book *The Wretched of the Earth*, regarded as 'a classic of third World politics.' **JP**.

FARNSWORTH, PHILO
1906-1971
American electrical engineer

Farnsworth was one of the independent innovators in the 1930s race for a practical TV system. He was particularly concerned with camera tubes which would produce the electrical analog of an optical image. Farnsworth realized this in his 'image dissector' tube but the later devices using charge storage techniques won the battle. **PW**.

FAROUK, KING
1920-1965
Egyptian monarch

Succeeding to the throne in 1936, Farouk lacked political experience. As Arab nationalism developed in the early 1950s, he could not cope with the pressure, retreating into a self-indulgent lifestyle which further alienated his people. Exiled following a military coup in 1952, he was officially deposed a year later. **JP**.

FAULKNER, WILLIAM [CUTHBERT]
1897-1962
American novelist

Born in Mississippi, Faulkner's first publication was a book of poems, *The Marble Faun* (1924), and his first novel, *Soldiers Pay*, about the return home and subsequent death of a disabled soldier, appeared in 1926. Two further novels were written between that and the appearance of *The Sound and the Fury* in 1929, justly one of his most famous novels. It was his first experiment with multiple points of view, and his second novel to feature the fictional Yoknapatawpha County, Mississippi was also the setting for the subsequent *As I Lay Dying* (1930), which showed his comic talents to be as considerable as his tragic vision of the decay of the American South. These and *Light in August* (1932), as well as the later *Absalom,*

ABOVE: *US novelist William Faulkner.*

Absalom! (1936) were all powerful works. However, his popularity was not as great as his literary reputation, and he was forced periodically to earn his living as a Hollywood scriptwriter over the years, on such films as *The Big Sleep* (1946). His later fiction bears little comparison with the earlier works, though he won two Pulitzer Prizes, for *A Fable* (1954) and for *The Reivers* (1962), his last novel. He was awarded the Nobel Prize for Literature in 1950. **AM**.

FAURÉ, GABRIEL
1845-1924
French composer

Ironically Fauré's most popular work, namely his *Requiem* (1887) is not the reason why he is cited as one of the greatest composers in the twentieth century. Rather, his greatest achievement lies in his songs. Here he creates an intense and intimate relationship between singer and accompanist which many believe is unrivaled in the history of song. **DK**.

FEIGENBAUM, MITCHELL
1945-
American mathematician

An eccentric with very wide intellectual interests, it was Feigenbaum's training as a particle physicist that led him to discover, using only a pocket calculator, the underlying similarity in the behavior of the equations describing a variety of diverse physical systems. Ironically, since he had published almost nothing when he was appointed to his post at Los Alamos National Laboratory, his findings were rejected by the mainstream scientific journals, but they became widely known throughout the scientific community. The underlying scaling invariance in apparently chaotic behavior such as turbulent flow which his chaos theory described, has been hugely influential in many scientific areas. **EB**.

FELLINI, FEDERICO
1920-
Italian film director

One of the most flamboyant artists of European cinema, Fellini's films reflect his early experience as a performer in the circus and as a cartoonist. His first big international success was *La Strada* (1954), starring his wife Giulietta Massina and Anthony QUINN, and he achieved world-wide notoriety with *La Dolce Vita* (1960), a sensational, satirical study of high-life decadence in modern-day Rome. Fellini's imagination is grotesque, mischievous, erotic, self-indulgent, but with an Italianate passion and love of life: in his films, nothing succeeds like excess. His best films are his most autobiographical, notably 8½ (1963), in which a film-maker in a creative crisis ransacks his past for inspiration, and *Amarcord* (1973), an affectionate remembrance of his own childhood. **NS**.

FERMI, ENRICO
1901-1954
Italian physicist

He was Professor of Theoretical Physics in his native Rome from 1926 to 1938. Then, with the rise of Fascism, he moved to America to become Professor at Columbia University and later at Chicago. His field was nuclear reactions and he realized the possibility of producing a nuclear bomb, urging President Roosevelt to develop one before Germany did. In 1942 he produced a controlled chain reaction in the first atomic pile, built in Chicago. He approved of the production and use of the atomic bomb, but opposed the later development of a hydrogen bomb. The Fermilab – the center for particle physics in Chicago – is named after him, as is the element fermium. **DD**.

ABOVE: *Italian physicist Enrico Fermi.*

FERRAGAMO, SALVATORE
1898-1960
Italian designer

At the age of 16 Ferragamo joined his brothers in California where he made shoes by hand for American film companies as well as for private clients. In 1936 he set up a workshop in Florence and became the first large-scale producer of hand-made shoes. He originated the wedge heel and platform sole, and experimented with a variety of materials. By 1957 Ferragamo had created some 20,000 styles and registered some 350 patents for his designs. **MC**.

FERRARI, ENZO
1898-1988
Italian motor manufacturer

The man whose name is now synonymous with motor racing and exciting sports cars apparently wanted to be an opera singer as a child. Despite being badly injured in World War I, Ferrari began his career as a racing driver, having a long and fruitful association with Alfa Romeo. He started Scuderia Ferrari – running Alfa Romeos – at the end of 1929. Even at this time, Ferrari had strong links with Fiat. Despite the outbreak of World War II, Ferrari first raced cars of his own manufacture at Bresica in 1940, and the first road car bearing the Ferrari name was built in 1947. The famous Prancing Horse symbol has been on many fabulous sportscars and achieved worldwide racing successes including Formula One and sportscar World Championships. After his only son died in 1956, Ferrari became rather more of a recluse within the factory and stopped attending races. Ford attempted to buy Ferrari in 1967, but Fiat increased its interest in the company. 'Il Commendatore', as he was known, exerted an immeasurable influence on the automotive business. **NF**.

FIELDS, W C [WILLIAM CLAUDE DUKENFIELD]
1879-1946
American actor

Fields was already a vaudeville star by the age of 20, and early movies brought him a modest following. He usually played the great drinker, all-time cynic and misanthrope, hen-pecked and persecuted, fighting back by bragging, griping, avoiding his enemies, speaking harshly to children, and weakly abandoning himself to pointless fits of temper. He was a cult hero as early as 1930, and shone when he stepped out of character to play Humpty Dumpty in *Alice in Wonderland* (1933) or Mr Micawber in *David Copperfield* (1934). Not only have his films survived, but today his reputation is greater than at the peak of his career. **DC**.

FINCH, PETER
1916-1977
British actor

Finch was a leading radio actor before his rugged appearance made him a respected stage and film actor. He received British Academy Awards for *A Town Like Alice* (1956) and *Sunday Bloody Sunday* (1971), and won the award for Best Actor for his last film, *Network* (1976), in which he played a crazed television commentator. **DC**.

FINNEY, ALBERT
1936-
British actor

Finney has been called the second Olivier; an illustrious stage and film actor, he comes as close as any to deserving the title. After the Royal Academy of Dramatic Art, he made his stage debut with the Birmingham Rep and for the next ten years did mainly Shakespeare. Fame came with *Billy Liar* on stage and *Saturday Night and Sunday Morning* (1960) on screen. *Tom Jones* won him a Best Actor Award at the Venice Film Festival in 1963, but he turned down lucrative parts to spend two seasons with the National Theatre enhancing his reputation as one of the finest actors of his generation. As a psychotic murderer in the remake of the classic *Night Must Fall* (1963) and the self-absorbed husband in *Two for the Road* (1967) through to recent films such as *Miller's Crossing* (1990) he has continued to show exceptional range on screen in a rather eccentric choice of roles. **DC**.

FISCHER-DIESKAU, DIETRICH
1925-
German opera and lieder singer

Fischer-Dieskau was long the leading baritone at the Berlin State Opera House after his debut in 1948, although he is known in the US only from recordings. Mozart and Strauss are specialities, as are twentieth-century roles such as Berg's *Wozzeck*. Fischer-Dieskau's musical intelligence and command of expression have caused his lieder interpretations to overshadow his operatic career. **JH**.

FISHER, RONALD
1890-1962
British statistician

Fisher reworked the theoretical foundations of mathematical statistics, and devised many of the modern techniques of experimental design and analysis, including random sampling and the analysis of variance, before publishing a theoretical account of natural selection in which he reconciled the views of Darwin with those of Mendel. While Galton Professor of Eugenics in London, Fisher laid the foundations of the genetic study of human blood groups, before returning to Cambridge where he became President of Gonville and Caius College. **EB**.

FITZGERALD, ELLA
1918-
American jazz singer

Sometimes criticized and dismissed as a jazz artist, Fitzgerald's early work with BASIE is evidence of her dedication to jazz, although she is probably now better known as an interpreter of classic American song. Her mid-1950s duets with Louis ARMSTRONG are characterized by a warmth and unpretentiousness, and although she has occasionally performed low-grade material, her bell-like clarity and range as well as her great ability to swing make her one of jazz's finest performers. **DC**.

FITZGERALD, F[RANCIS] SCOTT
1896-1940
American novelist

Born in St Paul, Minnesota, and educated at Princeton, Fitzgerald served briefly in the US Army during World War I, when he became engaged to the beautiful and neurotic Zelda Sayre. In 1919, he left the army for advertizing in New York, then returned home and finished the semi-autobiographical novel *This Side of Paradise* (1920); it was a great success. He also married Zelda that year, and published his first collection of short stories *Flappers and Philosophers*. The stories *Tales of the Jazz Age* and the novel *The Beautiful and the Damned*, with its prophetic story of alcoholic disintegration, both appeared in 1922 as the Fitzgerald lifestyle was speeding up. Life in privileged Great Neck, Long Island, provided the inspiration for *The Great Gatsby* (1924), his finest novel, published after they had moved to France in 1924. More short stories, more traveling, and a series of mental illnesses for the driven Zelda preceded and succeeded the appearance of *Tender is the Night* in 1934. Brief stints as a screenwriter led to a Hollywood contract in 1937, where he worked on *The Last Tycoon*, which was to remain unfinished at his death (it was edited for publication in 1941 by Edmund Wilson), and he was fired for the alcoholism that eventually killed him. **AM**.

FLAGSTAD, KIRSTEN
1895-1962
Norwegian opera singer

An outstanding Wagnerian soprano, Flagstad appeared in a wide range of opera and operetta in Scandinavia and was on the verge of retiring in 1933 when a small part at Bayreuth led to her Met debut as Sieglinde in *Rheingold* (1935), which created a sensation and was swiftly followed by Isolde and Brunnhilde. Her voice was already rich and mature, and she had the stamina to handle the most demanding roles. In San Francisco, Chicago, and London as well as New York, she sang all the great Wagnerian roles; Beethoven's *Fidelio* was her only major non-Wagner part. **JH**.

FLAHERTY, ROBERT J
1884-1951
American film maker

Known as the father of film documentary, largely for his ground-breaking study of Eskimo life, *Nanook of the North* (1922), Flaherty made documentaries that were more poetic than polemic. In *Man of Aran* (1934) and *Louisiana Story* (1948), he typically pitted man against nature, and paid homage to a vanishing way of life. **NS**.

FLECK, ALEXANDER, BARON
1889-1968
British industrialist

Fleck was chairman of Imperial Chemical Industries from 1953 to 1960. He also served on many government committees, some of which were highly influential. He is an example of an academic who, more or less by accident, rose high in the world of business. His working life had begun in chemistry research and it was only World

War I which drew him into the management of a chemical firm that was later absorbed by ICI. His greatest moments were in World War II when, as head of ICI's Billingham division, he kept chemical production going despite heavy bombing. **JW**.

FLEMING, SIR ALEXANDER
1881-1955
British bacteriologist

On his return to St Mary's Hospital, London, after World War I, Fleming resumed his study of antibacterial mechanisms. His most renowned discovery occurred in 1928 when he noted that a culture plate containing staphlococci bacteria had killed the bacteria around it. He identified the mold as *Penicillium notatum*, and noted that the antibacterial substance, penicillin, was effective against many other pathogenic species. In 1929 he reported that penicillin was non-toxic to animal tissue and 'may be an efficient antiseptic . . . against penicillin sensitive microbes.' Unable to produce a pure extract, Fleming's confidence that penicillin would one day be stabilized and purified was vindicated when in 1940 Ernst CHAIN and Howard FLOREY achieved this. Within two years the antibiotic's remarkable powers were established and the mounting war casualties ensured its use. Postwar, it revolutionized the fight against bacterial infection and Fleming received the Nobel Prize for Medicine jointly with Florey and Chain in 1945. **ES**.

ABOVE: Sir Alexander Fleming, the noted bacteriologist.

FLEMING, IAN
1908-1964
British novelist

Fleming worked as a journalist before publishing *Casino Royale* (1952), his first James Bond thriller. It was followed by 12 more, whose and jet-set ambiance made Bond the world's best-known secret agent. Many became successful films, notorious for their technological special effects. **AM**.

FLOREY, HOWARD WALTER, BARON
1898-1968
Australian pathologist

Florey was an outstanding experimental pathologist, remembered above all for his work on penicillin. In 1938 he focused on the problems of isolation and production as well as on the drug's therapeutic use. With Ernst CHAIN he made enough crude penicillin to treat the first patient in 1941. The efficacy of penicillin was obvious, but with resources for industrial production unavailable in wartime Britain, Florey visited the United States in 1941 to arouse interest. The first US patient was treated in 1942 and sufficient penicillin produced to treat the casualties of 1944. In 1945 Florey shared the Nobel prize with CHAIN and Alexander FLEMING. **GL**.

ABOVE: The swashbuckling Errol Flynn.

FLYNN, ERROL
1909-1959
Australian-American actor

Colorful, witty, and charming, Flynn was the dashing hero of some of Hollywood's finest adventure films, a comedian, and a more than competent actor. After starting to act in England, a contract with Warner Brothers brought him to Hollywood and instant stardom in the 1935 film *Captain Blood*. A series of costume pictures with Olivia De Havilland was immensely popular, and much-publicized bar-room brawls, three marriages, and scores of flamboyant affairs helped build the Errol Flynn 'Don Juan' legend. But by the late 1940s drugs and alcohol began to take their toll and his career never really recovered. **DC**.

Fo, Dario
1926-
Italian dramatist

Fo's stylized farces combine *commedia dell' arte* technique with Marxist philosophy in a social protest whose targets include the military, the church, government, the middle classes and the pompous self-importance of all figures of power. Probably best known for *Accidental Death of an Anarchist* (1969), his technique is best exemplified in the collection of short pieces *Mistero Buffo* (1977). **DC.**

Foch, Ferdinand, Marshal
1851-1929
French soldier

After enlisting in the infantry in the Franco-Prussian War of 1870, Foch was commissioned into the artillery in 1873. His promotion was slow, but he was well known as a strategist and a firm advocate of frontal attacks, a policy that was to lead to enormous French casualties during the early campaigns of World War I. Nevertheless by the end of 1914 Foch, commanding the 9th Army, had helped to win the vital Battle of the Marne, pushing the Germans back from Paris. Appointed to co-ordinate the Allied armies of the north in Flanders, Foch soon gained a reputation for parsimony in the commitment of reserves, something that contributed to the heavy losses experienced in the 2nd Battle of Ypres (1915) and on the Somme (1916). Removed to an administrative post in late 1916, Foch became Chief of the French General Staff in 1917. When the Germans launched their offensive in March 1918, Foch was appointed Allied generalissimo, in which capacity he supervised the counter-attacks of August-November 1918 and took the enemy surrender. **JPi.**

Fokine, Mikhail Mikhailovich
1880-1942
Russian dancer and choreographer

Although an excellent expressive dancer and technically very strong, Fokine's main contribution to twentieth-century ballet was as a choreographer and ballet reformer, transforming it from 'pretty entertainment' to a potent art form. He worked in Russia, France, and America, and with PAVLOVA and Diaghilev to create memorable and influential ballets. **MC.**

Fokker, Anthony Herman Gerard
1890-1939
Dutch aviation pioneer and engineer

A keen inventor, at 20 Fokker attended automobile school in Germany, where in 1910 he helped build and test two ill-fated airplanes. In 1911, with the help of Jacob Goedecker, he built a successful *Spider* monoplane. Fokker Aviation was founded in 1912, becoming theFokker Aircraft Factory in 1915, supplying Germany with

fighter planes in World War I. After the Armistice, Fokker re-established aircraft production in the Netherlands. **MT.**

Fonck, René Paul, Capitaine
1894-1953
French fighter pilot

The highest-scoring Allied fighter pilot of World War I, Fonck's officially-credited 75 air victories were 52 short of his own estimate. Joining the 11th Engineer Regiment of the French army in 1914, he began training in 1915 and claimed his first 'official' victory in 1916. Postwar, an attempted New York to Paris flight ended in tragedy on 21 September 1926, when the overloaded Sikorsky S-35 failed to take off from Roosevelt Field, and two of the crew were killed. **MT.**

Fonda, Henry
1905-1983
American actor

On stage and screen, Fonda began playing gauche young men and graduated to roles of amiable wisdom. By the time of his death, he had attained mythic proportions in America after a lifetime playing characters embodying the values of the Midwestern prairie which was his home. By 1934 he had become a respected Broadway performer, and the shy unassuming Fonda shot to stardom within a year of his first movie, appearing in westerns, comedies, and melodramas until the greatest role of his career, that of Tom Joad in *The Grapes of Wrath* (1940). After the war, his career alternated between screen and theater, and films such as *Twelve Angry Men* (1957), for which he won a British Film Academy Award, and *The Best Man* (1964), reflected his preference for scripts with a political and social content. In 1982 he was at last given an Academy Award for Best Actor for *On Golden Pond* opposite Katharine HEPBURN and his daughter Jane. **DC.**

Fonda, Jane
1937-
American actress

It was Lee STRASBERG of the Actors Studio who persuaded Fonda to become an actress, and a family friend gave her a big part in her first film, *Tall Story* (1960). That and her next film, *Walk on the Wild Side* (1961) were critically praised. She emerged as a sexpot in *La Ronde* (1964) for Roger VADIM, and after their marriage he proceeded to turn her into another BARDOT in *Barbarella* (1968). Fonda became deeply involved in radical, and later feminist, politics during the Vietnam era despite the risk of destroying her career, but still went on to win Academy Awards for Best Actress in *Klute* (1971) and *Coming Home* (1978). **DC.**

Fonteyn, Margot, Dame
1919-1991
British dancer

After studying ballet in Shanghai and London, Fonteyn made her debut as a snowflake in the 1934 Vic-Wells production of the *Nutcracker*, and the next year created her first major role in Ashton's *Baiser de la Fée*. By 1939 she had danced all the ballerina roles of the standard classics – Giselle, Odette-Odile, and Aurora – and created new roles in Ashton's works. She shared the fortunes of the Vic-Wells Ballet during World War II but in 1959 decided to become guest artist with the company, now the Royal Ballet. It was then that her dancing reached its peak in performances of *Sleeping Beauty* and *Swan Lake*. By 1960 retirement seemed near: she was over 40 years old but was provided with a new partner, Rudolf NUREYEV, who was able to match her in artistry and international fame. In effect, it was Nureyev who was instrumental in allowing Fonteyn to continue her dancing career until well beyond her 58th year. In 1956 Fonteyn met Panamanian politician Roberto de Arias whom she later married.

BELOW: Dame Margot Fonteyn partnered by Rudolf Nureyev.

Following an assassination attempt which left him paralysed, Fonteyn divided her time between caring for her husband at their Panamanian ranch and working as President of the Royal Academy of Dancing. Although she readily admitted to having weak feet and was unable to perform feats of virtuosity, her musicality and personality made her a greatly admired and one of the most famous, ballerinas of the twentieth century. **MC**.

ABOVE: Former US President Gerald Ford.

FORD, GERALD R
1913-
American politician and president

Ford became President in 1973 after the disgrace first of Vice-President Spiro Agnew, whom he replaced, and then of his patron, President Richard NIXON. A prominent conservative, after 25 years in the House of Representatives he had earned a reputation for honesty which helped him survive the Watergate Scandal. Initially villified for pardoning Nixon prematurely, Ford's decision to airlift thousands of Vietnamese refugees to the USA won him renewed public acclaim, although insufficient for his re-election in 1976. **CH-M.**.

FORD, HENRY
1863-1947
American motor manufacturer

Undoubtedly the father of mass production in the automobile world, Henry Ford's early days were involved in motor sport. He built his first car in 1901 and founded the Ford Motor Company in 1903. The famous Model T Ford, introduced in 1908, was the car that built Ford's reputation, and over 15 million were sold in an 18-year production run. This success allowed Henry Ford to buy out all his shareholders in 1919, giving himself sole control. In 1938 Ford introduced the V8 engine, a configuration that, in America at least, remains popular today. Henry Ford made the motor car affordable to a great number of people for the first time. The company was kept in the family after Henry's death by sons Edsel and Henry Ford II. **NF**.

FORD, JOHN
1895-1973
American film director

'My name's John Ford', he once said, 'I make Westerns.' Ford will always be associated with John WAYNE, whom he made a star in *Stagecoach* (1939), and Monument Valley, a location he made his own in such films as *Fort Apache* (1948), *She Wore a Yellow Ribbon* (1949) and *The Searchers* (1956). In a career stretching back to the silent era, no director did more to enshrine the spirit of pioneering America. Yet curiously his four directing Oscars were all for non-Western films: *The Informer* (1935), *The Grapes of Wrath* (1940), *How Green was My Valley* (1941), and *The Quiet Man* (1952). A notoriously cantankerous man who could intimidate actors, producers, and critics alike, he always eschewed deep analysis of his work. He was a meticulous craftsman whose films not only celebrated America's past, but also showed the cost of progress, exposed the shaky basis of some of the nation's myths, and confronted the unpleasant aspects of prejudice, injustice, and racial intolerance. **NS**.

de FOREST, LEE
1873-1961
American electronics engineer

In 1906, de Forest invented the triode radio valve which he put to innovatory use as an amplifier, magnifying weak radio signals to enormous power levels. He experimented with broadcasting, and established a radio station in 1916. During the 1920s, he tried to develop talking pictures with less success. **PT**.

FORSSMANN, WERNER
1904-1979
German surgeon

A graduate of Berlin University, Forssmann became an eminent and much-decorated surgeon but is principally remembered for his pioneering experiments on cardiac catheterization at the Eberswalde Surgical Clinic. In 1925, unable to persuade senior colleagues that the technique was safe to carry out on patients, Forssmann introduced a catheter into his own heart, via an

ABOVE: Motor manufacturer Henry Ford

arm vein. He viewed the procedure using X-rays. Thirty years later, when the relative safety of the technique was established, Forssmann shared a Nobel Prize for this work. **GL**.

FORSTER, E(DWARD) M(ORGAN)
1879-1970
British novelist and literary critic

After his graduation from King's College, Cambridge in 1897, Forster traveled in Greece and Italy, countries whose Mediterranean passion inspired him to write. In 1905 he published *Where Angels Fear to Tread*, followed by *The Longest Journey* (1907), *A Room with a View* (1908), and *Howard's End* (1910). *Maurice*, written during these prewar years, depicts Forster's personal desires; dealing as it does with a homosexual relationship, it was not published until after his death in 1971. During World War I Forster worked for the Red Cross in Alexandria after which, in 1921, he travelled to India as the private secretary to a maharajah, an experience which resulted in his greatest novel, *A Passage to India* (1924). Forster returned to England in 1927, and devoted his energies to writing and literary criticism (*Aspects of the Novel* [1927]). Always concerned with the liberty of the individual, in 1934 Forster became the first President of the National Council for Civil Liberties; in 1945 he was elected an honorary fellow of King's College, Cambridge. **CH-M**.

FOSSEY, DIAN
1932-1985
American zoologist

In 1963 Fossey took a seven-week safari in Tanzania and met the LEAKEYS. Captivated by the continent she founded the Karisoke Research Center in the Rwanda forest. Increasingly reclusive, she spent 18 years living with and studying gorillas, until she was murdered. Her moving plea for conservation, *Gorillas in the Mist* (1983), made her world famous. **MB**.

FOSTER, SIR NORMAN
1935-
British architect

Foster's buildings are characterized by high technology and sleek, austere surfaces. Foster himself has expressed his aesthetic: 'High technology is not an end in itself . . . rather it is a means to social goals and wider possibilities.' His headquarters for the Hong Kong and Shanghai Banking Corporation, Hong Kong (1986), embodies the essence of Foster's style. In England his major designs include the Sainsbury Centre for Visual Arts at the University of East Anglia (1978), the passenger terminal for Stansted Airport (1980-90), and the headquarters of Independent Television News, London, completed 1991. **DE**.

FOYT, AJ
1935-
American racing driver

A fierce competitor behind the wheel, AJ Foyt has won the USAC/CART championship seven times, more than anyone else. On four occasions he has sped to victory at the Indianapolis 500. Displaying great versatility, Foyt is the only racer ever to win the Indy 500, the Daytona 500, and 24 Hours of LeMans. **MD.**

FRANCO, FRANCISCO
1892-1975
Spanish statesman

Franco's 40-year rule spanned the heyday of the dictators and the growth of the Common Market. His skilful political juggling maintained the trappings of dictatorship, making Spain a pariah in postwar Europe, while laying the groundwork for prosperity. Having fought the Civil War 'for Spain, Church, and King,' he selected a Borbon, Juan Carlos, as his successor to preserve those values. The restored monarchy immediately killed off the Caudillo's repressive state and introduced a modern democracy which successfully applied to join the EEC but now faces the problems of regional autonomy, which Franco sternly suppressed. **JC.**

FRANKFURTER, FELIX
1882-1965
American lawyer

Frankfurter made his name as adviser to the 1919 Versailles Peace Conference and as founder of the American Civil Liberties Union in 1920. He turned down F D R ROOSEVELT's offer of the Solicitor Generalship but was appointed to the Supreme Court where he put into practice his belief 'that individual freedom in a complex society requires constant redefinition.' **JC.**

FRANKLIN, ARETHA
1942-
American soul singer

Franklin began recording gospel music for her preacher father until spotted by CBS, with whom she had a string of 1960s soul hits such as 'Natural Woman' and 'Respect'. 'Sisters Are Doin' It For Themselves' with the Eurythmics and a No. 1 with George Michael, 'Knew You Were Waiting', and her own 'Who's Zoomin' Who', revived her career in the 1980s. **DC.**

FRANKLIN, ROSALIND
1920-1958
English crystallographer

Franklin's untimely death from cancer prevented her sharing the Nobel Prize for determining the structure of DNA; her X-ray diffraction photographs (passed without her knowledge to Watson and Crick in 1952) showed the molecule to be helical. A Cambridge chemistry graduate (1941), Franklin specialized in the study of the physical structure of matter. From 1942 to 1951 she held posts at the British Coal Utilisation Research Association and the Laboratoire Central des Services Chimiques de l'Etat. Unhappy at King's College, London, Franklin moved to Birkbeck College, London, to study the polio virus. **MB.**

FRASER, DAWN
1937-
Australian swimmer

Dawn Fraser won gold medals in the 100 metres freestyle at three successive Olympic Games, 1956-64. At Rome in 1960 she set three new world records within an hour, and at Tokyo she was the first woman to swim 100 metres in under one minute. Highly popular with the public, her independent attitudes meant that she was not always as popular with officialdom. **DS.**

FREGE, GOTTLOB
1848-1925
German logician and philosopher

Perhaps the greatest influence on the study of logic and language since Aristotle, Frege developed a logic of quantification (albeit in a notation so idiosyncratic as to ensure its obscurity), and devised set-theoretic axioms from which he believed all mathematics could be derived. He revolutionized the theory of meaning by distinguishing between the sense and reference of expressions, giving a functional account of predication. He fell into a depression after Bertrand RUSSELL pointed out a contradiction in the first volume of his *magnum opus* just as the second volume was going to press. **EB.**

FREUD, ANNA
1895-1982
British psychologist

The youngest of Sigmund FREUD's children, Anna Freud developed and spread his theories after his death. In particular she systematized the theoretical understanding of psychological defenses, as spelled out in her most famous book *The Ego and the Mechanisms of Defence*. She was also interested in child development, and in legislation affecting children. After World War II she established a specialist nursery, as well as developing a major school of Freudian child psychoanalysis in London, which now bears her name. **MBe.**

FREUD, LUCIAN
1922-
British painter

Born in Berlin, a grandson of Sigmund Freud he lived in Britain from the early 1930s and was naturalized in 1939. Freud studied at the Central School of Art and Goldsmith's College, painting full-time from 1942. The central theme of his work is the human figure and during the 1940s and early 1950s he used a careful, linear form of realism which achieved acute psychological penetration. In the late 1950s he turned to a broader, more painterly style and his work became relentlessly objective. He is best known for his probingly intimate nudes, whose flesh appears almost palpable. **ER.**

FREUD, SIGMUND
1856-1939
Austrian psychiatrist and psychoanalyst

The undisputed 'father of psychoanalysis', Freud's early interest in neurology and hypnosis led him to believe that some neurological symptoms had psychological significance. He began to study the dreams and parapraxes (slips of the tongue) of his patients, and developed the notion that much thinking takes place outside our conscious awareness, in a part of the mind which he called the unconscious. Freud was

ABOVE: *Spanish dictator General Francisco Franco (left).*

ABOVE: *The psychoanalyst Sigmund Freud.*

also quick to understand that the evolving relationship between doctor and patient, which he called the transference, was an important diagnostic and therapeutic tool, in that the patient would always relate to the analyst in ways which shed light on his other important relationships. Freud encouraged the use of the couch, to enable the patient to free-associate. This has left us with an almost universal image of what a psychiatrist's room must look like. Also associated with Freud are well known terms such as the Oedipus Complex, and the ego, id, and superego. To escape Nazi persecution Freud moved to London in 1938. **MBe**.

FRIEDAN, BETTY
1921-
American feminist

Betty Friedan was a pioneering feminist of the 1960s, who took the view that women should demand different treatment by political campaign. Her book *The Feminine Mystique* (1963) was taken up by the feminist cause around the world, and provoked women to ask whether their lot could be improved. In 1966 she founded the National Organization of Women in the USA, and campaigned vigorously for legal recognition of equal rights. Her thinking shifted in the 1980s when she published *The Second Stage* (1981) and began to advocate partnership between the sexes. The change of emphasis has brought her into dispute with some militant feminists. **EMS**.

FRIEDMAN, MILTON
1912-
American economist

Professor at the University of Chicago from 1946, winner of a Nobel Prize in 1976, Friedman attracted attention in 1962 with his *Capitalism and Freedom*, written with his wife. This regarded government social welfare services as a threat to individualism and proposed a state-guaranteed income instead. Subsequent books examined monetary history, and he was later regarded as the begetter of 'monetarism', a theory which became an ideology applied with great enthusiasm but questionable success by the US and British governments in the 1980s. This, in the view of its more fervid practitioners, held that inflation could be cured by a rigorous control of the money supply. **JW**.

FRINK, DAME ELISABETH
1930-1993
British sculptor

Born in Suffolk, Frink studied at Chelsea School of Art. Her early works were craggy, expressionistic images of predatory birds and warrior figures. During the 1970s her work became smoother, centering on male nudes and horses. In 1977 she was elected a Royal Academician. **ER**.

FRISCH, KARL VON
1886-1982
Austrian zoologist

Frisch's most important work was on the behavior of the honey bee. He determined that the bee can use polarized light as a navigation aid, and can communicate information about foraging areas to workmates by means of dance. He shared the Nobel Prize with Konrad LORENZ and Nikolaas Tinbergen in 1973. **DD**.

FRISCH, MAX
1911-1991
Swiss writer

Influenced by BRECHT and PIRANDELLO, Frisch's central dramatic theme is the search for identity. In his most famous play and political parable, *The Fire Raisers* (1958), a businessman abets the arson of his own home; while his extraordinary novel *Homo Faber* (1957) examines the human cost of technologism. **CW**.

FRISCH, OTTO ROBERT
1904-1979
Austrian-British physicist

To Frisch is attributed the term 'nuclear fission,' this being his principal study. His early work was done in Vienna and Berlin but, being Jewish, he had to make a run for it and subsequently worked in London, Copenhagen, and Birmingham. Along with Sir Rudolph Peierls, he recognized the possibility of producing an immense explosion with a handful of uranium. The advice on the subject that he gave to the British government during World War II spurred the development of the nuclear bomb. Like most nuclear physicists of the time, he ended up working on the Manhattan Project. **DD**.

FROMM, ERICH
1900-1980
American psychologist

Born in Germany, Fromm worked mainly in the United States as a psychologist and psychoanalyst. He saw man's individual aspirations as being in conflict with the dehumanizing aspects of collective life. The appeal of his work was increased by his ability to write well – *The Art of Loving* is perhaps his best-known work. **MBe**.

FROST, DAVID
1939-
British television interviewer/producer

Frost started his television career with the satirical show *That Was The Week That Was* in 1962, going on to become a celebrated interviewer with his own show, *Talking with Frost*, as well as *The Nixon Interviews*. He was the joint founder of London Weekend Television and was involved in the launch of TV-AM. He is currently involved in several television consortia and still has an interview show. **DSl**.

FROST, ROBERT
1874-1963
American poet

Robert Frost was the closest thing to a 'national' poet that America possessed. Born in San Francisco, he returned to his roots in New England farm country. His first volumes – *A Boy's Will* (1913) and *North of Boston* (1914), which contained 'Mending Wall' and 'The Death of a Hired Man' – were published during his sojourn in England, where he was close to the Georgian poets. The New England celebrated with patriotic conservatism in these and following collections is one of everyday rural simplicity, self-reliance, and plain-dealing values which Frost himself popularly came to represent. **CW**.

FRY, C[HARLES] B[URGESS]
1872-1956
British cricketer

To describe C B Fry as a cricketer is in many ways misleading although he is rightly remembered as one of the game's finest players. His batting was said to rely on a comparatively limited range of strokes but he played them superbly well with feats including centuries in six successive matches in the 1901 season when he also scored over 3000 runs. Away from the cricket field he also played soccer for England and held the world record for the long jump for a time. Away from sport he stood several times for parliament, had a notable career as a diplomat at the League of Nations, and was offered and declined the crown of Albania. **DS**.

FUCHS, SIR VIVIAN
1908-
British explorer

Fuchs trained as a geologist, but from his student years went on many expeditions, and it is as a polar explorer that he is best remembered. He worked as a scientist in the Falklands and Antarctica until, in 1957, he led a Commonwealth team to the South Pole and to a famous prearranged meeting with a team led by Sir Edmund HILLARY – who reached the Pole from the opposite side. **RJ**.

GABIN, JEAN
1904-1976
French actor

This versatile actor was a cabaret entertainer before making his film debut in *Chacun sa chance* (1930). Within a few years he was an established star, and his stocky virility and world-weary features kept him there for over 40 years. By the time of his death Gabin was revered in France and admired worldwide. **DC.**

GABLE, CLARK
1901-1960
American actor

Gable's popularity spanned nearly 30 years, and his impudent grin won female hearts everywhere. He was box-office gold; a man who exuded sexual confidence, yet was comfortable trading wisecracks with co-stars like Myrna Loy and Jean HARLOW. Throughout the 1930s and into the 1940s Gable was in a class by himself. After a stint on Broadway and screen tests he first began playing supporting roles, usually gangsters, starting with *The Painted Desert* (1930). He achieved stardom in MGM's *A Free Soul* (1931). A well-publicized affair with Joan CRAWFORD, his co-star in *Possessed* (1932),

seemed to further his career, as did the joyous romping with Jean HARLOW in *Red Dust* (1932). But it took *It Happened One Night* (1934) to win Gable an Academy Award as Best Actor. In 1939 Gable played his most memorable role, as Rhett Butler in *Gone With the Wind* opposite Vivien LEIGH. After the death of his wife, actress Carole Lombard in 1939, he joined the Army Air Corps, and after the war returned to the screen in *Adventure* (1945). Perhaps his best performance was opposite MONROE in *The Misfits* (1961), but his insistence on doing his own stunts provoked a fatal heart attack. **DC.**

GABO, NAUM
1890-1977
Russian sculptor

Originally trained in physical science and engineering, Gabo began making sculptures around 1916. In 1917 he met Tatlin, with whom he developed Constructivism, expounding their theories in the *Realist Manifesto* (1920). Their non-representational constructions were intended as art for a new industrialized age and used novel materials like glass and plastic. In 1920 Gabo produced one of the first kinetic sculptures, wire set in motion by a motor. Gabo disagreed with Tatlin's belief that art should be

utilitarian, but this 'Productionism' was officially favored and in 1922 Gabo left Russia. He worked in Germany, France, and the USA and his more humanist theories were the basis for western Constructivism. **ER.**

GABOR, DENNIS
1900-1979
British physicist

A brilliant theoretical physicist, Hungarian-born Gabor made important contributions to the mathematical analysis of communications. He first achieved fame with his concept for a flat TV tube to 'hang on the wall.' In 1948 he devised a means of producing spatial three-dimensional images, or holograms, from flat surfaces by the interference effects of light waves. It requires light sources which emit light waves moving together, and the development of the laser in 1960 enabled Gabor's ideas to be realized. In 1971 he won the Nobel Prize for Physics for his invention of holography. **PW.**

GABRIEL, PETER
1950-
British pop singer

After leaving Genesis in 1975, Gabriel went on to produce a series of exploratory albums, the third, for example, using African rhythms and producing the angry tribute to murdered anti-apartheid activist Steve BIKO. Further albums continued to address political and environmental issues and to make use of non-Western influences. **DC.**

GADAFFI, MUAMMAR, COLONEL
1942-
Libyan politician

The stormy petrel of modern Arab politics, Gadaffi led the officers' coup which overthrew the monarchy in 1969 and attempted to merge Egypt and Libya. Although enforcing a strict observance of Islam, he has followed an idiosyncratic and violent form of nationalism, intervening in the politics of other Saharan states. He used the money from foreigners' oil concessions to buy massive quantities of Russian arms, and to fund terrorism, including the IRA. Since the Americans bombed his Tripoli base in 1986, Gadaffi has drawn in his political horns somewhat. **JC.**

GAGARIN, YURI
1934-1968
Soviet cosmonaut

The first man in space, Gagarin was rocketed into orbit on 12 April 1961, aboard the *Vostok I* spacecraft. Unable to steer the spacecraft, he orbited the earth once and after 108 minutes his craft parachuted safely down. Gagarin became involved in cosmonaut training, although he made no further flights. **PT.**

ABOVE: *Clark Gable dances with Vivien Leigh in* Gone with the Wind.

ABOVE: Hugh Gaitskell of the Labour Party.

GAITSKELL, HUGH
1906-1963
British politician

Misfortune marred Gaitskell's political career. Although a capable economist, his Treasury stewardship was dominated by a bitter battle with BEVAN over the introduction of National Health Service charges. On becoming Labour Party leader, Gaitskell found this personality clash overtaken by ideological conflict. Having struggled to reconcile and revitalize the party, Gaitskell's premature death proved the final misfortune. **JP**.

GALBRAITH, JOHN K[ENNETH]
1908-
American economist

Canadian born, Galbraith occupied a succession of academic and government posts. His persuasively written books drew public attention to new social problems. Especially influential was his 1958 *The Affluent Society*, which contrasted private opulence with 'public squalor' in its plea for less emphasis on production and more spending on public services. **JW**.

GALLUP, GEORGE
1901-1984
American pollster

Gallup is famous as a pioneer of public opinion polls. After teaching journalism and working in advertizing research, Gallup began taking opinion polls in 1933. In 1936 he conducted his first Presidential poll and predicted that Roosevelt would win. Gallup founded the American Institute of Public Opinion at Princeton and the Audience Research Institute, and his technique has spread worldwide. **DSl**.

GANDHI, INDIRA
1917-1984
Indian politician

Imprisoned by the British during the struggle for independence, Indira Gandhi learnt a great deal from her father NEHRU. After studying at Oxford she joined the All-India Congress Party in 1938, and was elected Congress president in 1959. Prime Minister on the death of her father in 1964, she pursued a policy of non-alignment in foreign affairs, made India self-sufficient agriculturally and an extremely strong industrial power. She responded to the worsening economic problems of the mid-1970s with a draconion clamp down on civil liberties. The unpopularity of her emergency measures lost her the 1977 election but she returned to power in 1979. Her second term of office was dominated by ethnic and religious unrest and she was assassinated by Sikh extremists a few months after the storming of the Sikh holy of holies, the Golden Temple at Amritsar. **JC**.

GANDHI, MAHATMA MOHANDAS
1869-1948
Indian politician

Gandhi opposed the might of the British Raj with the non-violent ethos of the ascetic. A London-trained barrister, he first used passive resistance in organizing Indian laborers against the racism of turn-of-the-century South Africa. But he deployed it on a vast scale in India, particularly in the salt march of 1930. As leader of the Congress

ABOVE: Indian political leader Indira Gandhi.

ABOVE: Mahatma Gandhi, Indian leader.

Party he tried to keep a dialogue with the British alive, suffering periods of imprisonment when it failed. When independence came, in 1947, it was to a divided India, and it was for urging tolerance for the Muslim minority in India that Gandhi was assassinated by a Hindu fanatic. **JC**.

GANDHI, RAJIV
1944-1991
Indian politician

The last of the Nehru 'dynasty,' Rajiv was propelled into politics in 1980 after his brother Sanjay's death in a flying accident. He won in the December 1984 election, following his mother Indira GANDHI's assassination, with a record majority, but further ethnic violence forced his resignation in 1989, and he was killed by a terrorist bomb while campaigning for re-election two years later. **JC**.

ABOVE: Indian leader Rajiv Gandhi.

GARBO, GRETA
1905-1990
Swedish actress

Hollywood has spawned no greater myth than that of Garbo. Beautiful and sensitive, Garbo was the most magnetic actress in the history of the movies. She was not MGM boss Louis B MAYER's idea of a sex symbol, but when her first film for the studio, *The Torrent*, was a huge success, she received top billing. A typical Garbo film had her acting outside the prescribed social code and suffering for it, as exemplified in *Anna Karenina* (1935). Moody and elusive she got more publicity than any other star simply by running away from it. 'I vant to be alone' was the life-long credo that made journalists and fans alike maniacally curious. She made the transition to sound easily, making some of her best films during the talkie era, notably *Ninotchka* (1939), which offered her a rare chance to show her comic talents. In the early 1940s, when some of her box-office appeal had faded and a new wind of puritanism was sweeping Hollywood, she simply retired. But her legend grew stronger, and for more than 40 years after her last movie was released, she remained the most famous star in the world. **DC**.

GARCÍA MÁRQUEZ, GABRIEL
1928-
Colombian novelist

Gabriel García Márquez is one of the foremost novelists of our time. Born in Aracataca, he was educated at a Jesuit college in Bogotà, and became a journalist at the age of 18. He came to Europe in 1954 for the newspaper *El Heraldo*, beginning his career as a novelist during this period with *Leaf Storm* (1955) and *No-one Writes to the Colonel* (1961). The imaginary town of Macondo — decaying, remote, surrounded by swamp — provides the setting and the subject for much of the work culminating in his most famous and immensely successful novel *One Hundred Years of Solitude* (1967). A classic work of magic realism, blending the fantastic and the concrete, the supernatural and the everyday, this is a richly allusive novel, drawing on sources from Biblical myth to other Latin American writers, at once grimly ironic and comic. In 1975 García Márquez published *The Autumn of the Patriarch*, a more cerebral yet comic exploration of myths of dicatorship. He has also published collections of short stories. He was awarded the Nobel Prize for Literature in 1982. **CW**.

GARDEL, CARLOS
1890-1935
French-born Argentinian singer

The first vocalist to adapt the melancholy rhythm of the tango to lyrics, Gardel achieved super stardom, selling 70,000 albums in the first three months of a Paris tour. When he died in an air crash, his funeral attracted the largest crowds in Argentinian history. **JH**.

GARLAND, JUDY [FRANCES GUMM]
1922-1969
American actress and singer

When her vaudeville act with two older sisters broke up, Garland, guided by her ambitious mother, continued to sing on her own, and made her way to Hollywood and an MGM contract by the tender age of 13. It was as Dorothy in *The Wizard of Oz* (1939) that she really shone, and she went on to star with Mickey ROONEY in a string of movies showing the rosy side of teenage life. During the 1940s she made some of MGM's greatest musicals, such as *For Me and My Gal* (1942) and *Easter Parade* (1948). But by the end of the 1940s she had acquired a reputation for unreliability due to her alleged

ABOVE: The ethereal look of Swedish movie star Greta Garbo.

dependence on pills, first prescribed by MGM moguls to keep her weight down and combat fatigue, and she abandoned or was fired from several pictures. The smash hit *A Star is Born* with James MASON, her finest dramatic performance, signaled a comeback in 1954. But though Garland continued to make fine films and give great concerts, her private troubles proved overwhelming. In 1960 she was nominated for an Oscar for her role in *Judgment at Nuremberg*, but just as she seemed on her way back she died of an overdose of sleeping pills, leaving a million dollars in debts. **DC**.

GASPERI, ALCIDE DE
1881-1954
Italian statesman

De Gasperi emerged in 1944 from Vatican City, where he had spent many of the Fascist years in self-imposed exile, to mold Italy's postwar democracy. He became an MP for Trento in 1921. De Gasperi firmly opposed MUSSOLINI and was involved in resistance to the Germans. As Foreign Secretary he won Italy fresh respect in Europe. He was Prime Minister 1945-53. **JC**.

GATES, BILL
1955-
American software designer

The son of a Seattle attorney, Bill Gates dropped out of Harvard in 1975 in order to co-found Microsoft with his schoolfriend Paul Allen. The company furthered his ambition of 'a computer on every desktop, running Microsoft software' by developing the languages needed to operate the early microcomputers. Collaboration with IBM led to the Microsoft Disk Operating System (MS-DOS) which dominated the market for personal computers. Following the lead of Xerox and Apple Microsoft, Gates launched the Windows operating system, which became a major influence on the computer market in its third version, launched in 1990. The new discipline made IBM-compatible computers easier to use, and in-

ABOVE: Bill Gates, co-founder of Microsoft.

creased the need for more powerful computers with more complicated software. Microsoft's own programming teams were well placed to exploit Windows, and allowed Microsoft to expand from being an operating systems and languages vendor to a supplier of major mainstream applications such as wordprocessors and spreadsheets. Despite the rapid growth of the company, Gates maintains close hands-on control of the day-to-day running of Microsoft; staff are expected to work long hours and generally do so gladly. **SR**.

GAUDI (I CORNET), ANTONI
1852-1926
Spanish architect and furniture designer

Trained under a Gothic Revival architect in Barcelona, Gaudi was much influenced by Viollet-le-Duc's advice to seek inspiration for structure and ornament in nature. Early work, like Casa Vicens (1878), is neo-Gothic in character, but later work (Palau Güell, 1885-90; Casa Batlló, 1904-05; Casa Milá, 1905-10) became increasingly organic with undulating façades, roofs, and columns recalling bones and musculature. His furniture is similarly asymmetric. Gaudi's later years were dominated by the Church of the Sagrada Familia (1883-1926; unfinished) whose openwork towers, decoration including religious inscriptions, and vaulted structure recall both neo-Gothic and natural forms. The building was Gaudi's personal statement of his passionate Christianity and Catalan nationalism. **AR**.

de GAULLE, CHARLES, GENERAL
1890-1970
French soldier-politician; President of France

A career soldier, de Gaulle served in World War I and later acquired a reputation as a military writer and theorist, advocating the need for mechanization. He commanded the 4th Armored Division in 1940 and was briefly Under-Secretary for War. Refusing to accept Pétain's capitulation to the Germans in June 1940, he escaped to England and declared himself leader of the Free French movement. In August 1944 he entered Paris in triumph and was President of the provisional government until 1946, when he resigned over the constitution of the new 4th Republic. He retired from public life, only to reappear during the Algerian crisis of 1958. De Gaulle was granted sweeping powers by the National Assembly and the constitution altered to provide for a presidential system. President of the 5th Republic until 1969, de Gaulle possessed an old-fashioned vision of France as one of the world's great powers. He followed a nationalist policy in Europe, granted independence to Algeria and presided over French economic recovery. The upheavals of 1968 and the loss of a referendum forced him out of office in 1969. **JPi**.

ABOVE: Judy Garland poses for a publicity shot with Mickey Rooney.

GAVASKAR, SUNIL
1949-
Indian cricketer

Sunil Gavaskar made more runs and more hundreds in test cricket than any other batsman in the history of the game. Although a very small man, he had impeccable technique and great concentration. Perhaps his best performance was his innings of 221 against England in 1979 which gained a draw for his team from a poor position and nearly paved the way to a sensational victory. **DS**.

GEHRIG, LOU [HENRY LOUIS]
1903-1941
American baseball player

The great New York Yankee teams of the mid-1920s to mid-1930s featured two contrasting heroes. One was the flamboyant Babe RUTH, known for his epic home runs and robust appetite for life. The other was strong, silent Lou Gehrig, a Columbia University-educated first baseman whose entry into the record books was both dignified and unassuming. Known as 'the Iron Horse,' Gehrig played a record 2130 consecutive games. He had a career batting average of .340, while slamming 493 home runs, including a record 23 grand slams. He died of amyotrophic lateral sclerosis, a rare nerve disorder that is now known as Lou Gehrig Disease. **MD**.

GEIGER, HANS WILHELM
1882-1945
German physicist

After studying electrical discharges for his PhD at Erlangen, he moved to Manchester in 1907 to work under Ernest RUTHERFORD. Between them, they developed the Geiger-counter – a device that measured radiation by detecting the momentary current created when the gas between charged electrodes is ionized by a radiated particle. **DD**.

GELDOF, BOB
1954-
Irish pop singer

Geldof's band The Boomtown Rats, one of the most vital groups to come out of the punk scene, attracted a huge and loyal following in Dublin before moving to London in 1976 to play the growing punk circuit. A debut album in 1977 launched them to chart success, and singles from the second album, including 'Like Clockwork' and 'Rat Trap', established them as mainstream. By 1980, however, their popularity was waning. Until the 1984-85 Live Aid project brought him to international prominence, Geldof's only real exposure came from the lead role in Pink Floyd's harrowing film *The Wall*, but two solo albums since have earned him praise from the critics. **DC**.

GELL-MANN, MURRAY
1929-
American theoretical physicist

His study was elementary particles, working for a time with Enrico FERMI, and becoming Professor of theoretical physics at the California Institute of Technology in 1956. With G Zweig, he introduced the concept of quarks – the fundamental constituents of all matter. He was awarded the Nobel Prize for Physics in 1969. **DD**.

GEMZELL, KARL
1910-
Swedish endocrinologist

Gemzell has made three major contributions to human well-being. A common cause of infertility is the deficiency of follicle-stimulating hormone (FSH), which stimulates

RIGHT:
*Bob Geldof
on stage at
Live Aid.*

the ovaries to mature the follicles that release eggs. He extracted this hormone from the pituitary glands of cadavers, and injected it into volunteer infertile women, two of whom conceived and later gave birth to twins. From this was developed the infertility drug clomiphene; though less potent than FSH, it is easier to manufacture and administer. Gemzell also showed that the pituitary produced a growth hormone, which he extracted and used to treat children with serious growth deficiencies. He also developed an immunological test for pregnancy that gave rapid results and superseded existing practices. **CR**.

GERSHWIN, GEORGE [JACOB GERSSHOVITZ]
1898-1937
American composer

Trained as a pianist, Brooklyn-born George Gershwin pulled himself out of his impoverished childhood by working as a song-plugger for a music publisher. With his brother Ira as librettist, he produced some great musicals (like *Lady Be Good*) and immortal songs like 'Fascinating Rhythm,' 'Stairway to Paradise,' 'A Foggy Day' and 'I Got Rhythm.' With *An American in Paris* and *Rhapsody in Blue* Gershwin successfully fused memorable melodies and intricate jazz harmonies with orchestral technique; but his masterpiece was the negro folk opera *Porgy and Bess*, which today retains its rightful place in the operatic repertoire. **DK**.

GETTY, JEAN PAUL
1892-1976
American industrialist

The son of a wealthy oil speculator, Getty entered the business in Oklahoma in 1914. In 1930 he inherited his father's company and during the Depression used his excellent cash position to buy up oil shares at low prices. In 1949 he obtained a 60-year oil concession in Saudi Arabia which vaulted him into the billionaire class. Divorced and

ABOVE: *George Gershwin (at piano) and movie folk.*

married five times, Getty owned a relatively modest art museum in Malibu. On his death he bequeathed his legendary wealth to the museum. With enormous buying power, the Getty Museum and associated research institutes played a controversial part in the international art market during the 1980s. In 1992 it was rehoused in a purpose-built building by Richard Meier. **PT**.

GIACOMMETTI, ALBERTO
1901-1966
Swiss sculptor and painter

Giacommetti studied painting and sculpture in Geneva, Italy, and Paris, experimenting with various styles, including Cubism. In 1930 he joined the Surrealists, producing witty constructions such as *The Palace at 4am* (1933), but in 1935 abruptly reverted to figurative work. He began exploring the phenomenon of perception, particularly how things appear when seen at a distance, and by around 1947 had developed the mature style for which he is best known. Working in plaster of Paris on a wire foundation, he created emaciated, skeletal figures which seem to embody the sense of alienation in modern society and aroused interest in Existentialist writers such as SARTRE, for whom they encapsulated modern man's sense of angst. **ER**.

GIAP, VO NGUYEN
1912-
Vietnamese revolutionary soldier

A schoolteacher by profession, Giap was active in the Communist underground in the 1930s, opposing French rule of Vietnam. Recruited by HO CHI MINH in the early 1940s to reorganize the Viet Minh, Giap created and led a highly effective revolutionary army which defeated the French at Dien Bien Phu in 1954. In independent North Vietnam, Giap was Minister of Defense and commander of the North Vietnamese Army; as such he masterminded attacks on American-backed South Vietnam. After failures in the 1968 Tet Offensive and the 1972 Easter Offensive, he was retired as Minister of Defense. **JPi**.

GIDDENS, ANTHONY
1938-
British sociologist

After his early work on class structure, Giddens became known for his prolific output on the history of classical social theory, accounts of the main institutions of industrialized countries, and on social theory and sociological methodology. Giddens is particularly notable for synthesizing a wide range of social theory into a general account of society which he calls 'structuration theory.' This is largely an account of the relation between human agency and social structures which emphasizes their mutual interaction rather than arguing that one or other is more causally important. Giddens' most recent work applies structuration theory to issues of modernity and the role of space and time in social organization. **DSI**.

GIDE, ANDRÉ
1869-1951
French novelist

Gide's first work, *Les Cahiers d'André Walter*, was published anonymously in 1891. In the 1890s he visited North Africa, shortly afterwards becoming aware of his own homosexuality; both these factors were to have a profound influence on his work. In *Les Nourritures Terrestres* (1897) Gide urged individual freedom rather than self-governance by the hypocrisy of moral restraint. In 1908 Gide and other writers founded the literary journal *La Nouvelle Revue Française*. Gide's prewar *récits* include *L'Immoraliste* (1902), *La Porte Étroite* (1909) and *Isabelle* (1911). After World War I Gide became increasingly introspective and concerned with the hypocrisy of religion, a preoccupation reflected in *La Symphonie Pastorale* (1919). Later works dealt with other concerns: homosexuality (*Corydon* (1924)), intergenerational conflict (*Les Faux-Monnayeurs* (1926)), and exploitative colonialism (*Voyage au Congo* (1927) and *Retour du Chad* (1928)). *Si le Grain ne meurt* (1926) is an autobiographical work. Gide was awarded the Nobel Prize for Literature in 1947. **CH-M**.

GIELGUD, SIR JOHN
1904-
British actor

Noted for his clear diction and distinctive voice, Gielgud is known primarily for his illustrious stage career which began in 1921. One of the great Shakespearean actors of the century, he has played all the major roles, some on screen as well as stage. His film work has embraced a variety of parts, from his hilarious Oscar-winning performance as the valet in *Arthur (1980)*, through cameos in *Chariots of Fire* (1981), *Gandhi* (1982) to the most recent *Prospero's Books* (1991). **DC**.

GIGLI, BENIAMINO
1890-1957
Italian opera singer

Gigli's beautiful tenor and secure technique led him to be regarded as CARUSO's successor when he made his debut at the Met in 1922. His roles there concentrated on the lyric repertoire and included Rodolfo in *La Bohème*, Des Grieux in both Massenet's and Puccini's *Manon*, and the Duke of Mantua in Verdi's *Rigoletto*. He left the US in 1935 in protest at Depression-induced salary cuts but returned in 1939 to sing Radames in *Aida*, a new and heavier role for him. His acting ability did not match his voice, and his stage style was robustly sentimental rather than subtle. **JH**.

GILL, ERIC
1882-1940
British sculptor and typographer

At the age of 22 Gill became a professional stone-cutter, and established a reputation for the elegant and original lettering of his inscriptions. Later in his career he designed a series of typefaces, some of which (such as Gill Sans-Serif) are among the most popular typefaces in use today. Gill's sculptural work was much affected by his passionate, if idiosyncratic, religious beliefs: the Stations of the Cross in Westminster Cathedral are among his most famous works. **RJ**.

GILLESPIE, DIZZY
1917-1993
American jazz trumpeter and composer

One of the great figures of be-bop, Gillespie's late 1940s big band played complex, convoluted orchestrations which marked a new beginning for jazz and a departure from its danceable good-time origins. He was already displaying characteristics of the be-bop style with Cab Calloway's band in the late 1930s. The blistering pace of his playing mellowed in the 1950s, and as be-bop began to lose popularity he took to working with a quartet, introducing influential Latin American rhythms. **DC**.

GINSBERG, ALLEN
1926-
American poet

Howl and Other Poems (1956), his first collection, established his status as a major poet. With Jack KEROUAC and William BURROUGHS he was one of the leading lights of the American Beats. His San Francisco publisher was tried for issuing Ginsberg's allegedly obscene work, and acquitted. There was some shock value at the time from his use of obscenities, which has now abated, and his poetry has become increasingly rambling and inchoate, without the power of the raw anger in his earlier works, such as 'Howl'. *Allen Verbatim*, his collected lectures published in 1974, won the National Book Award. **AM**.

GISCARD D'ESTAING, VALÉRY
1926-
French politician

Impeccable credentials, including war-time service with the Free French and graduation from the Ecole Nationale Administration, ensured Giscard's rapid rise under De Gaulle; he became France's youngest Minister of Finance at age 36. Under his presidency, from 1974 to 1981, France built Europe's second strongest economy. Giscard worked for closer British integration in Europe and cooperation with Germany. His defeat by MITTERAND in 1981 was due partly to intervention by his ex-Prime Minister Jacques Chirac. **JC**.

GISH, LILLIAN
1896-1993
American actress

Gish was a superb actress able to convey power and strength on screen despite her fragile appearance. An intelligent actress, she initially played either good girls who were rewarded, as in *Orphans of the Storm* (1922), or bad girls who repented, as in *Way Down East* (1920). Working with director D W GRIFFITH she became the queen of the silent screen. Sound was no problem for her excellent stage-trained voice, but changing fashions caught up with her, and she left Hollywood to return to the theater, appearing occasionally in character parts from the 1940s. **DC.**

GIUGIARO, GIORGIO
1938-
Italian designer

Giugiaro's work ranges from car design (Alfa Romeo Giulia GT; Volkswagen Golf, 1974) to the design for Vriello pasta (1983). All Giugiaro's product designs, including those for Necchi sewing machines, watches for Seiko, and cameras for Nikon share a standard 'technical' aesthetic; even the pasta is an exercise in industrial design. **DE.**

GIVENCHY, HUBERT
1927-
French designer

Born near Beauvais, Givenchy studied at the Ecole des Beaux-Arts in Paris, then also briefly studied law before beginning his fashion career with a number of Paris designers, notably Jacques Fath (from 1945-46) and Elsa SCHIAPARELLI (from 1949-52). In 1952 he opened his own fashion house. Many of the garments in his first collection were made of shirting, including the 'Bettina Blouse'. Named after Bettina Graziana, one of Paris's top models, the blouse featured a wide open neck and full ruffled broderie anglaise sleeves. During the 1950s Givenchy transformed the 'chemise' or 'sack' shape into an exaggerated kite outline that was wide at the top and tapered towards the hem. A favorite designer for prominent women and film stars, Givenchy designed for Jacqueline Kennedy Onassis and Audrey Hepburn, who wore Givenchy's outfits designed for the film *Breakfast at Tiffany's*. **MC.**

GLACKENS, WILLIAM
1870-1938
American painter

Trained at the Pennsylvania Academy of Fine Arts, Glackens worked as a newspaper illustrator throughout his career and began painting in 1894. He was associated with the Ashcan School of urban realists but his work, stylistically derived from the Impressionists, particularly Renoir, avoided serious issues, concentrating on picturesque middle-class scenes. **ER.**

GLENN, JOHN
1921-
American astronaut

Glenn became the first American in orbit when on 20 February 1962 he made three revolutions of the earth. His flight was significant in that Glenn used his hand controls to demonstrate that man could pilot a spacecraft in orbit. He returned to earth and was hailed a national hero. He never returned to space but instead entered the US Senate. **PT.**

GOBBI, TITO
1913-1984
Italian opera singer

Gobbi only began to exploit his natural but not outstanding baritone after studying law. First prize at an international contest in Vienna led to debuts in Rome (1939) and La Scala, Milan, as Belcore in Donizetti's *L'Elisir d'Amore* in 1942. He sang regularly with the Chicago Lyric Opera between 1954 and 1973, making his directorial debut there in 1965, staging Verdi's *Simon Boccanegra* with himself in the title role. He also regularly sang Scarpia in *Tosca* at the Met, frequently opposite Maria CALLAS. Gobbi's acting ability and penetrating musicianship made him one of the finest singing actors of his day. **JH.**

GODARD, JEAN-LUC
1930-
French film director

The most controversial director of the French 'New Wave', Godard was originally a combative film critic. By the mid-1960s he had become the most fashionable director on the art-house circuit because of his radical ideas and innovative techniques in films such as *Breathless* (1959) and *Une femme mariée* (1964). His work became increasingly political and obscure after his apocalyptic black comedy *Weekend* (1967), but he is still regarded as an influential avant-garde director. **NS.**

GÖDEL, KURT
1906-1978
American mathematician

While holding posts simultaneously at both Vienna and Princeton, Gödel shook the foundations of mathematics by proving (using recursive function theory, which he devised for this purpose) that any theory complex enough to model ordinary arithmetic cannot be both consistent and complete. it follows that RUSSELL's project of deriving all of mathematics from pure logic must be unattainable, as is HILBERT's program of proving the consistency of all mathematics. **EB.**

GOEBBELS, JOSEF
1897-1945
German propagandist

Evil genius of the art of modern state propaganda, Goebbels won HITLER's trust by capturing the leftist lager of Berlin for the Nazis by street violence. He edited the newspaper *Der Angriff* ('The Attack') and moved from managing Hitler's election campaigns to the Ministry for Propaganda and Public Enlightenment. From there he controlled the whole cultural life of the Third Reich, as well as its public relations during World War II. Goebbels was primarily responsible for the wholesale emigration of major figures in the German arts. He committed suicide with his family in the Berlin bunker. **JC.**

ABOVE: *Nazi Propaganda Minister Josef Goebbels.*

GOEPPERT-MAYER, MARIA
1906-1972
Polish-American physicist

In 1930 Maria Goeppert obtained her doctorate from Göttingen and married the chemist Joseph Mayer. They later emigrated to the USA where she became a university professor. At Johns Hopkins and Columbia she worked on the separation of uranium isotopes, and in 1945 she moved to the new Institute for Nuclear Studies at Chicago University. Here, under Enrico FERMI, she deepened her interest in nuclear physics. By 1948 she proposed the hypothesis that some atomic nucleae were more stable than others depending on the shell-arrangement of protons and neutrons within them. For this discovery she shared the Nobel Prize in 1963. Goeppert-Mayer was the first woman to win the Physics Prize since Marie Curie. **MB**.

GOERING, HERMANN
1893-1946
German politician

Number two in the Nazi leadership, Goering's flamboyant self-assurance won him the confidence of foreign leaders and diplomats but could not avert war; his record as a fighter ace did not prevent him from wrecking the Luftwaffe. Responsible for the first concentration camps and the initial organization of slave labor, Goering was also overseer of the Four-Year Plan, under which Germany prepared for war. He cheated the gallows at Nuremberg by swallowing a cyanide pill. **JC**.

GOFFMAN, ERVING
1922-1982
Canadian sociologist

Goffman is famous for analyzing the face-to-face interactions of people. Using the 'dramaturgical model,' Goffman focused on the way in which people construct roles, situations, and identities by putting on performances for themselves and others. In one of his best known books, *Asylums*, he showed how people managed their identities in total situations such as prisons and mental institutions. **DSl**.

GOLDING, WILLIAM
1911-
British novelist

Golding's first published work was poetry, but it was his first novel *Lord of the Flies* (1954), that brought him instant success. Among his other works the best known are *Pincher Martin* (1956), *The Spire* (1964), and *Rites of Passage*, winner of the 1980 Booker Prize. Most of his novels deal with profound moral questions, often focused on the fragility of 'civilized' values in extreme situations, and the rapidity of their breakdown into the primeval cruelty he detected beneath. He

ABOVE: Hermann Goering (with baton), chief of Hitler's Luftwaffe.

was awarded the Nobel Prize for Literature in 1983. *The Paper Men* (1984) tells of a famous author plagued by an American academic in search of material, Golding's revenge for his own hounding. **AM**.

GOLDMARK, PETER
1906-1977
American inventor

Between 1944 and 1948, Goldmark utilized recent advances in plastics technology to create an unbreakable long-playing record. The 'LP' had three times as many grooves per side as the old 78 records and, when combined with a running speed of 33⅓ rpm, gave a side length of 20 minutes. A huge success, his product lasted unchallenged for 35 years until the advent of cassettes and compact disks. **PT**.

GOLDWATER, BARRY
1909-
American politician

A charismatic right-winger from the Sunbelt who was the Republican contender against JOHNSON in the 1964 election, despite a high-profile, almost messianic, campaign Goldwater was heavily defeated. An outspoken conservative spokesman for over 40 years, he wrote the best-selling *The Conscience of a Conservative? Why not victory?* **JC**.

ABOVE: Nobel Prize-winning author William Golding.

GOLDWYN, SAMUEL
1882-1974
American film producer

Born Samuel Goldfish in Warsaw, Goldwyn emigrated to America at the age of 13. He became an independent producer in 1923 and formed a particularly productive relationship with director William WYLER, who made such quality films as *Dead End* (1937), *The Little Foxes* (1941), and *The Best Years of our Lives* (1946) for Goldwyn. Famous for his 'Goldwynisms', sayings such as 'Include me out', 'A verbal contract isn't worth the paper it's written on', he was also a great philanthropist. **NS**.

GOLITSYN, ANATOLY
1926-
Soviet spy

In December 1961 Anatoly Golitsyn, claiming to be a major in the KGB, knocked on the door of the American embassy in Helsinki and offered his encyclopaedic knowledge of Russian intelligence to the CIA. Golitsyn was arguably the most extraordinary piece of good fortune ever visited upon Western intelligence, and his information led to the uncovering of a number of important spies. However, the CIA remained suspicious that he was a double agent and his reports were never fully trusted. **RJ**.

GOLLANCZ, SIR VICTOR
1893-1967
British publisher

Gollancz rebelled against his eminent family until, in 1928, he founded his own publishing company. A man of enormous energy, he campaigned for political causes and in 1936 set up the Left Book Club. During World War II he worked to get Jewish refugees out of Europe. After the war he launched campaigns against capital punishment and for nuclear disarmament. **DSl**.

GOMUŁKA, WŁADYSLAW
1905-1982
Polish politician

A founder of the Polish Workers' Party, Gomułka led it out of Stalinism after he had served prison terms for insisting on Polish autonomy. A reformist breeze carried him to power in 1956 and he effectively scrapped collectivization and restored a measure of free speech. Failure to solve the underlying economic malaise led to his fall in 1970. **JC**.

GOODALL, JANE
1934-
British zoologist

Goodall began her research on primates in Africa in 1960 and gradually gained the trust of chimpanzee troupes. Her work showed that chimpanzees were partially car-nivorous, used tools, and indulged in inter-tribal rivalry – behavior traits never before suspected. Her books include *In the Shadow of Man* (1971). **DD**.

GOODMAN, BENNY
1909-1986
American clarinettist and jazz bandleader

Although it was as a bandleader that 'King of Swing' Goodman is best known, his best work can be heard on the small ensemble recordings he made from 1935. As big band became less popular in the 1950s he spent more time recording classical music, although he briefly reassembled a band in 1956 after the film *The Benny Goodman Story*. **DC**.

GORBACHEV, MIKHAIL SERGEYEVICH
1931-
Russian statesman

The youngest Soviet leader since STALIN succeeded LENIN, Gorbachev was a remarkable and forceful leader who changed the course of Russian history. General

BELOW: Deposed Russian President Mikhail Gorbachev.

Secretary of the Communist Party from 1985, he embarked on a radical program of reform based on two premises: *perestroika* (restructuring) and *glasnost* (openness). The Soviet people achieved greater freedom of expression than they had enjoyed for over 50 years, but *perestroika* introduced dramatic socio-economic changes which only gradually revealed their benefits. Gorbachev was well-received abroad and in foreign policy agreed major arms limitation treaties in 1987 and 1990, effectively ending the Cold War. His acquiescence to the dismantling of Communist regimes in eastern Europe in 1989 culminated in the reunification of Germany in 1990, but at the same time he refused to countenance the break up of the Soviet Union into its constituent republics. Facing growing criticism at home, he strengthened his personal powers as President in 1990 and in 1991 was overthrown in a hardline coup. He survived thanks to YELTSIN's resistance and to remain in power was forced to promise more rapid reforms and to disassociate himself from the now discredited Communist party. Gorbachev resigned all his offices in December 1991, announcing the official dissolution of the Soviet Union into independent republics. **JM**.

GORER, Peter Alfred
1907-1961
British biologist

A student of genetics under J B S Haldane, Gorer discovered the histocompatibility antigens through his study of the surface of mouse red blood cells and established the control of their expression at the genetic level. This was an outstanding result little appreciated in his lifetime but now used for the matching of human tissues, a vital factor in the success of transplantation surgery. **ES**.

GORKY, Maxim
1868-1936
Russian writer

Gorky is known as the inventor of socialist realism and unofficial laureate of post-revolutionary Russia. His early fiction exhibits a masterful use of reportage and the vernacular, while *The Mother* (1907), much favored by Lenin, is sentimental and didactic. The trilogy *Autobiography* (1913-23) represents the best of his later work. **CW**.

GRADE, Lew [Louis], Baron
1906-
British media chief

Born in Odessa, Grade came from a Jewish family that was to dominate British show-business for over 40 years. He started his career as a dancer before becoming a theatrical agent, alongside his brother, Bernard Delfont. With youngest brother, Leslie Grade, he put on shows and they became impresarios. In 1962 Lew became Managing Director of the commercial television company ATV; he also led several large film, entertainment, and communications companies. **DSl**.

GRAF, Steffi
1969-
German tennis player

Steffi Graf is one of the finest tennis stars of the modern period. She first made her mark in the major championships in 1987 and remarkably won the Grand Slam of singles titles in both 1988 and 1989, also adding an Olympic gold medal to her tally in the former year. Less dominant thereafter, she still won the Australian championship in 1990 and Wimbledon in 1991 and continues to compete successfully at top level. **DS**.

GRAHAM, Billy [William Franklin]
1918-
American evangelist

Billy Graham can claim to have personally preached the Christian gospel in more countries and to more people than anyone else in history. Ordained as a minister of the Southern Baptist Church in Carolina in 1940, he began his evangelical crusade in

ABOVE: *The grace of dancer Martha Graham.*

1949 in Los Angeles. An eloquent preacher, he has traveled widely offering a personal invitation to be 'born again'. Unlike so many religious leaders who have achieved a cult following, Graham has retained an integrity devoid of scandal as a great and good man. **ML**.

GRAHAM, Katharine
1917-
American newspaper proprietor

Katharine Graham is a newspaper woman through and through. She began as a reporter with the *San Francisco News*, moved to *The Washington Post* in 1938, and has stayed with the paper for most of her life. In 1969 she became President of the Washington Post Company and backed up her journalists BERNSTEIN and WOODWARD when they investigated the Watergate scandal. **DSl**.

GRAHAM, Martha
1894-1991
American dancer, teacher, choreographer and director

One of the founders of modern dance, Graham's American pioneer ancestry and west-coast childhood had a profound influence on her creative work. She studied and danced with Denishawn (Ted Shawn and Ruth St Denis) from 1916-23 and made her solo debut in 1926, after which she moved away from the St Denis style and began to develop her own ideas and classroom technique based on centering the movement impulse in the solar plexus. Graham's pivotal work of the early years was *Primitive Mysteries*, but the 1935 *Frontier* looked more like the Graham style to come. Replacing the totemic figures of earlier works, the dancer was now the archetypal 'American woman', and as such expressed the lives of women in all their forms. Her most memorable depiction was the Bride in *Appalachian Spring* (1946), but she later began to draw on Greek mythology and female protagonists for her themes: Medea (*Caves of the Heart*, 1946), Jocasta (*Night Journey*, 1947), and Clytemnestra (1958). Following two years of illness, Graham finally gave up dancing in 1973, and retired to head her school and company. Although nearly blind, she continued to teach and supervise reconstructions of her repertory. The long list of eminent dancers and choreographers to have emerged from her school includes Merce CUNNINGHAM, Paul Taylor, and Robert Cohan. **MC**.

LEFT: *Tennis star Steffi Graf.*

GRANGE, RED [HAROLD EDWARD]
1903-1991
American football player

'The Galloping Ghost,' Red Grange was football's greatest draw in the 1920s. He gained fame at the University of Illinois, where he was a three-time All-American halfback and led his team to startling upsets against some of the best teams in the country. In 1925 he joined the fledgling National Football League, lending credibility to a pro game that had not yet caught on with the public. Though slowed by injuries, he continued to be a big draw until his retirement from the Chicago Bears in 1935. He was a member of the first class of inductees into the Pro Football Hall of Fame in 1963. **MD**.

GRANGE, KENNETH
1929-
British designer

Grange's product designs are an integral part of British public life, from the Venner parking meter to British Rail's 125 train. Since the 1960s his work has reflected the influence of contemporary German rationalism in product design, most marked perhaps in his kitchen mixers for Kenwood and the design of the Kodak 'Instamatic' camera. **DE**.

GRANT, CARY
1904-1986
British-born American actor

Grant was one of the most famous screen personalities in the world, playing a succession of light romantic comic leads. He enjoyed modest success on Broadway before Hollywood beckoned, and got off to a good start opposite Mae WEST in She Done Him Wrong (1933). Soon he rivaled Gary COOPER in popularity, but it wasn't until the late 1930s that his gifts for screwball comedy flowered on screen, beginning with The Awful Truth (1937). By the late 1940s Grant was the established master of roles requiring a sophisticated man-about-town. When other leading men of his generation were turning to aging character roles, Grant was still handsome and in top form in films such as Charade (1963) at the age of 59. What set him apart from other actors was his air of never taking himself too seriously. Witty and urbane off screen as well as on, he once remarked 'I play myself to perfection.' **DC**.

GRAPPELLI, STEPHANE
1908-
French jazz and popular violinist

Best remembered for his swing recordings with the Quintette du Hot Club de France in the late 1930s, Grappelli's performances are marked by virtuosity coupled with an ability to stay just the right side of sentimentality. Frequent TV appearances have made him something of an institution, although he is still in demand by recording artists young enough to be his grandchildren. **DC**.

GRASS, GÜNTER
1927-
German novelist

Of partly Polish descent, Grass was born and educated in Danzig. The most internationally successful of all postwar German writers, Grass studied art, wrote rhymes, and experimental plays, but is most famous for his long experimental novels. His fondness for the grotesque, and the linguistic vitality of his work has led to them being labeled 'Rabelaisian'. Clever and amusing, they are also highly political. One of the world's greatest writers, Die Blechtrommel (The Tin Drum, 1959) is his most famous novel, and others include Hundejahre (Dog Years, 1963), Der Butt (The Flounder, 1977), and The Rat (1987). **AM**.

GRAVES, MICHAEL
1934-
American architect, theorist, and designer

Graves, a prominent exponent of Post Modernism in architecture and design, has taught architecture at Princeton since 1962 and worked as a designer for Alessi and Memphis. His projected additions to the Whitney Musuem, New York, caused considerable controversy as did the Public Services Building in Portland, Oregon, with its vivid colors and classical allusions (completed 1982). **DE**.

ABOVE: English novelist Graham Greene.

GREENE, [HENRY] GRAHAM
1904-1991
British novelist

Greene's conversion to Roman Catholicism in 1926 had a profound influence on the theme of his writings which he described dismissively as either novels or entertainments. His concern for spiritual issues, his exceptional talents as a storyteller, and the exotic settings of his works were a powerful combination. The superb Brighton Rock (1938) is noteworthy as the first embodiment of his central thematic concept, 'the appalling strangeness of the mercy of God.' The Power and the Glory (1940), The Heart of the Matter (1948), The Third Man (1950, originally written as a screenplay), The Quiet American (1955), and The Honorary Consul (1973) are his most famous novels, many of which have been filmed. **AM**.

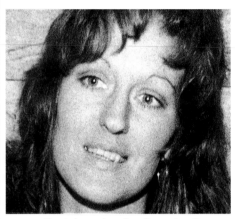

ABOVE: Feminist and author Germaine Greer.

GREER, GERMAINE
1939-
Australian feminist and writer

Greer attended university in Melbourne and Sydney before going to Cambridge in the 1960s. She was appointed English Lecturer at Warwick University (1968-1973) and it was during this time that she wrote The Female Eunuch (1970). An exposé of women's frustration and subservience in a male-dominated society, it was an international success. Greer wrote many feminist articles, gave talks and appeared on TV to put forward her case. However in her 1981 book, Sex and Destiny, Greer shows a change in attitude to the sexual revolution, emphasizing that men need a fair deal, too. While she is still a leading proponent of the feminist cause she is not always supported by militant feminists. **EMS**.

GRETZKY, WAYNE
1961-
Canadian hockey player

Wayne Gretzky dominated hockey in the 1980s as much as any North American athlete has ever dominated a decade of team sports. From 1980 through 1987 he won the Hart Memorial Trophy as the NHL's Most Valuable Player every year. During that time he set league records for most goals (92) and points (215) in a season, leading the Edmonton Oilers to four Stanley Cup titles. Traded to the Los Angeles Kings, he won the Hart Trophy for a record ninth time in 1989. Gretzky is hockey's all-time leading point scorer, and he may eclipse Gordie HOWE's record for most goals in a career. His nickname, 'The Great One,' is well deserved. **MD**.

GRIFFITH, ARTHUR
1871-1922
Irish nationalist

A journalist with a strong belief in the right of Irishmen to rule themselves rather than submit to the British, Griffith founded a political movement known as *Sinn Féin* ('Ourselves Alone') in 1905, disseminating his ideals through a newspaper of the same name. Imprisoned on a number of occasions, he helped to organize the campaign against the British in 1919, being part of the delegation which negotiated the Free State Treaty in 1921. When this produced a split with Republicans intent on full Irish independence, Griffith headed a provisional Free State government during the last few months of his life. **JP**.

GRIFFITH, D[AVID] W[ARK]
1875-1948
American film director

A pioneer of the silent film era and one of the most important figures in American film, Griffith made the most celebrated and controversial of all silent movies, *The Birth of a Nation* (1915), and followed it with *Intolerance* (1916), a film that intertwined four stories and whose technique was to prove massively influential. Later films failed to match the promise of these works, and his career was virtually over by the time sound arrived. However, he was an innovator who encouraged a new subtlety and realism in screen performances. **NS**.

GRIS, JUAN
1887-1927
Spanish painter

Born in Madrid, Gris moved to Paris in 1906. Initially he was influenced by PICASSO and BRAQUE, following their experiments with papier collé, but from 1912 his tightly composed, strongly colored images played a central role in the second 'synthetic' phase of Cubism. He also produced stage sets and costumes for Diaghilev (1922-23). **ER**.

GRIVAS, GEORGIOS
1898-1974
Greek-Cypriot soldier

During the Axis occupation of Greece during World War II, Grivas organized and led resistance units, gaining experience of mountain fighting and unconventional warfare. In the late 1940s he fought the Communists during the Greek Civil War and in 1951 returned to his homeland of Cyprus, ruled by the British. Between 1955 and 1959 he commanded EOKA guerrilla groups trying to force the British to accept *Enosis* (union of Cyprus with Greece). Although *Enosis* was not achieved – in 1960 Cyprus became independent – Grivas returned to Cyprus from self-imposed exile in 1964 to command Greek-Cypriot troops. **JP**.

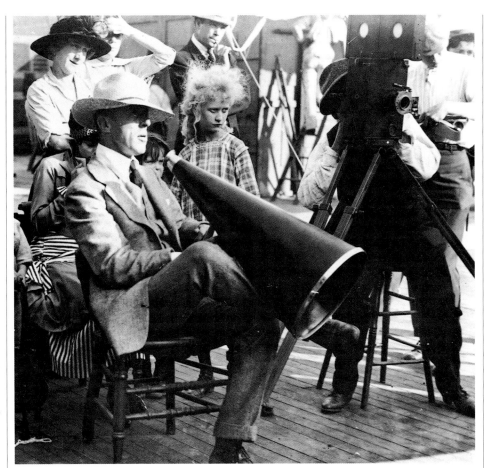

ABOVE: Movie director D W Griffith.

GROMYKO, ANDREI
1909-1989
Russian politician

'Mr Nyet' to two generations of Western diplomats, Gromyko was appointed Ambassador to Washington in 1943 at 34 and promoted Foreign Minister by KHRUSCHEV in 1957. Implacable in his opposition to the West, he nevertheless backed GORBACHEV as Communist Party leader, only to be dismissed by him and given the nominal Presidency. In 1988 he left the Politburo. **JC**.

GROPIUS, WALTER
1883-1969
German architect and educator

Gropius trained in the influential Berlin office of Peter BEHRENS. He set up on his own in 1910 and in 1914 designed the Fagus shoelace factory at Alfeld-an-der-Leine. This landmark building was steel-framed, the walls merely a skin of brick and plate glass. In 1919 Gropius founded Das Staatliche Bauhaus, Weimar, a school which followed his precept of the unity of craft, art, and technology; after the Bauhaus moved to Dessau in 1925 Gropius designed the new buildings on the same principles as the Fagus factory. His first influential housing project was at Dammerstock (1927-28) where five-story glass-walled blocks of flats were arranged in parallel rows perpendicular to the street with large areas of greenery in between allowing maximum access to light and air. In 1937, after four years in

ABOVE: German architect Walter Gropius.

London, Gropius emigrated to the US as Senior Professor of Architecture at Harvard. Alone, with Marcel BREUER (1937-41), or with the collective, The Architects Collaborative (founded 1946), Gropius built private houses and public buildings including housing (New Kensington project near Pittsburgh, 1941), all reflecting his ideas about standardization and prefabrication, glass walls to admit maximum light, careful siting according to landscape, refined proportioning and design restraint. A whole generation of his pupils propagated these ideas. **AR**.

GROSZ, GEORGE
1893-1959
German painter

Born in Berlin, Grosz began his career as a caricaturist. A prominent member of the Berlin Dada group from 1918, he began using Dadaist montage as a vehicle to highlight social abuses. During the 1920s drawings such as *The Face of the Ruling Class* (1921) made his reputation as a biting social satirist and his violent social criticism led to prosecutions for blasphemy and obscenity. A Communist party member since 1918, Grosz became disgusted by political developments in Germany and in 1932 left for the USA, where he settled. Largely abandoning satire, his work became rather romantic until around 1946 it took on a nightmarish, apocalyptic quality. **ER**.

GUDERIAN, HEINZ, GENERAL
1883-1954
German soldier

After World War I, Guderian remained in the German Army, where he experimented with mechanized forces. With HITLER's support, by 1935 he had developed the first of the Panzer Divisions, all-armored units that were the key to *Blitzkrieg*. Guderian spearheaded the lightning panzer advance across France and the Low Countries in May-June 1940 and in 1941 his tanks almost reached Moscow. He was sacked for disagreeing with HITLER in late 1941, and was not reinstated until 1944. He was Chief of the General Staff until March 1945. **JPi**.

GUEVARA, CHE [ERNESTO]
1928-1967
Argentine revolutionary

From a middle-class Argentine family, Guevara trained as a doctor before travels through Latin America in the 1950s convinced him that violent revolution was the only way for the masses to overcome their poverty. He fought with CASTRO in Cuba from 1956, eventually becoming a member of his government, and with LUMUMBA in the Congo during the 1960s. In 1966 his efforts to train guerrillas in Bolivia led to his death. A legendary figure, Guevara became a model for radical students the world over. **JM**.

GUINNESS, SIR ALEC
1914-
British actor

This London-born actor has continued his career in the theater right through and beyond his years as a major screen attraction. He played eight different characters in *Kind Hearts and Coronets* (1949) and appeared in two of Ealing Studios' best comedies, *The Lavender Hill Mob* and *The Man in the White Suit* in 1951. He was the mad mastermind undone by a sweet old lady in *The Ladykillers* (1955) and won a Venice Film Festival Award for *The Horse's Mouth* (1958). He has continued to maintain his reputation through a series of fine supporting roles in film and further stage and television appearances. **DC**.

GULBENKIAN, CALOUSTE
1869-1955
Armenian oil magnate and philanthropist

Gulbenkian was one of the first to appreciate the huge oil potential of the Middle East. Although in 1928 his Iraq Petroleum Co gave up its near monopoly in the Middle East to the British, Dutch, Anglo-Persian, and Americans, Gulbenkian maintained a 5% stake – hence his nickname 'Mr 5%'. He bequeathed much of his fortune to Armenian religious and educational institutions and his magnificent art collection to the foundation which bears his name. **PT**.

GUNN, THOM[SON]
1929-
British poet

A Cambridge contemporary of Ted HUGHES, in 1954 he published *Fighting Terms*, his first collection, and moved to California. Then regarded as a Movement poet, he was also influenced by the American Beats. An increasing emphasis on homosexual themes led to *The Man with Night Sweats* (1992), whose last section deals with AIDS. **AM**.

GUTHRIE, WOODY
1912-1967
American folk singer, songwriter, and guitarist

Guthrie was immensely influential on the 1960s generation of folk singers. He took to the road aged 16 with his harmonica in his pocket and arrived on the West Coast in 1935, where he became involved in radical politics. He began to record in 1941 after a meeting with Pete SEEGER, and worked with many of the leading vocalists of the day, including Leadbelly and Sonny Terry. After war service, he returned to recording with the Folkways label. He wrote over 1000 songs, including classics such as 'This Land is Your Land' and 'This Train is Bound for Glory'. **JH**.

GUTIERREZ, GUSTAVO
1928-
Peruvian liberation theologian

In many respects the father of liberation theology, Gutierrez has avoided the Marxism of many of his colleagues. His main works include *The Theology of Liberation* and *The Power of the Poor in History*. His theology and his practical example are a living challenge to the Church and the world to relieve the poverty of the poor. **ML**.

BELOW: Argentinian revolutionary Che Guevara.

HAAS, EARLE C
1885-1981
American inventor

In the early 1930s Haas set about adapting the conventional surgical technique of tamponage (the insertion of cotton wool into haemorraged orifices) for intra-vaginal use. His efforts culminated in the creation of the modern compressed tampon which, when combined with an extensive educational program, has achieved worldwide acclaim. **PT**.

HABER, FRITZ
1868-1934
German physical chemist

In 1908-09, with Carl Bosch, Haber developed the Haber process for converting atmospheric nitrogen into ammonia that could be used for artificial fertilizers. This meant that the world's agriculture was no longer dependent on the supply of natural nitrogenous fertilizers from Chile. In 1911 he became the Director of the Kaiser Wilhelm Institute for Physical Chemistry in Berlin. His work on poison gases during World War I led to protests against his award of the Nobel Prize for Chemistry in 1918. In 1933 he resigned and fled Germany in protest at the growing anti-semitism, but died shortly afterwards. **DD**.

HABERMAS, JURGEN
1929-
German social scientist

The most important representative of the Frankfurt School of critical theory, Habermas has attempted to produce a sociology with 'critical intent.' His early works, such as *Knowledge and Human Interests* (1968), argued, against positivism, that facts and values, theory and practice, cannot be kept separate in human knowledge but that science should have an interest in furthering human freedom. Habermas developed these philosophical arguments within a series of sociological works, culminating in the massive *Theory of Communicative Action* which argues that the potential for freedom is implicit in the very structure of language and communication. However, this potential remains unrealized because modern society has developed human interaction in the direction of increasing technical control and power. Against postmodernists, however, Habermas argues that modern rationalization has produced not only domination, but also increases in communicative freedom such as civil rights and democracy. In works such as *Legitimation Crisis*, Habermas has tried to outline these developments more concretely in terms of political and economic analysis. Habermas continues to be a massive figure within international sociology, attempting to carry out his belief in free human communication by engaging in debates with all the major currents of social thought as well as fostering empirical social research. Most recently he has been a central figure in debates about both Postmodernism and Neoconservatism. **DSI**.

HADLEE, SIR RICHARD
1951-
New Zealand cricketer

Hadlee played a leading part in the development of New Zealand cricket to top-class status during the later 1970s and 1980s. He was himself also unquestionably one of the game's great players and remains the leading wicket taker in tests, with 431 successes. His bowling featured a unique combination of pace, control, and tactical acumen. **DS**.

HAIG, DOUGLAS, 1ST EARL, FIELD MARSHAL
1861-1928
British soldier

Commissioned into the 7th Hussars, Haig saw service in Sudan and the Boer War before being posted to India in 1903. Nine years later he was appointed GOC Aldershot, and in 1914 he commanded the British 1st Corps in France. He replaced Sir John French as Commander-in-Chief in December 1915. He launched the Somme offensive in 1916, achieving considerable advances only at the cost of terrible casualties, and used similar tactics at Passchendaele in 1917. Despite severe criticism Haig retained his command until the end of the war. After the war, he devoted himself to the welfare of ex-servicemen, and founded the British Legion. **JPi**.

ABOVE: *Military commander Sir Douglas Haig.*

HAILE SELASSIE, EMPEROR
1892-1975
Ethiopian ruler

Ras Tafari was son of the principal adviser to Emperor Menelik II. In 1916 he was made regent and heir to the throne of what was then Abyssinia, becoming emperor in his own right in 1930 and adopting the title Haile Selassie ('Might of the Trinity'). Five years later his country was invaded by the Italians and, after making an impassioned (but fruitless) plea for support to the League of Nations in Geneva on 30 June 1936, he went into exile in Britain. Restored to the throne by British troops in 1941, he was deposed in a coup in 1974. **JP**.

HALAS, GEORGE STANLEY
1895-1983
American football coach

A charter member of the Pro Football Hall of Fame in 1963, Halas essentially defined the Chicago Bears – as a player, as an owner, and most of all as a combative and highly successful coach. He coached the team almost every year from its inception (as the Decatur Staleys) in 1920 until his retirement in 1967. No one has matched his 40 years of coaching or his 325 wins. Six times he led Chicago to the NFL championship. He was also responsible for numerous tactical innovations that helped to transform the game. **MD**.

HALDANE, JOHN BURDON SANDERSON
1892-1964
British geneticist

Haldane was an exceptionally wide-ranging scholar in both arts and sciences who became the leading figure in human genetics for many decades. Educated at Eton and Oxford, he was initially a classical and mathematical scholar who went on to study and hold senior posts in biochemistry, biometrics, physiology, and genetics. In science he was a great self-experimenter, even undergoing hazardous procedures. Haldane's greatest impact was in human genetics. He made important discoveries concerning the X chromosome, including, with Julia Bell in 1937, the first measurement of linkage (for haemophilia and color blindness). He made major contributions to statistical aspects of human genetics, publishing his theories in *The Causes of Evolution* (1932), and to the relationship between heredity and environment. Haldane was an ardent advocate of the 'one gene, one enzyme' hypothesis, and of the biochemical basis of genetics. A man of strong views and unconventional opinions, Haldane was a Marxist for many years. He emigrated to India in 1957 in protest at the Suez invasion. **GL**.

HALE, GEORGE E
1868-1938
American astronomer

Hale was a pioneer of astrophysics, the application of physics to astronomy, with particular reference to the sun. In 1904 he built a solar observatory on Mount Wilson, California, where he discovered that sunspots are cooler areas on the sun's surface associated with strong magnetic fields. He raised money to build the famous 100-inch (2.5-meter) reflector on Mount Wilson and then the great 200-inch (5-meter) on Palomar Mountain, which is named after him. **IR**.

ABOVE: Rock-and-roller Bill Haley and his Comets.

HALEY, BILL
1925-1981
American singer, guitarist and bandleader

The pioneer of rock and roll, Haley's early work was with country and western and rhythm and blues bands. The classic 'Rock Around the Clock' (1954) flopped at first but went on to top the charts when used in the film *Blackboard Jungle* (1955). **JH**.

HALL, STUART
1932-
British Sociologist

Originally from the Caribbean, Hall has been an influential figure since the late 1950s when he was one of the founders of the New Left in Britain. In the 1960s Hall was involved in, and eventually headed, the Birmingham School of Contemporary Cultural Studies through which he played a key role in defining and founding the entire field of cultural studies. Hall was notable for bringing American and British sociology into contact with European sociological (particularly Marxist) traditions. He has written prolifically on ideology, racism, the media, and political theory. **DSl**.

HALLSTEIN, WALTER
1901-1982
German politician

President of the EEC Commission 1958-67, Hallstein's championing of British entry to the EEC provoked de GAULLE into ordering the French 'empty chair boycott' and calling for a revision of the Treaty of Rome. A pugnacious champion of a federated Europe, he came to the EEC from the West German Foreign Office. There he had formulated a doctrine under which any country other than the USSR which recognized East Germany risked boycott. **JC**.

HALSEY, WILLIAM, FLEET ADMIRAL
1882-1959
American sailor

Halsey served on destroyers during World World I, but in 1935 transferred to aircraft carriers. In December 1941 his ships of Task Force 2 were fortunately at sea and missed the Japanese attack on Pearl Harbor. By April 1942 Halsey was Commander, Carriers, Pacific Fleet and in October became Commander, South Pacific. As such, he supervised the Solomons counter-offensive. By 1944 he was commanding the Third Fleet, and although his actions at Leyte Gulf in October were criticized, the Japanese were defeated. Halsey conducted operations around Okinawa before witnessing the Japanese surrender in August 1945. **JPi**.

HAMILTON, RICHARD
1922-
British painter

Hamilton was a founder member of the Independent Group, which met between 1952 and 1955 for informal discussions about modern technology and mass-media culture. In 1956 they organized the exhibition *This Is Tomorrow* for which Hamilton made the collage *Just What is it That Makes Today's Homes So Different, So Appealing?* Practically an inventory of popular culture, it was a key work in the development of British Pop Art. He went on to explore the social psychology of advertising in works such as *Hommage à Chrysler Corps* (1957) and *She* (1958/61) and the impact of photography in *Hugh Gaitskell as a Famous Monster of Filmland* (1964). **ER**.

HAMMARSKJÖLD, DAG
1905-1961
Swedish diplomat

Hammarskjöld greatly expanded the

ABOVE: Former Secretary-General of the UN, Dag Hammarskjold.

authority of the General Secretaryship of the United Nations, which he held from 1953 until his death. An exponent of UN intervention to preserve world peace, he personally persuaded NASSER to accept a force which held the Middle East peace line for a decade. He died in an air crash, probably sabotaged, on his way to arrange for another cordon sanitaire, in the Congo. **JC**.

HAMMER, ARMAND
1898-1990
American entrepreneur and philanthropist

Hammer journeyed to Russia in 1921 where he became the one capitalist LENIN could deal with. Importing medical and food supplies to a Soviet Union blighted by famine, he exported furs, minerals, and Tsarist treasures, thus amassing a modest fortune. His purchase of the rundown Occidental Petroleum Company in 1956 and a lucky wildcat oil strike increased his fortune immeasurably. Hammer became an international fixer, helping to maintain US-USSR links during the Cold War and earning a reputation as a generous philanthropist. **PT**.

HAMMETT, [SAMUEL] DASHIELL
1894-1961
American novelist

An ex-Pinkerton private detective turned crime writer, he created the famous detective Sam Spade. His were the essential hardboiled heroes, tough men in a violent world, as immortalized by Humphrey BOGART. Many of his books became films, like *The Maltese Falcon* (1930). Imprisoned in the MCCARTHY era, his longtime companion was the playwright Lillian HELLMAN. **AM**.

HAMMOND, WALTER
1903-1965
British cricketer

Wally Hammond was a star of English cricket throughout the 1930s. A slow starter in the first-class game, he came to the fore with the England team in Australia in 1928-29, unfortunately for him at a time when his remarkable performances were overshadowed by BRADMAN's unique talent. Hammond was not always popular with team mates and personal problems saw him leave the game in 1947. **DS**.

BELOW: *Philanthropist Armand Hammer greets Mikhail Gorbachev.*

HANBURY-TENISON, ROBIN
1936-
British explorer

Hanbury-Tenison has been an explorer for most of his life, although for many years he has also worked a farm in Cornwall between journeys. He has traveled across most of the remoter regions of the world, including the Sahara and the Amazon, showing a particular interest in the way of life of native peoples, especially hunters and gatherers. In 1969 he helped to found the organization 'Survival International', which campaigns on behalf of indigenous peoples all over the world. **RJ**.

HARDIE, KEIR
1856-1915
British Labour politician

Easily recognised by his beard, and widely known as 'the man in the cloth cap', Keir Hardie is the figure most associated with the emergence of the British Labour Party. Behind this symbolism lies the substance of the Scottish miner who became the first independent representative of the working classes in Parliament, and then helped secure powerful trade-union support. A committed but non-denominational Christian, his greatest legacy, however, belongs not to institutions but to ideals – due to him Labour's socialism espoused brotherly love rather than class war. **JP**.

ABOVE: *Oliver Hardy (right), and partner in comedy, Stan Laurel.*

HARDING, WARREN
1865-1923
American politician

The Ohio country boy Harding's watchword of 'normalcy' won him the presidency from war-weary American voters in 1920. He kept the United States out of the League of Nations, introduced a Budget Bureau into the Treasury, and refused to pay a bonus to returning war veterans. He called an international conference in Washington to stop naval expansion, but Germany circumvented the treaty by building pocket battleships and Japan eventually repudiated it, claiming naval parity with Britain and the United States. Harding's administration was overshadowed by corruption in his Cabinet. **JC**.

HARDY, OLIVER
1892-1957
American actor

Hardy, the tie-twiddling fat half of the Laurel and Hardy team, had bit parts in films before he began to appear with Stan LAUREL, the acknowledged creative force behind their mayhem. Together they romped their way through the 1920s and 1930s, still making occasional films as late as the 1940s. **DC**.

HARLOW, JEAN
1911-1937
American actress

Harlow was the shimmering light of the silver screen, a wisecracking sexy platinum blonde who made brunette vamps obsolete overnight. First appearing in *Moran of the Marines* in 1928, her natural comic talent and saucy vulgar charm emerged after she signed with MGM in 1932, when she made *Red Dust* with Clark GABLE, who became a lifelong friend. She stole *Dinner at Eight* from a cast of veterans in 1933, as well as making her finest film, *Bombshell*, in which she gleefuly satirized her sex-driven image. While filming her last picture, *Saratoga* (1937), she became ill and died of cerebral edema. **DC**.

HARMSWORTH, ALFRED, BARON NORTHCLIFFE
1865-1922
British newspaper proprietor

Viscount Northcliffe started his newspaper career on the *Hampstead and Highgate Gazette*. He launched a string of newspapers and magazines in the 1880s and 1890s, culminating in the *Daily Mail* in 1896 which used American-style presentation and revolutionized British mass-circulation newspapers. Having purchased *The Times* in 1908, he proceeded to used it to express his political views, particularly during World War I when he attacked Kitchener and ASQUITH. An autocratic and energetic man, he created the largest newspaper empire of his day and transformed British journalism. **DSl**.

HARRIS, SIR ARTHUR, MARSHAL OF THE ROYAL AIR FORCE
1892-1984
British airman

A pilot in World War I, 'Bomber' Harris remained in the RAF and by 1939 was an advocate of strategic bombing. Appointed AOC Bomber Command in 1942, with CHURCHILL's support he organized the massed bombing of German cities, including Hamburg (1943) and Dresden (1945). When the scale of civilian casualties became clear, the morality of Harris's policy was repeatedly questioned and still arouses controversy. **JPi**.

HARRISON, ROSS GRANVILLE
1870-1959
American biologist

One of the pioneers of experimental embryology, Harrison's single most important contribution was the innovation of the technique of tissue culture. He realized that biological changes occurring within animals could be studied directly by growing cells and tissues outside the body. At the John Hopkins Medical School, he studied the mode of development of nerve cell fibers in embryonic tissue through the modification of the hanging drop method. He established that nerve fibres are formed from outgrowths of the nerve cell itself. This work gave impetus to the further use of tissue and cell culture and established it as a technique adaptable to the solution of a wide variety of problems in biology and medicine. **ES**.

HART, WILLIAM S
1870-1946
American actor

Hart was one of the giants in the history of the Western. He took it from short one and two reelers, and made it into full-length stories that depicted the old West with realism and poetic feeling, making silent films which appealed to adults and children alike. His influence on the Western cannot be exaggerated. **DC**.

HARTMANN, ERICH, MAJOR
1922-
German fighter pilot

Hartmann became the highest-scoring fighter pilot ever, gaining 352 victories on the Eastern Front from 5 November 1943 to May 1945, with Jadgeschwader 52. He was awarded the Knight's Cross on 29 October 1943, after 148 'kills', adding the coveted Diamonds after 301 victories in 1944. He led 11 Gruppe, JG 52, from February 1945, which retreated westward under Soviet pressure and surrendered to American forces in Czechoslovakia in May. After serving a 10-year prison sentence in the USSR, he returned to West Germany in 1955 and commanded JG 71 *Richthofen*, flying F-86 Sabres within the reformed Luftwaffe. **MT**.

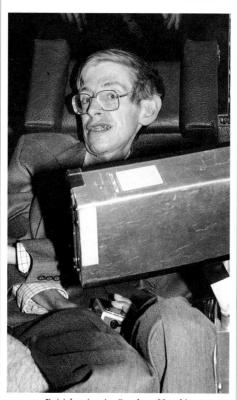

ABOVE: British scientist Stephen Hawking.

HARTNELL, NORMAN, SIR
1901-1979
British designer

Having left Cambridge University without a degree, Hartnell first began designing clothes in the 1920s, when he worked briefly for Lucille. In 1930 his Paris show brought him success and acclaim, but he is best known as the dressmaker to the British Royal family, a position to which he was appointed in 1938. In addition to making clothes for the Queen Mother, Hartnell also made Queen Elizabeth II's wedding and 'going-away' dresses and, in 1953, her Coronation robe. Hartnell's reputation rested on his creations of ballgowns and wedding dresses, although he also produced tailored suits and tweed garments. In the 1940s he designed a ready-to-wear line for Berketex. In addition to being the creator of 'In Love' perfume, Hartnell also redesigned the uniform of British women police officers. **MC**.

HAUSHOFER, KARL [ERNST]
1869-1946
German political geographer

One of the leading exponents of the study of geopolitics, Haushofer was greatly influenced by Japanese expansionism and was influential in the development of German military theory between the wars. He argued for an alliance with the Soviet Union, and for the policies of the Axis powers, but was compromised by having a Jewish wife. His son, also a Professor of geopolitics, was executed for his activities in the Resistance, and when he was accused of war crimes by the Allies, he and his wife committed suicide. **EB**.

HAVELANGE, JOÃO
1916-
Brazilian sports administrator

João Havelange competed for Brazil in the 1936 and 1952 Olympics as a swimmer and water polo player. A lawyer by profession, he then moved into various posts in sporting administration until becoming, in 1974, President of FIFA, soccer's governing body worldwide. His presidency, often controversial, has seen great development of the game outside its traditional strongholds including the decision to hold the 1994 World Cup in the USA. **DS**.

HAWKE, ROBERT
1929-
Australian politician

Bob Hawke made the Australian Labor Party electable by arranging with the Australian Council of Trade unions to keep down their wage demands for the national good. Labor duly won in 1983 and Hawke served four terms. His unashamed populism endeared him to the Australian worker, despite his unsocialist record of deregulating banking and privatising state monopolies like telecommunications. **JC.**

HAWKING, STEPHEN WILLIAM
1942-
British physicist

Graduating from Oxford, Hawking obtained a doctorate at Cambridge and remained there to become a Fellow of the Royal Society and Lucasian Professor of Mathematics. His research field was Einstein's theory of relativity, which he found did not account for such concepts as black holes – points in space where gravitation is so strong that even light rays cannot escape – or the 'big bang' – the theory that the universe was created by expansion from a single point of infinite mass. His subsequent work has developed both these concepts considerably, proving mathematically that black holes can actually radiate heat. He has also sought to find a unified field theory, uniting the nuclear forces, electromagnetic force, and gravitational force – a quest that defeated Einstein. In his student days he contracted the severely disabling motor neuron disease which has confined him to a wheelchair ever since. All the complex mathematics of his work are carried out in his head. He is also a popular communicator. His book *A Brief History of Time* (1988) has been very successful in bringing the complex concepts of cosmology and theoretical physics to a wider audience. **DD.**

HAWKINS, COLEMAN
1904-1969
American jazz saxophonist

Hawkins was instrumental in popularizing the tenor sax. He gave the instrument a warmth of tone and color which kept him ahead of imitators throughout the 1930s, and in the mid-1940s assembled an all-star band including PARKER and GILLESPIE for the first be-bop sessions. Losing out to 'cool' players such as Stan Getz in the 1950s, he nevertheless continued playing right up until his death. **DC.**

HAWKS, HOWARD
1896-1977
American film director

Hawks's films are particularly characterized by an undemonstrative visual style, strong female roles, and the situation of the group pulling together under crisis. He produced excellent films in every major genre, including *Scarface* (1932), *Bringing up Baby* (1938), *The Big Sleep* (1946), *Red River* (1948), and *Gentlemen Prefer Blondes* (1953). **NS.**

HAWORTH, SIR WALTER NORMAN
1883-1950
British organic chemist

Haworth was a Fellow of the Royal Society and held academic posts in several universities including London, St Andrews, and Newcastle and was director of chemistry at Birmingham from 1924 to 1948. In 1933, with O Paul Karrer, he synthesized vitamin C. Both were awarded the Nobel Prize for Chemistry for this work in 1937. **DD.**

HAYEK, FRIEDRICH
1899-1992
British economist

Austrian-born, Hayek held successive academic posts in Vienna, London, and Chicago. In his *Road to Serfdom* (1944) he warned that government intervention in the economy leads to totalitarianism. This gave intellectual respectability to opponents of socialism, but his thesis was, and remains, quite unsupported by twentieth-century history, although he was joint winner of the 1974 Nobel Prize for Economics. **JW.**

ABOVE: Distinguished economist Friedrich Hayek.

HEANEY, SEAMUS
1939-
Irish poet

Born into a Catholic family in Northern Ireland, Heaney's first major collection, *Death of a Naturalist* (1966) was of rural and nature poems which bore comparison with the work of Ted HUGHES. Heaney taught at Queen's University, Belfast, for some years, then settled in Eire in 1972. His work became progressively more sophisticated and verbally complex, as his interests in language and the vexed questions of Irish identity and politics became major themes in his poetry, as in *Wintering Out* (1972) and *North* (1975). Further collections include *Selected Poems* (1975) and the prose selection *Pre-occupations* (1980). **AM.**

HEARST, WILLIAM RANDOLPH
1863-1951
US publisher

Hearst was a multimillionaire publisher whose enjoyment of power and lavish lifestyle inspired Orson WELLES' film *Citizen Kane*. He became editor of his father's paper, the *San Francisco Examiner*, in 1887, and increased circulation by publishing sensational and salacious stories until it was profitable in 1890, after which he gradually acquired a chain of newspapers. Hearst's name became a byword for the power of the media to make or break careers and influence the course of world events. He unsuccessfully tried to enter politics. He began his long affair with actress Marion Davies in 1917, and in 1919 he began building a castle at San Simeon, which he furnished with works of art. By the 1930s, his empire on the brink of bankruptcy, Hearst was forced to sell off his assets, but was still able to leave a vast fortune, estimated at over $200 million. **DSI.**

HEARTFIELD, JOHN
1891-1968
German painter and journalist

A founder member, in 1919, of the Berlin Dada group, Heartfield was a pioneer of photomontage. He used this medium to express his strongly held Communist and pacifist views in bitingly satirical illustrations and posters. After spending 12 years in London he moved to East Germany in 1950 where he lived until his death. **ER.**

HEATH, EDWARD, SIR
1916-
British politician and statesman

Hard-working, pro-Common Market and an ardent modernizer, Heath seemed an ideal Conservative champion against Harold WILSON. In government, however, he was no better treated by economic crisis and industrial unrest than Wilson. Although EEC entry was achieved, two defeats by the miners lost Heath the 1974 election. Ruthlessly replaced by Margaret THATCHER, Heath's outpoken counter-attacks made him very unpopular in the party. It was ironic, therefore, when pressure for a more positive European policy saw his successor replaced by John MAJOR. Mellowed by age, Heath's happiest days in politics appeared to have begun when he was elected Father of the Commons in 1992. **JP.**

HEFNER, HUGH
1926-
American magazine publisher

Hefner began his career as subscription and promotion writer for *Esquire* magazine. In 1953 he became editor of *Playboy* magazine and turned it into one of the most popular men's magazines with a raunchy mixture of centerfold naked women and light-hearted articles. Changing tastes led to falling sales and Hefner passed the editorship of the magazine to his daughter in 1988. **DSI.**

HEIDEGGER, MARTIN
1889-1976
German philosopher

After studying theology as a Jesuit novice, Heidegger studied phenomenology under Husserl, whom he succeeded in his post at Freiburg. His major work *Sein und Zeit [Being and Time]* explored the notion of 'Being' and greatly influenced other existentialist thinkers. He saw human existence as characterized by apprehension of a future filled with inescapable choices and death; living conventionally is an escape, but authenticity is possible if one faces up to death and consciously exercises freedom of choice. The obscurity of his prose is exacerbated by his fondness for wordplay, exemplified by his later dictum that 'Nothing noths'. A supporter of HITLER, his inaugural address as Rector of Freiburg was on the role of a university in the *Reich*; after the war, he was banned from teaching but was exonerated of active Nazism in 1951. **EB**.

HEIFETZ, JASCHA
1901-1987
American violinist

Heifetz graduated at the remarkably early age of eight from the Vilnius School of Music to begin a long and successful career on the concert platform. Subsequently his popularity spread throughout the world helped by the large number of recordings he made. He was greatly admired by his contemporaries and had many works written specially for him including violin concertos by Walton, Gruenberg, and Achron. **DK**.

ABOVE: *The acclaimed American novelist Ernest Hemingway.*

ABOVE: *American playwright Lillian Hellman.*

HELLMAN, LILLIAN
1907-1984
American playwright

Born in New Orleans but essentially a New Yorker, Hellman's first play, *The Children's Hour* (1934), dealt controversially with a malicious charge of lesbianism by a schoolgirl against her teachers. *The Little Foxes* (1939), a perceptive study of greed and power, is perhaps her best-known work. Dashiell HAMMETT was her companion. **AM**.

HEMINGWAY, ERNEST
1899-1961
American novelist

Born in Illinois, Hemingway began his lifelong passion for hunting and fishing in northern Michigan, and worked as a journalist both before and after serving with an ambulance unit during World War I. He then settled in Paris in 1921, among the other American expatriates like Ezra POUND and Gertrude STEIN. *Three Stories and Ten Poems*, his first book appeared in 1923, followed by more stories and a novel. His reputation was established with the publication in 1926 of *The Sun Also Rises* (initially published as *Fiesta* in England). From the beginning, his renowned technique with its brevity of sentences and sharpness of observation, created works of immense power, some of the literary importance of which has been obscured by the macho myth to which he heavily contributed, and which probably eventually cost him his life. *A Farewell to Arms* (1929) is a wartime love story, and *Death in the Afternoon* (1932) is based on bullfighting; the remarkable short story 'The Snows of Kilimanjaro' appeared in a 1938 collection, and his finest work *For Whom the Bell Tolls* in 1940. He was a war correspondent in World War II, and in 1952 *The Old Man and the Sea* showed he had recaptured his earlier powers; he was awarded the Nobel Prize in 1954. In failing health, he committed suicide by shooting himself. **AM**.

HENDRIX, JIMI
1942-1970
American rock guitarist

Hendrix was working as a session musician with names such as Jackie Wilson, the Isley Brothers, and Little Richard when he was persuaded to come to England in 1966. Success was practically instant, and he was soon fêted as a guitar hero along with CLAPTON, Beck and Townshend after hits such as 'Hey Joe' and 'Purple Rain'. But after the classic double album *Electric Ladyland* he abruptly quit his band The Jimi Hendrix Experience. An attempt to reform a year later, and two solo albums were followed by his death from an overdose of barbiturates in 1970. **DC**.

ABOVE: *Jimi Hendrix, pictured with his legendary guitar.*

HEPBURN, KATHARINE
1907-
American actress

Hepburn may well be the most respected actress ever to emerge from Hollywood because she has never confused her star image with her strong individualism. Educated at Bryn Mawr, she stormed Broadway and then Hollywood, where she wore trousers and no make-up in an era where carefully applied allure was an actress's stock in trade. An instant success in *A Bill of Divorcement* (1932), several popular movies followed, including *Morning Glory* (1933) for which she won her first Academy Award. She hit her stride as a screwball comedienne in *Bringing Up Baby* with Cary GRANT in 1938; *Woman of the Year* (1942) was the first of many very successful films with her companion Spencer TRACY, including *State of the Union* (1948) and *Desk Set* (1957). Their final film, completed shortly before Tracy's death, was *Guesss Who's Coming to Dinner* (1967). Hepburn and BOGART scored a triumph with *The African Queen* (1951), one of her best spinster characterizations, and she won the Best Actress Award at Cannes for a fine performance as the hopelessly drug-addicted mother in *Long Day's Journey Into Night* (1962). Opposite the ailing Henry FONDA in *On Golden Pond* (1982) she proved she still had that touch of greatness after more than 50 years of making films. **DC**.

HEPWORTH, BARBARA, DAME
1903-1975
British sculptress

Hepworth trained at the Royal College of Art, 1921-24, and like MOORE, her contemporary and close associate, she was an advocate of direct carving, her early works in wood and stone attesting to her sensitivity to materials. During the 1930s her work developed from combinations of geometric and organic forms to complete abstraction. She went on to explore contrasts created between painted and natural wood surfaces and strings stretched tautly across hollowed-out curves, and began tunneling into her carvings, creating an interplay between interior and exterior surfaces. In the late 1950s she also produced bronzes and her works reached monumental proportions. **ER**.

HERRERA, HELENIO
1916-
Argentinian soccer coach

Helenio Herrera spent most of his playing career in France but is best known as the coach of the highly-successful Inter Milan club in the 1960s. He also managed the Spanish national team in 1962. **DS**.

HESS, HARRY HAMMOND
1906-1969
American geologist and geophysicist

Working from Princeton University, and using his expertise in underwater sensing gained in the US Navy during World War II, Hess was at the forefront of the surge of interest in oceanography in the 1960s. He proposed the theory of seafloor spreading, in which new material from the Earth's mantle is constantly welling up to form surface material along ocean ridges. This provided part of the mechanism for the old idea of continental drift, and was later refined to the concept of plate tectonics. **DD**.

HESS, DAME MYRA
1890-1965
British pianist

After her sensational debut in London in 1907 under Sir Thomas BEECHAM she continued her success as one of the leading interpreters of piano concertos. She is perhaps best remembered for her lunchtime concerts given at the National Gallery during World War II and for her many piano transcriptions including Bach's *Jesu, Joy of Man's Desiring*. **DK**.

ABOVE: *Rudolf Hess, Hitler's deputy until 1941.*

HESS, RUDOLF
1893-1987
German politician

Hess was HITLER's official deputy until he flew to Scotland in May 1941 in an attempt to end the war. The 50-year mystery surrounding it was cleared up recently by the release of the case papers, which showed that Hess, who was deranged as GOEBBELS had said, flew on his own initiative. He had taken down *Mein Kampf* in dictation from Hitler in prison and promulgated the Nazi racial decrees. Sentenced to life imprisonment at Nuremberg, he served 46 years in all and allegedly committed suicide just before he was due for release from Spandau Prison. **JC**.

ABOVE: *Sculptress Barbara Hepworth and U Thant in front of her abstraction 'Single Form.'*

HESTON, CHARLTON
1923-
American actor

Tall, muscular, and strong-jawed, Heston looks every inch the hero that he has played through most of his film career. After *The Greatest Show on Earth* was a box-office success in 1952, his big breakthrough came as Moses in the epic *The Ten Commandments* (1956). He received an Academy Award for *Ben Hur*, another De MILLE epic, in 1959, although some of his best performances have come in smaller pictures, notably *Touch of Evil* (1958), directed by Orson WELLES. His popularity declined in the 1960s, although he scored a hit with *Planet of the Apes* in 1968, and he regained popularity in the 1970s in sci-fi films such as *Earthquake* (1974). **DC.**

HEWLETT, WILLIAM
1913-
PACKARD, DAVID
1912-
American inventors

Hewlett and Packard set up their first workshop in a garage to market a variable frequency oscillator in 1939. World War II stimulated the market for electronic goods and after the war Hewlett and Packard concentrated on producing precision electronic items. Their greatest success has been with computers, particularly inventions that reduced the size of the components, and their company has played a great part in the computer revolution of the last 20 years. **PT.**

HEYERDAHL, THOR
1914-
Norwegian explorer

Heyerdahl has spent much of his life trying to demonstrate one fundamental point – that the early civilizations were connected, rather than separated, by the sea. His first and most famous attempt to prove this point was in his balsa-wood raft, the *Kon-Tiki* in which, in 1947, he sailed from Peru to the Marquesas Islands. He then made a study of the ancient culture of the Easter Islands in an attempt – rejected by most archaeologists – to find archaeological evidence to support his theories. In 1969 he built the reed-boat *Ra*, and later *Ra II*, in a successful attempt to prove that it would have been possible to sail from Europe to the West Indies in ancient times. Heyerdahl set fire to his final reed-boat, *Tigris*, in Djibouti as a protest against both maritime pollution and the political unrest that had brought her voyage through the Red Sea and Indian Ocean to an abrupt end. **RJ.**

HILBERT, DAVID
1862-1943
German mathematician

One of the most influential mathematicians ever, Hilbert published authoritative accounts of algebraic number theory, and of the axiomatization of geometry, while his work on functional analysis, in which he studied infinite-dimensional spaces (now called 'Hilbert spaces'), contributed to the development of mathematical physics. His views on the foundations of mathematics gave rise to 'Hilbert's program' of proving the consistency of finitistic mathematics by purely formal methods, and although this was later proved impossible by Gödel's theorem, he nonetheless thereby laid the foundations of the study of metamathematics, proof theory, and computability. In 1900 he published a list of 23 then-unsolved problems (of which many still remain unsolved), which greatly influenced the direction of twentieth-century mathematics. **EB.**

HILLARY, EDMUND, SIR
1919-
New Zealand mountaineer

Hillary learned to climb in the New Zealand Alps, but in the early 1950s graduated to climbing in the central Himalayas. In 1953 he joined a British expedition led by Colonel John Hunt, which aimed to conquer Mount Everest. On the morning of 29 May, Hillary and the Sherpa Tensing Norgay traversed the last ridge and became the first men to climb the world's highest mountain. **RJ.**

HIMMLER, HEINRICH
1900-1945
German politician

As HITLER's top policeman, Himmler crushed Röhm's Stormtroopers and turned his rival SS into the instrument of enforcing the Führer's will, as well as a model of Aryan racial 'superiority.' He put into practice the politico-eugenic theories he had formulated then on a European scale, with horrifying results. Himmler exercised overall control of the concentration camps and the Final Solution, of which he told his staff; 'it is a page of glory in our history which will never be written.' Himmler swallowed poison on capture in 1945. **JC.**

HINAULT, BERNARD
1954-
French cyclist

Bernard Hinault shares the record of five Tour de France wins, in his case between 1978 and 1985. Among his other successes he was world champion in 1980. Known as 'The Badger' to his many fans, he had made his competitive debut in 1971 and retired in 1986. **DS.**

HINDENBURG, PAUL VON, FIELD MARSHAL
1847-1934
German soldier and President

By 1914 Hindenburg was a retired general, having joined the Prussian Army in 1858. Recalled to service, with Erich Ludendorff as his Chief of Staff, he was sent to East Prussia, where his victory at Tannenberg (August 1914) made him a national hero. Transferred to the Western Front in 1916, Hindenburg and Ludendorff (the latter the strategic brain) planned the offensive of March 1918 which nearly won the war. After Germany's defeat Hindenburg retired from public life until 1925 when he became President of the Weimar Republic. Re-elected in 1932, he was forced to appoint HITLER Chancellor in 1933. **JPi.**

HINDEMITH, PAUL
1895-1963
German composer

A violinist and viola virtuoso, Hindemith's music reflects his Lutheran Gothic heritage and his view of music as 'an agent of moral elevation,' expressed in strongly contrapuntal textures and latterly in neoclassical forms. He settled in the USA after attracting Nazi disfavor in the 1930s, and composed prolifically thereafter. **DK.**

HINSHELWOOD, SIR CYRIL NORMAN
1897-1967
British chemist

Hinshelwood spent his whole career in Oxford and his work included studies in the chemistry of bacterial growth. In 1956 he shared the Nobel Prize for Chemistry with Nikolay Semenov for their simultaneous work on chain reactions. He was a talented artist and linguist, and an expert on oriental ceramics. He was President of the Royal Society and of the Classical Association. **DD.**

HIRSHHORN, JOSEPH H
1899-1981
Canadian businessman

Hirshhorn's life took him from poverty on the back streets of Brooklyin to a nine-figure millionaire in his adoptive Canada. A successful entrepreneur and stockbroker, he struck lucky in the early 1950s when he and a geologist Franc Joubin combined forces to make the greatest uranium strike in Canadian history. During the course of his life Hirshhorn amassed a vast art collection of nineteenth and twentieth century works which he donated to the United States in 1966. At the time it was valued at $50,000,000. It is housed in Hirshhorn Museum, part of the Smithsonian Institution in Washington. **PT.**

HISS, ALGER
1904-
American diplomat

Whether Hiss was the most prominent victim of the McCarthyite hysteria or a highly-placed traitor, remains an open question. This highflyer of the New Deal – he was assistant to the Assistant Secretary of State in 1936 and Director of the Office of Special Political Affairs – went to jail for perjury in 1950 after a *Time* magazine editor, Whittaker Chambers, denounced him to the House Committee on UnAmerican Activities, claiming to have found microfilms of State Department documents, hidden in a pumpkin, which the FBI testified had been typed on Hiss's typewriter. **JC**.

HITCHCOCK, SIR ALFRED
1899-1980
British film director

Hitchcock began directing in the 1920s and made the first important British 'talkie', *Blackmail* (1929). After a series of exciting thrillers in the 1930s, including *The Thirty-Nine Steps* (1935) and *The Lady Vanishes* (1938), his first Hollywood success was *Rebecca* in 1940. His prestige increased during the 1950s when he made some of his most profound and suspenseful films, including *Rear Window* (1954), *Vertigo* (1958), and *Psycho* (1960). He was regarded as not only as a master entertainer, but as a major artist whose sensibilities were acutely attuned to the modern age of anxiety and paranoia. **NS**.

HITLER, ADOLF
1889-1945
Austrian-born German politician

Hitler came to power legitimately as an answer to the rise of Communism and to the great slump in Germany. But he soon assumed dictatorial powers and began to rearm in contravention of the Versailles treaty. The triumph of his will in creating a Greater Reich, as outlined in *Mein Kampf*, also brought about his downfall. He miscalculated in attacking Poland, thus starting World War II before he was ready; further errors were invading his idealogical enemy Russia, and declaring war on the United States. His single-minded pursuit of his other foe, the Jews, diverted the war effort and lost Germany some of her finest scientific talent, including nuclear physicists. The German General Staff, who had had their misgivings about the war quelled by the lightning conquest of France, almost invariably deferred to Hitler in the strategy for the Eastern Front. This led to the disaster of Stalingrad. Failure of the Officers' Bomb Plot in July 1944 tightened Hitler's grip on command and eventually, totally isolated, physically and mentally, he committed suicide in his bunker as the Red Army broke into Berlin. The war he started sounded the death knell of the British empire, replacing it with an American economic one; ironically it also helped create another, the Communist empire in Eastern Europe. **JC**.

RIGHT: The master of suspense, film director Alfred Hitchcock.
BELOW: Adolf Hitler, erstwhile Führer of Germany.

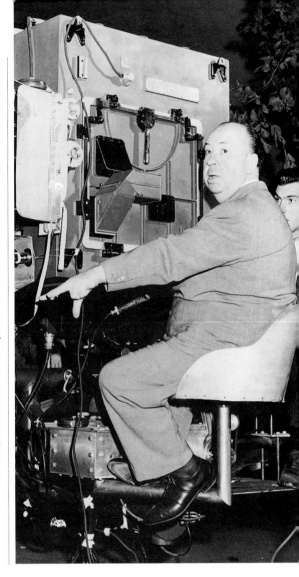

HOBBS, SIR JOHN
1882-1963
British cricketer

Throughout the 1920s Jack Hobbs was known simply as 'The Master' and although he remarkably made 98 of his 197 hundreds after the age of 40, he had probably been still better in the 'golden age' of cricket immediately before World War I. He made his first-class debut in 1905 and retired in 1934. He was the first professional sportsman to be knighted, not only for his great skills but also for standards of behavior that would put modern stars to shame. **DS**.

HOCKNEY, DAVID
1937-
British painter

Hockney is easily the best-known British artist of his generation, often for his flamboyant personality and the homo-erotic content of his work. After a brilliant prize-winning student career at the Royal College of Art, London, Hockney became identified as a Pop artist through the jokey mood of his early work. Paintings in the later 1960s, often portraits in a smoothly painted technique, timeless and almost classical in style (*Mr and Mrs Clark and Percy*, 1970-71), were more substantial. California, Hockney's home for much of his life, has provided many subjects especially the swimming-pool paintings. Hockney's fame has brought many opportunities for diversifying, including series of etched illustrations and opera stage sets for Glyndebourne and the Metropolitan Opera, New York. Work in the 1980s and 1990s has included photomontage and prints produced on a photocopier or sent by fax. **AR**.

ABOVE: *Innovative British painter, David Hockney.*

HODGKIN, ALAN LLOYD
1914-
HUXLEY, ANDREW FIELDING
1917-
British physiologists

Their original collaborative experiments in Cambridge after the end of World War II contributed significantly to the understanding of how nerve impulses are transmitted. They showed that during the conduction of nerve impulse, the potential inside the nerve cell membrane, the action potential, changed rapidly (and reversed). With Bernhard Katz, Hodgkin developed the 'voltage clamp method' to measure electrical currents across the nerve membrane. Their findings were pursued by John ECCLES with whom they shared the 1963 Nobel Prize for Physiology. **ES**.

HODGKIN, DOROTHY
1910-
British crystallographer

Dorothy, the daughter of archaeologist John Winter Crowfoot, was born in Cairo and spent much of her childhood in the Middle East. After obtaining a chemistry degree at Oxford, she studied x-ray diffraction at Cambridge under J D BERNAL. In 1937 she married Africa historian Thomas Hodgkin (cousin of physiologist Alan HODGKIN) by whom she had three children. During the war Dorothy determined the structure of penicillin, and by 1956 had, aided by several of her graduate students, unravelled the structure of vitamin B-12. In the 1960s Hodgkin made a decisive contribution to uncovering the structure of insulin: while she identified its unique three-dimensional structure, Frederick SANGER

determined the exact order of amino acids in the molecule. In 1964 Hodgkin was the sole recipient of the Nobel Prize for Chemistry and decided to use the money to create a scholarship and to further the cause of peace and relief of famine. Many of her peers felt that this accolade ought to have been hers earlier. The next year she was awarded the Order of Merit becoming the only woman to be so honored since Florence Nightingale. **MB**.

HOFF, TED [MARCIAN E]
1937-
American inventor

After a decade in academe, Hoff went to work at Intel, where most computer designers were producing mainframe computers rather than domestic instruments. Hoff, however, ignored conventional practice, and packed all the central processing unit (CPU) functions into a single chip, using other chips to drive the first chip and to provide a memory. In January 1971 the first microprocessor chip, the '4004' was launched, enabling Intel to sell a single microprocessor for thousands of different applications. **PT**.

HOFFMAN, ABBIE
1936-
American radical

An opponent of American involvement in Vietnam, Hoffman came to prominence in 1967 when he led an antiwar march on Washington which culminated in an attempt to levitate the Pentagon. In the same year, he founded the Youth International Party, or 'Yippies', and in the summer of 1968 took part in violent protests at the Democratic National Convention in Chicago, joining forces with such disparate groups as Students for a Democratic Society and the Black Panthers. Hoffman was found guilty of conspiracy to riot by a Federal Grand Jury in 1969, but in November 1972 the verdict was overturned. **JP**.

HOFFMAN, DUSTIN
1937-
American actor

Talent and brains have made Hoffman a superstar, bold in his choice of roles and willing to take chances. Having worked in odd jobs and small parts, he was chosen by Mike Nichols to play a young man floundering in a cynical world in *The Graduate* (1967). He proved he wasn't a flash in the pan in *Midnight Cowboy* (1969). Essentially a character actor, he went on to choose challenging, rather than charismatic roles in his films. In *Little Big Man* (1970) he aged on screen from adolescence to over 100 years old. Deftly playing a father who learns to nurture his son in *Kramer vs Kramer* (1979), he at last earned a much-deserved Academy Award for Best Actor. Then came his sensitive,

ABOVE: Hoffman in Midnight Cowboy.

subtle performance as a man pretending to be a woman in the extraordinarily popular *Tootsie* (1982). Hoffman won his second Best Actor Academy Award for *Rain Man* (1988). **DC.**

HOGAN, BEN [WILLIAM BENJAMIN]
1912-
American golfer

For much of the 1940s and 1950s this Texan was the state of the art in professional golf. He won 62 tournaments, including nine 'Majors.' Four times he captured the US Open title, one of only four golfers who can make that claim. **MD.**

HOLDEN, WILLIAM
1918-1981
American actor

Holden became a star in his very first picture, *Golden Boy*, in 1939. He went on to play nice guys in a series of films, but in 1949 *The Dark Past*, in which he played a psychotic killer, was the first of several pictures which broke his mold, and he followed this by the role of creepy gigolo in *Sunset Boulevard* (1950) with Gloria SWANSON, then the unheroic hero of *Stalag 17* (1953) which won him an Academy Award. A low-key, understated actor, he appeared in the box-office successes *S.O.B.* and *The Earthling* in the year of his death. **DC.**

HOLIDAY, BILLIE
1915-1959
American jazz singer

The first and arguably the greatest, Holiday possessed unique timing and the ability to turn even a hackneyed lyric into an emotional experience. Born Eleanora Fagan, she had a disrupted childhood and was entertaining in Harlem clubs in her early teens. She made her first record with Benny GOODMAN in 1933, and had a sensational success with her stage debut in 1935. Early records included 'They Can't Take That Away From Me' with Count BASIE (1937) and 'Any Old Time' with Artie Shaw (1938), while 'Lover Man' (1944) is perhaps her most famous. By the time she toured Europe in 1954 and appeared at the first Newport Jazz Festival, her voice had coarsened and her range narrowed; she died from a kidney infection after years of alcohol and drug abuse. Jazz fans, and fellow singers recognized her greatness instantly, but she did not attract a wide public during her lifetime. **JH.**

HOLLY, BUDDY
1936-1959
American pop singer and guitarist

Several unsuccessful early recordings eventually bore fruit for Holly with the 1957 hit 'That'll Be The Day'. By the end of the year 'Oh Boy' and 'Peggy Sue' gave Holly three top ten hits on both sides of the Atlantic, and his distinctive vocal style and pioneering guitar technique (he was one of the first to use the new Fender solid bodied guitar) made 1958 an even bigger year, with tours to Europe and Australia amid further chart success. Ballads and orchestral arrangements followed a split with backing group, The Crickets, and thus it was that they escaped the 1959 plane crash that cut short Holly's blossoming career. **DC.**

HOLM, ELEANOR
1913-
American swimmer

The multitalented and controversial Eleanor Holm rose and fell with great fanfare in the 1930s. In 1932 she won Olympic gold in the 100-meter backstroke. Four years later she was expelled from the Olympic team after drinking champagne and breaking training rules on the ship to Germany. She later gained fame as a singer. **MD.**

HOLST, GUSTAV
1874-1936
British composer

Unlike his contemporary and close friend VAUGHAN WILLIAMS, Holst never enjoyed much popularity in his day. His was an unusual character; rather than conform to public taste he strove to produce the music

ABOVE: Celebrated jazz singer Billie Holiday – 'Lady Day'.

within him no matter how unpopular. One can see this insular quality in his best known work *The Planets* where there is a strong feeling of mysticism. After its performance in 1919 at a Philharmonic concert conducted by Sir Adrian BOULT, Holst received the recognition he deserved and consequently many festivals commissioned new works from him, including his three operas. **DK.**

HOMMA, MASAHARU, LIEUTENANT-GENERAL
1887-1946
Japanese soldier

Commander of the Japanese 14th Army in 1941, Homma led the invasion of the Philippines. He lacked battle experience and his campaign dragged after December 1941; Homma was sacked but remained as a figurehead. He was therefore held responsible for the infamous Bataan Death March in which 16,000 prisoners died. **JPi.**

HOOVER, HERBERT
1874-1964
American politician and president

Hoover rose from day laborer in a California mine, through mining engineering to become the 31st President of the United States. He achieved world fame with his World War I Commission for Relief in Belgium which sent five million tons of food and clothing to German-occupied Flanders. In 1917 he was made the US Food Administrator with sweeping powers which were extended eventually to a famished Europe. After the Armistice Hoover started a European Children's Fund, giving free meals to eight million children and supervised relief in the Great Russian Famine. He was HARDING's Secretary of Commerce and in 1929 succeeded him in the presidency. He was overwhelmed by the Wall Street crash and was defeated by ROOSEVELT in 1932. **JC.**

HOOVER, J EDGAR
1895-1972
American lawyer and FBI director

For over 50 years, from 1924 until his death, Hoover was synonymous with the FBI (Federal Bureau of Investigation). His national security policing concentrated on making the FBI the most efficient law-enforcement administration ever. From the gangsters of Prohibition, to the Communist subversives of the 1950s to the Civil Rights protesters of the 1960s, Hoover's officers surveyed every aspect of national security. **JC**.

ABOVE: J Edgar Hoover, director of the FBI.

HOPE, BOB
1903-
American actor and entertainer

Hope first won national attention as a radio comedian. In 1939 he starred in the comedy/mystery movie *The Cat and the Canary* with Paulette Goddard, and his popularity became firmly established when he teamed up with Bing CROSBY and Dorothy Lamour in a series of 'Road' pictures, beginning with *The Road to Singapore* (1940). Hope's many television and cabaret appearances, as well as his concerts to entertain the troops have ensured lasting popularity. **DC**.

HOPKINS, SIR FREDERICK GOWLAND
1861-1947
British biochemist

As the first professor of biochemistry at Cambridge, for 20 years Hopkins headed a world-famous school of biochemistry and made an immeasureable contribution to biochemical thought and experimental biochemistry. With S W Cole, he isolated the amino acid tryptophan and thus introduced the concept of the essential amino acid as dietary components for many animals. His study of the diets of rats in 1912 led him to conclude that certain 'accessory factors', later termed vitamins, were indispensable for normal growth and maintenance. This research earned him the Nobel Prize in 1929 which he shared with Christian Eijkmann. His other contributions included demonstrating (with Walter Fletcher) that contracting muscles accumulated lactic acid. This led others to develop the detailed knowledge that exists of muscle metabolism today. Oxidizing enzymes became his next interest which led to the discovery of the tripeptide glutathione, important as a hydrogen carrier in the intracellular use of oxygen. His impressive achievements have ensured that Hopkins is regarded as the father of modern biochemistry. **ES**.

HOPKINS, HARRY LLOYD
1890-1946
American diplomat

As ROOSEVELT's trusted aide in the New Deal, Hopkins was called 'the world's greatest spender.' Heading the Federal Emergency Relief Administration, he dispensed between $8 billion and $10 billion in five years and helped organize the Works Progress Administration (WPA) relieving the poverty of over 15 million Americans. He became Secretary of Commerce in 1938 and when illness forced his resignation from the Cabinet Roosevelt sent him overseas on important diplomatic missions, culminating in his appointment to head Lend-Lease and to 'the little War Cabinet.' He was at Roosevelt's side at every major wartime conference, except for Potsdam, which he arranged during a mission to STALIN. **JC**.

HOPKINS, MICHAEL
1935-
British architect

Michael Hopkins has evolved his erstwhile partner Norman FOSTER's Hi-Tech to newly expressive and humane levels. His Schlumberger Cambridge Research Centre (completed 1985) and Mound Stand, Lord's Cricket Ground, London (completed 1990), both utilize teflon-coated fiberglass fabric stretched by trusses and cables to create roofs of much-imitated tent-like shapes. **AR**.

HOPPER, EDWARD
1882-1967
American painter

Hopper studied at the Chase School of Art, New York under the urban realist Robert Henri. Between 1913 and 1923 he worked as a commercial illustrator, but continued producing watercolors and, from 1915, etchings, realistic portrayals of everyday America. During the 1920s, in an intellectual climate which favored American Scene painters such as BENTON, his oil paintings were widely acclaimed. He himself felt these artists caricatured America and his own aim was simply 'the most exact transcriptions possible' of nature. His urban scenes, either deserted, as in *Early Sunday Morning* (1930), or containing single or a very few non-communicating figures, as in *Nighthawks* (1942), are haunting evocations of the boredom and loneliness of city life. **ER**.

HOPPER, GRACE, REAR ADMIRAL
1907-1992
American mathematician and programmer

Two of the fundamentals of computing were devised by Grace Hopper: the first high-level language COBOL and the term for a flaw in a computer program – the 'bug'. She joined the United States Navy as a Lieutenant in 1943, and worked on the Mark 1, the first large digital computer. Folklore reports that she found a moth trapped in a relay, causing the system to crash. From then on all faults in programs were attributed to 'bugs'. Hopper's invention of COBOL allowed programmers the freedom to program computers in a way which was more like a natural language than the mathematical notation used by machine code. In recognition of this she was awarded the US National Medal of Technology in 1991. She rose through the ranks in the Navy and left in 1986 as its oldest member of staff. She then joined DEC as a consultant, a post which she held until her death in 1992. **SR**.

ABOVE: Comic actor Bob Hope (center) in The Road to Morocco.

HORNBY, FRANK
1863-1936
British inventor and manufacturer

Hornby was one of Britain's great toy manufacturers, producing miniature trains, Meccano, and Dinky toys in his Liverpool factory. Aware that children loved constructing toys themselves, he patented a design for strips of metal with regular perforations which could be bolted together, and Meccano was born. **PT.**

HORNEY, KAREN
1885-1952
American psychoanalyst

Horney was born in Germany and worked as a psychoanalyst in the United States. Unlike FREUD she stressed the importance of environmental influences; like Freud she wrote well, and her books were accessible to the general public. She also introduced some early feminist notions into psychoanalytical literature. **MBe.**

HOROWITZ, VLADIMIR
1904-1989
Russian-American pianist

Horowitz began his concert career at the relatively late age of 20 but was quick to make an impact on London six years later, with a sensational performance of Rachmaninov's D minor concerto. His career was interrupted by three years of illness, starting in 1936, from which he recovered and resumed his former position and prestige. He won many awards for his artistry, including the Royal Philharmonic Society Gold Medal (1972). **DK.**

HOUNSFIELD, SIR GODFREY
1919-
British engineer

Hounsfield shared the 1979 Nobel Prize for Physiology and Medicine (with the American Allan Cormack) for his development of the EMI computerized X-ray scanner. This enables greatly refined images to be obtained all over the body and has revolutionized diagnostic radiology. Computerized Transverse Axial Tomography, as it is called, is now in general use in hospitals throughout the world. **PW.**

HOUSMAN, A[LFRED] E[DWARD]
1859-1936
British poet and scholar

A brilliant classical scholar, Housman published work on Propertius, Ovid, and Juvenal, and a definitive edition of the works of Manilius. He paid for the publication of *A Shropshire Lad* (1896), the collection of poems for which he is most famous which idealize the English countryside. The *Collected Poems* was published in 1939 after his death. **AM.**

HOWARD, LESLIE
1890-1943
British actor

Sensitive, intellectual, with a dreamy air, Howard was America's ideal as the model Englishman, establishing himself on both sides of the Atlantic after the film *Outward Bound* (1930). Beginning with Norma Shearer in *A Free Soul* (1931) he played opposite many of Hollywood's most glamorous leading ladies. *The Scarlet Pimpernel* (1935) brought him a Picturegoer Gold Medal, and he went on to play his most famous role, that of Ashley Wilkes in *Gone With the Wind*, only under pressure, preferring *Intermezzo* (1939) with Ingrid BERGMAN. Howard went on making fine films until his plane was shot down during World War II. **DC.**

HOWARD, TREVOR
1916-1988
British actor

Howard was not one of the glamorous stars, yet his performance opposite Celia Johnson in *Brief Encounter* (1946) placed him in the first rank of movie actors. He quickly established a reputation as a polished actor of understated style, playing the other man in the sparkling romance *The Passionate Friends* (1948) and helping make *The Third Man* (1949) a superb spy picture. From the mid-1950s he was seen in American as well as British films, and *Sons and Lovers* (1960) brought him an Academy Award nomination. His last film, *White Mischief*, appeared in 1988, the year of his death. **DC.**

HOWE, GORDIE [GORDON]
1928-
Canadian hockey player

When Gordie Howe retired from the National Hockey League at the astonishing age of 52, he was already a legendary figure. Few athletes in any sport will ever equal his sustained brilliance. Howe played in a record 2186 games over 32 years, 26 in the NHL and six in the World Hockey Association, and no one has matched his total of 975 goals. Six times he won the Hart Memorial Trophy, awarded to the Year's Most Valuable Player of the NHL. **MD.**

HOYLE, SIR FRED
1915-
British astronomer

Hoyle showed that the chemical elements are built up from hydrogen and helium by nuclear reactions inside massive stars, and then distributed into space when the stars explode. Hoyle was an instigator of the Steady State Theory, not now widely supported, which denied that the Universe began in a Big Bang. Hoyle has written science fiction, including *The Black Cloud*, and in recent years has made controversial

ABOVE: L Ron Hubbard, founder of the Church of Scientology.

suggestions about the origin of life in space, reminiscent of his science-fiction novels. **IR.**

HUBBARD, L. RON
1911-1986
American cult theologian and writer

Possibly the first and certainly among the most notorious of the twentieth-century cult founders, Hubbard published his *Dianetics* and in 1954 opened his first Scientologist Church in Los Angeles. Dianetics, a form of psychotherapy, boasted the ability to release people from themselves, from events in their past and even their pre-existence by sharing their fears with a counsellor. With aggressive recruiting and financial techniques, Scientology spread internationally, but so too did the scandals. It is hard to disagree with the notorious denouncement of Hubbard in 1984 by a judge as a 'pathological liar gripped by avarice and a lust for power.' **ML.**

HUBBLE, EDWIN
1889-1953
American astronomer

Hubble was a law student who turned to astronomy. He joined Mount Wilson Observatory in California where he worked with the newly opened 100-inch (2.5-meter) reflector and, in the 1920s, made two of the most significant discoveries in astronomy. First he proved that so-called spiral nebulae were actually separate galaxies beyond our Milky Way from the faintness of stars they contained. Then, in 1929, he announced his shattering conclusion that the universe is expanding like a balloon being inflated. The galaxies are moving apart at speeds that increase with distance; this is known as Hubble's law and is the foundation of modern cosmology. **IR.**

H

HUGHES, CHARLES EVANS
1862-1948
American lawyer

A reforming governor of New York, Hughes ran unsuccessfully against President WILSON in 1916. He was made Secretary of State by HARDING, when he refused to trade with the USSR. He was chairman of the Washington Conference on arms limitation and led the unsuccessful fight to bring the US into the League of Nations. HOOVER made him Chief Justice of the United States in 1930. His tenure is memorable for his civil rights' decisions and his liberal interpretation of the commerce clause of the Constitution, although he declared some of ROOSEVELT's reforming statutes unlawful, thus leading to a 'packing' of the Supreme Court in 1937. **JC**.

HUGHES, HOWARD
1905-1976
American entrepreneur and eccentric

After taking over the family company, Hughes Tools, Hughes moved to Hollywood in 1926. He financed some notable movies and introduced several stars, including Jean HARLOW and Jane Russell, to film. From 1948 he was usually in control of RKO Pictures. Meanwhile he founded Hughes Aircraft in 1935 and, flying an aircraft of his own design and construction, reached a world-record of 352 mph. From 1942 he was obsessed with the design of a wooden 750-passenger flying boat, but this barely got into the air. From 1950 his refusal to appear in public led to all kinds of speculation. **JW**.

RIGHT:
American
entrepreneur
Howard
Hughes.

HUGHES, TED [EDWARD]
1930-
British poet

Born in Yorkshire, Hughes went to Cambridge, where he met Sylvia PLATH whom he married in 1956. *Hawk in the Rain* (1957), his first collection of poems, was well received. His emphasis on the beautiful savagery of predatory wildlife in particular in his various volumes has much to do with the projection of selected human traits on to animal life and nature. Dark, occult imagery, and vague mythologizing, powerful and energetic but rather empty, characterize his work, which also reflects a fear of the feminine. He has also written for children. Poet Laureate since 1984, his prolific output includes some very poor occasional verses. **AM**.

HULL, BOBBY
1939-
Canadian hockey player

Bobby Hull was a prolific scorer throughout his 23-year career, and his son Brett is currently a dominant scoring force in the NHL. Hull joined the Chicago Black Hawks in 1957 and immediately impressed fans with his vicious slapshots, which traveled well over 100 miles per hour. In his 16 seasons in the NHL and seven in the World Hockey Association, Hull scored 913 goals and 895 assists. This 1808-point total is third on the all-time list. A left wing with blond hair and blazing speed, he was known as 'The Golden Jet.' **MD**.

HULL, CORDELL
1871-1955
American politician

Hull was prominent in income and inheritance tax legislation in the House of Representatives, of which he was a member from 1907 until 1931 when he was elected to the Senate. He was quickly selected by ROOSEVELT as his Secretary of State, having to deal with the rise of Japanese militarism. On December 7, 1941, he struck the first counter-blow on the Day of Infamy. He ordered the Japanese negotiators out of his office calling them 'scoundrels and pissants' for covering up for 'the infamous falsehoods and distortions' contained in the last Note from Tokyo. He resigned the secretaryship in 1944 and was awarded the 1945 Nobel Peace Prize for his contribution to setting up the United Nations' Organization. **JC**.

HUSSEIN, KING
1935-
Jordanian monarch

Educated in England, Hussein succeeded to the Hashemite throne of Jordan in 1952 following the assassination of his grandfather, King Abdullah, and the abdication of his father through ill health. In 1967 Hussein went to war with Israel, losing control of the West Bank and Jerusalem, and as Jordan became a refuge for Palestinian exiles he fought for power against the Palestine Liberation Organization (1970). Even so, by the early 1990s Jordan's population was predominantly Palestinian, leaving Hussein vulnerable and obliging him to maintain precarious neutrality in the Gulf War (1991), which alienated Western powers. Surprisingly, he survived the crisis. **JP**.

ABOVE: Iraqi President Saddam Hussein (left) with Egyptian counterpart, President Mubarak.

HUSSEIN, SADDAM
1937-
Iraqi politician

Saddam Hussein emerged as a key figure after the Ba'athist coup of 1968 and became Iraqi President in 1979. He consolidated his dictatorship with a war against the Ayatollah KHOMEINI's fundamentalist Iran. This eight-year struggle was followed by the invasion of Kuwait in 1990 and the American-led United Nation's counterattack to liberate it. The most dangerous maverick in Middle East politics especially since surviving the Gulf War, he continues to have the upper hand in the psychological war which has followed, particularly over dismantling his chemical arsenal. **JC**.

HUSTON, JOHN
1906-1987
American film director

A maverick film-maker who was noted for his association with Humphrey BOGART on such films as *The Maltese Falcon* (1941), *The Treasure of the Sierra Madre* (1948), and *The African Queen* (1952), and for some of the screen's most intelligent literary adaptations, like *Moby Dick* (1956), and *The Dead*

(1987). Huston was intrigued by over-reachers, who pursue their dreams to the point of obsession: even when they fail, he is impressed by the grandeur of their aspiration. He, too, was a character, a former actor who was the subject of numerous film biographies and books. His direction helped win Oscars not only for himself (*Sierra Madre*) but his family: his father Walter HUSTON (*Sierra Madre*) and his daughter Anjelica (*Prizzi's Honor*). **NS**.

HUSTON, WALTER
1884-1950
American actor and director

This distinguished American character actor came to films when he was already in

ABOVE: Film director John Huston.

his mid-40s. Even in small roles he could outshine the greatest stars, and in *The Treasure of the Sierra Madre* (1948) he was awarded a long-overdue Oscar. He ended his career playing roguish and eccentric characters. **DC**.

HUTTON, SIR LEONARD
1916-1990
British cricketer

Len Hutton began a successful international career before World War II and, despite a wartime injury that left his left arm shorter and much weaker than his right, he recovered to carry a series of poor England teams until his retirement in 1955. His innings of 364 against Australia in 1938 was for many years the highest individual test score. He was the first professional to captain England and never lost a series as captain. **DS**.

HUXLEY, ALDOUS
1894-1963
British writer

Plans for a scientific career were changed by a serious eye problem at Eton which left Huxley nearly blind. Instead he read English at Oxford, became a journalist, and wrote volumes of poetry and short stories before his first novel, *Crome Yellow* (1921). *Brave New World* (1932), a prophecy of the

ABOVE: Aldous Huxley, author of Brave New World.

science-dominated future was a major success. He went to California and continued to publish novels, including the utopian *Island* (1962), and other works. His interest in philosophy, mysticism, and altered states of consciousness grew in the California climate, and his hallucinogenic drug experiences are described in *The Doors of Perception* (1954) and *Heaven and Hell* (1956). **AM**.

ABOVE: *Christopher Isherwood (left) with fellow playwright Tennessee Williams.*

IBARRURI, Dolores 'La Pasionaria'
1895-1989
Spanish revolutionary

During the Spanish Civil War (1936-39), Ibarruri became a symbol of the Republican cause through her radio broadcasts and newspaper articles. Born in the Basque region, she discovered Marxism through the activities of her husband, a miner frequently imprisoned for his views. In 1930 she was elected to the Central Committee of the Spanish Communist Party and, six years later, became a Parliamentary Deputy for the Popular Front. During the Civil War she appeared at Republican rallies, where her oratory was renowned, but in 1939 she fled to Moscow. Following the death of General FRANCO, she eventually returned to Spain. **JP**.

IBN SA'UD, Abdul 'Aziz, King
c1880-1953
Saudi Arabian monarch

In 1902 Ibn Sa'ud seized Riyadh as a base for his revival of the Wahabis, a puritanical Muslim sect. During World War I, although he refused to join the Arab Revolt, he did throw off Turkish rule, being recognized in 1921 as Sultan of Nejd. Five years later he overthrew the King of Hejaz and seized Mecca, acquiring both wealth and religious prestige. In 1932 he declared himself King of Saudi Arabia, maintaining his position through the huge influx of American money from oil concessions, which he distributed principally to members of his own family to ensure their loyalty. **JP**.

IONESCO, Eugene
1912-
French playwright

Born in Romania, Ionesco was educated in Bucharest and Paris, and has lived in France for most of his life. He published only poetry and criticism until writing his first play in 1948. This was *La Cantatrice chauve (The Bald Prima Donna)*, first seen in 1950 and translated into English in 1958. One of the leading exponents of the 'Theater of the Absurd,' along with BECKETT, CAMUS, GENET and others, Ionesco played an important role in broadening the horizons of postwar theater. While he has written extensively for the theater and other media, only *The Lesson* (1951) and *Rhinoceros* (1959) are well known. **AM**.

ISAACS, Alick
1921-1967
British virologist

Isaacs studied medicine in his native city of Glasgow. After completing a research fellowship in Sheffield, he moved to the Walter and Eliza Hall Institute in Melbourne – possibly the world's leading center for immunology research – where he worked under

ABOVE: *American composer, Charles Ives.*

Macfarlane BURNET. His particular interest was the interaction of viruses and specifically why a cell infected with one virus is resistant to infection by another. In 1957 Isaacs identified the 'interfering' chemical as interferon. At first interferon was hailed as a wonder drug; then it became a wonder drug in search of a disease. He returned to Britain in 1961, becoming head of Virology at the National Institute for Medical Research, and was elected a Fellow of the Royal Society in 1966. Since his death, interferon has found its therapeutic role, for example in eradicating persistent infection in people with hepatitis B, who are at risk of developing liver cancer if the virus remains in their bodies. **CR**.

ISHERWOOD, Christopher
1904-1986
British-American writer

Associate of W H AUDEN, Isherwood is best known for his Berlin novels and sketches reflecting life on the eve of Hitler's rise to power, an experience dramatized in the musical *Cabaret*, and for the later novelistic accounts of his own homosexuality. He became an American citizen in 1946. **CW**.

ISSIGONIS, Alex[ander], Sir
1906-1988
British car designer

Issigonis introduced the modern small car to the world. He is especially remembered for the design of the Mini, undoubtedly one of the most significant cars ever built, on a par with the Model T Ford and Volkswagen Beetle. Born in Turkey to a German mother and Greek father, he nearly failed his degree at Battersea Polytechnic before starting his apprenticeship in the motor industry. He joined Jack Daniels, head of engineering at Morris, in 1936, Daniels later commenting that Issigonis was the 'inspiration to his perspiration'. In simple terms, Issigonis was the man behind the Morris Minor, working on the 1100 project before the stunning inspiration of the front-wheel drive, transverse-engined, Mini in 1959. He was working on a new project before it was quashed by Lord Stokes. The project? A replacement for the Mini, complete with opening rear hatch. Had he been permitted, Issigonis would have also been father of the hatchback - many years before the term had been conceived! His significance to the modern era of motoring cannot be underestimated, the car he designed remaining in production 33 years after it went into production. **NF**.

IVES, Charles
1874-1954
American composer

Ives has been hailed as a 'pioneer' of modern music. It is true that many of his experimental ideas can be seen in the works of later composers, especially his ideas on polytonality and atonality. Whether he will be regarded as an inventor of compositional techniques or as a composer in his own right remains to be decided. **DK**.

JACKLIN, TONY
1944-
British golfer

Tony Jacklin won the British Open in 1969 and the US Open the following year. He was the first Briton in the modern era to have such success and provided the inspiration for a whole generation of younger British and European players. After his own period as a top competitor was over, his leadership as non-playing captain was instrumental in the European team's success in the Ryder Cups of 1985 and 1987. **DS**.

JACKSON, GLENDA
1936-
British actress and politician

Cool strength and keen intelligence are the hallmarks of Jackson's performances. After joining the Royal Shakespeare Company in 1964 she turned in an unforgettable performance in Peter Brook's *Marat/Sade*, and, turning to films, she went on to win the New York Film Critics Award and Academy Award for Best Actress for *Women In Love* (1970). Critics also praised her work in *Sunday Bloody Sunday* (1971) and *Stevie* (1978). Tall and angular, she has a range to rival the best in the business. The embodiment of her brittle genius was her *tour de force* performance in the title role of the BBC production *Elizabeth R*. In 1992 she abandoned her first career for politics. **DC**.

JACKSON, MICHAEL
1958-
American pop singer

After eight years with the Jackson Five the young Michael had limited success with his first two solo efforts. However, both the next two albums missed the top forty altogether, and it wasn't until the 1979 album *Off The Wall* that he found his feet. *Thriller* in 1982 made No 1 on both sides of the Atlantic and showed he had made the transition

ABOVE: the hugely popular star, Michael Jackson.

from precocious teenager to mature recording artist once and for all. The 1987 album *Bad* enjoyed similar success, and he was soon established as one of the most successful entertainers ever, grossing over $100 million in 1990 alone. **DC**.

JAMES, C L R
1901-1992
Trinidadian writer

James was a novelist, historian, and cricket enthusiast who pioneered the idea of an autonomous black movement. Interned at the height of McCarthyism, in the 1970s he lectured extensively, and was Professor of the Humanities at Columbia University. His most outstanding work is *The Black Jacobins*. **CW**.

JANÁČEK, LEOS
1854-1928
Czech composer

Janáček was the epitome of a late developer. He was in his forties before he composed his first major work of any significance, in his sixties before he reached public acclaim with a performance of his opera *Jenufa* in Prague, and in his seventies before one could say his works had settled into any particular style. He had a deep affection for his native country and for Moravian folk music. Of particular importance is the influence of the Czech language. He studied the rhythms and intonations of Moravian speech and used their characteristics to create the unique melodic style apparent in his operas. **DK**.

JANNINGS, EMIL
1886-1950
German actor

Before the talkies, Jannings had a peerless international reputation, playing a series of historical characters on screen including Henry VIII in *Ann Boleyn* (1920). Voted Best Actor for *The Way of All Flesh* (1927) and *The Last Command* (1928), he made Nazi propaganda films from 1933, but with World War II his career came to an end. **DC**.

JANSKY, KARL
1905-1950
American radio engineer

Working at the Bell Telephone laboratories in the early 1930s, Jansky investigated the sources of interference encountered by long-distance short-wave radio signals. He identified one type of 'static' as directional, with a persistent hissing sound. Jansky deduced that the source of this static was the center of the Milky Way – the faint signals reached a maximum every 24 hours less four minutes – sidereal, rather than solar time. Jansky published his results in 1932, but they were largely ignored until after World War II when they became the basis for the science of radio astronomy. **PW**.

JEKYLL, GERTRUDE
1843-1932
British landscape gardener

Gertrude Jekyll was a horticultural designer, journalist, and author who, between 1890 and 1910, designed some of the finest English gardens of the period – such as Hestercombe in Somerset (1904). She worked closely with the architect Edwin LUTYENS, and through her writing helped to popularize the planting of old-fashioned varieties of flowers. **RJ**.

ABOVE: British actress and politician, Glenda Jackson (left).

JELLICOE, JOHN, 1ST EARL, ADMIRAL
1859-1935
British sailor

After rising through the ranks of the Royal Navy, Jellicoe received his first major command in 1900, when he led an Allied expedition to relieve Peking during the Boxer Rebellion. A member of the committee which produced designs for the *Dreadnought*, he served as Second Sea Lord (1912-14) before gaining command of the Grand Fleet. His actions at Jutland (1916) were criticized at the time, but it is now accepted that they were effective, forcing the German Fleet to remain in port for the rest of the war. Jellicoe was Governor-General of New Zealand from 1920 to 1924. **JPi.**

JINNAH, MUHAMMAD ALI
1876-1948
Pakistani statesman

An urbane lawyer and frequenter of Western social circles, Jinnah founded the Muslim state of Pakistan after breaking with his long-standing Hindu allies in the Congress Party. At first he tried to win a measure of autonomy for his co-religionists (30 per cent of the population) in a future independent India, but he fell out with GANDHI and from 1940 was committed to a separate Pakistan. It was born in an orgy of bloodshed, as whole populations were exchanged, and Jinnah's health collapsed under the strain. **JC.**

ABOVE: *Muhammad Ali Jinnah, Pakistani statesman.*

JOBS, STEVE
1955-
American computer designer

'Apple is going to be the most important computer company in the world, far more important than IBM'. Famed for his vision, Jobs left school in Los Altos and dropped out of college in 1972 to design video games for Atari. But when he and Steve WOZNIAK teamed up in Jobs' parents' garage to build the Apple II he became the marketing man, and was responsible for purchasing. His reputation for being self-centred is reenforced by arguments over who should be the boss at Apple. However, it was this nature which led to the success of the Macintosh (at the expense of the Lisa), and which caused him to sell his shares at a low price in order to set up NeXT Inc, making powerful and stylish home computers. **SR.**

JOFFRE, JOSEPH, MARSHAL
1852-1931
French soldier

Appointed chief of the French General Staff in 1911, Joffre became French Commander in Chief in 1914 and, by his actions on the Marne (September 1914), saved Paris. His strategy thereafter led to heavy casualties and in December 1916 he was replaced. **JPi.**

JOHN XXIII, POPE
1881-1963
Italian Pontiff

Angelo Guiseppe Roncali was 77 when he became Pope, but his brief papacy was one of the most energetic in the Catholic Church's history. Often referred to as 'Good Pope John', he called the Second Vatican Council in 1959 to discuss the modernization of the Church. His encyclical *Pacem in Terris* (Peace on Earth) urged peaceful coexistance and was welcomed by both American and Soviet governments. It is interesting to speculate if he would have chosen the rigid interpretation of his successor PAUL VI on birth control. **ML.**

JOHN, ELTON [REGINALD DWIGHT]
1947-
British pop singer and pianist

John was working with blues artist Long John Baldry in the late 1960s when he decided to go solo. A newspaper ad put him in touch with Bernie Taupin, who became his lyricist partner, and his eponymous debut album reached the US top five. For the next six years he toured with his newly-formed band, breaking off to record such classics as 'Goodbye Yellow Brick Road' and 'Captain Fantastic and the Dirt Brown Cowboy', but after two collapses in 1975 he retired briefly from touring. A handful of less successful albums was followed in 1983 with *Too Low For Zero*, and this and subsequent albums have established him as a consistent and enduring artist. **DC.**

JOHN PAUL I, POPE
1912-1978
Italian Pontiff

Born into a poor family of nine children, Albino Luciano's election as Pope came as a surprise. His brief 30-day pontificate brought a joyful humility to the Papacy, but his sudden death fueled sensational speculation of reactionary plots against the liberal Pope who threatened to reverse the Church's teaching on birth control. **ML.**

JOHN PAUL II
1920-
Polish Pontiff

The election of Karol Wojtyla as the first non-Italian Pope since 1523 stunned the world and he has since become the most traveled Pontiff of all time. He studied poetry and philosophy at Kracòw University in 1938 and fought in the student Polish resistance. He also studied theology in secret and was ordained as a priest in 1946. Before being appointed Cardinal in 1967 he could boast two PhDs in theology and a wealth of pastoral, diplomatic, and political experience in the constant conflict between Poland's Catholics and its Communist government. The early popularity which greeted his appointment as Pope, peaked after his survival of an assassination attempt in 1981 but has since waned as he has stuck rigidly to orthodox Catholic teaching, alienating many liberal critics. His total con-

ABOVE: *Frequently outrageous pop star, Elton John.*

demnation of artificial birth control, refusal to countenance married clergy or the question of women priests suggests that, like Pope PAUL VI, the impact of his sincere appeals for a worldwide respect of the dignity of man – a subject which after his personal experience of Nazi and Communist oppression he is well-qualified to talk about – will be lessened. Historically, however, the election of the Polish Pope will be seen as a major contributory nail in the coffin of the eastern bloc, given his active sponsorship of the Polish Solidarity movement and continual attacks against the Kremlin. **ML**.

JOHNS, JASPER
1930-
American painter and sculptor

In 1954 Johns began his famous *Target, Flag,* and *Numbers* paintings. Choosing subjects with no aesthetic associations, his two-dimensional paintings of two-dimensional objects precluded artistic artifice. In the late 1950s he also made sculptures of everyday objects, such as his 1960 hand-painted bronze cast of two ale cans. Johns sense of pictorial irony and choice of subject matter paved the way for Pop Art. His fusion of object and art in a way which makes questions of reality meaningless, forcing his works to be viewed as objects in themselves, prefigured Conceptual Art. His later paintings often incorporated real objects, challenging artistic preconceptions through visual contradictions. **ER**.

JOHNSON, CLARENCE
1910-1990
American aircraft engineer

An aeronautical engineering graduate of the University of Michigan, Johnson joined Lockheed Aircraft in 1933 and later became head of the advanced development projects group which produced many aircraft, from the wartime prototype P-80 Shooting Star, to the secret U-2 and SR-71 cold-war spy-planes in the famous Burbank 'Skunk Works'. He retired in 1975. **MT**.

JOHNSON, MAGIC [EARVIN]
1959-
American basketball player

Magic Johnson led Michigan State to the 1979 NCAA title, sparked the Los Angeles Lakers to five NBA crowns, and starred on the US gold medal-winning 'Dream Team' in 1992. At 6'9", Johnson seemed too big to be a point guard, but his quickness and brilliant passing made him one of the greatest ever to play that position. He is the NBA all-time assist leader and a three-time MVP. Johnson sat out the 1991-92 season after disclosing that he had the HIV virus, but he returned briefly in dramatic fashion to win the all-star game MVP and to play in the 1992 Olympics. **MD**.

JOHNSON, JACK [JOHN ARTHUR]
1878-1946
American boxer

It was the day after Christmas in 1908 when Jack Johnson knocked out Tommy Burns to become the first black man ever to win the world heavyweight title. Despite considerable public protest, Johnson defended his crown nine times, before losing in 26 grueling rounds to Jess Willard in 1915. Johnson continued to fight in exhibition matches almost until his death in 1946. **MD**.

JOHNSON, LYNDON BAINES
1908-1973
American politician and president

The quicksand of Vietnam dragged down a President who had a reputation as a tough and astute Democratic Senate Whip. KENNEDY's Vice-President, Johnson tried to continue the 'New Frontier' reform program after his sudden acquisition of the presidency in 1963. He fought through substantial reforms, among them the Civil Rights Act. Re-elected in 1964 with a large majority, he scrapped his election manifesto on foreign policy, pouring large numbers of troops into Vietnam. As the protests grew stronger, Johnson did not seek re-election in 1968. **JC**.

JOHNSON, PHILIP
1906-
American architect

Johnson turned to architecture late having read a journal article on modern architecture. As a curator at the New York Museum of Modern Art he co-wrote *The International Style* (1932) and the first book on MIES VAN DER ROHE (1947). Johnson's designs from the late 1940s onward, such as his own house at New Canaan, Connecticut (1949), reflect MIES's influence, especially of the Edith Farnsworth house, in their not-so-simple steel- or concrete-framed glass forms. The Theater of the Dance, Lincoln Center, New York (1960s), although of steel, glass, and concrete construction, shows clear classical allusions in drum-like form and steel columns, which prefigure Johnson's so-called 'conversion' to postmodernism since the late 1970s. His direct use of historical allusion in recent work such as the AT&T building, New York, can be seen as a natural evolution of the inherent romanticism of his modernist designs. **AR**.

BELOW: Lyndon Johnson (center), US President in the 1960s.

JOHNSON, Virginia
1925-
American sexologist

Graduate of Missouri University, Virginia Eshelman embarked in 1954 on a career at Washington University that would make her and her research collaborator, William Masters, household names. The first of their many books *Human Sexual Response* (1966) continues to be a bestseller and the sex therapy techniques they pioneered at St Louis in 1959 have shaped modern views on the treatment of sexual problems. **MB**.

JOLIOT-CURIE, Irène
1897-1956
French physicist

Irène was destined to inherit her mother, Marie CURIE's mantle. In 1918 she became her assistant at the Radium Institute where she met and married co-worker Frédéric Joliot. The couple were pipped to the post

ABOVE: *Champion amateur golfer, Bobby Jones.*

in the discovery of the neutron by James CHADWICK and the positron by Carl ANDERSON in 1932. But Nobel glory would be theirs in 1935, for their discovery of artificial radiation, the result of bombarding aluminum with alpha particles causing it to emit positrons. Irène's solo work on radio-elements produced by the irradiation of uranium with neutrons was of crucial importance to Lise MEITNER's and Otto HAHN's discovery of nuclear fission. Irène found that the bombardment products behaved chemically like thorium but did not identify them as radium. Meanwhile Frédéric established the chain reaction. Realizing the implications of his work, he and Irène stopped publishing papers in 1939. They recorded the principle of nuclear reactors and deposited their paper at the Academy of Sciences where it remained secret till 1949. After the war Irène succeeded her mother as Director of the Radium Institute and with Frédéric was appointed scientific commissioner of the Atomic Energy Commission. Irène devoted herself to pacifist causes until her death from leukemia. **MB**.

JOLSON, Al
1886-1950
Russian-American singer and songwriter

Inventor of the catchphrase 'You ain't heard nothing yet!', Jolson is remembered above all for his performance of songs such as 'Mammy' and GERSHWIN's 'Swanee', delivered blacked up and kneeling. He starred in the first talking movie, *The Jazz Singer* (1927), but his own style was vaudeville. **JH**.

JONES, Robert Trent
1906-
American golf-course architect

Golfers who have marveled at the beauty and challenge of many of the world's top courses owe their gratitude and frustration to Robert Trent Jones. He helped to design more than 400 golf courses, and won numerous awards for his work. He also wrote widely about the game. **MD**.

JONES, Bobby [Robert Tyre]
1902-1971
American golfer

Jones spent the 1920s earning three academic degrees (including Literature at Harvard and Law at Emory) while establishing himself as the greatest golfer of his time. He played his entire career as an amateur, winning 13 major titles. In 1930 he won the US and British Opens, as well as the US and British Amateurs, the only acknowledged 'grand slam' in the history of the sport. He then retired from tournament play at the age of 28, established a successful law practice in Atlanta and founded the Masters Tournament, now one of the crown jewels of the pro tour. **MD**.

JOPLIN, Janis
1943-1970
American blues singer

Starting out as a folk and country singer, it was with Big Brother and the Holding Company that Joplin acquired both the raucous and powerful delivery and the lifestyle of drink, drugs, and sexual excess for which she is equally famed. After the 1968 *Cheap Thrills* album she began to spend more time on the road touring and living up to her public image, where trouble with authority was matched only by the electrifying and unpredictable brilliance of many of her performances. The album *Pearl*, considered to be her finest, was released after her death from a heroin overdose in 1970. **DC**.

JOPLIN, Scott
1868-1917
American ragtime musician

Born in Texas, Joplin won lasting fame as a pianist and the composer of short works he called rags, a precursor of jazz. The first black rag composer to write down his music, Joplin's attempts at larger-scale works failed, but he will always be remembered for his 'Maple Leaf Rag' and 'The Entertainer.' **DK**.

JORDAN, Michael
1963-
American basketball player

Including the 1991-92 season, Jordan has led the NBA in scoring for six straight years. A three-time league MVP, he has sparked the Chicago Bulls to the last two NBA titles. He was a member of the team that won an NCAA crown for the University of North Carolina in 1982, and of the teams that won Olympic gold medals for the US in 1984 and 1992. He is generally acknowledged as the best player in the world today. **MD**.

JOYCE, James
1882-1941
Irish writer and poet

Although his output was comparatively small, his experimental writing made Joyce one of the major figures of literary modernism; no-one has had more influence on the development of the modern novel. He was born in Dublin, educated at Jesuit schools and studied modern languages at University College, Dublin, from which he graduated in 1902 and went to Paris for a year. He returned on his mother's death, and met Nora Barnacle, with whom he lived from 1904 and married in 1931; they left for Trieste where he taught English, and subsequently for Zurich in 1915. *Chamber Music* (1907), a collection of poems, was his first published work, followed by the short stories of *Dubliners* in 1914, admired by EZRA POUND, who published the autobiographical *A Portrait of the Artist as a Young Man* in

JUAN CARLOS, KING
1938-
Spanish monarch

In 1975 Juan Carlos assumed the Spanish throne, having been specifically chosen by General FRANCO as his successor. Any right-wing hopes that the new king would continue Franco's policies were dashed as Juan Carlos pursued democracy, holding free elections in 1977 and surviving an attempted military coup in 1981. **JP**.

JUNG, CARL GUSTAV
1875-1961
Swiss psychologist

Jung was an early disciple of FREUD, but separated from him over the issue of infantile sexuality. He argued that, in addition to the 'personal unconscious', there was a 'collective unconscious', the latter relating to racial experiences and collective beliefs, built up over generations. He also stressed the importance of religion and symbolism. His influence was considerable, and led to the development of the school of Analytical Psychology. Jung emphasized the importance of the quality of parent-child relationships, and the effect of parental disorder on children. He was one of the first psychiatrists to attempt a psychological understanding of schizophrenia. **MBe**.

*ABOVE: The electrifying blues singer Janis Joplin.
RIGHT: Carl Jung, the influential Swiss psychologist.*

serial form in *The Egoist* before it appeared as a whole in 1916. His one play, *Exiles* (1918), was never a success. The brilliant *Ulysses*, his greatest novel, and one of the finest of the century was published in Paris in 1922, where the family had settled. Banned for obscenity, it was hailed by ELIOT and POUND among others as a masterpiece, though Virginia WOOLF was famously disdainful. *Finnegans Wake*, his last and most difficult work, written in spite of terrible eye problems which left him almost blind, was published complete in 1939. **AM**.

JOYCE, WILLIAM ['LORD HAW-HAW']
1906-1946
Irish-American fascist

Born in New York to an Irish father, Joyce arrived in England in 1923, immediately joining the fascists. He was appointed Propaganda Officer in Oswald Mosley's British Union of Fascists in the 1937, but in 1939 he fled to Berlin, traveling on a British passport. Throughout World War II he broadcast radio propaganda to Britain, gaining the nickname 'Lord Haw-Haw' for his distinctive drawling voice. Captured in May 1945, he was tried as a traitor, his entry 'British by birth' on his passport application in 1939 bringing him within British jurisdiction. Found guilty, he was hanged in July 1946. **JP**.

KADAR, JANOS
1912-1982
Hungarian politician

Imprisoned and tortured under the Rakosi regime of the 1950s Kádár seemed to back NAGY during the 1956 uprising and then, as Party leader, swung behind the Red Army's suppression of the revolt. Generally execrated for his duplicity, he still won a great measure of acceptance for the relatively liberal policies – releasing some political prisoners and decentralizing and strengthening the economy – he pursued thereafter. When Hungary emerged from Communism only a few months after his death it was as the most viable economy in the former Eastern bloc, and possibly the most stable state. **JC**.

ABOVE: Franz Kafka, the Czech writer.

KAFKA, FRANZ
1883-1924
Czech novelist

Kafka is one of the most outstanding writers of the century, though if he had been granted his request, his three unfinished novels would have been destroyed after his death. His friend Max Brod published *The Trial* (1925), *The Castle* (1926), and *Amerika* (1926) against his wishes, bringing Kafka worldwide posthumous renown. A writer whose work possesses an oneiric quality, both disturbing and comic, his central themes are those of the alienated self, guilt-ridden and inexplicably humiliated, in a nightmarish – apparently totalitarian – world of powerful institutions and bewildering bureaucracy. For all its almost allegorical symbolism, it is nevertheless a world precisely conveyed, overwhelmingly ordinary and recognizable, wherein lies its fascination and sinister nature. Kafka's characteristic mode is that of irony, derived, perhaps, from the Jewish traditions from which he came, and a skepticism informed by Freud. His most successful work is arguably to be found in his short stories, such as *Metamorphosis* (1912), the story of Gregor Samsa, who awakes one morning transformed into a giant insect, embodying the self he has, in a form of bad faith, always been. **CW**.

KAHN, LOUIS
1901-1974
American architect

Although Kahn's major work spans only 15 years, it has become a legend of modern architecture. Such monumental buildings as the Yale University Art Gallery (1951-53), the Richards Medical Research Building for the University of Pennsylvania (1957-65), and the Salk Institute in La Jolla, California (1959-65), were a powerful influence on a whole generation of architects. Kahn's architecture is a compelling mixture of the progressive use of technology with a poetic structuring of space and form. Kahn's cryptic theories are extraordinarily influential, particularly his concept of the division of architectural space into 'served and servant spaces' and the idea of the architect's task as 'searching for what a material wants to be.' **DE**.

KAISER, HENRY
1882-1967
American industrialist

Kaiser moved from the gravel business into construction by buying, on borrowed money, a highway-building company. He steadily enlarged it into a main contractor for such big projects as the Hoover and Grand Coulee dams, and entered other industries. His greatest hour came in World War II, when he introduced assembly-line methods at seven shipyards to achieve astonishingly short construction times. The 'Liberty Ship,' a standardized general-purpose freighter, was built by the hundreds using these methods and was a key element in the Allied victory. In 1942 he introduced a health plan for shipyard workers, and this was copied elsewhere in the USA. **JW**.

KANDINSKY, WASSILY
1866-1944
Russian painter

Originally trained in law, Kandinsky began painting in 1896, and studied in Munich. Influenced by Fauvism he began simplifying his images until line and color, rather than subject matter, became the vehicle with which he expressed emotion. In 1911 he founded Der Blaue Reiter, a group of artists sharing his belief that 'the creative spirit is conceived in matter', and in 1912 published *Concerning The Spiritual In Art*, which set out his theories of a non-objective art based on harmonies of color and form which could appeal directly to the senses, like music. He finally rid his work of any representational connotations around 1913, working only with color and basic geometric shapes which he endowed with different spiritual values, yellow, for instance, being sensual and earthly. In 1914 he returned to Russia and after the 1917 Revolution worked in the Visual Arts Section of the Peoples' Commissariat for Enlightenment. Disillusioned by

official attitudes to art, he left for Germany in 1921, securing a teaching post at the Bauhaus through which his ideas were widely disseminated. On its closure by the Nazis in 1933 he moved to France, developing a highly personal pictorial language of invented amoeba-like symbols. Perhaps the first truly abstract artist, his legacy to later twentieth-century artists was immense. **ER**.

KANTOROVICH, LEONID
1912-
Russian economist

Kantorovich, trained as a mathematician, suggested ways of making the planned economy, especially the Soviet planned economy, work better. Considered reckless by his colleagues but winning a Nobel Prize in 1975, he developed linear programing and maintained that in a planned economy decentralized decision-making was impossible without rational prices. **JW**.

KAPITZA, PETER LEONIDOVITCH
1894-1984
Russian physicist

Kapitza left Russia in 1921 having lost his wife and children in the famine following the Revolution. He worked with Ernest RUTHERFORD at the Cavendish laboratory in Cambridge, specializing in magnetism. He discovered that helium displayed superfluidity – having no resistance to flow – when cooled to $-271°C$. In 1934 he returned to Russia but was not allowed to leave. Although he did valuable research which helped Soviet industry, he suffered house arrest because of his opposition to nuclear weapons development. He gained the 1979 Nobel Prize for Physics. In his later years he worked on satellite research and nuclear fission. **DD**.

KARAJAN, HERBERT VON
1908-1989
Austrian conductor

Karajan received high acclaim after his performance of *Tristan and Isolde* at the Berlin State Opera in 1937. He earned many prestigious appointments including lifelong concert director of the Vienna Symphony Orchestra (1949) and principal conductor of the Berlin Philharmonic Orchestra (1955). He is remembered as an outstanding exponent of Beethoven, Brahms, Wagner, Verdi, Bruckner, and Richard Strauss. **DK**.

KARAN, DONNA
1948-
American designer

Born in Forest Hills, NY, Karan's father was a haberdasher and her mother a model and saleswoman. During her second year at Parsons School of Design, Karan worked during the summer as a sketcher at Anne Klein, one of the most popular sportswear (daywear and separates) designers in the United States. Karan returned to Anne Klein after graduating, left to join the company Addenda, later returning to Klein in 1968. The following year she was appointed Anne Klein's successor and, following Klein's death in 1974, she and Louis dell'Olio became codesigners for the company. In 1984 Karan left to design under her own name, producing a couture range and the DKNY (Donna Karan New York) line. The most enduring of her designs to date has been the 'Body', a leotard-like garment that forms the basis of each outfit. **MC**.

KARLOFF, BORIS [WILLIAM HENRY PRATT]
1887-1969
British actor

An actor of sensitivity and skill, Karloff was rarely given a chance to appear in movies other than horror films. Invariably a villain, he was first cast as Frankenstein's monster in 1931 and became a star, remaining firmly identified with this role although he played it only three times. **DC**.

BELOW: *Boris Karloff as Frankenstein's monster.*

ABOVE: *Canadian photographer Yousuf Karsh.*

KARSH, YOUSUF
1908-
Canadian photographer

This great photographer of eminent people was born in Armenia, settled in Canada in 1924, and opened his own studio in Ottawa in 1932. His intention was 'to photograph the great in heart, in mind and in spirit, whether they be famous or humble'. His subjects – statesmen, artists, and healers – appear cherished by a finely graduated light. **IJ**.

KAUNDA, KENNETH
1924-
Zambian statesman

As the first president of independent Zambia (1964-91), Kaunda misjudged economic developments, saddling his country with the world's highest foreign debt per head. He backed freedom movements in Zimbabwe, Mozambique, and South Africa through the African National Congress, yet made Zambia a one-party state in 1973. **JC**.

KAYE, DANNY [DAVID DANIEL KAMINSKI]
1913-1987
American actor

A likeable comedian whose trademark was the fast patter song, Kaye left the New York stage to make his first film, *Up in Arms*, in 1944. An instant star, he followed with similar films such as *Hans Christian Anderson* (1952), a sentimental hit, and *White Christmas* (1954) opposite Bing CROSBY. **DC**.

ABOVE: *Elia Kazan, film director and author.*

KAZAN, ELIA
1909-
American film director

Turkish-born Kazan established a reputation as one of Broadway's finest theater directors in the 1930s and 1940s. He began working on films, winning an academy award for *Gentleman's Agreement* in 1947. He co-founded the Actor's Studio with Lee Strasberg in 1947 and is credited with the introduction of 'Method' acting, particularly through his association with Marlon BRANDO in *A Streetcar Named Desire* (1951), *Viva Zapata* (1952); and *On the Waterfront* (1954). *East of Eden* (1955) is widely regarded as his finest film and until the 1960s he was a superb interpreter of the works of playwrights such as Arthur MILLER and Tennessee WILLIAMS. **NS.**

KEATON, BUSTER [JOSEPH FRANCIS]
1895-1966
American actor and director

Abandoning vaudeville to make films with Fatty ARBUCKLE, Keaton soon went on to make his own film shorts in which his lithe acrobatic body expressed whirlwind activity as he was caught in the clutches of machinery or dogged by confusion and misunderstanding. In *One Week* (1920) he was a bridegroom trying to assemble a portable home. *Sherlock Junior* (1924), about a projectionist lost between reality and dreams on the screen and *Our Hospitality* (1923) are among his greatest full-length films. His troubles began when he gave up his own studio. Devoured by studio bosses, he lost control of his movies just as the talkies arrived. **DC.**

KELLOGG, WILL
1860-1951
American businessman and philantropist

Kellogg's brother, Dr JH Kellogg, devised a method of making cornflakes palatable for the patients of the Battle Creek sanatorium that he directed. They set up a company for marketing this product and in 1906 Will bought out his brother to form the Kellogg Toasted Corn Flakes Company. Despite competition from Post Toasties (Post had been a patient at the sanatorium and obviously had not wasted his time there), he developed new cereal products, then acquired other food businesses and by 1930 was rich enough to found the WK Kellogg Foundation, a charitable trust with a major interest in child welfare. **JW.**

KELLY, GENE
1912-
American actor, dancer, choreographer, and film director

Kelly was taught by his mother in her Pittsburg dance school before entering Pittsburg University, where he directed the annual graduation 'Cap and Gown' shows. In 1939 he went to New York and appeared in musicals, but his big break came in 1949 in *Pal Joey*, which was almost immediately recreated for the screen in Hollywood. The most ambitious of his dance productions were for the movies: *An American in Paris* (1952) and *Invitation to the Dance* (1956), in which he duetted with the animated cartoon character 'Jerry the Mouse'. Less well known, however, is his ballet *Pas de Deux* (1960) for the Paris Opera Ballet, set to music by George GERSHWIN. **MC.**

KELLY, GRACE
1928-1982
American actress

Kelly's first major role was opposite Gary COOPER in *High Noon* (1952). HITCHCOCK used her to perfection in his thrillers, and she proved herself a serious actress winning an Academy Award for Best Actress in *The Country Girl* (1954). She retired from movies after *High Society* (1956), marrying Prince Rainier III of Monaco at the height of her career. **DC.**

ABOVE: *Petra Kelly, former leader of the German Green Party.*

ABOVE: *Actress turned princess, Grace Kelly, with Cary Grant.*

ABOVE: *Buster Keaton and friend in* Our Hospitality.

KELLY, Petra
1947-1992
German environmentalist

A fervent pacifist, feminist, and anti-nuclear power protestor, Kelly was leader of the West German Green Party (1980-83), before being elected to the Bundestag in 1983 and 1987. As such, she was the first Green Party representative in any European parliament, symbolizing a growing public awareness of environmental issues. **JP**.

KENDREW, Sir John
1917-
British biochemist
PERUTZ, Max
1914-
Austrian-British biochemist

Perutz set up the Molecular Biology Laboratory in Cambridge in 1946 where he was joined shortly afterwards by John Kendrew. Both worked on determining the 3D crystalline structure of proteins using X-Ray diffraction techniques. Kendrew analysed the muscle protein myoglobin and Perutz the blood protein haemoglobin that he had first studied for his PhD. By 1959, despite seven years of little progress, Perutz had shown haemoglobin to be a four-chain tetrahedral structure with four haem groups near the molecule's surface and Kendrew was able to pinpoint the position of most of the atoms in myoglobin, the first protein to reveal its three-dimensional structure. They received the Nobel Prize for Chemistry in 1962. **ES**.

KENNAN, George
1904-
American diplomat

Kennan was 'X,' the anonymous author of an article on how to 'read' Russian moves in the great chess game of the Cold War, which had a profound influence on ACHESON and DULLES' diplomacy. He became Acheson's chief adviser in 1949, moving to Moscow in 1952 as Ambassador, until being declared persona non grata. He moved from recommending containment of the Soviet Union to advocating American disengagement from Europe, which he suggested should be demilitarized. **JC**.

KENNEDY, John Fitzgerald
1917-1963
American politician and president

The first Roman Catholic and youngest man to be elected President of the USA, Kennedy produced a vision of social justice and freedom which inspired his countrymen. From a wealthy and politically ambitious family, once in office Kennedy surrounded himself with an articulate, glittering governing elite whose idealist rhetoric barely disguised a forceful foreign policy. Keen to stand up to the Soviet menace, he was embarrassed by the 1961 failure of the CIA-backed Bay of Pigs insurrection in Cuba. His tough reaction to the erection of the Berlin Wall, however, and the Cuban Missile crisis of 1962 which brought the world to the brink of war, earned him international respect and improved East-West relations. In domestic affairs his reform program promised federal help for education, healthcare for the elderly, and an ambitious space program, but achievements were limited. His assassination in Dallas shocked the world and rumors still abound over who shot him and why. Despite posthumous revelations about his private life, Kennedy's glamorous image has been largely untarnished in the years since his death. **JC**.

KENNEDY, Robert Francis
1925-1968
American politician

Bobby Kennedy is considered by some as the lost great hope of liberal America, who might have proved even more effective than his brother. He masterminded JFK's 1960 election campaign and earlier, as chief counsel of the Senate Select Committee on Improper Activities in the Labor or Management Field, he led the investigation and prosecution of James R Hoffa, the Teamsters' leader, for corruption, leading to the latter's imprisonment. In JFK's administration Bobby promoted Civil Rights and fought the racketeers. He remained as Attorney-General under JOHNSON, was elected senator in 1964, and assassinated while celebrating his victory in the vital California primary for the Democratic presidential nomination. **JC**.

BELOW: John Fitzgerald Kennedy, the US President tragically assassinated in 1963.

KENYATTA, JOMO [KAMAN NGENGI]
1898-1978
Kenyan statesman

Kenyatta rose from the secretaryship of the Kikuyu tribal association and presidency of the Kenya African Union. He was jailed in 1952 on perjured evidence that he had masterminded the Mau Mau terror campaign. Ten years later the British had no alternative but to call on him to ease Kenya's passage to independence, a transition he managed so successfully that it became a model African state. After independence Kenyatta did not make the mistake of basing his power solely on his own tribe, and he achieved a rare harmony with the white settlers who had branded him as a 'terrorist.' **JC**.

KENYON, KATHLEEN, DAME
1906-1978
British archaeologist

Kathleen Kenyon was a specialist in the archaeology of Palestine, and directed the British School of Archaeology, Jerusalem, between 1951 and 1963. Her most famous series of excavations were those at Jericho (1952-58), where she uncovered a walled town dating to about 7000 BC – which made it perhaps the earliest town in human history. Kenyon also excavated in Jerusalem and contributed much to Biblical archaeology. In 1962 she returned to England to become Principal of St Hugh's College, Oxford. **RJ**.

KENZO, [KENZO TAKADA]
1940-
Japanese designer

Born in Kyoto, Kenzo studied art in Japan and, after graduating, designed patterns for a Tokyo magazine. In 1964 he moved to Paris where, working as a freelance designer, he sold collections to Louis Feraud. 'Jungle Jap', Kenzo's own shop, was opened in 1970 and, by 1972 he was well known for his ability at mixing prints and colors and as a leading ready-to-wear knitwear designer. **MC**.

KERENSKI, ALEXANDER
1881-1970
Russian politician

The last leader of pre-Communist Russia, Kerenski joined the first Provisional Government after the February 1917 Revolution as Minister of Justice. On May 5 he was appointed first War Minister and then Prime Minister with the task of restoring the Army's morale and returning to the offensive. In this role he was overtaken by the Bolshevik Revolution. His attempts to overthrow the revolution failed and he fled to western Europe and in 1940 settled in the United States, where he taught at Columbia University, New York. **JC**.

KERN, JEROME
1885-1945
American composer

Writer of over 1000 songs, many for films, Kern was instrumental in establishing the American musical as the successor to the European operetta, with songs forming an integral part of the action. His most influential work, *Showboat*, set sail in 1927 and contained many hit songs, such as 'Ol' Man River.' **DK**.

KEROUAC, JACK
1922-1969
American novelist

More than anyone else, Kerouac's writings epitomized the philosophy of the Beat Generation. Born in Lowell, Massachusetts, he spent time at sea and traveling around the USA before publishing his first novel, *The Town and the City* (1950), which was followed by his most famous work, the semi-autobiographical *On the Road* in 1957. A tale of a trio of traveling Beats, thinly disguised portraits of himself, Allen GINSBERG and Neil Cassady, with its loose style and lack of structure it captured perfectly the mood of the time. *The Dharma Bums* (1958), *The Subterraneans* (1958), and *Big Sur* (1962) among his other works provided more of the same. **AM**.

KERR, DEBORAH
1921-
British actress

Kerr, a dancer with the Sadlers' Wells company, made her film debut with *Major Barbara* (1940), and went on to star in a series of British films in which she was properly prim. *Black Narcissus* (1946) produced critical acclaim, and she was recognized as a serious actress, winning the New York Film Critics' Award. But she continued to play the long-suffering heroine in films such as *The Hucksters* (1947) and *Quo Vadis* (1951). Her most popular role was probably as tutor to the King of Siam's children in *The King and I* (1956) in which she played opposite Yul Brynner. **DC**.

KERTÉSZ, ANDRÉ
1894-1984
American photographer

Kertész worked as a clerk in the Budapest Stock Exchange, photographing only as an amateur in Budapest and then later in the Austro-Hungarian army. He moved to Paris in 1925 and after working as a freelance began, in 1928, to work for Lucien Vogel's new magazine, *Vu*. The work of those early years is summed up in his picture book of 1934, *Paris vu par André Kertész*. More than any other artist, he established a French style of photography, at once humorous and philosophical. His conversation and bitter-sweet manner was ousted only in the 1960s by the more melancholic and romantic photography of Robert Frank, for instance. **IJ**.

KESSELRING, ALBRECHT, FIELD MARSHAL
1885-1960
German soldier and airman

As an artilleryman, Kesselring saw service in World War I before becoming a staff officer. By 1935 he had transferred to the Luftwaffe, specializing in tactical air support. He commanded Luftwaffe units in Poland (1939), France, and the Battle of Britain (1940), and the invasion of Russia (1941), before moving to Sicily where he organized the air assaults on Malta. Between 1943 and March 1945 he conducted a masterful defensive campaign in Italy, but spent the last months of the war as Commander-in-Chief West. Sentenced to life imprisonment for war crimes, he was released in 1952. **JPi**.

ABOVE: John Maynard Keynes, British economist.

KEYNES, JOHN MAYNARD, 1ST BARON
1883-1946
British economist

A Cambridge lecturer from 1908, Keynes took a special interest in monetary problems. As a member of the British delegation at the 1919 Peace Conference, he saw the danger of forcing the defeated powers to pay reparations and wrote the biting *The Economic Consequences of the Peace*. This had little effect, but its lessons were remembered by the victorious powers in 1945. His 1936 *General Theory of Employment, Interest, and Money* revolutionized both economic theory and policy-making. In it he ascribed the damaging fluctuations of the business cycle to a difference between savings and investment, with both determined not by interest rates (as classical theory held) but by the current feelings of savers and industrialists. At times of depression the government should increase its own spending programs, he advised. Such investment had a 'multiplier effect' on incomes and employment because the money spent was repeatedly re-used for other transactions. The beneficiaries would consume more (encouraging businessmen to invest) and save more (providing the funds for that investment). Thus in depressions governments should intervene rather than hope for falling prices, wages, and employment to maintain equilibrium. Conversely, reduced government spending or higher taxation could control booms. **JW**.

KHAN JAHANGIR
1963-
Pakistani squash racquets player

Jahangir Khan was squash's top player for most of the 1980s. He was unbeaten in all competitive matches for more than five years beginning in 1981; among his enormous total of title wins was the record tally of 10 successes in the British Open. He announced during the 1992 season that it would be his last. **DS**.

KHOMEINI, RUHOLLAH [RUHOLLAH HENDI], AYATOLLAH
1900-1989
Iranian politician and theologian

The turbulent priest who unseated the Shah, Khomenini confined himself to teaching theology in the holy city of Qom until the beginning of the imperial secularization program led him to take an increasingly radical political stance. He soon became the focal point for unrest and in 1964 was banished to Iraq. In 1978 he was again declared persona non grata and took refuge in France from where he unleashed a propaganda campaign which in 1979 brought down the Shah. The Ayatollah's theocracy became a byword for doctrinaire extremism and the many thousands who died in his prisons were matched by the losses in the long war he waged with Iraq. **JC**.

KHORANA, HAR GHOBIND
1922-
Indian-American biochemist
HOLLEY, ROBERT
1922-
American biochemist
NIREMBERG, MARSHALL WARREN
1927-
American biochemist

The separate work of all three during the sixties led to the cracking of the genetic code and to their sharing the Nobel Prize in 1967. Khorana's role was his synthesis of the 64 nucleotide triplets that comprise the code. He is also known for having synthesized the first artificial gene. Holley discovered a molecule now called transfer RNA that carried the information from the DNA to the protein being formed and in 1965 he solved the complete structure of the trans-

fer RNA for alanine. Nirenberg identified the first of the base triplets (uracil UUU) that coded for an amino acid (phenylalanine). Once this was known others were quick to unravel the rest of the code. Their combined achievements was undoubtedly a major step forward in scientists' understanding of how genes function. **ES**.

KHRUSHCHEV, NIKITA
1894-1971
Soviet politician

As Soviet Prime Minister (1958-64) Khrushchev dismantled the Stalinist system which he had survived by becoming clown prince to the tyrant. But similar clowning, as at the United Nations, did not delude foreign statesmen about his propensity for dangerous brinkmanship. His adventurism twice threatened war: in Hungary in 1956, and more seriously in the Cuban missile crisis in 1962. He was the first publicly to confirm the Stalinist Terror and he and his temporary colleague BULGANIN became, in their travels, the embodiment of the new Thaw of peaceful co-existence. He was toppled in 1964 by arch conservatives in the Politburo. **JC**.

KIEFER, ANSELM
1945-
German painter

Born in the Bavarian town of Donaueschingen, Kiefer studied with BEUYS in Düsseldorf. His earth-toned images fuse idiosyncratic materials such as straw, with oil paint. Drawing on German history and Teutonic myth, he creates apocalyptic visions of the past striving for conciliation with present-day Germany. **ER**.

KILLY, JEAN-CLAUDE
1944-
French skier

Born in the ski resort of Val d'Isère, Killy excelled particularly in the 1968 Winter Olympics held at nearby Grenoble where he won all three gold medals in Alpine skiing: downhill, slalom, and giant slalom. He had previously won gold medals at the 1966 World Championships in Chile. After his Olympic triumph he turned professional and now has many business interests in winter sports equipment and related fields. **DS**.

KIM IL SUNG [KIM SONG JU]
1912-
Korean politician

Founder of the Democratic People's Republic of Korea in 1948, Kim Il Sung is the personification of the Cult of Personality. He has ensured that his isolated country remains free of any taint of the capitalism which has transformed South Korea, which he is pledged to unite with, despite the seemingly permanent division caused by the 1950s' war. **JC**.

ABOVE: *Soviet Premier Nikita Khrushchev (left)*.

ABOVE: American blues guitarist, B B King.

membered for his leadership of civil rights protests on behalf of the American Blacks in the late 1950s/early 1960s. His campaign began in 1957, when he organized a protest in Montgomery, Alabama, against the prevailing policy of segregated buses, and when this led to widespread desegregation throughout the South, his reputation spread. In 1960 he led a campaign to allow Black students free access to public libraries and parks; a year later he organized 'freedom rides' to end segregation in interstate travel. By then, his mixture of success and evangelical speech-making had won him a substantial following, not just among Blacks but also among more liberal Whites. He believed fervently in non-violent protest, following the ideas of Mahatma GANDHI, and his campaigns climaxed in a march on Washington in August 1963, attended by over 200,000 people; it was at the end of this that he made his famous speech which began 'I have a dream'. He never achieved such intense support again, but did force fundamental change in US laws concerning civil rights, being awarded the Nobel Peace Prize in 1964. Four years later, he was assassinated in Memphis, Tennessee. **JP**.

BELOW: Martin Luther King, the charismatic civil rights leader.

KING, B B
1925-
American blues guitarist

A vital link between blues and rock, B B King recorded his first material in the early 1950s, mainly big band arrangements featuring his own virtuoso guitar playing. Cited as an influence by 1960s guitarists such as CLAPTON, his music began to reach a wider audience than the mainly black following he had hitherto enjoyed. **DC**.

KING, BILLIE-JEAN
1943-
American tennis player

As a young girl in California, Billie-Jean King worked at odd jobs to save for her first tennis racket; she went on to become one of the top players in the history of the women's game. She won 12 Grand Slam singles titles, including three in 1972, and she won 20 Wimbledon championships, including six in singles play. In 1971 she became the first woman tennis player to make $100,000 in a year. **MD**.

KING, ERNEST, FLEET ADMIRAL
1878-1956
American sailor

When America entered World War II, King was commanding the US Atlantic Fleet, the culmination of a naval career which had en-

compassed every type of warship, including aircraft carriers. He was therefore well suited to the post of Chief of Naval Operations, which he assumed in March 1942. Although he favored an emphasis on the Pacific and disagreed with both Admiral NIMITZ and General MACARTHUR about the conduct of that campaign, he was flexible enough to change his mind when presented with their successes. **JPi**.

KING, (WILLIAM LYON) MACKENZIE
1874-1950
Canadian politician

A university don, King was Minister of Labour in Sir Wilfrid Laurier's Administration in 1909 and became Prime Minister in 1921. He was elected for a third term in 1935 after surviving scandals involving his colleagues. He copied ROOSEVELT in setting up a national commission to tackle unemployment and in his extensive use of public works programs to get men off the dole. He pushed through his conscription for overseas service legislation against strong opposition and collaborated closely with CHURCHILL and Roosevelt in the strategy of World War II. **JC**.

KING, MARTIN LUTHER
1929-68
American civil rights campaigner

By profession a Baptist preacher, King is re-

KINNOCK, NEIL
1942-
British politician

An MP since 1970, Kinnock became chief Opposition spokesman on education in 1979 and party leader in 1983. He set in motion a campaign to make Labour electable, ruthlessly excluding the extreme left-wing. Kinnock staked his political future on the outcome of the 1992 election; he resigned the Labour leadership on his defeat. **JC.**

KIPLING, RUDYARD
1865-1936
British writer

Poet, novelist, and short-story writer, Kipling was born in Bombay and educated in England. Much of his early work such as *Plain Tales from the Hills* (1887), reflects life in India under the British raj, although *Stalky and Co* (1899) owes much to his schooldays in Devon. He worked briefly in England, 1889-92, and settled temporarily near his American wife's family in Vermont where he completed *The Jungle Book* (1894) and its sequel. In 1896 he returned to England where anti-imperialist feeling lessened his popularity and he concentrated largely on children's books in the early years of the century – *Just So Stories* (1902), *Puck of Pook's Hill* (1906), and *Kim* (1901), his picaresque novel of India. He was the first British writer to be awarded the Nobel Prize in 1907. During World War I he produced patriotic work that became increasingly somber in tone after the death of his only son in 1915. **AM.**

KISSINGER, HENRY
1923-
American politician

Kissinger's years as US Secretary of State (1973-77) saw diplomatic relations resumed with China, the end of the Vietnam War, and the start of the SALT (strategic weapons limitation) agreements with Russia. His peripatetic diplomacy, the Pax Americana, was less effective, however, in pacifying the Middle East after the 1973 war and his 'preemptive' strike against Cambodia in 1975 has been widely blamed for leading to the Khmer Rouge coup and resulting holocaust. **JC.**

KLEE, PAUL
1879-1940
Swiss painter

Paul Klee was one of the most inventive and influential of twentieth-century painters. He trained at the Munich Academy of Fine Art (1898-1901) and, after traveling to Italy and Paris, returned there in 1906. He made contact with the Blaue Reiter group of painters in 1911 and exhibited with them in 1912. He made a trip to North Africa with August MACKE in 1914 which invested his work with a new sense of color. After war service in the German army he had an exhibition of 362 works in 1919 which led Walter GROPIUS to invite him to teach painting at the Bauhaus (1921-31). Klee left there in 1931 to teach at the Düsseldorf Academy but Nazi pressure saw him return to Switzerland in 1933. His last years were plagued by ill-health and depression and his work was included in the notorious Nazi exhibition of 'degenerate art' in 1937. Klee was a hugely prolific painter, producing around 8000 works, and, apart from the late paintings, his tone is unusually positive and joyous among twentieth-century artists. It is notable because although he moved frequently from figuration to abstraction, adapting a wide variety of artistic influences to his own uses, it is always clearly his. **AR.**

KLEIN, CALVIN
1942-
American designer

Born in New York, Klein graduated from the Fashion Institute of Technology in 1962 and spent the next five years in New York working for a number of coat and suit manufacturers. In 1968 he started his own business, also specializing in coats and suits. In the mid-1970s he began to attract attention for his daywear and separates and, by the late 1970s his designs were becoming increasingly sophisticated, featuring long, slim lines and broad shoulders in materials such as linens, silks, and wools. In the mid-1970s, Klein launched his 'designer jeans', the publicity for which brought to public attention the teenage model Brooke Shields. While many other designers followed suit with their own less successful 'designer jeans', Calvin Klein's have continued to remain a respected brand. Recently the Klein range has been extended to include underwear for both men and women. **MC.**

KLEIN, CHRISTIAN
1849-1925
German mathematician

A leading popularizer of science and founder of an encyclopaedia of mathematics, Klein greatly influenced the modern conception of geometry with his *Erlangen Programm*, which applied group theory to the generalization and classification of the invariant properties of spaces. He actively encouraged women to enter higher education, and was a leading member of the International Commission of Mathematics Education. **EB.**

ABOVE: American fashion designer, Calvin Klein.

KLEIN, LAWRENCE
1920-
American economist

Klein won a Nobel prize in 1980, his reputation resting mainly on his creation of detailed models of economic activity. These enabled economists to make somewhat better forecasts of gross national product, investment, consumption, international trade, and capital flows. **JW.**

KLEIN, MELANIE
1882-1960
Austrian psychoanalyst

An early disciple of FREUD, Klein was born in Vienna, and moved to Berlin before settling in London. She quickly established herself in the British psychoanalytical world, where she was drawn into conflict with Anna FREUD. She was a pioneer in attempting to analyse children, and her influence in this particular area has been considerable. **MBe.**

KLEIN, YVES
1928-1962
French painter

Klein had no artistic training and continually challenged accepted ideas about art. His bizarrely original works were presented as theatrical events and included his *Anthropometrie* (1960) in which paint-covered nude models were dragged over canvas, *Peintures de Feu* (1962), produced with a blow torch, and his controversial *Void* (1958), an empty gallery painted white. **ER.**

KLEIST, EWALD VON, FIELD MARSHAL
1881-1945
German soldier

A top Panzer commander throughout World War II, Kleist commanded the Panzer arm that crossed the Meuse at Sedan in 1940 with such ruthless and devastating speed. After service in the Balkans and Russia, Kleist commanded Army Group A in the abortive attack on the Caucasus. Fighting a long retreat in southern Ukraine, Kleist was captured in 1945 and died in jail. **JPi.**

KLERK, F(REDERICK) W(ILLEM) DE
1936-
South African politician

Assuming the presidency of South Africa in 1989, de Klerk, considered a cautious politician, confounded many by initiating reforms that chipped away at the edifice of apartheid, including recognizing the African National Congress and freeing Nelson MANDELA. However de Klerk remains caught between greater calls for majority Black rule and a right-wing Afrikaner backlash, and he and his country face an uncertain future. **JC.**

KLINE, FRANZ
1910-1962
American painter

In 1948, influenced by De KOONING, Kline abandoned his earlier urban landscapes for abstraction. Using black strokes on a white ground, his stark images were suggestive of oriental calligraphy but, unlike calligraphy, the black-and-white forms he created had equal weight in the composition. In the late 1950s he began to introduce vivid color. **ER.**

KOCH, MARITA
1957-
East German track athlete

Marita Koch was one of the greatest ever performers at 200m and 400m. She set or improved world records at both distances a total of 11 times and also participated in highly successful relay teams. She was beaten only once at 400m from 1977 through 1985. She retired in 1987 and there are now suspicions that her performance, like that of many East German athletes, may have been drug-enhanced. **DS.**

KODÁLY, ZOLTAN
1882-1967
Hungarian musicologist and composer

Kodály is perhaps best known as a teacher and musicologist rather than a composer although several of his compositions remain immensely popular in today's concert repertoire, such as his *Háry János* suite. Most of his life was devoted to researching, collecting, and publishing Hungarian folk music, much of which influenced his own compositions. **DK.**

KOESTLER, ARTHUR
1905-1983
British writer

Born in Budapest, he came to England in 1940 and thereafter wrote in English. His finest work of fiction was the anti-totalitarian, anti-Stalinist *Darkness at Noon* (1940). He also wrote numerous works of non-fiction reflecting his wide range of interests, including famously, parapsychology (*The Roots of Coincidence*, 1972). He committed suicide. **AM.**

KOHL, HELMUT
1930-
German politician

Kohl was elected Chancellor in 1982, winning Federal Democratic Party support by making its leader, Hans-Dietrich Genscher, Foreign Minister. Kohl twice won at the polls, in 1983 and 1987, and deployed Nato Cruise and Pershing II missiles in Germany, despite protests. He was saved from political disaster by the revolution in East Germany, paving the way for reunification, which had been the Christian Democrats' rallying cry.

The man who said it was his 'good fortune to be born too late' (to have experience of the Third Reich) was in 1989 called upon to act as godfather to a newly united Germany. **JC.**

KOKOSCHKA, OSCAR
1886-1980
Austrian painter

Kokoschka studied in Vienna, developing a highly individual Expressionist style which he practiced throughout his career, steadfastly unaffected by modern movements. From 1906 he produced portraits, using a nervous wiry line and luminous colors, overlaid by his own personal torments. His paintings were received badly and in 1909 his play *Murderer, Hope of Woman* caused outrage. Severely wounded in World War I, he became eccentrically exhibitionist and began extensive travels through Europe and North Africa, producing restlessly vigorous landscapes and town 'portraits' employing almost birds-eye viewpoints. Condemned as degenerate by the Nazis, from 1937 he lived in London, in 1953 settling in Switzerland. **ER.**

KONEV, IVAN, FLEET MARSHAL
1897-1973
Russian soldier

Having joined the Red Army in 1918, Konev was commander of the 2nd Ukranian Front in 1942 and liberated the Ukraine in 1943. In early 1945 he spearheaded the advance to the Oder River, linking up with US-British forces outside Berlin. After World War II he commanded Soviet Land Forces and in the 1950s, the Warsaw Pact. **JPi.**

KOONING, WILLEM DE
1904-
American painter

Born in Rotterdam, de Kooning emigrated to the USA in 1926. In the 1930s he began producing vaguely biomorphic abstractions and by the mid-1940s had developed a hectic, gestural style with which he became one of the leading exponents of Abstract Expressionism. At the same time he was virtually alone among the avant-garde in continuing the figurative tradition, and he became notorious for his semi-abstract female figures, particularly his *Woman* series of the early 1950s. He used lurid color, grimy black, and expressive slashing brushstrokes to present women variously as erotic symbols, vampires, or fertility goddesses. **ER.**

KORBUT, OLGA
1955-
Russian gymnast

Olga Korbut's influence was largely responsible both for transforming the nature of her sport and for making it into a major spectator attraction. She caught world attention at the Munich Olympics in 1972 when her slight figure, happy personality, and daring new techniques charmed a vast audience. She won two gold medals and one silver but was only seventh in the overall competition. The emphasis her style placed on acrobatic tumbling rather than on balletic grace was of questionable long-term benefit to the sport, however, being criticized particularly for encouraging harsh and often illegal training methods involving very young gymnasts. **DS**.

KORNBERG, ARTHUR
1918-
American biochemist

Born and educated in New York, Kornberg became Professor of microbiology at Washington University in 1953. There Kornberg and his associates, while investigating the synthesis of coenzymes in 1956, discovered DNA polymerase I and how it is replicated in the cell. It catalyses the formation of DNA and now is commonly used to synthesize short DNA molecules in a test tube. It took Kornberg and his colleagues almost 10 years to purify the enzyme to homogeneity and to characterize it in detail. He won the Nobel Prize in 1959 which he shared with Severo Ochoa who discovered RNA polymerase. **ES**.

KORNER, ALEXIS
1928-1984
British blues guitarist

Korner's Blues Incorporated influenced many of rock 'n' roll's finest – among others the ROLLING STONES, Cream, and Fleetwood Mac. While remaining a blues player first and foremost, Korner's nurturing influence meant that many of his protégés went on to achieve greater fame as artists in their own right, while his importance was often overlooked. **DC**.

KOSYGIN, ALEXEI
1904-1980
Soviet politician

Kosygin rose to power under STALIN and his support of KHRUSHCHEV in 1953 earned him the post of Deputy Prime Minister. Elected to full membership of the Politburo in 1960, he succeeded KHRUSHCHEV as Prime Minister in 1964. Overshadowed by BREZHNEV, he remained a member of the ruling troika until his death. **JC**.

KRAUS, KARL
1874-1936
Austrian journalist

Kraus's main influence was as a satirist and cultural critic of Austrian society. At first he wanted to be an actor but turned more successfully to journalism. He wrote extensively and in 1899 founded *Die Fackel* (The

Torch). He was deeply pessimistic about the survival of civilization and railed against the decay of language. He bitterly attacked the Nazis and their simplistic statements. **DSL**.

KREBS, SIR HANS
1900-1981
German-British biochemist

Born and educated in Germany, Krebs gained a medical degree before beginning his distinguished career in biochemical research. He is famous for his outstanding work in elucidating the series of chemical reactions fundamental to the metabolisms of living organisms – a pathway now known as the tricarboxylic acid or Krebs cycle. Interested initially in the way in which the body degrades amino acids, he found that during this process nitrogen atoms are removed (deamination) and are then excreted in the urine as urea. By 1932 he had worked out the basic steps in what is now known as the urea cycle. In 1937 at Sheffield University, he discovered the tricarboxylic acid cycle, by which food is converted to usable energy. The energy from this chemical pathway is the main source of energy for the cell and therefore of the entire organism. His research also showed its vital involvement in the metabolic break-down of fats and amino acids, and in the provision of substrates for the biosynthesis of other compounds. **ES**.

KREISLER, FRITZ
1875-1962
American violinist

Kreisler was admitted to the Vienna Conservatory at the unusually early age of seven and won the gold medal when he was only ten. His reputation and popularity grew to such an extent that Elgar dedicated his violin concerto to him with Kreisler giving its first performance in London (1910). **DK**.

KRUPP, ALFRIED
1907-1967
German industrialist

Briefly imprisoned for war crimes, Alfried Krupp inherited what was left of the Krupp engineering and armament empire after World War II. Exploiting the Cold War atmosphere, he slowly put together the old company. However, he was wary of armaments production, and initially concentrated on building factories in underdeveloped countries. **JW**.

KUBRICK, STANLEY
1928-
American film director

A major postwar director, Kubrick's work has divided the critics. Called pretentious and self-indulgent, he has also been hailed as an artist with a brilliant visual style. *Paths of Glory* (1957) established his reputation, but it was *2001: A Space Odyssey* (1968) that

showed his potential for stunning imagery. His penchant for black comedy and his underlying pessimism showed most clearly in *Dr Strangelove* (1964) and the masterful *A Clockwork Orange* (1971). **NS**.

KUNDERA, MILAN
1929-
Czech novelist

Kundera taught at the Prague Institute for Advanced Cinematographic Studies until the 1968 invasion, settling in Paris in 1975. His novels *The Joke* (1967), *The Book of Laughter and Forgetting* (1979), and *The Unbearable Lightness of Being* (1984) are painful, satirical evocations of the cultural, political and sexual life of postwar Europe. **CW**.

KUROSAWA, AKIRA
1910-
Japanese film director

With *Rashomon* (1951), Kurosawa became the first Japanese director to make a major impact with Western audiences. His subsequent movies such as *The Seven Samurai* (1954), which was remade in Hollywood as *The Magnificent Seven*; his Shakespeare adaptations, *Throne of Blood* (1957), based on *Macbeth*, and *Ran* (1985), based on *King Lear*, share a pulsating visual style which matches the psychological extremes of his characters, and makes for uniquely powerful cinema. **NS**.

ABOVE: *Akira Kurosawa, the Japanese film director.*

LADD, ALAN
1913-1964
American actor

Despite diminutive stature and a total lack of expression Ladd became one of Hollywood's top stars after his first major role as the cold-eyed killer in *This Gun for Hire* (1942). His most successful performance was in *Shane* (1953). An alcoholic by the 1960s, he died apparently from a combination of alcohol and sedatives. **DC.**

LAKER, SIR FREDDIE
1922-
British businessman

A self-confessed wheeler-dealer in the aviation industry, the crash of Laker's business in 1982 yielded donations adding up to a million pounds from a grateful public. His career as the provider of cheap air travel for the masses began after the war and reached its height with the launch of Skytrain in 1977. Victory in the courts against the conglomerates made possible Transatlantic travel at half the prices of the competition. Based now in the Bahamas, Laker has recently tried to revive his operations. **PT.**

LALIQUE, RENÉ
1860-1945
French designer

Trained as a goldsmith and jeweler in Paris, Lalique had his own jewelry workshops by 1885. He had 30 employees by 1890 supplying Cartier, Boucheron, and Vever. He exhibited his lushly naturalistic Art Nouveau designs widely. Lalique continued to design for all media but, after 1906, when he was commissioned to design pressed-glass scent bottles for Coty, glass became his main interest. He took over one glass factory near Paris in 1909 and founded another near Alsace in 1918. Commissions included glass panels and chandeliers for the liner *Normandie*. His style remained naturalistic but geometrically inclined and, especially after the 1925 Exposition des Arts Décoratifs, this Art Deco mode was highly influential. **AR.**

LANCASTER, BURT
1913-
American actor

This athletic leading man's fine physique and radiant smile made him a star of 1950s adventure films. He took control of his own career and became a distinguished actor, never allowing himself to be trapped in typical leading parts. In 1952 he starred in *The Crimson Pirate*, a rousing swashbuckling spoof, and in the same year played an alcoholic husband opposite Shirley Booth in *Come Back Little Sheba*. The beach love scene with Deborah KERR in *From Here to Eternity*, remains one of the most sensual and memorable in film history. He received an Academy Award for Best Actor as the

*RIGHT:
Actor Alan
Ladd.*

crooked evangelist in *Elmer Gantry* (1960), but the 1960s and 1970s were barren years for him. Then in 1980 his touching and subtle portrayal of an aging gambler in *Atlantic City* began a new phase as a character actor, and won him new roles such as the elderly train robber in which he played alongside Kirk DOUGLAS in *Tough Guys* (1986). **DC.**

LAND, EDWIN
1909-1991
American inventor and businessman

While a student at Harvard, Land developed a filter which could polarize light. By reducing sun glare his invention had a wide variety of uses in scientific and optical equipment like cameras and sunglasses. Showing an astute business sense, he set up the Polaroid corporation in 1937 to market his invention. Continuing his research, he produced the Polaroid Land Camera in 1947. Land was a distinguished scientist who found a practical and lucrative outlet for his discoveries. **PT.**

LANDAU, LEV DAVIDOVITCH
1908-68
Russian theoretical physicist

Landau studied in Baku, Leningrad, and Copenhagen before becoming Professor of physics at Kharkov in 1936. He survived arrest as 'an enemy of the state' by the intervention of Peter KAPITSA. His fields were statistical physics, thermodynamics, and quantum mechanics. He was awarded the Nobel Prize for Physics in 1962, just before the road accident that eventually led to his death. **DD.**

LANDIS, KENESAW MOUNTAIN
1866-1944
American judge and baseball commissioner

After gaining fame as a judge, Landis became baseball's first commissioner, restoring public trust in the game by banning for life eight players implicated in the 'Black Sox scandal,' the plot to 'fix' the 1919 World Series. He continued to rule the game with a firm, just hand until his death in 1944. **MD.**

LANDSTEINER, KARL
1868-1943
Austrian pathologist

Landsteiner's doctorate was in general medicine, but immunology and serology became life-long preoccupations. He discovered the major human blood groups and developed the ABO System of blood typing which became routine practise before blood transfusions. He was awarded the Nobel Prize in 1930. **GL.**

LANE, SIR ALLEN
1902-1970
British publisher

Allen Lane served his apprenticeship in publishing at The Bodley Head before founding Penguin Books in 1936. He pioneered paperback books by reprinting novels in soft covers for sixpence. This expanded to cover children's books (Puffin) and non-fiction (Pelican). Penguin Books became highly successful and Allen Lane received a knighthood in 1952. **DSL.**

LANG, FRITZ
1890-1976
American film director

Lang was a major director of the German silent cinema (*Metropolis*, 1926) who fled to Hollywood when the Nazis came to power, and infused popular cinema with his Teutonic brand of fate and pessimism in thrillers like *Fury* (1936), *The Woman in the Window* (1944), and *The Big Heat* (1953), and even in Westerns like *Rancho Notorious* (1952). **NS**

LANGE, DOROTHEA
1895-1965
American photographer

Crippled by polio as a child, Lange trained as a teacher in New York, learning photography from Arnold Genthe and later, in 1917, from Clarence White at Columbia University. She worked as a portrait photographer in San Francisco, before, under the influence of the Depression, beginning to take pictures of the disadvantaged and unemployed. The compassionate documentary work for which she became famous began in California in 1935 with a report on impoverished migrants for the economist Paul Taylor, who later became her husband.

In that year she also began to work for the Resettlement Administration, set up to report on the progress of ROOSEVELT's 'New Deal'. That work continued for five years, during which time she secured 'Migrant Mother', the most sensitive and eloquent documentary portrait ever. **IJ**.

LANGEVIN, PAUL
1872-1946
French physicist

Langevin first postulated that magnetism was due to electrons. In World War I he devised a method of detecting submarines using the reflection of ultrasonic beams. This was developed into SONAR in World War II. He was an outspoken anti-fascist in occupied France, lost his immediate family in the concentration camps, and escaped to Switzerland. **DD**.

LANGLEY, SAMUEL PIERPONT
1834-1906
American mathematician, solar radiation physicist, railroad surveyor and engineer

Langley began experimenting with model airplanes in the 1890s, and demonstrated sustained heavier-than-air flight. A state subsidy led to a full-sized piloted version with petrol engine, but the *Aerodrome* was damaged on take-off. Much criticized, Langley died after a long illness. **MT**.

LANGMUIR, IRVING
1889-1957
American engineer

Langmuir joined the General Electric Company (US) in 1909 and made many scientific contributions of great importance especially in the development of electric light bulbs and radio valves. The former owe their inert gas filling and coiled filaments to his discoveries, and valves their improved performance from his studies of electron emission. He won a Nobel prize in 1932 for his work on the surface behavior of materials in liquid, gaseous, and solid states. **PW**.

LANSBURY, GEORGE
1859-1940
British politician

One of the first Labour politicians to attain national prominence after an apprenticeship in East End London local government, Lansbury became a powerful spokesman for Christian socialism. Elected party leader after MACDONALD's defection, Lansbury's pacifism, although highly respected, was increasingly out of tune with the needs of the times, and he resigned in 1935. **JP**.

LARKIN, PHILIP
1922-1985
British poet

Poet, novelist, and jazz expert, Larkin was born in Coventry and after graduating from Oxford became a librarian, eventually of the Brynmor Jones Library at the University of Hull. His first collection, *The North Ship*, appeared in 1945, followed by two novels, *Jill* (1946) and *A Girl in Winter* (1947). *The Less Deceived*, a collection of poems published in 1955 featured the famous 'Toads', familiar to thousands of schoolchildren. The wry and self-deprecating landscapes of English provincial life, *The Whitsun Weddings* (1964) is probably his best known collection, and he edited the *Oxford Book of Twentieth Century English Verse* (1973). **AM**.

LASKI, HAROLD JOSEPH
1893-1950
British political theorist

A prominent member of the left wing of the Labour Party, of which he was Chairman when it won power in 1945, Laski's radical views won him few friends in McGill and Harvard, and he returned to teach political science at the London School of Economics for most of his life. He regarded democratic socialism as the only defense against fascism and published critical studies of both the British and American postwar democracies. **EB**.

LATTRE DE TASSIGNY, JEAN DE, MARSHAL
1889-1952
French soldier

After fighting the Germans in 1940, de Lattre served the Vichy government until 1942, when he fled to Britain. He returned to North Africa as commander of the Free French First Army which, in 1944-45, he led into southern France, then into Germany. He commanded French forces in Indochina 1950-52. **JPi**.

LAUDA, NIKI
1949-
Austrian racing driver

Lauda won three Formula One World Championships, yet will always be remembered for surviving an horrendous accident at the Nurburgring when his Ferrari crashed and caught fire. Against the odds he returned to racing in a remarkably short time. An astute business man, he has built up his own airline, Lauda Air. Lauda returned to motor sport in 1992 to manage the Ferrari team. **NF**.

LAUGHTON, CHARLES
1899-1962
British actor

Laughton was one of the most popular and brilliant character actors of the 1930s. He played mainly villains at first, such as Captain Bligh in *Mutiny on the Bounty* (1935), and in 1933 he won an Academy Award for Best Actor in the British film *The Private Life of Henry VIII*. He returned to England in 1936 for the title role of *Rembrandt*, and his most outstanding role was as Quasimodo in *The Hunchback of Notre Dame* (1939), in which he was able to communicate the human being behind the grotesque make-up. His last role, as Senator Cooley in *Advise and Consent* (1962), was one of his best. **DC**.

ABOVE: Stan Laurel (left) attracting the attention of Oliver Hardy.

LAUREL, STAN
1890-1965
British-American actor

Laurel was the thin half and chief gag deviser behind the Laurel and Hardy team. He made his first shorts in 1915, making over 50 before teaming up with Oliver HARDY in 1926 under the supervision of producer Hal Roach. A typical Laurel and Hardy film would show them wreaking havoc with figures of authority in a series of essentially visual gags, and so sound caused hardly a ripple; they made the transition to full-length features equally smoothly, but the team broke up after Laurel's disputes with Roach. Although he worked with Hardy again in the 1940s and received a Special Academy Award in 1960, Laurel died in relative poverty. **DC**.

LAUREN, RALPH
1939-
Austrian designer

Enrolled at night school at City College in New York as a business studies student, Lauren worked during the day as a glove salesman, until 1967. Then he joined Beau Brummel Neckwear for whom he created the 'Polo' division, creating handmade neckties. The following year he established the Polo range of menswear, featuring Ivy League styles. In 1972 the Ralph Lauren label was launched, with a complete range of garments for women featuring traditionally styled jackets and knitwear in quality fabrics. **MC**.

LAURIER, WILFRED
1841-1919
Canadian politician

Laurier was the first French-Canadian to become Premier, a post he held from 1896 to 1910. In this period he brought Alberta and Saskatchewan into the union, constructed a second transcontinental railway, and reached an important tariff agreement with the United States. He fought hard for the racial and political integration of Canada. **JC.**

LAVAL, PIERRE
1883-1945
French politician

An advocate in the 1930s of the containment of HITLER's Germany, he proved its most loyal collaborator after the fall of France. He was Premier and Foreign Minister in 1931-32 and again in 1935-36, when he signed the secret Hoare-Laval Pact, offering to appease MUSSOLINI over Ethiopia, ostensibly to keep him out of Hitler's arms. As Premier under PÉTAIN's puppet regime, Laval sanctioned the deportation of French workers to Germany, as a quid pro quo for the release of prisoners of war, and also allowed the persecution of Vichy's Jews. He was sentenced to death for treason and executed. **JC.**

LAVER, ROD
1938-
Australian tennis player

Rated by many as one of the best male tennis players ever, Rod Laver won the Grand Slam twice, in 1962 as an amateur and in 1969 when the sport had become 'open'. Laver also won the first open Wimbledon in 1968 and two US titles. He had turned professional in 1963, and became the first tennis millionaire. **DS.**

LAWRENCE, D(AVID) H(ERBERT)
1885-1930
British writer

The son of a coalminer and a schoolteacher, initially Lawrence followed his mother into teaching. However, after the success of his first novel, *The White Peacock* (1911), he devoted himself to writing. Eloping with Frieda Weekley, the wife of his former tutor at Nottingham University, Lawrence travelled in Germany and Italy, during which time he wrote *The Trespasser* (1912), *Love Poems and Others* (1913), and *Sons and Lovers* (1913). A pacifist, World War 1 proved a period of great unhappiness for Lawrence. Furthermore the publication of *The Rainbow* (1915) caused him to face prosecution for indecency. In 1917 the Lawrences left England for Italy, later moving on to Australia and the United States, where *Women in Love* (1920) was privately printed. During this nomadic existence Lawrence wrote prolifically, his work frequently influenced by the countries in which he lived. After his ill health forced him to return to Italy, Lawrence wrote *Lady Chatterley's Lover* (1928). The book caused a scandal, and indeed it was not until 1960 that the unexpurgated version was allowed to be published in Britain. **CH-M.**

LAWRENCE, T(HOMAS) E(DWARD)
1888-1935
British soldier and author

'Lawrence of Arabia' was an outstanding scholar, and the research for his thesis on medieval military architecture (*Crusader Castles* [1936]) enabled him to travel to the Middle East and immerse himself in the Arab culture. On the outbreak of World War I he was assigned to military intelligence in Egypt, his empathy and understanding of the Arab world making him the ideal candidate for such sensitive work. In 1916 Lawrence became adviser to Prince Faisal in Arabia, to assist in his revolt against the Arabs' Turkish rulers and thus also to protect the right flank of the British advance into Syria. Lawrence helped seize the port of Wajh and, in co-operation with the Howaitat tribe, routed the Turks near Ma'an, before capturing Aqaba in 1917; in 1918 the Arabs occupied Damascus. At the resulting peace conference Lawrence attempted to obtain a just settlement for the Arabs, but became disillusioned by the great powers' lack of interest. In 1922 Lawrence joined the ranks of the Royal Air Force in order to escape his renown and live as anonymously as possible. Soon after his retirement in 1935 he was killed in a motorbike accident. Lawrence was also a writer, his most famous work being *The Seven Pillars of Wisdom* (1926). **CH-M.**

LEACH, BERNARD
1887-1979
British potter

Leach was born in Hong Kong and the influence of oriental ceramics was paramount in his work. After studying in Japan he established the Leach Pottery in an artists' workshop at St Ives, Cornwall, in 1920. Leach's work succeeded in establishing in England the idea of the potter as an autonomous artist, and pots as individual works of art. **DE.**

LEAKEY, LOUIS
1903-1972
Kenyan archaeologist

Leakey displayed a brilliant talent for discovering the tools and fossils of early man, most often at the famous sites of Olduvai Gorge. He made his first significant fossil discoveries in 1932, but really made his name in 1959 when he and his wife Mary unearthed the partial remains of what is now known as *Australopithecus boisei* – an ancestor of man, dating from about 1,750,000 years ago, with massive jaws and eyebrow ridges. There followed an unequaled series of early hominid discoveries, including the remains of *Homo habilis*. However Leakey's interpretation of his fossils was not always accepted by the academic community – the essential points of contention being that Leakey had a tendency to classify his discoveries as separate species, and that he believed that many early fossils (*Australopithecus, Homo erectus*) were the remains of extinct hominids and were not directly ancestral to man. **RJ.**

LEAKEY, MARY
1913-
British archaeologist

Mary Leakey moved to Kenya after marrying the archaeologist LOUIS LEAKEY in 1936. While working with Leakey on his quest to discover evidence of the earliest hominids, she made a series of important finds, including *Proconsul africanus* (1948), and *Australopithecus boisei* (1959), and helped to excavate the remains of *Homo habilis* (1960). After Leakey's death she continued in the field, and her team at Laetoli uncovered a unique hominid footprint trail dating back perhaps 3.5 million years. **RJ.**

LEAN, SIR DAVID
1908-1991
British film director

Lean established his reputation as a director with adaptations of Noel COWARD (notably, *Brief Encounter*, 1945) and still unsurpassed screen interpretations of Dickens, *Great Expectations* (1946) and *Oliver Twist* (1948). He won Oscars for his international productions, *The Bridge on the River Kwai* (1957) and *Lawrence of Arabia* (1962), which aligned epic vistas with intimate characterization. Dismissed by the intelligentsia for 'bourgeois impersonality', his reputation revived with *A Passage to India* (1984), and, at his death, he was acknowledged as one of the great story-tellers of popular cinema, as well as an acute observer of the English character. **NS.**

LEAVIS, F[RANK] R[AYMOND]
1895-1978
British literary critic

As a student Leavis was influenced by the Practical Criticism teachings of I A Richards at Cambridge. One of the major figures in twentieth-century literary criticism, his re-evaluations of the canon of English literature from *New Bearings in English Poetry* (1932) to *The Great Tradition* (1948) have had enormous influence, though his intransigence in support of his own views, and rejection of those that conflicted made him a controversial figure. He believed passionately in the importance of literature and an intellectual élite and represented these views in the journal *Scrutiny* of which he was co-editor (1932-53). **AM.**

LEAVITT, HENRIETTA
1868-1921
American astronomer

Leavitt was one of a group of female 'human computers' employed at Harvard College Observatory to catalogue stars on photographic plates. In 1912 she discovered a law that allowed the brightness of certain stars, called Cepheid variables, to be calculated from the time they took to vary. This provided astronomers with a powerful new method for measuring distances in space, using Cepheids as 'standard candles.' **IR**.

LEBESGUE, HENRI-LÉON
1875-1941
French mathematician

One of the main influences on twentieth-century mathematical analysis, Lebesgue is best known for his contribution to abstract measure theory, as developed by his teacher BOREL, and its application to generalize (Riemann) integration so that most functions can be integrated. He also contributed to topology and the Fourier Series, and became a Fellow of the Royal Society of London. **EB**.

LED ZEPPELIN
PLANT, ROBERT
1943-
PAGE, JIMMY
1944-
JONES, JOHN PAUL
1946-
BONHAM, JOHN
1948-1980
British rock group

The best-known exponents of the heavy-metal genre, Led Zeppelin produced albums of uniformly high quality. Their 1968 debut album, *Led Zeppelin*, was an astonishing display of virtuosity, and *Led Zeppelin II* made No. 1 on both sides of the Atlantic, giving them singles chart success with 'Whole Lotta Love'. A shift to more acoustic material on the third album in 1970 kept them ahead, and their fourth yielded their most famous track, 'Stairway to Heaven'. Record-breaking tours followed the fifth album, yet in 1977 after more successful releases they were beset by tragedy amid rumors of occult involvement. In 1979 the album *In Through The Out Door* entered the US chart at No. 1, evidence of their continuing popularity, but in 1980 just before a planned tour, drummer Bonham was found dead after a drinking session. They retired soon after, although Plant and Page continued with successful solo careers. **DC**.

LEE KUAN YEW
1923-
Singaporean politician

Creator of modern Singapore as one of the three financial capitals of the East, this Cambridge-educated lawyer turned from a socialist into a passionate defender of capitalism. After he became its first Premier in 1965 he practically ran Singapore as an autocrat and the fabulous economic boom has been purchased at the cost of a restriction in liberties. He established diplomatic links with China and chose the man who inherited his mantle. **JC**.

LEE, PEGGY
1920-
American singer, songwriter, and actress

She had a number one hit with Benny GOODMAN in 1942 with 'Somebody Else is Taking My Place', and began writing her own material with Dave Barbour, whom she married in 1943; they took 'Mañana' to number one in 1948. Hits continued into the 1950s, with 'Lover' (1952) and 'Fever' (1958), a perennial favorite which perfectly exploited her smokey voice and vulnerable sexuality. Nominated for an Oscar for her searingly convincing portrayal of a breakdown in *Pete Kelly's Blues* (1955), she staged a comeback to the Top 40 in 1969 with 'Is That All There Is'. **JH**.

LÉGER, FERNAND
1881-1955
French painter

Originally trained in architecture, from 1909 Léger was associated with the Cubists and by 1911 was experimenting with non-representational painting. After active service in World War I he returned to human themes, the socially leveling experience of the trenches determining him to create an art accessible to all levels of society. The simplified forms of his monumental, static style, characterized by strong, unmodulated color and bold black outlines, had the polished precision of machinery. During World War II he lived in the USA and taught at Yale University. Returning to France in 1945, his work increasingly reflected his political interest in the working classes, as in *The Builders* (1950). **ER**.

LEIBOVITZ, ANNIE
1950-
American photographer

A Californian pioneer of 'swagger' portraiture, Annie Leibovitz took her first pictures for *Rolling Stone* magazine in New York in 1970. By 1973 she was that magazine's chief photographer, and became the prime celebrity portraitist of the postmodern era. After an existential and realist phase in the 1970s, she turned to a more theatrical and conceptual manner in the 1980s. **IJ**.

LEIGH, VIVIEN
1913-1967
British actress

A delicate and graceful woman, Leigh be-

came a talented stage and screen actress, a complex and ambitious performer who won Hollywood's plum role as Scarlett O'Hara in *Gone With the Wind* (1939) after a talent hunt that rivaled a political convention. Although she was British, she played the part of the Southern belle to perfection, a feat she achieved again as Blanche du Bois in Tennessee Williams' *A Streetcar Named Desire* (1951). Those two sterling performances alone would qualify her for film immortality, and she won Academy Awards for Best Actress for both. An off-screen romance with and subsequent marriage to Laurence OLIVIER created a stir in 1936, after which she played Juliet to Olivier's Romeo on Broadway, and Emma to his Horatio Nelson in *That Hamilton Woman* (1941), going on to tour with him in the Old Vic, London's venerable repertory company. But there were complications. Always frail, Leigh saved her limited stamina for her frequent stage appearances. Bouts of physical illness and mental breakdowns also cast a tragic shadow over the brightness of her many achievements. One of her finest performances came in her last movie, *Ship of Fools* (1965). **DC**.

ABOVE: Airman Curtis LeMay (left) and comrades.

LEMAY, CURTIS, GENERAL
1906-1990
American airman

An advocate of strategic bombing, LeMay participated in campaigns against both Germany and Japan during World War II, culminating in command of B-29s in the Marianas carrying out low-level incendiary raids on Japanese cities. As commander of Strategic Air Command (1948-57), he developed the concept of nuclear bombers. **JPi**.

LEMMON, JACK
1925-
American actor

Lemmon made his first Broadway appearance in the 1953 revival of *Room Service*, and his film debut, opposite popular comedienne Judy Holliday, followed with *It Should Happen to You* (1954). His portrayal of Ensign Pulver in *Mister Roberts* (1955) won him an Oscar as Best Supporting Actor; he won another as Best Actor in 1973 for *Save the Tiger*. He became known as the best young comedian in Hollywood, but he proved spectacularly that his talents weren't confined to comedy in *Wine and Roses* (1962), a grim and touching story of an alcoholic couple. In 1986 he returned to Broadway as the father in Eugene O'Neill's *Long Day's Journey into Night*. **DC**.

LEMOND, GREG
1962-
American cyclist

In 1986 Greg LeMond became the only American ever to win the Tour de France, the world's premiere cycling event. Nine months later he lay near death after a hunting accident. (Shotgun pellets remain in the lining of his heart.) He returned to the Tour in 1989 and won with a blazing finish from Versailles to Paris. He won it again in 1990. **MD**.

LENGLEN, SUZANNE
1899-1938
French tennis player

In many respects the first great tennis player, Lenglen's record can be summarized by saying that she lost only one singles match between Wimbledon in 1919 and 1926 when she turned professional. As well as the accuracy of her play, she was also known for the style of her dress, causing a sensation during that first Wimbledon win by appearing in a short-sleeved, knee-length outfit. **DS**.

LENIN, VLADIMIR ILYICH
1870-1924
Russian statesman

The revolutionary and founder of the Bolshevik party, Lenin was upheld for over 65 years as the founder of the Soviet Union. Having studied Marxism at the University of St Petersburg, his involvement with revolutionary politics earned him three years exile in Sibera from 1897. He moved to Switzerland in 1900, becoming leader of the Bolsheviks in 1903, and returning briefly to Russia during the abortive revolution of 1905. After the deposition of the Tsar, Lenin returned to Russia with German connivance in March 1917 in a 'sealed train' and won power in the October Revolution that year. During the Civil War (1918-21) he commanded the Bolsheviks and fought off foreign intervention as well as the White army. Successful in establishing Bolshevik power, he founded the Comintern in 1919 to spread the revolution, and also instituted the New Economic Policy in 1921 which permitted limited free enterprise. A shrewd political operator, Lenin devoted his life to the furtherance of Marxism, his writings and action making a significant contribution to the ideology. **JC**.

LEONE, SERGIO
1921-1992
Italian film director

Leone was responsible for the phenomenal popularity of the 'Spaghetti Western' during the 1960s. The Westerns that he filmed in Italy with Clint EASTWOOD, *A Fistful of Dollars*, (1964), *For A Few Dollars More* (1966), and *The Good, the Bad, and the Ugly* (1967) were box-office smashes and brought a new violence, cynicism, and stylisation to the genre. **NS**.

LESSING, DORIS
1919-
British novelist

Born in Persia, Lessing and her parents moved to Southern Rhodesia when she was five. Her early novels, such as *The Grass is Singing* (1950), were set in colonial Africa. Having settled in Britain in 1949, later works such as the Martha Quest novels and *The Golden Notebook* (1962) dealt with a run-down 1960s Britain. Always concerned with social and political questions, particularly the changing position of women and the possibility of technological disaster, she has frequently explored mental breakdown and its parallels with social disintegration. She broke away from realism in the science fictional *Canopus in Argus Archives* series (1979-83), but has since returned, with *The Good Terrorist* (1985). **AM**.

LEVI-MONTALCINI, RITA
1909-
Italian biochemist

Anti-Semitic laws prevented Rita from continuing her neuroembryological research at the University of Turin. Undeterred she transferred her laboratory to her bedroom. She escaped the Nazis by fleeing to Florence during the war and in 1947 she took up a

ABOVE: British author Doris Lessing.

ABOVE: Vladimir Ilyich Lenin, father of the Soviet Union.

research post at Washington University. By 1952 she was convinced that a stimulating substance regulated growth in nerve cells; she called it nerve growth factor (NGF). In 1953 she was joined at Washington by Stanley Cohen with whom she collaborated to establish that NGF was a protein. She continued working on the structure, action, and therapeutic uses of NGF, effectively pioneering an entire new field in the biochemistry of growth factors. After becoming a full professor in 1958, Rita began to spend more time in Italy and in 1969 she established the Laboratory of Cell Biology in Rome where she now works. In 1986 she and Cohen shared the Nobel Prize in Medicine and Physiology. **MB**.

LEVI-STRAUSS, CLAUDE
1908-
French social anthropologist

Levi-Strauss studied law and philosophy in Paris before beginning his career as an anthropologist by investigating the Brazilian Indians. In 1949 he introduced a new element into the study of kinship, stressing the concept of alliance over that of descent. He developed the linguist SAUSSURE's theory of structuralism – essentially the search for underlying organizational principles in human thought and behavior. This concept came to dominate much of social anthropology, particularly in the areas of kinship, totemism, symbolism, and myth. **RJ**.

LEWIS, CARL
1961-
American track and field star

Carl Lewis's sustained brilliance in track and field is one of the great accomplishments in twentieth-century sports. He won eight gold medals in three Olympiads (1984, 1988 and 1992). A great sprinter, Lewis is also the only man ever to win three golds in the long jump. **MD**.

LEWIS, C[LIVE] S[TAPLES]
1898-1963
British academic and writer

Scholar, literary critic, novelist, and Christian apologist, Lewis was Professor of Medieval and Renaissance English at Cambridge 1954-63. His works include *The Allegory of Love*, a critical text, religious writings such as *The Screwtape Letters*, highly moralistic allegorical science fiction and children's books, such as the Narnia stories. *Surprised by Joy* and *A Grief Observed* are autobiographical. **AM**.

LEWIS, [HARRY] SINCLAIR
1885-1951
American novelist and journalist

A graduate of Yale, Lewis briefly joined Upton Sinclair's socialist Helicon Home Colony in New Jersey. After writing several minor novels, *Main Street* (1920) brought him wide recognition. This critique of small-town Midwestern life, was continued in *Babbitt* (1922), the satirical but affectionate portrait of a complacent businessman and his mid-life crisis. In 1926 he refused a Pulitzer prize for *Arrowsmith* (1925). His finest novel, *Elmer Gantry* (1927), is a brilliant evocation of religious hysteria, with the monstrous fake evangelist preacher Gantry at its core. Later novels lack this power, but in 1930 he became the first American to win a Nobel Prize for Literature. **AM**.

LEWIS, JOHN L
1880-1969
American labor leader

Of Welsh immigrant background, Lewis was elected President of the Union of Mineworkers in 1920, from where, over the next 40 years, he fought to extend union power in heavy industry. In 1935 he helped found the Committee for Industrial Organization, a move for which his mineworkers were expelled from the conservative American Federation of Labor. As President of the reorganized and militant Congress of Industrial Organizations, Lewis led the unionization of the steel and automobile industries, with its violence-ridden strikes. He turned against ROOSEVELT and a series of wartime strikes led to the passing of the Smith-Connally and Taft-Hartley Acts, both designed to hobble the unions. When in 1946 Lewis called his men out on strike in defiance of a court injunction, the Government seized the mines. He was twice heavily fined for defying the courts. In 1952 he was responsible for establishing federal safety standards for mines. **JC**.

LEWIS, SIR THOMAS
1881-1945
British physiologist

Beginning his research career while still a medical student, Lewis made a series of important observations in 1921 of the vascular reaction of the skin to various forms of injury. He described the red line, flare and wheal produced by the skin as the so-called 'triple response.' He postulated that this was due to vasodilatation and increased vascular permeability caused by the release by the injured tissue of a humoral histamine-like substance (H-substance). He thus established the concept that chemical substances locally induced by injury mediate the vascular changes of inflammation. This formed the basis of the important discoveries of chemical inflammatory mediators and of potent anti-inflammatory agents. **ES**.

LIBBY, WILLARD FRANK
1908-1980
American chemist

He taught at the University of California at Berkeley until 1941 when he joined the Manhattan Project to develop the atomic bomb. At the end of World War II, he taught at the University of Chicago and, in 1959, returned to California. His work on nuclear weapons led him to discover the technique of carbon-14 dating by which archeological and natural remains can be dated by determining the proportion of the radioactive isotope carbon-14 remaining in them. This technique can date remains up to 40,000 years old. He was awarded the Nobel Prize for Chemistry for this work in 1960. **DD**.

LICHTENSTEIN, ROY
1923-
American painter

Lichtenstein is one of the best-known American Pop artists. His most characteristic works are magnified images from comic strips on a seemingly printed ground of Benday dots. He later brought this ironic and impersonal treatment to bear on images from 'high art,' including the abstract expressionist style with which he began his career. **ER**.

ABOVE: *Leading exponent of Pop Art, Roy Lichtenstein.*

LIE, TRYGVE
1896-1968
Norwegian politician

From acting as legal adviser to the Norwegian Trades Union Organization (1922-35) Lie was appointed Minister of Trade in 1939, moving with the wartime government in exile to London where he became Foreign Minister (1940-45). First Secretary-General of the United Nations (1946-52), Lie committed it to the Korean War, and the resulting refusal of the Russians to recognize him led to him stepping down at the beginning of 1953. **JC.**

ABOVE: Charles Lindbergh and the Spirit of St Louis.

LINDBERGH, CHARLES, BRIGADIER-GENERAL
1902-1974
American engineer and pilot

Tall and handsome, Lindbergh became a celebrity overnight after making the first nonstop solo flight from New York to Paris, crossing the North Atlantic on 20-21 May 1927, and winning a $25,000 prize. Then an advisor to US Airlines, he flew surveys with his wife over the North Pacific, North Atlantic, and Arctic. The kidnap and murder of their son and their subsequent press hounding led to their move to England in 1935. He campaigned for American neutrality but later helped improve warplanes and flew Pacific combat missions. Postwar, he worked with PanAm and the USAF ballistic missiles program. He died of leukemia. **MT.**

LIPMANN, FRITZ ALBERT
1899-
German-American biochemist

While with the Carlsberg Foundation in Copenhagen, Lipmann made one of the most fundamental but important advances in cell biochemistry. During his work on the metabolism, the means by which a cell acquires energy, in 1937, he discovered, quite fortuitously, that the process could not proceed without the addition of phosphate. He realised that the molecule adenosine triphosphate or ATP delivered both phosphate and energy to the cell and that this was the real purpose of metabolism. Surprisingly, it was not for this work that he won the Nobel Prize for Physiology in 1953, but for his discovery of the molecule coenzyme A and its importance in intermediary metabolism. **ES.**

LIPPMANN, WALTER
1889-1974
American journalist

Lippmann is famous for his column 'Today and Tomorrow,' which he produced for more than 40 years. He began as a journalist before getting involved in politics, publishing books and working on the *New Republic*. Lippmann became increasingly influential and helped to draft President WILSON's Fourteen Points. Returning to journalism he wrote about public opinion and came to doubt that citizens could make informed decisions in elections. In 1931 he began his column in the New York *Herald Tribune* and gained a wide audience for his views, which became increasingly conservative. In the late 1960s he became widely popular for opposing the Vietnam War. **DSI.**

LISSITZKY, EL[IAZIR]
1890-1947
Russian painter and designer

Trained as an architect, Lissitzky was also a printmaker and his book *The Story of Two Squares* (1922) was a landmark in typography and book design. In 1919 he met MALEVICH and began a series of geometric paintings called Proun (object), reminiscent of aerial views of modern architecture. During the 1920s he was the spokesman for Russian Constructivism in Western Europe. **ER.**

LITTLE RICHARD
1938-
American rock singer and pianist

Hits such as 'Tutti Frutti' and 'Lucille' established Little Richard as the champion of brash, pounding, 12-bar rock in the late 1950s and laid the foundations for a generation of rockers. But by the 1960s inspiration was running dry, and it was not until the 1970s that the nostalgia bandwagon returned him to the public eye. **DC.**

LLOYD, HAROLD
1893-1971
American actor

Once the most popular of the Hollywood silent clowns, Lloyd was a mixture of bold daredevil and ordinary American optimist. Usually dressed blandly in everyday clothes and peering at the world through horn-rimmed spectacles, his athletic prowess and feats of daring were amazing. He claimed never to use a double, and in movies such as *Safety Last* (1923), dangling atop a skyscraper hanging onto the hand of a clock, he had audiences screaming with laughter and terror. By the mid-1920s he was a huge star, and although his career declined after the arrival of the talkies, he received a Special Academy Award in 1952. **DC.**

LLOYD GEORGE OF DWYFOR, DAVID, 1ST EARL
1863-1945
British politician and statesman

Short on scruples but long on vision, full of innovation and overflowing with energy, Lloyd George ranks with CHURCHILL as the pre-eminent British leader of the century. Both had greatness bestowed by military crisis, both could demonstrate domestic achievement, and both suffered a long period in the political wilderness – unfortunately for Lloyd George, this comprised the last two decades of his life. A Welsh speaker of artisan origins, Lloyd George built his political career as a man of the people. Starting out a Celtic nationalist, radical causes brought public notoriety and led him to work for reforming legislation. If his People's Budget of 1909 had popular appeal, the humbling of the House of Lords that followed was a political masterstroke for the Liberals, while the National Insurance Act it financed proved a welfare watershed. Lloyd George was triumphant, but he was not trusted. While peace reigned ASQUITH held him in check. However when total war demanded governmental direction rather than liberal consciences, backbench Conservative pressure pushed Lloyd George into the premiership and Asquith into a bitter and unforgiving rivalry. Lloyd George proved the decisive war leader. He also appeared the man best suited to channel domestic unrest into peacetime reconstruction. With each adventure, however, these feelings faded and, in 1922, the backbench Conservatives now consigned him to years of Liberal Party feuding. When the nation faced economic crisis in 1931 it turned not to Lloyd George – yet retrospectively, he appears to have been the only politician with any answers. **JP.**

LLOYD WEBBER, SIR ANDREW
1948-
British composer

Lloyd Webber's partnership with the lyricist Tim Rice first produced two pop oratorios,

Joseph and his Amazing Technicolor Dreamcoat and *Jesus Christ Superstar*, before a string of hit musicals (starting with *Evita* in 1978) catapulted him to global fame and fortune. His *Variations*, written for his cellist brother Julian, showed his undoubted talents as an orchestrator of symphonic rock, but while the success of *Cats* and *Phantom of the Opera* testify to the popular appeal of his shows, the musical establishment has derided his forays into 'classical' waters (as with his *Requiem*), and continues to revile his music as shallow. **DK**.

LODGE, HENRY CABOT
1850-1924
American politician

Known as 'the scholar in politics,' Lodge, a Republican Senator (1893-1924), led the opposition in the Senate to President WILSON's peace covenant as part of the Versailles Treaty. Aware that he could not prevent Wilson from backing the treaty directly, he attached 15 reservations to it which rallied opposition in the Senate and ensured its defeat by seven votes, in March 1920. The United States failed to ratify the League of Nations and went isolationist. Ironically his grandson became the most celebrated American Ambassador to the United Nations. **JC**

LOMBARDI, VINCE[NT THOMAS VINCE]
1913-1970
American football coach

A legendary National Football League coach, Lombardi never piloted a losing team. He started with the Green Bay Packers in 1959, instantly transforming a 1-10-1 team into a winner. His Packers claimed five NFL titles in nine seasons, including victories in the first two Super Bowls. Lombardi came to Washington in 1969 and led the Redskins to their first winning season in 14 years. An inspirational leader, he was reputed to coin the phrase, 'Winning isn't everything; it's the only thing.' The trophy that is given annually to the Super Bowl champion bears his name. **MD**.

LONG, HUEY PIERCE
1893-1935
American politician

'The Kingfish''s personal rule in Louisiana was an American reflection of the fascism in prewar Europe. Long was admitted to the bar after studying between periods as a door-to-door salesman. His defense of the poor rural whites, particularly against the Standard Oil Company, made him a working-class hero and he was elected Governor in 1928. He anticipated ROOSEVELT's New Deal with his public works initiative but his term was marred by widespread corruption. With his 'Share the Wealth' campaign he entered the Senate in 1932 and having

ABOVE: Senator Huey P Long.

become practically a dictator in Louisiana he announced his candidature for the presidency. He was assassinated however in September 1935. **JC**.

LONG, RICHARD
1945-
British land artist

Born in Bristol, Long studied at St Martin's School of Art, London (1966-68). Throughout his career the central theme of his art has been the walk, an activity he first utilized in a work entitled *A Line Made by Walking England* (1967). He documents his walks with photographs, maps, and objects found in the countryside. He also produces sculptures which, like those of ANDRE, are earthbound, removing sculpture from its pedestal. These use sticks and stones to create patterns with simple forms, and may be arranged either in galleries or outdoors, where they are photographed. In 1976 he was chosen to represent Britain at the Venice Biennale. **ER**.

LONSDALE, DAME KATHLEEN
1903-1971
Irish physicist

A postmaster's daughter, Kathleen was the proverbial scholarship girl, graduating at 19 with the highest first at London University and becoming in 1945 the first woman FRS. As a member of W H BRAGG's X-ray diffraction team at University College, then at the Royal Institution, she worked on spacegroup tables. In 1927 she married fellow student Thomas Lonsdale whose job took the couple to Leeds where Kathleen succeeded in proving the planarity of the benzene ring. Back in London, her study of meteoric diamonds resulted in 'lonsdaleite' being named for her. **MB**

LORCA, FEDERICO
1898-1936
Spanish poet and playwright

Born in Andalucia, and educated at Granada and Madrid universities, Lorca's gypsy songs *Canciones* (1927) and *Romancero Gitano*

(1928) were and are probably his best-known works. A visit to New York in 1929 is recorded in the powerfully surreal and haunted *Poeta in Neuva York* (1940). His three best plays are the rural tragedies *Bodas de sangre* (*Blood Wedding*, 1933), *Yerma* (1934), and *La casa de Bernarda Alba* (*The House of Bernarda Alba*, 1945). Although he also wrote comedies, tragedy brought out the depths of passion and poetry for which he is most celebrated. He was killed by Nationalist troops early in the Spanish Civil War. **AM**.

LOREN, SOPHIA
1934-
Italian actress

At the age of 15 Loren won a beauty contest and came to the attention of her future husband, producer Carlo Ponti. She went to Hollywood in 1958, where her talents for both comedy and dramatic roles provided a counterpoint to her image as a sex symbol. In 1961 she won the Academy Award for Best Actress for *Two Women*, and her intelligence and beauty have ensured that she continues to enjoy international fame. **DC**.

ABOVE: Kathleen Lonsdale, Irish physicist.

LORENZ, KONRAD
1903-1989
Austrian zoologist

After graduating in medicine and teaching anatomy in Vienna, he developed an interest in animal psychology. He first recognized imprinting in birds – the way that a hatchling will follow the first moving object it sees – and determined that much behavior is genetically fixed rather than learned. He spent World War II in the German Army and a Soviet prisoner of war camp, returning to his studies afterwards. He founded ethology – the study of animal behavior in its natural environment – and shared a 1973 Nobel Prize with Karl von FRISCH and Nikolaas Tinbergen. **DD**.

LORRE, PETER
1904-1964
German actor

Best remembered for 1940s films such as *The Maltese Falcon* (1941) and *Casablanca* (1942), Lorre rose to fame as the psychopathic child murderer in Fritz LANG's *M* (1930). After the war he returned to Germany to make the film *The Lost One* (1951), but he ended his career in Hollywood playing mainly comic villains. **DC.**

LOSEY, JOSEPH
1909-1984
American film director

Losey worked in England in the 1950s after being blacklisted in America, and made several superb movies analyzing the class corruption and sexual mores of English society, notably in three films scripted by Harold PINTER, *The Servant* (1963), *Accident* (1967), and *The Go-Between* (1970). **NS.**

LOUIS, JOE [JOSEPH BARROW]
1914-1981
American boxer

With a calm ferocity Joe Louis fought his way to the world heavyweight championship and held it longer than any man who has ever lived. Louis knocked out James Braddock in 1937, becoming the youngest fighter ever to win the title. He then defended it a record 25 times. Perhaps his most famous bout was a ruthless one-round knockout of former champion Max Schmeling in 1938, thus avenging Louis's only professional loss up to that time. In 1949 Louis, known as 'the Brown Bomber,' retired. Later coaxed back into the ring, he dropped two decisions, finishing with a lifetime record of 68-3. **MD.**

LOUIS, MORRIS
1912-1962
American painter

Louis' early work was concerned with Cubism and collage but changed direction abruptly in 1953 when he was introduced to Helen Frankenthaler's method of applying color directly to unprimed canvas. In Louis' *Veil* series, 1954-59, thinned acrylic paint was poured on to unprimed canvas, which was moved to direct the flow, resulting in vivid, striated patterns of color. Later works introduced areas of bare canvas as positive forces in the design. His technique of staining rather than coating the support eliminated gestural and tactile qualities from the paint and perhaps produced the first fully autonomous abstract paintings. **ER.**

LOVELL, SIR BERNARD
1913-
British astronomer

After working in radar during World War II, Lovell turned to the new science of radio astronomy, of which he became an influential pioneer. He was head of the Nuffield Radio Astronomy Observatory at Jodrell Bank, near Manchester, England, where he built the 250-feet (76-meter) radio dish, the largest in the world when it opened in 1957. **IR.**

LOW, SIR DAVID
1891-1963
British cartoonist and caricaturist

From 1911 Low worked for *The Sydney Bulletin* before emigrating to Britain in 1919. His greatest cartoons, produced for the Beaverbrook Press between 1933 and 1945, are now often regarded as visual summations of British opposition to the Axis. The absence of subjects such as Hitler, Mussolini, and similar targets took the bite out of Low's postwar work. Low benefited from Beaverbrook's policy of using leftwing contributions to his rightwing newspapers. His two most enduring characters are reactionary Colonel Blimp, and the honest carthorse – symbol of the best trade-union values. **FM.**

LOWELL, ROBERT
1917-1977
American poet

Born in Boston and educated at Harvard and Kenyon College, Lowell served a term of imprisonment as a conscientious objector during World War II and was later to find fame as an opponent of the Vietnam war. His early poems reflect his interest in New England and family history, and later themes include nostalgia for cherished traditions, values, and relationships. His conversion to Catholicism was the cause of some conflict. He won the Pulitzer Prize for *Lord Weary's Castle* (1946). Later work was less formalist and tended toward the confessional, especially *The Dolphin* (1973). **AM.**

LUBITSCH, ERNST
1892-1947
American film director

Lubitsch produced a number of successful German silent films before moving to Hollywood in 1921. He became an elegant purveyor of sophisticated sex-comedies, who, in

ABOVE: *American film director, Ernst Lubitsch (left).*

ABOVE: Henry Luce, founder of Time *magazine.*

Billy WILDER's phrase, 'could do more with a closed door than most modern directors can do with an entire bedroom.' His most famous films are *Ninotchka* (1939), and the anti-Nazi satire, *To Be or Not To Be* (1942). **NS**.

LUCE, HENRY ROBINSON
1898-1967
American publisher

Luce was famous for founding *Time* magazine which he launched with Briton Hadden in March 1923. Its circulation rose steadily until by 1960 it was selling 2.5 million copies per issue. In 1930 Hadden and Luce launched *Fortune* magazine, followed by *Life* in 1936, and *Sports Illustrated* in 1954. He continued as editor-in-chief of his magazines until 1964. His publishing empire extended to films, radio, and television, including such well-known series as *The March of Time* and Time-Life books. In the 1930s he caused a sensation throughout every part of US society when he divorced his wife and married the playwright Clare Boothe Brokaw. **DSL**.

LUMUMBA, PATRICE
1925-1961
Zairean politician

The Belgian Congo had barely achieved independence when it was torn apart in internal strife which killed Lumumba, its first Prime Minister. A clerk in the colonial administration, in 1958 Lumumba gave the rallying cry that independence 'was not a gift to be given by Belgium' – triggering a wave of agitation which caused the Belgians 'to scuttle' in 1960. He called for UN protection when the Belgians backed the breakaway province of Katanga but was arrested and murdered by the secessionists. **JC**.

LURIA, ALEXANDER ROMANOVICH
1902-1977
Russian neuropsychologist

Luria was the pioneer of neuropsychology. He applied psychoanalytic, behaviorist, and Marxist ideas in his great effort to examine the relationships between brain structure and brain function. Patients with head injuries provided a valuable source of empirical information. In his later years he was particularly interested in brain damage and speech disorder. **MBe**.

LUTYENS, SIR EDWIN
1869-1944
British architect and designer

Trained by the London firm of George and Peto, by 1900 Lutyens had established a successful practice designing country houses in a sophisticated and massive, rather than rustic, Arts and Crafts style. With the exception of Castle Drogo (1910-30) which is in a simplified medieval style, all Lutyens's work after 1906 (Thiepval Arch, 1926; scheme for Liverpool Cathedral, 1929-41) was in a heroic Mannerist classical style, sometimes showing appropriate local influences (Viceroy's House, New Delhi, 1912-31). Lutyens's work has excited much interest among traditionalist architects in recent years. **AR**.

LUXEMBURG, ROSA
1870-1919
German revolutionary

Born in Russian-ruled Poland to Jewish parents, Luxemburg completed her education in Switzerland, where she first encountered Marxism. She then moved to Germany, where she became a leading figure in left-wing politics before World War I. Imprisoned for opposing that conflict, she joined Karl Liebknecht in founding a Communist group known as the Spartacists, which she led in an uprising in Berlin (January 1919). She was beaten to death by German troops sent to put down the revolt. Renowned for her oratory and, ironically, her belief in peaceful revolution, she became a heroine of the European Communists. **JP**.

ABOVE: Heroine of the Communist movement, Rosa Luxemburg.

LYNN, LORETTA
1935-
American country and western singer and songwriter

The first woman in country music to become a millionaire, Lynn took up singing after marriage at age 13. She was signed by Decca in 1962; hits included 'Blue Kentucky Girl', 'Coal Miner's Daughter' and 'You're Looking at Country'. Her autobiography, a bestseller in 1976, was filmed in 1980. **JH**.

MacARTHUR, Douglas, General
1880-1964
American soldier

In 1937 MacArthur retired from the US Army. Commissioned from West Point in 1903, he had served in the Philippines (1903-06), at Vera Cruz (1914), had commanded a division in France (1918), served as Superintendent of West Point (1919-22) and as US Army Chief of Staff (1930-35), and attained the rank of General. He was also Field Marshal in the Filipino Army. An intelligent and gifted strategist, MacArthur was recalled to duty as commander of US forces in the Far East in July 1941. When the Japanese invaded the Philippines, MacArthur fought a delaying action; although his troops surrendered in May 1942, he was evacuated on President ROOSEVELT's orders, leaving with the pledge 'I shall return.' Appointed Supreme Allied Commander, South-West Pacific, MacArthur planned the island-hopping advance from New Guinea to the Philippines, liberating Manila in early 1945. He took the Japanese surrender in September 1945, before spending five years as Supreme Commander of the Allied occupation force in Japan. In 1950, when the North Koreans invaded the South, he became commander of United Nations' forces; in September he drove the Communists back at Pusan and Inchon. A year later, he was sacked by President Truman for criticizing US/UN policy. **JPi.**

MacDONALD, Ramsay
1866-1937
British politician and statesman

Although he masterminded Labour's transformation from pressure group to alternative government, the party remembers MacDonald for splitting the Cabinet over unemployment benefit cuts, rather than as their most inspirational Prime Minister. Believing domestic political compromise to be the best way to build working-class parliamentary strength, he was willing to agree electoral pacts with the Edwardian Liberal Party, and to govern by financial orthodoxy during the 1920s. However in foreign policy fraternal socialist principles predominated, whether promoting global disarmament or fostering improved international relations through the League of Nations. As Depression struck many people found comfort in MacDonald's contradictions. Unfortunately Labour's grassroots were only alienated. **JP.**

Mach, David
1956-
British sculptor

Born in Methil, Fife, Mach studied at the Duncan of Jordanstone School of Art, Dundee, and the Royal College of Art, London. His work uses large quantities of industrially

ABOVE: General Douglas MacArthur, military commander during World War II.

manufactured goods, such as milk bottles or newspapers, arranged in temporary installations. The sheer amount of material parallels contemporary over-production. **ER.**

MacIVER, Robert
1882-1970
American social theorist

An exponent of a conceptual rather than an empirical approach to sociology, MacIver distinguished society from state, and insisted on the possibility of individualism and specialization within a pluralist state. He taught at Toronto and Columbia before becoming President and then Chancellor of the New School for Social Research, New York. **EB.**

Macke, August
1887-1914
German painter

A member of the Blaue Reiter group, Macke utilized elements of Fauvism and Cubism, encountered on visits to Paris in 1907 and 1912, for expressionist ends in his gay park and street scenes. His jewel-like watercolors, made on a trip to Tunisia with KLEE in 1914, are considered the high point of a career cut short by World War I. **ER.**

MacKINDER, Sir Halford John
1861-1947
British political geographer

An exponent of the 'new geography', MacKinder was the first Director of the Oxford School of Geography, and later of the London School of Economics. He made the first ascent of Mount Kenya, but is best

known for his division of the globe between the 'heartland' of Eurasia and the inferior 'maritime lands' of the other continents, and his insistence on the strategic importance of Eastern Europe. After a period as an MP, he served as British High Commissioner in South Russia after World War I, and his theories influenced German military thinking in World War II. **EB.**

MACKINTOSH, Charles Rennie
1868-1928
British architect and designer

Mackintosh trained as an architect in Glasgow. His domestic architectural works (eg Windyhill, 1899; Hill House, Helensburgh, 1903) combine traditional Scottish-influenced exteriors with his distinctive Art Nouveau interiors: stark elongation and abstraction of forms in black and white contrasted with vivid, ornate stylized details. Other major Glasgow works were various Tea Rooms for Miss Cranston, and his masterpiece, the School of Art (1897-99, 1907-09). Mackintosh's work was very influential in Austria. His last work, remodeling and furniture at 78 Derngate, Northampton (1916-17), is more rectilinear and with stronger colors, prefiguring much Art Deco design of the 1920s and 1930s. **AR.**

MacLAINE, Shirley
1934-
American actress

MacLaine made her film debut in the Hitchcock movie *The Trouble with Harry* (1955) and was decorative and funny in many subsequent films. She was finally taken seriously as an actress after a heartbreaking perform-

ABOVE: Actress Shirley MacLaine.

ance as Ginny Moorehead in *Some Came Running* (1958). In the 1970s she fought for complex roles, such as in *The Turning Point* (1977) and *Being There* (1979), but was often cast as the soft-hearted female. She also appeared in cabaret and one-woman shows on Broadway and in London. She won an Academy Award for Best Actress in *Terms of Endearment* (1983), and is today considered to be one of Hollywood's finest actresses.

MacLeish, Archibald
1892-1982
American poet and dramatist

One of the expatriate Americans in Paris in the Twenties, he was influenced by TS Eliot and Ezra Pound. Winner of three Pulitzer Prizes, including one for the *Collected Poems* (1953), he also held eminent public and academic positions, as Librarian of Congress (1939-44), Assistant Secretary of State (1944-45), and as Boylston Professor at Harvard (1949-62). **AM**.

Macmillan, Harold, 1st Earl of Stockton
1894-1986
British politician and statesman

Having been overlooked in the 1930s, Mediterranean ministerial success in war, and responsibility for record house-building in the 1950s, established Macmillan in government. Emerging from the Suez débâcle as premier, his public panache and private calmness proved a winning combination. While the 'winds of change' brought international prestige, and Britons at home had 'never had it so good', Macmillan's achievements had a hint of illusion which evaporated in 1963 with the Profumo affair

and failure to enter the EEC. His long retirement was well used, however. An inspiring Chancellor of Oxford University, Macmillan's greatest parliamentary performance was saved for entry to the House of Lords in 1984. **JP**.

Macmillan, Sir Kenneth
1929-1992
British dancer and choreographer

Trained at Sadler's Wells Ballet School, MacMillan graduated into the Sadler's Wells Theatre Ballet at its inception in 1946. His first choreographic works were two apprentice pieces for the company's choreographic group in 1953-54: *Somnambulism* and *Laiderette*. His first professional work was the lively and witty *Danses Concertantes* in 1955 while, in 1958, in *The Burrow* he was to discover the exceptional dance skills of Lynn Seymour, for whom he created the roles of Juliet (1965) and Anastasia (1971). MacMillan's first major choreographic achievement was undoubtedly *Le Baiser de la fée* (1960), set to a score by Igor Stravinsky. Next came a sequence of magnificent ballets: *Invitation* (1960), *Diversions* (1961), and the massive *Rite of Spring* (1962), with the unforgettable Monica Mason as the Chosen Maiden. In 1966 MacMillan was invited to direct the Berlin Opera Ballet and for the next three years, with Seymour as ballerina, he extended the range and repertory of the company. In 1970 he returned to London to succeed Ashton as Director of the Royal Ballet and where his major ballets have since demonstrated the increasing strength of the company. Most important have been his full-length ballets *Anastasia* and *Manon*, while one-act ballets like *Elite Syncopations* continue to delight audiences worldwide and demonstrate the virtuosity of the Royal Ballet. **MC**.

ABOVE: Harold Macmillan, British statesman.

MacNeice, Louis
1907-1963
British poet and writer

Born in Belfast, MacNeice was educated at Sherborne, Marlborough and Oxford, where he published *Blind Fireworks*, his first collection. A minor poet, he was technically resourceful but limited in scope. In his last volume, *The Burning Perch* (1963), he attempted painfully to record a depth of feeling his earlier facile sophistication had witheld from him. **AM**.

ABOVE: Provocative singer and actress, Madonna.

Madonna [Madonna Ciccone]
1958-
American pop singer

Madonna's debut album of 1983 brought her instant success in the US; popularity in the UK came in 1984 with the film *Desperately Seeking Susan* and the single 'Like a Virgin'. The accompanying video brought her sexually provocative image to the fore, and her next single, 'Into The Groove' made No. 1 in the UK. In 1985 she entered the record books with eight top-ten hits, and *True Blue* (1986) and *Like A Prayer* (1989) established her as a leading female artist. Beaten in record sales only by Presley and the Beatles, cited by sections of the feminist community as a positive role model for women, she is also the arch foe of America's 'moral' right with her outrageous stage antics. **DC**.

MAGRITTE, RENÉ
1898-1967
Belgian painter

Magritte trained as a painter in Brussels, experimenting with various styles until in 1922 he discovered the work of de CHIRICO. In 1924 he collaborated in the Dadaist review *OÉsophage*, which spawned a group whose activities were similar to the Surrealists in Paris, where he worked in close association with BRETON and DALI in 1927-30. His precise, highly finished style conferred a specious reality on the mysterious, improbable situations he presented. With anachronisms of scale and lighting, odd juxtapositions of objects and inappropriate words used as labels, as in *The Key of Dreams* (1930), his work forced the spectator to question the nature of perception, visual and mental, and the relationship between language and vision. **ER**.

MAILER, NORMAN
1923-
American writer

Raised in Brooklyn and educated at Harvard, Mailer served in the Pacific with the US army, an experience which provided the raw material for *The Naked and the Dead* (1948), one of the best books to emerge from World War II. It was followed by other novels, including his most ambitious work, *Ancient Evenings* (1983), about which critical opinion is divided. A polemical writer who utilizes many different styles, including a hybrid genre of faction, he has won two Pulitzer Prizes (*The Armies of the Night*, 1968, and *The Executioner's Song*, 1979). He remains one of modern America's most colorful, exasperating, and exhilarating writers. **AM**.

MAINBOCHER, [MAIN ROUSSEAU BOCHER]
1891-1976
American designer

Born in Chicago, from 1911 Mainbocher studied and worked in Munich, Paris and London and, during World War I, served with the American hospital unit in France. In 1922 he joined Condé Nast as a fashion artist and the following year became fashion editor, then editor-in-chief to French *Vogue*, a position he held until 1929. In 1930 Mainbocher became the first American to open a successful couture salon in Paris, becoming famous for his evening wear. He created a fashion for 'Wallis Blue', following his designs for the wedding gown for Mrs Simpson on her marriage to the Duke of Windsor. His collection in 1939 just before the outbreak of World War II featured small waists and tightly laced corsetlike garments which would not be seen again until Dior's 'New Look' in 1947. Returning to the United States in 1940, Mainbocher opened his salon in New York which closed only in 1971. **MC**.

MAJOR, JOHN
1943-
British politician and prime minister

Major entered parliament in 1979 and quickly rose to ministerial rank. A Cabinet minister for only three years prior to his selection as THATCHER's successor in 1990, he had been Chancellor of the Exchequer and, briefly, Foreign Secretary. A mild-mannered man, he abandoned several Thatcherite policies, taking a more pro-European stance and winning respect for his handling of the 1991 Gulf War. After his election victory in April 1992, his administration was plagued by economic problems and a succession of scandals. **JM**.

ABOVE: Colorful US writer, Norman Mailer and friend.

MAKARIOS III, MIKHAIL
1913-1977
Cypriot archbishop and politician

Inspirer of *enosis*, the movement for union with Greece, Makarios canvassed the idea widely in Greece, the Middle East and the United States in the 1950s as an alternative to British proposals for Cypriot independence within the Commonwealth. With Greek support from 1954, he backed the EOKA guerrilla campaign in 1955 and was exiled by the British the following year. He abandoned *enosis* in 1959, Cyprus was granted independence, and Makarios was elected President, remaining in power until a coup in 1974. After the Turkish invasion of northern Cyprus, Makarios returned to power, but found difficulty in asserting Greek dominance. **JC**.

MAKAROVA, NATALIA ROMANOVA
1940-
Russian dancer

A student at the Leningrad Choreographic School, Makarova graduated in 1959 and joined the Kirov ballet, becoming one of its most outstanding ballerinas. During the company's visit to Covent Garden where she made her debut as Giselle, Makarova decided to remain in the West and since then has followed a freelance career, mostly dancing with the American Ballet Theater, but often dancing as a guest ballerina throughout the world. Her interpretation of the role of Giselle is regarded as one of the finest, celebrated for its expressiveness and exceptional Kirov style. With improvements in relations between the West and the USSR in the 1980s, Markarova returned to St Petersburg to dance again with her beloved Kirov Ballet. Non-ballet roles have included the lead in the stage revival of *On Your Toes*, and presenting a series of documentaries about dance and dancers for BBC television. **MC**.

ABOVE: Daniel Malan, architect of Apartheid.

MALAN, DANIEL
1874-1959
South African politician

Architect of Apartheid, Malan put in place the legislation, from his Afrikaner National Party's victory in 1948, which established a racial division of South Africa. His first taste of government was in 1924, after he had been his party's newspaper editor for many years. When Smuts founded the United Party Malan stayed in the Nationalist lager from which he gained, and kept power until 1956. **JC**.

LEFT: Malcolm X.

RIGHT: Nelson Mandela.

MALCOLM X
1925-1965
American political activist

After serving a seven-year term of imprisonment for 'hoodlum activities,' Malcolm X discovered Islam. Erasing his original surname as a symbol of his slave ancestors, he preached Black Power to congregations in search of new identity within a racist society. In 1965 he was assassinated by rival Black Muslims. **JP**.

MALENKOV, GEORGI
1902-1988
Soviet politician

The liquidation of many old Bolsheviks could be laid to Malenkov's door. Chairman of the Committee for the Rehabilitation of Formerly Occupied Territories in 1944, he became Deputy Prime Minister in 1946. Immediate successor to STALIN, he lost power to BULGANIN and KHRUSCHEV. He favored peaceful coexistence with the West, was expelled from the Central Committee in 1957 and sent to manage a power station. **JC**.

MALEVICH, KASIMIR
1878-1935
Russian painter

Malevich experimented with various styles, including Cubism, before formulating Suprematism, a system of abstraction which did not derive from observed reality, but depended on the basic geometric forms of square, rectangle, triangle, and cross. First exhibited in 1915, his Suprematist works were initially in black and white. He later introduced color and began stretching and fragmenting his shapes into bars, rhomboids, and ellipses, but by 1918 was using only squares, for him the purest form, painted in white on white. Having reached the ultimate distillation of his ideas, he largely abandoned painting to teach. In the late 1920s he returned to figurative painting but his radical, innovatory Suprematist ideas continued to exert widespread influence. **ER**.

MALINOWSKI, BRONISLAW
1884-1942
Polish anthropologist

Malinowski trained as an anthropologist in London before traveling to the Trobriand Islands to carry out a now classic piece of fieldwork, published as *Argonauts of the Western Pacific* (1922). He recommended that anthropologists should practice 'participant observation', whereby the observer immerses himself almost unnoticed in the culture he is studying, and this has become standard in the discipline. Malinowski's work emphasized that even apparently meaningless activities by groups possessed some kind of social function. **RJ**.

MALLOWAN, MAX
1904-1978
British archaeologist

Mallowan was one of the most successful of the European archaeologists who worked to illuminate the origins of civilization in the Near East in the 1930s and after. His excavations at Chagar Bazar, a Syrian tell site, provided an invaluable sequence of prehistoric wares, but perhaps he is best remembered for his work at the spectacular ruined city of Nimrud, last capital of the Assyrian empire. He was married to Dame Agatha CHRISTIE. **RJ**.

MALRAUX, ANDRÉ
1901-1976
French novelist

A youthful adventurer, Malraux was involved in revolutionary activities in China, Spain, and wartime France. His action novels, *Man's Estate* (1933), set in communist China, and *Days of Hope* (1937), on the Spanish Civil War, established his reputation for cinematic writing. He became a Minister in De GAULLE's governments. **CW**.

MAMET, DAVID
1947-
American playwright

Born in Illinois, Mamet helped found the Chicago St. Nicholas Theater Company, which produced many of his early plays. Works such as *Sexual Perversity in Chicago*, *Duck Variations*, and *American Buffalo* (1977) have brought him considerable acclaim for their ironic wit. His work is increasingly adapted for film. **CW**.

MANDELA, NELSON
1918-
South African political leader

Committed to converting South Africa to an equitable multi-cultural nation, Mandela has worked since his youth to end the apartheid laws of his homeland. He established the country's first black law practice and was an activist with the ANC from his 20s. Charged with treason for organizing protests during the 1950s, and advocating the use of violence in what he regarded as a just cause he was hounded by the authorities. Finally tried in 1964, he was sentenced to life imprisonment and during the next 27 years, he became a symbol of black South Africa's struggle for equality, and the world's most famous political prisoner. Released in 1990 by President F W De KLERK, Mandela's triumph has been marred by violence between rival factions of the Zulu Inkatha movement and the ANC. **JM**.

MANDELBROT, BENOIT
1924-
French mathematician

Twice a refugee from the Nazis, Polish-born Mandelbrot found the rigor of French mathematics at odds with his geometrical intuition, and moved to the United States to become a research scientist at IBM. He was always a scientific outsider, but his wide knowledge of the history of science led him to recognize the existence of similar problems in fields as disparate as economics, engineering, physiology, and meteorology. In *The Fractal Geometry of Nature* he uses the notion of fractional dimensionality to describe how superficial orderliness can be compatible with underlying chaotic behavior in a wide variety of scientific contexts. **EB**.

MANKIEWICZ, JOSEPH L.
1909-1993
American film director

Mankiewicz first worked as a screenwriter, then as an MGM producer, finally graduating to writer-director, winning Oscars in both fields for *A Letter to Three Wives* (1949) and his witty, eloquent masterpiece *All About Eve* (1950). His career sadly ground to a virtual halt after the mammothly expensive *Cleopatra* (1963). **NS.**

MANLEY, MICHAEL
1924-
Jamaican politician

Twice Prime Minister, Manley has been a strong advocate of more equality in trade between the First and Third World countries and is a past Chairman of the Socialist International Economic Commission. In 1972 he had led the People's National Party to a landslide victory, winning again in 1976, and regaining power again in 1989. He tried to strengthen Jamaica's economy through the encouragement of local industry, and introduced a free education system. **JC.**

MANN, THOMAS
1875-1955
German novelist

Born in Lübeck, Mann achieved extraordinary success at an early age with *Buddenbrooks* (1901), the story of the decline of a great bourgeois family; the book was later banned by the Nazis. His finest work, a novella rather than a novel, is *Der Tod in Venedig (Death in Venice*, 1912), which became an exquisite film. *Der Zauberberg (The Magic Mountain)* appeared in 1925, and he was awarded the Nobel Prize in 1929. To avoid the Nazis he left for Zurich, then the USA having written an attack on Facism, which also featured in *Dr Faustus* (1947). A major theme of his work was the relationship of the artist to society. **AM.**

MANNERHEIM, CARL, BARON VON, MARSHAL
1867-1951
Finnish soldier and president

As commander of the Finnish Army, Mannerheim organized the defense of the country during the 'Winter War' with Russia (1939-40); after being forced to cede territory, he committed Finnish troops to the Russo-German War from 1941 until an armistice was signed in 1944. Mannerheim was President of Finland 1944-46. **JPi.**

MAN RAY, [EMMANUEL RUDNITSKY]
1890-1976
American photographer

After studying art at the National Academy of Design in New York, Man Ray took up photography and between 1921 and 1949 worked as a freelance artist and film-maker in Paris. His early career was gathered together in 1934 in *May Ray Photographies, 1920-34*. He gave his name to the rayograph, in which images were achieved by resting objects on unexposed film. In his Parisian years he was an exemplary modern photographer, noted for ambiguous close-ups of natural and mechanical details, and for dispassionate portraits of beautiful women and art-world celebrities. **IJ.**

MANSELL, NIGEL
1954-
British racing driver

Mansell established himself as a national hero due to his gutsy driving. Brought into Grand Prix racing by CHAPMAN of Lotus, Mansell has driven for Lotus, Ferrari, and Williams. He came close to winning the Formula One World Championship on a number of occasions, before his victory in 1992, driving a Williams-Renault. **NF.**

MANSFIELD, KATHERINE
1888-1923
New Zealand novelist

Katherine Mansfield settled in London in 1903. Married to the critic John Middleton Murry, she contributed stories to his journal, publishing her first collection, *Bliss, and other stories* in 1920. An exceptional experimental writer of short stories influenced by Chekhov, she earned the envy of the reviewers, among them Virginia WOOLF. She died of tuberculosis. **CW.**

MANSTEIN, ERICH VON, FIELD MARSHAL
1887-1973
German soldier

One of the most innovative generals of World War II, in 1940 Manstein persuaded HITLER to support a Panzer advance through the Ardennes to catch the Allies in France by surprise. Its stunning success ensured that Manstein was promoted: in 1941 his corps almost took Leningrad, after which he led the 11th Army to victory in the Crimea. As commander of Army Group South in 1943, he initiated 'mobile defense' to slow the Russian advance, but could do little to stop the enemy entirely. In April 1944 he was sacked by HITLER. **JPi.**

MANTLE, MICKEY CHARLES
1931-
American baseball manager

The long New York Yankees dynasty (26 pennants in 39 seasons from 1927 through 1964) saw its last true superstar in Mickey Mantle. Mantle slugged 536 home runs, tops on the all-time list for switch hitters. A Hall of Fame center fielder, Mantle won three MVP awards and swatted a record 18 World Series homers. **MD.**

MAO TSE-TUNG
1893-1976
Chinese statesman

A Hunan peasant's son, Mao was a founding member in 1921 of the Chinese Communist Party in Shanghai. His election as Chairman of the first All-China Congress of Soviets in December 1931 coincided with the Manchuria Incident and the beginning of Japanese aggression against China. Mao, who had turned his home province into a Red enclave, called for a common front with the Kuomintang against the Japanese but CHIANG KAI-SHEK, obsessed with destroying the Communists, forced them into the Long March to northern Shansi [Kiangsi]. The alliance of convenience with Chiang

ABOVE: Mao Tse-tung, the first Chairman of Communist China.

did not survive the war and Mao drove the Nationalists off the mainland. Theories worked out when he was a guerrilla in the fastnesses of Shansi did not survive the realities of transforming the economy of China. The Great Leap Forward of 1958, an attempt to increase industrial production by molding China's vast population into rural 'people's communes,' cost millions of lives. The Cultural Revolution of 1966, in which Mao tried to revive the old revolutionary spirit by destroying bureaucracy and culture, was another disaster. China still suffers from the effects of his cult of personality. **JC**.

MAPPLETHORPE, ROBERT
1946-1989
American photographer

Mapplethorpe came to photography from underground filmmaking in the 1960s, and soon established himself as an unsettling vanguardist in whose work taboo subjects were beautifully and delectably presented. A photographer of flesh, flowers, and fine materials, he was always seen as a threat to establishment values. A fine printmaker, his work was collected by such institutions as the Museum of Modern Art, New York. **IJ**.

MARADONA, DIEGO
1960-
Argentinian soccer player

Diego Maradona was regarded as the world's best soccer player for much of the 1980s, but despite his undoubted skills, his behavior on and off the field was often con-troversial. As well as his domestic and international career for Argentina, he also played for the Barcelona and Napoli clubs in Europe. During his time in Italy he became associated with criminal groups and drug scandals and was accordingly banned from all football for 15 months from 1991. In late 1992 he was said to be planning a comeback. **DS**.

MARC, FRANZ
1880-1916
German painter

After studying theology Marc became a painter, hoping to create a new religious unity through art. Animals, particularly horses, were his main theme, as he believed them more spiritual than humans. A member of the Blaue Reiter group, his expressionist style simplified forms and used color symbolically. His work was approaching abstraction before his death at Verdun. **ER**.

MARCIANO, ROCKY [ROCCO FRANCIS]
1923-1969
American boxer

Not many professional athletes can make Rocky Marciano's claim: they never lost. Marciano won all 49 of his pro bouts. In 1951 he knocked out former champ Joe LOUIS, and the next year he won the heavyweight crown by flooring Jersey Joe Walcott. Four years and six title defenses later, he retired. **MD**.

MARCONI, GUGLIELMO
1874-1937
Italian electrical engineer

Following early research in his native Bologna, Marconi traveled to England in 1896 to demonstrate his wireless apparatus to the British Post Office. Convinced, in the face of 'expert' opposition, that radio waves could follow the curvature of the earth's sur-face, Marconi made history in 1901 by transmitting the letter "S" in morse code from Poldhu, Cornwall, to St Johns, Newfoundland. The Marconi Wireless Telegraph Company established radio stations on land and sea throughout the world to receive and transmit radio waves. Showered with honors, Marconi won the Nobel Prize for Physics in 1909. **PW**.

MARCOS, FERDINAND
1917-1989
Filipino politician

The Philippines paid a heavy price for the 20-year rule of this ex-lawyer, who, with his extravagant wife Imelda, played out a fantasy. At its most innocuous it portrayed him as a war hero and Olympic athlete. But it also led to him raiding the national finances to maintain his opulent lifestyle, and to declaring martial law in 1972. He made the mistake of using fraud to win the 1986 election over Cory Aquino, as a result of which he was deposed and exiled. **JC**.

MARCUSE, HERBERT
1898-1979
American political theorist

One of the founders of the Frankfurt Institute for Social Research, Marcuse re-established it in Columbia University after fleeing from Germany when HITLER came to power. After working for American Intelligence during World War II, he returned to academic life, arguing the need for revolutionary change to liberate the working classes from economic and psychological repression. His *One-Dimensional Man* made him a cult figure in the student movements of the 1960s, because he saw students and the alienated poor as the only people immune from manipulation by the capitalist media. **EB**.

BELOW: Ferdinand and Imelda Marcos.

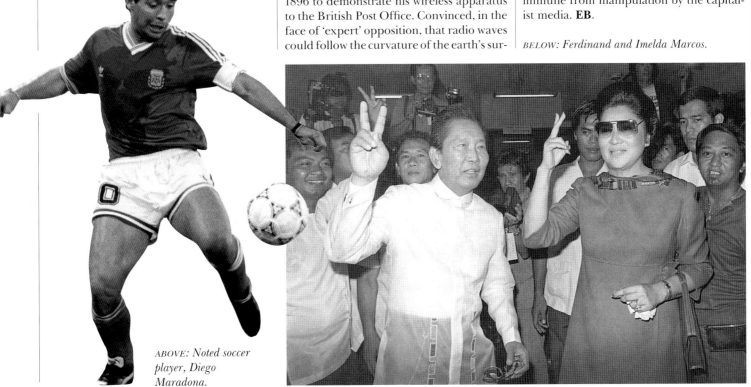

ABOVE: Noted soccer player, Diego Maradona.

MARIGHELA, CARLOS
1909-1969
Brazilian revolutionary

Son of an Italian immigrant, Marighela joined the Brazilian Communist Party in 1925. Thereafter he dedicated his life to left-wing revolution, initially following an orthodox Communist line. In 1968, however, he broke with the official Communist Party to found *Acção Libertadora Nacional*, a group intent on forcing revolutionary change from within the cities. In 1969 he produced the influential *Minimanual of Urban Guerrilla Warfare*, in which he advocated the use of armed action to polarize society and create a 'climate of collapse' preparatory to political takeover. On 4 November 1969 Marighela was killed in a gun battle with police. **JP**.

MARITAIN, JACQUES
1892-1973
French philosopher

Maritain is regarded as the foremost neo-Thomist philosopher of the century, bringing the thinking of Thomas Aquinas into the twentieth century. He converted to Catholicism after his education at the Sorbonne. As well as many distinguished academic appointments including a Chair at Princeton, Maritain was French Ambassador to the Vatican and in 1970 joined the Little Brothers of Jesus in Toulouse. Despite being highly regarded by Pope PAUL VI, he was a stern critic of Vatican II and its attempts to move the Church into the modern age. **ML**.

MARKOVA, DAME ALICIA [LILIAN ALICIA MARKS]
1910-
British dancer

A Governor of the Royal Ballet and co-founder (with Anton Dolin) of the London Festival Ballet (now the English National Ballet), Markova entered Diaghilev's company at the age of 14, creating the title roles in BALANCHINE's *Le Rossignol*. After Diaghilev's death, she danced for Ballet Rambert, the Camargo Society, and the Vic-Wells Ballet, where she was not only the first British dancer to appear as Giselle and to dance Odette-Odile, but also to create a great number of roles in ASHTON's ballets. She continued to appear as a guest ballerina with many international companies and as prima ballerina with Festival Ballet until her retirement from dancing in 1963. She continues to teach master classes at the Royal Ballet School and is a familiar figure to audiences at Covent Garden. **MC**.

MARKS, SIMON, LORD
1888-1964
British retailer

Marks joined his father's firm, the Marks and Spencer penny bazaar chain, in 1907, and in 1916, after military service, he became chairman. With his partner and friend Israel Sieff he transformed the firm into a highly successful public company specializing in clothing and with a commitment to quality at reasonable prices. He was able to exploit volume buying to obtain low-cost goods from manufacturers, and set standards that other retailers had difficulty in following. In World War II and after he served on official bodies, and much of his wealth was donated to medical research and the Zionist movement. **JW**.

ABOVE: Reggae legend Bob Marley.

MARLEY, BOB
1945-1981
Jamaican reggae singer

The Wailers were already a sensation in Jamaica when they came to prominence in the US and UK with the 1973 album *Catch a Fire*. The single 'No Woman No Cry' brought limited success in the singles charts, but a move towards more generalized pop brought wider acceptance in the late 1970s. Marley's Rasta faith and political activity in his homeland remained undiluted, however, and his last album, *Uprising* (1980) was more strident than earlier releases. The following year he died of cancer, his death ironically assuring him of by far his greatest commercial success, the compilation album *Legend* in 1984. **DC**.

MARSHALL, GEORGE, GENERAL
1880-1959
American soldier and diplomat

Between September 1939 and November 1945 Marshall held the post of US Army Chief of Staff, acting as close adviser to the president on military affairs. He was well suited to the task, having been a staff officer since World War I, when he was largely responsible for planning the St Mihiel offensive in 1918. During World War II he supervised the expansion and training of the US Army and was present at the inter-Allied planning conferences. As US Secretary of State (1947-49), he was responsible for the Marshall Plan of economic aid to war-torn Europe. **JPi**.

MARSHALL, THURGOOD
1908-1993
American lawyer

The first black person to be United States Solicitor-General as well as the first to be a Justice of the Supreme Court, Marshall's law degree course was funded from clerking and waiting at table. He made his name in Civil Rights cases, becoming special counsel for the National Association for the Advancement of Colored People. He had 23 years' service with the organization as head of its legal services' division, famously winning blacks voting rights in Texas primary elections and, by the Brown v Board of Education case of 1954, establishing that racial segregation in public schools was denying black pupils their rights under the Fourteenth Amendment. **JC**.

MARTIN, MARY
1913-1991
American actress and singer

After a top ten hit with 'My Heart Belongs to Daddy' in 1939, she starred on Broadway in *One Touch of Venus* (1943) and *Lute Song* (1946), and wrote herself into the history books by making both the stage and screen versions of the all-time great *South Pacific*. **JH**.

MARTINU, BOHUSLAV
1890-1959
Czech composer

In order to avoid political disruption in Czechoslovakia Martinu found himself travelling constantly throughout his life, spending time in France, the United States, and Switzerland. Despite all this upheaval, Martinu was a prolific composer whose works have been described as eclectic in that they combine concerto grosso form with Czech melodies. **DK**.

THE MARX BROTHERS
CHICO
1886-1961
HARPO
1888-1964
GROUCHO
1890-1977
American comic actors

The Marx Brothers were quite possibly the funniest team ever to appear on screen. Their films are as fresh and hilarious as they were half a century ago. Born in New York, they were thrown into vaudeville by an

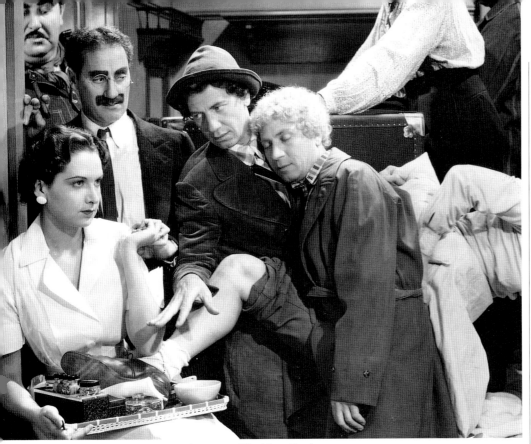

ABOVE: *Groucho, Chico and Harpo – The Marx Brothers.*

ambitious mother who initially appeared with them. Their brand of inspired lunacy caught on, and they became Broadway successes before moving on to Hollywood. At first there were five brothers, but the three everyone remembers were Chico, who played piano eccentrically and spoke with an impossible Italian accent, Harpo, the child-like girl-chasing mute who played the harp, and Groucho, with his painted moustache, cigar, loping walk, and most of the wisecracks. They began making films for Paramount in 1929; *Duck Soup* (1933) is considered to be one of their finest, and *A Night at the Opera* (1935) was enormously popular. By 1950 they had stopped making films together, although Groucho went on to a successful television career. **DC**.

MASARYK, TOMAS
1850-1935
Czech statesman

Father of Czechoslovakia, Masaryk was a Prague University Professor who made a reputation defending Slav nationalists against the Hapsburg authorities both in and out of the courtroom. During World War I he campaigned tirelessly for a united Czech and Slovak state and became its first President in 1918, remaining so until shortly before his death in 1935. **JC**.

MASON, JAMES
1909-1984
British actor

A polished performer who added luster to every film he was in, suave and handsome Mason played villains and gentlemen with equal ease. After *The Man in Grey* (1943), a Regency melodrama, he made a career out

of playing nasty evil men who browbeat sensitive heroines, but once in Hollywood he broke away from playing villains and cads. Although he hoped to become a recognized leading man, it never happened. His range was simply too great, although he left such a mark on many important films that he achieved the kind of stardom most character actors can only dream of. **DC**.

MASSEY, RAYMOND
1896-1984
American actor

Massey's first film role was as Sherlock Holmes in *The Speckled Band* (1931). Widely respected as a character actor, he played the lead in the stage and screen versions of *Abe Lincoln in Illinois* (1940). On television he is best remembered as Dr Gillespie in the *Dr Kildare* series. **DC**.

MASSINE, LÉONIDE
1896-1979
French dancer, choreographer, ballet master and teacher

Born in Russia, and trained at the Bolshoi School in Moscow, Massine graduated into the company in 1912. The following year Diaghilev invited him to join the Ballets Russes to dance the leading role in FOKINE's *The Legend of Joseph*. Massine's own first ballet in 1915 was *Soleil du Nuit*, set to a score by Rimsky-Korsakov, and for the next 16 years he was Diaghilev's principal choreographer, creating *Femmes de bonne humeur*, *Parade*, *Boutique fantastique*, *Tricorne*, and *Sacre du printemps*. In 1921 he left Diaghilev, but returned for three further years in 1925 to compose several more ballets. During the 1920s Massine also worked in England, and

in New York as solo dancer and ballet master at the Roxy Theater. In 1932 he began his association with the Ballets Russes de Monte Carlo and after the war staged revivals of his ballets for Sadler's Wells Ballet at Covent Garden. As well as studying the dances of North American Indians, Massine also worked on films: *The Red Shoes* (1946), *Tales of Hoffmann* (1951), and *Carosello Napoletano* (1954). As a dancer, his greatest successes were in character roles; as a choreographer his enormous contributions to the comedy genre and origination of the Symphonic ballet (ballets danced to complete symphonies) have made him an important figure. **MC**.

MASTROIANNI, MARCELLO
1923-
Italian actor

Mastroianni could have become a Hollywood star any time he wished over the past 20 years, a fate he has resisted. He rose steadily after the war both on stage and screen until he won international success in *La Dolce Vita* (1959) in which he was broodingly brilliant as a man trapped by luxury and decadence. ANTONIONI's *La Notte* (1961), Pietro Germi's clever *Divorce Italian Style* (1962), which won Mastroianni a British Film Academy Award, and FELLINI's *8½* solidified his fame. In the years that followed, Mastroianni became such a staple ingredient in films by great directors that he seemed almost to personify the European male. **DC**.

ABOVE: *Italian actor Marcello Mastroianni.*

MATISSE, HENRI
1869-1954
French painter

Matisse began to paint in 1890 having trained as a lawyer. He worked through a variety of influences, including the Neo-Impressionists, van Gogh, and Gauguin, gradually developing a personal style in which naturalistic color was suppressed in favor of apparently arbitrary hues. His aim was to 'transpose feelings into color', and he attempted to enhance its emotive force by distortions of form. In 1905 this bold use of color and seemingly clumsy execution earned him, and like-minded associates such as VLAMINCK, the sobriquet Fauve, or wild beast. His increasingly flat, decorative style reached a high point of expressive abstraction in the brilliant, pure color of *La Dance* and *La Musique* (1909-10). From 1914 he lived on the Riviera and returned to a more naturalistic style. Working mainly on the themes of Mediterranean interiors, Odalisques and still-life, he made free use of textile patterns as a subsidiary decorative element. He had been making sculpture since 1900 and he also produced theater designs, illustrated books, and murals. His decorative scheme for the Chapelle de Rosaire, Vence, was a major late work and the first religious building to be decorated in a modern idiom. From 1948 arthritis forced him to work in colored cut-paper and these simple, bright compositions are a fitting testimony to perhaps the greatest master of color in the twentieth century. **ER**.

MATTHAU, WALTER
1920-
American actor

An ordinary-looking man with an elastically lugubrious face, Matthau won stardom in Neil Simon's *The Odd Couple* after a steady career on stage, film, and television. He won an Academy Award for Best Supporting Actor for the ambulance-chasing lawyer 'Whiplash' Willy Gingrich in Billy WILDER's *The Fortune Cookie* (1966) and became Hollywood's leading grouch with the heart of gold. **DC**.

ABOVE: Henry Matisse working on a cut-out.

MATTHEWS, SIR STANLEY
1915-
British soccer player

Stanley Matthews is one of the folk heroes of English soccer. He was a master of the old-fashioned close control skills of the winger's position. He played 54 times for England and, in an astonishingly long-lasting career, made his last appearance in a senior game shortly after his 50th birthday. **DS**.

MAUGHAM, W[ILLIAM] SOMERSET
1874-1965
British writer

Novelist, short-story writer, and playwright, Maugham's first real success came with the autobiographical novel *Of Human Bondage* (1915). An extensive traveler, many of his works have exotic locations, like the Samoa of the atmospheric 'Rain', by far his best-known short story, which has been both staged and filmed. **AM**.

BELOW: British novelist Somerset Maugham.

MAURIAC, FRANÇOIS
1885-1970
French writer

A novelist, dramatist, and leading commentator on current affairs, Mauriac was awarded the Nobel Prize in 1952. His early tales, such as *A Kiss for the Leper* (1922) and *Thérèse Desqueyroux* (1927), are powerful, pessimistic explorations of a theme central to Mauriac's stern Catholicism: the inability of natural man to find salvation. **CW**.

MAXWELL, ROBERT
1923-1991
British media magnate

Born in Slovakia to a Jewish family, Maxwell fled to England in the wake of the Nazi roundup of Jews in Europe. He served in the British Army in World War II before setting himself up as a publisher, founding Pergamon Press. He served briefly as a Labour MP (1964-70) and launched a Buy British campaign. In the 1970s he suffered business setbacks as the Department of Trade investigated his companies but he bounced back and with the backing of many banks, bought the ailing British Printing Corporation in 1980. He turned its financial fortunes around and set about buying publishing, media, film, and other companies. He purchased the *Daily Mirror* and was hailed as its savior. He died in mysterious circumstances after falling from his yacht. After his death it was discovered that his business empire had been maintained by plundering the pension funds of the many companies he owned. **DSL**.

MAYAKOVSKY, VLADIMIR
1893-1930
Russian poet

Mayakovsky was the foremost poet of the Russian avant-garde, central to the Futurist movement, and renowned for his vital public performances. Born in Georgia, he joined the Moscow Bolshevik Party in 1908, and was arrested: in prison he began to write. In 1911 he entered the Moscow Institute of Painting, Sculpture, and Architecture, signing the Futurist manifesto, 'A Slap in the Face for Public Taste' with his fellow artists and poets in 1912. He met his great love, Lili Brik, wife of the critic Osip Brik, in 1915. Mayakovsky's work addresses the grand themes of human fate and impossible love, and searches for a language and form with which to celebrate and express a revolutionary future. Thousands of his poems were published in newspapers. Yet the authorities, LENIN among them, favoring nineteenth-century realist models of literature, found his staccato rhythms and form incomprehensible, his vigorous polemic too anarchic for comfort. Instrumental in setting up the short-lived LEF (the Left Front of the Arts) in 1923, Mayakovsky wrote the long narrative poem *Vladimir Ilyich Lenin*

(1924) on Lenin's death. His work was boy-cotted and, increasingly disillusioned, he committed suicide in 1930. Ironically STALIN was to claim him, suitably interpreted, as an official laureate. **CW**.

MAYER, LOUIS B.
1885-1957
American film executive

A ruthless quick-tempered businessman, Mayer combined an astute financial sense with an intuitive feeling for public taste. He was Vice-President and General Manager of MGM from 1924 until 1951, and the most powerful magnate in 1930s and '40s Hollywood. With 'more stars than there are in the heavens', MGM produced wholesome escapist entertainment that reflected Mayer's tastes and moral convictions. **NS**.

MAYS, WILLIE HOWARD JR
1931-
American baseball player

Mays's explosive combination of power, speed, and defense made him one of the game's greatest players. In 22 seasons (mostly with the New York and San Francisco Giants), the 'Say Hey Kid' blasted 660 home runs, third on the all-time list. He had 3283 hits and finished with a .302 batting average. A two-time Most Valuable Player in his league, he also came up with one of the most famous catches in history, a breathtaking over-the-shoulder grab in distant center field of a shot by Vic Wertz in the 1954 World Series. **MD**.

McBRIDE, WILLIE JOHN
1940-
Irish rugby union player

Willie John McBride's international rugby career spanned 1962-75, when he gained 63 Ireland and 17 British Isles test appearances. A powerful lock forward, he was a central figure in the development of forward play in Britain, achieving standards that for a time surpassed those of the previously dominant southern hemisphere teams. He captained the 1974 British Lions in South Africa, the most successful British Isles side ever. **DS**.

McCARDELL, CLAIRE
1905-1958
American designer

Born in Maryland, McCardell is considered to have been one of America's most influential designers. Having studied for two years at Hood College, in 1927 she transferred to Parsons' School of Design in New York, and later to their Paris school. She began her career in New York in the 1920s, working as a sketcher in a dress shop before joining designer Richard Turk in 1929 and moving with him to the manufacturers Townley Frocks. After Turk's death, McCardell took

over as designer and introduced the 'Monastic Dress', a highly successful, free-flowing, waistless dress cut on the bias. In the next years McCardell was influential in the field of daywear and separates, designing practical clothing for the growing number of working American women. The McCardell signature was the use of large patch pockets, metal rivets, and shoestring shoulder ties in simple fabrics such as gingham, denim and jersey. Throughout the 1940s and 1950s she continued to introduce innovative designs, including the American classic 'Popover', an unstructured, wrap-round dress, flat pump shoes based on ballet slippers, the 'diaper' style one-piece swim suit, and elasticated strapless tube tops. **MC**.

McCARTHY, JOSEPH
1908-1957
American politician

The junior Senator from Wisconsin used his witchhunt against 'Reds under the bed' to advance his career in the 1950s. His system was to proclaim the 'guilt' of his victims, usually by innuendo, and create an atmosphere of paranoia, inside and outside the House Committee on UnAmerican Activities. Celebrities in science and showbusiness were seen denouncing their friends on camera. The bubble, which had been kept inflated by the moral cowardice of his senatorial colleagues, finally burst at the televised trial hearings in 1954 and McCarthy was discredited. **JC**.

McCLINTOCK, BARBARA
1902-1992
American geneticist

McClintock's early interest in science was initially discouraged by her parents as 'unfeminine,' but they relented allowing her to study botany at Cornell in 1919. Her doctoral study of maize cytology won her immediate acclaim, but fellowships rather than a tenured post were her reward until she took up a position in 1941 at Cold Spring Harbor Laboratory, Long Island where she worked until her death. Hailed as an intuitive, even 'mystical' scientist, McClintock's ability to understand cell differentiation now never failed to impress her peers. But her discovery of 'jumping genes' which demonstrated that chromosomes were not stable and that genetic material could shift unpredictably over generations, appeared heretical in 1948. Though the discovery of the structure of DNA leant support to her theories, years of neglect by the scientific community awaited McClintock; by her own testimony 'they called me crazy.' Though given a chair at Cornell in 1956, McClintock always preferred working in isolation. It took almost 20 years for her work to be acknowledged. Awards then flowed, among them the Albert Lasker Basic Medical Research Award and the Columbia University

Horwitz Prize in 1982 and the Nobel Prize in Medicine and Physiology in 1983. **MB**.

McCULLERS, CARSON
1917-1967
American writer

Carson McCullers was born in Georgia. She is best known for her novella *The Ballad of the Sad Café* (1951), which Edward ALBEE dramatized in 1963. This grotesque tale and its eccentric characters places McCullers in the Southern Gothic tradition, but it nevertheless presents an affirmative vision of the world of the crippled individuals she represents. Among her other works *The Heart is a Lonely Hunter* (1940) stands out, an extraordinary allegorical story of the life of a deaf-mute, and his enigmatic presence in the life of four people. **CW**.

ABOVE: The controversial American senator, Joe McCarthy.

McCULLIN, DON
1935-
British photographer

Working as a photographer for *The Sunday Times* (London), McCullin took pictures of armed conflict in Biafra, Bangladesh, the Congo, Vietnam, and Cambodia. Those pictures were collected in *The Destruction Business* (1971), and established McCullin as an unforgettable photographer of war's bleakness. Previously he had worked for *The Observer* (London), and he subsequently turned to landscape photography. **IJ**.

McGILLICUDDY, CONNIE [CORNELIUS ALEXANDER]
1862-1956
American baseball manager

As a baseball manager, nobody won more games, lost more games or even approached the longevity of Connie Mack; he was a regal fixture of the American sporting world all through the first half of the twentieth century. Mack managed the sometimes splendid, sometimes pathetic Philadelphia Athletics from 1901 to 1950, into his 87th year. He also served as President, Treasurer and co-owner of the team, twice having to fire star players to save money. His teams won nine pennants and five world championshps. All told, he managed for 53 years, compiling a record of 3731-3948. **MD.**

McINDOE, SIR ARCHIBALD
1900-1960
New Zealand surgeon

An outstanding plastic surgeon, McIndoe is best known for his work at Queen Victoria Hospital, East Grinstead, rebuilding the faces of airmen badly burned during World War II. He was apparently able to restore not only appearances but also the will to live. McIndoe made further important contributions to plastic surgery in peacetime devising several new operations. **GL.**

BELOW: Canadian media guru Marshall McLuhan.

McLUHAN, MARSHALL
1911-1980
Canadian writer

McLuhan became a media guru in the 1960s for espousing his controversial views on communications and its effect on civilization. He argued that shifts in media technology – such as that from print to electronic media – cause fundamental changes in consciousness and social relations, coining the phrase 'global village' to describe a world where television makes everyone instant participants in public events. **DSL.**

McMAHON, SIR WILLIAM
1908-1988
Australian politician

A lawyer, he held successively the ministries of Navy and Air, Social Services, Primary Industry, Labour and National Service, Federal Treasury, and Foreign Affairs in the Liberal Government (1951-71). He became Deputy Leader of the party in 1966 and Leader when Gorton was deposed in 1971. He automatically succeeded as Prime Minister, being defeated by Labor the following year. **JC.**

McNAMARA, ROBERT
1916-
American politician

McNamara became a focus of controversy because of the central role he played in the Vietnam War. Defense Secretary in KENNEDY's administration, he advised the President that the American role in Vietnam would be completed by 1965. In 1967 disillusioned and aware that he was wrong, he resigned to become President of the World Bank. **JC.**

McQUEEN, STEVE
1930-1980
American actor

McQueen was one of the hottest stars of the 1960s and 1970s, the natural heir to BOGART and CAGNEY, with a cool self-awareness, ice-blue eyes and a strong sense of independence. He got his first break in Hollywood with the starring role of the bounty hunter in the TV series *Wanted Dead or Alive*. He performed his own stunts in *The Great Escape* (1963) with its spectacular motorcycle chases, but it wasn't until *Bullitt* (1968), with its pace-setting car chases, that he really carried a film on his own. After that, he was a superstar, and films like *Papillon* (1973) and *Tom Horn* (1980) followed. **DC.**

MEAD, MARGARET
1901-1978
American anthropologist

Mead's fieldwork was mainly in Samoa and New Guinea, where she was particularly interested in investigating how the behavior of the individual is influenced by the surrounding culture. Her work aroused especial interest because it seemed to demonstrate that many of the behavioral patterns adopted by human beings in accordance to their age and sex were defined by the culture they happened to belong to, rather than being biologically determined. Some of her fieldwork has since been strongly criticized, but Mead remains one of the few anthropologists successfully to exploit her work in the field to encourage reform (particularly educational reform) in modern Western society. **RJ.**

MEADS, COLIN
1936-
New Zealand rugby union player

Colin Meads played a record total of 55 international matches and 133 games in all for New Zealand in the period 1957-71. He epitomized the type of powerful, uncompromising forward play for which All Black teams are known and he was described by one New Zealand writer as playing with a 'total dislike of the opposition'. His abrasive style and physique were also indicated by the nickname 'Pine Tree', and during his career he was involved in several controversial on-field incidents. **DS.**

MEDAWAR, SIR PETER
1915-1987
British biologist

As Professor of Zoology and Comparative Anatomy at University College, London University, Medawar conducted the work that won him the Nobel Prize in 1960 (sharing it with Frank McFarlane Burnet). In the early 1950s his experiments showed that the ability of an animal to produce a specific antibody developed during its lifetime and was not inherited. The implications of this discovery were far-reaching, indicating that an animal's immune system could be influenced by external factors. **ES.**

MEINHOF, ULRIKE
1934-1976
German terrorist

Educated at Marburg University, Meinhof embraced the anarchist student politics of the 1960s, initially expressing her views through journalism. In May 1970, however, she adopted more direct methods, mounting a spectacular prison rescue of her lover, Andreas Baader. Together they founded the Red Army Faction, popularly known as the Baader-Meinhof Group, which carried out terrorist attacks on 'Establishment' targets in the early 1970s in what was then the Federal Republic of [West] Germany. Captured in Hanover in 1972, Meinhof was put on trial with other members of the group; found guilty, she was imprisoned by the German authorities but committed suicide in 1976. **JP.**

MEIR, Golda [Goldie Mabovitch]
1898-1978
Israeli politician

Emigrating from Russia to the United States to escape a Cossack pogrom, she met BEN-GURION in Milwaukee and started working for the Zionist cause at 15. She emigrated to Palestine in 1921 and in 1940 took over the political department of Histadrut, the labor federation. The political campaign for a Jewish national state benefited by $50 million from her fundraising in the United States and when Israel was founded she was appointed first Ambassador to the Soviet Union and then Labor Minister. She was Foreign Minister in 1956 and became Prime Minister on Eshkol's sudden death. She was blamed for delaying mobilization in the Yom Kippur War and resigned. In 1974 she wrote the bestselling *My Life*. **JC**.

MEITNER, Lise
1878-1968
Austrian physicist

In 1912 Meitner, her physics doctorate in hand, joined Otto HAHN at the Kaiser Wilhelm Institute in Berlin, although as a woman she was not allowed in the main building. Together they discovered numerous radioelements, but their best research occurred in the 1930s, when nuclear chemistry was born. They repeated the JOLIOT-CURIES' neutron bombardment of uranium and set about investigating the products. After Jewish-born Meitner fled to Sweden from the Nazis in 1938, Hahn discovered that the bombardment products were isotopes of radium. Using this discovery Meitner and her nephew Otto FRISCH developed the theory of nuclear fission. **MB**.

MELLON, Andrew
1855-1937
American financier and administrator

Mellon, a Pennsylvania financier, used his inherited millions to undermine President WILSON's foreign policy after World War I, helping to secure American rejection of the League of Nations. He headed the aluminum price-fixing trust and in 1921 became treasury secretary in HARDING's notoriously corrupt government. He reduced taxes for the rich, and turned a blind eye to tax evasion. He remained in office until 1932, despite having helped to set the scene for the 1929 slump. Having used his bought influence to do his country no good, he secured his posthumous reputation by substantial gifts to universities and art foundations. **JW**.

MENDELSOHN, Erich
1887-1953
American architect

Berlin- and Munich-trained Mendelsohn set up practice in 1912. His projects up to the 1920s reflect his interest in Expressionism, in the bold sketchiness of his drawings and the extraordinarily sculptural form of the Einstein Observatory, Potsdam (1920). His later buildings, such as the Schocken stores at Stuttgart (1927), and Chemnitz (1928), reflect this in the way form expresses function, but they are very refined and considered in their use of steel and glass, with alternating bands of windows and opaque panels. After leaving Germany in 1933 Mendelsohn developed these ideas on a larger scale, often employing concrete, in projects in Palestine (Haifa hospital, 1927), England (De la Warr Pavilion, Bexhill-on-Sea, 1934) and America (Maimonides Hospital, San Francisco, 1946-50). **AR**.

MENDES, Chico
1944-1988
Brazilian environmentalist

Coming to prominence in the 1980s as an opponent of deforestation in the Amazon basin, Mendes organized his fellow rubber-tappers against land speculators who were intent on the destruction of the Amazonian rain forests. His assassination in December 1988 led to significant changes in government policy toward the ecology of Brazil. **JP**.

MENDES-FRANCE, Pierre
1907-1982
French politician

Minister of national economy in de GAULLE's provisional government from 1944-45, Mendès-France was elected Prime Minister in 1954 and negotiated with Vietnam to end French involvement in Indochina. Possibly as a result of the débâcle at Dien Bien Phu, he lost the 1955 election. Often a maverick, the teetotaller Mendès-France is best remembered as the Prime Minister who tried to persuade the French to drink milk, in the process outraging the wine trade. **JC**.

MENNINGER, Karl
1893-1990
American psychiatrist

Karl Menninger developed the internationally renowned Menninger Clinic in Topeka, Illinois. He set up a number of psychoanalytical training institutes around the United States, and had a considerable influence on the training and practice of American psychiatrists in the middle part of the twentieth century. He created a model village for abused and deprived children in an effort to prevent the development of delinquency and criminality, and campaigned against nuclear war and for prison reform. Latterly Menninger's influence has waned, as biological psychiatry has become more prominent on both sides of the Atlantic. **MBe**.

MENUHIN, Sir Yehudi
1916-
British violinist and conductor

Menuhin was a child prodigy who at the age of seven made his first public appearance in San Francisco and made his European debut at age eleven. Although his technical abilities were astounding, most impressive at this early stage was his maturity of interpretation. Menuhin adored BARTOK's music and commissioned a solo violin sonata from him in 1944. He also performed ELGAR's violin concerto in 1932 for which Elgar coached him and conducted the performance. Latterly Menuhin has turned his talents toward conducting and has set up a specialist music school in the west of England for gifted pupils which bears his name. **DK**.

ABOVE: Sir Robert Menzies, Australian statesman.

MENZIES, Sir Robert
1894-1978
Australian politician

A storekeeper's son, Menzies became the grand old man of Australian politics after a stormy political career. A brilliant lawyer, he was appointed Attorney-General and Minister for Industry immediately on entering the House of Representatives in 1934 and succeeded JA Lyons as leader of the Liberal Party and Prime Minister in 1939. The Labor Opposition vetoed Menzies' suggestion of a wartime coalition and he embarked on a tour of Britain and North America which many saw as a bid for the leadership of a projected Imperial War Cabinet which would displace CHURCHILL. His neglect of his Australian electors forced his resignation in August 1941. He turned round an apparently hopeless political position to win the 1949 election and stayed in power until 1966. A prime mover in the establishment of the South-East Asian Treaty Organization, he was made a Knight of the Thistle. **JC**.

MERCKX, EDDY
1945-
Belgian cyclist

Eddy Merckx recorded five wins in cycling's most grueling event, the Tour de France, a distinction he shares with two other riders. During his first win in 1969 he also demonstrated his all-round abilities by winning both the points competition and the 'king of the mountains' in addition to the overall title. **DS.**

MERMAN, ETHEL
1909-1984
American singer and actress

One of the great ladies of the American musical, with her immensely powerful voice and personality to match, Merman got her big break with GERSHWIN's *Girl Crazy* (1930). Other hit shows included Cole PORTER's *Anything Goes* (1934) and Irving Berlin's *Annie Get Your Gun* (1946). **JH.**

MERTON, THOMAS
1915-1968
American Trappist monk, theologian and poet

Merton's New Zealand-American background perhaps holds the key to an understanding of his life. Educated in Europe and America, he converted to Catholicism in 1938, taking the radical step of joining the Trappist monastery of Our Lady of Gethsemane in Kentucky. His autobiography, *The Seven Storey Mountain*, won international acclaim and attracted many to the contemplative life. He was strongly influenced by the Orient and he emphasized the importance of monastic life being grounded firmly in sound scholarship and social concern. He was in certain respects a victim of his own success, often being forced away from his own contemplation by many admirers seeking guidance. **ML.**

MESSERSCHMITT, WILLY
1898-1978
German aircraft engineer

Designer of gliders from 1921, Messerschmidt founded Messerschmitt Flugzeugbau in 1925. After a period of collaboration with BFW, in 1928 he became one of its managers and then, in 1933, a director. After designing the Bf 108 cabin monoplane, he produced his greatest work, the Bf 109 fighter. **MT.**

MESSIAEN, OLIVIER
1908-1992
French composer

Following Olivier Messiaen's success as a student at the Paris Conservatoire, his position as principal organist at La Trinité gave him the opportunity to explore the expressive range of the organ. This forty-year in-cumbency was to shape his compositional style in all media and produce some of the finest organ music composed since J S Bach, such as *La Nativité du Seigneur* and *La Transfiguration*. World War II saw Messiaen conscripted into the French army and captured by the Germans; undaunted, he composed his *Quartet for the End of Time* in his prison camp in Silesia and performed it with three fellow-inmates in front of 5000 other prisoners. On his release he became a Professor at the Paris Conservatoire, but the quality of his compositon overshadows his legacy as a great teacher. Deriving inspiration from diverse sources, including Gregorian chant, medieval modes, Hindu rhythms, and twelve-note scales, Messiaen's music has an extraordinary richness. His passion for birdsong is clearly evident, while his concept of death, informed by a devout Catholic faith, provides the strong spiritual impetus which drives his music. Profound, but capable of levity, exuberant or contemplative, Messiaen's works exude a freshness and originality which few composers have matched, as can be seen on an orchestral scale in his epic *Turangalila Symphony*. **DK.**

MESSNER, REINHOLD
1944-
Italian mountaineer

Of German descent, Messner was born at Villnoss in the Italian Tyrol, where he still lives. He began rock climbing in the Dolomites and was soon joining major expeditions to the highest peaks of the Andes and Himalayas, including a 1970 trip to Nanga Parbat when his brother Günther was killed descending with Reinhold after their successful summit bid. In 1975 Messner and Peter Habeler (Austria) made the first 'Alpine style' (ie lightweight, without oxygen supplies, fixed ropes, high-altitude porters) ascent of the 8000-meter Hidden Peak. Messner has since climbed all 14 peaks over 8000 meters in this fashion, including the first ascent of Everest without oxygen (also with Habeler in 1978), and a later solo trip to Everest in which his whole equipment weighed only 40 pounds. As well as the magnitude of his own achievement, his example has helped to ensure that a more ecologically responsible approach, using less artificial assistance, has become generally preferred by participants in his sport. **DS.**

MESTRAL, GEORGES DE
1902-1990
Swiss inventor

While millions of people over the years must have noticed the seed heads that stick to ones clothes on country walks it was de Mestral who first looked at them scientifically and invented Velcro. This revolutionary fabric fastener uses two strips of material, one containing myriads of little hooks and the other 'eyes' to catch into them. **PW.**

MEYER, ADOLF
1866-1950
American psychiatrist

Meyer had a great influence on psychiatry in the English-speaking world, especially in the United States. He thought that psychiatric conditions had multiple causes, and developed a psychobiological approach as a way of understanding the interplay between mind and body. Like FREUD he also emphasized the importance of early influences upon the child. **MBe.**

MIES VAN DER ROHE, LUDWIG
1886-1969
German-American architect and designer

After training with his master-mason father, Mies spent a formative three years in Peter BEHRENS's office. Early, unbuilt, projects show the influence of the heavy neoclassical aspect of Behrens's buildings. But a more lasting influence was the variety of metal-product design Behrens did for AEG, and the metal framing with glass infill which he also used in his buildings. From 1919 Mies began designing revolutionary steel- or reinforced-concrete-framed skyscrapers, one (1922) with the first continuous ribbon windows. Other 1920s' designs show the influence of De Stijl (see MONDRIAN), as in the German pavilion at the 1929 Barcelona International Exhibition, a composition of concrete slab and sheet-glass wall. Mies succeeded GROPIUS as head of the Bauhaus Architecture School but Nazi interference forced him to emigrate to the United States in 1938. There he designed a whole campus of vigorously metal-framed buildings (begun 1940) for the Illinois Institute of Technology, Chicago, where he taught. Mies's famous aphorism 'less is more' is as elegantly exemplifed by the steel-and-glass monolith of the Seagram Building, New York (1958), as by the glass-walled Edith Farnsworth House, Fox River, Illinois (1946-50), a single story structure whose thin concrete-slab roof appears to float. **AR.**

MIFUNE, TOSHIRO
1920-
Japanese actor

Mifune, the internationally respected Japanese actor, first came to the attention of the West with *Rashomon* (1950), winning the Venice Grand Prix and the American Academy Award for Best Foreign Language Film. Director Akira KUROSAWA was recognized as a great artist, and their partnership was legendary. He brought sanity, sexiness, and a world-weary air to historical adventures like *Seven Samurai* (1954), one of the first of its kind to catch on in the West. He formed his own company in 1963, and made *Grand Prix* (1966), his first Hollywood film. He is best known for the lead in the popular television mini-series *Shōgun*. **DC.**

MIKOYAN, ARTEM IVANOVICH, COLONEL-GENERAL
1905-1970
Soviet aircraft engineer

Born in Sanaïne, Armenia, Mikoyan attended college at Tbilisi before becoming an engineer at the railway works at Rostov-on-Don in 1923 and then elsewhere. After military service, he returned to Moscow in 1930 and joined the Jukouski Academy in 1931, qualifying as a pilot. From 1939 until his death in 1970, he headed the experimental construction bureau OKB, responsible for MiG fighters designed with the collaboration of his countryman, Mikhail Iosifovich Guryevich. Mikoyan's first aircraft was the Oktyabryonok of 1935, which incorporated an American 22hp engine. He assisted Polikarpov with the I-153 biplane, before producing the first fighter to bear the famous Mikoyan and Guryevich (MiG) name, the MiG-1 monoplane, which flew as a prototype piston-engined fighter in 1940. The team was responsible for the MiG-9, an early jet fighter that won the designers a Stalin Prize and, more importantly, the MiG-15, the first outstanding Soviet jet fighter which entered service from 1948-49. Subsequent MiGs became the most operated jet fighters in the world, introducing level supersonic flight and variable-geometry wings to Soviet fighter units for the first time. **MT.**

DE MILLE, AGNES
1909-
American dancer and choreographer

Niece of the legendary film director Cecil B de Mille, and a graduate of the University of California, de Mille studied dance with Marie RAMBERT and danced in London in the 1930s. Her first important choreographic work was *Black Ritual*, set to Darius Milhaud's *Creation du Monde* for the American Ballet Theater in 1940. Later ballets included *Rodeo*, with music by Aaron COPLAND for the Ballets Russes de Monte Carlo in 1942. She is best remembered, however, as a leading figure in American musical-comedy, choreographing *Oklahoma!* (1943), *Carousel* (1945), *Brigadoon* (1947), *Gentlemen Prefer Blondes* (1949), *Paint Your Wagon* (1951), and *110 in the Shade* (1963). **MC.**

DE MILLE, CECIL B.
1881-1959
American film director

De Mille's name is synonymous with sex, sadism, sanctimoniousness, and spectacle. Sometimes known as the 'founder of Hollywood' after the success of *The Squaw Man* in 1914 he is probably best remembered for epic productions such as *Samson and Delilah* (1949) and *The Ten Commandments* (1956) which were massively successful and vulgar. **NS.**

MILLER, ANN
1919-
American actress

Miller was a professional dancer when she broke into movies at the age of 17, but it wasn't until the late 1940s in some of MGM's finest musicals that her ability was fully recognized. She later performed in night clubs and on television, delighting Broadway audiences with Mickey ROONEY in *Sugar Babies* in the early 1980s. **DC.**

MILLER, ARTHUR
1915-
American playwright

Born in New York, Miller came to prominence in 1947 with *All My Sons*, a strong drama succeeded in 1949 by the far more impressive *Death of a Salesman* for which he won a Pulitzer Prize. *The Crucible* (1953) uses the Salem witch trials of 1692 as a powerful parable for McCarthyism; Miller himself later refused to name names to the House Un-American Activities Committee investigating Communism in 1956. Fame came too from his 1956 marriage to Marilyn MONROE to which *After the Fall* (1964) makes reference; they were divorced in 1960. His later plays are less noteworthy. **AM.**

MILLER, [ALTON] GLENN
1904-44
American bandleader

Raised in a middle-class home in Iowa, Glenn Miller started his musical career as a passable trombonist before deciding to form his own band in 1937. Initially unsuccessful, Miller tried again in 1938 and created the world's most famous big band. Playing such immortal numbers as *Moonlight Serenade*, *In the Mood*, and *Tuxedo Junction*, Glenn Miller brought his distinctive swing sound before a global audience during World War II when he joined the US Army. Miller died when the plane carrying him to France after D-Day crashed in heavy fog over the English Channel. **DK.**

LEFT: Arthur Miller.

RIGHT: Glenn Miller.

ABOVE: *Iconoclastic writer, Henry Miller.*

MILLER, HENRY
1891-1980
American writer

Novelist, essayist, and painter, Henry Miller was born in New York and lived in Paris in 1930-39, where he wrote his most famous book, the notorious *Tropic of Cancer* (1934), an explicit, autobiographical account of a sexually promiscuous lifestyle which was banned for years as pornographic, as were others of his works. An extraordinary travel book, perhaps his best work, *The Colossus of Maroussi*, appeared in 1941 after a trip to Greece. In 1944 he settled in Big Sur, California, and continued to fight censorship, publishing novels, essays, and correspondence. Rebel and iconoclast, he was naturally an inspiration to the Beat Generation writers. **AM**.

MILLER, LEE
1907-1977
American photographer

Lee Miller is best known for her pictures of the death camp at Dachau, liberated in the spring of 1945. She reported on the closing phases of World War II for *Vogue*. She began her career in 1927 as a fashion model in New York for the same magazine, before moving to Paris in 1929 to live and work with MAN RAY. **IJ**.

MILLET, KATE
1934-
British painter, sculptor, and feminist

Millet attended Catholic schools before studying at Minnesota, Oxford, and Columbia. Her doctoral thesis entitled 'Sexual Politics', was published in 1970. In it she examined the notion of patriarchy detailing the implications, in literature and life, of the pattern of dominance and subordination in male-female relationships. She taught at Columbia University for a time, and was involved with the Civil Rights movement, but her radicalism lost her the appointment. In the aftermath of the revolution in Iran, she went to agitate for women's rights but was expelled by the Khomeini government. Millet remains a powerful influence in the women's movement. **EMS**.

MILLS, C. WRIGHT
1916-1962
US sociologist

In his book *The Sociological Imagination* Mills championed the cause of a sociology that was politically and socially relevant and that would help people to understand the forces that shaped their lives. It was also an attack on the narrow horizons of the sociological establishment with whom he was in constant battle. Mills pursued his ideas through books on power and social stratification such as *White Collar* and *The Power Elite*. **DSL**.

MILLS, SIR JOHN
1908-
British actor

Mills made his film debut in *The Midshipmaid* in 1932, and during the war gained popularity playing stoic heroes. He has since presented moviegoers with a fine portfolio of screen portraits, winning an Academy Award for the mute village idiot in *Ryan's Daughter* (1970). Although his acting style is low-key, he is extremely versatile. **DC**.

MILSTEIN, CÉSAR
1927-
Argentinian molecular biologist

Milstein was engaged on research into the immune system in Cambridge in 1975 when he and his colleague George Kohler developed monoclonal antibodies (MABs), cloned cells which can assist in the diagnosis and treatment of the immune system. The full potential of this research has still to be realized, and Milstein was awarded the Nobel Prize for Medicine in 1984. **ES**.

ABOVE: *Kate Millet, feminist artist.*

HO CHI MINH [NGUYEM THAT THANKH]
1890-1969
Vietnamese statesman

'Uncle' Ho's was the second successful post-war revolution in the Orient, but unlike MAO he was a sophisticated cosmopolitan figure who only returned to his country in 1945. He declared himself First President of the Democratic Republic of Vietnam (1946-54). He had spent many years from 1917 in Paris, helping to found the French Communist Party and by proxy, its Indo-Chinese equivalent. As the Viet-Minh it swept the French from Indo-China in 1954 after eight years of bloody conflict and established a people's republic in the north of which he became President (1954-69). His last eight years were spent in the increasingly bloody struggle to unify Vietnam, as the Americans poured in troops and aid to shore up the rival Saigon regime. He did not live to see his dream turn sour in a destitute, albeit united Vietnam. **JC**.

ABOVE: *Vietnamese statesman, Ho Chi Minh.*

MINNELLI, VINCENTE
1910-1986
American film director

Minnelli was most closely identified with the MGM musicals, and directed many of the most distinguished: *Meet Me in St Louis* (1944), *The Pirate* (1948), *An American in Paris* (1951), and *Gigi* (1958). He was also a skilful director of intense melodramas, such as his Hollywood saga, *The Bad and the Beautiful* (1952) and his van Gogh biopic *Lust for Life* (1956). **NS**.

MINTOFF, DOM
1916-
Maltese politician

Twice Prime Minister of Malta (1955-58 and 1971-83), Mintoff instituted a republic in 1974, and further strained relations with Britain by restricting the use of Malta's naval base. He formed close and controversial links with Libya, and also hoped to increase Soviet investment in the country. **JC**.

MIRÓ, JOAN
1893-1983
Spanish painter

Miró began painting seriously in 1911, from 1919 visiting Paris regularly and in 1924 joining the Surrealists. Fascinated by their exploration of the unconscious, he began using the hallucinations brought on by extreme hunger to unlock his imagination. He developed a highly personal, pictorial language of cryptic signs and fantastic forms which have a delightfully playful exuberance. The insect characters at play in *Carnival of Harlequin* (1924/25), have a deliberately child-like character, for he tried to stimulate basic sensations of humor, fear, and excitement through his art, and from the 1940s produced murals, ceramics, and prints to make this art more accessible to the public. His output and international reputation were rivaled only by PICASSO. **ER**.

MITCHELL, JONI
1947-
American pop singer

It wasn't until 1969 and the album *Clouds* that Mitchell, already a successful songwriter, achieved recognition as a singer. The follow-up, *Ladies of the Canyon*, held the public's interest partly due to the single 'Big Yellow Taxi', an early green anthem, and in 1976 her first all-electric albums were followed by *The Hissing of Summer Lawns*, a perceptive parody of middle America. The rhythmic flavor of this album bore witness to an increasingly jazz-oriented style, and throughout the 1980s she continued to make interesting contributions backed by an array of influential names from the jazz community. **DC**.

MITCHELL, REGINALD J
1895-1937
British aircraft engineer

Designer of the legendary Spitfire, Mitchell died before it helped win the Battle of Britain. After an apprenticeship to a locomotive company, in 1916 he joined Pemberton Billing as an aircraft draftsman, but ended the war as chief designer and engineer with Supermarine, with which he worked on many aircraft, including Schneider Trophy racers. **MT**.

BELOW: Spanish Surrealist artist, Joan Miro (left).

ABOVE: Joni Mitchell, the singer-songwriter.

MITCHELL, WILLIAM E, GENERAL
1879-1936
American air commander

Controversial advocate of air power and a separate air force, Mitchell was court-martialed for his views in 1925, and resigned in 1926. Proved correct, in 1946 Congress authorized a Medal of Honor. Originally an infantry private, he graduated from Staff College in 1909 and joined the aviation section in 1915. **MT**.

MITCHUM, ROBERT
1917-
American actor

A durable actor, Mitchum broke into films in a series of Hopalong Cassidy westerns. *The Story of GI Joe* (1945) made him a star and earned him an Oscar nomination. *River of No Return* (1954) with Marilyn MONROE was a box office hit, and Mitchum was superb as the vicious, relentless pursuer in the first version of *Cape Fear* (1962). **DC**.

MITSCHER, MARC, ADMIRAL
1887-1947
American sailor

Mitscher was the US Navy's main aviation expert and a commander of carrier forces in the Pacific throughout World War II. He commanded USS *Hornet* which was used to launch the bomber raid against Tokyo in April 1942, and was present at the Battle of Midway. Air Commander of Guadalcanal from April 1943, Mitscher went on to lead the powerful Task Force 58 in 1944. **JPi**.

ABOVE: The first Socialist President of France, François Mitterand.

MITTERAND, FRANÇOIS
1916-
French politician and president

An inscrutable and highly skilled political operator, Mitterand is one of the great survivors of French politics. Active in the Resistance during World War II, he also worked briefly for the Vichy government. He held a number of ministerial posts during the 1950s and 1960s, first standing as presidential candidate for the Federation of the Democratic and Socialist Left in 1965. Having been defeated by GISCARD D'ESTAING for the presidency in 1974, he finally achieved his aim in 1981, becoming the first socialist President of the Fifth Republic. His presidency has not delivered the 'rupture with capitalism' that he promised, but he has nationalized key firms, increased the minimum wage and played a major role in formulating EC policy. **JM**.

MIYAKE, ISSEY
1935-
Japanese designer

After graduating from Tama University in 1964, Miyake went to Paris where, in 1966, he worked first for Guy Laroche and later, GIVENCHY. By 1969 Miyake was in New York working with Geoffrey Beene. His first show was held in New York in 1971, followed in 1973 with a Paris show, by which time he had developed his hallmark style: a layered and wrapped look using geometric shapes of textured fabrics that mix Western and oriental influences. **MC**.

MOBUTU, SESE SEKO
1930-
Zairean politician and president

President of Zaire since 1965, when he also became Commander-in-Chief of the Armed Forces, Mobutu was Minister of Defense until 1989. A former journalist and colleague of LUMUMBA's until he seized power for three months in 1960, he was Chairman of the Organization of African Unity in 1967. **JC**.

ABOVE: President Mobutu of Zaire.

MOHAMMED REZA PAHLAVI, SHAH
1919-1980
Iranian monarch

Succeeding his father REZA SHAH in 1941, Mohammed Reza lacked the strength to prevent a resurgence of nationalist and Shi'ite opposition in Iran. In 1951 he was forced to accept Mohammed MOSADDEQ as Prime Minister, who alienated Western powers by nationalizing the Iranian oil industry. Mohammed Reza reasserted his power in 1955 with US help, after which he turned to his armed forces for protection. High spending on arms, coupled to policies of Westernization and modernization, led to public opposition, crudely suppressed. In January 1979, Mohammed Reza left Iran, opening the way to fundamentalist Shi'ite rule under the Ayatollah KHOMEINI. **JP**.

MOLOTOV, VYACHESLAV [VYACHESLAV MIKHAILOVICH SERIABIN]
1890-1986
Russian politician

Nicknamed 'stone backside' by STALIN, he was the perfect factotum for the dictator, sitting through endless party congresses and top-level international conferences to interpret his master's wishes. He didn't even protest when his Jewish wife was sent to the gulag. As so many first-rank Bolsheviks were in exile when the February 1917 Revolution broke out he rose rapidly in the Petrograd Party and in 1921 was appointed Secretary of the Central Committee by LENIN. He was Prime Minister of Russia from 1930 to 1941 and Foreign Minister of the USSR from 1939, doubling as Deputy Head of Government. Molotov helped Stalin create the postwar Eastern Bloc at the Yalta Conference but was dismissed by KRUSHCHEV in 1957 and appointed Soviet representative at

LEFT: *Vyacheslav Molotov (center), Soviet statesman.*

the International Atomic Agency in Vienna 1960. He was expelled from the Communist party in 1962 but was rehabilitated shortly before his death. **JC**.

MONDRIAN, PIET
1872-1944
Dutch painter

Mondrian trained in Amsterdam. His early subdued landscapes gave way to brightly colored Expressionist paintings until, in 1911 he went to Paris and encountered Cubism. His aesthetic asceticism attracted him to abstraction for its own sake and in his *Arbre* series and the seascapes he produced on returning to the Netherlands in 1914, he carried Cubist principles much further toward abstraction than the Cubists themselves. Eventually his works were no longer abstractions from nature but autonomous abstract constructions. On a white ground a black scaffolding, constructed from verticals and horizontals alone, contained blocks of primary color. In 1917 Mondrian founded the De Stijl movement with DOESBURG, based on the theory behind his style, which he called Neo-Plasticism. Believing that humankind was entering a new age in which order was all-important, he felt the artist should reject representation in favor of the expression of order by strictly limited means. In 1919 he returned to Paris, continuing to pursue his formula rigorously. Moving to London in 1938, in 1940 he settled in New York and a new vigor entered his work. Without abandoning Neo-Plasticism, his work became more colorful, eliminating black, and works such as *Broadway Boogie-Woogie* (1942-43) appear infused with the syncopated rhythms of jazz music and New York life. **ER**.

MONK, THELONIOUS
1920-1982
American jazz composer and pianist

Monk was something of a hardliner in the be-bop of the 1940s; uncompromising in his angular and alienating keyboard style, he worked with a familiar group of musicians, refusing to discuss his work with critics as he struggled for acceptance. In later years however, he was acknowledged as one of the most important composers since ELLINGTON. **DC**.

MONROE, MARILYN
1926-1962
American actress

More than 30 years after her death, the public is still fascinated by Monroe. She was the world's favorite blonde, cuddly and vulnerable, whose image quickly tarnished, leaving her a frustrated, neurotic, and tragic victim of the Hollywood that created her. The pity was that she had real talent as well as sex appeal. She was just another blonde bit-part actress until her first noteworthy roles in *The Asphalt Jungle* and *All About Eve* (1950). A born scene-stealer with a genius for self-promotion, the news that she had posed nude for a calendar in 1948 only enhanced her image. The ultimate in her sex-pot roles came in *Gentlemen Prefer Blondes* (1953), and her most ethereal, heart-stopping performance was in *Bus Stop* (1956). But one of her best was *Some Like It Hot* (1959), in which she played a brilliant comedic parody of herself. Sadly she failed in her quest to be taken seriously, never receiving an Academy Award nomination. Her last film, *The Misfits*, written by her then husband, playwright Arthur MILLER, and co-starring Clark GABLE, was excellent, but by then things had gone drastically wrong. Divorced from Miller, in and out of psychiatric hospitals, she died of an overdose of barbiturates. **DC**.

BELOW: The eternally alluring Marilyn Monroe.

MONTAGINIER, LUC
1932-
French virologist
GALLO, ROBERT C
1937-
American biochemist

Montaginier and Gallo are likely to be remembered for the controversy surrounding the discovery of the HIV virus as much as the discovery itself. It is now accepted that both reported the isolation of the same virus (now called HIV) from AIDS patients in May 1983. Gallo's group at the National Cancer Institute, Maryland, USA, and Montaginier's at the Pasteur Institute in Paris have made separate claims of having been the first to identify the causative agent of AIDS. Revelations of cross-contamination of the French and American viral samples have complicated the question of who had the virus first. While Montaginier made the first identification, he demonstrated its viral character at the same time as Gallo and it is therefore probable that the two will ultimately be credited jointly with its discovery. **ES**.

ABOVE: *Field Marshal Montgomery – 'Monty'.*

MONTGOMERY, BERNARD, 1ST VISCOUNT, FIELD MARSHAL
1887-1976
British soldier

After distinguished service in World War I, Montgomery gradually gained promotion until, in 1939, he was commanding a division. His calm actions during the retreat to Dunkirk in 1940 enhanced his reputation and he was rewarded with promotion to corps command. In August 1942 he took over the 8th Army in North Africa, boosting morale by preparing for a counter-offensive against ROMMEL's forces in Egypt. At Alam

Halfa in September he fought a defensive battle, but at Alamein in October-November he achieved a decisive victory. He then pursued Rommel into Tunisia before commanding British troops in the invasions of Sicily and Italy. Recalled to Britain in December 1943, Montgomery was given command of all land forces for the invasion of North-West Europe, and supervised both the D-Day landings and the subsequent breakout operations. In September 1944 when EISENHOWER arrived in Europe as Supreme Commander, Montgomery commanded the Anglo-Canadian 21st Army Group, leading it through Belgium and Holland, across the Rhine into northern Germany. A cautious strategist, popular with his men, his superiors often found 'Monty' difficult and high-handed. CHURCHILL summed him up as 'indomitable in retreat; invincible in advance; insufferable in victory.' **JPi**.

MOODY, HELEN WILLS
1906-
American tennis player

Helen Wills was a successful painter, but she made her mark primarily as an artful tennis player, the top woman in the game for most of the 1920s and early 1930s. She won a total of 19 Grand Slam singles titles (second on the all-time list), including eight crowns at Wimbledon and seven at the US Open. **MD**.

MOON, SUN MYUNG
1920-
South Korean founder of the Unification Church

Little is known of the controversial founder of the Unification Church's early life, but in his book *The Divine Principle*, he claimed a vision at the age of 16 to carry on Christ's unfinished work. In 1954, following expulsion from the Presbyterian Church and imprisonment in North Korea, he founded the Unification Church and has courted controversy ever since both through his spurious commercial and political activities, as well as his alleged brainwashing of gullible youngsters. Known derogatorily as Moonies, his followers have retained great faith in him despite a series of scandals, as proven by the mass wedding he presided over in 1992 of over 100,000 couples many of whom had not even met before. **ML**.

MOORE, BOBBY
1941-1993
British soccer player

Bobby Moore played 108 times for England, over 90 of them as captain of the team. The highlight of his career was leading the side to victory in the 1966 World Cup final but he also won honors in English and European club competitions, playing for most of his career with the West Ham club in London. **DS**.

MOORE, GEORGE EDWARD
1873-1958
British moral philosopher

A leading member of the Bloomsbury Group and a Fellow of Trinity College, Cambridge, Moore influenced Bertrand RUSSELL away from idealism, and an entire generation of British philosophers towards analytical philosophy. His major work *Principia Ethica* argued that moral goodness cannot be defined in terms of 'naturalistic' properties but is known by direct intuition, and that the right action is that which maximizes good. His 'Ideal Utilitarianism' is thus opposed to the classical utilitarianism of Mill, which he accused of committing the 'Naturalistic Fallacy'. His belief that philosophy is wrong wherever it conflicts with common sense is deployed against both idealists and skeptics, and is at its clearest in his 'Proof of an External World'. **EB**.

MOORE, SIR HENRY
1898-1986
British sculptor

The son of a Yorkshire miner, Moore was for 40 years considered Britain's greatest living artist. After war service he attended Leeds School of Art and the Royal College of Art, London (1919-23). He taught at the Royal College (1925-32) and Chelsea School of Art (1932-39), and from 1940 until his death he lived and worked in Much Hadham, Hertfordshire. Early on Moore rejected classical precepts of beauty and proportion, preferring to charge his work with expressive variety and formal vigor. These were qualities he found in ancient meso-American and Middle-Eastern sculpture seen in the British Museum, as well as in the work of Italian quattrocento painters such as Masaccio. Another theme found throughout his life's work was a truth to the material, so that the inherent physical qualities of wood, bronze, or stone were always a major part of the finished work. Although Moore flirted in the 1930s with European-influenced abstraction, most of his work was inspired by natural forms: the female figure and mother and child were much-explored subjects. The poignant drawings he made of

ABOVE: *British soccer captain Bobby Moore.*

ABOVE: *Sculptor Sir Henry Moore at work.*

war-time figures sheltering in the London Underground made him a household name. His postwar work was often on a massive scale partly because of his many public commissions. **AR**.

MOORE-BRABAZON, JOHN, LORD BRABAZON OF TARA
1884-1964
British pioneer aviator

Learning to fly in France in 1908, in 1909 Moore-Brabazon became the first Englishman to make a recognised airplane flight in England. In the following year he was awarded the Royal Aero Club's aviator certificate No 1. During World War II he chaired the committee which formulated Britain's postwar commercial aircraft requirements. **MT**.

MOREAU, JEANNE
1928-
French actress

Moreau made her debut in *Last Love* (1949), the first of many roles as sexually aware, if not liberated, characters, but it was a decade before Louis MALLE recognized her genius with *Elevator to the Scaffold* (1958). She went on to work with many great directors, including TRUFFAUT, whose *Jules et Jim* (1961) highlighted her on-screen charisma. **DC**.

MORGAN, JOHN
1837-1913
American financier

John Pierpont Morgan, inheritor of a family banking business, specialized in railroad reorganizations, thereby stabilizing the chaotic competition that had deterred foreign investment. Having won control of a substantial part of the eastern railroad network he turned his attention to steel and created by merger the US Steel Corporation, the world's biggest company. In 1912 he was investigated by Congress and criti-

cized for his financial domination of so much of US industry, but his work was mainly beneficial, bringing order into the competitive system and ousting many a robber-baron. **JW**.

MORISON, STANLEY
1889-1967
British typographer

Morison was the twentieth century's leading expert on the design and use of typography. He spent much of his career as advisor to the Cambridge University Press and the Monotype Corporation, but his most enduring memorial is the Times New Roman typeface; created for *The Times* in 1932, this has now established itself as perhaps the leading modern typeface. **RJ**.

MORITA, AKITO
1921-
Japanese electronic engineer and businessman

Morita is the imaginative mind behind the highly-successful Sony Corporation which he co-founded in 1946. A physics graduate, Morita was interested in radios and sound, and this, combined with his passion for miniaturization, has led to innovations such as the world's first transistor radio and the Sony Walkman. **PW**.

MORO, ALDO
1916-1978
Italian politician

Moro aroused fierce controversy as Prime Minister when he tried to form a broad political front with the Communists. He was kidnapped and murdered by the Red Brigades in 1978 and his own Christian Democratic party has since been criticized for apparent dilatoriness in their response to the crime. He had successively held the portfolios of Justice, Education, and Foreign Affairs. **JC**.

MORRIS, WILLIAM, 1ST VISCOUNT NUFFIELD
1877-1963
British motor manufacturer

William Morris made his company a success by learning from the work and experience of Henry FORD in America with regard to mass production and marketing. Morris had actually spent time in America studying the industry, and used American engines in the early 1915 Morris Cowley. Ironically what he learnt led him to undercut prices in the UK on cars like the Model T Ford. His aggressive pricing policy sent some companies into liquidation – Wolseley for one had been the largest car manufacturer in 1914, yet was taken over by Morris in 1926. Morris joined Herbert AUSTIN in 1952 to set up BMC. **NF**.

MORRISON, JIM
1943-1971
American rock singer

Teen poet Morrison first met keyboard player Ray Manzarek at UCLA in 1965, and by 1967 the Doors' first album had hit the charts giving them international success on the back of the single 'Light My Fire.' But before 'Hello I Love You' from the third album made it to the top in 1969, Morrison had been charged with 'lewd and lascivious behavior' resulting from his stage act, one of many such incidents which marked him out as a role model for the young and antisocial. The last album, *LA Woman* appeared in 1971 shortly before Morrison's death from a heart attack while in his bath in Paris, an event which did nothing to diminish his cult status. **DC**.

MORRISON, TONI
1931-
American novelist

Toni Morrison is arguably the foremost black woman writer working in the United States today, and a major influence on the development of the American novel. Born in Lorain, Ohio, her fiction has an extraordinary epic range and is rich in allegory. It is often placed within a tradition that includes Hawthorne, Melville, and FAULKNER. It draws on a number of forms, from oral narratives and African folk-tales, to the syncopated rhythms of improvised jazz; it attempts to excavate the forgotten and silenced histories of black culture and experience, and celebrates the desires and energies discovered there, while exploring the cost of psychic and racial violence. Her most recent novels are undoubtedly the finest: *Beloved* (1987) is set in the last days of slavery, the story of a mother who is haunted by the child she has killed rather than return her to captivity; *Jazz* (1992) is a formally daring narrative, using musical improvisation as a model to capture the experience of life in Harlem after the Armistice. **CW**.

M

ABOVE: Jelly Roll Morton.

MORTON, JELLY ROLL
1885-1941
American jazz pianist, composer, and singer

Morton came to New Orleans just as jazz was exploding on the scene, and it is on his early work, first as a solo artist and then with the Red Hot Peppers, that his reputation rests. He took ragtime and expanded it to include greater expressiveness and dynamic range, incorporating Caribbean rhythms to create the essential flavor of 1920s New Orleans. Rich and successful throughout the 1920s, he fell from grace in the 1930s and ended his days running a Washington club amid legal wrangles which he instituted to prove that he had 'invented' jazz and that his many imitators had stolen his work. **DC.**

MOSER-PRÖLL, ANNEMARIE
1953-
Austrian skier

Annemarie Moser (neé Pröll) was the top women's Alpine skier throughout the 1970s. Her total of 62 individual wins in major events is unsurpassed. She was overall World Cup champion six times and also won record numbers of titles in the downhill and giant slalom disciplines. **DS.**

MOSLEY, SIR OSWALD
1896-1980
British politician

An establishment maverick, Mosley's defection from the Conservative to the Labour Party was followed in 1930 by his resignation from the Cabinet over the government's unimaginative response to unemployment. On forming the British Union of Fascists his policies became anti-Semitic and his methods intimidatory. Legislation curbed his campaigns in 1936, but Mosley was not detained until 1940. Although he stood at the 1959 Election, now campaigning against immigration, most of his postwar years were spent in self-imposed exile. **JP.**

MOSS, STIRLING
1929-
British racing driver

Moss was the first racing driver to become a household name in Britain. He began racing in 1948 and later drove for Vanwall, Maserati, Cooper, Lotus, and Mercedes-Benz in Grand Prix racing, besides a whole host of other formulae. Often called the greatest-ever driver never to have won the World Championship, Moss came second in 1955, 1956, 1957, and 1958. **NF.**

MOSSADEQ, MUHAMMAD
1880-1967
Iranian politician

Mossadeq was a millionaire landowner who became an unlikely street hero as the first Middle Eastern politician to nationalize his country's oil, despite Western boycott. At 64 he became a spokesman on popular causes in parliament, checkmating a Soviet oil claim and calling on the government to cancel the Anglo-Iranian oil company's concession. Carried to power by the popular will in 1951, he wrecked Iran's economy by his nationalization program. He tried to dominate the Shah and was toppled in a CIA plot in 1953. **JC.**

MOTHER THERESA, [AGNES GONXA BOJAXHIU]
1910-
Albanian nun

Undoubtedly one of the most heroic characters of the century, this tiny nun has gained universal respect for her work amongst the poorest of the poor in Calcutta. After personal experience of the horrific living conditions in Calcutta as a teaching member of the Sisters of Loretto, she founded her own order, the Missionaries of Charity, in 1948 designed specifically to offer practical aid to the dying and destitute of Calcutta. The work of her order has now spread internationally and despite her age she is still highly active building hospitals, schools, orphanages, and leper colonies. When photographed with world leaders she continues to provide a poignant reminder of the inadequacy of the northern hemisphere's response to the third-world crisis. **ML.**

MOTHERWELL, ROBERT
1915-1991
American painter

Motherwell entered the Otis Art Institute, Los Angeles, in 1926, but was equally active as a theorist. He studied philosophy at Stanford and Harvard Universities, and in 1945 became Director of the *Documents of Modern Art* series. His first one-man exhibition, in 1944, included brilliantly colored collages, a medium developed throughout his career. His paintings became increasingly abstract, while retaining figurative overtones. In 1949 he began his *Elegy to the Spanish Repub-*

lic series, employing a motif of vertical bands framing oval shapes, in stark black and white. His 1968 *Open* series, explored the effect of color used on a grand scale. **ER.**

MOTT, SIR NEVILL FRANCIS
British physicist
1905-

Like his parents, Mott worked at Cambridge. His most famous research was on the electronic properties of metals and semiconductors. He was awarded the Nobel Prize for Physics with Philip Anderson and John van Vleck for their work on the electronic properties of disordered systems in 1977. **DD.**

MOUNTBATTEN, LOUIS, 1ST EARL, ADMIRAL
1900-1979
British sailor and Viceroy of India

A great grandson of Queen Victoria, Mountbatten followed his father, Prince Louis of Battenberg, into the Royal Navy. By 1939 he was a captain on destroyers; in May 1941 his ship, *HMS Kelly*, was sunk off Crete. Later that year he was appointed Chief of Combined Operations, and organized a number of successful commando raids. Between 1943 and 1945 he was Supreme Commander South-East Asia, responsible for the defense of India and the expulsion of the Japanese from Burma. In 1947 he oversaw Indian independence as the last Viceroy of India. He was murdered by Irish Republican terrorists in 1979. **JPi.**

MUBARAK, HOSNI
1928-
Egyptian politician

The Six-Day War of 1967, the nadir of Egyptian military fortunes, also saw the beginning of Mubarak's rise to power as he was given the job of rebuilding a shattered Air Force. As Commander in Chief he masterminded the Egyptian revenge in the Yom Kippur War of 1973 and two years later became Vice President. In 1981 he was elected President after SADAT's assassination and negotiated the return of Sinai to Egypt in 1982. He has acted as broker in peace negotiations between the West, Israel, and the Palestinians. Economic and religious problems, however, remain unresolved. **JC.**

MUDDY WATERS
1915-1983
American blues guitarist

Born McKinley Morganfield, Muddy Waters was an experienced blues guitarist by the 1940s, and after the war began recording hits such as 'Rollin' Stone'. However, he began to fade in the mid-1950s, and it was only with the emerging rock'n'roll movement that his influence was recognized, leading to a renewed interest in his work in the mid-1960s. **DC.**

MUGABE, ROBERT
1924-
Zimbabwean statesman

The 'Sea-green incorruptible' of the African independence movements, Mugabe transformed Ian SMITH's rebel Rhodesia into a new state with a broadly Marxist ethos but one in which the white settlers kept much of their economic power. Made President of the Zimbabwe African National Union (ZANU) in 1977, he beat Nkomo, leader of the Zimbabwe African People's Union (ZAPU), at the polls in 1980 to gain a mandate to remodel Zimbabwe. This he did with state planning, while stopping short of imposing a one-party state. His reputation has suffered since he paid off old scores against the Matabele in a bloody campaign. Since ZANU and ZAPU merged in 1987 Zimbabwe has been effectively a one-party state. The worst drought for a century in 1992 put Zimbabwe's increasingly shaky economy under almost unendurable strain. **JC**.

MUHAMMED, ELIJAH
1897-1975
American religious leader

Abandoning his 'slave name' of Poole in the 1930s, Muhammed led the American Nation of Islam movement from 1934 until his death. It combined elements of Islam, Christianity, and Black Nationalism, and thanks in part to the activities of Malcolm X, had a following of half a million at its height, a reaction to postwar America's inability to fulfil its promises to its Black citizens. **ML**.

ABOVE: *Zimbabwean politician, Robert Mugabe.*

MULLER, HERMANN
1890-1967
American geneticist

Muller was educated at Columbia University, where he resolved to study genetics. After further training at Cornell University, and at the Rice Institute in Houston, Texas with Sir Julian Huxley, he then specialized in analyzing the rate at which mutations occur. His career took him around the world several times, and he worked in Leningrad, Moscow, Edinburgh, Amherst, and finally at Indiana University. Muller made careful quantitative studies of mutation rates under both natural and artificial conditions, first showing that temperature increased the mutation rate, and then that radiation had a marked effect of up to *150. His knowledge of the far-reaching effect of irradiating germ cells led him to campaign against irradiation for humans. **CR**.

MULLER, PAUL HERMANN
1899-1965
Swiss chemist

Muller spent his career with the Swiss company J R Geigy with whom his most famous achievement was the development of DDT. The chemical had already been synthesized in 1873, but he patented it and produced it as a synthetic insecticide, for which he gained the Nobel Prize for Physiology and Medicine in 1948. It was widely used to prevent epidemics and in agriculture after World War II before it became discredited because of its environmental impact. He is also credited with the addition of lead to petrol to improve car performance, and the development of CFCs as a refrigerant and a propellant for aerosols. He committed suicide in 1965. **DD**.

MUNTHE, AXEL
1857-1949
Swedish physician and writer

Munthe was a highly competent high-society physician and his successful career included being physician to the Swedish royal family. He retired to Capri, where he built the Villa San Michele, which is the subject of his account, *The Story of San Michele*, published in 1929. It has been translated into 44 languages and remains a bestseller. Capri's sanctuary for migrating birds was established mainly through Munthe's influence. **CR**.

MURDOCH, DAME IRIS
1919-
Irish-born writer and academic

Irish Murdoch, novelist, and philosopher of note, has written many successful novels that explore her abstract concerns: good and evil, religious belief, and the nature of sexuality. Her most famous works – *The Bell* (1958), *A Severed Head* (1981), *The Black Prince* (1973) and Booker Prize-winning *The Sea, The Sea* (1978) – are formally complex psychological dramas. **CW**.

MURDOCH, RUPERT
1931-
Australian media magnate

Born in Melbourne, Murdoch started out with *The News* in Adelaide and soon built up a publishing empire in Australia. He moved to Britain where he bought *The Sun, The News of the World, The Times*, and *Today*, thus dominating the British press. He has been controversial both for the down-market style he has brought to his papers and for his antitrade union policies, notably in the News International strikes of the early 1980s. Murdoch expanded his activities during the 1980s to the United States, taking American citizenship to acquire the *New York Post* and *Chicago Sun*. He also has substantial interests in television in Australia and the United States and founded the Sky (now British Sky Broadcasting) satellite channel. **DSL**.

MUSIL, ROBERT
1880-1942
Austrian novelist

Robert Musil is renowned for his huge unfinished work *The Man Without Qualities* (1930-32), a rich, ironic narrative set in 1913. It is a sceptical, satirical meditation on the demise of the Austro-Hungarian Empire, on the indifferent universe of human action, and the violent dreams of the collective unconscious. Musil also wrote beautifully realized short stories and a shorter novel, *The Confusions of Young Törless* (1906). **CW**.

MUSSOLINI, BENITO
1883-1945
Italian statesman

Mussolini's fascism grew from his early socialism, a circle from which he had been expelled for advocating Italy's entry into World War I. But it was also a violent response to the Communist threat in the chaotic aftermath of that war. He borrowed freely from the ideas of the post-revolutionary Gabriele D'ANNUNZIO, particularly those concerning a revival of ancient Roman glories, linked to passionate nationalism. Ironically this lust for glory proved his downfall for it linked him inexorably with HITLER in the new fascist era envisaged for Europe. His 'March on Rome' in 1922 led the King to appoint him Prime Minister, a role which soon became dictatorial. But his office was always at the disposal of Vittorio Emmanuele, who dismissed him when the war turned against the Axis. He introduced economic and social reforms, reclaiming marshland in the Romagna and redistributing it for settlement, but they were at the cost of political freedom. He was executed by partisans. **JC**.

MYRDAL, GUNNAR
1898-1919
Swedish economist

Myrdal, previously interested in economic theory, in 1944 published his *An American Dilemma*, about American blacks. This showed that poverty breeds poverty, and Myrdal's later work on underdevelopment took this further by suggesting that poor countries might get poorer and the rich richer. This influenced, though not enough, aid programs for the Third World. He won the 1974 Nobel Prize for Economics jointly with HAYEK. **JW**.

NABOKOV, VLADIMIR
1899-1977
American writer

Novelist, short-story writer, and poet, Nabokov was born into a prominent St Petersburg family which emigrated in 1919. He studied modern languages at Cambridge, and lived in both Berlin and Paris before leaving for America, where at first he taught Russian literature at Wellesley College. When later appointed Professor at Cornell (1945) Nabokov had already published two novels and many stories and poems. His most famous novel, *Lolita* (1955), brought him such success (and notoriety) that he became a full-time writer and settled in Montreux. Critically acclaimed and financially successful, *Pale Fire* (1962) is the best known of his other novels. **AM**.

NADER, RALPH
1935-
American campaigner

Epitomizing the ordinary citizen fighting the big conglomerates, Nader began campaigning in the 1960s, forcing the American car industry to accept improved safety legislation. His supporters, known as 'Nader's Raiders,' exposed connexions between government agencies and industry, while he went on to campaign against unregulated car-insurance rates in California. **JP**.

NAGUMO, CHUICHI, ADMIRAL
1886-1944
Japanese sailor

In December 1941 Nagumo was commander of Japan's Carrier Fleet, responsible for executing the attack on Pearl Harbor. Following his loss of four carriers at Midway in June 1942, he was given the sinecure title Commander-in-Chief Central Pacific; in July 1944, as US forces closed in on Saipan, he committed suicide. **JPi**.

NAGY, IMRE
1896-1958
Hungarian politician

Hero of the Hungarian Rising of 1956, Nagy breached the one-party rule under Communism, permitting four-party pluralism in his brief period in power (1953-55). Noted for his 1945 land reforms, when he became Premier he introduced his New Course reforms and lifted the Stalinist yoke. The party leader Rakosi sacked him, falling in turn to KHRUSHCHEV's de-Stalinization program. When the Russians invaded he requested help from the United Nations. He was tried secretly and shot. **JC**.

NAIPAUL, V S
1932-
Trinidadian novelist

Born to a Hindu family, Naipaul settled in England following his education at Oxford. Strongly influenced by the English literary tradition, especially CONRAD, his stance has led to criticisms of his portrayal of Caribbean life and heritage in novels such as *A House for Mr Biswas* (1961). Increasingly pessimistic in political terms, his novels – including *Guerrillas* (1975) and *A Bend in the River* (1979) – have become more nihilist in outlook. They are usefully read alongside his political journalism, not least his controversial account *India: A Wounded Civilization* (1977), and his essay on Eva Perón. **CW**.

ABOVE: Abdul Nasser, Egyptian statesman.

NAMIER, SIR LEWIS BERNSTEIN
1888-1962
British historian

Born in Poland of Ukranian Jewish parents, Namier emigrated to England in 1906 and was to achieve a fearsome reputation as the most meticulous of scholars and the most savage of reviewers. As a fluent linguist and one whose native tongue was not English, he was intolerant of those who struggled to master their historical sources. Professor of Modern History at Manchester University from 1931-1953, the range of subjects at his command was vast: from Oliver Cromwell to twentieth-century diplomacy. *The Structure of Politics at the Accession of George III* changed the interpretation of British eighteenth-century history, asking the pertinent questions of who politicians actually were, what they did and said, as well as examining the family and regional influences they were prey to. **ML**.

NANSEN, FRIDTJOF
1861-1930
Norwegian explorer

At the age of 27 Nansen skied across Greenland, and five years later he deliberately forced a ship into the pack ice and drifted with it across the Arctic. He subsequently pursued an academic career as an oceanographer, and a diplomatic career as an Ambassador (to Britain). He won the Nobel Peace Prize in 1922 for his work repatriating prisoners-of-war and organizing relief for refugees immediately after World War I. **RJ**.

NASSER, ABDUL GAMAL
1918-1970
Egyptian statesman

Nasser not only revolutionized Egypt but was a standard bearer for Arab and African nationalism. He was behind the Free Officers Movement which deposed Farouk in 1952. He made Egypt a one-party state, introduced radical land reform, ensured British withdrawal from the Nile Valley, and nationalized the Suez Canal in 1956. Following the humiliation of Britain in the Suez invasion his stock rose greatly in the Third World and he formed close links with the USSR. He became President of the United Arab Republic in 1958 and brought on the disastrous 1967 War with Israel when he closed the Tiran Straits to her shipping. **JC**.

NAUDÉ, BEYERS
1915-
South African campaigner

As a minister in the Dutch Reformed Church, Naudé became aware of the suffering of his Black congregation and concluded that the South African policy of apartheid ('separate development') was wrong. Resigning from his ministry in 1963 to form the multiracial Christian Institute, he has campaigned effectively against Afrikaner insularity. **JP**.

NAVRATILOVA, MARTINA
1956-
American tennis player

One of the all-time greats in women's tennis, Navratilova went to the United States from Czechoslovakia in 1975 and quickly became a dominant force on the pro tour. She has won well over 100 tournaments, including 18 grand slam titles. She has won nine singles titles at Wimbledon, more than anyone in history. **MD**.

NEHRU, JAWAHARLAL
1889-1964
Indian statesman

An Inner Temple barrister, Nehru was at first a moderate on home rule but became a

ABOVE: *Indian Premier Jawaharlal Nehru (right) with Chou En-Lai.*

committed nationalist after the Amritsar massacre of 1919. As Mahatma GANDHI's second in command he took a major role in talks with the British on independence, and refusing to shelve the issue while the Japanese threatened India, he was imprisoned from 1942 to 1945. As President of the Indian National Congress he supervised the handing over of power and became the new dominion's first Prime Minister, subsequently building a reputation, when India became a republic, as the political guru of the non-aligned countries. The 'dynasty' he founded with his daughter Indira GANDHI perished with the assassination in 1991 of his grandson Rajiv GANDHI. **JC**.

NELSON, WILLIE
1933-
American country singer, guitarist, and songwriter

Raised by grandparents in Texas, Nelson served in Korea before settling in Nashville in 1960, where he wrote a number of country hits including 'Hello Walls' and 'Crazy', a number two for Patsy Cline in 1961. He joined RCA in 1964 and made 18 albums in eight years, characterized by his conversational singing style and relatively complex technique. Increasingly disillusioned with the slickness of the Nashville scene, he moved back to Texas and his 1975 album *Redheaded Stranger* was his first to make the pop album chart; his single 'Blue Eyes Cryin' in the Rain' made the top 20 as well as the top of the country chart. By the late 1970s he had achieved superstar status, made a series of record-breaking tours and duets with Waylon Jennings, and moved into films, notably *Honeysuckle Rose* (1980). **JH**.

NEPIA, GEORGE
1905-
New Zealand rugby union player

George Nepia is remembered as one of the finest full backs in the history of rugby. He excelled in the traditional defensive skills of his position as well as in attacking moves which have only become commonplace in much more recent times. The highlight of his career was probably the 1924 tour by New Zealand's 'Invincibles' to Australia, Britain, Ireland, and France. As a Maori he was regarded as 'not eligible' for his country's 1927 tour to South Africa. **DS**.

NERVI, PIER LUIGI
1891-1979
Italian architect and engineer

Nervi's engineering knowledge enabled him to exploit the use of reinforced concrete to produce some of the most spectacular modern buildings. He achieved eminence in the early 1930s with the municipal stadium in Florence. One of his greatest successes was the UNESCO assembly hall in Paris. Latterly his three sons joined his enterprises. **PW**.

NEUMANN, JOHN VON
1903-1957
American mathematician

While studying chemical engineering, von Neumann published what is now the standard definition of ordinal numbers, and went on to make significant contributions to many branches of pure and applied mathematics, including the standard text on quantum mechanics, and various aspects of computation and computer design. A member of the Institute for Advanced Study at Princeton from 1933, he is best known as the founder of Games Theory, the mathematical study of strategy in situations of conflict and uncertainty, and its application to economic behavior. **EB**.

NEUTRA, RICHARD
1892-1969
American architect

Trained in Vienna, Neutra emigrated to the US in 1923, and he came under the influence of Frank Lloyd WRIGHT. Neutra's austere Southern Californian regional style is exemplified by the Elementary Training School at the University of California, LA and the Fine Arts Center, for the Californian State University, San Fernando. **DE**.

NEVELSON, LOUISE
1900-1990
Russian-American sculptor

Born in Kiev, and brought up in the USA, Nevelson studied at the Art Students' League, New York, and worked with RIVERA in Mexico City in 1932-33. In the late 1950s she became internationally famous for her 'sculptured walls', reliefs built up of compartments containing both abstract shapes and commonplace objects. From the 1960s she also executed large open-air sculptures. **ER**.

NEWMAN, ARNOLD
1918-
American photographer

Associated with the development of 'environmental portraiture' in the 1940s, Arnold Newman worked as a portraitist in Philadelphia during the 1930s, before moving to Florida and, in 1946, to New York. In his portraits he habitually finds a match between site and subject, most especially in his celebrated pictures of such artists as Piet MONDRIAN and Francis BACON. **IJ**.

NEWMAN, BARNETT
1905-1970
American painter

Newman led the development of Color Field painting in the late 1940s. His characteristic style was first achieved in *Onement* (1948) in which a dark red canvas is intersected by an orange-red vertical band or 'zip.' His work gradually increased in scale and he also experimented with shaped canvases. **ER**.

NEWMAN, PAUL
1925-
American actor

Newman's first film, *The Silver Chalice* (1954), a costume epic, only served to embarrass him. But he won the Cannes Film Festival Award for Best Actor for *The Long Hot Summer* (1958) and has since been showered with Oscar nominations for, among others, *Cool Hand Luke* (1967) and *The Verdict* (1982). He won a British Film Academy Award for *The Color of Money* (1986). **DC**.

NEWTON, HELMUT
1920-
Australian photographer

Newton's career began in Berlin in 1936, in the studio of the fashion photographer Yva. During the 1960s he worked mainly for *Vogue*, and brought to fashion photography an aura of violence and eroticism which recalled the art of Otto DIX and of other Weimar artists. With AVEDON, PENN, and BAILEY, he helped dissolve the boundaries between art and fashion. **IJ**.

NICHOLAS II, CZAR
1868-1918
Russian Emperor

A weak, smallminded man, Nicholas succeeded to the Russian imperial throne in 1894 on the death of his father, Alexander III. He inherited a vast, unruly empire, riven by political and social discontents, which required a ruthless autocratic ruler to control it. Nicholas could not provide the strength or political acumen to hold his realm together. Resentment boiled over into revolution in 1905, during the disastrous Russo-Japanese War, and although Nicholas was quite prepared to order his troops to suppress the uprising, he also accepted the creation of an elected *duma* (parliament). Unfortunately he refused to allow it any power to introduce reforms, further alienating his people. At the same time, he lost the support of the aristocracy when his wife Alexandra came under the influence of the 'mad monk' Rasputin, reportedly the only man who could cure the hemophilia of Nicholas' son and heir. By 1917, in the midst of another disastrous war, revolution broke out again, this time with more success. In March, faced with implacable and almost universal opposition, Nicholas abdicated; in July 1918 he and his entire family were executed by the Bolsheviks at Ekaterinburg. **JP.**

NICHOLSON, BEN
1894-1982
British painter

Nicholson's earliest works were Dutch-inspired still lifes. The influence of Cubism from around 1914 saw his work simplify into flat shapes parallel with the picture plane. After toying with abstraction and primitivism for many years, in 1933 he produced the first of his famous *White Reliefs*: white-painted panels of simple, geometric shapes cut in shallow relief, which were partly inspired by MONDRIAN. He was in the forefront of English modernism promoting exhibitions and publications. In 1940 he moved to St Ives, Cornwall, which he had been visiting for many years, and established a colony of artists there, including John Piper and his second wife, Barbara HEPWORTH. **AR.**

NICHOLSON, JACK
1937-
American actor

After over a decade making cheap horror movies, Nicholson by chance wound up in *Easy Rider* (1969), a box-office smash. The irreverent Nicholson was in tune with the mood of the 1960s and 1970s, and *Five Easy Pieces* (1970) made him a star, who has collected Academy Award nominations with some regularity. Although *Chinatown* (1974) earned him a New York Film Critics Award, it was not until *One Flew Over the Cuckoo's Nest* (1976) that he won an Oscar for Best Actor. In 1979 he gave an eccentric and electrifying performance in Stanley Kubrick's *The Shining*, another horror movie, but a brilliant one this time. **DC.**

NICKLAUS, JACK WILLIAM
1940-
American golfer

The 'Golden Bear' has won 20 major championships, seven more than any other man in history. That total includes six titles at the Masters and five at the PGA. Nicklaus grew up in Ohio, where he was a golfing prodigy, shooting 51 over nine holes in his first round, played at the age of 10. When he was 13 he shot a 69, and went on to a stellar amateur career before turning pro in 1961. His first professional win came in a dramatic playoff against Arnold Palmer in the 1962 US Open. **MD.**

NIEMEYER, OSCAR
1907-
Brazilian architect

Walter GROPIUS designated Niemeyer 'The Bird of Paradise of the architectural world' in 1940. Niemeyer's richly visual architecture draws on the spirit and imagery of his native country. For his masterwork, the new capital of Brasilia, Niemeyer refused to accept fees beyond his civil servant's salary. His work includes office building at the Tour de la Défense, Paris. **DE.**

NIJINSKY, VASLAV FOMICH
1888-1950
Ukrainian dancer and choreographer

From 1898 to 1907 Nijinsky was a student at the Imperial Ballet School in St Petersburg and later danced at the Maryinsky Theater, both in works of the old repertory and in the

ABOVE: Jack Nicklaus (left) and fellow golfer Arnold Palmer.

RIGHT: Jack Nicholson.

early works of FOKINE. In 1908 he met Serge Diaghilev who became his mentor and creator of the Nijinsky legend. A much publicised scandal over the 'inadequacy' of his costume in *Giselle* in 1911 led to Nijinsky's dismissal from the Maryinsky theatre and he left Russia for good, joining Diaghilev's now independent Ballets Russes as 'premier danseur.' Most of his famous roles, almost all of which were created for him, were in the new Fokine works: *Scheherezade* (1910) *Spectre de la Rose, Carnaval, Petrushka, Le Dieu Bleu*, and *Daphnis et Chloë*. He was nearly always partnered by Tamara Karsavina. An incredible technician, Nijinsky's greatest quality however was his interpretive genius, his ability to transform himself completely into each of his roles, from the comic Harlequin in *Carnaval* to the tragic puppet figure of Petrushka. He devised his own new style of choreography, inspired by Greek friezes, and his first ballet *L'Après-midi d'un faune* was a succès de scandale because of his erotic gestures as the Faune. His greatest achievement was the choreography for *Sacre du printemps*, which outraged audiences who fought with supporting intellectuals on the first-night performance. On the Ballets Russes American tour in 1913, Nijinsky married the Hungarian dancer Romola de Pulszky. The jealous Diaghilev dismissed him from the company, but was instrumental in securing his release from Hungary during World War I, where he had been interned as an alien. For the Ballets Russes' second American tour in 1916, Nijinsky took over as Artistic Director. His last ballet *Till Eulenspiegel* had been conceived while he was a prisoner, and he was now suffering from illness and demonstrating some unpredictable behavior. Nijinsky's paranoia grew worse, and he gave his last performance with Diaghilev's company in Buenos Aires in 1917. He returned to Switzerland where, after a dance recital in 1919 in St Moritz, he was pronounced insane and spent most of the next 20 years in sanatoria. Once again interned in Budapest during World War II, the Nijinskys escaped to Austria in 1945 and moved to England in 1947. He died in London in 1950, his illness cutting short not only a memorable dancing career, but also an important choreographic talent. He was undeniably a pioneer of modern dance. **MC**.

NIMITZ, CHESTER, FLEET-ADMIRAL
1885-1966
American sailor

Chief of the US Navy Bureau of Navigation, on 31 December 1941 Nimitz was appointed Commander-in-Chief of the US Pacific Fleet and retained this post until the end of the war. An outstanding strategist, he succeeded in restoring the morale of the Pacific Fleet and took it to a position of initiative and offense in the first year of the war in the Far East. In May 1942 the US victory at the Battle of the Coral Sea secured communications with Australia, and the Battle of Midway the following month ensured that US bases on Hawaii were protected. With command in the Pacific now split with MAC-ARTHUR, in 1943 Nimitz assumed control of the Central Pacific from 160° East Longitude, which included Guadalcanal, the site of his next offensive in August. A strong believer in amphibious operations, Nimitz decided to attack less well-defended islands behind Japanese lines, a strategy known as leapfrogging, which cut off the main Japanese troop concentrations. His Central Pacific offensive began at Tarawa in November 1943 and culminated at Iwo Jima and Okinawa, February-June 1945. Nimitz and MACARTHUR received the Japanese surrender on board his flagship *USS Missouri* on 2 September 1945. **JPi**.

NIRO, ROBERT DE
1943-
American actor

De Niro frequently chooses roles of artistic merit over commercial success. He first came to critical attention as a not-too-bright baseball catcher in *Bang the Drum Slowly* (1973), following with *The Godfather Part II* (1974) and *Raging Bull* (1980) for which he received an Academy Award. De Niro remains one of Hollywood's outstanding talents. **DC**.

NIVEN, DAVID
1909-1983
British actor

By the start of World War II Niven was already a seasoned professional, having made his debut in *Dodsworth* (1936). After serving in the British Army during the war, he moved comfortably between London and Hollywood, continuing in debonair and urbane roles. In the 1950s he branched out into television and also starred in the most successful film of his career, the costume epic *Around the World in Eighty Days* (1956), playing Phileas Fogg. Long overdue for an Oscar, he at last won an Academy Award for Best Actor and the New York Critics Best Actor Award for his touching performance in *Separate Tables* (1958). **DC**.

NIXON, RICHARD
1913-
American politician and president

A Republican politician and 37th President of the USA (1969-1974), Nixon rose to fame during the late 1940s as a member of the House UnAmerican Activities Committee.

He was appointed Vice-President by EISENHOWER in 1956, but his own presidential bid was defeated by KENNEDY in 1960. He revived his political career in the late 1960s, winning the Republican nomination in 1968, and the election itself. His term of office was overshadowed by the Vietnam problem, Nixon advocating 'peace with honor' – a gradual withdrawal of American troops from the region. His conservative domestic and economic policies boosted US trade, and Nixon was elected for a second term in 1972. His tenure was shortlived, however; implicated in the 'Watergate Scandal', Nixon was found to have links with seven men found guilty of breaking into the Democratic Party headquarters during his election campaign. Taped transcripts of White House conversation convinced Congress that Nixon was lying about his involvement and they voted to impeach him. On 9 August 1974 Nixon resigned. **JC**.

NKRUMAH, KWAME
1909-1972
Ghanian politician

The first President of independent Ghana (1957-66), Nkrumah was a leader of the campaign for independence for the Gold Coast from 1947. His Convention People's Party was the first mass-appeal party to emerge in Black Africa, and his activities as leader earned Nkrumah a brief jail sentence in 1950. Having declared Ghana a republic in 1960, he announced that he would be President for life in 1964 and banned all opposition parties. While on a visit to Peking in 1966 he was deposed amid scenes of public jubilation. **JC**.

BELOW: US politician Richard Nixon.

NOBILE, UMBERTO
1885-1978
Italian aviator and explorer

As a result of his study of aeronautical engineering, Nobile succeeded in building himself a series of airships. In the *Norge* he flew across the North Pole in 1926 in the company of the famous explorer AMUNDSEN; as a polar aviator his achievements may be compared to those of his famous contemporary Richard BYRD. Nobile indirectly caused Amundsen's death, for it was during the search for Nobile in 1928, after the Italian had wrecked his airship *Italia* in the Arctic, that Amundsen disappeared. Nobile himself survived, but was held responsible for the catastrophe. **RJ**.

NOLAN, SIR SIDNEY
1917-1992
Australian painter

Nolan, largely self-taught, was the first Australian painter to achieve international recognition. His early abstract works included experiments with collage. Becoming increasingly interested in Australian folk history however, he developed a powerful folk-native style. Using brilliant color and bold designs he combined historical events with the stark beauty of the Australian landscape, achieving a hallucinatory intensity. His fluid brushwork is often accentuated by unusually smooth supports; for example, his 1949 series of paintings about the 1854 Eureka Stockade were executed on glass. His best-known works are a series of paintings, begun in 1946, on Ned Kelly, the notorious nineteenth-century bushranger and folk hero. **ER**.

NOLDE, EMIL
1867-1956
German painter

Born Emil Hansen, Nolde called himself after his birthplace in Schleswig. Originally a furniture carver and designer, he began painting in the mid 1890s. After visiting Paris and Copenhagen he settled in Berlin in 1906. His Expressionist style used intense, violent color and grotesque distortions, in an attempt to communicate the most primary human emotions. From 1910 he produced a number of large, ecstatic, religious works which caused violent controversy. In 1941 he was declared degenerate by the Nazis and forbidden to paint, but produced small watercolors in secret, which he called 'unpainted pictures.' **ER**.

NORDHOFF, HEINZ
1899-1968
German motor manufacturer

A trained engineer, Nordhoff developed Opel into Europe's biggest truck producer by 1936. After World War II he was responsible for rebuilding Volkswagen, and introducing the VW Beetle. VW's postwar success played a major part in Germany's industrial recovery and by 1967 VW was the fourth largest motor manufacturer in the world. **NF**.

NUREYEV, RUDOLF
1938-1993
Tartar dancer and director

Nureyev's dance career began with studies of folk dancing before his first ballet lessons with local teachers at his home in Ufa. In 1955 he auditioned for both the Bolshoi Ballet School, Moscow, and the Kirov Ballet School in St Petersburg. Accepted by both, he chose the Kirov, but his relatively late start in dancing and his somewhat 'nonconformist' attitude at first created problems. Nevertheless under his teacher Aleksandr Pushkin Nureyev was to graduate with distinction, and joined the Kirov Ballet in 1958. For the next three years he danced the leading roles in most of the nineteenth-century classics and several modern works. Outstanding success followed his first visit to Paris in 1961, but he was ordered back to the USSR. Fearing official disapproval might end his career, he sought and was granted asylum in France. His Covent Garden debut in 1962 began the historic partnership with Margot FONTEYN. Admired for his interpretation of classic heroes, he also showed his versatility in the comedy ballet *La Fille mal gardée*, and asserted that his favorite partner was the Muppet Show's Miss Piggy in their television performance of *Swine Lake*. Later becoming Director of the Paris Opera Ballet, he staged his version of *Cinderella*, where, instead of the traditional Prince, Nureyev danced the role as a Hollywood producer. **MC**.

NURMI, PAAVO
1897-1973
Finnish track athlete

Paavo Nurmi was perhaps the first track and field athlete to become an international household name. He won nine Olympic gold medals and held numerous world records throughout the 1920s. His first successes were in the 1920 Olympics (10,000 metres and cross country) and he might have added to his tally at his fourth games in 1932, but was ruled a professional. He carried the Olympic torch on its final leg for the 1952 Helsinki Olympics. **DS**.

NUVOLARI, TAZIO GIORGIO
1892-1953
Italian racing driver

Nuvolari had a unique driving style, still admired today. Born into a land-owning Italian family, the majority of his Grand Prix victories were with Alfa Romeo, although he also had success with Maserati and two notable Grand Prix victories in 1938 with the rear-engined Auto Union. Nuvolari drove his last race at the age of 58 – only three years before his death. **NF**.

NYERERE, JULIUS
1920-
Tanzanian politician

Nyerere can be seen as a well-meaning Socialist whose economic experiments ruined Tanzania, the country he had founded. A former school teacher, he formed the Tanganyika African National Union, gaining independence through it in 1961. His notorious Arusha Declaration of 1967 remodeled the country along utopian Socialist principles and forced 11 million Tanzanians to resettle on cooperatives in the bush. He proclaimed liberty for other African peoples but imprisoned large numbers of political opponents. Nyerere retired as head of state in 1985, leaving his party's chairmanship in 1990. **JC**.

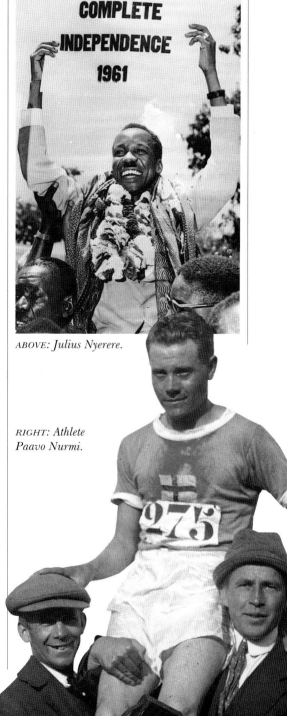

ABOVE: Julius Nyerere.

RIGHT: Athlete Paavo Nurmi.

ABOVE: *Sean O'Casey, the Irish playwright.*

O'CASEY, SEAN
1880-1964
Irish playwright

Born in the Dublin slums and self-educated, O'Casey's best plays are three of his earliest major works: *Shadow of a Gunman* (1923), *Juno and the Paycock* (1925), and *The Plough and the Stars* (1926), which caused a riot in the nationalistic audience. Its brilliant portrayal of the tragedy of Ireland aroused enormous anger because of his depiction of the 'heroes' of the Easter Rising as rather less than heroic. In the wake of this rejection, O'Casey moved to London and his later plays were never as successful nor as powerful. His six volume autobiography, published 1939-54, was well received. **AM**.

O'CONNOR, FLANNERY
1925-1964
American writer

Flannery O'Connor was born in Georgia. Her works – the novels *Wise Blood* (1952) and *The Violent Bear it Away* (1960), and the short fiction collections *A Good Man is Hard to Find* (1955) and *Everything that Rises Must Converge* (1965) - exemplify the grotesque humor and perverse violence of characterization that marks the Southern Gothic tradition. What makes her fiction distinctive is her use of dialect, and a curious critique of Christianity deriving from her own brand of Catholicism, one sympathetic to Teilhard de Chardin. **CW**.

ODETS, CLIFFORD
1906-1963
American playwright

Odets was a founder member of the Group Theater and a radical writer. *Waiting for Lefty* (1935) first brought Odets to prominence. Briefly a member of the Communist Party, he did not so much champion the working class as reject middle-class hypocrisy, and later in *The Big Knife* (1949), Hollywood corruption. **AM**.

ABOVE: *Advertising mogul David Ogilvy.*

OGILVY, DAVID MACKENZIE
1911-
American advertising executive

Born in Britain, Ogilvy emigrated to the United States in 1938. In 1948 he founded the advertising company Ogilvy & Mather, which soon became champion of the 'soft-sell,' creative approach to advertising, characterized by the use of humor and emotional appeals. An unashamed self-promoter, Ogilvy has written many books on advertising, including *Confessions of an Advertising Man*. **DSL**.

O'KEEFFE, GEORGIA
1887-1986
American painter

In 1915 O'Keeffe broke with her academic training to experiment with abstraction, deriving images from an intense, direct study of nature and emphasizing the formal qualities she discerned in organic things. During the 1920s she produced works based on magnified botanical subjects, particularly flowers, as in *Black Iris III* (1926). From 1929 she found inspiration in the majestic terrain of New Mexico and also became fascinated by the forms of bones. The stark, monumental *Cow's Skull: Red, White, and Blue* (1931), is among the first isolated studies, while later works placed skulls or pelvic bones in a desert setting, where they float surreally. A strikingly original artist, O'Keeffe was a pioneer of modernism in the USA. **ER**.

BELOW: *American artist Georgia O'Keefe.*

OLDENBURG, CLAES
1929-1990
American sculptor

Swedish born, Oldenburg spent much of his childhood in the USA. In 1950 he graduated from Yale University and in 1952 began attending the Chicago Art Institute. From 1960 he was involved in Happenings, an art form in which the spectator participates in plotless, theatrical 'events'. Among the first Pop artists, in 1961 he opened 'The Store' in New York, which sold his large vinyl or plaster sculptures of food, such as *Giant Hamburger* (1962). He also produced soft sculptures of normally hard objects, as with *Soft Typewriter* (1963), and designed colossal public monuments, in 1969 executing a giant lipstick for Yale University. **ER**.

OLDFIELD, MIKE
1953-
British guitarist and multi-instrumentalist

Mike Oldfield's *Tubular Bells* was at the top of the required listening list for progressive rock enthusiasts in the 1970s. Using the latest techniques the overdubbed display of virtuosity was followed by a handful of similar works throughout the 1970s, but later releases, while broadening his range, never achieved the same success. **DC**.

OLDS, RANSON ELI
1864-1950
American motor manufacturer

A true American automobile pioneer, a non-smoking, non-drinking Baptist, Olds built his first steam-powered horseless carriage in 1887, and founded the Olds Motor Vehicle Company in 1897. He moved to Detroit before falling out with his partner and starting the Reo Motor Car Company in 1907 which was one of the largest in the US by 1915. **NF**.

OLIVIER, LAURENCE, BARON OLIVIER OF BRIGHTON
1907-1989
British actor and director

Olivier is regarded by many as the finest actor of the century. Distinguished, handsome, and gifted, his most outstanding work was probably on the stage. He made his stage debut in 1924, and although he did not go unnoticed, he did not achieve instant fame. He divided his time between London, Broadway, and Hollywood in the 1930s, making his first film, *Too Many Crooks*, in 1930. He appeared with John GIELGUD in *Romeo and Juliet* in 1935, and two years later joined the Old Vic, where he played one great Shakespearean role after another to public and critical acclaim. Returning to America in 1939, he married Vivien LEIGH and they became Hollywood's golden couple. Olivier established himself as a superb romantic lead with a series of suc-cessful films: *Wuthering Heights* (1939), *Rebecca* (1939), and *Pride and Prejudice* (1940). In 1944 he became co-director of the Old Vic with Ralph RICHARDSON and produced some of his most powerful performances, many of which were filmed: *Henry V, Hamlet*, and *Richard III*. Olivier became the first theatrical knight in 1947 and worked to establish Britain's Royal National Theatre. He continued to appear in films and on television until the end of his life. **DC**.

O'NEILL, EUGENE
1888-1953
American playwright

Born in New York, O'Neill had a varied career, including journalism and service as a seaman, before becoming associated with the Provincetown Players (1916), for whom he wrote a series of plays drawing on his many experiences. His finest plays are the trilogy *Mourning Becomes Electra* (1931), a re-working of Aeschylus' *Oresteia* adapted to post-Civil War America, *The Iceman Cometh* (1946), set in a Bowery bar, and his masterpiece, the autobiographical tragedy *Long Day's Journey into Night* written 1940-41, and first produced and published in 1956. Few twentieth-century playwrights, and none in America have written so powerfully. He received four Pulitzer Prizes, and the Nobel Prize in 1936. **AM**.

OPPENHEIMER, SIR ERNEST
1880-1957
British financier

Born in Germany, naturalized in England, Oppenheimer flourished in South Africa. With American finance in 1917 he founded the Anglo American Corporation to develop the East Witwatersrand goldfield, and two years later he founded Consolidated Diamond Mines. His acquisition of the largest diamond producer, de Beers, and formation of his Diamond Corporation gave him virtual control of the industry. He was a member of parliament 1924-38, supporting the Smuts government, and while his domination of mining was of questionable benefit, the political power it gave him was wielded responsibly. He was a great philanthropist, with African housing and Oxford University being among the beneficiaries. **JW**.

OPPENHEIMER, JULIUS ROBERT
1904-1967
American theoretical physicist

Born of a wealthy German immigrant family, he studied at Harvard, Göttingen and Cambridge. When World War II broke out, he was appointed Director of the Manhattan Project to develop the first atomic bomb. He successfully assembled a compe-

ABOVE: *Sir Laurence Olivier, as Henry V.*

ABOVE: Brilliant physicist, Julius Robert Oppenheimer (left).

tent and skillful team of brilliant physicists, and drove it forward with the urgency required. Despite his success, he ran into political trouble afterwards. This was partly to do with his opposition to the hydrogen bomb, and partly due to the left-wing sympathies of his immediate family. He was conferred with the Fermi Award in 1963. **DD**.

OPPER, FREDERICK
1857-1937
American cartoonist

Opper's record 58 years of uninterrupted production began in 1876, with the magazine *Wild Oats*, and ended in 1932 as a result of failing eyesight. Among his best work for HEARST-owned New York newspapers were several antitrust caricatures published separately as *Willie and his Poppa* (1901) and *Alphabet of Joyous Trusts* (1902). Opper's line, developed early on for wood-engraved reproduction, retained its density and was once characterized as being like 'barbed wire and chicken scratches'. **FM**.

ORBISON, ROY
1936-1988
American country, pop singer and songwriter

A notable survivor, Orbison's first work was in dance-band style, then he moved into rockabilly mode in the mid-1950s. After a slow start, he hit the big time and established his personal style with 'Only the Lonely', which made number two in the US and one in the UK with its R&B/country style and emotional, high-register vocals. Other hits included 'Running Scared', 'Dream Baby', 'It's Over' and 'Oh, Pretty Woman'. He was as successful in the UK as the US and, with Elvis PRESLEY, was the only American vocalist to survive the British pop explosion of the 1960s. **JH**.

OROZCO, JOSE CLEMENTE
1883-1949
Mexican painter

One of the great Mexican muralists, Orozco worked as a cartoonist before beginning to paint in 1909. His first major murals were produced in 1922. Working in Mexico and the USA, he developed a monumental narrative style which, unlike that of his contemporary RIVERA, had a humanitarian rather than a directly political mission. **ER**.

ORR, BOBBY
1948-
Canadian hockey player

Bobby Orr was the first of the real 'offen-sive-minded defensemen,' shattering scoring records for the position. In the early 1970s he won three straight Hart Memorial Trophies as the league's MVP, twice leading his Boston Bruins to the Stanley Cup championship. **MD**.

ORTEGA Y GASSET, JOSÉ
1883-1955
Spanish philosopher

A leading figure in the intellectual life of Spain and founder of the Institute for the Humanities in Madrid, Ortega y Gasset founded a number of periodicals in which he also published his work. He believed there was no truth beyond the circumstances of each individual, and no reason other than historical reason. He left Spain during the Civil War and did not return until 1945. **EB**.

ORTON, JOE
1933-1967
British playwright

Noted for his black comedies, Orton was born in Leicester and first trained as an actor. A powerful mixture of sophistication and vulgarity, the farcical element in his work narrowly escapes complete tastelessness, and is redeemed by a scintillating wit. Violent, sexually perverse, cynical, they have been a commercial and critical success. From *Entertaining Mr Sloane* (1964), to *Loot* (1965), to *What the Butler Saw*, first performed two years after his death in 1969, the plays are both extremely funny and extremely transgressive. In a macabre and tragic incidence of life imitating art, he was beaten to death by his lover Kenneth Halliwell, who then killed himself. **AM**.

ABOVE: Roy Orbison (center), with fellow pop stars, John Lennon and Ringo Starr.

O

ABOVE: *George Orwell, the British writer.*

ABOVE: *War poet Wilfred Owen.*

periences in the trenches of World War I. He enlisted in the Artists' Rifles in 1915, and was in the thick of the fighting for two years. Invalided home with shell-shock in 1917, he met Siegfried SASSOON who boosted his self-confidence as a poet. He wrote his most memorable poems during the remaining months of his life, most of which were pulished posthumously. Their forceful language and consummate technical skill capture the mental and physical horrors of war perfectly. Owen returned to France in August 1918, to be killed a week before the Armistice. **AM**.

ORWELL, GEORGE [ERIC BLAIR]
1903-1950
British writer

Born in Bengal and educated at Eton, Orwell served with the Indian Imperial Police in Burma from 1922 to 1927, resigned to escape imperialism and returned to Europe and an unsuccessful writing career, funded by various poorly paid jobs. A commission from Gollancz in 1936 on unemployment in the north of England produced *The Road to Wigan Pier* (1937), and the Spanish Civil War prompted *Homage to Catalonia* (1938). Less a novelist than a social commentator, his satires of the threat of totalitarianism, *Animal Farm* (1945) and *Nineteen Eighty-Four* (1949), are his most enduringly popular works. **AM**.

OSBORNE, JOHN
1929-
British playwright

Most celebrated for his *Look Back in Anger* (1956), which established him as one of the 'Angry Young Men' of the fifties, Osborne initiated a new and exciting movement in the theater when the realism of the 'kitchen sink' drama replaced the drawing room comedy. Arguably he has never quite equalled this deeply passionate play, although anger, increasingly vitrolic, has continued to be one of the main weapons in his dramatic arsenal. *The Entertainer* (1957), *Luther* (1961), and *Inadmissable Evidence* (1964) are probably the best of his other plays. His forthright autobiography, *A Better Class of Person* (1981), attracted a great deal of attention. **AM**.

OSTWALD, FRIEDRICH WILHELM
1853-1932
Russian-born German chemist

Ostwald moved from Riga Polytechnic to Leipzig University in 1887. He developed a process for producing nitric acid, and his work on catalysts became important in the petrochemical industry. Despite his brilliance, he did not believe in the existence of atoms until 1908, long after the concept was accepted by the scientific establishment. He was awarded the Nobel Prize for Chemistry in 1909. **DD**.

OSWALD, LEE HARVEY
1939-1963
American assassin

Lee Harvey Oswald made himself the most infamous of American assassins on 22 November 1963 in Dallas, Texas, when he fired on the open-top car carrying President John F KENNEDY. Kennedy was hit by two bullets and died in hospital immediately afterwards; a policeman was also killed. Oswald was arrested, but only two days later was shot dead himself by the night-club owner Jack Ruby as he was being moved from one prison to another. Oswald had lived in the USSR for a short period, and had been involved in Communist fringe groups, but most of the conspiracy theories that have sprouted since his death have suggested that he was employed by a faction of the American right-wing or the Mafia; in fact, it seems most likely that he was simply a deluded psychopath. **RJ**.

OWEN, WILFRED
1893-1918
British poet

Owen's poetry was inspired by his ex-

OWENS, JESSE [JAMES CLEVELAND]
1913-1980
American track and field star

Jesse Owens, a black American who had grown up on a tenant farm in Alabama, proved to be the dominant athlete of the Olympics held in Berlin in 1936. He sprinted to victories in the 100 and 200 metre dashes and also helped the US 400-metre relay team blaze to a world record, but his most dramatic victory came in the long jump, where Owens was pitted against Luz Long, a German who seemed to embody Adolf HITLER's claim of Aryan racial supremacy. During the preliminaries Hitler walked out of his box before Owens's jumps in a show of disrespect, and Owens nearly failed to qualify for the finals, fouling and then jumping short on his first two attempts. Getting some advice from Long, Owens adjusted his approach and sailed into the finals, where he won with an Olympic record. Long and Owens became fast friends and maintained an active correspondence until the former's death in World War II. Owens's performance made him one of the most celebrated athletes in US history. **MD**.

ABOVE: *Jesse Owens (center), American champion at the 1936 Olympic Games.*

PALACH, JAN
1948-1969
Czechoslovak student

The reform movement which developed in Czechoslovakia under Alexander DUBCEK was suppressed in 1968 when Warsaw Pact tanks entered the country. In January 1969 Palach, a student activist, set himself on fire in Wenceslas Square in Prague in protest. His death was a powerful symbol of continued resistance to repression. **JP**.

PALME, OLAF
1927-1986
Swedish politician

The darling of left-wing intellectual circles in the 1960s and 1970s, Palme was assassinated on a Stockholm street and speculation about his death is still rife. As Prime Minister, 1968-76, and again from 1982, Palme worked to create a strong society – a radical leveling movement with high taxes funding uniformly high state benefits. A supporter of pacifist causes, Palme had strong views on European disarmament. **JC**.

PALMER, ARNOLD DANIEL
1929-
American golfer

One of the most popular figures in American sports, this Pennsylvania native is still followed around golf courses by 'Arnie's Army,' a group of particularly rabid fans. The son of a pro golfer, he took to the game at a young age, carving out great success as an amateur. He turned pro himself in 1954. By 1967 he had amassed $1 million in prize money, the first golfer ever to do so. He has won over 90 tournaments, including eight major championships. Four times he has won the coveted green jacket at the Masters. In his heyday, Palmer's trademark was roaring from behind for dramatic victories. **MD**.

PANKHURST, EMMELINE
1857-1928
British suffragette

After the death of her husband in 1898, Pankhurst (née Goulden) devoted herself to gaining the vote for women in Britain. In 1903 she and her daughters Christabel, Sylvia, and Adela founded the Women's Social and Political Union (WSPU). Known as 'suffragettes,' they and their followers adopted extreme measures, which included chaining themselves to lamp-posts and assaulting the police, to gain publicity. Many were arrested, put on trial, and imprisoned. Although other women were alienated by such actions, Emmeline Pankhurst did succeed in bringing the issue of female suffrage to the fore, not least through her personal record of eight terms of imprisonment, during which she refused to eat and suffered the indignity of forced feeding. During World War I Pankhurst diverted the

ABOVE: *Emmeline Pankhurst (left), imprisoned in 1908.*

energy of the women's movement to the war effort, encouraging women to enter male-dominated occupations. By 1917, confident that enough had been done to show that women had as much right as men to the vote, she reformed the WSPU as the Women's Party, fielding 16 candidates for the 1918 election. None was elected, but in that year women over the age of 30 gained the vote; 10 years later they achieved full suffrage. **JP**.

PARETO, VILFREDO
1848-1923
Italian economist and social scientist

Trained in mathematics and physics, Pareto first worked as an engineer, but his mathematical analyses of economic problems won him the Chair of Political Economy at Lausanne. His argument that inequality of income follows a universal pattern ('Pareto's Law') was much criticized. He then turned to constructing an elaborate general theory of the relationship between economics and sentiment and ideology, including an account of social stratification involving the 'circulation of elites'. His abiding contributions to economics were indifference curves, and the 'Pareto optimality' of welfare theory, an equilibrium in which no one could become better off without someone becoming worse off. **EB**.

PARKER, CHARLIE
1920-1955
American jazz saxophonist and composer

A leading figure in be-bop, Parker had a unique ability for taking a simple melody and embroidering it, delving into different keys, rhythms, and syncopations and miraculously arriving back at the theme. Still more remarkable was his ability to do this while under the influence of drugs; towards the end of his career Parker, or 'Bird,' as he

was popularly known, would be admitted to hospital midway through recording sessions which produced records hailed as masterpieces of avant-garde invention. He acquired both a musical facility and a narcotics habit on leaving school, working fitfully with various bands in the late 1930s, and in 1941 recording on his own, meeting Dizzy GILLESPIE for the first time. Soon after his style began to crystalize, and in recordings with Gillespie in the mid-1940s he set the pace for the new be-bop generation with an improvizational ability which provided new goals for modern jazz. **DC**.

PARKER, DOROTHY
1893-1967
American writer

Parker's legendary caustic wit as a critic is present also in her poetry and short stories. Sardonic, ironic and sophisticated, she could compress a wealth of malicious observation into one carefully crafted sentence. *Enough Rope*, her first collection, was a best-seller. The collected poems, *Not So Deep as a Well*, appeared in 1936. **AM**.

PARSONS, TALCOTT
1902-1979
American sociologist

Parsons was a social theorist who dominated American sociology from the post at Harvard which he held from 1927 until his retirement in 1973. An influential teacher, he attempted to integrate WEBER and DURKHEIM's social theories with American positivism to produce a grand theory of human action, which was known as structural-functionalism. His work has fallen into disfavor (though there are signs of a revival), most frequently being criticized as focusing on the way action and institutions function to maintain social order, rather than on conflict and change in society. **DSL**.

BELOW: *Saxophonist Charlie 'Bird' Parker.*

LEFT: US General, George Patton.

PARTON, DOLLY
1946-
American country singer, songwriter, and actress

She moved to Nashville in 1964 and was originally promoted as a pop singer; part of her success has been her ability to appeal to both markets. Her breakthrough hit in the US was 'Mule Skinner Blues' (1970), while 'Joelene' (1974) took her into the international scene, where she has remained ever since. Immensely promotable, with her outsize personality, figure-hugging clothes, and blonde wig, she has toured with Kenny Rogers, filmed with Burt Reynolds (*The Best Little Whorehouse in Texas*, 1982) and Sylvester Stallone (*Rhinestone*, 1984) and has continued to produce a stream of hits. **JH**.

PASTERNAK, BORIS
1890-1960
Russian novelist and poet

Pasternak is renowned for his anti-Stalinist epic *Doctor Zhivago* (1957), the Western cold war reception of which has obscured his avant-garde past and anti-fascism. His early poetry appeared under a futurist imprint, the best published in *My Sister Life* (1922) and *Themes and Variations* (1924), and in fragments appended to *Zhivago*. **CW**.

PATON, ALAN
1903-1988
South African novelist

This vociferous opponent of the apartheid regime was President of the South African Liberal Party until it was banned in 1968. His huge bestseller, *Cry the Beloved Country* (1948), makes a plea for racial understanding; his better, less ambiguous novel, *Too Late the Phalarope* (1953), attempts a complex analysis of Afrikaner mentality. **CW**.

PATTON, GEORGE, GENERAL
1885-1945
American soldier

Patton led the 1st US Tank Brigade in 1918 and became a firm believer in armored mechanized warfare. In November 1942 he led the armored forces that took Morocco and Tunisia in May 1943. In July 1943 he commanded US forces in Sicily, although his reputation was marred when he publicly slapped a battle-shocked soldier. A flamboyant general, in March 1944 he assumed command of the US 3rd Army, taking it to Normandy in August. Thereafter, he advanced across the Seine and into Alsace-Lorraine before crossing the Rhine and sweeping through southern Germany into Czechoslovakia. He died in a jeep accident in late 1945. **JPi**.

PAUL VI, POPE
1897-1978
Italian Pontiff

Born into a landowning legal family, Giovanni Battista Montini overcame frailty to be ordained in 1920 and to progress steadily through the Catholic hierarchy. He was appointed a cardinal in 1958 by JOHN XXIII. As Pope, his implementation of many of the reforms of the Second Vatican Council alienated many conservatives in the Church, but his firm reiteration of the Catholic Church's condemnation of artificial birth control in the encyclical *Humanae Vitae* ('Of Human Life') in 1967 alienated him completely from the liberal wing of the Church. Thus, in trying like his patron St Paul to be all things to all men, he succeeded only in pleasing none. His papacy was completely overshadowed by the impact of *Humanae Vitae* which eclipsed entirely his more progressive ideals for social justice, peace in the world, and ecumenicalism. **ML**.

PAULI, WOLFGANG
1900-1958
Austrian physicist

Born into a scientific family, Pauli's most famous work was the Pauli Exclusion Principle which related quantum theory to the structure of the atom – work which brought him the Nobel Prize for Physics in 1945. He also predicted the existence of neutrinos. **DD**.

PAULING, LINUS CARL
1901-
American chemist

Pauling's vast range of expertise embraced inorganic chemistry, organic chemistry, theoretical chemistry, mineralogy, biology, and the development of practical equipment. His work on the chemical structure of minerals, particularly the complex silicates, led to his PhD in 1925. He worked on the structure of molecules, and was the first to suggest that the atoms in a protein molecule may be arranged in a helix. Much later, Francis CRICK and James WATSON were to use this idea in their work on the structure of DNA. In 1949 he discovered that the disease sickle-cell anemia was caused by a molecular fault in the hemoglobin of blood. This was the first time that a disease was traced to a molecular factor. His book *The Nature of the Chemical Bond*, published in 1939, led to his award of the Nobel Prize for Chemistry in 1954. His insistence on the importance of vitamin C in a healthy diet – an idea still not wholly accepted – resulted in a great deal of controversy, as did his pacifist politics. He was awarded a second Nobel Prize in 1962 – the Nobel Prize for Peace for his work with the nuclear disarmament movement. **DD**.

PAVAROTTI, LUCIANO
1935-
Italian opera singer

Pavarotti's sweet and powerful tenor voice, natural musicianship, and extrovert stage presence have earned him immense popular success as a recitalist and television personality as well as in operatic performances. He established his repertoire in the 1960s, and has returned to the New York Met almost every season since his debut there in 1968. In 1981 he founded a competition for young singers based at the Philadelphia Lyric Opera. In the last 15 years his voice has deepened and darkened, and he has extended his range into more dramatic roles. **JH**.

PAVESE, CESARE
1908-1950
Italian writer

Pavese was a major Italian poet, novelist, and translator, whose suicide was seen to mark a crisis in the conscience of postwar cultural life. His novellas, in particular the exceptional *The Moon and the Bonfire* (1950), are lyrical, mythic evocations of the past which offer an anguished critique of the present. **CW**.

PAVLOV, IVAN PETROVITCH
1849-1936
Russian physiologist

Pavlov was training for the priesthood, when he read Darwin's *On the Origin of*

Species. Its profound effect caused him to leave the seminary and go to St Petersburg University, from which he graduated in natural sciences and medicine and won gold medals for his research on nerves of the pancreas and the nervous control of the heartbeat. He then spent three years researching in Germany but, on his return to Russia found himself unemployed. He and his family lived in poverty in the cold Russian winter, while he carried out research on animals in his apartment. However in 1890 he was made pharmacology Professor at St Peterburg's military academy. Pavlov constantly sought to discover 'windows' on the digestive system, developing surgical procedures for animals which were modeled on those used for humans, with the same high standards of operation. He developed an operation in which a small area of a dog's stomach was isolated in a pouch, so that its activity could be studied while the rest of the stomach contained food. From this experiment he discovered that gastric juices began to flow shortly after the dog began to eat, even when the food never reached the stomach. He also discovered, to his irritation, that the dog's saliva began to flow when it heard the dinner bell, before food was even served. This finding pointed the way to the rest of his career, despite exhortations to return to 'real physiology'. Pavlov was miserable under Communist rule and, a socialist to the core, refused the government's offer of privileges, preferring instead to continue his work on conditioned reflexes. **CR**.

PAVLOVA, ANNA [ANNA MATVEYEVNA]
1881-1931
Russian dancer

After seeing a performance of *Sleeping Beauty* at the Maryinsky Theatre in St Petersburg in 1890, the young Pavlova was so impressed that she resolved to become a dancer. The following year she entered the St Petersburg Theatre School and, two years before her graduation, danced on the Maryinsky stage in the Pas des Almées in *La Fille du Pharaon*. Her superb graduation performance of 1899 brought her to the attention of the critics. In 1903 she danced the role of Giselle and the Fairy Variations in the Prologue of *Sleeping Beauty*, before achieving the role of Aurora in 1908 – her goal since she saw her first ballet performance. Having danced 18 leading roles on the Maryinsky stage, in 1907 FOKINE created for her the role of Cygne (the Dying Swan) which became her most famous solo. She began touring abroad with the Russian Imperial Ballet in 1908, and settled at the Ivy House in London in 1912, her home for the rest of her life. Fragments of her dancing the Dying Swan were filmed in Hollywood by Douglas Fairbanks in 1924-25. Never strong, Pavlova died of pneumonia at the relatively young age of 49. **MC**.

PAZ, OCTAVIO
1914-
Mexican writer and critic

Paz, a well-known poet and intellectual, is the leading Latin American poet-critic, best known for his critical work *The Labyrinth of Solitude* (1950). Son of one of Zapata's representatives, his early Trotskyist sympathies have been supplanted by a staunch defense of modernization and liberal-democratic reform in Latin America, and attacks on Cuba and Nicaragua. His poetry is marked by an erotic mysticism that embraces material from a number of sources – pre-Conquest Mexico, BRÉTON's surrealism, aspects of Spanish colonial culture – through the revelatory poetic truth of the sexual act. **CW**.

PEAKE, MERVYN
1911-1968
British writer and artist

A nervous breakdown during World War II saw Peake invalided out of the army, after which he became a war artist, and as such visited Belsen in 1945. Best known for the bizarre Gothic fantasy trilogy *Titus Groan, Gormenghast* and *Titus Alone*, he also illustrated his own and other works. **AM**.

PEARY, ROBERT
1856-1920
American explorer

Peary, a naval officer by profession, is the first explorer known to have reached the North Pole. He made numerous attempts to reach the Pole between 1898 and 1906, losing all his toes to frostbite in the process. He finally succeeded in February-April 1909, by means of a remarkably speedy journey by dog-sled across difficult ice. **RJ**.

PECK, GREGORY
1916-
American actor

A leading man who projects strength, sincerity, and conviction, Peck became an easy-to-love box-office star. His first film, *Days of Glory* (1943), was a war movie, and he went on to star in a variety of genres – Hitchcock's *Spellbound* (1945), the Western *The Gunfighter* (1950), the romantic comedy *Roman Holiday*, the adventure *Moby Dick* (1956). He won an Oscar for his role as the liberal southern lawyer in *To Kill a Mockingbird* (1963), after which his career nose-dived. It recovered with his role in *The Omen* (1976), the most lucrative film he ever made. **DC**.

PECKINPAH, SAM
1925-1984
American film director

A descendant of pioneer settlers, Peckinpah was arguably the most important director of Westerns since John FORD. He was particularly associated with scenes of violence and harbored a vision of America's past as brutal and anti-heroic. His best film is *The Wild Bunch* (1969), though *Straw Dogs* (1972) also explored the moral ambiguity of violence with particular ferocity. **NS**.

PEDDLE, CHUCK
1937-
American chip and computer designer

At Motorola Peddle was responsible for developing many of the accepted industry approaches to microcomputer I/O systems. At Commodore he designed a new processor chip – the 6502 – which was demonstrated in a home computer, the Commodore PET, which rapidly became one of the dominant computer systems. Peddle then co-founded Sirius Technology (later Victor Technologies), whose Sirius I and Victor 9000 were the premier MS-DOS computers before the IBM XT. Subsequently Peddle transformed disk-drive manufacturer Tandon into a major producer of personal computers. His latest project – THStyme Inc – is a pioneering co-venture with post-Soviet Russia, manufacturing low-price computers in Moscow. **SR**.

PEI, I[EOH] M[ING]
1917-
Chinese-American architect

Pei's use of pure geometric forms is seen at its most typical in the spectacular glass entrance pyramids in the courtyard of the Louvre, Paris. Earlier designs include the 'Chinese puzzle' of the east wing of the National Gallery, Washington, DC (completed 1978), and the triangular design of the huge Bank of China, Hong Kong. **DE**.

ABOVE: Actor Gregory Peck holding his Oscar in 1963.

PELE, [EDSON ARANTES DO NASCIMENTO]
1940-
Brazilian soccer player

Pele's remarkable talents were early recognized by the Santos club of São Paolo and the Brazilian national team. As a teenager he was a star of the Brazil side that won the World Cup in Sweden in 1958 and retained it in 1962. In 1966 he was fouled unmercifully by opponents who could see no other way to match his abilities, but in 1970 his mature talent was central to another superb Brazilian win. He made 110 appearances for Brazil and scored 97 international goals. In the twilight of his career he also played briefly for the New York Cosmos. His autobiography *My Life and the Beautiful Game* sums up his commitment to the highest sporting values. Many people would regard him as soccer's greatest ever player. **DS**.

PENKOVSKY, OLEG, COLONEL
1919-1963
Russian spy

Penkovsky was a decorated and high-ranking artillery officer, an expert on rocketry, who revealed crucial military information to Western intelligence from 1960 – information that was vital to KENNEDY in his bluffing of KHRUSHCHEV during the Cuban missile crisis. Penkovsky's motives were essentially idealistic, for he despised the Communist system and believed KHRUSHCHEV might provoke a nuclear war. He was caught and executed by the KGB in 1963. **RJ**.

PENN, IRVING
1917-
American photographer

One of a new generation of photographers who made the crossover between art and fashion, Penn was student of the great Alexey Brodovitch in Philadelphia in the 1930s. He began to work for *Vogue* in New York in 1943. His studio portraiture, begun in Peru in 1948, took him all over the world (*Worlds in a Small Room*, 1974). Emphatically formal, and elegantly lit, his portraits ask for admiration rather than for sympathetic understanding. **IJ**.

PENZIAS, ARNO ALLAN
1933-
American astrophysicist

Born in Germany, Penzias, fled with his family to America in the late 1930s and was educated in New York. He worked at the Bell Telephone Laboratories from 1961, and studying the sky with a radio telescope he detected radio signals that led to proof of the 'big bang' theory of the origin of the universe. **DD**.

RIGHT: Israeli politician, Shimon Peres.

ABOVE: The legendary Brazilian soccer star, Pele.

PERES, SHIMON
1923-
Israeli statesman

Consistently advocating a more conciliatory line to the Palestinian problem, Peres has been a leading left-wing politician since 1959. Leader of the Israeli Labour party since 1977, he led protests against the 1982 massacre of Palestinians in Beirut refugee camps. Prime Minister in 1984 as part of a power-sharing deal with the right-wing Likud, Peres withdrew Israeli forces from Lebanon in 1985. The coalition collapsed in 1990. **JM**.

PERÓN, JUAN
1895-1974
Argentinian politician

Perón was the charismatic Tribune of the Plebs who put his stamp on postwar Argentina. After seeing fascism at work when he was military attache in Rome, he introduced his own model, 'Peronism,' when his officers' junta overthrew President Castillo in 1943. From Minister of War he was elected President in 1946, a position he held until he in turn was ousted in a coup in 1955. His Peronista party was run by his glamorous wife Eva until her early death in 1952

ABOVE: *President Juan Peron of Argentina, and glamorous wife, Eva.*

and folk sentiment about her memory helped Perón back to power from his Spanish exile in 1973. The economic crisis which he failed to solve before his death a year later helped usher in a military dictatorship. **JC**.

PERRET, AUGUSTE
1874-1954
French architect

Perret's family firm specialized in re-inforced concrete construction, and he was among the first to exploit and express the material in his buildings. His rue Franklin Apartment Block (Paris, 1902-03) shows the stark rectilinearity of contrast between post-and-lintel reinforced concrete framing and infill which characterized most of his later work. This approach, which differed from the more romantic and visually inventive sweeps of such architect-engineers as Pier-Luigi NERVI, was internationally influential from the 1930s to the 1970s. **AR**.

PERRY, FRED
1909-
British tennis player

Fred Perry was the most successful British tennis player ever. He was already an international table-tennis player when he began to play tennis seriously. He won Wimbledon three times in a row (1934-36) and also had successes in the US, French, and Australian championships. He played professionally from 1936 and later became an American citizen. **DS**.

PERSHING, JOHN, GENERAL
1860-1948
American soldier

A soldier of distinction, Pershing served in the Spanish-American War of 1898, in the Philippines in 1899-1903, and in Mexico in 1916. He was appointed commander of the US Expeditionary Force to France in 1917 and his operations established the credibility of US troops. Universally known as 'Black Jack,' Pershing was US Army Chief of Staff, 1921-24. **JPi**.

ABOVE: *British tennis champion, Fred Perry.*

PÉTAIN, PHILIPPE, MARSHAL
1856-1951
French soldier-politician

Pétain did not command troops in battle until 1914-15. His belief in strong defense was well suited to the Western Front and in 1916 he became a national hero for his defense of Verdun, despite the loss of 542,000 French lives. In June 1940, he was called upon to negotiate an armistice with Nazi Germany, by which France was partitioned; Pétain became head of a puppet state of the initially unoccupied region centered on Vichy. Tried as a collaborator in 1945, he was sentenced to death, later commuted to life imprisonment. **JPi**.

PETRIE, FLINDERS, SIR
1853-1942
British archaeologist

Petrie is often regarded as the founder of modern archaeology. He began his career with a careful survey of Stonehenge, but went on to become one of the foremost Egyptologists of his day. It was in Egypt that he realized the extreme importance of a careful recording of stratigraphy – the accumulated horizontal layers that comprise an archaeological site. He also helped to develop the art of seriation, which charts the stylistic development of artefacts, such as pottery, through time. **RJ**.

PHILBY, KIM
1912-1988
British spy

Philby is regarded as having been the most damaging of the agents that the KGB recruited in Cambridge in the 1930s. For 29 years he supplied information gained through his jobs at the Russia desk of MI6 and as the SIS representative at the Washington embassy. After BURGESS and Maclean fled to Russia in 1951, Philby came under suspicion and was obliged to leave his sensitive post – but did not feel the need to flee himself until 1963. **RJ**.

ABOVE: *Edith Piaf (left) in the company of Marlene Dietrich.*

PIAF, EDITH
1915-1963
French cabaret singer

Born Edith Gassion, she was a street singer at age 15 and was nicknamed *piaf*, sparrow. By the mid-1940s she was the most popular singer in France, with her husky, melancholy voice, tough songs and soul-baring delivery. 'La Vie en Rose' became an international standard, but her most characteristic material did not translate well. **JH**.

PIAGET, JEAN
1896-1980
Swiss psychologist

Piaget was a Swiss psychologist, biologist, and philosopher whose particular contribution was to identify the ways in which children's cognitive understanding of their world develops with age. He showed how children move from the physical and the concrete, to the abstract and the rational in an orderly and predictable way. He also described how children actively seek to make sense of their environment, fitting new experiences into existing mental models where possible (assimilation), and developing their thought processes to cope with challenging new information (accommodation). **MBe**.

PICASSO, PABLO
1881-1973
Spanish painter

The son of a drawing-master, Picasso showed a precocious talent for art. From 1901 he produced austere, predominantly blue, images of the poor, but on settling in Paris in 1904, he began to use warmer, more varied colors and the mood of his work softened, with circus figures a predominant theme. Increasingly interested in primitive art, he attempted to achieve a similar emotive force in *Les Desmoiselles d'Avignon* (1907). The stylized figures combined profiles with frontal views and are locked into their surroundings, creating a very flat image, foreshadowing Cubism, which he began to develop with BRAQUE. Rejecting the assumption that painting uses a single, fixed viewpoint, they attempted to show various physical aspects of their subjects simultaneously. The fragmentary images produced moved swiftly towards abstraction, but this was counteracted by stencilled lettering, recognizable details, and the introduction of collage. Picasso's *Still-life with Chair-Caning* included a piece of oil-cloth printed with a cane pattern, heightening the realism of the image. During the 1920s he became increasingly preoccupied with the themes of the Minotaur and the dying horse and this emotional intensity culminated in *Guernica* (1937), an angry response to the horrors of the Spanish Civil war. His later work was abundant though sporadic, including prints and sculpture and he died the most famous and influential artist of the twentieth century. **ER**.

PICKFORD, MARY
1893-1979
Canadian actress

Pickford's audiences loved her as the plucky innocent young girl, rich only in spirit, for whom a happy ending waits. Married to Douglas FAIRBANKS during the 1920s, she was a canny actress who negotiated the best deals possible from movie moguls. She be-

ABOVE: Pablo Picasso, the most famous artist of the century.

came a star in *A Poor Little Rich Girl* (1917) in which she played a child, although she was 24. By 1928 she was 34 and sick of ingenue roles, and appeared in her first talkie, *Coquette* (1929). She won an Academy Award, but the public stayed away, and she retired from films in the early 1930s. **DC**.

PIERCE, JOHN ROBINSON
1910-
American radio and electrical engineer

In 1962 the first active telecommunications satellite, Telstar I, was launched by NASA. It was designed by the Bell Company, and Pierce's work was fundamental to its success, particularly his 'traveling wave' electron tube which amplified the feeble signals involved and made the satellite transmission of speech, TV, and data a reality. **PW**.

PIGGOTT, LESTER
1935-
British jockey

Lester Piggott is certainly the leading British jockey of the modern era with 29 wins in the 'Classic' races and well over 4000 other successes in Britain and more in other countries. His reputation was tarnished by imprisonment for a substantial tax fraud in 1987. He made a comeback to riding after his release. **DS**.

PINCUS, GREGORY
1903-1967
American endocrinologist

Although prominent in mammalian reproductive physiology and endocrinology research for more than 35 years, Pincus is best known for the development of the birth control pill which he began work on in 1951. With M C Chang he found that certain progestational compounds, administered orally, could prevent pregnancy mainly by inhibiting ovulation. 'The pill' proved to be virtually 100% effective and from the mid-1960s transformed family planning worldwide. **ES**.

PININFARINA, SERGIO
1926-
Italian coachbuilder

The father of Italian styling has to be Battista 'Pinin' Farina, who established the company Carrozzeria Pininfarina to produce a series of highly innovative car bodies, notably the Cistalia coupe of 1947, and worked with numerous manufacturers in Europe and America. He died in 1966 but his son Sergio continued the family tradition. Perhaps best known for his work with Ferrari, it is worth underlining that the design company has been linked strongly with Cadillac in the United States and Rolls Royce in Britain, notably with the 1975 Rolls Royce Camargue. This family epitomizes Italian style in the automotive arena. **NF**.

PINOCHET, Augusto
1915-
Chilean politician

Responsible for the notorious post-ALLENDE repression, Pinochet was at first a lukewarm adherent of the coup which toppled the Marxist regime. Thereafter he rigorously persecuted the Left in defiance of world opinion. Many Leftists were tortured and shot and censorship was imposed. He scrapped ALLENDE's nationalization and survived bad recessions to retire in 1990. **JC.**

PINTER, Harold
1930-
British playwright

Born and educated in Hackney, East London, Pinter first trained as an actor. *The Birthday Party* was his first full-length play in 1958, since when a series of successful dramas of the impossibility of relationships and communication, conveyed in a realistic and demotic language, attended by his celebrated pauses and silences, have ensured that the adjective 'Pinteresque' has passed into the language. The erotic, madness and alienation, obsessionality and pathological family dynamics are powerful themes in his work which includes *The Caretaker* (1960), *The Homecoming* (1965), and *Betrayal* (1978). He has also written extensively for film and television. **AM.**

ABOVE: British playwright Harold Pinter.

PIRANDELLO, Luigi
1867-1936
Italian dramatist and novelist

Pirandello is a major influence upon European drama. His 44 plays – including *Six Characters in Search of an Author* (1921), *Henry IV* (1922), *Each in his Own Way* (1924), and *Tonight We Improvise* (1930) – challenge the conventions of naturalist theater in a manner that prefigures BRECHT and BECKETT. A central theme of his work is the probing of identity: the relation between self and role, actor and character, face and mask. Despite the anti-political skepticism of his work,

Pirandello was a member of the fascist party, which had poured cash into the Italian theater. He won the Nobel Prize in 1934. **CW.**

PIUS XII, Pope
1876-1958
Italian Pontiff

Eugenio Pacelli came from an aristocratic family and was ordained in 1899. Elected Pope in 1939, political circumstances forced him to adopt a studied neutrality during World War II, and he has since been criticized for his failure to condemn Nazi atrocities and antisemitism. **ML.**

PLANCK, Max
1858-1947
German physicist

Planck's discovery of quantum theory, for which he received the Nobel Prize for Physics in 1918, transformed twentieth-century physics. From 1889 until his retirement in 1927 Planck held the post of Professor of Physics at Berlin University, and it was here that he did his most important work. In 1900 his paper 'On the Theory of the Law of Energy Distribution in the Continuous Spectrum' caused a sensation, with the formula that energy is radiated in discrete quanta of magnitude hf, where f is the frequency of the radiation emitted and h is a constant (later called Planck's constant). **CH-M.**

PLATH, Sylvia
1932-1963
American poet

Born in Boston and educated at Smith College, Plath won a Fullbright Scholarship to Cambridge, where she met and married Ted HUGHES. *The Colossus and Other Poems*, her first volume of poetry, appeared in 1960, the only one to be published before her death. Her only novel, the semi-autobiographical *The Bell Jar*, was published under a pseudonym in 1963, shortly before her suicide. Her intense, self-revelatory poetry has created a considerable, highly partisan following, many of whom see Hughes, from whom she separated in 1962, as the villain of the piece. *Ariel*, her most passionate and finest collection, was published in 1965. **AM.**

PLAYER, Gary
1935-
South African golfer

Gary Player stands high on the all time list of golfing success with nine wins in the 'Majors', and is the only non-American to have won each of the four. He was the first overseas player to make an impact on the modern US golf circuit, and with PALMER and NICKLAUS made up the 'Big Three' in the 1960s. His short game was perhaps the strongest feature of his play. **DS.**

PLISETSKAYA, Maya Michailovna
1925-
Russian dancer

Plisetskaya is just one member of a veritable artistic dynasty: she is the niece of Asaf and Sulamith Messerer, the cousin of designer Boris and dancer Mikhail Messerer, the sister of dancer Azari Plisetsky and the wife of Rodion Shchedrin. She first came to public attention when she danced solo roles with the Bolshoi Ballet before graduating in 1943. She became ballerina in 1945 and, during the following years, danced many of the standard ballerina roles, but was particularly admired as Odette-Odile, Raymonda, the Dying Swan, and the Tsar-Maiden in *The Humpbacked Horse*. A dazzling technician and actress, in 1962 Plisetskaya was considered the leading dancer in the Soviet Union. **MC.**

POINCARÉ, Jules Henri
1854-1912
French mathematician and physicist

A prolific and influential writer on most branches of pure and applied mathematics, Poincaré became President of the French Academy of Science. His early interest in differential equations led him to crucial results on planetary orbits, and he also wrote extensively on the philosophy of mathematics and science, thermodynamics, probability, and topology. **EB.**

POINCARÉ, Raymond
1860-1934
French politician

Poincaré was the French President who invoked the Entente Cordiale with Britain to present a united front to Germany on the eve of World War I. He had already faced down the Kaiser in the Agadir Incident of 1911 and together with CLEMENCEAU he led France throughout the war. Claiming that Germany had failed to honor the coal reparations agreement he ordered the occupation of the Ruhr in 1923. **JC.**

POITIER, Sidney
1927-
American actor and director

Poitier was the handsome black actor who broke many racial barriers and made it easier for others to achieve commercial success in films. In 1958 he appeared with Tony Curtis in *The Defiant Ones*, a film about two convicts chained together but divided by racial bigotry. Both were nominated for Best Actor Academy Award; Poitier eventually won an Oscar for *Lilies of the Field* (1963). He starred with Spencer TRACY and Katharine HEPBURN in *Guess Who's Coming to Dinner* (1967), a blockbuster dealing with the touchy subject of white/black romance. As a director his credits include the 1977 film *A Piece of the Action*. **DC.**

POLLOCK, Jackson
1912-1956
American painter

Pollock began painting in 1929, studying at the Art Students' League, New York, under BENTON, and working in a Regionalist style. In the early 1940s his increasingly abstract work utilized mythic imagery stemming from his Jungian analysis and his interest in Surrealism. His influential Action Paintings were first produced around 1947. Working on a large scale, with his canvas on the floor, he poured and dripped his colors, manipulating them with sticks or palette knives. He often used materials such as metallic and enamel paint, sand, and broken glass. His seemingly random technique was actually carefully controlled, with the final composition often a chosen section cut from the original canvas. **ER.**

POMPIDOU, Georges
1911-1974
French politician

A former literature teacher, Pompidou was director of DE GAULLE's Cabinet 1958-59. De Gaulle's successor as President in 1969, he established his credentials as Prime Minister from 1962 in the aftermath of the retreat from Algeria by containing the threat from the OAS. He was also notably skilful in his assertion of Gaullism in international diplomacy. **JC.**

PONIATOFF, Alexander M
1892-1980
American electronic engineer

Russian-born Poniatoff constructed the first practical video tape recorder in 1956. Marketed by his company AMPEX (his initials and EX for 'excellence') this invention radically changed TV program production and dissemination. His system was adopted as the norm in the industry and made possible the instant editing and playback of recorded material. Later Poniatoff invented 'the instant replay' machine used widely in sports programs. **PT.**

POPPER, Karl, Sir
1902-1989
British philosopher

Educated in mathematics, physics, philosophy, and psychology in Vienna, Austrian-born Popper was an associate of the Vienna Circle of Logical Positivists, which published his first book, although he disagreed with many of their doctrines. He opposed the positivist view of science as proceeding by generalization from observation with his own doctrine of 'conjecture and refutation'. In *The Open Society and its Enemies* he attacked Marxism and Freudian psychology as superstitious 'pseudoscience', on the grounds that they advance claims that are not amenable to falsification. **EB.**

PORSCHE, Ferdinand
1875-1951
German motor manufacturer

Germany's motor industry was strongly directed by the Nazi Party in the early 1930s. Ferdinand Porsche was asked to build a vehicle for the masses, and the result was the Volkswagen Beetle in 1934, a car which outsold the Model T Ford. Highly innovative and a pioneer in the German industry, it is very ironic that Ferdinand Porsche was 73 years old before a car bearing his name was produced. After his death the company was left in the hands of his son Ferry, who has been responsible for sports-car development, both for the road and in international motorsport. **NF.**

PORTAL, Charles, 1st Viscount, Marshal of the Royal Air Force
1893-1971
British airman

After distinguished service in World War I, Portal rose steadily through the ranks of the RAF; in 1940 he commanded Bomber Command before being appointed Chief of Air Staff. As such, he served on the Anglo-American Joint Chiefs of Staff Committee 1942-45, helping to formulate Allied strategy. **JPi.**

PORTER, Cole
1891-1964
American songwriter

Raised in an affluent Indiana family, Cole Porter began writing songs as a law student before joining the French Foreign Legion during World War I. He came to live at the center of a social whirl in Europe, unhindered by snobberies attached to race or background, and hiding his homosexuality

ABOVE: *Prolific songwriter Cole Porter.*

behind his marriage to the socialite Linda Lee Thomas. His brilliantly written songs, for which he unusually wrote both words and music, include 'Let's Do It,' 'Night and Day,' and 'Anything Goes.' There were many others from 27 shows and revues such as *Kiss Me Kate* and *Rosalie*. **DK.**

POT, Pol
1928-
Cambodian politician

Pol Pot was responsible for the Killing Fields, the mass transfer of population from city to countryside which resulted in two million Cambodian deaths from starvation and brutality between 1975 and 1978. Having defeated the American-backed Phnom-Penh regime with his Khmer Rouge forces in 1975 he was able to impose his crazed, bloodthirsty brand of Marxism unchecked, until the Vietnamese invaded and ousted him. **JC.**

ABOVE: *The infamous dictator, Pol Pot.*

POULENC, Francis Jean Marcel
1899-1963
French composer

A gifted pianist, Poulenc came to prominence in the artistic life of Paris after World War I, being one of a celebrated group of composers called Les Six. Following a renewal of his Roman Catholic faith, Poulenc composed sacred choral works of great cogency, the most notable of which is his magnificent *Gloria*, but he by no means confined himself to this genre. His ballet *Les Biches*, commissioned by Diaghilev, remains very popular, as does his organ concerto. But of all his works, perhaps the most worthwhile are his solo songs, which combine pathos with levity, whimsy, with tragedy, and earn him the soubriquet of heir to Schubert and Schumann, in his own very French idiom. **DK.**

POULSEN, VALDEMAR
1869-1942
Danish engineer

Although the idea of recording sounds magnetically was mooted by one Oberlin Smith in 1888, Poulsen was the first to achieve it. His 'Telegraphone,' demonstrated at the Paris Exposition of 1900, was the forerunner of the now ubiquitous tape recorder. It used a moving steel tape which was magnetized in sympathy with electric currents from a microphone to store and reproduce messages. Poulsen worked for the telephone company in Copenhagen and conceived it as a message-taking device for telephones. He also had the idea of using a length of wire or a strip of flexible material covered with magnetizable powder in place of the steel tape. The reddish-brown plastic recording tape is the modern equivalent. In 1903 Poulsen and some US associates formed the American Telegraphone Company to exploit the device, but success for this type of recording was years off and the company failed. Poulsen's other contributions included pioneering work in the use of the high-frequency currents from electric arcs in wireless transmitters. **PW**.

POUND, EZRA
1885-1972
American poet

Born in Idaho and educated in Pennsylvania, Pound left for Europe in 1908, and published *A Lume Spento (With Tapers Quenched)*, his first of many collections of poems, in Venice. He also lived in London, where he taught, and published more poetry and a volume of critical essays, *The Spirit of Romance* (1910). He was one of the founders of the Imagist movement, whose characteristics were brevity, precision, and the rejection of symbolism and abstraction, from which he gradually moved away in search of greater poetic freedom. The first three of his major project, the *Cantos*, appeared in 1917. He went to live in Paris, then Italy again in 1924, continuing to work on the epic *Cantos* which eventually numbered 117, meanwhile publishing *A Draft of XVI Cantos* in 1926. His politico-economic theorizings led him to anti-semitism and won the admiration of MUSSOLINI; he made wartime radio broadcasts in support of the dictator. He was arrested in 1945, returned to the USA and held in an insane asylum until 1958, when he returned to Italy. The last part of the *Cantos* was published in 1970. A powerful supporter of other writers, his undoubtedly great influence on the development of modern poetry is of more literary significance than his own avant-garde poetry. **AM**.

TOP: American icon, Elvis Presley.

RIGHT: Ezra Pound, the eccentric Imagist and poet.

PRESLEY, ELVIS
1935-1977
American rock and pop singer

Presley was the prototype teen idol of the rock 'n' roll explosion of the 1950s, a potent combination of rebellion and sex which inspired so many great performers. Spotted by producer Sam Phillips at Sun Studios recording a birthday greeting to his mother, his first single, 'That's All Right Mama', was a Memphis sensation in 1954. But it was Colonel Tom Parker who supplied the aggressive management for Presley's rise to international stardom with his first record for RCA in 1955, 'Heartbreak Hotel', a US No 1 for eight weeks. TV appearances followed where he captivated the nation's youth and outraged their parents, and his debut album was RCA's biggest selling ever. Film deals followed: *Love Me Tender* and *Jailhouse Rock* were huge successes, but later films in the 1960s were invariably banal. In the 1960s he lost ground to the UK invasion led by the BEATLES and the ROLLING STONES, but from 1969 made an effort to re-enter the limelight. But after the break-up with his wife Priscilla, he gradually became a recluse, eventually found dead from a cocktail of drugs prescribed for depression in 1977, leaving record and memorabilia sales as a reminder of his status as rock's most potent cultural phenomenon ever. **DC**.

ABOVE: The multitalented Prince.

PRINCE
1958-
American rock singer

Although the single 'I Wanna Be Your Lover' and the 1980 album *Dirty Mind* made the charts, it wasn't until the 1984 film and album *Purple Rain* that the talented multi-instrumentalist Prince Rogers Nelson began to achieve his current popularity. The single 'When Doves Cry' made it to the top in the US charts, and the next two albums kept him there. Tours acquainted UK audiences with his sexually provocative stage show in the late 1980s and in 1991 the movie, *Graffiti Bridge* was further evidence of his musical talents and his status as one of contemporary rock's greatest performers. **DC.**

PRINCIP, GAVRILO
1895-1918
Serbian assassin

Princip was an active member of the Serbian nationalist group, the 'Black Hand'. This organization was committed to freeing the Slavs from the decrepit Austro-Hungarian Empire. On 28 June 1914 Princip assassinated the Archduke Francis Ferdinand of Austria and his wife Sophie while they were visiting the Bosnian capital of Sarajevo; this action provoked a series of diplomatic and military responses that culminated in World War I. **RJ.**

PROCTER, WILLIAM
1862-1934
American businessman

Procter devoted his life to Procter and Gamble, an Anglo-Irish soap-making company founded in the USA in 1837. He headed the company from 1907 to 1934, during which it expanded to dominate the market. Before becoming President he had organized a profit-sharing scheme, and in 1887 he introduced the Saturday half-day, believed to be the first in America. He also admitted worker-representatives on the board of directors. Much of the success of the company was in marketing, making Tide, Oxydol, and other products into household names. In 1932 the company sponsored a radio drama serial for advertising purposes, resulting in the term 'soap opera.' **JW.**

PROKOFIEV, SERGEI
1891-1953
Russian composer

Although Prokofiev began composing at a very early age he was first noted for his outstanding piano playing. While studying at the St Petersburg Conservatory under Rimsky-Korsakov he won the Rubenstein Prize for performing the first of his own piano concertos. Then followed the success of his 'Classical Symphony' (1917) which revealed his talent for pastiche work. Like many Soviet composers Prokofiev found the political pressure to conform too restricting and so fled to the United States. Here he was warmly received as a pianist but had more difficulty being accepted as a composer. Finally he had a breakthrough in Chicago in 1921 with his opera *The Love for Three Oranges*. After the United States, Prokofiev moved to Paris where he struck up an exciting new relationship with the renowned Diaghilev, writing music for his ballets. In 1934 Prokofiev returned to Russia where some say his style mellowed. According to the Central Committee of the Communist Party his style did not mellow enough and they criticized his work in 1948 as being 'modernistic and anti-melodic.' In Prokofiev's reply he pledged to use a more 'lucid melody' and a 'simple harmonic language' but others say he really continued to compose exactly as he liked. **DK.**

ABOVE: Russian composer, Sergei Prokofiev.

PROST, ALAIN
1955-
French racing driver

Triple World Champion, Prost's driving style earned him the nickname 'The Professor'. A 'thinking' race driver, he has won an astonishing number of Grand Prix and has driven for Renault, McLaren, and Ferrari. Prost took a year off in 1992 rather than drive what he considered to be an uncompetitive car. **NF.**

PROUST, MARCEL
1871-1922
French novelist, essayist, and critic

Marcel Proust is held by some to be the greatest writer of the century. Born to a distinguished doctor and a Jewish mother, Proust suffered from chronic asthma throughout his life. In 1896 he published a collection, *Pleasures and Regrets*, and about this time began an early draft of *Remembrance of Things Past* that was to be published as *Jean Santeuil* (1952), also translating Ruskin's art criticism. He was actively involved in the Dreyfus case of 1897-9 against a rising tide of anti-semitism. In 1907 Proust became a virtual recluse from fashionable circles, dedicated to the life-long project of finishing his seven-volumed masterpiece, and suffering from a neurosis partially caused by an ambivalent attitude to his own homosexuality. *Swann's Way* (1913), the first volume of *À la recherche du temps perdu (Remembrance of Things Past)*, found little success. Despite the intervening war years, Proust's reputation grew, and his acclaimed second volume was published by *La Nouvelle Revue Française*, winning the Prix Goncourt. Set in the Paris of his time, his great novel explores the self's complex, multi-layered relation to the processes of time, and the creative wealth of the unconscious, an aesthetic defined in his critical essays, *By Way of Saint-Beuve* (1954). **CW.**

PUSKAS, FERENC
1927-
Hungarian-born Spanish soccer player

Ferenc Puskas was a leading member of the highly successful Hungarian national side of the early 1950s. He was playing abroad during the Soviet invasion of his country in 1956 and chose to join Real Madrid and become a Spanish national. The strongest club in European soccer at the time, Real Madrid won the European club championship each year from 1956-60, with Puskas' contribution to the fore (including four goals in the 1960 final). Puskas was also later a successful coach. **DS.**

PYNCHON, THOMAS
1937-
American novelist

One of the most remarkable writers of modern fiction, Pynchon is an enigmatic figure. He received a scientific education at Cornell University and worked for the Boeing Corporation, facts which may explain the fascination for technology that characterizes his work. His complex novels such as *V* (1963), *Gravity's Rainbow* (1973), and *Vineland* (1990) elaborate on a monumental scale the apocalyptic, hi-tech universe of postwar America, their theme the search for historical meaning and identity in an overdetermined late-capitalist world. **CW.**

QUANT, MARY
1934-
British designer

The quintessential designer of the 1960s, Quant's bright, simple, and coordinated clothes epitomized young British fashion of the decade. Born in London, Quant studied at Goldsmith's College of Art in 1950-53. In 1955 she spent several months with a London milliner before leaving to open 'Bazaar', a shop on the King's Road, with her partner Alexander Plunkett-Greene (later to be Quant's husband) and Archie NcNair. Although Quant first began by selling clothes, she soon started to design and to achieve success. In the 1960s she formed the Ginger Group, and designed in the United States for the JC Penny chain. Quant made the mini-skirt popular with both the young and the not-so-young, produced a 'Wet' collection in PVC, and designed a range of co-ordinating hosiery and underwear. Although she continues to design, Quant's name and the stylised daisy trademark will always be synonymous with the 1960s. **MC**.

QUINE, WILLARD VAN ORMAN
1908-
American logician and philosopher

Based in Harvard, Quine was influenced by the Vienna Circle and went on to influence an entire generation of Anglo-Saxon philosophy. Trained as a mathematician, his first work was in symbolic logic, for which he devised a number of elegant axiomatizations. At the same time he addressed fundamental questions in the philosophy of logic and, in his paper 'Two Dogmas of Empiricism', attacked the view that there is a difference of kind between 'logical truths' and empirical propositions, and that the latter are verified by experience. He opposed this with his metaphor of the 'Web of Belief': experience impinges on the edges, but it is open to us to maintain anything in the face of experience, though only at the cost of consequential adjustments elsewhere in the net, including even the truths of logic at the center. One casualty of Quine's argument is meaning, and in *Word and Object* he further undermined the traditional view, by arguing that an anthropologist could not determine to which of a number of incompatible types of entity a native language referred. This pointed to a new formal approach to metaphysics, which leads him to reject his own preference for an ontology of physical objects, since the mathematics required by science makes irreducible reference to abstract entities: sets. **EB**.

QUISLING, VIDKUN
1887-1945
Norwegian politician

So notorious was his collaboration with the Nazis that Quisling's name became a synonym for treason. A member of the pre-war government, he founded a Norwegian fascist party and when the Germans invaded he was made Minister President of the State Council under the Reichkommissar Terboven. He was condemned for treason in 1945 and shot. **JC**.

RABI, ISIDOR ISAAC
1898-1988
Austrian-American physicist

Rabi was educated at Cornell and Columbia Universities, and became a Professor at the latter in 1937, remaining there for the rest of his working life. He is best known for his work on magnetism, quantum mechanics, and molecular beams. He invented the techniques of atomic-beam and molecular-beam magnetic resonance, in which the magnetic properties of molecules and atoms can be calculated by observing their reactions to magnetic fields and radio waves. During World War II, he worked on microwave radar. Later, he was the Chairman of the General Advisory Committee of the Atomic Energy Commission, and was instrumental in founding CERN in Geneva. **DD**.

RACHMANINOV, SERGEI
1873-1943
Russian composer and pianist

Many think of Rachmaninov as the composer of the ever-popular second piano concerto or of the *Rhapsody on a Theme of Paganini*. However few realize that he was also the composer of the most exquisite songs and, although not as popular as his piano concertos, they give a valuable insight into the more intimate side of his character. Sadly these songs are not performed as often as they deserve. It has also become apparent from recordings that Rachmaninov was an exceptional pianist of virtuosic quality and probably one of the finest pianists the twentieth century will ever see. **DK**.

ABOVE: C V Raman, namesake of the Raman Effect.

RAMAN, SIR CHANDRASEKHARA VENKATA
1888-1970
Indian physicist

Raman gained a brilliant degree from Madras Presidency College, but India was a dead-end as far as scientific employment was concerned and so he worked as a civil servant for 10 years while researching in his spare time. Eventually, he became Professor of Physics at Calcutta University. His most important research was on the scattering of light. He realized that the blue color of seawater was due to the refraction of light by the water molecules rather than by the suspended material. This Raman Effect gained him the Nobel Prize for Physics – the first ever awarded to an Indian researcher – in 1930. **DD**.

RAMANUJAN, SRINIVASA
1887-1920
Indian mathematician

Having little formal education, Ramanujan discovered for himself much of the prevalent knowledge in number theory before he was brought to Cambridge by G H Hardy in 1914. In 1918 Ramanujan was elected the first Indian Fellow of the Royal Society, but contracted tuberculosis and returned to India where he died the following year. He used mainly intuitive methods to make significant contributions to number theory and the theory of functions, and his work is still a rich source of material for mathematicians. **EB**.

RAMBERT, DAME MARIE
1888-1982
British dancer and teacher

Sent by her parents to Paris to study medicine after the 1905 Warsaw Uprising, Rambert soon became interested in dance. In 1910 she went to study at Emile Dalcroze's Summer School in Geneva where she remained for three years, later becoming an assistant teacher of Dalcroze Eurythmics at the Dresden school. It was here that she met Diaghilev, whose company she joined, and NIJINSKY, whom she helped overcome the difficulties of rhythm of *Le Sacre du Printemps*. At the outbreak of World War I, Rambert left for London, where she created the ballet *La Pomme d'Or* (1917), in which she danced and first attracted critical attention. Continuing her studies with Enrico Cecchetti, Rambert opened her own studio and among her first pupils was Frederick ASHTON. The first performance of the Marie Rambert Dancers (soon to become Ballet Rambert) was in 1930. In addition to a gift for finding and encouraging designers she had a sharp eye for dance and choreographic talent. Alongside Dame Ninette de VALOIS, Rambert is considered one of the great pioneers of modern British ballet, and was a much loved teacher and personality. **MC**.

RAMS, DIETER
1932-
German designer

Rams's designs for electrical and kitchen appliances for the Frankfurt electrical company Braun are, in their pared-down elegance, efficiency and reliability, the epitome of postwar German industrial design. Rams believes that 'one of the most important and most responsible tasks of a designer today is to help clear the chaos we are living in.' **DE**.

RANK, ARTHUR, BARON
1888-1972
British industrialist

Rank's work as a Sunday school teacher prompted his interest in films as a means of education. In 1934 he formed British National Films, whose first production failed not through lack of merit, but because distributors did not want to take it. After inheriting the substantial family flour business in 1943 he had the means to acquire an interest in films and bought film studios as well as the Gaumont and Odeon cinema chains. This enabled him to create a substantial all-British film industry as part of his Rank Organisation. **JW**.

RASPUTIN, GRIGORI YEFIMOVICH
1871-1916
Russian monk and charlatan

Rasputin was undoubtedly one of the key factors contributing to the fall of the last Tsar of Russia, Nicholas II. He rose to influence in 1907 through his miraculous ability as a starets or holy man to cure the Tsarvitch Alexis' haemophilia, succeeding where the best surgeons had failed. This gave him an entrée to court which he ex-

BELOW: The Russian monk, Grigori Rasputin.

ploited greedily in a scandalous life of debauchery, arousing the jealousy of the aristrocracy and dragging the image of royal family and court further into the mud. The Tsarina Alexandra was completely under his hypnotic spell and as she guided the Tsar, Rasputin's political influence soon grew. Key political and military personnel were chosen or dropped according to his whim. He was assassinated by a group of monarchists led by Prince Felix Yusupov. **ML**.

RATHENAU, WALTHER
1867-1922
German industrialist and statesman

By 1914 Rathenau headed the electrical engineering conglomerate AEG, founded by his father. In World War I he persuaded the German government that state control of economic resources was necessary, and in the difficult post-war period helped to found the German Democratic Party. He believed that unfettered capitalism was damaging and recommended a combination of industrial self-government, employee participation, and state supervision. As Foreign Minister he initiated a reconciliation with Russia, signing the Rapallo Treaty in 1922. This contact with Bolshevism aroused nationalist extremists and, already at risk because he was a Jew, he was murdered the same year. **JW**.

RATTIGAN, SIR TERENCE
1911-1977
British playwright

Critics emphasize the careful craftsmanship of his quintessentially middle-class plays, which still find an audience for their exploration of moments of crisis and moral dilemma. A comedy, *French Without Tears* (1936), was his first success, but he is remembered more for his serious plays *The Winslow Boy*, *Ross*, and *The Deep Blue Sea*. **AM**.

RAUSCHENBERG, ROBERT
1925-
American painter

Rauschenberg studied at Black Mountain College with ALBERS, who influenced his early work. In the mid 1950s he began producing 'combine' paintings, fusing outrageously incongruous real objects with his abstract oils, such as *Bed* (1955), a paint-splashed quilt. His iconoclastic approach to art included acquiring a drawing from de KOONING, which he erased and exhibited as *Erased de Kooning by Robert Rauschenberg*. His stated aim was to 'act in the gap beween art and life' and like JOHNS, his work linked Abstract Expressionism and Pop Art. During the 1960s he used silkscreen to produce complex conflations of imagery drawn from current events, art history, and literature, interspersed with abstract passages of painting. **ER**.

ABOVE: Maurice Ravel at the piano.

RAVEL, MAURICE
1875-1937
French composer

Most of Ravel's orchestral works first appear in a piano version which is surprising since Ravel did not profess to being a particularly gifted pianist himself. However this did not pose a problem, for what Ravel may have lacked in his ability as a pianist he more than made up for in his talent for orchestration. He has become famous for his richly orchestrated scores and for the kaleidoscope of colors and variety of textures he achieves. A perfect example of this can be seen in his orchestration of Mussorgsky's *Pictures from an Exhibition*. He composed a great variety of works including many with a Spanish flavor as well as his masterpiece *Daphnis et Chloe* written for Diaghilev's Ballets Russes. **DK**.

RAWLS, JOHN
1921-
American philosopher

Rawls's influential *Theory of Justice* (1971) elaborates his doctrine of 'Justice as Fairness'. His substantive ethical view consists in the liberal 'maximum principle', that given a choice of distributions of benefits, the morally correct one is that with the highest baseline. This he derives from a thought experiment in which he considers which rules the founders of a society would adopt were they ignorant of their individual strengths and weaknesses. **EB**.

RAY, SATYAJIT
1921-1992
Indian film director

Ray made the Apu trilogy, *Pather Panchali* (1955), *Aparajito* (1957), and *The World of Apu* (1959) which really introduced Indian film to the West. His films were influenced by the social concern of Italian neo-realism, as evidenced in *Bicycle Thieves*, and by the natural lyricism of a director like Jean RENOIR, for whom Ray had worked as an assistant. His main subject was India – the conflict between tradition and progress, and the relationship with the British Empire. His best films include: *The Music Room* (1958), *Charulata* (1964), *Days and Nights in the Forest* (1970), *The Chess Players* (1977). **NS**.

RAYBURN, SAMUEL T.
1882-1961
American politician

Known as 'Mr Sam,' Rayburn served a record 17 years as Speaker of the House of Representatives. A lawyer, he was reelected to the House 24 times, for a total of 48 years' service - another record. Elected Democratic leader in 1937, he was responsible for pushing through a lot of ROOSEVELT's New Deal legislation. His strength lay in his integrity and his political wisdom was sought by a succession of presidents up to John F KENNEDY. **JC**.

REAGAN, RONALD
1911-
American politician and president

Ronald Reagan was the Hollywood star who landed the West's number one political role. It was the California conservatives who launched him in politics as state governor (1967-80) with a mandate to reverse the liberal tide and kick-start the economy. He did both so effectively that he swept into the White House in 1980, an endorsement which a failed assassination bid only enhanced. This 'Teflon' President survived the Iran-Contra scandal, and the calling to account of several former staff for underhand dealings, but his image was damaged. His brand of prosperity was based on an over-inflated economy and it was left to his successor from 1988, George BUSH to face the consequent recession. **JC**.

REBER, GROTE
1911-
American radio engineer

A keen amateur radio astronomer, Reber, influenced by Karl Jansky's work in 1932, built the world's first radio telescope. He used a dish some 10 meters across to focus radio waves on to a sensitive aerial and with this relatively primitive equipment he detected radiation from the sun and several constellations. **PW**.

REDFORD, ROBERT
1936-
American actor

The good-looking Redford has turned out to be much more than the standard Hollywood leading man. He scored an early success on Broadway with *Barefoot in the Park* (1963) but had to fight for challenging roles. *Butch Cassidy and the Sundance Kid* made him a superstar, and he and NEWMAN were great together again in *The Sting* (1973). Thousands of women fell in love with Redford and by 1974 he was the number one box-office star in America. He also won an Academy Award as Best Director for the film *Ordinary People* (1980), his directing debut. **DC**.

REDGRAVE, MICHAEL
1908-1985
British actor

Versatility and intelligence marked Redgrave as a consummate performer from the start – witness his performance in HITCH-

BELOW: Ronald Reagan, the first actor to become US President.

ABOVE: Actor Robert Redford, who won an Oscar for Ordinary People.

COCK's *The Lady Vanishes* (1938). A man who preferred challenging roles, such as his sensitive portrayal of the schoolteacher in *The Browning Version* (1950), he had a distinguished stage and screen career, as an actor director, producer, and playwright. **DC**.

REDGRAVE, VANESSA
1937-
British actress

Redgrave is one of Britain's most powerful and celebrated actresses. The daughter of Michael REDGRAVE, she is a controversial presence off-screen, well-known for her espousal of left-wing causes. She began her career with the Royal Shakespeare Company and came to international recognition with movies like *Morgan* and *Blow Up* (both 1966). Nominated for several Academy Awards, she won the Best Supporting Actress Award in 1977 for *Julia*. More recently she has appeared in *Wetherby* (1985), *Comrades* (1987) and *Howards End* (1992). **DC**.

REICHSTEIN, TADEUS
1897-
Swiss chemist and pharmacologist

Reichstein identified steroids from the cortex of the adrenal gland, subsequently used for the treatment of Addison's disease. He was one of the recipients of the 1950 Nobel Prize for Physiology and Medicine. **DD**.

REITH, JOHN CHARLES WALSHAM, BARON REITH OF STONEHAVEN
1889-1971
British statesman and broadcaster

Born in Scotland, Reith became an engineer and entered broadcasting as a technician. He became the first general manager of the British Broadcasting Corporation in 1922 and its Director General in 1927-38. In this position, Reith pioneered the concept of public service broadcasting with the idea that radio's duty was to both educate and entertain. He later became an MP and government minister. In 1948 the BBC started the annual Reith lectures in honor of his services to broadcasting. **DSL**.

RENAULT, LOUIS
1877-1944
French motor manufacturer

Formed by three brothers – Louis, Marcel, and Fernand – Renault Frères was established in 1898. Two brothers died, leaving Louis in sole charge by 1908. Louis Renault had to fight Citroën's imaginative marketing methods and did so through a strong mass-market production facility. After World War II Renault was accused of being a collaborator and his company was nationalized in 1944. **NF**.

ABOVE: French director Jean Renoir.

RENOIR, JEAN
1894-1979
French film director

Born in Paris, son of the great French Impressionist painter, Renoir's distinguished film career spanned nearly 50 years, with a spell as an exile in Hollywood, and even a film in India. His greatest period of creativity (and one of the great periods of French cinema) was the 1930s, made especially memorable by two prewar masterpieces: *La Grande Illusion* (1937), a pacifist war film set in a POW camp, and *La Règle du jeu* (1939), a scintillating denunciation of the moral corruption of French society on the eve of World War II. **NS**.

ABOVE: Syngman Rhee, South Korea's first President.

RESNAIS, ALAIN
1922-
French film director

Resnais began as a documentarist making a powerful film about Nazi concentration camps, *Night and Fog* (1956). He achieved international renown with his features, *Hiroshima mon amour* (1959) and *Last Year in Marienbad* (1961), mesmerizing films about time, memory, and imagination. Probably the most important director of the 'New Wave,' Resnais is highly regarded by critics. **NS**.

REYNAUD, PAUL
1878-1966
French politician

Prime Minister during the Fall of France, Reynaud's favorable response to CHURCHILL's offer of an Anglo-French Union provoked a concerted attack in the National Assembly by the defeatists which led to his resignation on June 16, 1940. He was a Deputy Prime Minister in the 1953 Laniel government and chairman of the Economic Committee of the Council of Europe from 1952. **JC**.

REZA SHAH PAHLAVI
1878-1944
Iranian monarch

In 1921 Reza Shah, commander of the Persian Cossack Brigade, joined other reformers to seize power from the Qajar dynasty. Made Prime Minister in 1923, he tried to introduce reforms but, when these were blocked, responded by overthrowing the last Qajar shah in 1925. Taking the dynastic name Pahlavi, he modernized Persia (renamed Iran in 1935), breaking the stranglehold on power enjoyed by the Shi'ite clergy and tribal chiefs. Pro-German in World War II, he was forced to abdicate in 1941 when British and Soviet forces invaded. He died in exile. **JP**.

RHEE, SYNGMAN
1875-1965
Korean politician

Methodist layman and Princeton alumnus whom the Americans chose as their man in Seoul, Rhee changed from Jekyll to Hyde and instituted a ruthless and repressive regime. He became South Korea's first President in 1948 and the Korean War only committed the United States further to supporting the discredited regime of a divided state, a support finally removed in 1960 when Rhee went into exile. **JC**.

RIBBENTROP, JOACHIM
1893-1946
German politician

Ribbentrop affected an aristocratic past to gain entry as ambassador (1936-38) into British ruling circles. When he was rejected as a vulgar parvenu he misled HITLER on Britain's willingness to fight, thereby making war more certain. He negotiated the Anglo-German Naval Treaty of 1935, and as Foreign Minister the Anti-Comintern Pact with Japan and Italy and the so-called Ribbentrop Pact with STALIN in August 1939. He was hanged at Nuremberg in 1946. **JC**.

RICHARDS, SIR GORDON
1904-86
British jockey

Sir Gordon Richards was the most successful jockey ever in British flat racing with a total of 4870 wins, including 14 in 'Classic' races. He was also champion jockey 26 times with his first success in 1925 and his last in 1953. He rode with an unorthodox upright style and although he habitually kept a long, loose rein still maintained good control of his mounts. **DS**.

RICHARDSON, SIR RALPH
1902-1983
British actor

One of Britain's greatest actors, Richardson was admired around the world for his versatile and memorable characterizations. He produced his finest work on stage, earning a reputation as a fine Shakespearean actor at the Old Vic during the 1930s. He appeared in many films, among them *Anna Karenina* (1948) with Vivien LEIGH, *Richard III* (1955), *Dr Zhivago* (1965) and *Greystoke* (1984), released after his death. **DC**.

RICHTHOFEN, MANFRED, RITTMEISTER VON
1892-1918
German pilot

During World War I Richthofen became known as the 'Red Baron', his 80 'kills' making him the most successful pilot of any combatant nation. He became a living legend through his exploits and skill, nurtured by German propaganda. The son of an aristocratic Silesian family, Richthofen first served as a cavalry officer in the Uhlan Regiment Nr 1 Kaiser Alexander III, almost losing his life on the Eastern Front. In 1915 he transferred to the Imperial German Air Service, later joining Feldfliegerabteilung Nr 69 operating reconnaissance two-seaters in the East. His potential was not at first obvious, but in 1916 he was chosen to join Jagdstaffel 2, a scouting unit. Richthofen's first 'kill' was on 17 September 1916, flying an Albatros DII to shoot down an RFC FE2b. In January 1917 he was awarded the *Ordre pour le Mérite* and then given command of Jagdstaffel 11. By June he led a group of four squadrons, Jagdgeschwader Nr 1, known as 'Richthofen's Flying Circus' because of its highly decorated fighters. Occasionally he flew a red Fokker Dr I triplane, and it was while flying such a machine that he was shot down. **MT**.

RICKENBACKER, EDWARD VERNON, CAPTAIN
1890-1973
American fighter pilot

R

A prewar racing driver, in 1917 Rickenbacker became General Pershing's chauffeur in France but later transferred to the army's Aviation Section, where he became an engineering instructor. Taking advantage of available flying and gunnery classes, he learned the skills of a combat pilot and in March 1918 achieved a transfer to the 94th Aero Squadron on the Western Front, taking part in the first American air combat patrol over enemy lines of World War I. From 29 April he claimed 26 victories. Postwar he worked with the airline and car industries, becoming Chairman of Eastern Air Lines in 1953. **MT**.

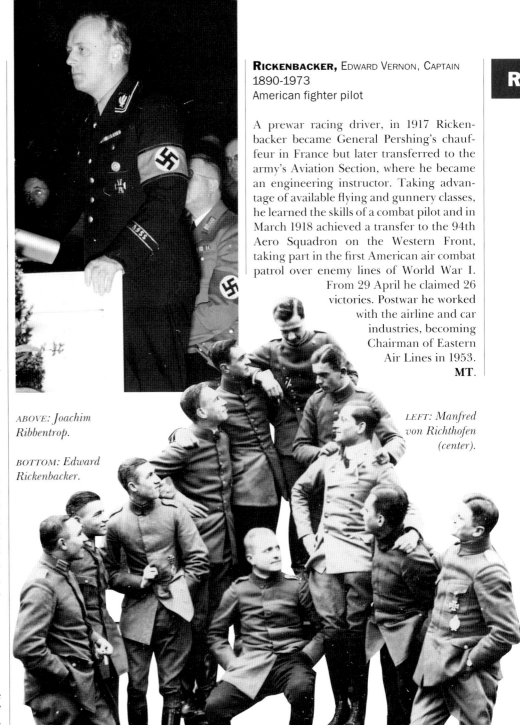

ABOVE: Joachim Ribbentrop.

BOTTOM: Edward Rickenbacker.

LEFT: Manfred von Richthofen (center).

RIDGWAY, MATTHEW, GENERAL
1895-
American soldier.

As commander of 82nd Airborne Division, Ridgway participated in the invasion of Normandy in June 1944 before being promoted to lead XVIII Airborne Corps. In 1950 he took over the 8th Army in Korea, succeeding MACARTHUR as Supreme Commander Far East in 1951. He was US Army Chief of Staff 1953-55. **JPi**.

RIEFENSTAHL, LENI
1902-
German actress and film director

Reifenstahl was responsible for some of Nazi Germany's most powerful propaganda. Having attracted Hitler's attention, she was entrusted with filming the 1934 Nuremburg rally, and produced the remarkable documentary, *Triumph of the Will*. She followed it with the impressive *Olympiad*, a dramatic, though morally dubious, celebration of the 1936 Berlin Olympics and Nazi ideology. **NS**.

BELOW: Controversial film director Leni Riefenstahl.

RILEY, BRIDGET
1931-
British painter

Riley studied at Goldsmith's College (1949-53) and the Royal College of Art (1952-55). In the early 1960s she made her first Op Art paintings, in black and white and, from 1965, in color. These exploit the optical effect of pattern and juxtaposed colors, provoking visual disturbance. **ER**.

RILKE, RAINER MARIA
1875-1926
German poet

Rilke is regarded as the most important lyric poet of twentieth-century Germany. His first work of note was *The Book of Hours* (1905), a romantic meditation on death in a series of poetic 'prayers' to an almost Nietzschean God. In *New Poems* (1907-8) Rilke found his mature style, moving towards a more objective and autonomous poetic form which employed 'the child's wise incapacity to understand'. His great works *The Duino Elegies* (1912-22) and *Sonnets to Orpheus* (1923) explore an extreme personal crisis, marking the movements between the pagan poet's despair and acceptance of a world that offers no religious certainty nor prospect of immortality. **CW**.

RIVERA, DIEGO
1886-1957
Mexican painter

Rivera studied in Mexico City and Madrid before moving to Paris in 1909, where he worked in a Cubist style. Returning to post-revolutionary Mexico in 1921, he was, with OROZCO, one of the founders of the Mexican mural renaissance. Rejecting European modernism he developed a realistic monumental style, which allowed him to present more clearly and directly his strong socialist beliefs to a largely illiterate populace. He produced murals at several Mexican government buildings, the best known being at the Ministry of Education, 1923/27, as well as several major works in the USA. While his political opinions were often unpopular, as an artist he was highly influential **ER**.

ROBESON, PAUL
1898-1976
American actor

Robeson's most famous role was that of Joe, the slave in *Show Boat* (1936), leaving audiences thunderstruck with his singing of *Ol' Man River*. In the late 1940s he stunned theater audiences with his portrayal of Shakespeare's *Othello*, after which his career fell apart due to his espousal of Communist causes. **DC**.

LEFT: Paul Robeson.

RIETVELD, GERRIT
1888-1964
Dutch furniture designer and architect

Rietveld's fame rests on a few modern classics like the 1918 Red-Blue chair, the planes of simple square-section wood painted in primary colors, close in spirit to De Stijl (see MONDRIAN). Buildings like the Schröder House, Utrecht (1924), replicate this in the contrast of artfully composed concrete slabs, and brightly painted metal balconies. **AR**.

ABOVE: Edward G Robinson in Little Caesar.

ROBINSON, EDWARD G
1893-1973
American actor

Robinson was the quintessential tough-guy actor who became a star in the gangster film *Little Caesar* (1930). This stocky man could never have the sheer physical appeal of a BOGART, but the power he radiated was more than adequate compensation. In 1972 he received a Special Academy Award. **DC**.

ROBINSON, JACKIE [JACK ROOSEVELT]
1919-1972
American baseball player

One of the most important moments in twentieth-century sports came in 1947 when Jackie Robinson debuted with the Brooklyn Dodgers, breaking the color barrier and paving the way for generations of blacks to play Major League baseball. Branch Rickey, president of the Dodgers, had signed Robinson – a former four-sport star at UCLA – to a minor league contract for the 1946 season. Robinson had played that year at Montreal (AAA), enduring some vicious racism, but still leading the league in hitting with a .349 average. The next year he came up to the Dodgers amid much fanfare and controversy. Some of his opponents on the field tried to spike him, and in St Louis, he was not allowed to stay in the team hotel. Robinson remained stoic, and played brilliantly, winning Rookie of the Year Honors. Two years later he was voted the league's Most Valuable Player. Over a 10-year career Robinson hit .311. He was inducted into the baseball Hall of Fame in 1962. **MD**.

ROBINSON, SIR ROBERT
1886-1975
British organic chemist

Robinson's work on naturally occurring chemicals, particularly alkaloids, led to his discovery of the importance of electronic forces in chemical bonds. This formed the basis for modern physical chemistry. He was awarded the 1947 Nobel Prize for Chemistry. He also studied plant pigmentation, penicillin, and sex hormones. He was a great instigator, in that much of the work that he started was completed by others. In a wide-ranging career, he was Professor at Sydney, Liverpool, St Andrews, Manchester, London, and Oxford. He was also famed as a chess player, mountaineer, and traveler. He had an active old age, with 20 of his 700 scientific papers being published after his 80th birthday. **DD**.

ROBINSON, SUGAR RAY [WALKER SMITH]
1920-1989
American boxer

After a storied amateur career, Robinson turned pro in 1940. A welterweight champion from 1946 to 1951, Robinson won the middleweight crown five separate times during the 1950s. Pound for pound, he was one of the greatest fighters ever. **MD**.

ROCKEFELLER, JOHN D
1839-1937
American industrialist and philanthropist

Brought up by religious parents to be painstaking and unscrupulous, John D Rockefeller was well-equipped to succeed. Still in his 20s, he helped to establish an oil refinery in the backwoods of Ohio which in 1870 became his Standard Oil. He realized that he would do better without competition, and when bullying failed he set up interlocking directorships to control other refineries and virtually monopolize the American market. Eventually the Supreme Court invoked the anti-trust laws, but well before then Rockefeller had relinquished close control of his empire and spent most of his time organizing great philanthropic projects through his Rockefeller Foundation. **JW**.

ROCKEFELLER, NELSON
1908-1979
American politician

A stalwart of Republican party politics, Rockefeller was Governor of New York State (1958-73) and twice narrowly missed the Republican presidential nomination in 1964 and 1968. He was appointed vice-president by Gerald FORD in 1973. A keen patron of the arts he used some of his family's wealth to found the Museum of Primitive Art in New York. **JM**.

ROCKNE, KNUTE
1888-1931
American football coach

Even now, more than 60 years after his tragic death in an airplane crash, Knute Rockne remains a symbol of coaching brilliance, an innovative, and inspirational leader. First as a player and then as a coach, he helped bring football into the modern age by emphasizing the forward pass. He coached at his alma mater, Notre Dame University, from 1918 to 1931, lifting the Fighting Irish to the highest level of the college game. He compiled a record of 105-12-5 and went undefeated five times. During Rockne's reign the team produced the most famous backfield in football history: 'The Four Horsemen of Notre Dame.' **MD**.

BELOW: Sugar Ray Robinson (right).

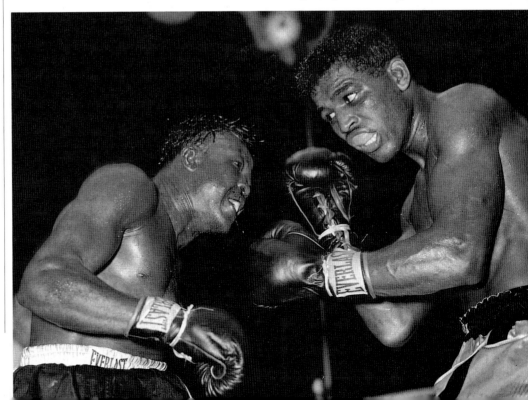

ABOVE: American painter Norman Rockwell.

ROCKWELL, NORMAN
1894-1978
American painter and illustrator

Rockwell achieved enormous popularity in the USA through the illustration work he executed in oils, particularly his *Saturday Evening Post* covers (1916-63). His humorous, sentimental evocations of small-town life and edifying, patriotic images embodied what many wished to imagine as the spirit of America. **ER**.

RODDICK, ANITA
1943-
British businesswoman

A woman who professes that finances 'bore the pants' off her, Roddick has, with the aid of her husband Gordon, made her Body Shops the UK's biggest overseas retailers. Founded in Brighton in 1976, the Roddick's shop catered for and developed a desire for simple products not tested on animals. Careful exploitation of the media made advertising unnecessary and a stock market flotation in 1984 turned the Roddick's into multi-millionaires overnight. **PT**.

ROGERS, GINGER
1911-
American actress

Rogers, sassy and sexy, was a clever comedienne who longed for dramatic roles, but was swept into film immortality in the arms of Fred ASTAIRE instead. Their 1930s musicals were the best Hollywood ever made. In *Flying Down to Rio* (1933) they stole the show dancing the 'Carioca' and were top box-office stars from then. Rogers made other films during the years with Astaire, and afterwards tackled various roles, winning an Academy Award for *Kitty Foyle* (1940). In the 1950s and 1960s she pulled in the crowds on Broadway and on the London stage played the lead in, among others, *Hello Dolly!* and *Mame*. **DC**.

ROGERS, SIR RICHARD
1933-
British architect

Rogers's buildings are controversial, particularly the Centre National d'Art et de Culture Georges Pompidou, Paris (more popularly known as Beaubourg), completed in 1976. The idea of the working parts (electrical conduits, plumbing, escalators etc) being put on show is an essential part of Rogers's design aesthetic: 'Each single element is isolated and used to give order. Nothing is hidden, everything is expressed.' The idea of the flexible kit of parts, or 'giant meccano set,' as Rogers has described it, is also to be seen in his headquarters for Lloyds of London (completed in 1986). **DE**.

ROGERS, ROY
1911-
American actor

Rogers was one of the most famous western stars of all time. Copying the Gene Autry 'singing cowboy' formula in the late 1930s, his pleasant voice and personality soon made him the idol of millions of children, and in the 1950s he moved to television and his own show where his popularity remained undimmed. **DC**.

ROKOSSOVSKY, KONSTANTIN, MARSHAL
1896-1968
Russian soldier

In 1941 Rokossovsky defended Moscow against German attack and in 1942 he led part of the counter-offensive which encircled Stalingrad. By 1944 he was commanding forces which advanced to the Vistula, but did nothing to aid the Warsaw Uprising. His troops reached Lübeck in May 1945. **JPi**.

RIGHT: Roy Rogers with faithful friend Trigger.

THE ROLLING STONES
JAGGER, MICK
1943-
RICHARDS, KEITH
1943-
JONES, BRIAN
1942-1969
WYMAN, BILL
1936-
WATTS, CHARLIE
1941-
TAYLOR, MICK
1948-
WOOD, RON
1947-
British rock group

The Stones were first spotted by the aggressive young promoter Andrew Oldham, who carefully nurtured their bad-boy image through the early years, and songwriting problems were finally overcome with the single 'Satisfaction' in 1965, a statement of rebellion which caught the British mood of the times. Through the flower power movement of the late 1960s, their occasionally lukewarm efforts were marked by constant drug busts and conflicts with authority, but the 1969 album *Let It Bleed* kept them on top. After the sacking and subsequent death of Brian Jones, and the notoriety of the stabbing of a fan by Hell's Angels at a concert, the Stones tried to improve their public image. *Sticky Fingers* and *Exile on Main Street* were both classic albums, but thereafter

ABOVE: *The British bad boys of rock – The Rolling Stones.*

Richards' drugs involvement and Jagger's elevation to the jet-set left them directionless until the 1978 best-selling album *Some Girls*, when ex-Faces guitarist Ron Wood joined them. Their excessive concerts hid a somewhat tired mediocrity amidst constant feuds and solo projects through the 1980s, but in 1989 Richards and Jagger patched up their differences to record *Steel Wheels*, hailed as their best work for a decade. They followed it with massive world tours, demonstrating that at their best they are still one of the finest live acts around. **DC**.

ROLLS, CHARLES STEWART, HON.
1877-1910
British motor manufacturer

Rolls was an entrepreneur running a number of motor agencies when he became interested in producing a quality British car and joined forces with engineer Henry ROYCE. He agreed to sell the cars Royce built and the Rolls-Royce company was formed in 1906. Rolls was responsible for the 'Best car in the World' marketing policy, before dying in a flying accident. **NF**.

ROMMEL, ERWIN, FIELD MARSHAL
1891-1944
German soldier

A brave and resourceful leader, Rommel won Germany's highest award for bravery, *Ordre Pour le Mérite*, on the Italian front in 1917. Between the wars he wrote an important textbook on infantry tactics, extolling his theory of 'forward control'. In 1940 he commanded the 7th Panzer Division in the attack through the Ardennes, successfully putting into practice his theories on leading from the front. He exploited this habit to the full in North Africa, 1941-43, where, as commander of the Afrika Korps, he received the nickname 'the Desert Fox' for his ability to mount fast-moving flanking attacks. His conduct of the North African campaign has become almost legendary and he retained the initiative until October 1942. Defeated at Alamein by MONTGOMERY partly because he had over-extended his supply and reinforcement lines, Rommel retreated as far as Tunisia. Ordered home by HITLER to serve as Inspector of Coastal Defenses, in 1944 he assumed command of Army Group B in northern France opposing the Allied invasion. He was wounded in an air attack on 17 July and three days later he was implicated in the July bomb plot against Hitler. Rather than face certain disgrace and execution, he committed suicide on 14 October 1944. **JPi**.

BELOW: Erwin Rommel (left), the 'Desert Fox.'

ROONEY, MICKEY
1920-
American actor

After a series of short features at the tender age of six, Rooney went on to star as Andy, the painfully typical teenager of the Hardy family, in some 17 full-length MGM productions. He won a Special Award in 1938 for the tough kid in *Boys' Town*, made musicals with Judy GARLAND, and much, much more. Finally, at the age of 28 he left off being a child actor and began just being an actor, appearing in everything from comedy to serious drama, and his credits include *Girl Crazy* (1943) through to the frantic treasure hunt *It's a Mad Mad Mad Mad World* (1963). **DC**.

ROOSEVELT, FRANKLIN DELANO
1882-1945
American statesman and president

As 'that man in the White House,' Roosevelt was detested by the Republicans, not only for ending their 13-year rule but almost as a crypto-Communist. Yet he alone held the Presidency for three terms, despite the crippling effects of polio, and with the battlecry 'the only thing we have to fear is fear itself,' he launched his New Deal to banish the worst effects of the Great Depression. With his 'alphabet agencies' he introduced a revolutionary interventionist style of government; public works including great dams and highways, the Tennessee Valley Authority, and credit for the destitute farmers of the Dust Bowl. Roosevelt was returned on a landslide vote in 1936. When his New Deal ran into opposition in the Supreme Court he threatened to pack it with six nominees, thus forcing a compromise, with the acceptance of his Social Security measures and the Wagner Act which set up a National Labor Relations Board, guaranteeing workers' rights. His decision to approve Lease-Lend in the face of American isolationist prejudice was an enlightened and courageous move in the blackest days of the war. Roosevelt formed a close working relationship with CHURCHILL to win the war but in his negotiations with STALIN, particularly at Yalta in February 1945, he has been accused of losing the peace. By then he was seriously ill and he died April 1945. **JC**.

ROOSEVELT, THEODORE
1858-1919
American statesman and president

Perhaps the most popular President in American history, 'Teddy' was a complex character. An early environmentalist who secured the first national parks, he was also a big-game hunter. A sickly youth, he spent some time as a cowboy. Author of a book on the Naval War of 1812, he served in 1897 as Assistant Secretary of the Navy. However, the cornerstone of his fame was a land engagement of the Spanish-American War, the charge up San Juan Hill, in which he led his privately raised regiment of 'Roughriders.' He was immediately elected Governor of New York, but so outraged his colleagues with his reforms that they shunted him into the Vice-Presidency. On 14 September, 1901, President McKinley succumbed to an assassin's bullet and Roosevelt moved into the White House as 26th President. He moved against big money interests, indicting 30 corporations for breaking the anti-trust laws. He created the Department of Commerce and Labor and brought in the Pure Food and Drugs Act. In foreign policy he 'spoke softly and carried a big stick.' Elected President again in 1905, he was awarded the Nobel Peace Prize in 1906 for helping end the Russo-Japanese War, and he persuaded the new state of Panama to cede a Canal Zone for the construction of the waterway. Roosevelt retired in 1909 but ran again in 1912 for President as an independent, being defeated by Woodrow WILSON. **JC**.

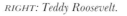

BELOW: F D Roosevelt.   *RIGHT: Teddy Roosevelt.*

ROOT, ELIHU
1845-1937
American lawyer

Root was the leading figure in the American movement to establish international peace before and after World War I. Having been instrumental, as Theodore ROOSEVELT's Secretary of War, in reforming the Army and drawing up a Constitution and code of laws for the Philippines, he became Secretary of State. His role in solving several international disputes, including one over fishery rights between Britain and the United States, won him the Nobel Peace Prize in 1912. He helped set up the International Court of Justice at the Hague but the Senate vetoed American involvement. He secured the banning of poison gas weapons and restrictions on submarine warfare under the Washington Arms Limitation Treaty in 1921 and drafted the Four Power Pacific Treaty which followed it. **JC**.

ROSE, PETE [PETER EDWARD]
1941-
American baseball player

Pete Rose smacked 4256 hits in his 24-year career (mainly with the Cincinnati Reds), more than anyone in Major League history. Owner of the National League record 44-game hitting streak, he won three batting titles. Known as 'Charley Hustle' for his hell-bent playing style, Rose was banned from baseball for life in 1989 after betting on the game. **MD**.

ROSS, DIANA
1944-
American pop and soul singer

After leaving the Supremes in the late 1960s Ross produced a series of hits, from 'Ain't No Mountain High Enough' (1970) to the disco chart-topper 'Chain Reaction', moving from Motown to embrace more commercial pop styles. In 1973 a starring role in the Billie Holiday biopic *Lady Sings the Blues* earned her praise from critics. **DC**.

ROSSELLINI, ROBERTO
1906-1977
Italian film director

A major figure in the Italian neo-realist movement, Rossellini made films on a shoestring budget, on location, and in hazardous conditions, such as filming the anti-Fascist *Rome-Open City* (1945) in Fascist-occupied Rome. His private life, notably his relationship with Ingrid BERGMAN, overshadowed his work in the 1950s, but his reputation recovered in the 1960s. **NS**.

ROTH, PHILIP
1933-
American novelist

Philip Roth made his mark with his novella

Goodbye Columbus (1959), a caustic, witty portrait of affluent Jewish life. His novels, from *Portnoy's Complaint* (1969) and *The Great American Novel* (1973), to *The Counterlife* (1986), test the boundaries between fact and fiction, the reportorial and the fantastic, his theme the Jewish writer in crisis. **CW**.

ROTHEIM, ERIC
1898-1938
American inventor

Eric Rotheim, a passionate nature lover, filed his patent for the aerosol can as early as 1926. The aerosol was developed commercially after 1941 as an insect spray and was widely used by US troops in the Pacific. After the war a whole host of uses was found for Rotheim's invention. However in recent years alternative means of propulsion have been developed as a result of evidence showing that fully halogenated chlorofluorocarbons (CFCs) used as the propellent have a harmful effect on the ozone layer. **PT**.

ROTHKO, MARK
1903-1970
American painter

Born in Latvia, Rothko went to the USA in 1913. He began painting in 1925 and was largely self-taught. His early urban scenes gave way to a primordial imagery influenced by Surrealism which, in turn, became increasingly abstracted. He reached his mature style as one of the earliest Color Field painters in the late 1940s. His characteristic format consisted of vertically stacked rectangles of intense, vibrant color, often on such a large scale that they engulf the spectator. In the late 1950s his palette darkened, echoing his mental state. His somber mural for St Thomas University Chapel, Houston, in black, dark brown, and purple, was executed the year before his suicide. **ER**.

ROYCE, SIR FREDRICK HENRY
1863-1933
British motor manufacturer

Royce was the dour perfectionist in the RR alliance, an engineer who thrived on detailed perfection. He built his first car in 1904 after which it was only a couple of years before the Silver Ghost was produced. When Royce died in 1936 the RR emblem was changed from red to black in his honor. **NF**.

RUBENSTEIN, ARTUR
1887-1982
Polish-American pianist

A pupil of Paderewski, Rubenstein made his debut at the age of twelve and continued to enjoy a successful career. He is most admired for the clarity he achieved in his performances of Chopin, Beethoven, Schubert, Schumann, and Brahms. He also wrote an autobiography, *My Young Years*. **DK**.

RUNDSTEDT, GERD VON, FIELD MARSHAL
1875-1953
German soldier

After service in World War I, Rundstedt remained in the postwar German Army until 1938, when he retired as a full general. Recalled a year later, he commanded Army Group A in the successful campaigns in Poland (1939) and France (1940), and Army Group South in the invasion of Russia (1941). Sacked in the great purge of commanders in December 1941, he was recalled in March 1942 by HITLER, who admired his calm professionalism, to become Commander-in-Chief West; he held this post until July 1944, then again from September 1944 until March 1945. **JPi**.

BELOW: The great pianist, Artur Rubenstein.

RUNYON, [ALFRED] DAMON
1884-1946
American writer

Short-story writer and journalist, he was a war correspondent in World War I. The underworld and *demi-monde* of New York provided the inspiration for his humorous, slang-ridden stories of show business, athletes, gamblers, and assorted hangers-on. The most famous collection was *Guys and Dolls*, which inspired the Broadway musical. **AM**.

RUSHDIE, [AHMED] SALMAN
1947-
British novelist

Born in Bombay, and educated at Rugby and Cambridge, Rushdie is one of the foremost exponents of magic realism. In his colossal novels he has explored the post-colonial world of the Indian subcontinent, alongside his interest in the creative process and the human need for myth in an increasingly secular world. His first book, *Grimus*, appeared in 1975, and *Midnight's Children* (1981) won the Booker Prize. *The Satanic Verses* (1988) brought him an undesired renown when its alleged blasphemies prompted Ayatollah KHOMEINI of fundamentalist Iran to declare a *fatwa* or death sentence upon him. **AM**.

RUSSELL, BERTRAND, LORD
1872-1970
British philosopher, mathematician, and political activist

One of the most outstanding figures in British philosophy, Russell received no formal education, being brought up in the home of his grandfather, the Liberal Prime Minister Lord (John) Russell, after the death of his parents. At Cambridge he studied mathematics and philosophy and was elected to a Fellowship at Trinity College for his dissertation on the foundations of geometry, whose idealism he soon repudiated under the influence of G E MOORE. Instead his seminal work on the foundations of mathematics, which culminated in the three-volume treatise, *Principia Mathematica*, written jointly with A N WHITEHEAD, argued that mathematics could be entirely deduced from logic. He reached this conclusion independently of FREGE, in whose work he detected the flaw which is universally referred to as Russell's Paradox. After he brought WITTGENSTEIN to Cambridge and arranged for the publication of his *Tractatus* while he was a prisoner of war, his interest turned mainly to epistemology, on which he published a number of books. He wrote widely on other philosophical and educational topics, and in 1945 published the *History of Western Philosophy*. He lectured throughout the world, and in 1950 received the Nobel Prize for Literature. A life-long radical, Russell was im-

ABOVE: Streetwise journalist, Damon Runyon (left).

ABOVE: Lord Bertrand Russell, philosopher, mathematician and radical.

prisoned and dismissed from his first Cambridge post for his pacifism during World War I; he then refused an offer of reinstatement after the war, just as he later refused to use the title he inherited. Married four times, he scandalized society by leaving his wife for Lady Ottoline Morrell in 1912, and in 1940 was barred from teaching in New York because of his public views on sexual libertarianism. In 1960 he led the Committee of 100 out of the CND, and the following year, at the age of 89, he was again arrested for demonstrating against nuclear weapons. **EB**.

RUSSELL, BILL [WILLIAM FENTON]
1934-
American basketball player

The consummate team player, Bill Russell sparked the Boston Celtics to eight consecutive NBA titles, and 11 in his 13 years with the team. He was a monumental rebounder (22.5 per game during his career) and a stellar defender. In 1966 he became the Celtics' player/coach, the first black man to pilot a major pro team. Russell also won NCAA and Olympic titles. **MD**.

RUTH, BABE [GEORGE HERMAN]
1895-1948
American baseball player

No one is more responsible than Babe Ruth for the vast popularity of the game of baseball, for it was he who essentially introduced fans to the majesty of the home run. In 1920, his first season with the New York Yankees, Ruth slugged 54 homers; the next highest total in the major leagues was 19. As

BELOW: *Baseball's fabled Babe Ruth, of the New York Yankees.*

the centerpiece of the Yankees' 'Murderer's Row' in 1927, he swatted 60, a single-season record surpassed only once (when Roger Maris hit 61 in 1961). All told, Ruth scored 714 homers, a figure finally eclipsed (by Henry AARON) only in 1974. Born in Baltimore, Ruth began his career as a pitcher with the Boston Red Sox in 1914. He helped to pitch Boston to the World Series three times, then was made an outfielder so that his vast hitting talent could be used every day. After the 1919 season the Sox sold Ruth to the Yankees (Boston has not won a World Series since), and the Yanks went on to become the sport's greatest dynasty. In 1923 the Yanks opened a new stadium that became known as 'The House that Ruth Built.' Notable among the many legends surrounding his career is one that relates to the incident in which he apparently predicted precisely when and where he would hit a home run in the 1932 World Series. **MD**.

RUTHERFORD, SIR ERNEST, LORD RUTHERFORD OF NELSON
1871-1937
British physicist

Regarded as the founder of modern nuclear theory, Rutherford saw his work as totally academic and having no useful application whatsoever. While still at Canterbury College, Christchurch, New Zealand, he built a radio wave detector not long after HERTZ

and MARCONI did their pioneering radio work. Later, working in Cambridge and Montreal, he studied the phenomenon of radioactivity recently discovered by the late nineteenth-Century physicists and defined the three types of radiation – alpha rays consisting of helium nuclei, beta rays consisting of electrons, and gamma rays which are electromagnetic. He first postulated the presence of a dense nucleus at the center of the atom when he observed that a certain proportion of alpha radiation bounced off a substance that it should pass cleanly through. This was the first correct idea of the structure of the atom, and was subsequently developed by Niels BOHR. This was all before World War I, and during the war he worked on devices for detecting submarines by sound. He returned to nuclear physics afterwards and his work culminated in the involvement with M Oliphant and P Harteck in the first fusion reaction in 1934. He was awarded the Nobel Prize for Chemistry in 1908. **DD**.

RYAN, LYNN NOLAN
1947-
American baseball player

With blazing speed and amazing longevity, Nolan Ryan has pitched his way to baseball greatness. In 1992 he was still going strong at age 45 with a 90-plus fastball. A 300-game winner, Ryan owns records for no-hitters (7) and most strikeouts in both a career (over 5500) and a season (383). **MD**.

RYLE, SIR MARTIN
1918-1984
British radio-astronomer

During World War II Ryle worked at the Telecommunications Research Establishment on the development of radar. He joined J A Ratcliffe in the Cavendish laboratory in 1945 and built a radio telescope to investigate the radio sky; his third survey (1959) remains a standard. In 1955 the Mullard Radio Astronomy Observatory was established at Cambridge, enabling the construction of bigger aerials of the interferometer type which Ryle had developed. The Observatory, of which Ryle was director, tracked the path of the Soviet Sputnik I in 1957. It also attracted publicity in 1967 when the team discovered the existence of small, but very strong sources of radio emissions; these were called pulsars, because they were heard in regular bursts and gave rise to speculation that they might be communications from other worlds. The Observatory's work on exploring the outermost reaches of the universe provided support for the 'Big Bang' theory of its beginnings, rather than the 'steady state' theories of HOYLE, Bondi, and Gold. The first professor of radio astronomy at Cambridge in 1959, Ryle was knighted in 1966, created Astronomer Royal in 1972 and shared a Nobel Prize in 1974 with Anthony Hewish. **PW**.

SAARINEN, EERO
1910-1961
American architect

Saarinen emigrated with his parents from Finland to the United States in 1923 and worked closely with his architect father Eliel (1873-1950). His first major work on his own, the General Motors Technical Center, Warren, Michigan (completed 1955), based on the purist Modernist principles of MIES and GROPIUS, is composed of numerous cubic shapes of varying sizes, but with greater variety of individual detailing and surface modulation than the prototypes. Saarinen's most famous buildings, the domical Kresge Auditorium at Massachusetts Institute of Technology (completed 1955) and the Yale University Hockey Rink (completed 1958), with its sweeping whale-like roofline, reveal modern architects' difficulty in resolving their desire to make striking formal statements and classical allusions with fulfilling a building's essential and often complex functional requirements. **AR**.

SAATCHI, CHARLES AND MAURICE
Born 1943 and 1946
British communications executives

The Saatchi brothers set up their advertising agency in 1970, while in their mid-20s. Over the next few years they built up an impressive list of clients, largely because Charles was adept at publicizing the company. In 1978 Saatchi & Saatchi became a household name when it started working for the Conservative Party, devising the effective 'Labour Isn't Working' slogan for the 1979 election. Meanwhile the brothers embarked on an ambitious aquisition program, swallowing up many smaller companies and expanding into the US and European markets to create one of the world's largest and most successful advertising businesses. **DSL**.

SABIN, ALBERT BRUCE
1906-1993
American virologist

Born in Russia, Sabin graduated with a medical degree from New York University and dedicated his career to the production of vaccines. Known in particular for his development of the oral poliomyelitis vaccine, he began working on it at about the same time as Jonas SALK was working on an inactive one. Sabin was convinced that the use of a dead virus could only confer temporary protection. After many years of painstaking research, he produced a live virus in 1957 that could be taken orally and that conferred immunity rapidly. The 'sugar lump' as it is now called has become an easy and accepted method of vaccination against polio and has resulted in the marked decline of this once prevalent disease around the world. **ES**.

ABOVE: *President Anwar Sadat of Egypt, murdered in 1981.*

SABIN, FLORENCE
1871-1953
American physician

The first woman to graduate from and teach at Johns Hopkins Medical School, Sabin became Professor of Histology in 1917. She set up the renowned Cellular Studies department at the Rocketed Institute (1925-38). She received 15 honorary degrees and at 73 saw the Sabin Health Bills passed which included the tuberculosis X-ray survey. **MB**.

SADAT, ANWAR
1918-1981
Egyptian politician

Sadat broke ranks with the Arab bloc to sign the first peace treaty with Israel and defied Islamic sentiment to suppress Islamic Fundamentalism. He became Vice-President in 1969 and succeeded to the Presidency on NASSER's death in 1970. He tried to regain the Sinai by attacking the Israelis during Yom Kippur festival in 1973. But having asserted his own charismatic leadership, and having turned from his predecessor's pro-Communist and Arab Nationalist path, he opened the way to a peace treaty with Israel, which was reached after talks in Jerusalem in 1977. The Camp David Accords followed and he and the Israeli Premier Menachem BEGIN shared the 1979 Nobel Prize for Peace. In 1981 he arrested hundreds of Muslim fundamentalists and political opponents and as a direct result of this in October he was assassinated while reviewing a military parade. **JC**.

SAGAN, FRANÇOISE
1935-
French novelist

Sagan is known above all for her novels *Bonjour Tristesse* (1954) and *Aimez-vous Brahms?* (1959), both of which were made into films. The appeal of her prose style is lucidity, though this has not been sustained. Her novels portray bored, superficial people who seek an escape from mediocrity through brief sexual liaisons. **CW**.

BELOW: *Françoise Sagan in 1956.*

SAINT LAURENT, YVES
1936-
French designer

Algerian-born Saint Laurent's first success came while he was still a student: at 17 he won a competition sponsored by the International Wool Secretariat. Shortly afterwards he was hired by Christian DIOR and took over the house when Dior died. Here Saint Laurent created considerable controversy since his designs were not what the fashion world or the public had come to expect of the House of Dior. 1958 saw the 'Little Girl Look' of a narrow-shouldered dress with a semifitted bodice and short flared skirt; 1959 saw him revive a short version of the 'Hobble Skirt', and in 1960 he introduced black leather jackets. Under Saint Laurent's direction, the House of Dior redesigned street fashion into couture design. In 1960 he was required to do his national service and was called up to serve in the war in Algeria. Some months later he was invalided out of the army, and returned to Dior to find he had been replaced as head designer by Marc Bohan. Undaunted and with new business partner Pierre Berger, Saint Laurent opened his own house in 1962. Year after year Saint Laurent produced innovative designs that were widely copied: thigh boots in 1963; the 'Mondrian' dresses in 1965; the 'Smoking' or tuxedo jacket for women in 1966. 1966 also saw the opening of a string of Rive Gauche boutiques, and throughout the 1970s and 1980s Saint Laurent continued to reign in Paris as one of the kings of design. **MC**.

SALAZAR, ANTÓNIO
1889-1970
Portuguese politician

The longest-serving dictator of the century, Salazar maintained Portugal as the calm backwater of Western Europe for 40 years. He was a Professor of Economics at Coimbra University (1918-21) and became a Catholic Center deputy in Parliament in 1921. Salazar left politics after only one session in disgust at republican corruption. When the 1926 Army coup occurred, his terms for bailing the Army leaders out of their financial crisis was to be given complete independence. From Finance Minister he became in 1932 de facto head of state and was as good as his word in balancing the budget, something that was done annually for nearly half a century, at some cost to political liberty. The revolution which followed his death in 1970 cleared the way for Portugal's entry into the EC. **JC**.

SALINGER, J[EROME] D[AVID]
1919-
American writer

Fueler of a thousand adolescent fantasies of rebellion, Salinger was born in New York. Having published several stories, his first and only novel, *The Catcher in the Rye* (1951), was a great success. He caught perfectly the tone of adolescent alienation in the first person narrative of Holden Caulfield, and it became a cult book; the success was not to be repeated. His collection of short stories *Nine Stories* (1953, published in England as *For Esme – With Love and Squalor*) and other volumes of long short stories about the eccentric Glass family are darker, less engaging and deservedly less popular. **AM**.

SALK, JONAS EDWARD
1914-
American microbiologist

The son of Polish-Jewish immigrants, he developed the first safe, and effective attenuated vaccine against poliomyelitis in 1952 at the University of Pittsburgh. Previous attempts had failed and caused several deaths and cases of paralysis. He made use

ABOVE: *J D Salinger, American author.*

of ENDERS' virus culture method and took extra precautions to ensure that he produced a safe vaccine. Despite many objections from other researchers he tested the vaccine in mass clinical trials where it was shown to be 80-90% effective. His courage and persistence were rewarded by the results between 1956-1958 during which 200 million injections were administered without a single case of vaccine produced paralysis. **ES**.

SANCHEZ, ILYICH RAMIREZ ['CARLOS THE JACKAL']
1949-
Venezuelan terrorist

The son of a Marxist millionaire, Sanchez was trained in Cuba and Moscow before fighting with the Palestinians against the Jordanian Army in 1970. Moving to Lebanon, he joined Wadi Hadad's Popular Front for the Liberation of Palestine (PFLP) and was sent to London to mount terrorist attacks on Jewish-related targets. In 1973-75 he was in Paris, avoiding capture only by killing two policemen in a shoot-out. He gained international notoriety in December 1975 when he kidnapped oil ministers attending a meeting of the Organization of Petroleum Exporting Countries (OPEC) in Vienna. Since then, he has gone underground. **JP**.

SANDBURG, CARL
1878-1967
American poet

Sandburg was a journalist and socialist organizer before his use of colloquialism and free verse in *Chicago Poems* (1916) caused critical controversy. His interest in idiom is evident in the ballad compilation *The American Songbag* (1927), while prose works include a life of Abraham Lincoln and the family chronicle *Remembrance Rock* (1948). **CW**.

ABOVE: *American poet Carl Sandburg, with wife and admirers.*

SANGER, FREDERICK
1918-
British biochemist

He graduated from Cambridge in 1939 and continued his work there. In 1951 he joined the staff of the Medical Research Council laboratories. He was awarded the Nobel Prize for Chemistry twice – the first person ever to do so. The first award was in 1958 for his work on determining the exact structure of insulin. This was achieved by using a compound – Sanger's reagent - that split up the insulin protein chain and attached itself to particular components. He was able to determine the sequence of the 51 amino acids in insulin's two-chain molecule. He also found differences between pig, horse, sheep, and whale insulin. His second Nobel Prize was in 1980 for his work on the chemicals that formed genes – determining the sequence of nucleotides in DNA. Eventually, by 1984, he and his team were able to work out the sequence of 150,000 nucleotides in the entire genetic makeup of certain viruses. The second Nobel Prize was shared with the American scientists Paul BERG and Walter GILBERT. His work has been fundamental in the understanding of genes and proteins. **DD**.

SANGER, MARGARET
1883-1966
American doctor

Leader of the birth-control movement, Sanger braved indictment and arrest to further her cause. She toured the world teaching birth control and authored many books including the classic *What Every Girl Should Know* (1916). She received the American Women's Award in 1931. **MB**.

SANT'ELIA, ANTONIO
1880-1916
Italian architect

Sant'Elia built little before his death in World War I. His importance lies in his theoretical project for a *Città Nuova* of towering buildings with internal elevators, multilevel road bridges, vast stations and factories, exhibited in 1914. It was lauded by Marinetti and the Futurists although Sant'Elia despised their right-wing, nationalist aspirations. **AR**.

SANTOS-DUMONT, ALBERTO
1873-1932
Brazilian aviation pioneer

This diminutive Brazilian was educated in France, where he lived and worked until 1928. His first aircraft was a balloon (1898) followed by a series of airships. His *No. 6* airship won a F100,000 prize on 19 October 1901 after a controled flight around the Eiffel Tower in Paris. Turning to airplanes, his tail-first *14-bis* boxkite biplane made the first recognized European flight on 12 Novem-

ABOVE: Leading existentialists Jean-Paul Sartre (center) and Simone de Beauvoir.

ber 1906, covering 722 feet (220m) in 21.2 seconds, while his little *Demoiselle* monoplane was the precursor of cheap and simple lightplane for the masses. **MT**.

SARTRE, JEAN-PAUL
1905-1980
French philosopher and writer

Best known for his plays and novels, Sartre's literary works were closely linked with his philosophy. He was influenced by Husserl, but his major existentialist work, *Being and Nothingness*, owes much to HEIDEGGER; here the *pour-soi* embodies the human condition, able to make authentic, unconditioned choices, or escape to the 'bad faith' of convention. The nephew of Albert SCHWEITZER, Sartre taught philosophy in schools for many years, joined the Resistance, founded the political and literary journal *Les Temps Modernes* with his mistress Simone de BEAUVOIR, and was a member of the Communist Party until the invasion of Hungary in 1956. He was offered the Nobel Prize for Literature in 1964, but followed his principle of refusing all honors. **EB**.

SAUNDERS, DAME CICELY MARY STRODE
1918-
British physician

Trained as a nurse, Saunders graduated in medicine in 1957 and devoted her medical career to improving conditions for the dying. Regarded as the founder of the hospice movement in Britain, her pioneering work at St Christopher's Hospice, Sydenham, established outstanding standards of physical and spiritual care for terminally ill patients. **GL**.

SAUSSURE, MONGIN-FERDINAND DE
1857-1913
Swiss linguist

Saussure is commonly held to be the founder of modern linguistics. His posthumously published book, *Course in General Linguistics*, argued that language should be studied as a system of signs (rather than as individual speech acts) in which individual words get their meanings not from their relation to objects in the world or from the intentions of speakers but rather from their relations to other signs in the system. Saussure's massive impact on twentieth-century thought is evident not only in linguistics but even more in the adoption of his methodology as 'structuralism' which dominated sociology, anthropology, literary studies, and other fields through much of the postwar era. **DSL**.

SCARGILL, ARTHUR
1938-
British trade unionist

A coalminer from the age of 15, Scargill was elected President of the Yorkshire branch of the National Union of Mineworkers (NUM) in 1973 and NUM President in 1982. In 1984 he led a strike against pit closures, only to see it fail amid violent confrontations with the police. **JP**.

SCHACHT, HJALMAR
1879-1970
German banker

Schacht was seconded to the German finance ministry in 1923, charged with quelling the runaway inflation. He proposed a new issue of currency backed by the value of land, a confidence trick that restored people's faith in money. He was appointed president of the Reichsbank, but resigned in 1930 in protest at the continuing burden of the World War I reparations demanded by the victorious Allies. From 1934 as HITLER's economics minister he provided the financial expertise for rearmament. In 1937 he resigned in protest at GÖRING's interference, and was dismissed from the Reichsbank two years later. **JW**.

SCHEER, REINHOLD VON, ADMIRAL
1863-1928
German sailor

In January 1916 Scheer was appointed Commander of the German High Seas Fleet. As such, he fought the Battle of Jutland in May, claiming victory in what was, in reality, a drawn contest. Promoted to Chief of the Naval Staff in August 1918, he witnessed the disintegration of the Fleet. **JPi**.

SCHIAPARELLI, ELSA
1890-1973
Italian designer

Schiaparelli spent her early married life in America before moving to Paris in 1920. Her business started when one of her designs – a black sweater with a *trompe-l'oeil* – effect bow at the neck – was seen by a store buyer. Her own shop, 'Pour le Sport', was opened in 1928 and was followed a year later by a salon which produced smart, sophisticated designs but which were often eccentric and shocking. She used hessian for evening dresses, put *trompe-l'oeil* drawers and padlocks on suits, used a fabric printed to resemble newspaper (complete with headlines about herself) and sold handbags that lit up or played tunes when opened. Her interest in the unusual led her to design using the new synthetic materials, such as cellophane and a glasslike fabric called Rhodophane. Influenced by art movements such as Cubism and Surrealism, Schiaparelli commissioned leading artists including Jean COCTEAU and Salvador DALI to design fabrics and accessories. Among her most famous items were hats made in the shape of shoes, lamb chops, and ice-cream cones. An outstanding colorist, she took one of the artist Christian Berard's pinks, called it 'Shocking Pink', and promoted it vigorously. With a penchant for names that began with her own initial, she called her two fragrances 'Sleeping' and 'Shocking', the bottle for which was created by Surrealist artist Léonore Fini and was based on the hourglass silhouette of Hollywood actress Mae WEST. During World War II Schiaparelli lectured in the United States and in 1949 opened a branch of her business in New York. She held her last show in 1954 but the Surrealist aspects of her designs continue to influence a great number of designers. **MC**.

SCHIELE, EGON
1890-1918
Austrian painter

Schiele studied at the Vienna Academy of Fine Arts 1906-09. In 1907 he met Gustav Klimt, whose ornamental figure paintings deeply influenced him, but from 1909 he evolved a highly individual style, characterized by intense visual richness and superb draftsmanship. His work is dominated by female nudes and self-portraits, often nude, and his preoccupations with sexuality and the self paralleled those same concerns of the emerging psychoanalytical movement in Vienna. The open sexuality of his art and his unconventional lifestyle led to Schiele's imprisonment in 1912, charged with immorality. He achieved acceptance and recognition shortly before his death, after exhibiting at the Vienna Secession in 1918. **ER**.

SCHLEMMER, OSKAR
1888-1943
German painter, sculptor and stage designer

Schlemmer was head of the stage workshop at the Bauhaus from 1920 to 1929. He viewed theater, particularly dance, as a medium to express moving forms and colors within an abstract space. His painting attempted to recreate the transitory movements of dance, while in sculpture he explored the rhythmic interplay of forms. **ER**.

SCHMIDT, HELMUT
1918-
West German statesman and chancellor

The fifth postwar Chancellor of West Germany, Schmidt succeeded Willy BRANDT in 1974. Born in Hamburg, Schmidt joined the Social Democratic Party (SDP) in 1946, having served in the army during the war. Defense Minister from 1969, and Finance Minister from 1972 until he became Chancellor, he was defeated at the polls by KOHL in 1982. **JM**.

SCHNABEL, JULIAN
1945-
American painter

Born in Brooklyn, Schnabel studied at the University of Houston (1969-72), and on the Whitney Museum Independent Study Program (1973). He made a rapid and controversial rise to fame in the 1980s. His works are extravagant in scale and have hyper-elaborate titles. Those best known employ shards of broken china, embedded in impasto. **ER**.

ABOVE: Elsa Schiaparelli, influential fashion designer.

ABOVE: *The creator of 'Peanuts', Charles Schulz.*

SCHOENBERG, ARNOLD
1874-1956
German-American composer

Schoenberg is probably the most important figure in the history of twentieth-century tonality, for he revolutionized the orthodox system of key relationships and introduced what he referred to as a 'pantonal' one. He also introduced a new technique called 'Sprechstimme' or speech-song in his melodrama *Pierrot Lunaire* (1912). To begin with he composed several highly successful works which are intensely chromatic and lean towards the postromantic style influenced by Brahms and Wagner. Examples of this earlier approach to composition can be seen in the monodrama *Verklärte Nacht* (1899) and in *Gurrelieder* (1900-11) for solo voices, chorus, and large orchestra. The real revolution, however, came in 1921 with the birth of serialism and SCHOENBERG's twelve-note system of composition. Basically Schoenberg believed that an entire piece could be built around a pre-determined set of twelve notes. The piece would maintain its interest by varying the treatment of the twelve notes such as changing their order, inverting them, transposing them and using them in retrograde. Schoenberg's influence on contemporary composers and those after him cannot be overemphasized. He altered the paths of tonality and molded the way ahead for many composers including BERG and WEBERN. **DK**.

SCHOLL, WILLIAM
1882-1968
American podiatrist

Dr Scholl's name is now a household word, thanks to the many footcare products marketed in his name. Scholl started out as a shoemaker's apprentice at 16 in Indiana, later establishing his own business in Chicago. By 22 he had put himself through medical school, invented and patented his first arch support, and had started the manufacturing company that was to lodge over 200 patents. **CR**.

SCHULZ, CHARLES
1922-
American cartoonist

Schulz is the creator of *Peanuts*, the world's most successful comic strip. *Peanuts*, originally entitled *L'il Folks*, first appeared in 1950. Charlie Brown, the central character, an anxious and rather dull child, suffers life's misfortunes with resignation. Other characters include Sally, Lucy, Lucius, Woodstock, and Charlie's dog, Snoopy – a perpetual dreamer. Schulz's humor is wry, never ribald or dark, and is essentially comforting. The strip's appeal across so many cultural boundaries is in part the result of its blandness. The TV, film, and toy spin-offs from his characters have become major multi-million dollar industries. **FM**.

SCHUMACHER, ERNST
1911-1977
British economist

Schumacher's very influential *Small is Beautiful* (1973) urged that economic development, especially in underdeveloped countries, should be helped by the provision of simple equipment that could be handled by local people. This contrasted with the prevailing economic ideology that favored big schemes involving expensive technology and high capital investment. **JW**.

SCHUMPETER, JOSEPH
1883-1950
American economist

Schumpeter began his academic career in his native Austria, where he was briefly (1919) Finance Minister. After moving to the USA his main field of study was the business cycle, and he established his reputation as an economic theorist with his two-volume *Business Cycles* in 1939. This was quoted in economics textbooks for decades afterwards. His 1942 *Capitalism, Socialism and Democracy* had less of a long-term impact, though was notable in its time. In it, he visualized capitalism rendering itself archaic by its very success, and being replaced by a system under stronger public control, even by socialism. **JW**.

SCHWARZKOPF, ELISABETH
1915-
Polish opera singer

Schwarzkopf began her career in Berlin and Vienna in coloratura roles in Verdi and Strauss, moving gradually to more lyric parts. She sang at Covent Garden, London, in 1947-53; in Salzburg (1947-64) she specialized in a limited group of roles – Mozart's Countess, Donna Elvira and Fiordiligi, Verdi's Alice Ford and Strauss's Marschallin – which she made entirely her own. **JH**.

RIGHT: *Soprano Elisabeth Schwarzkopf.*

ABOVE: *Gulf War commander, General Norman Schwarzkopf.*

SCHWARZKOPF, NORMAN, GENERAL
1934-
American soldier

Commissioned from West Point in 1956, Schwarzkopf completed two tours in South Vietnam (1965-66 and 1969-70). After service in Grenada (1983) and the Pentagon, he took over US Central Command in 1988 and in 1991 commanded coalition troops in the Desert Storm operation to liberate Kuwait from Iraqi occupation. **JPi**.

SCHWEITZER, ALBERT
1875-1965
German missionary

Having devoted the first 30 years of his life to scholarship and music, Schweitzer spent the rest in service to humanity. He qualified as a doctor in 1913, and set up a missionary station at Lambarene in French Equatorial Africa, building a hospital to combat leprosy and sleeping sickness. Apart from periodic fund-raising trips to Europe, he remained in Africa, demonstrating by example his 'reverence for life'. **JM**.

SCHWITTERS, KURT
1887-1948
German painter and sculptor

While Schwitters's early work was Expressionist, he later attempted to free art from striving for 'expression.' In 1918 he began producing collages, compositions built up from urban detritus, including bus tickets, stamps, and nails. He invented the meaningless term *Merz* for his work and Merzbau for his large constructions of discarded rubbish. A founder of the Hanover Dada group, he instigated an influential Dada magazine entitled *Merz*. Schwitters's work was declared degenerate by the Nazis and his publications burnt. Forbidden to seek employment he fled to Norway and in 1940 to Britain where he was interned for a year before settling in Ambleside. **ER**.

SCOFIELD, PAUL
1922-
British actor

Although he won an Academy award and a British Film Academy Award for the role of Sir Thomas More in *A Man For All Seasons* (1966), a repeat of his stage success, Scofield's films have been infrequent. A successful and wide-ranging stage actor, recent films include Kenneth Branagh's *Henry V* (1989) and *Hamlet* (1990). **DC**.

SCORSESE, MARTIN
1942-
American film director

A volatile filmmaker whose movies are characterized by restless camera movement, extreme violence, religious overtones, and troubled masculinity. Scorsese has formed a particularly productive partnership with actor Robert de NIRO on such films as *Taxi Driver* (1976), *Raging Bull* (1980), and *Cape Fear* (1991). **NS**.

SCOTT, ROBERT FALCON
1868-1912
British explorer

Despite an earlier successful attempt to explore the Ross Ice Shelf, Scott is largely famous for having failed to become the first man to reach the South Pole, and for having

ABOVE: Dr Albert Schweitzer and friend at his missionary station.

ABOVE: Director Martin Scorsese (right) with Robert De Niro on the set of Taxi Driver.

died in the attempt. He set out on the 1500km trek from Cape Evans on 1 November 1911, reaching his goal on 18 January, only to find that the Norwegian explorer AMUNDSEN had beaten him to it. The suffering endured by the team on their attempted return journey, and the heroism of the injured Captain Oates who staggered out to die in the blizzards rather than slow down his companions, are revealed in Scott's journal, discovered next to his frozen body in their final camp – which was within 10 miles of the closest supply depot. **RJ**.

SEABORG, GLENN THEODORE
1912-
American physical chemist

During World War II Seaborg worked on the Manhattan Project to build the nuclear bomb and was responsible for isolating uranium-233. For his work on transuranic elements – radioactive artificially-produced elements with an atomic number higher than that of uranium – he shared the Nobel Prize for Chemistry with Edwin McMillan in 1951. **DD**.

SEEGER, PETE
1919-
American folk singer and songwriter

Eminence grise of the 1960s' folk revolution, Seeger was a natural rebel and first put his talents at the service of the Communist Party, forming Almanac Singers in 1940, which also included Woody GUTHRIE. After war service he formed a new quartet, the Weavers, in 1948 and had a huge success, but was blacklisted as a Communist during the McCarthy years. Instead he toured outside the US and finally had a hit with 'Little Boxes' in 1964. Among his classic folk songs are 'If I Had a Hammer', 'Where Have All the Flowers Gone', 'Turn, Turn, Turn', 'We Shall Overcome' and 'Guantanamera'. **JH**.

SEGOVIA, ANDRÉS
1893-1987
Spanish guitarist

It is hard to believe that Segovia, who has been hailed as the world's greatest classical guitarist of the twentieth century, was self-taught. His technique of using finger tips and nails to provide a broader spectrum of tone-color was extremely influential. He did much to increase the popularity of the instrument and commissioned works by composers such as Villa-Lobos, Rodrigo, Falla, and Castelnuovo-Tedesco. **DK**.

SELYE, HANS
1907-
Canadian physician

Born in Vienna and educated in most of the countries of Europe, Selye joined McGill University in Montreal in 1932, finally becoming Professor and Director of the Institute of Experimental Medicine and Surgery. In 1936 he published an epic letter to the scientific journal *Nature*, in which he argued that all ill people have features in common and that various harmful events trigger the same set of body changes, which he called the 'general adaptation syndrome'. He then went on to coin the concept of 'stress' (he should have called it 'strain' but, as he later admitted, his knowledge of engineering was poor at the time). The stress concept caught the popular imagination, and Selye became one of the world's best-known scientists. His concept – that stress was an overreaction by the pituitary-adrenal system to the stress of modern life and environment, and that this caused diseases ranging from rheumatoid arthritis, hypertension, heart attacks and stroke – was appealing in its intellectual simplicity, but was never supported by any valid experimental work. **CR**.

BELOW: Spanish guitarist Andrés Segovia.

SELZNICK, DAVID O.
1902-1965
American film producer

A dynamic personality, for a while Louis B. MAYER's son-in-law, Selznick founded his own company in 1936, which made the hugely successful *Gone with the Wind* (1939), a large part of which he wrote and directed himself. He also made a number of successful films with Alfred HITCHCOCK, including *Rebecca* (1940) and *Spellbound* (1945). **NS**.

SENNA, AYRTON
1960-
Brazilian racing driver

Senna arrived in Europe as Ayrton da Silva before taking his mother's maiden name. He first drove at a Grand Prix for the under-budget British Toleman team in 1984, and later moved to McLaren to win two World Championships. Fiercely self-confident, Senna is one of the fastest drivers of any generation. **NF**.

SENNETT, MACK
1880-1960
American film maker

Born Michael Sinnott, Sennett began his career as an actor. He founded the Keystone Company in 1912 and under his fun-loving direction it became Hollywood's leading comedy studio whose stars included Fatty ARBUCKLE, Charlie CHAPLIN and the Keystone Kops. The arrival of sound marked the end of Sennett's career as 'King of Comedy', although his lasting contribution was acknowledged with a special Academy Award in 1937. **NS**.

THE SEX PISTOLS
ROTTEN, JOHNNY
1956-
JONES, STEVE
1955-
MATLOCK, GLEN
1956-
COOK, PAUL
1956-
VICIOUS, SID
1957-1979
British punk rock group

The nucleus of the group which marked a watershed in the history of rock was found in London in the mid-1970s working in Malcolm McLaren's music shop, Let It Rock. Taking their cue from Johnny Rotten's ripped T-shirt, safety pins, and spiky hair, the Pistols' first untutored musical offerings were heard at an art college in 1975. With the punk fanzine *Sniffin' Glue* proclaiming that 'all you need is three chords', other bands were encouraged by their example. Soon they were hot property; EMI's advance of £40,000 was accepted and 'Anarchy in the UK' was released. The band then vomited and cursed their way to national

notoriety under McLaren's guidance and were soon paid off handsomely by an embarrassed EMI. When first Matlock then Rotten left, their roles were filled by Sid Vicious, one of the more violently exhibitionist of their followers, who was discovered dead from a drug overdose while awaiting trial for the murder of girlfriend Nancy Spungen. Various relaunches were attempted amid hordes of imitators, but their influence was soon absorbed into rock, and while the Pistols' importance cannot be overestimated, only ex-vocalist Rotten maintained chart success under his real name John Lydon with the group Public Image Limited. **DC.**

SHACKLETON, ERNEST, SIR
1874-1922
British explorer

Shackleton started his career as a merchant seaman, but was selected by the explorer Robert SCOTT as an officer on his boat *Discovery* during Scott's investigation of the Ross Ice Shelf. He then found a sponsor for his 1909 attempt to reach the South Pole, and managed to come within a 100 miles of Scott's last fatal goal. His next expedition, to cross the Antarctic continent, nearly ended in complete tragedy when the team's ship was crushed by ice, but 'Shackles' fought his way across bitter seas in a tiny whaleboat to get help. Shackleton died of heart failure during a final expedtion to explore Graham Land. **RJ.**

SHAFFER, PETER
1926-
British playwright

Five Finger Exercise (1958), his first play brought him fame, as did *The Royal Hunt of the Sun*, a spectacular treatment of the conquest of Peru. *Equus*, a fascinating psychological study, and *Amadeus*, based on the creative rivalry between Mozart and Salieri, brought further critical acclaim. The last three all became successful films. **AM.**

SHAMIR, YITZAK
1915-
Israeli statesman

Born in Poland, Shamir emigrated to Palestine in 1935, joining the underground Zionist movement, the Irgun, in 1940. He worked for Mossad from 1955 and was elected to the Knesset in 1973. Speaker and then Minister of Foreign Affairs in Begin's Likud government (1977-83) he acquired a reputation as a hardliner on issues such as the occupied territories. He became Prime Minister on Begin's retirement in 1983, but elections the following year produced a coalition government and Shamir shared power with the Labour leader PERES until 1990 when they split over US plans for an Israeli-Palestinian peace conference. Shamir's restraint during the 1991 Gulf War in

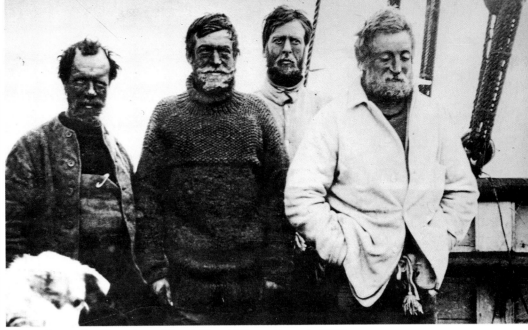

ABOVE: *Ernest Shackleton (second from left) and fellow explorers in 1909.*

not retaliating against Iraqi attacks won him international praise. **JM.**

SHANKAR, RAVI
1920-
Indian musician

A naturally gifted musician and dancer, Ravi Shankar has become India's premier cultural ambassador, fusing western musical techniques with those of his native land. His global fame as a sitarist came during the late 1950s when he toured Europe and America, since when he has performed with numerous international celebrities. **DK.**

SHAPLEY, HARLOW
1885-1972
American astronomer

At Mount Wilson Observatory, California during World War I, Shapley measured the size of our galaxy using a technique devised by Henrietta LEAVITT. He found that the galaxy was far bigger than had previously been supposed and that the sun lay in the suburbs, not at the center as then believed. This was a major advance in our understanding of the structure of the universe and our place in it, although Shapley failed to realize that other galaxies existed outside our own. Shapley later became director of Harvard College Observatory and helped found UNESCO. **IR.**

SHAW, GEORGE BERNARD
1856-1950
Irish playwright

Born in Dublin, Shaw left Ireland for London in 1876. In 1882 he became a socialist and became one of earliest members of the Fabian Society in 1884. He worked as a journalist, and first published novels and writings on political and ethical issues. Influenced by Ibsen, he is most famous as a playwright and wrote over 50 plays dealing with intellectual and moral rather than

ABOVE: *Indian musician Ravi Shankar.*

ABOVE: *George Bernard Shaw, Irish writer.*

emotional conflicts, including *The Devil's Disciple* (1897), *Major Barbara* (1905), *Pygmalion* (1916), and his masterpiece *Saint Joan* (1923). He won the Nobel Prize in 1925, and was in constant demand as a columnist until his death. **AM.**

SHAW, PERCY
1890-1976
British inventor

The son of a Yorkshire laborer, Shaw was the inventor of one of the greatest aids to road safety: the 'cat's eye'. Shaw devised an aluminum-backed glass prism to replicate the cat's eye in reflecting a beam of light in the direction from which it came, and used a rubber cone to wipe clean the prisms when the stud was depressed. **PT**.

SHEPARD, ALAN
1923-
American astronaut

On 5 May 1961 Shepard made a 15-minute suborbital space flight, and became the first American in space. His trajectory was a simple up-down one beyond the atmosphere and back again aboard the Mercury capsule. Although a relatively modest flight of only 116 miles (as opposed to the GAGARIN orbital flight of two weeks earlier) Shepard was, nonetheless, able to steer his spacecraft and made observations of the Earth and sky. **PT**.

SHERRINGTON, SIR CHARLES
1857-1952
British physiologist

Sherrington's major contribution was to the understanding of the nervous system. He described its basic functional units of neurones interacting at synapses (his term), thus explaining phenomena such as reflex action. For this and much further neurological work he shared a Nobel prize with E D ADRIAN in 1932. **GL**.

SHERWOOD, ROBERT
1896-1955
American dramatist

Sherwood was a New Yorker and radical, whose World War I service made him a convinced pacifist until he worked for ROOSEVELT in the Forties. Most celebrated for *The Petrified Forest* (1935), filmed with Humphrey BOGART, he won four Pulitzer prizes, and an Academy Award in 1946 for the screenplay of *The Best Years of Our Lives*. **AM**.

SHEVARDNADZE, EDUARD
1928-
Georgian politician

The Foreign Minister of perestroika, Shevardnadze collaborated with GORBACHEV in calling off the Cold War and rolling up the Soviet Eastern Empire. He had a good reforming record as head of the Georgian Party and he was entrusted with much of the negotiation for the nuclear disarmament agreements, particularly for the 1988 dismantling of the intermediate-range ballistic missiles. The Start treaty which he negotiated in 1990 cut Intercontinental ballistic missiles by 50 per cent. Shevardnadze's resignation was a perhaps fatal blow to Gorbachev. He returned to Georgia where he has been markedly less successful in dealing with the after-effects of the dismemberment of the imperial system which he had feared would become a dictatorship. **JC**.

SHIRER, WILLIAM LAWRENCE
1904-
American journalist

Shirer worked as a foreign correspondent for US newspapers in Europe, India and the Middle East. He was based in Berlin in 1940-41 and published an account of life under Nazi rule, *Berlin Diary*. From 1942 to 1946 he was a columnist for the New York *Herald Tribune*, and later wrote the best-selling *The Rise and Fall of the Third Reich*. **DSL**.

SHOCKLEY, WILLIAM BRADFORD
1910-1989
American physicist

Born in London, the son of an American family, he was educated in California and Massachusetts. He worked on anti-submarine research before and during World War II. After the war, he worked in the Bell Telephone Laboratories and collaborated with John Bardeen and Walter Brattain in developing the transistor. These devices soon replaced vacuum valves, and as a result electronic equipment became much smaller and more compact. Although his qualifications were in physics, Shockley regarded himself as something of a geneticist, and his theories on the heredity of intelligence and on race led him into deep trouble. **DD**.

ABOVE: Finnish composer, Jean Sibelius.

SHOEMAKER, BILL [WILLIAM LEE]
1931-
American jockey

No North American jockey ever rode more winners than Bill Shoemaker. In 41 years he posted 8833 wins. Four times he won the Kentucky Derby, including a 1986 triumph aboard Ferdinand at the age of 54. He won seven other Triple Crown races and earned well over $100 million in career purses. **MD**.

SHOENBERG, ISAAC
1880-1963
British engineer

As director of research at EMI in 1931 Shoenberg recruited a powerful scientific team which gave Britain the world's first public electronic TV service. It began regular transmissions on 2 November 1936. Shoenberg put his faith in an all-electronic system, which proved immensely superior to the rival mechanical system of Baird. **PW**.

SHOSTAKOVICH, DMITRI DMITRIIEVICH
1906-1975
Russian composer

Born and educated in St Petersburg, Shostakovich showed early promise as both pianist and composer, but chose to dedicate most of his career to writing music. In the Soviet Union this creative urge was far less easy to indulge than elsewhere, and Shostakovich, ironically a committed Communist, found himself perpetually struggling under a regime which dictated even the sort of music that should be composed. His memoirs provide a fascinating insight into the tensions an artist faces in a totalitarian society, and confirm all the worst reports of life under Stalin. Yet he produced some of the most powerful music of the century, full of pathos, irony, and energy. His 15 symphonies cover the whole spectrum of orchestral textures, some (like the Tenth) attaining a level of rare brilliance within conventional structures, while his chamber music is among the finest written since the eighteenth century. His opera *Lady Macbeth of Mtsensk District* was greeted as a masterpiece in 1934 and two years later condemned as too modernist. With six concertos, plus a wealth of excellent vocal music and solo works, Shostakovich was one of the most prolific composers of the age. **DK**.

SIBELIUS, JEAN JOHAN JULIUS CHRISTIAN
1865-1957
Finnish composer

A law student until he turned to a musical career at the age of 21, Sibelius's is the definitive voice of music in Finland. Drawing inspiration from the Nordic landscape in which he ensconced himself, he expressed the spirit of his country in a wealth of orchestral music, most notably in his symphonies and numerous tone poems. From the exuberance of the *Karelia Suite* and the Violin Concerto to the immense melodic waves created in the symphonies, Sibelius used conventional classical structures as a framework for his momentous harmonic creations. For the last thirty years of his life he composed nothing. **DK**.

SICA, VITTORIO DE
1902-1974
Italian film director

De Sica began his career as an actor, but his reputation rests on a series of poignant post-war films he directed about poverty (notably *Bicycle Thieves* (1948)) which were shot in a 'neo-realist' style, using actual locations and non-professional actors. **NS**.

ABOVE: Actress Simone Signoret.

SIGNORET, SIMONE
1921-1985
French actress

After powerful portrayals largely of prostitutes and lovesick women, *La Ronde* (1950) made Signoret an international star. She won a British Film Academy Award for Best Foreign Actress for *Casque d'Or* (1952) and another for *Room at the Top* (1958), which also brought her a Cannes Film Festival Award and an American Academy Award as Best Actress. She allowed herself to grow older and gain weight without a battle, switching comfortably to character roles and winning fresh acclaim for *Le Chat* (1972) with Jean GABIN and *Madame Rose* (1978), which earned her a César, the French equivalent of an Oscar. **DC**.

SIKORSKI, WŁADYSŁAW
1881-1943
Polish politician

Sikorski was Premier of the wartime Polish government-in-exile and died in an air crash over Gibralter in 1943. The timing of this event, at a critical juncture in relations with Russia, has given rise to allegations, never proved, that he was murdered. He tried to overcome his colleagues' suspicion of the Russians, and helped form a Polish Army in Russia. He died soon after the discovery of the Katyn Wood massacre of Poles by the Russian NKVD ended cooperation. **JC**.

SIMENON, GEORGES
1903-1989
Belgian-French novelist

Simenon was enormously popular and prolific in both his professional and private lives. His famous detective, Maigret, was created in 1931, and the series of thrillers featuring him have been adapted for film and television. His prose is noted for its detailed observation of location, evocation of atmosphere, and objective treatment of extreme passions. Despite his impressive output of over 500 novels, he also found time for a fulfilling love-life, of which he was inordinately proud. **CW**.

SIMON, PAUL
1941–
American pop singer

Success with Simon's high-school friend Art Garfunkel eventually came with the single 'Sounds of Silence' in 1966. Continuing with classics of the folk-rock genre from *Parsley,*

ABOVE: The creator of Maigret, Georges Simenon.

Sage, Rosemary and Thyme to the 1970 album *Bridge Over Troubled Water*, it was only after his split with Garfunkel that Simon was able to expand his horizons as a musician and songwriter, assimilating styles from reggae to jazz and latin, finally utilizing South African township jive on the 1986 best-selling album *Graceland* which confirmed his steady and not inconsiderable influence in the world of pop. **DC**.

ABOVE: Paul Simon (right), reunited with Art Garfunkel in 1981.

ABOVE: 'Ol' Blue Eyes', the sophisticated Frank Sinatra.

SINATRA, FRANK
1915-
American singer and actor

Sinatra made it to the top as lead singer with the Tommy Dorsey Band in 1941; when he appeared live with Benny GOODMAN in New York, the fans went wild and modern pop hysteria was born. Determined to make it as a soloist rather than a big-band vocalist, he followed Bing CROSBY in transforming the art of pop singing, with his natural baritone and elegant phrasing. Films in the 1940s included *Anchors Aweigh* (1945) and *On the Town* (1949), but a stormy marriage to Ava Gardner preluded a disastrous slide in Sinatra's popularity. He turned his career around with his Oscar-winning role as Maggio in *From Here to Eternity* (1953) and went on to conquer the album market with his arranger, Nelson Riddle, making 13 top five LPs in seven years. Other films have included *High Society* and *The Manchurian Candidate*, as well as the notorious 'Clan' movies; 'Strangers in the Night' topped the charts in 1966; and his 75th birthday tour in 1990 was a sellout. **JH**.

SINCLAIR, SIR CLIVE
1940-
British inventor

Clive Sinclair never attended university; his basic grounding in electronics was self-taught, much of it as the result of his job as a technical writer and later as the editor of an electronics magazine. He recognized the potential of microelectronics early on, initially selling matchbox-sized radios. He is credited with the invention of the pocket calculator, and also produced the 'black watch', a notoriously unreliable digital watch. Sinclair's major success was his move into computers. The low-cost ZX80 was launched in 1979 at half the price of rival systems. This was superseded by the ZX81, the first home computer for most British users. The first color machine, the Spectrum, was launched in 1981 and Sinclair was elevated from his popular name of 'Uncle Clive' to Sir Clive. As rival systems caught up with the price and performance of the Spectrum, Sinclair strove to stay ahead with the QL (Quantum Leap) computer. Like all Sinclair products this suffered massive produc-

tion delays from which the company never recovered and, when the bank failed to extend any more credit, the computer line was sold to Amstrad plc. Other Sinclair ventures included the C5, an electrically-powered recumbant tricycle and the Zike, launched in 1992, a small-wheeled city bicycle with an electric motor. **JR**.

SINGER, ISAAC BASHEVIS
1904-1991
American writer

Born in Poland, Singer emigrated to New York in 1935 and became the most important Yiddish writer. His many novels, including *The Family Moskat*, short story collections like *The Spinoza of Market Street*, and memoirs vividly recapture Polish Jewish history, infused with the mystical. Internationally highly regarded, in 1978 he was awarded the Nobel Prize. **AM**.

SKIDMORE, LOUIS
1897-1962
American architect

Louis Skidmore established the architectural practice of Skidmore and Owings in 1936 and the multidisciplinary partnership of Skidmore, Owings, and Merrill, arguably the most powerful of its time, in 1939. Skidmore, famed for his organizational ability, claimed to be able to 'produce the people who produce the architecture.' Influential buildings include Lever House, New York, 1952. **DE**.

SKINNER, B[URRHUS] F[REDERICK]
1904-1990
American psychologist

B F Skinner was an ardent exponent of behaviorism, arguing that all behavior can be explained in terms of genetic predispositions and simple rewards and punishments, and that emotions, beliefs, and thoughts stand for nothing. He developed the 'Skinner Box', an extraordinary construction which allowed an animal to press a lever to obtain food. It was used to identify the optimum schedules of reinforcement, behavior which Skinner applied to humans as well as animals. **MBe**.

SLIM, WILLIAM, 1ST VISCOUNT, FIELD MARSHAL
1891-1970
British soldier

Arguably the most able British General of World War II, 'Bill' Slim joined the army as a temporary officer in 1914, serving in Gallipoli, Mesopotamia, and France before transferring to a permanent commission in the British-Indian Army. Slim led 10th Indian Brigade into Eritrea against the Italians in 1940, then commanded 10th Indian Division in Syria, Iraq, and Persia. In March 1942 he arrived in Burma to take over 1st Burma Corps, under pressure from the invading Japanese, but could do little to prevent a long and painful British retreat to the Indian border. When the 14th Army was created in 1943, Slim became its commander, concentrating on the build-up of morale and supplies. By early 1944 his troops were able to enjoy some success in Arakan, but the real turning-point came when 14th Army turned back a Japanese offensive at Imphal. In 1945 Slim advanced south into Burma, fighting a bold encircling action at Meiktila in March to isolate Mandalay and, two months later, liberating Rangoon. Promoted to Commander-in-Chief Land Forces South-East Asia, he went on to become Chief of the Imperial General Staff in 1948 and Governor-General of Australia 1953-60. **JPi**.

SLOAN, ALFRED
1875-1966
American engineer and executive

Sloan headed the Hyatt Roller Bearing Company when it was bought by General Motors, and rose to become President of GM in 1923. He reorganized the corporation with a highly centralized adminstration supervising geographically decentralized production units, and before he retired as chief executive in 1956, GM had won half the US automobile market. **JW**.

SMITH, BESSIE
1894-1937
American blues singer

Hailed as 'Empress of the Blues', Bessie Smith sang in the streets and worked as a chorus girl before establishing her own revue in 1918. Her posthumous reputation rests on the recordings she made with Columbia between 1923 and 1933, including 'Downhearted Blues' (1923), 'St Louis Blues' (1925, accompanied by Louis ARMSTRONG) and 'Nobody Knows When You're Down and Out' (1929). By the time she died of car-crash injuries she was already being overtaken by a new generation, including Billie HOLIDAY. **JH**.

SMITH, DAVID
1906-1965
American sculptor

An innovatory and influential artist, in the early 1930s Smith began constructing non-representational sculptures from scrap metal and machine parts, utilizing a knowledge of metalwork techniques gained through employment in the car industry. His open, linear works of the 1940s and 1950s, such as *Hudson River Landscape* (1951), appear like three-dimensional drawings and many were intended to be set outdoors, where their skeletal structure allowed the landscape to be viewed through them. Always large-scale, in the 1960s his work became more massive and volumetric while retaining its dynamic qualities. **FR**.

SMITH, IAN
1919-
Zimbabwean politician

In 1962 Smith became the leader of the white diehards of the Rhodesian Front Party. After the break-up of the Central African Federation in 1964, Smith made a Unilateral Declaration of Independence (UDI) and maintained this white suprematist government despite UK and UN sanctions and a bloody civil war (1972-74) until 1979. He finally found himself isolated, even from South Africa, and his compromise of multiracial government (1979-80) led by Bishope Muzorewa failed. He could not prevent the foundation of an independent Zimbabwe but he is believed to harbor ambitions of making a political return. **JC**

ABOVE: *Bessie Smith, 'Empress of the Blues'.*

SMITH, WILLIAM EUGENE
1918-1978
American photographer

Careers in photojournalism sometimes lose momentum, but Smith ended his with his greatest achievement, which was an exposé of industrial pollution at Minamata on the southern Japanese island of Kyushu. *Minamata*, published in 1975, contains one of his most celebrated images, of a mother cradling her deformed child. In 1937 he began to work for *Newsweek*, and in 1938 joined the Black Star agency, shortly before signing for *Life* and then for war service in the Pacific. His reportage, much of it for *Life*, is theatrically composed, dramatically lit, and compassionate throughout. He epitomized American photoreportage in the years after the war. **IJ**.

ABOVE: *Jan Smuts, a major figure in South African history.*

SMUTS, JAN
1870-1950
South African statesman

The Cambridge law student turned Boer guerrilla leader who in 1910 played a major role in founding the Union of South Africa, Smuts had already been largely responsible for gaining self-government for the republics of Transvaal and Orange Free State. Together with President Louis Botha, he risked the fragile new racial unity by suppressing a rising by their former comrades-in-arms on the eve of World War I. In the East African bush he pitted his guerrilla skills against the German Lettow-Vorbeck and won and in 1917, already seen as an Imperial elder statesman, he was the first to suggest a British Commonwealth, and also an independent, unified Royal Air Force. As Prime Minister (1919-24) he tried reconciliation with the Nationalist ultras, but failed and resigned. He took South Africa into World War II, becoming a British Field Marshal, and he wrote the introduction to the United Nations' Charter. But MALAN beat him against the odds in the 1948 election and Smuts died two years later, well aware that the political and ethnic bonds he had worked so hard to forge were about to break. He was spared the sight of South Africa's withdrawal into its racial lager. **JC**.

S

SOBERS, SIR GARFIELD
1936-
Barbadian cricketer

Gary Sobers was cricket's greatest ever all-rounder. He made his debut for the West Indies in 1954 when only 17, playing 93 tests before his retirement in 1974. He was a devastating batsman (most runs in tests by a West Indies player), bowled effectively in a variety of styles, and did it all with enormous style and panache. His 365 not out against Pakistan in 1957/58 remains the highest individual score in test cricket. **DS**.

SOLZENHITSYN, ALEXANDER
1918-
Russian novelist

Born in Kislovodsk in the Caucasus and educated at the University of Rostov, Solzenhitsyn fought in the Red Army during the Second World War, was arrested for criticizing Stalin and sent to a labor camp in 1945. Released in 1953, he subsequently became a teacher. *One Day in the Life of Ivan Denisovich* (1962) is his stark account of life in the camp. *Cancer Ward* (1968) and *The First Circle* (1969) were published abroad, and in 1969 he was expelled from the Writers' Union. He was awarded the Nobel Prize in 1970. Publication of *The Gulag Archipelago* prompted his deportation in 1974, and he emigrated to the USA where his reputation has perhaps been inflated by his dissident status. **AM**.

ABOVE: *Alexander Solzenhitsyn.*

SORGE, RICHARD
1895-1944
Russo-German spy

Posing as a Nazi spy in Japan, Sorge sent back high-grade information to the Soviet Union – most crucially that Japan intended to launch its initial attack against South-East Asia, not the USSR. He warned the Soviets of the impending attack on their allies at Pearl Harbor, but he was betrayed by a Japanese dancing girl with whom he had become infatuated. **RJ**.

SPAAK, PAUL-HENRI
1899-1974
Belgian politician

'Mr Europe,' the first great advocate of a united Continent, Spaak chaired the commission from six nations which drew up the Treaty of Rome in 1957. He had been the first Belgian Socialist prewar Prime Minister, as well as Foreign Minister, a spot to which he returned in 1945 and which he used to lay the foundations of European unity. His persuasive powers first cemented the treaty and were then used to great effect in his term as Secretary General of NATO (1957-61). He passionately but unsuccessfully defended Britain's EEC candidacy against De GAULLE. His political career was marred by the gory Belgian withdrawal from the Congo in 1961, necessitating UN intervention. **JC**.

SPARK, MURIEL
1918-
British novelist

Muriel Spark began her literary career as editor of *Poetry Review*. She is best known for her novel *The Prime of Miss Jean Brodie* (1961), a disturbing study of the relationship between an Edinburgh teacher and her elite group of girls. Her distinctive fiction has a sophisticated comic style, often verging on the perverse. **CW**.

SPECTOR, PHIL
1940-
American record producer

Phil Spector's 'Wall of Sound' technique, featuring the trademark huge orchestral arrangements, made him arguably the most innovative producer of the 1960s. First with The Crystals, then the Ronettes and the Righteous Brothers, it seemed he could do no wrong. But after a lukewarm US reception to Ike & Tina Turner's 1966 hit 'River Deep, Mountain High' he gradually withdrew from the music business until work with various Beatles in 1969 began a second, though less successful phase of his career. By the 1980s he was something of a recluse, with occasional co-writing credits the only evidence of a continued interest in the music business for which he had created so many hits. **DC**.

SPENCER, STANLEY
1891-1959
British painter

Christianity was, for Spencer, a living reality and using a simplified, sculptural style, he produced biblical scenes set firmly in his native village of Cookham. He drew on his experiences in World War I in his murals for the Burghclere Memorial Chapel (1927-30) which dwell on the humdrum activities of war rather than its horror and culminate in a scene of mass resurrection. In later work his unhappy personal life was manifest as an obsession with sex and he depicted sexual encounters between all manner of people, in the belief that all desire was holy. This fusion of literal description with the visionary was the source of his originality. **ER**.

SPIELBERG, STEVEN
1947-
American film director

Spielberg is the most successful director in the modern cinema, with three of the most financially profitable films of all-time to his name, *Jaws* (1975), *Close Encounters of the Third Kind* (1977), and *ET: The Extra-Terrestrial* (1982). Born in Cincinnati and a film fanatic at an early age, Spielberg was directing TV films at the age of 22 and made his feature film debut at 27. In one sense, he is the modern screen's new Disney, making sentimental films about innocence of particular appeal to children. But he also makes films of Hitchcockian suspense, like *Duel* (1971), and recent work, such as *Empire of the Sun* (1987), suggests that Hollywood's *Wunderkind* is growing up. **NS**.

ABOVE: *Successful film director, Steven Spielberg.*

SPITZ, MARK
1950-
American swimmer

In the 1972 Summer Olympics Mark Spitz won seven gold medals, a figure never matched before or since. He also won a pair of golds, a silver, and a bronze in the 1968 Games. Dominant in the freestyle and the butterfly, Spitz set 23 world records during his career. **MD**.

SPOCK, BENJAMIN MCLANE
1903-
American paediatrician

Spock has specialized in paediatrics and psychiatry, working in New York, at Cornell University, the Mayo Clinic in Rochester, Minnesota, Pittsburgh University and Case Western Reserve University, Ohio. His research has been on preventive psychiatry and the emotional development of children, but it is his books for parents that have made him deservedly famous. His major work, *Baby and Child Care*, overthrew an entire regime of childraising philosophy, rejecting authoritarian rules in favor of a more intuitive and child-centred approach. Before Spock, parents were expected to follow a set of arbitrary rules about when to feed children and when to put them to bed; parents were warned not to spoil children by feeding them on demand or responding to their crying. Spock gave parents the confidence to listen to their children and to respond more instinctively. He taught that each child should be treated as an individual, so that its innate character can be allowed to develop. Critics have complained that Dr Spock was responsible for a generation of spoiled, undisciplined children, and Spock has conceded that at one stage he erred too much on the side of flexibility. *Baby and Child Care* has gone through a number of editions, evolving somewhat from its most permissive stance, and has sold 30 million copies in over 30 languages. In his later years Spock has become a close supporter of the United States peace movement, speaking at anti-Vietnam War demonstrations, and at one stage was sentenced to two years' imprisonment, overthrown on appeal, for helping young men avoid the draft; this brought him additional blame, for supposedly producing a generation of spineless men. **CR.**

SPRINGSTEEN, BRUCE
1949-
American rock singer

Hailed as the new Bob Dylan after the early album *Greetings From Asbury Park NJ*, his 1975 album *Born To Run* promoted a rather rockier image of 'The Boss' with the accompanying legendary three-hour live shows. More pensive and considered work throughout the late 1970s culminated in *Nebraska* in 1982, a solo acoustic effort, but the 1984 release *Born In The USA* stayed at the top of the US charts for seven weeks and cemented his superstar status. A live album two years later marked a lull until he took the unusual step of releasing two studio albums simultaneously in 1992. **DC.**

SPRUANCE, RAYMOND, ADMIRAL
1886-1969
American sailor

Spruance assumed command of Task Force 16 (the carriers *Enterprise* and *Hornet*) in 1942, leading it in the decisive Battle of Midway in June. He went on to command the US Fifth Fleet at the Battle of the Philippine Sea two years later. In 1945-46 he was Commander-in-Chief of the Pacific Fleet. **JPi.**

STALIN, JOSEF [JOSEF DZHUGASHVILI]
1879-1953
Russian statesman

The failed priest and bank robber who made the Soviet Union a superpower, from 1903, Stalin was successful as a propagandist for Bolshevism in his native Caucasus, and in raising funds at gunpoint. LENIN dubbed him 'the wonderful Georgian,' and coopted him on to the party's Central Committee. As a political commissar he helped his future chief of the armed forces, Voroshilov, defend Tsaritsyn (later Stalingrad, now Volgograd) against the Whites. In 1922 Lenin appointed him Secretary of the Central Committee of the Party, the key post he held for the next 30 years. Lenin soon regretted the promotion and in his pre-deathbed 'Testament' specifically warned the other old Bolsheviks against him. Stalin brought trumped-up charges against them at the Moscow Show Trials of 1936 and had them shot. He had already caused over a million deaths by collectivizing the farms, against the Old Comrades' advice. He went on to purge the Army, leaving it almost fatally weakened to resist HITLER's 1941 invasion. A combination of the strong industrial infrastructure produced by successive five-year plans and the talent of generals like ZHUKOV threw the Nazis back to Berlin and annexed their eastern empire. The Yalta

BELOW: Josef Stalin, who ruled the Soviet Union by terror.

peace conference (April 1945) confirmed his conquests, which were held by extending his secret police terror and slave-labor system. Paranoia affected his judgment; he miscalculated over the Korean War and the Berlin Airlift and died in 1953 as he was about to arrest more 'plotters' against him. His memory still has an uncomfortable resonance in his demolished empire. **JC.**

STANWYCK, BARBARA
1907-1990
American actress

After stints as a dancer Stanwyck made her film debut in *Broadway Nights* (1927). Her hardbitten, sensuous appearance made her typecasting inevitable in such films as *Ten Cents a Dance* (1931). By 1932 and *So Big* she was a big box-office draw, and by the late 1930s she was a durable leading lady. In 1937 she made *Stella Dallas*, a tear-jerker and classic so-called 'woman's movie', but she was equally good at comedy in *The Mad Miss Minton* (1938). Her best performance was in *Double Indemnity* (1944) for which she was nominated for an Academy Award. **DC.**

STARK, FREYA
1893-1993
British explorer

Freya Stark only began to travel seriously in her mid-thirties, when she first experienced the deserts of Arabia. Her earliest major trip took her across Persia, seeking out the castles of the medieval sect of the Assassins. But it was her account of a dangerous journey across the deserts of Yemen, in 1935, that made her famous. Stark continued to travel, often in Turkey, and to write, until she was well into her eighties. **RJ.**

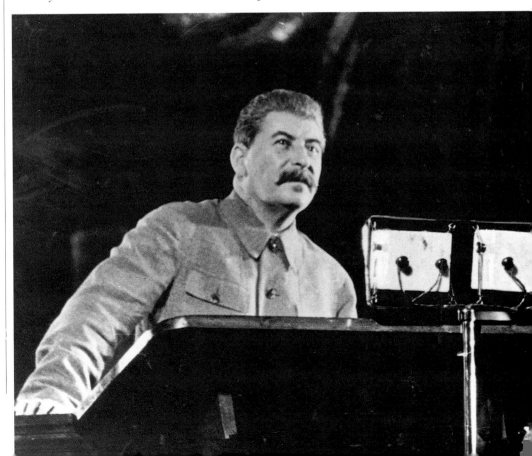

STARLING, ERNEST HENRY
1866-1927
British physiologist

Starling received his degree in medicine from Guy's Hospital in 1889 where he studied the mechanism of lymph secretions, the blood circulation through small capillaries. With Bayliss he demonstrated the nervous control of peristalsis (waves of muscle contractions along the gut) and in 1902 they detected a substance secreted by the duodenum into blood, which they named secretin. Starling devised the generic term 'hormone' for all similar endocrine secretions to the blood. He also carried out important research into factors affecting heartbeat, establishing that the strength of a contraction depends on the extent to which the muscles of the chambers are stretched during filling (Starling's Law). **EMS.**

STAUDINGER, HERMANN
1881-1965
German organic chemist

Worked on albumen and cellulose, but his principal interest was the structure of plastics, which he recognized as early as 1920 as being polymers – molecules bonded together to form long chains. Until his work, it was thought that substances like rubber had no chemical structure – and consisted merely of a jumble of molecules. His theories were opposed for a long time. His work in the field led to the growth of the modern plastics industry, and the development of synthetic polymers like rubbers, plastics, fibers, and adhesives. It also gained him the Nobel Prize for Chemistry in 1953. **DD.**

ST DENIS, RUTH
1877-1968
American dancer, choreographer, teacher, and actress

With little formal training, St Denis created for herself a 'Hindu' ballet, *Radha*, in 1906, curiously set to the music of French composer Délibes. The Indian theme continued with *Cobras* and *Incenses* (1906) and *Nautch and Yogi* (1908); St Denis toured these in Europe and the United States. She founded Denishawn School and company with her partner and husband from 1914, Ted Shawn; their pupils included Martha GRAHAM and Doris Humphrey. Even after she was obliged to give up the school, St Denis continued to perform many of her early dances well into her eighties. **MC.**

STEFANO, ALFREDO DI
1926-
Argentinian soccer player

Alfredo di Stefano won his greatest fame as a player with Real Madrid who were, by a considerable margin, the strongest club in Europe in the later 1950s and early 1960s.

Real won five consecutive European Cups 1956-60, with di Stefano leading their tactics and scoring many of their goals. Before coming to Spain in 1953 di Stefano had already played successfully in Argentina and Colombia and for Argentina in internationals. Later he also played for Spain. **DS.**

STEIN, GERTRUDE
1874-1946
American writer

Gertrude Stein originally planned to become a psychologist, and was influenced by William James. In 1902 she settled in Paris, where her home and collection of modern art became a focus for the avant-garde. Stein named her life-long companion Alice B Toklas as the author of her popular memoir *The Autobiography of Alice B Toklas* (1933). Apart from her essays and collection of poetry, *Tender Buttons* (1914), she wrote experimental prose noted for its non-representational form. Her masterpiece, and most accessible work, *Three Lives* (1909), contains the extraordinary 'Melanctha', hailed as unique for its serious treatment of a black woman's life. **CW.**

STEINBECK, JOHN
1902-1968
American novelist

John Steinbeck was born in California. The lives of rural workers in his home state provides the material for his early work, in which his characteristic blend of a semi-mystical relation to the land and a realist critique of the exploitation of labor is evident. First achieving success with *Tortilla Flat* (1935), his following novels *In Dubious Battle* (1936) and *Of Mice and Men* (1937) are more explicitly concerned with migrants' conditions. His greatest work is *The Grapes of Wrath* (1939), an epic saga of the fortunes of a refugee family from the dust bowl, in California. He won the Nobel Prize in 1962. **CW.**

BELOW: John Steinbeck, author of The Grapes of Wrath.

STEINEM, GLORIA
1934-
American journalist and feminist

Granddaughter of a prominent feminist leader, Steinem graduated from Smith College in 1956, after which she studied in India for two years. She started as a writer of photocaptions on Harvey Kurtzman's magazine *Help!* and made her name with an article 'I was a Playboy bunny' (based on undercover work in one of Hugh HEFNER's clubs). She was attracted to the women's movement in 1968, becoming a major fundraiser and spokesperson. In 1971 she founded the magazine *Ms*, which is the most widely read feminist periodical. Not much of its early influences remain but it has spawned many imitators. **EMS.**

STELLA, FRANK
1936-
American painter

A leader of Post-Painterly Abstraction in the 1960s, Stella embarked on this road after seeing JOHNS' flag paintings in 1958. Working only in black, to avoid the expressive connotations of color, he created flat patterns with stripes and orthogonals, rejecting any suggestion of three-dimensionality. From 1960 he used shaped canvases which echoed his designs, so that support and image were necessarily viewed as a unified object. Later introducing color, from around 1967 he produced more complex designs of curved bands. In the 1970s he began experimenting with three-dimensional supports, and the exuberant, painterly quality of works such as *Guadalupe Island, Caracara* (1979), is in marked contrast to his earlier images. **ER.**

STENGEL, CASEY [CHARLES DILLON]
1890-1975
American baseball manager

Quirky and homespun, Casey Stengel was one of baseball's most successful managers. 'Stengelese,' the dizzy inversion of English spoken by 'The Old Perfessor,' delighted and exasperated generations of fans. Stengel's greatest fame as a manager came with the New York Yankees, a team he piloted from 1949 to 1960. During that span the Yanks won 10 pennants and seven World Series titles. Earlier he managed weak teams in Brooklyn and Boston. He finished his career as the beloved manager of the laughably bad New York Mets in the early 1960s. Stengel also played in the majors for 14 years, batting .284. **MD.**

STENMARK, INGEMAR
1956-
Swedish skier

Ingemar Stenmark was a highly successful competitor in Alpine skiing events, specializing in the slalom disciplines. Among his record total of race wins were two Golds in the Lake Placid Olympics in 1980 and three World Championships. **DS**.

STEPTOE, PATRICK
1913-1988
British obstetrician

Patrick Steptoe is best known for his work with Robert Edwards on infertility problems and the development of a successful IVF technique. After the first birth of a baby from *in vitro* fertilization in 1979 their methods were adopted worldwide. He was also a pioneer of laparoscopy (a method of examining the abdomen through a small incision). **EMS**.

STEVENS, GEORGE
1904-1975
American film maker

An underrated classical Hollywood filmmaker, Stevens began his career photographing Laurel and Hardy shorts and, as a young director, was associated mainly with stylish, slow-burning comedies of the sex war, like *Woman of the Year* (1941) and *The More the Merrier* (1943). His war experience, particularly being part of the American force that liberated Dachau, brought a new seriousness and sadness into his work. Arguably his greatest, certainly his grandest, works are three films that celebrate the outsider while offering a poignant re-assessment of the American Dream: *A Place in the Sun* (1951), *Shane* (1953), and *Giant* (1956). **NS**.

STEVENS, WALLACE
1879-1955
American poet

This distinguished poet was educated at Harvard, and after Law School made his business career with an insurance firm in Hartford, Connecticut. Most of his poetry was written after he was 50, his earlier poems collected in *Harmonium* which was published in 1923. His poetry, including the collections *Ideas of Order* (1935), *The Man with the Blue Guitar* (1937), and *The Auroras of Autumn* (1950), is renowned for its rich exploration of tropic forms, its striking intellectual meditations on order and the imagination, and investigations of the nature of artistic experience. His aesthetic philosophy is contained in the prose essays of *The Necessary Angel* (1951) **CW**.

STEVENSON, ADLAI
1900-1965
American politician

Stevenson was a Democratic front-runner who never gained the Presidency. One of ROOSEVELT's New Deal team, he toured the country in the 1930s, filtering farmers' problems through to Washington. He was appointed US delegate to the United Nations' General Assembly at its first session in 1946, and returned there in 1961 as Ambassador for John KENNEDY, who had eclipsed him, but only narrowly, in the third round of the fight to win back the White House for the Democrats. Stevenson had twice been their choice, in 1952 and 1956, but 'the intellectuals' candidate' fell on both occasions before the popular image of EISENHOWER. **JC**.

ABOVE: American actor James Stewart.

STEWART, JAMES
1908-
American actor

This leading actor with his inimitable slow drawl and gangly walk has been playing honest heroes for more than 50 years. Stewart's sincerity and slightly embarrassed air caught on with the public in *You Can't Take It With You* (1938), *Mr Smith Goes to Washington* (1939), and *The Philadelphia Story* (1940), which brought him an Academy Award. He moved smoothly into a variety of roles after the war with a wonderful performance in the classic *It's a Wonderful Life* (1946), and the gentle *Harvey* (1950). He has also played detectives, western heroes and the lead in HITCHCOCK blockbusters such as *Rear Window* (1954) and *Vertigo* (1958). **DC**.

STEWART, JACKIE [JOHN YOUNG]
1939-
Scottish racing driver

Setting the standard for Grand Prix driving throughout his career, Jackie Stewart drove for BRM and Matra before fully establishing his dominance with Tyrrell. He won the World Championship three times and took 27 Grand Prix victories before retiring in 1973. Also a champion at clay-pigeon shooting, Stewart is still involved with motorsport promotion. **NF**.

STIEGLITZ, ALFRED
1864-1946
American photographer

Stieglitz began his career conventionally enough as a photographic enthusiast in the 1880s and 1890s, but after the establishment of his own magazine, *Camera Work* in 1903, went on to become one of the most charismatic and influential artists in photography. From 1905 he staged around 80 exhibitions at The Little Galleries of the Photo-Secession at 291 Fifth Avenue in New York. 291 ended in 1917, as did *Camera Work*, after 50 issues. In 1917 he began to photograph the painter Georgia O'KEEFFE; and between 1929-46 ran the gallery An American Place, at 509 Madison Avenue. He was responsible for the encouragement of the photographers Ansel ADAMS and Paul Strand, and for the promotion of European modernist art in New York. He was, in effect, a symbolist photographer who believed in, or hoped for, an affinity with the appearance of things in the world: the movement of clouds and light in landscape. Dedicated to the idea of an art of photography, he believed, towards the end of his life that the battle had been lost to photo-journalism. However his insistence on personal significance and print quality established photography's credit as a major medium in the arts, and led to its subsequent standing as a leading art form. **IJ**.

STILWELL, JOSEPH, GENERAL
1883-1946
American soldier

After military service in France (1917-18), Stilwell studied Chinese, being appointed military attaché in Peking 1932-39. When war against the Japanese began in 1941, he was sent back to China as Chief of Staff to CHIANG KAI-SHEK, assuming command of Chinese armies in Burma. He could do little to stem the Japanese tide, and his difficulties were made worse in 1943, when he was given additional responsibilities as Deputy Commander South-East Asia. Despite success recapturing Myitkyina in August 1944, Vinegar Joe's relations with Chiang deteriorated and he was recalled by his superiors. In 1945 he commanded US 10th Army in the Pacific. **JPi**.

STIRLING, SIR JAMES
1926-1992
British architect

Stirling first came to public notice with his History Faculty Building for Cambridge University (1959-64). However his best-known works in England are the two buildings designed for the Tate Gallery: – the Clore Gallery, built to house the Turner Collection, London (1980-87) and the conversion of the Albert Dock, in Stirling's native Liverpool to accommodate the 'Tate in the North.' In partnership with Michael Wilford, Stirling designed the new building and chamber theater for the Staatsgalerie, Stuttgart (completed 1984), distinguished, like the Tate buildings, by their innovative use of interior and exterior space and decorative use of bright color. **DE**.

STOCKHAUSEN, KARLHEINZ
1928-
German composer

Stockhausen is undoubtedly the world's leading exponent of electronic music. Many of his works involve the use of generators and transformers while others explore the modern technique of aleatory music and spatial effects. Latterly such works as *Goldstaub* and *Stimmung* reveal a stronger influence from Eastern mysticism and philosophy. **DK**.

ABOVE: *Dr Marie Stopes, campaigner for birth control.*

STOPES, MARIE
1880-1958
British pioneer of birth control

A scientist, but not medically qualified, Marie Stopes made knowledge of reliable contraceptive techniques available to ordinary women. Trained as a botanist at University College, London, with a PhD from Munich, she became the first woman on the scientific staff of Manchester University (1904). The physical failure of her first marriage apparently convinced Stopes of the need for reliable information on sex and contraception accessible to the ordinary reader. In 1918 she published *Married Love*, which dealt frankly with sexual matters, and later that year *Wise Parenthood*, advocating birth control in marriage to space out pregnancies and limit overall family size. Her advocacy of contraception and her frank discussion of sexual matters outraged orthodox opinion, especially in religious circles. However she thrived on opposition, taking up her cause with almost missionary zeal. Helped by her second husband and the royalties from her books she opened the 'Mothers' Clinic for Constructive Birth Control' in North London in 1921 – the first of its kind in Britain. Clinics in Leeds, Aberdeen and many other centres followed, some independently run. They were eventually united under the Family Planning Association. **GL**.

STRASBERG, LEE
1901-1982
American actor

One of the founders of the Actors Studio in 1948, he also established the Lee Strasberg Institute in 1969. Instrumental in the development of countless screen stars, he finally made his screen debut in 1974 as the mobster Hyman Roth in *The Godfather Part II* at the age of 73. **DC**.

STRAUSS, RICHARD
1864-1949
German composer

Strauss quickly rose to public acclaim with his colorful and vivacious tone-poems. He had a remarkable talent for orchestration and a powerful imagination. In writing the popular *Don Juan*, *Till Eulenspiegel's Merry Pranks*, and *Don Quixote* he revived programmatic writing, raising its credibility as a worthy musical form. His operas *Salome* and *Elektra* were no less powerful but were met with some controversy. Many labeled them obscene, brutal, and even anti-vocal. Today thankfully it is a different story and no one would dream of describing them, or his hundred-odd songs, as anti-vocal. His *Four Last Songs* for soprano and orchestra are of sublime beauty. **DK**.

ABOVE: *Russian composer Igor Stravinsky.*

ABOVE: *Richard Strauss, the noted German composer.*

STRAVINSKY, IGOR
1882-1971
Russian composer

Stravinsky first attracted public attention as a composer for Diaghilev's Ballets Russes in Paris. His first ballet *The Firebird* (1910) met with overnight success as did his second ballet *Petrushka* a year later. Unfortunately this was not the case with his third attempt, *The Rite of Spring* which in 1913 caused an uproar in the musical world with its iconoclastic harmonies and instrumentation, not to mention its ruthlessly bold rhythms. Stravinsky has often been compared with the artist PICASSO because like him his compositional style changed throughout his life. The first real change came with the *Pulcinella* suite in 1919 which was based on Pergolesi. This marked the beginning of his neoclassical period which included much pastiche work. Other examples of compositions in this period include *The Fairy's Kiss*, based on Tchaikovsky, and even his later opera *The Rake's Progress* where he composed using the standard classical forms of the eighteenth century. Ironically Stravinsky had always been strongly opposed to the theories of Schoenberg and yet the next change which was to take place during the 1950s saw him experimenting with the use of serial techniques. Such techniques are quite prominent in his work *In Memorian Dylan Thomas* (1954). **DK**.

STREEP, MERYL
1951-
American actress

Streep is one of the brightest stars to appear in years, a winner of numerous awards and great critical acclaim. She made her screen debut in *Julia* (1977), rising to the top in films such as *The Deer Hunter* (1978), *Kramer vs Kramer* (1979), and *Sophie's Choice* (1982), for which she was awarded an Oscar. **DC**.

ABOVE: Indonesian President, Achmad Sukarno.

SUKARNO, ACHMAD
1901-1970
Indonesian statesman

Co-founder of the struggle for Indonesian independence from the Dutch, Sukarno achieved his aim in 1949 when he became first President of the Indonesian republic. He assumed almost dictatorial powers, but succeeded in uniting the scattered peoples of the Indonesian islands into a single nation. Adopting a diluted form of Chinese Communism, Sukarno nevertheless brutally crushed a Communist coup in 1965. His powers declined, however, and he surrendered office to Suharto in 1967. **JC**.

SUMNER, JAMES
1887-1955
American biochemist

Undeterred by the loss of his left arm in an accident Sumner was the first to successfully purify an enzyme and to demonstrate its protein nature. He purified the enzyme urease in the form of a crystalline protein in 1926. Even then, his evidence that urease was a protein was not accepted until 1930 when J H Northrop isolated another enzyme, pepsin, also in the form of a crystalline protein. **ES**.

SUN YAT-SEN
1866-1925
Chinese statesman

Sun was the American-trained Christian chosen to create a new China out of the ashes of the world's oldest empire. His idealism lay behind the one-party system with which the new republic was launched in 1911. Sun's Kuomintang party embraced his Three Principles of national unity, people's rights, and a guaranteed livelihood. In practice this meant trying to reconcile benign, Western-oriented authoritarianism with nascent Communism. By the time of his death from cancer in 1925, his heir CHIANG KAI-SHEK was already preparing a militaristic state, alien to Sun's principles, although Chiang's heirs still venerate the founding father. **JC**.

SUTHERLAND, DAME JOAN
1926-
Australian opera singer

With her staggeringly powerful and flexible soprano and effortless control and delivery, Sutherland was one of the great coloraturas, reviving single-handedly the taste for full-throated florid singing. The lead in Donizetti's *Lucia de Lammermoor* (1959) launched her career; other favorites included Norma, Violetta in *La Traviata*, and Gilda in *Rigoletto*. **JH**.

SWANSON, GLORIA
1897-1983
American actress

Starting as a Mack SENNETT bathing beauty, Swanson became Hollywood's leading box-office draw from 1918 to 1926. A genius at self-promotion, fans went mad over her high-fashion clothes, her marriage to a genuine marquis, and her sultry beauty. Dramas and suggestive comedies were her forte, and it was Cecil B De MILLE who made her a star in films such as *Male and Female* (1919). She was less in evidence in the 1930s and 1940s until she reappeared triumphant in *Sunset Boulevard* (1950), which earned her her third Academy Award nomination. **DC**.

SYNGE, J[OHN] M[ILLINGTON]
1871-1909
Irish dramatist

Born near Dublin and educated at Trinity College, Synge spent some years in Paris where he met W B YEATS, who persuaded him to write about Irish peasant life. *The Aran Islands* (1907) was the first play to tackle the subject, and the theme recurs in many of his plays, both tragedies and comedies. *In the Shadow of the Glen*, his first play, was performed in 1903. In 1906 he became a director of the Abbey Theatre, where most of his plays were staged. The most controversial and now best regarded of his works, *The Playboy of the Western World*, was performed in 1907. The *Collected Works* appeared in four volumes, 1962-68. **AM**.

SZILARD, LEO
1898-1964
Hungarian-American physicist

Szilard's expertise covered a number of fields in physics – and even in molecular biology and biochemistry – but his main contribution to the history of science was the recognition of the significance of nuclear fission as an energy source. He moved from Hungary to Britain in 1933 and to America in 1938. With Albert EINSTEIN, he advised President Franklin ROOSEVELT about the possibility of atomic weapons, and subsequently became involved in the Manhattan Project to build the first atomic bomb. Along with Enrico FERMI, he worked on the first fission reactor in Chicago in 1942. **DD**.

BELOW: Dame Joan Sutherland, pictured with colleague Luciano Pavarotti.

TAFT, WILLIAM HOWARD
1857-1930
American politician

Taft held not only the highest executive office, as 27th President of the United States, but also, later, the top legal post, as Chief Justice of the Supreme Court. Appointed Solicitor-General in 1890 he moved in 1900 to the newly conquered Philippines where he became the first Governor, pacifying the Church over its confiscated lands with a payment of $7 million. As Secretary of War from 1904 he supervised the construction of the Panama Canal and in 1908 succeeded ROOSEVELT as President. His special excise tax on corporations passed as the 16th Amendment. Theodore Roosevelt stood against him in 1912 and split the vote, as a result of which Taft ran third. Taft became Chief Justice in 1921. **JC**.

TAKAMINE, JAKICHI
1854-1922
Japanese-American chemist

Educated in Tokyo, Takamine's work followed the demonstration in 1896 that an injection of an extract from the center of the suprarenal gland caused blood pressure to rise rapidly. In 1901 he isolated and purified the substance involved. This was adrenaline (epinephrine), the first hormone to be isolated and purified from a natural source. **ES**.

TANGE, KENZO
1913-
Japanese architect

Tange's work epitomizes the changing Japanese economic and political climate since 1945. Throughout the 1950s he played a leading part in the 'traditional debate' in Japanese architecture, which culminated in his National Gymnasia for the Tokyo Olympics of 1964. Tange's celebration of technology can be seen in his Press and Broadcasting Center, Yamanashi (1961-67) and in recent buildings outside Japan, including the Arabian Gulf University, Bahrain. **DE**.

TARKOVSKY, ANDREI
1932-1986
Russian film maker

Tarkovsky's spiritual and surrealist, rather than socialist, movies brought him into conflict with the Soviet authorities, particularly *Andrei Rublev* (1966) and *Mirror* (1974). His final film, *The Sacrifice* (1985) – a religious dream-drama of nuclear holocaust – ends on a moving note of affirmation. **NS**.

TARSKI, ALFRED
1902-1983
American mathematician and logician

Unable to obtain a permanent university

ABOVE: *Jacques Tati (far left) in* M Hulot's Holiday.

post in Poland because he was Jewish, Tarski fled to the United States in 1939. Although he also published in algebra and measure theory, Tarski is best known for his work on the logical and philosophical foundations of mathematics, and especially on model theory and decidability. His formal account of truth laid the foundations for modern semantics and has been a great influence on the subsequent history of philosophy. **EB**.

TATI, JACQUES
1908-1982
French actor and director

Tati became a cabaret and music-hall entertainer in the early 1930s, and several of his routines were turned into short films, such as *Oscar Champion de Tennis* (1932). After the war he hit his prime, appearing in movies such as *M Hulot's Holiday* (1953) and *My Uncle* (1958) which emphasized visual humor. **DC**.

TATUM, EDWARD
1909-1975
American geneticist

Edward Tatum won a Nobel prize in 1958 for his work (with George Beadle) proving that genes regulate definite chemical processes. He concluded that the production, specificity and action of individual enzymes

was controlled by a particular gene and therefore every biochemical reaction could be altered by genetic mutation. His research into single genes was useful in increasing the production of penicillin after World War II. **EMS**.

TAWNEY, R H
1880-1962
British economic historian

The description of historian hardly does justice to this influential scholar and pioneer of the Fabian Movement. Tawney dedicated his life to the cause of social justice, and his humanitarian influence was particularly evident in the field of Adult Education where as President of the Workers' Educational Association he campaigned vigorously for equal opportunities in education. His blossoming academic career at Glasgow University from 1908 to 1914, was interrupted and very nearly ended by the war, when he was seriously wounded at the Battle of Somme. Tawney continued his scholarship as a Fellow of Balliol in 1918 and as Professor of Economic History at London in 1931-49. A sincere Christian as well as a socialist, he was a staunch critic of the immoral premise which he saw at the heart of the Capitalist system, and this permeates his scholarship, particularly his masterful *The Acquisitive Society* and *Religion and the Rise of Capitalism*. **ML**.

TAYLOR, A J P
1906-1990
British historian

Taylor was acknowledged on his death as the most well-known and controversial historian in the English-speaking world. The first historian to bring history to the masses through the medium of television in the 1950s, he brought history alive with his epic unscripted lectures. Unquestionably his journalistic skills, honed on *The Manchester Guardian*, greatly assisted him as a historian but it would be wrong to minimize just how much his brilliantly simple but effective historiographical approach contributed to his success. Taylor was acutely aware that the duty of a historian is to find out what happened and why. This fundamental premise is evident throughout his vast litany of publications, including his most famous work, *The Origins of the Second World War*, which outraged many with its provocative revisionist onslaught on the accepted version of events. A lifelong socialist and short-lived member of the Communist Party, Taylor was never afraid of courting controversy in either his public or personal life. He was married three times and in 1980 resigned his fellowship of the British Academy following its expulsion of Anthony Blunt. He lectured at Manchester University in 1930-38 under one of his great mentors Lewis NAMIER before ensconcing himself at Magdalen College, Oxford. **ML**.

TAYLOR, ELIZABETH
1932-
American actress

Groomed by her mother to be an actress, Taylor was just 12 when she starred in *National Velvet* (1942), and she matured quickly, playing romantic roles well beyond her years, such as Amy in *Little Women* (1949). She began taking her acting seriously in 1951 with *A Place in the Sun*, co-starring Montgomery CLIFT and Shelley Winters, and was soon a top box-office superstar and one of the best-publicized women in the world. While her private life and many marriages fueled public interest, she won an Academy Award for *Butterfield 8* (1960), and another for *Who's Afraid of Virginia Woolf?* She has emerged as a magnificent character and now works tirelessly for charities. **DC**.

TEDDER, ARTHUR, 1ST BARON, MARSHAL OF THE ROYAL AIR FORCE
1890-1967
British airman

After service as a pilot during World War I, Tedder remained in the RAF, and became Director-General of research in 1938. In 1941 he became RAF Commander Middle East, successfully co-ordinating the air war against Axis forces in the desert. In February 1943 he was appointed Allied Air

ABOVE: One of the world's best-known actresses, Elizabeth Taylor.

Commander-in-Chief for the Mediterranean, serving under General EISENHOWER. The partnerhsip was continued in 1944-45, when Tedder acted as Eisenhower's deputy and commanded all Allied air forces during the campaign in North-West Europe, destroying enemy supply lines and ensuring the availability of maximum airpower. **JPi**.

TE KANAWA, DAME KIRI
1944-
New Zealand opera singer

She made her Covent Garden debut in 1971 and had a well-established career in the UK before making her first appearance at the New York Met at three hours' notice as Desdemona in Verdi's *Otello*. Other roles have included Mozart's Donna Elvira and the Countess, STRAUSS's Arabella and the Marschallin, and Verdi's Violetta. Te Kanawa's rich and creamy lyric soprano and dramatic, poised stage presence, despite a certain lack of subtlety, have brought her immense success both on stage and in the recording studio. **JH**.

TELLER, EDWARD
1908-
Hungarian-American physicist

Teller is regarded as being the father of the hydrogen bomb. Educated in Budapest and Germany, he quickly left Europe for America in the face of rising fascism. There, he became involved in the Manhattan Project to build the first atomic bomb, but at the time he was seeing further to the development of the more powerful hydrogen bomb. This was achieved in 1952. Since then he has been active in nuclear armament and the Strategic Defense Initiative. **DD**.

BELOW: Dr Edmund Teller receives an award from President Kennedy.

ABOVE: Child actress Shirley Temple.

BELOW: U Thant, Secretary-General of the UN.

TEMPLE, SHIRLEY
1928-
American actress

Curly-headed Shirley Temple became a Hollywood star at the age of six. She made 19 films for Fox between 1934 and 1937, usually appearing as an orphan who found a new family, or the child of a single parent who found a new mate for them. Her films were immensely popular and she became the center of a remarkable cult: there were Shirley Temple dolls, dresses, plates, even a cocktail. She made several successful films as a teenager, and as an adult (now Shirley Temple Black) she has had a distinguished career in politics and diplomacy. **DC**.

THANT, U
1909-1974
Burmese diplomat

The first UN representative of the Burmese republic, Thant became a permanent representative to the UN in 1957. After HAMMARSKJÖLD's death, Thant became Secretary-General in 1961, helping to resolve crises from the Cuban Missile Crisis (1962) to the Six Day War (1967). **JM**.

THARP, TWYLA
1942-
American dancer and choreographer

A student of such famous teachers as Merce CUNNINGHAM, Martha GRAHAM and Matt Mattox, Tharp made her debut in 1963 with the Paul Taylor Dance Company. In 1965 she formed her own company and choreographed her first work. *Tank Dive*. Throughout the 1960s Tharp's work was performed almost entirely without musical accompaniment, and usually in venues not associated with dance: art galleries, outdoors, and in gyms. Pieces such as *Dancing in the Streets of Paris and London, Continued in Stockholm and Sometimes Madrid* involved performances in multiple spaces viewed on a closed circuit television system, with the audience free to move between performance areas. A turning point in Tharp's career came in 1971 with *Eight Jelly Rolls*, eight pieces set to music by jazz pianist Jelly Roll MORTON, and the first of a number of dances using American jazz and popular music, including *Sue's Leg* (music by Fats WALLER) and *Ocean's Motion* (music by Chuck BERRY). In 1976 Tharp choreographed *Push Comes to Shove* for American Ballet Theatre and became the first American choreographer to create a work for Mikhail BARYSHNIKOV. **MC**.

THATCHER, MARGARET, BARONESS
1925-
British politician and prime minister

After studying at Oxford and practicing as a lawyer Thatcher entered parliament in 1959. Appointed education secretary by HEATH in 1970, she supplanted him as party leader in 1975 and won the 1979 general election for the Conservatives. She advocated a reduction in state controls and encouragement to private enterprise, and the 1980s saw the consolidation of fiscal caution, privatization, and self-help, policies which came to be known as 'Thatcherism'. Combative in foreign affairs, her decisive handling of the 1982 Falklands Campaign undoubtedly contributed to the landslide election victory of 1983. The second term nearly came to an abrupt end when an IRA bomb came close to wiping out the Cabinet at the party conference in Brighton in 1984. She was relentless in her pursuit of the trade unions, considerably reducing their power, particularly after the year-long miners' strike (1984-85). Unemployment bugged her administration but the economy boomed until 1987. Elected for a third term in 1987, she became the longest-serving Prime Minister this century and was a respected world leader. Disaffection with policies such as health cuts, the poll tax, and her hostility to Europe served to undermine Thatcher's standing in both the country, and within the ranks of the Conservative party, and in November 1990 she was replaced by John MAJOR. **JM**.

THOMPSON, E P
1924-
British historian

As both a Radical historian and political campaigner Thompson has made his mark on the century as a thorn in the flesh of the establishment. His greatest academic achievement was the seminal, *The Making of the English Working Class* (1963) which changed the way social history, particularly working-class history was written. Thompson was an unwilling academic who only published because he was penniless, preferring work in adult education to the lofty corridors of academia. Socialism prompted his convinced unilateralism and his leadership of the European nuclear disarmament movement. His brilliant riposte to the Thatcher government's 'Protect and Survive' leaflet, 'Protest and Survive' earned widespread publicity and the condemnation of both NATO and the Kremlin. **ML**.

THOMPSON, ROY, 1ST BARON THOMPSON OF FLEET
1894-1976
Canadian newspaper proprietor

Canadian-born Thompson began as a radio salesman and in 1931 set up his own transmitter thus launching a press and broadcasting empire. In 1953 he moved to Britain where he purchased *The Scotsman*. His biggest acquisition was the Kelmsley Newspapers group in 1959, followed in 1966 by the purchase of *The Times*. He was noted for being a proprietor who did not interfere with his editors' running of the newspapers. **DSL**.

ABOVE: Welsh poet Dylan Thomas.

THESIGER, WILFRED PATRICK
1910-
British explorer

Thesiger is perhaps the most famous recent explorer of Arabia, and has recorded his travels in the deserts and elsewhere in a series of popular and widely read books. He was actually born in Addis Ababa in Ethiopia, where in 1930 he witnessed the coronation of the Emperor Haile SELASSIE. In 1935 he began his exploration of the Sahara and used his expertise during World War II when he served with the special services, including the Special Air Service (SAS), of the British Army in the Western Desert. After the war he explored the Empty Quarter of Saudi Arabia, and for some time lived with and later wrote about the Marsh Arabs of Iraq. During the 1960s he increasingly traveled in, and wrote about, East Africa. **RJ**.

ABOVE: 'Iron Lady', Margaret Thatcher.

THOMAS, DYLAN
1914-1953
British poet

Born and educated in Swansea, South Wales, Thomas lived a very public and flamboyant life. A charismatic and chaotic bohemian, his lifestyle finally killed him with alcoholic poisoning. His poetry is imbued with vitality, full of powerful, sometimes obscure imagery, deeply religious and pantheistic. *18 Poems* (1934) was his first publication in the year he moved to London. During his lifetime his reputation was over-inflated, and it has suffered, unjustly, the reverse since his death. At his best magnificent, at his worst self-indulgent, he was always a craftsman. His most famous work was the play for voices *Under Milk Wood* (1952). **AM**.

THORPE, JIM [JAMES]
1888-1953
American athlete

His Indian name was 'Bright Path,' and Jim Thorpe made a brilliant journey through the sporting world, exceling in football, baseball, and track and field. At the Carlisle Indian School he was a two-time All-American in football, leading his team to startling victories over the top college squads in the country. Thorpe burst on the international scene in the 1912 Olympics in Stockholm, Sweden. There he finished first in both the decathlon and pentathlon. He was forced to surrender the gold medals, however, when it was learned that he had played semipro baseball a few years before. (Thirty years after Thorpe's death, the International Olympic Committee restored his amateur status, and presented his heirs with the medals.) Thorpe went on to play Major League baseball and NFL football. He was the first President of the NFL when it debuted in 1920 as the American Professional Football Association. Thorpe's multi-faceted successes earned him the honor of being the best athlete of the half-century, as voted by the Associated Press. In his later years, Thorpe became an active leader in Indian affairs. **MD**.

THURBER, JAMES
1894-1961
American humorist

Thurber published numerous essays, sketches, stories, and reminiscences, often in *The New Yorker*. These include the well-known short story *The Secret Life of Walter Mitty* (1932), which has lent its gently melancholic name to those who indulge in the delusions of escapist fantasy. Thurber also wrote fantasies for children. **CW**.

TILDEN, BILL [WILLIAM TATEM II]
1893-1953
American tennis player

In the 1920s 'Big Bill' was an overpowering force in the world of tennis. He won the US Open six straight times from 1920 through 1925 and then again in 1929. He also claimed three Wimbledon titles. In his prime Tilden was the dominant player on the US Davis Cup team. Primarily a baseline player, Tilden wore opponents down with his precise groundstrokes. His tennis success spanned virtually his entire life: a local singles title at age seven, a national doubles crown at 52. In 1950 the Associated Press voted Tilden the greatest tennis player of the first half of the twentieth century. **MD**.

TILLICH, PAUL JOHANNES
1886-1965
American theologian

Born in Germany, a student at Tübingen, Berlin, and Breslau and like many of the

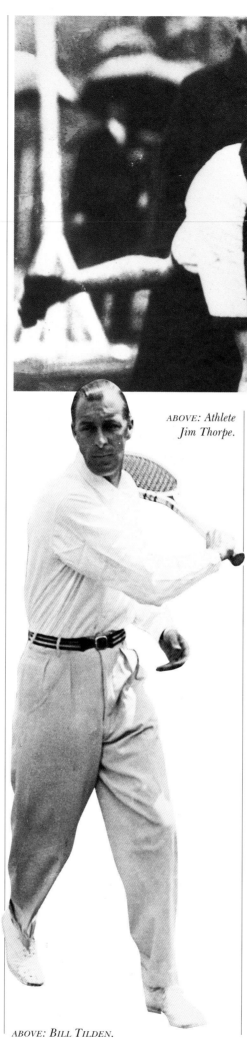

ABOVE: Athlete Jim Thorpe.

ABOVE: BILL TILDEN.

great theologians of his generation an outspoken critic of the Nazi regime, Tillich was the first Gentile to be removed from a teaching post. He emigrated to the USA where he produced the three volume *Systematic Theology* (1951-63) which combined elements of existentialist philosophy with the ontological tradition of Christian thought. Critics have regarded him as a crypto-atheist, although such spurious aspersions have not prevented works such as his *Courage to Be* and *The Dynamics of Faith* reaching a wide audience. **ML**.

TINBERGEN, NIKOLAAS
1907-1988
Dutch zoologist

Tinbergen graduated and taught in Leiden, but after World War II he moved to Oxford and researched animal behavior. He found that much animal behavior was based on ritual patterns – the display gestures of aggressive sticklebacks, and the dances of rival gulls – as an alternative to physical combat. **DD**.

TING, SAMUEL CHAO CHUNG
1936-
American physicist

Born in America but educated in China and Taiwan, and later at the University of Michigan, Ting became Associate Professor at Columbia University at the early age of 29. In an experiment in the synchrotron in the Brookhaven National Laboratory in 1974 he detected a new particle called the J particle. Burton Richer discovered it at the same time at Stanford, calling it the psi particle, and the two shared the Nobel Prize for Physics in 1976. The newly discovered particle is now known as the J/psi particle. **DD**.

TIPPETT, SIR MICHAEL KEMP
1905-
British composer

Even in his late eighties, Michael Tippett has shown himself to be an energetic and original voice in world music. Fascinated by the whole range of sounds around him, his music shows influences from traditional English songs to jazz, to Indonesian music, even to parodies of monkeys chattering (as in his magnificent oratorio *The Mask of Time*). His powerful operas, his song cycles, his intricate chamber music, his solo sonatas, all exude a vibrance, humor, and color which characterize this passionate and idealistic man, pacifist, and humanist. Tippett's life and music have greatly enriched the world. **DK**.

TISELIUS, ARNE WILHELM KAURIN
1902-1971
Swedish physical biochemist

He worked mostly on proteins and with his former teacher Theodor Svedberg, in 1937 he discovered that an electric current passed through a solution of proteins would move the molecules of different proteins at different speeds. Consequently he developed the process of electrophoresis by which different proteins can be separated in this way, and was awarded the Nobel Prize for Chemistry for it in 1948. Among his discoveries was the fact that blood serum could be separated into four distinct groups – albumens, alpha-globulins, beta-globulins, and gamma-globulins. Most of his work was done in Uppsala. **DD**.

TITO, JOSIP (BROZ)
1892-1980
Yugoslav politician

Tito owed his rise initially to STALIN's liquidation of the rest of the Yugoslav Communist leaders, but thereafter to his own vision and political cunning. From being benevolently neutral towards Germany as demanded by the 1939 non-aggression pact, he turned his party into a bastion of anti-Fascism after winning the admiration and armed support of CHURCHILL for his epic guerrilla campaign. Narrowly escaping capture in one of the sweep-and-destroy operations which the Germans mounted, Tito led his Partisans out of the trap and by 1945, as a self-appointed Marshal, he was on the borders of Italy, where his claims on Trieste nearly led to war with his recent allies, the British. Stalin tried unsuccessfully to bring Tito to heel and condemned him through the Cominform, whereupon the Marshal left the Eastern alliance. He gained new stature and allies among the Non-Aligned Nations. In the 1950s and 1960s Tito became the West's favorite Communist, and Yugoslavia a popular holiday destination and investment center, but as subsequent events have proved, the unity was fragile

ABOVE: *Josip Tito, Yugoslavia's Communist leader.*

and the Yugoslav union only survived the Marshal's death by a decade, the ethnic hatreds which he had suppressed, dissolving it in blood. **JC**.

TODD, BARON ALEXANDER ROBERTUS
1907-
British organic chemist

Todd synthesized certain vitamins and determined the chemical structure of nucleic acids, thus paving the way for the later understanding of the action of genes in the reproduction of cells. He was awarded the Nobel Prize for Chemistry for this work in 1957. **DD**.

TOGLIATTI, PALMIRO
1893-1964
Italian politician

Leader of the Italian Communists from 1926, Togliatti spent the war years in Moscow, returning to Italy in 1944 to become a Cabinet member until 1947. He made his the largest Communist party in the West, committed to obtaining power by constitutional measures. **JC**.

TOJO, HIDEKI
1884-1948
Japanese politician

Tojo turned Japan's search for economic elbow room into a full-scale world war

ABOVE: *Japan's Prime Minister from 1941 to 1944, Hideki Tojo.*

against her strongest Pacific competitor, the USA. Prime Minister from 1941, he controlled all political and military decisions, but could not prevent the succession of military defeats from 1942. The army forced him to resign in 1944 and after his suicide attempt failed, he was tried for War Crimes by the Allies. **JC**.

ABOVE: *J R R Tolkien.*

TOLKIEN, J[OHN] R[ONALD] R[EUEL]
1892-1973
British academic and writer

Scholar, critic, and Merton Professor of English Language and Literature at Oxford (1945-59), Tolkien's international fame has sprung not from his studies of *Beowulf* and philology, but from his fictional world of Middle Earth, with its complete mythology of the eternal battle of good against evil, in *The Hobbit* and *Lord of the Rings*. **AM**.

TOSCANINI, ARTURO
1867-1957
Italian conductor

Toscanini must surely be one of the finest conductors the world has ever seen. When largely unknown he conducted Verdi's *Aida* entirely from memory. He then went on to become musical director of La Scala, Milan, where he conducted the first performance of Puccini's *Turandot* in 1926. **DK**.

BELOW: *Italian conductor Arturo Toscanini.*

TOYNBEE, ARNOLD
1889-1975
British historian

A distinguished historian, Toynbee's magnum opus, the 12-volume *A Study of History* (1934-61), remains one of the most influential and controversial works of the century. It focused on the rise and fall of various civilizations and rejected outright the naive theory of inevitability in history. Toynbee saw history as being shaped primarily by spiritual factors rather than by political and economic considerations, but many critics felt this to be proof of his own Christian convictions clouding his historical judgment. Nevertheless he was internationally acclaimed as an expert in Middle Eastern affairs both as Professor of Byzantine and Modern Greek Studies at London University and as a journalist during the Greco-Turkish War of 1920-22. **ML**.

TOYODA, KIICHIRO
1894-1953
Japanese motor manufacturer

Considered the father of the Japanese motor industry, Toyoda studied mechanical engineering, qualifying in 1921 and going to work in the family Automatic Loom Works. Toyoda visited the United States and was impressed by Ford's conveyer-belt produc-

ABOVE: *Spencer Tracy collars Freddie Bartholemew in* Captain Courageous.

tion process, developed for the Model T. In 1930 he started a research department in the family business in order to look at automobile production, the Model A1 passenger car being introduced in 1935. 'Toyoda' became 'Toyota' after the company ran a competition to design a logo for the new department. The first factory was completed in 1936 and the Toyota Motor Co Ltd began trading a year later. **NF**.

TRACY, SPENCER
1900-1967
American actor

During his extraordinary movie career, Tracy rarely received a bad review. His low-key style and ability to react to other actors has rarely been bettered. His craggy, rugged appearance let him play a variety of roles, from gangsters, to priests, to comic heroes, yet he was never a typical leading man. He received several Oscar nominations, winning two in succession for *Captain Courageous* (1937) and *Boys Town* (1938). He played some memorable parts in films with his lifelong companion Katharine HEPBURN, among them *Adam's Rib* (1949) and his last movie, *Guess Who's Coming to Dinner* (1967). **DC**.

TREVELYAN, GEORGE MACAULAY
1876-1962
British historian

Regius Professor of Modern History at Cambridge, Trevelyan's genuine love of history was displayed by his insistence that historical works had a duty to appeal to the general reader as well as the scholar. His *History of England* (1926) certainly succeeded in this respect as did his *British History in the Nineteenth Century* (1922), and *English Social History* (1944). His memory lives on through his scholarship, his sterling work with the National Trust, and as an early President of the Youth Hostels Association. **ML.**

TROTSKY, LEON
1879-1940
Russian politician

A leader of the Russian Revolution, Trotsky was the most powerful man after LENIN in the Soviet Union. He helped organize the October Revolution in 1917, and when the Bolsheviks took control became commissar for foreign affairs. He established the Red Army as an effective force during the civil war (1918-21), but his influence declined after Lenin's death in 1924. A ruthless, energetic man Trotsky was distrusted by STALIN who him into exile. He formed an anti-Stalin opposition from his base in Mexico, articulating theories which have inspired a romantic brand of workers' socialism ever since. He was murdered by a Stalinist agent. **JC.**

TRUDEAU, PIERRE ELLIOTT
1919-
Canadian politician

A trend-setter of the liberated sixties, Trudeau made his reputation first as a lawyer, fighting civil liberties cases, and then representing Canada at the United Nations in 1966. Elected leader of the Liberal Party in April 1968, he won that year's general election. He faced increasing demands from separatist Quebec, and lost power in 1979 in the wake of economic problems. During his second administration of 1980-84 Quebec rejected independence in a referendum. **JC.**

TRUFFAUT, FRANÇOIS
1932-1984
French film director

Perhaps the best-loved of the directors of the French 'New Wave', whose first feature *The 400 Blows* (1959) drew on his own childhood in its study of adolescence and delinquency. He was one of the most sensitive directors of childhood experience (see also *L'Enfant Sauvage*, 1970). Truffaut's infectious love of movies was especially evident in his published letters and reviews, his book-length interview with Alfred HITCHCOCK, and his affectionate film about the trials and tribulations of film-making, *Day for Night*

ABOVE: *Leon Trotsky, the revolutionary whose fortunes declined after Lenin's death.*

ABOVE: *François Truffaut (left), and Alfred Hitchcock.*

(1973). His masterpiece is probably *Jules et Jim* (1961), an unusual love story shot in an alternately lyrical, exuberant, and tragic style. **NS.**

TRUMAN, HARRY S
1884-1972
American statesman

Truman's tough, courageous response to the challenges posed by the dawn of the nuclear era turned him from ROOSEVELT's understudy into one of the great presidents. He gave the order to drop the A-bombs; promulgated the Truman Doctrine, giving aid to countries fighting Communism; provided economic means to the same end with the Marshall Plan; faced down STALIN over the Berlin blockade; was godfather to Nato and committed the USA to the Korean War. Less successful in domestic politics, he failed to get his 'Fair Deal' reforms through Congress, which in 1947 passed the Taft-Hartley Act, curbing workers' rights, over his veto. Lurid spy cases like those of HISS and the Rosenbergs, and public fears of both Communist subversion (culminating in the McCarthyite trials) and about the Soviet nuclear threat, undermined Truman's resolve. He declined to run for re-election in 1952 and retired to be a revered Democratic elder statesman. **JC.**

TSHOMBE, MOISE
1919-1969
Congolese politician

Tshombe led the bloody and unsuccessful Katanga breakaway from the Congo in 1960 which was backed by the Belgians and saw fighting between UN troops and mercenaries. In August 1960 he was made head of state by the secessionists, but was exiled in 1963. Recalled in 1964, he became Prime Minister of the Congo, but his presence failed to stop the civil war. MOBUTU seized power in 1965 and Tshombe was kidnapped

ABOVE: President Harry S Truman (left) advising his successor, Dwight D Eisenhower.

and charged with treason. He died in captivity in Algeria. **JC.**

TSIOLKOVSKY, KONSTANTIN
1857-1935
Russian physicist

Regarded as the father of rocketry, Tsiolkovsky recognized the limitations of solid fuel such as gunpowder for powering heavy rockets, and proposed the use of liquid fuels, such as liquid hydrogen and liquid oxygen, instead. The suggestion was made in 1903 but he had to wait until R H Goddard fired a liquid-fueled rocket in 1926 to see his ideas put into action. He also postulated that a multi-stage rocket would be the most practical means of overcoming the Earth's gravitational field. He also foresaw the development and use of space stations as part of a space exploration program. **DD.**

TUCHMAN, BARBARA
1912-1989
American historian

Twice a Pulitzer prize winner, for *August 1914* and *Sand Against the Wind*, Tuchman had the rare quality of being able to make a historical period come alive, be it the eve of World War I in the *Proud Tower* or the fourteenth century in *A Distant Mirror*. What made her achievements more remarkable was that she could hardly be described as a conventional academic, allowing the role of housewife and mother to interrupt her promising journalistic career. Perhaps this enhanced her ability to appeal both to the scholar and the general reader. **ML.**

TUPOLEV, ANDREI NIKOLAYEVICH
1888-1972
Soviet aircraft engineer

One of the outstanding Soviet aircraft designers, Tupolev's name will always be associated with large bombers and airliners, although his input into several small single- and multiseat biplanes in the latter 1920s helped free the Soviet forces from their dependence on foreign-designed aircraft. He joined the Higher Technical School in Moscow in 1909 and became the Assistant Director of the Central Aero-Hydrodynamic Institute (TsAGI) in that city after its formation in 1918, leading the design department from 1921. In 1938, under STALIN's purges, he was arrested as an enemy of the people, but this situation was reversed in 1943, and he became a Lieutenant General in the Soviet Army. From 1944 until 1956 he served as a deputy to the Supreme Soviet and in 1952 was awarded a Stalin Prize for 'new work' connected with aircraft design. In 1953 he became a member of the Academy of Sciences and in 1957 won a Lenin Prize for his contribution to the development the Tu-104 turbojet airliner. Other honors included a Gold Medal from the FAI for this airliner, and an Honorary Fellowship of the Royal Aeronautical Society in 1970. **MT.**

TURING, ALAN
1912–1954
British mathematician

The father of modern computing, Turing was an eccentric mathematician. He began work for the British army at the start of World War II at Bletchley Park. His major achievement in the war effort was cracking the Enigma code used by German U-boats, contributing directly to the Allied victory. A brilliant seer, Turing foretold of the time when computers would appear intelligent and is credited with the Turing Test, where a person asks a computer questions. The computer is deemed to have passed the test, and thus be intelligent, if the human cannot tell if the responses are emanating from another person at a distant keyboard or from the computer. Turing devised the process of using binary mathematics for computing, which has had a profound effect on the industry. **SR.**

TURNER, TED [ROBERT EDWARD III]
1938-
American television magnate

Turner became one of the world's major media magnates by seizing on the opportunities of cable and satellite technologies. Starting with his Atlanta-based 'Superstation', Turner went on to develop Cable News Network (CNN), a 24-hour news station, received around the world and watched by business and political leaders. **DSL.**

ULANOVA, Galina Sergeyevna
1910-
Russian dancer and teacher

Ulanova studied dance with her mother at the Maryinsky School, and later with Agrippina Vaganova, the so-called 'Queen of Variations' and the perfector of a ballet method where the aim is to bring the body to a state of perfectly coordinated harmony. On graduation in 1928 Ulanova danced the waltz and mazurka in *Chopiniana* and also the role of the Sugar-Plum Fairy. She went on to extend her repertory to include the roles of Aurora, Giselle, Juliet, Raymonda, and Cygne. After 1959 she limited her stage appearances to *Sylphides* and *Fountain of Bakhchisary* but passed on her stage experience to younger dancers when she became ballet mistress and Artistic Director of the Bolshoi Ballet. The refinement and musicality of her performances in *Romeo and Juliet*, *Giselle*, and *Le Cygne* have been preserved on films made in the 1950s in Russia and Britain. **MC**.

ULBRICHT, Walter
1893-1973
East German statesman

Co-founder of the German Communist party in 1919, Ulbricht was elected to the Reichstag in 1928, but was forced to leave the country in 1933 when HITLER came to power. He founded the Socialist Unity Party on his return to Germany in 1945 and proclaimed the German Democratic Republic in 1949. As chairman of the Council of State from 1960 until his retirement in 1971, he combined political leadership with military control, and the following year erected the Berlin Wall to stem the flow of refugees from East Germany to the West. **JM**.

UPDIKE, John
1932-
American novelist

Novelist, short story writer, and interesting poet, Updike was born in Pennsylvania and graduated from Harvard. Work for the *New Yorker* and volumes of poetry and stories preceded his first critical and popular success, *Rabbit Run* (1960); *Rabbit Redux* (1972), *Rabbit is Rich* (1981), and *Rabbit at Rest* (1990) completed the small-town story of Harry Angstrom. As well as volumes of poetry, short stories and essays, his output of novels has been considerable, including *The Centaur* (1963), which combines mythology and realism, and *The Witches of Eastwick* (1984), which was made into a highly successful film. **AM**.

UREY, Harold Clayton
1893-1981
American physical chemist

Urey qualified as a zoologist but his main interest soon turned to chemistry. In 1932 he isolated heavy water and duterium, for which he received the Nobel Prize for Chemistry in 1934. He went on to be director of the War Research Atomic Bomb Project in World War II, leading to the development of nuclear weapons. Later, in 1952, with Stanley Miller, he investigated the Earth's primitive atmosphere and proposed a mechanism by which the basic chemicals of living things could be created from this atmosphere's constituents. He published several books on atomic structure and on the origin of the Earth and life. **DD**.

ABOVE: American novelist, John Updike.
BELOW: Screen legend Rudolph Valentino in The Sheik.

VALENTINO, Rudolph
1895-1926
Italian-born American actor

Valentino was the great Italian-American leading man of the 1920s, typecast as a Latin lover. His animal magnetism, flashing dark eyes, elegant clothes, and aura of mystery and wickedness made him a great idol and sex symbol of the silent era. Contacts and luck brought him the lead in *The Four Horsemen of the Apocalypse* (1921), a record-breaking smash hit. *The Sheik* (1921) made women swoon and started an Arabian fad in interior decorating. In 1926 he was rushed to hospital with a perforated ulcer. When it was reported that he had died, American women became hysterical, suicides were reported, and his funeral was a national event at which rioting broke out **DC**.

VAN ALLEN, James Alfred
1914-
American physicist

Van Allen was educated at the University of Iowa where he became Professor in 1951. In World War II he worked with the US Navy, and developed radio-proximity fuses. His subsequent experience in rocketry with discarded V2 rockets and with balloon-mounted equipment helped him to develop miniaturized instruments and study the upper atmosphere. His detectors in the first successful American satellite, Explorer 1, discovered the Van Allen Belts – the doughnut-shaped regions of radiation produced by solar particles trapped in the upper atmosphere by the Earth's magnetic field. They are a hazard to astronauts and to satellite instruments. **DD**.

VALERA, EAMON DE
1882-1975
Irish politician

De Valera took part in the Irish Easter Rising in 1916 and only his American citizenship saved him from execution. Following imprisonment (and escape), he traveled to the USA to rally support for the cause of Irish Republicanism and campaigned against the Anglo-Irish Treaty of 1921. In 1926 he founded the Fianna Fáil Party which he led to victory in 1932, eventually severing links with Britain. From 1959 he served two terms as President of the Irish Republic. **JC**.

VALOIS, DAME NINETTE, DE
1898-
Irish dancer and choreographer

A soloist in Diaghilev's Ballets Russes from 1923 to 1925, Valois founded her own school, the Academy of Choreographic Arts, in London in 1926. In the same year she met Lillian Bayliss, a meeting which was to lead to the founding of the Vic-Wells Ballet (later Sadler's Wells Theatre Ballet and, in 1956, the Royal Ballet) of which she was a director in 1931-63. Only at the age of 73 did she retire from her official duties, but continued to supervise revivals of her own ballets such as *Checkmate*. Furthermore, Valois was also responsible for founding the National Ballet of Turkey and was instrumental in the early planning of the National Ballet of Canada. Together with RAMBERT she is regarded as one of the pioneers of new British ballet and, thanks to her, the Royal Ballet and its school have achieved international renown. **MC**.

VAN DER POST, LAURENS, SIR
1906-
South African explorer and writer

Van der Post served as a soldier in World War II in the Middle East and the Far East until he was captured by the Japanese. He was subsequently employed by the British government on a number of missions in Africa, which led to his famous description of the Bushmen of southern Africa – *The Lost World of the Kalahari* (1958). He has since published a series of neophilosophical books about his various travels and prisoner-of-war experiences. **RJ**.

VARAH, [EDWARD] CHAD
1911-
British clergyman

The course of Chad Varah's life was changed when as a young priest he buried a 14-year-old girl who had committed suicide because she thought the onset of menstruation meant she was terminally ill. Appalled by suicide rates, Varah set up the non-religious Samaritans in the crypt of his London church, which recruited volunteer counsellors to listen to people's problems. The Samaritans now receive over 2½ million calls a year in the UK. The umbrella organization, Befrienders International, exists in 20 different countries, with over 6000 helpers. **PT**.

VARDON, HARRY
1870-1937
British golfer

Along with his notable contemporaries James Braid and J H Taylor, Harry Vardon pioneered professional golf and was instrumental in the development of the game in Britain, and to some extent in the USA. He won six British Open titles, the last in 1914, and also the 1900 US Open. He is still remembered in golf for the 'Vardon grip', the method of holding the club that is still the most commonly used by amateurs and top players alike. **DS**.

VAUGHAN, SARAH
1924-
American singer

Like Ella FITZGERALD, there is argument as to whether she is a jazz singer or simply a unique vocalist, with her warm, mellow voice, wide range, and perfect pitch. A founder member of the Billy Eckstine band, she soon went solo, touring variously with a piano trio, a symphony orchestra and a jazz band, and recorded with all the great jazz musicians of the day. **JH**.

VEBLEN, THORSTEIN
1857-1929
American economist

Veblen's writings had enormous impact on social thought, undermining the extraordinary prestige accorded to businessmen in the USA. He taught economics at several US universities, invariably arousing hostility that resulted in frequent changes of employer. This hostility was perhaps due less to his brilliant dissection of society than to his unorthodoxy in daily life, which included numerous extramarital successes with admiring women students. In his 1899 *The Theory of the Leisure Class* he pointed out that, just as in ancient barbaric times, high position was won not by creators and producers, but by predators. In both modern and ancient times such men were marked by freedom from industrial toil, acquisitiveness, force, and fraud. For them, lavish consumption was a sign of success. Five years later he published *The Theory of Business Enterprise*, which contrasted the almost infinite productive capacity of machine technology with the fact that the most successful industrialists were those who reduced that productivity by, for example, limiting output to maintain prices. He wrote several other books, all having the same destructive effect on complacency. He had a knack of inventing vaguely disrespectful terms; some, like 'conspicuous consumption' and 'captains of industry' still play a valuable role in the English language. **JW**.

VENTRIS, MICHAEL
1922-1956
British linguist

Ventris practiced as an architect, but his most relevant training was his work as a code-breaker during his war service. In 1952 he succeeded in deciphering the Linear B texts of the Minoan and Mycenaean civilizations, brilliantly revealing that Linear B was an early form of Greek. Ventris died in a road accident. **RJ**.

VENTURI, ROBERT
1925-
American architect, designer, and academic

Venturi is the leading American architect and theorist of Postmodernism. In his own words: 'I like elements that are hybrid rather than pure, compromising rather than clean, distorted rather than straight-forward.' He has designed furniture for Knoll and metalwork for Alessi but is best known for his architecture: Seattle Art Museum (1984) Philadelphia Orchestral Hall (1987), and the controversial Sainsbury Wing of the National Gallery, London (1986). **DE**.

VICTOR EMMANUEL III, KING
1869-1947
Italian monarch

Coming to the throne in 1900, Victor Emmanuel earned the respect of his people during World War I, when he chose to live in the combat zone. In 1922, fearful of the spread of Communism, he acquiesced to Benito MUSSOLINI's demands for power and acted as a figurehead and spokesman to the fascist government, even when Italy entered World War II in 1940. On 25 July 1943, with defeat inevitable, Victor Emmanuel dismissed Mussolini, opening the way to surrender in September. In 1944 he transferred royal power to his son Crown Prince Umberto, but in 1946 the Italians voted to abolish the monarchy and to establish a republic. **JP**.

VIGNEAUD, VINCENT DU
1901-1978
American biochemist

While head of Biochemistry at Cornell University Medical College, du Vigneaud discovered that one of the hormones of the pituitary gland, oxytocin, was composed of eight amino acids. In 1954 he bcame the first to synthesize artificially a protein using oxytocin. He showed it to be as effective as the natural hormone in inducing labor and milk flow in mothers, and received the Nobel Prize for Chemistry a year later. **ES**.

VILLA-LOBOS, HEITOR
1887-1959
Brazilian composer

A protégé of the great pianist Artur RUBIN-STEIN, Villa-Lobos made his name in Europe as a composer, having received great acclaim as a cellist and tutor in his homeland. His musical legacy includes 12 symphonies, 14 string quartets, and the ever-popular *Bachianas Brasileiras*, among a wealth of other works. **DK**.

VIONNET, MADELEINE
1876-1975
French designer

Vionnet was apprenticed at an early age as a seamstress and worked in the Paris suburbs until her late teens, when she joined dressmaker Kate O'Reilly in London. In 1901 she returned to Paris and worked for the Callot Sisters, who specialized in elaborately tiered lace and beaded dresses. Her own shop opened in 1912, closed during World War I reopening shortly afterwards to become one of the most innovative design houses of the day. Conceiving her designs on miniature models, and draping the fabric in sinuous folds, Vionnet is credited with the invention of the bias cut, the cowl, and halter necklines. Many of Vionnet's garments looked limp and lifeless until they were worn, when the crêpe-de-chine and satin dresses clung and draped elegantly against the body. **MC**.

VISCONTI, LUCHINO
1906-1976
Italian film director

Visconti began his career as a neo-realist with such films as *Ossessione* (1942) – the Italian version of *The Postman Always Rings Twice* – and a study of Sicilian fishermen, *La Terra Trema* (1948). He went on to make sumptuous operatic dramas, notable for their magnificent recreation of the past and their atmosphere of voluptuous doom: the best of them include *Senso* (1954), *Rocco and his Brothers* (1960), *The Leopard* (1963), *Death in Venice* (1971), and *Ludwig* (1972). **NS**.

VLAMINCK, MAURICE DE
1876-1958
French painter

Born in Paris, Vlaminck had no formal artistic training. His early violent use of color was encouraged by the 1901 van GOGH exhibition and he exhibited with MATISSE and the Fauves in 1905. His later works, mainly landscapes, utilized a more somber palette and sudden transitions from dark to light for dramatic effect. **ER**.

BELOW LEFT: King Victor Emmanuel III of Italy (in uniform).

WAJDA, ANDRZEJ
1926-
Polish film director

Wajda grew up in Poland during the Nazi occupation, and his famous trilogy – *A Generation* (1954), *Kanal* (1956), and *Ashes and Diamonds* (1958) – records the suffering and sacrifice of those years. He has never been afraid of tackling contemporary issues and politically sensitive material: *Man of Marble* (1976) is a bold study of history, censorship, and cinematic responsibility, while *Man of Iron* (1980) celebrated the rise of Solidarity. **NS**.

WALESA, LECH
1943-
Polish politician

The trade-union leader who turned a shipyard strike in Gdansk into a national revolution and survived to become the first President of a democratically elected government in Eastern Europe, Walesa's leadership of the Solidarity movement won him the Nobel Peace Prize in 1983. Premier in 1989, and since then, President Walesa has seen his revolution run into the economic quicksands. **JC**.

BELOW: Lech Walesa, the electrician who became President of Poland.

WALLACE, DEWITT
1889-1981
American publisher

Wallace was the founder of the *Reader's Digest*. After serving in World War I he worked in public relations before he and his wife Lila Bell Acheson thought of producing a digest of articles. The first issue of *Reader's Digest* appeared in 1921. It grew slowly both in the USA and abroad until it became the largest single publication in the world. **DSL**.

WALLENBERG, RAOUL
1912-?1947
Swedish diplomat

A diffident member of a wealthy banking family, Wallenberg made it his mission to rescue Hungarian Jews who were threatened by EICHMANN's mass deportations to Auschwitz. Ignoring Nazi threats, he persuaded the Hungarian authorities to let him issue four times the number of protective Swedish passports authorized and may have saved up to 100,000 lives. Arrested by the Soviets in 1945, he disappeared without trace. **JC**.

ABOVE: *Swedish diplomat Raoul Wallenberg.*

WALLER, FATS [THOMAS]
1904-1943
American jazz pianist, singer, and songwriter

The best-known and best-loved of the Harlem-style stride piano players, Waller wrote over 300 tunes and several Broadway shows before his early death, including classics such as 'Ain't Misbehavin'' and 'Honeysuckle Rose.' By 1934 he was approached to record some of his party-atmosphere performances, including as always several sub-standard Tin Pan Alley tunes through which his infectious good humor and keen rhythmic sense still shone. However just as his prowess was becoming legendary, a hard drinking lifestyle finally caught up with him. Despite his reputation as something of a comic performer, his influence as a major early jazz composer can hardly be overestimated. **DC**.

WALTER, BRUNO
1876-1962
German-born American conductor

As a conductor Walter is almost unrivaled in the music of Mozart, Mahler, and Bruckner. He devoted much of his life toward conducting opera and gave a sensational performance of Mahler's *Song of the Earth* at the very first Edinburgh Festival in 1947 with Kathleen Ferrier and the Vienna Philharmonic. **DK**.

WALTON, SIR WILLIAM TURNER
1902-1983
British composer

One of the Bloomsbury set and particular friend of the Sitwells, Walton was something of an original composer, being largely self-taught. His grasp of orchestral technique was remarkable, as displayed in his two symphonies, concertos for violin, viola and cello, and the coronation marches *Crown Imperial* and *Orb and Sceptre*. His oratorio *Belshazzar's Feast* is one of the most accessible and impressive large-scale works of the century, while his firm scores evince a majesterial style which some would say 'out-Elgar Elgar.' **DK**.

BELOW: *Extrovert jazz musician, Fats Waller.*

WANKEL, FELIX
1902-1988
German engineer

Wankel's ingenious design for a rotary piston engine eliminates both the valve gear and oscillating piston masses of conventional petrol engines thus allowing higher rotational speeds to be attained. Despite its sale to manufacturers around the world, the Wankel Rotary Engine's design problems have prevented widespread use. **PWO**.

WARHOL, ANDY
1930-1987
American painter and film maker

Warhol was the most internationally known Pop artist of the 1960s. His multiple images of dollar bills, Campbell's soup cans, Coca-Cola bottles and Marilyn MONROE epitomized an era overwhelmed by consumer madness, the mass media and exaggerated star cults, of whom he was one. Obsessed by the idea of mass-production, he called his studio The Factory and adopted silkscreen printing, which eliminated any trace of the artist's hand. His work neither projects nor demands emotion, and images such as *Electric Chair* (1965), are a subtle comment on the emotional bankruptcy of a society numbed by media bombardment. **ER**.

ABOVE: Andy Warhol escorts cult star Candy Darling.

RIGHT: John Wayne in True Grit.

WARREN, ROBERT PENN
1905-1984
American poet and novelist

The first US Poet Laureate, he won two Pulitzer Prizes for poetry and one for his most famous work, the novel *All the King's Men* (1946). Other works of fiction and nonfiction were numerous, and most frequently are centered on issues of Southern history and set in Southern locations. **AM**.

WATSON-WATT, SIR ROBERT
1892-1973
British physicist and engineer

A noted research engineer, Watson-Watt filed a patent concerned with radio direction finding in 1919. He became superintendent of the radio section of the National Physical Laboratory and in 1935 was appointed head of a team recruited by the Air Ministry to design practical systems of locating aircraft by radio waves – or radar. Working at Bawdsey, Suffolk, by 1939 they had developed a radar system which could detect on a radio screen attacking aircraft in all weathers, by day or night. The Battle of Britain was won as much on the radar screens as in the air. **PW**.

WAUGH, EVELYN
1903-1966
British novelist

Educated at Lancing and Oxford, Waugh's first, frustrating, job as a schoolmaster inspired his first novel, *Decline and Fall* (1928). He converted to Catholicism in 1930 and continued to write sophisticated, satirical, and successful novels which caught the cynical mood of the interwar years. After military service during World War II, Waugh's later novels such as *Brideshead Revisited* (1945), *The Loved One* (1948), and the acclaimed war trilogy, *The Sword of Honour* (completed 1962), set out to recreate a golden image of the world he had once satirized. A superb stylist, his critics accused him of eccentricity, a charge he answered in *The Ordeal of Gilbert Pinfold* (1957). **AM**.

WAVELL, ARCHIBALD, 1ST EARL, FIELD MARSHAL
1883-1950
British soldier and Viceroy of India

During World War I, Wavell served with distinction. By 1939 he was Commander-in-Chief Middle East, responsible for an area from Egypt to the Horn of Africa. In 1940 he co-ordinated a series of campaigns against the Italians in Libya, Somaliland, and Ethiopia, but was less successful in Greece and North Africa against the Germans. Replaced by AUCHINLECK in July 1941, Wavell was sent to India and, in December, appointed Supreme Commander of Allied Forces facing the Japanese. Again, he could do little to prevent enemy success. He was Viceroy of India 1943-47. **JPi**.

WAYNE, JOHN
1907-1979
American actor

Although his most fervent admirers would agree that the only part 'Duke' could play was himself, to millions he personified rugged masculinity. Wayne shot to stardom in the film *Stagecoach* (1939), changing the image of the western from a kids' entertainment to a vehicle for a real story. His most successful non-western was *The Quiet Man* (1952), about an Irish American boxer who returns to the old country. Stricken with lung cancer in 1964, after a serious operation he went back to making films, including *True Grit* (1969), for which he received an Oscar. Although he never really recovered his health, he continued making pictures right up to the end. **DC**.

WEBB, SIDNEY
1859-1947
WEBB, BEATRICE
1858-1943
British social theorists and political
activists

Amongst the founders of the Fabian
Society, the Webbs together wrote histories
of British trade unionism and of local
government, set up the *New Statesman*, and
established the London School of Economics. Beatrice contributed to Booth's *Life and
Labour of People in London*, and laid the foundations of the welfare state in a minority report of the Royal Commission on the Poor
Laws, while Sidney, as a member of the
Commission on the Coal Industry, drew up
a plan for its nationalization. While a
London County Councillor, he was instrumental in educational reform, contributing
to the restructuring of London University,
was elected to Parliament, and served as
President of the Board of Trade and (as
Baron Passfield) as Secretary of State for the
Colonies. **EB**.

WEBER, BRUCE
1946-
American photographer

As clothes became simpler during the 1980s,
fashion photography became increasingly
involved with manners and tone. The
photographer projected and even invented
the 'look' of a season or even an era, none
more so than Bruce Weber, with his taste for
relaxed athleticism. He worked with the designers Karl Lagerfeld, Ralph LAUREN and
Calvin KLEIN. Athletes were the subjects of
his first book, *Bruce Weber*, in 1984. **IJ**.

WEBER, MAX
1864-1920
German sociologist

Weber is considered to be, like DURKHEIM
and Marx, one of the founding fathers of
modern sociology. His original studies were
in law but he soon moved on to economic
history. After holding posts at Freiburg and
Heidelberg, Weber suffered a nervous
breakdown, in 1896, which incapacitated
him for four years. He only returned to a
university post three years before his death.
Weber stressed the role of individual action
in social life, arguing that sociologists must
understand the meaning of an action to the
actor. In his most famous book, *The Protestant Ethic and the Spirit of Capitalism*, Weber
demonstrated this methodology by arguing
that the rise of capitalism can be partly explained by attitudes towards worldly wealth
and human fate which were fostered by
Protestant sects. This book was part of his
lifelong project to understand why capitalism arose in the west, a project which drew
on a wide range of cultural sources, such as
Chinese, Jewish, and Indian civilization,
and which led him to major achievements in

comparative sociology, the sociology of religion and of law, economic sociology, and
many other areas. He received much support from his remarkable wife, Marianne,
who ran a *salon* for sociologists and wrote his
biography. **DSl**.

WEBERN, ANTON VON
1883-1945
Austrian composer

Webern's main sources of inspiration came
from a detailed study of the fifteenth-
century polyphonic music of Isaacs and his
teacher SCHOENBERG. So taken was Webern
with Schoenberg's theory of serialism that
he remained the most loyal of all his pupils.
Although his first composition shows the influence of Mahler, the rest of his output
demonstrates a strict adherence to the principles of serialism. Most of his works are surprisingly short with his longest composition
Passacaglia for Orchestra lasting a mere ten
minutes. Aside from being influenced by
Schoenberg, Webern himself became an influence on other leading composers. His introduction of the technique *Klangfarbenme-
lodie* influenced both BOULEZ and
STRAVINSKY. **DK**.

WEGENER, ALFRED LOTHAR
1880-1930
German meteorologist, geophysicist and
astronomer

Educated at Heidelberg, Innsbruck, and
Berlin, Wegener is famed for proposing
the idea of continental drift – the theory that
the continents have not always been in the
position that they are now but are gradually
moving. Although he was not the first to
suggest such an idea, he was certainly the
first to put it on a scientific footing and cite
evidence. His work was largely rejected by
the scientific establishment and, dying on an
expedition to Greenland, he did not live to
see it vindicated with the general acceptance
of plate tectonics in the 1960s and 1970s.
DD.

WEIL, SIMONE
1909-1943
French philosopher and social critic

Although Jewish by birth, Weil's philosophical work was mainly influenced by Christian gnosticism, being concerned to integrate the sacred human expectation of good
with a mechanistic determinism. This led
her to her critique of industrial society as
offering no place for the spiritual aspirations of humanity. She published almost ex-
clusively in obscure left-wing journals,
fought in the Spanish Civil War, and joined
the French Resistance, but refused to join
any formal religious or political group. Her
ascetic existence was always controversial,
and she died in exile in England while on
hunger strike in sympathy with the victims
of the Nazis. **EB**.

ABOVE: *Johnny Weismuller, Olympic gold-
medallist and screen Tarzan.*

WEISMULLER, JOHNNY
1904-1984
American swimmer and actor

Johnny Weismuller was famous for both
swimming in pools and swinging on vines. A
ferociously powerful freestylist, he won
three gold medals in the 1924 Olympics and
two more in the 1928 Games. He is perhaps
better known, however, for his portayal of
Tarzan in 12 movies. **MD**.

WEIZMANN, CHAIM
1874-1952
Israeli statesman

Israel's founding father, Weizmann was Russian-born, German-educated, and a British subject. His involvement with the Zionist movement enabled him to join in negotiations for the Balfour Declaration of 1917 which advocated British support for a Jewish homeland in Palestine. Elected President of the World Zionist Organization in 1920, holding office (as well as the presidency of the Jewish Agency) until 1931 and again from 1935 to 1946, his concept of a peaceful transition to nationhood, with roots in the soil and guaranteed rights for the Arabs was destroyed by the latter's intransigence and Zionist militancy. He was Israel's first President after independence in 1949. **JC.**

ABOVE: Israeli statesman Chaim Weizmann, Israel's first President after the country gained its independence in 1949.

WELLS, H[ERBERT] [GEORGE]
1866-1946
British writer

Author of a huge body of work including histories of the world and social commentary, Wells is perhaps best known for his scientific romances such as *The Time Machine* (1895) and the apocalyptic *The War of the Worlds* (1898), allegories of technological progress in which he found both utopian promise and extreme danger. From novels dealing with the manners of lower-middle-class suburbia of his childhood, such as *Love and Mr Lewisham* (1900), to the suffragism of *Ann Veronica* (1909), and the entrepreneurial society of *Tono-Bungay* (1909), Wells measured the scale of social and economic change. In *Experiment in Autobiography* (1934) he depicts the Fabian and bohemian world of his contemporaries. **CW.**

ABOVE: British writer H G Wells, author of The War of the Worlds.

WELLES, ORSON
1915-1985
American actor and director

A child prodigy, Welles shot to fame in 1938 with his frighteningly realistic radio production about a Martian invasion of Earth, *The War of the Worlds*. He made the most sensational Hollywood debut in movie history with his first film, *Citizen Kane* (1941), still widely regarded as the best film ever made. His career, like Kane's, could only go downhill. It did, but with many impressive achievements along the way, such as *The Magnificent Ambersons* (1942), *Lady from Shanghai* (1948), with its much-imitated shoot-out in a hall of mirrors, and *Touch of Evil* (1958), with its virtuoso three-minute opening shot. Welles was also a powerful actor, most memorably as Harry Lime in Carol REED's *The Third Man* (1949), and as Falstaff in *Chimes of Midnight* (1966). Even with his career disappointments and frustrations, he remained a giant of the cinema. **NS.**

WELTY, EUDORA
1909-
American writer

A Mississippi-born novelist and short-story writer, Eudora Welty is an inheritor of the Faulknerian Southern Gothic tradition. At her best in the economy of form offered by the short story and novella, in collections such as *The Curtain of Green* (1941) and *The Golden Apples* (1949) she observes the small-town life of her region with an idiosyncratic eye for the grotesque and comic. Her condensed form of characterization is much richer, in its sense of existential dislocation, than the caricature it is often compared with. Her novels, such as *The Robber Bridegroom* (1942) and *The Ponder Heart* (1954), often draw on legend and fantasy. **CW.**

ABOVE: Orson Welles – a remarkable actor and director.

ABOVE: *Mae West beguiles W C Fields in* My Little Chickadee.

WEST, MAE
1892-1980
American actress

West, of the half-mast eyelids, come-hither voice, and no-nonsense seductiveness, was a living American institution. Her aggressive sexuality and comic genius established her as the archetypal sex symbol, splendidly vulgar, mocking, overdressed and endearing. Arriving in Hollywood in 1932 after theater success, she appeared with George Raft in *Night After Night* and began breaking box-office records. Lines like 'Come up and see me' passed into common usage. She made Cary GRANT a star with *She Done Him Wrong* (1933) and vied with W C FIELDS in *My Little Chickadee* (1939), but by then American puritanism was on the upswing and censorship ended her movie career. **DC**.

WEST, DAME REBECCA [CICILY FAIRFIELD]
1892-1983
Anglo-Irish writer

Influenced by the Pankhursts, from 1911 Rebecca West wrote her shrewd, vigorous pieces for a number of feminist journals. In addition to her now-admired novels, she reported from the Yugoslav nation in 1937, and from the Nuremberg war trials in 1946, continuing to write until her death. **CW**.

WESTMORELAND, WILLIAM, GENERAL
1914-
American soldier

After service in World War II and Korea, Westmoreland was appointed Commander of Military Assistance Command Vietnam (MACV) in 1964. As such, he commanded US combat forces in South Vietnam until 1968 when, in the aftermath of the Tet Offensive, he was promoted US Army Chief of Staff. **JPi**.

WESTWOOD, VIVIENNE
1941-
British designer

Westwood studied for a single term at Harrow Art School before she left to train as a teacher. In the 1960s she and partner Malcolm MacLaren opened a shop on London's King's Road and during the 1970s both the shop and MacLaren's group the SEX PISTOLS attracted a great deal of attention for their representation of an anarchic urban youth culture. Westwood's shop, which was known by a number of names, sold garments in leather and rubber and catered primarily to clients interested in

RIGHT: *General William Westmoreland.*

punk. The 1980s saw Westwood's launch of the 'Pirate' and 'New Romantic' looks, which brought her to the attention of the mainstream fashion world and set a new trend for huge petticoats and baggy coats. Despite acclaim as one of the leading British fashion designers, her clothes are often met with both outrage and curiosity. Her garments frequently appear to have been torn, have extra armholes, or sleeves of exceptional length. The 'vandalized' appearance of some of her clothes has been enhanced by her employment of graffiti artists to paint on sweatshirts. Her most recent designs have included the 'Mini-Crinoline' skirt and the reintroduction of corsets, and platform and wedge-heeled shoes. **MC**.

WHARTON, EDITH
1867-1937
American novelist

Edith Wharton came from an affluent New York family and was educated in Europe. Her career, encouraged by an unhappy marriage, began with the publication of poems and stories in *Scribners Magazine*. Like her friend and mentor Henry James her novels – from *The House of Mirth* (1905) which established her fame and *Ethan Frome* (1911) to her most achieved work, *The Age of Innocence* (1920) – are concerned with an ironic scrutiny of aristocratic mores from the point of view of a single, complex consciousness. **CW**.

WHEELER, SIR MORTIMER
1890-1976
British archaeologist

Wheeler established himself as one of

the most meticulous excavators of his generation, conducting masterly excavations at the Roman site of Verulamium (St Albans) and at Maiden Castle. After serving in World War II, he became Director of Antiquities for India and excavated a famous series of sites of the Indus Valley civilization. From the 1950s he became perhaps the most successful popularizer of archaeology on the new medium of television. **RJ**.

WHITE, PATRICK
1912-1990
Australian writer

This Nobel Prize winning novelist, born and educated in England, returned to Australia after serving in World War II. His early novels *The Tree of Man* (1955) and *Voss* (1957) won him an international reputation, exploring the epic, Dostoevskian themes that mark his work: the atheist's search for identity and meaning. **CW**.

WHITEHEAD, ALFRED NORTH
1861-1947
British philosopher and mathematician

While a Fellow of Trinity College, Cambridge, Whitehead collaborated with his pupil Bertrand RUSSELL on the three-volume *Principia Mathematica* in which they attempted to show how all of mathematics could be derived from pure logic. He was to have contributed a fourth volume on geometry but, although he did publish some such material, the project was never concluded. After 10 years as Professor of Applied Mathematics at Imperial College, at the age of 63 Whitehead was appointed Professor of Philosophy at Harvard, and devoted the remainder of his life to developing his organic philosophy of science, influenced by Heraclitus and field theory, in opposition to the mathematical mechanism of Newton. **EB**.

WHITLAM, GOUGH
1916-
Australian politician

Australia's first Labor Prime Minister for 23 years when he won the 1972 elections, Whitlam plunged into a reforming program which included reducing the voting age, abolishing the death penalty and conscription, introducing welfare payments for single parents and the homeless, and establishing Aboriginal rights. He was sacked by the Governor-General in 1975 amid great controversy and resigned from politics in 1978. **JC**.

WIENER, NORBERT
1894-1964
American mathematician

After receiving a Harvard PhD at the age of 18 for a thesis on the logic of Bertrand RUSSELL, Wiener worked as an engineer before obtaining a post in mathematics at MIT, where he remained for the rest of his life. An analyst and applied mathematician, he made significant contributions to a wide range of topics, but is best known as one of the founders of the science of cybernetics (communication theory). Although he was well known as a popularizer of science, his lectures were famed for their disorderliness. He also wrote on ethical and theological aspects of cybernetics, and published autobiographical accounts of his life as a child prodigy. **EB**.

WILDER, BILLY
1906-
American film director

A Viennese-born writer-director, Wilder emigrated to Hollywood and became a director to protect his own scripts. He made some of Hollywood's most acerbic movies, including the film-noir *Double Indemnity* (1944); a study of an alcoholic, *The Lost Weekend* (1945); and a macabre masterpiece that dissected Hollywood itself, *Sunset Boulevard* (1950). Wilder's most famous film is probably his classic comedy, *Some Like it Hot* (1959). He has had a particularly rewarding association with the actor Jack LEMMON, with whom he has made seven films, including *The Apartment* (1960) and *Avanti!* (1972). Renowned as one of the wittiest men in Hollywood, Wilder has made some of the most entertaining, intelligent, and meticulously constructed films of the sound era. **NS**.

WILDER, THORNTON
1897-1975
American writer

Academic, novelist and playwright, Wilder first found success with his Pulitzer Prize-winning novel *The Bridge of San Luis Rey* (1927). His plays, such as *Our Town* (1938), *The Skin of Our Teeth* (1942), and *The Merchant of Yonkers* (1938), were also well received, the latter now famous through its musical adaptation *Hello, Dolly!* (1963). **CW**.

WILLIAMS, HANK
1923-1953
American country singer and songwriter

Williams took his songs to Nashville and had a sensational success on Grand Ole Opry singing 'Lovesick Blues' (1949), ironically not one of his compositions. Chart-toppers that he wrote included 'Your Cheatin' Heart', 'Hey Good Lookin' and 'I's so Lonesome I could Die', but his own recordings never moved beyond the country chart. **JH**. **JP**.

WILLIAMS, RALPH VAUGHAN
1872-1958
British composer

To some Vaughan Williams epitomizes the classic English music of this century, evoking images of rural idylls on sunny summer days. But this is to underestimate the achievements of a master of color and form, whose grounding in Tudor music (an interest he shared with HOLST), as well as in English folk and church music, provided a basis for some great works. Vaughan Williams used traditional forms to create impressionistic works containing a whole range of moods and textures. Although he composed nine symphonies, his *Fantasia on a Theme of Thomas Tallis* and folksong arrangements are perhaps his finest works, while his choral pieces stand alongside those of his teachers. **DK**.

WILLIAMS, TENNESSEE
1911-1983
American playwright

This outstanding dramatist was born in Mississippi. After an unhappy childhood in St Louis, he struggled to establish himself, first achieving success with his twelfth play *The Glass Menagerie* (1944), a painful, tender account of a crippled girl's emergence from a fantasy world. This was followed by *A Streetcar Named Desire* (1947), an exploration of Southern sexual tension and familial violence marked by the themes of emotional alienation and perversity that characterize his work, which is generally expressionist in style. Pulitzer Prize-winning *Cat on a Hot Tin Roof* (1955), a Freudian family drama, hints at the latent theme of homosexual anguish that preoccupies many of his most famous plays. **CW**.

WILLIAMS, RED [THEODORE SAMUEL]
1918-
American baseball player

Many baseball fans consider Ted Williams to be the greatest hitter in the game's history. Though his career was twice interrupted by military service (1943-1945, 1952-1953), Williams still managed to hit .344 and slug 521 home runs. He had a flair for the dramatic. In 1941 he insisted on playing a doubleheader on the last day of the season despite entering the game with a .400 average: he bashed hits all over the ballpark and finished at .406. (No one has broken the .400 barrier since then.) Williams ended his career in 1960 with a home run in his final at bat. A two-time American League MVP, he played his entire career with the Boston Red Sox. **MD**.

WILSON, CHARLES ERWIN
1890-1961
American automobile industrialist

A trained electrical engineer, Wilson became Vice President of manufacturing at GM in 1929. He directed GM's immense war effort, and is credited with saying: 'What's good for GM is good for the country.' He served as Secretary of Defense from 1953-57. **NF**.

WILSON, CHARLES THOMSON REES
1869-1959
British physicist

He was born on a Scottish sheep farm, and although most of his academic work was done in Cambridge, it was inspired by atmospheric effects observed in the Scottish highlands. In trying to replicate cloud formation in the laboratory, he found that water droplets condensed on ionized particles produced by radiation. As a result he developed the cloud chamber used in the study of radiation and won the Nobel Prize for Physics for it in 1927. He postulated the presence of radiation from space – a theory that was subsequently proved by the discovery of cosmic rays in 1911. **DD**.

WILSON, EDMUND
1895-1972
American writer and critic

Edmund Wilson was educated at Princeton, after serving in World War I. Best known for his influential and wide-ranging critical work, including his symbolist study, *Axel's Castle* (1931), he was also editor of *Vanity Fair* and *The New Republic*, and author of numerous reviews, experimental plays, and novels. **CW**.

WILSON, HAROLD, BARON WILSON OF RIEVAULX
1916-
British politician

Academic economist turned politician, Wilson's career began with ministerial experience in, and principled resignation from, ATTLEE's government. Offering leftist credentials as well as administrative competence, Wilson was well placed to succeed GAITSKELL and lead Labour into the 1964 election. Unfortunately success with the 'white heat of the technological revolution' slogan turned sour as first a series of sterling crises and the then fiasco over industrial-relations reform undermined the government. Conservative misfortune and his debating prowess saw Wilson back at Number 10 by 1974, but, reduced in confidence and lacking a strategy for power, he resigned two years later. **JP**.

WILSON, JOHN TUZO
1908-
Canadian geophysicist

He worked for the Canadian Geological Survey and was appointed professor of geophysics in Toronto in 1946. He provided proof of the seafloor spreading effect of plate tectonics and proposed the existence of hot-spots in the Earth's mantle to account for island chains like Hawaii. **DD**.

RIGHT: Former US President Woodrow Wilson.

WILSON, WOODROW
1856-1924
Australian statesman and president

This university professor's crusade to establish world peace after World War I was dismissed as Utopian by the Allies at the Paris Peace Conference and by his fellow-countrymen. Elected 28th President of the USA in 1913, Wilson was pushing through a reform program, under the title 'New Freedom' when he was faced with the provocations of all-out European war. Woodrow maintained American neutrality until 1917 and declared war on Germany after the sinking of several US ships. Wilson was set to become the supreme arbiter at the end of the war, with his 'Fourteen Points,' designed 'to make the world safe for democracy.' His idealism was ignored by Europeans making their own territorial deals and when he tried to rally support in the USA for the League of Nations the Senate twice voted against it. He had hopes to turn the 1920 election in to 'a solemn referendum' on the Versailles Treaty but ill-health forced him to retire. He was awarded the Nobel Peace Prize in 1919. **JC**.

WITTGENSTEIN, LUDWIG
1889-1951
British philosopher

The son of an Austrian industrialist, Wittgenstein came to England to continue his study of engineering at Manchester, but after he was advised by FREGE to contact RUSSELL, he moved to Cambridge to study mathematics. He returned to Austria to join the army, but was taken prisoner by the Italians in 1918. While in a PoW camp Wittgenstein completed the *Tractatus Logico-Philosophicus*, containing his 'picture theory' of meaning, an idiosyncratic form of Logical Positivism; this was smuggled in a diplomatic bag to Russell, who eventually arranged its publication in 1921. Having concluded that philosophy itself fell foul of his dictum that 'whereof one cannot speak, thereof one must be silent', Wittgenstein abandoned the subject to teach in a rural primary school. However after he was contacted by the Vienna Circle, he returned to philosophy and to Cambridge, where his eccentric behavior and philosophical intensity made him a cult figure; he succeeded G E MOORE as Professor in 1939 but spent part

of the war working as a hospital porter and resigned in 1947. Becoming increasingly dissatisfied with his earlier views, Wittgenstein subjected them to a sustained attack in his lectures; although he died while still preparing the *Philsophical Investigations* for the press, his views werre already widely known through the illicit circulation of notes of his lectures and the writings of his disciples. Since his death a veritable industry of publishing his fragmentary notes on various topics has sprung up, and the *Remarks on the Foundations of Mathematics* and *On Certainty* have been particularly influential. Opposed to all forms of essentialism, Wittgenstein denied that his views constituted a theory, but the underlying approach is that since philosophical problems stem from linguistic confusions, they are resolved by 'assembling reminders' about proper usage, drawing conceptual maps 'to show the fly the way out of the flybottle'; otherwise philosophy 'leaves everything as it is'. Wittgenstein stresses the diversity of 'language-games', that there need be no one criterion met by all things called by the same term (the doctrine of 'family resemblances'), and that language, which is part of 'the natural history of our species', must be capable of being learned in terms of public 'agreement in responses'. Hence a 'private language' of experience is unintelligible, because there can be no rules to distinguish correct from incorrect usage. **EB**.

WOLFE, THOMAS
1900-1938
American writer

This novelist from North Carolina is best-known for his autobiographical works *Look Homeward, Angel* (1929) and *Of Time and the River* (1935), about the adolescent fortunes of Eugene Gant and his quarrelling family. Popular with the young, his passionate and often unpleasantly egocentric narratives were pared into shape by his editors, who also produced the continuation of the Gant story in *The Web and the Rock* (1939) and *You Can't Go Home Again* (1940) from posthumous material. An immensely prolific writer, his reputation has now declined, though some have found a romantic patriotism in his work that rises above the self-fascination. **CW**.

WONDER, STEVIE
1950-
American keyboard player and pop singer

Keyboard whizz-kid Wonder had his first million-selling chart hit, 'Uptight', at the tender age of 16 with Motown, the in-house team which penned most of his early songs. His career peaked in 1977 with the album *Songs in the Key of Life*, and he continued throughout the 1980s to release a steady amount of successful material. **DC**.

RIGHT: Stevie Wonder.

WOOD, GRANT
1892-1942
American painter

Born in Anamosa, Iowa, Wood studied at the Chicago Art Institute, (1912) and in Paris (1920). Originally working in an Impressionist style, he was deeply impressed by early Flemish painting while visiting Munich in 1928. He began to work in a sharp, meticulous style, as in his best-known work, *American Gothic* (1930). Originally considered an insulting caricature of plain country people, it is now among America's most popular paintings. Numbered among the Regionalist painters, Wood saw the ordinary people and landscape of Iowa as fitting subject matter for a truly American art, but his insight and wit raise his work above the folksy. **ER**.

WOOD, SIR HENRY
1869-1944
British conductor

Wood is best known for his close association with the annual London Promenade Concerts; he conducted the inaugural concert in 1895 and continued to conduct them throughout his life. He is particularly noted for his enthusiasm to introduce contemporary music into the 'Proms' (such as DEBUSSY and BARTÓK) and in so doing he helped increase the popularity of many notable composers. **DK**.

WOODWARD, ROBERT BURNS
1917-1979
American organic chemist

Something of a prodigy, Woodward entered the Massachusetts Institute of Technology at the age of 16 and gained his PhD at 20. Thereafter, at Harvard, he synthesized many complex molecules including quinine (1944), cholesterol (1951), strychnine (1954), chlorophyll (1960) and vitamin B12 (1971). He received the Nobel Prize for Chemistry in 1965. **DD**.

WOODWARD, BOB [ROBERT]
1943-
American journalist

Woodward served as a reporter on *The Washington Post* from 1971 to 1979. During that time he covered the Watergate story with CARL BERNSTEIN and co-wrote with him *All the President's Men* and *The Final Days*. Since 1981 he has been Assistant Managing Editor of *The Washington Post* and in 1987 wrote *The Secret Wars of the CIA*. **DSL**.

WOOLF, [ADELINE] VIRGINIA
1882-1941
British novelist

She was born in London, daughter of Leslie Stephen and Julia Duckworth, and educated at home. On her father's death in 1904 the children moved to 46 Gordon Square, which became the first meeting-place of the Bloomsbury Group. The death of her brother Thoby in 1906 triggered a severe breakdown, and all her life she was subject to attacks of the mental illness which had begun with her mother's death when Virginia was 13, culminating in her suicide by drowning. She married Leonard Woolf in 1912, and her first novel *The Voyage Out* appeared in 1915. She later developed away from the realism of her early work into the impressionistic technique, based on stream-of-consciousness and her own vision of the nature of character and event. A writer of critical works, essays, and biography as well as fiction, she was at the forefront of modernism. Her own feminism has made her works of particular interest to that school of literary criticism, to which she contributed the classic *A Room of One's Own* (1929) and *Three Guineas* (1938). Her finest novels are *Mrs Dalloway* (1925), *To the Lighthouse* (1927), her richest work, drawing heavily on her childhood, *The Waves* (1931), her most experimental book, and *Between the Acts*, which was published posthumously in 1941. **AM**.

WOOLLEY, LEONARD, SIR
1880-1960
British archaeologist

Woolley developed his famed excavation skills at a number of significant sites in Egypt, Syria, and Turkey – including the great Hittite ruin of Carchemish – before conducting his most outstanding work at the ancient city of Ur in Iraq (1922-29). At Ur Woolley discovered a spectacular royal cemetery, dating to about 2800 BC, which contained a wealth of stone and gold jewellery, as well as evidence of human sacrifice; he also skilfully excavated the great Ziggurat to the Moon God of about 2100 BC. His book describing the excavations at Ur, *Ur of the Chaldees*, was a huge popular success. **RJ**.

WOOLWORTH, FRANK
1852-1919
American retailer

A self-educated farm boy, Woolworth set up a 5-cent store in 1879 which immediately failed, but the same year his second try, a 5- and 10-cent store in Lancaster, Pennsylvania, was a great success. He soon expanded, often finding management and financial resources for new stores by entering into local partnerships. By 1904 he had 120 stores; in 1909 he founded the Woolworth Company to supervise his British operations and in 1911 he initiated a merger with most of his bigger US competitors to form a statewide chain of almost 600 stores. The success of his organization was based on three concepts: volume buying, which meant that he might contract for the entire output of a factory at appropriately low prices; counter display of all items for sale, a sure bait for impulse buying; and lastly, business was on a strict cash-and-carry basis, with none of the extra trouble and cost associated with delivery and credit. In 1913 his prestige and fortune were suitably reflected in his new headquarters, the new 792ft Woolworth Building in New York, the tallest building in the world at that time. **JW**.

WOZNIAK, STEVE
1955-
American computer designer

'Woz' was the technical genius behind Apple. He sold his Hewlett Packard Calculator to help finance the creation of the Apple II, designing the hardware, and writing most of the system software and its BASIC interpreter. He produced a specification for other companies wishing to add cards on to the Apple II, and so gave the machine a major asset in the face of competition from Radio Shack and Commodore. When Dan Bricklin wrote Viscalc for the machine it became a tool that all small businesses wanted. Famed for organizing rock concerts which personally cost him millions of dollars, Wozniak has dropped out of mainstream computing. **SR**.

WRIGHT, FRANK LLOYD
1869-1959
American architect

Frank Lloyd Wright never lost faith in traditional American homespun ideals and aesthetic. In his 'Prairie' houses of 1900-1910 such as the Bradley and Hickox houses in Kankakee, Illinois (1900), the Robie House, Chicago, and the Mrs Thomas Gale House, Oak Park (both 1909), he developed a whole vocabulary and philosophy of home building. Characteristically they have X, L, or T-shaped plans with space freely flowing between different areas, inside and outside, low sweeping roofs, bands of windows, prominent hearths and porches, and little or no decoration. They revolutionized American house design. Wright adapted new materials to his own purposes at Falling Water, Bear Run, Pennsylvania (1936), with great shallow concrete boxes and terraces cantilevered out over a waterfall. At the other end of the scale were his 'Usonian' houses, low-cost, prefabricated wooden houses, often with built-in furniture, with his favored flexible planning arrangements. Wright's interest in the possible uses of new materials and the expression of geometric forms are seen most in public buildings such as AC Johnson Administration Building Racine, Wisconsin (1936-39), the Price Tower, Bartlesville, Oklahoma (1955), and the spiral-ramp-based Guggenheim Museum, New York (1943-59). Wright was tirelessly prolific and hugely influential, especially in America. **AR**.

BELOW: Computer designer Steve Wozniak.

BELOW: US architect Frank Lloyd Wright.

ABOVE: Orville Wright flying the United States Army's first military aircraft in 1909.

ABOVE: Richard Wright.

WRIGHT, RICHARD
1908-1960
American writer

This foremost Black American novelist was born in Mississippi to a Seventh Day Adventist family, migrating to Chicago as the Depression began. Largely self-educated, he joined the Communist Party in 1932 until 1944, as he documents in *The God That Failed* (1950). He made his reputation as heir to the naturalist tradition with the seminal *Native Son* (1940), a powerful, nihilistic account of the murderous life of a boy from the Chicago slums. Among numerous works his autobiographical novel *Black Boy* (1945) also stands out, in part for its critique of a black culture that was seen to collaborate with white oppression. **CW**.

WRIGHT, ORVILLE
1871-1948

WRIGHT, WILBUR
1867-1912
American pioneer aircraft engineers and pilots

The most famous names in aviation, on 17 December 1903 the Wright brothers' *Flyer* made the first piloted (by Orville), powered, sustained and controled air flight. Originally bicycle makers from Dayton, Ohio, from 1900 the Wrights built man-carrying gliders and gained knowledge from a 10-month research program testing wing airfoils on rigs and in a simple wind tunnel. So great was their lead that they demonstrated a 24-mile flight in 1905 before anyone else had even flown. Incredibly, the brothers then gave up flying until 1908, but in 1909 built the first military airplane for the United States Army. Wilbur died from typhoid in 1912, and in 1915 Orville sold the Wright Aeronautical Company. **MT**.

WYLER, WILLIAM
1902-1981
American film director

Born in France, Wyler emigrated to America in the 1920s and had a close association with producer Sam GOLDWYN, which culminated in their Oscar-winning *The Best Years of our Lives* (1946). Wyler was noted for his ability to elicit brilliant performances from his casts – more than a dozen were rewarded with Oscars – and for his painstaking, even tyrannical methods on the set. Although he could handle the epic canvas, as *The Big Country* (1958) and *Ben-Hur* (1959) show, his particular forte was for family or marital dramas in a confined setting, such as *The Letter* (1940), *The Little Foxes* (1941), and *The Heiress* (1949). **NS**.